Economics of Religion in the Mycenaean World

Resources Dedicated to Religion in the Mycenaean Palace Economy

Lisa Maria Bendall

Oxford University School of Archaeology, Monograph Number 67
Published by Oxford University School of Archaeology

2007

Front cover:
Photo of Linear B tablet from Knossos: E 777.

Back cover:
Photo and line drawings of Linear B tablets from Knossos (counter-clockwise from top left): Fs 3, V 52, Gg(1) 702, M(1) 1645, Fp(1) 1.

Photos of E 777 (ASHM 1910.214) and M(1) 1645 (ASHM 1938.711) are reproduced with permission of the University of Oxford Ashmolean Museum. The line drawings from *CoMIK* I (1, 3, 31, 267) are reproduced with permission of Professor J.T Killen and the Cambridge University Press.

ISBN 978-1-905905-02-7

Designed and produced by the author
Cover design by Production Line
Printed in Great Britain

CONTENTS

LIST OF TABLES

CHAPTER 2

CHAPTER 3

CHAPTER 4

CHAPTER 5

CHAPTER 6

CHAPTER 7

CONVENTIONS

1 DOCUMENT TRANSLITERATIONS

Linear B document transliterations used in the present work are drawn from the following standard editions unless otherwise stated.

Chania	Hallager, Vlasakis & Hallager 1990; 1992
Knossos	*KT*[5]; Olivier & Killen 1992 (corrigenda to *KT*[5]); *CoMIK* I–IV
Mycenae	*TITHEMY*
Pylos	*PTT* I; *PTT* II
Thebes	*TITHEMY*; *Thèbes* I; *Thèbes* III (replacing Godart & Sacconi 1978); *Thèbes* IV
Tiryns	*TITHEMY*

For most sites the document transliterations are unproblematic, but for Knossos and Pylos – our major sources – the current situation is unusually complex due to the valuable recent and on-going work on tablet joins. New editions are planned, but they are still in progress. Most of the joins and new readings have been published in a series of articles, listed below. These references appear also in the bibliography, but it is useful to have a list to hand; note they are given here (being more useful for the purpose) in order of date of publication rather than alphabetically by author name. In addition, I have been able to consult the new editions in progress (*KT*[6]; *PoN* IV) through the kind permission of the general editor J.L. Melena, to whom I am very grateful for the privilege. Every effort has been made to use the most up-to-date published transliterations with reference to the new volumes; sources for individual documents, especially where they diverge from *KT*[5], *CoMIK* or *PTT* are normally indicated either in the footnotes or in notes to the tables.

It may also be noted here that apparatuses to document transliterations are normally included, but a few have been omitted in cases where the readings are not affected or are not germane to the main argument.

Further sources for Knossos and Pylos texts

Knossos

BENNETT, E.L., DRIESSEN, J.M., GODART, L., KILLEN, J.T., KOPAKA, C., MELENA, J.L., OLIVIER, J.-P. & PERNA, M. 1989. '436 raccords et quasi-raccords de fragments inédites dans *KT* 5.' *Minos* 24: 199–242.

GODART, L., KILLEN, J.T., KOPAKA, C., MELENA, J.L., OLIVIER, J.-P. 1990–1. '501 raccords et quasi-raccords de fragments dans les tablettes de Cnossos post-*KT V*.' *Minos* 25–26: 373–411.

MELENA, J.L., OWENS, G. & SERRANO, M. 1990–1. '55 raccords de fragments dans les tablettes de Cnossos.' *Minos* 25–26: 413–17.

GODART, L., KOPAKA, C., MELENA, J.L. & OLIVIER, J.-P. 1992–3. '175 raccords de fragments dans les tablettes de Knossos.' *Minos* 27–28: 55–70.

MELENA, J.L. 1996–7c. '19 raccords et quasi-raccords de fragments dans les tablettes de Cnossos.' *Minos* 31–32: 417–22.

Pylos

BENNETT, E.L. JR. 1992. 'A selection of Pylos tablet texts.' In OLIVIER, J.-P. (ed.) *Mykenaïka. Bulletin de correspondance hellénique* Suppl. 25. Athens: 103–28.

MELENA, J.L. 1992–3a. '167 joins of fragments in the Linear B tablets from Pylos.' *Minos* 27–28: 71–82.

MELENA, J.L. 1992–3b. '244 joins and quasi-joins of fragments in the Linear B tablets from Pylos.' *Minos* 27–28: 307–24.

MELENA, J.L. 1994–5a. '28 joins and quasi-joins of fragments in the Linear B tablets from Pylos.' *Minos* 29–30: 95–100.

MELENA, J.L. 1994–5b. '133 joins and quasi-joins of fragments in the Linear B tablets from Pylos.' *Minos* 29–30: 271–88.

BENNETT, E.L. JR. 1996–7. 'Junctions, restorations, and reconstructions in Pylian and related texts.' *Minos* 31–32: 135–44.

MELENA, J.L. 1996–7a. '40 joins and quasi-joins of fragments from the Linear B tablets from Pylos.' *Minos* 31–32: 159–70.

MELENA, J.L. 1996–7b. '13 joins and quasi-joins of fragments from the Linear B tablets from Pylos.' *Minos* 31–32: 171–8.

MELENA, J.L. 2000–1a. '24 joins and quasi-joins of fragments in the Linear B tablets from Pylos.' *Minos* 35–36: 357–69.

MELENA, J.L. 2000–1b. '63 joins and quasi-joins of fragments in the Linear B tablets from Pylos.' *Minos* 35–36: 371–84.

2 LINEAR B MEASURES AND EQUIVALENCIES

The values below are used throughout as the most reliable equivalencies. They should not be taken as exact, but are likely to be of the correct order of magnitude.[1]

DRY MEASURES

1 MU	=	10 T
1 T	=	6 V
1 V	=	4 Z

1 MU	=	96.0 litres
1 T	=	9.6 litres
1 V	=	1.6 litres
1 Z	=	0.4 litres

LIQUID MEASURES

1 MU	=	3 S
1 S	=	6 V
1 V	=	4 Z

1 MU	=	28.8 litres
1 S	=	9.6 litres
1 V	=	1.6 litres
1 Z	=	0.4 litres

MEASURES OF WEIGHT

1 L	=	30 M *
1 M	=	4 N
1 N	=	12 P
1 P	=	6+ Q

1 L	=	30 kg
1 M	=	1 kg
1 N	=	250 g
1 P	=	20.8 g?
1 Q	=	3.4 g??

Notes
MU = 'major unit' e.g. GRA, OLE, LANA (see *Documents*, 53–5).
* Except for wool, where M 3 = LANA 1 (Bennett 1950, 218; *Documents*, 55, 57; Killen 1964, 9; de Fidio 1998–1999).

Figures in the present study are usually given without rounding them off (except for percentages), for two reasons. First, this enables the reader to see at a glance what the numbers are if the calculations are done. Second, rounding implies a statement about the margin of error and no such statements are warranted for the Linear B evidence: we simply do not know in many cases how flawed the figures are. Rounding off would thus be misleading, but it must be understood that no exactitude is thus intended.

Modern equivalencies are used only where it is helpful to give a sense of the scales involved. The arguments in no way depend on the correctness or otherwise of such equivalencies, because all data are processed in Mycenaean measures in the first instance. Equivalencies *within* the Mycenaean measurement systems have been securely worked out, with the exception that the exact value of Q and its relation to P remain uncertain – but these measures do not happen to appear on tablets relating to religion so need not concern us here.[2]

3 COUNTING CONVENTIONS

The Linear B documents are often imperfectly preserved and in many cases numbers are incomplete or lost altogether. The tables below indicate the counting conventions normally followed where this has happened.[3] It is agreed that different schemes are possible, but the essential point is consistency. So long as the system is sensible and all figures are treated in the same way, we may at least be confident that we are comparing evidence derived in a uniform manner.

---

[1] The basic sources are: Bennett 1950; *Documents*, 394 (superseding values given p. 60); Chadwick 1976, 102–8. See also *Documents*, 53–5 (for equivalent values of V and Z in both solid and liquid systems), 55–8 (for weights), and Chadwick 1988, 74 (for notes on rations); see also recently Bartoněk 2003, 126–8. Lang's proposed figures (1964) are probably too low.

[2] See *Documents*, 55.

[3] In a few instances, slight modifications are made based on considerations of document content and structure. It is clearly indicated when this has been done.

The conventions were developed with attention to the internationally agreed principles for Linear B document transliteration .[4] Where possible, doubtful readings were checked against photographs of the tablets as a guide to interpretation. For the Knossos tablets, this was done using *CoMIK*; for the Pylos tablets I am grateful for access to the photographs held in the Mycenaean Epigraphy Room, University of Cambridge.

In the case of commodities counted as units (for example, animals and textiles), if an ideogram appears at all it means that at least one unit must have originally been present. Thus, where a number is lost altogether we are justified in counting at least '1', to which a plus sign (+) is appended to indicate that more may have originally been present. Strictly speaking, a plus sign and question mark (+?) would be better since we do not know *whether* more would have been present. But this would have rendered some already complex tables less legible, and it is preferable simply to note the issue here. The conventions are shown as below.

COMMODITIES COUNTED AS UNITS

transliteration		counted as
OVIS 1 [	=	1
OVIS 1[	=	1+
OVIS 1̣[	=	1+
OVIS [	=	1+
OVIS 2̣6[	=	2̣6+
OVIS 2̣6̣[	=	2̣6̣+
OVIS 26̣[	=	26̣+

In the case of commodities counted in dry or liquid measures (for example, wheat or oil), the tables give both the straightforward transliteration s, then show the figures converted to the unit V, which is thought to have the same value for both types of measure. Conversion to V is commonly done in Mycenaean studies because it is necessary in comparing different figures to represent them in the same (or a readily comparable) unit. The smaller unit Z could just as well have been chosen for this purpose but V is more frequently used both because it appears more often than Z and, being larger, produces less cumbersome figures.

COMMODITIES COUNTED IN DRY OR LIQUID MEASURES

transliteration	=	V
GRA 1 T 2̣[	=	72+
GRA T[	=	6+
GRA Ṭ[	=	6̣+
GRA [	=	1+
GRA[ ] T 2	=	12+
GRA]V 4	=	4+
GRA]1 T 1 V 1	=	67+

In the case of commodities given in measures of weight (for instance wool), figures are converted to the standard unit M. The counting conventions are the same as for dry and liquid measures.

4 A NOTE ON 'SETS'

The term 'set' is used throughout in the technical sense established for Mycenaean studies, meaning a group of tablets written by the same scribe which were filed together and meant to be read in tandem as a single document.[5] This understanding is often important for the interpretation of the documents.

[4] Commonly known as 'The Wingspread Convention' (Bennett 1964a, 253–62), with subsequent modifications as agreed by the Comité International Permanent des Études Mycéniennes (CIPEM), an international scholarly body convened under UNESCO. See *CoMIK* I, x–xii, esp. xi for numbers; *PTT* I, 10–11; also *Documents*, 153–4 and resolutions in publications of the proceedings of the Mycenological colloquia held by CIPEM approximately every five years.

[5] For the basic definition of the term see Chadwick 1966, 27 with n 1; 1968a, esp. 12–17; 1968b, 490–2.

PREFACE & ACKNOWLEDGEMENTS

This book began as Chapter 3 of my doctoral thesis 'The economic relations of religious and political organisations and social groups in the Mycenaean world' (Cambridge 2000). The aim of the thesis was to examine economic relations in general, but it became apparent early on that before any progress could be made certain fundamental questions had to be addressed. The thesis thus ended up laying groundwork rather than being the sort of research I had originally envisaged, but this had to be done in order to proceed. The central question asked by Chapter 3, and which is the subject of this book, was: What proportion of the Mycenaean palace economy was invested in support for religion?

Some of the research relating to the other two main questions addressed by the thesis has already been published (Bendall 2003; 2004). The questions were: What was the role of banqueting in relation to religion and Mycenaean society more widely? And what was the nature of the supposed connection between religion and workshops in the Mycenaean world? The second in particular is relevant to the present study and a brief further word is warranted. The question of religion and workshops turned out to be an issue different to what I had expected. A possible connection between the two is frequently mentioned in the literature, and I thought I would be investigating the *nature* of what the relationship was. I ended up, however, doubting whether there was any special link at all. The supposed connection was based on two main pieces of evidence: first, an apparent connection between workshops and shrines at some sites and, second, the appearance of deities in Linear B alongside obscure figures known as 'Collectors', who among other things appear to have some connection with craft production. With regard to the workshop-shrine connection, a detailed re-examination of the Northeastern Building at Pylos (Bendall 2003), found that neither the published archaeological nor the epigraphic material supported the long-standing notion that the building had functioned as a workshop. Further, evidence for a shrine in the building was tenuous. These findings prompted reconsideration of other supposed examples of workshop-shrine connections and on further examination none appeared to be particularly compelling. Work on this issue remains the only part of my thesis still unpublished (Chapter 5), and I hope to return to it eventually. What was to an extent lacking in the thesis and still remains to be done is an investigation of the second sort of evidence, the appearance of deities as 'Collectors'. Section 2.5 of this book makes clear why I do not feel that this factor will turn out to lend significant support for the religion-workshop hypothesis, but I am aware that we are far from a consensus about the nature of 'Collectors' and there is much still is to be done. It may be noted that there does seems to be much stronger evidence for a craft-cult connection in Crete and Cyprus and if the Mycenaean link did turn out to be illusory this would not argue against such a connection in other cultural contexts.

The religion-workshop connection is of relevance here because it has implications for the question of the economic significance of religion. With regard to the question asked in this book, a central conclusion is that the proportion of economic resources invested in support for religion was not substantial. It is further argued that the motivation for Linear B documentation of religious offerings was rooted not in economic concerns such as tracking resource expenditure, but was bound up with social and political objectives. This conclusion was unexpected as were the general conclusions about Linear B administration: I was not working specifically on administration, and certainly did not see at the outset that the work might relate to some long-standing issues about the extent of palatial involvement in the wider Mycenaean economy, the nature of Mycenaean accounting systems or the notorious scarcity of documents relating to trade. I was simply working through the records, commodity by commodity, document by document; the results emerge from these data.

Integrating the various questions and formulating a new approach is work that remains to be done. I hope that clarification of some of the issues involved may eventually lead to an improved methodology for the study of Mycenaean religion, above all with regard to integrating the epigraphic and archaeological data, still one of the major challenges in the field of Aegean Prehistory. It is hoped that the present volume may contribute to this larger project through setting out in systematic form and attempting to clarify the nature of the Linear B documentation relating to religion.

In terms of overall structure, Chapters 3–7 of the book are based on Chapter 3 of the thesis, while Chapters 1 and 2 correspond to thesis Chapters 1 and 2. Discussions especially with John Killen and Sophia Voutsaki first helped clarify that a reworked version of Chapter 3 might be suitable as a monograph and further discussions with John made clear that Chapters 1–2 should also be included. The first is needed because the issues of 'redistribution' and 'temple economies' have become somewhat conflated and clarification is essential. The second was required because our understanding of documents relating to religion had not been updated in many years, particularly with regard to those concerning banqueting. It was not easy to bring these chapters, originally written with a different purpose in mind, into a form which would make them appropriate as introductions to the present book and much more could be said in all areas than is done here. Chapter 2 in particular is in no sense intended as a 'definitive' account of Linear B records related to religion. It simply attempts to define various tablets in the corpus according to categories useful to the present study. It was originally envisaged that this chapter might form the basis of a further work integrating Linear B and archaeological data and I hope eventually to return to such a project.

Much scholarship has appeared since the original research for this book was undertaken. I have attempted to take it into account, but have by no means done so as thoroughly as I would wish. A major task was the incorporation of the new Thebes tablets, published after submission of my thesis. The material does not turn out to alter any of the original conclusions – on the contrary – but was essential to include. Literature from 2004 onwards was difficult to include in any systematic way. I would especially have liked to have made fuller use of Massimo Perna's book on Mycenaean fiscality (2004) and the proceedings of his 2004 conference held in Naples to which I was invited but was unable to attend. I received Del Freo's important new book on land tenure (2005) too late in 2006 to refer to and the land tenure section of the present book (Section 2.4) should be read with this in mind. It was only ever intended as an overview and does what it needs to do in this sense; certain details may be altered by Del Freo's work but it is unlikely that the overall picture would change substantially. I was never able to obtain a copy of Susan Lupack's unpublished Ph.D. thesis on economics of religion (2002, Austin), which is not available through the usual channels. Susan kindly provided copies of some of her forthcoming articles, although these again were received too late to make reference to.

This book has essentially the same title as my M.Phil. thesis (1996), as I recollected with a bit of a shock at an advanced stage of the work. I cannot remember when I first encountered the term 'economics of religion', but it is a broadly useful expression and there are a number of things that it might mean. On the most general level it could apply to anything having to do with both cult and economy. One might ask, for instance, how shrines are funded, who funds them, through what sorts of means, involving what sorts of goods, or how their internal supply system works and is managed. Or 'economics of religion' could refer to the effect of religion on the wider political and social economy. This might involve study of the effect of religion as a symbolic system, or more concretely in cases where temples had independent wealth how they affected and interacted with the wider economy.

In recent years attempts have been made to link 'economics of religion' to a specific type of research pioneered by I. Iannacone (see e.g. 1998), whose essential idea is to apply economic perspectives including microeconomic theory to the study of religion. Thus, a typical question of this school would be how religious 'consumers' make 'rational economising choices' in 'religious market places'. The approach is interesting and I have read more or less widely in the area but, apart from reservations about the way in which theorists of this school commonly take insufficient account of psychological and social aspects of religious behaviour (see e.g. Bruce 2000 for a critique), it is an essentially modernist perspective and few of the questions one might want to ask about the ancient world are accommodated. My own study advocates a very different perspective as will become apparent, and I see no need to relinquish a broadly useful phrase such as 'economics of religion' to a specific line of research.

'Religion' and 'economics' are themselves of course modern (scholarly) categories. This does not mean that they cannot be applied to the study of the ancient world (cf. e.g. Finley 1985), but to apply narrowly defined modern notions would be a mistake. Ancient societies should be viewed, insofar as possible, in their own contexts. This book attempts to do just that for the world of the Mycenaean Greek speakers of the Aegean Late Bronze Age.

This book is one outcome of many years of research: I therefore have very many people to thank. I fear I have not given all the weight they deserve.

All first thanks must go to my thesis supervisors, John Killen and John Bennet, for invaluable advice, kindness, care, attention and support over many years – the debt I owe them cannot be overestimated. Both also kindly offered comments on drafts of the new chapters, often in the middle of busy and difficult schedules. I cannot adequately express how deeply grateful I am.

I am also grateful to my thesis examiners, Sophia Voutsaki, who created a stimulating research environment for Aegean Prehistory at Cambridge at the time, and Cynthia Shelmerdine for helpful comments plus general inspiration on combining archaeology and Linear B. I again grateful to all other commentators on and helpers with the original thesis, especially Ralph Anderson, Vicky Jackson, Jean-Pierre Olivier, Rupert Thompson, Alan Hajèk, Coulter George, Ellen Adams, Tim Stevens and Isabella Image.

In preparing the new draft, some of my former readers helped again and I have many new obligations to acknowledge. What is presented here has been substantially improved through their generous input. Several readers generously read more than one chapter, more than one draft of a given chapter or particularly long chapters. In addition to John Killen and John Bennet I owe many thanks to Silvia Ferrara, Philomen Probert, Nicoletta Momigliano, Yannis Hamilakis, Isabella Image, Ralph Anderson, Anna Morpurgo Davies, Marc Van de Mieroop, Stephanie Dalley, Andreas Willi, Richard Hitchman, Rupert Thompson and Camilla Briault. Silvia gave feedback on the overall structure; Bella brought her outstanding Linear B numeracy to bear in checking my tables, contributing incalculably to the accuracy of what is printed here.

I would like to stress that none of the above are responsible for the views expressed, and the fault for any remaining errors, infelicities, or deficiencies is entirely my own.

I am further grateful to those who gave advice at crucial stages, particularly Anna Morpurgo Davies and Jean-Pierre Olivier for advice on tablet transcriptions, and Anna for more general advice. Sue Sherratt and Martin Jones advised on overall structure at a final point of decision. I was unable for technical reasons to incorporate all of their suggestions, but the final copy was improved by those that could be taken into account. Most particularly, I am grateful to José Melena for his kindness and patience over many years, and for granting me access to copies of the new Pylos and Knossos editions in progress. In addition to those who commented or offered specific advice, I would also like to thank those who gave important moral and other general support while I was working on the final copy, particularly Irene Lemos, Helen Hughes-Brock, John Baines, Maria Vlazaki, Richard Firth, Paul Halstead, Barbara Kowalzig, Bert Smith, Chris Gosden and Barry Cunliffe.

Permission to cite forthcoming articles was kindly granted by John Killen, John Bennet, José Melena, Carlos Varias Garcia and Kevin Pluta. I am grateful for additions to the bibliography at final stages to Peter Warren, Vangelio Kiriatzi, Ian Whitbread, Karen Croxon, Barbara Kowalzig, Richard Firth, Bob Arnott, Yannis Mylonopoulos and Helen Hughes-Brock. Andrew Bayliss and Vicky Jackson commented on formatting and layout; Sonya Hymer helped with final copy-editing. Rupert Thompson and Charles Crowther advised on fonts and Rupert kindly supplied the font used for the dedication, which is based on Ventris's own hand.

I am very grateful to several graduate helpers, especially my research assistant, Jessica Miller, who aided with the bibliography, indexing, typing-out of tablet transliterations and general administrative support. Olympia Bobou and James Kelly did the main formatting of the bibliography. Olympia also helped with indexing and the bulk of the final task was carried out heroically by Lucy Wadeson, for which I will be ever grateful. The indexers were not subject specialists and they achieved wonders; it is due to them that there is an index at all. Philomen Probert and Yannis Fappas kindly brought their Linear B expertise to bear in helping with final checking. A subject index was not possible given the time and space available; the division of the chapters by commodity type to some extent obviates the need. Also due to time constraints, apparatuses to the tablet transliterations were not indexed.

In 2004 I was honoured to be appointed to the Sinclair and Rachel Hood Lecturership in Aegean Prehistory at Oxford, and I am grateful to all who facilitated my work while I have been here. Particular thanks go to the School of Archaeology, Faculty of Classics and Governing Body of Keble College for permission to take sabbatical leave in Michaelmas Term 2006, and to those who covered my administrative and teaching duties (Nellie Phoca-Cosmetatou, Adrian Hollis, Maria Stamatopoulou, Ioannis Galanakis, Lucy Wadeson, Chris Gosden and Averil Cameron). Due to the technical difficulty of type-setting Linear B tablet transliterations (which in the end had to be set in four different fonts), it was agreed that I should type-set the manuscript myself, which took most of Summer 2007. I am very grateful to Barry Cunliffe and Charlie Webster for help, advice, encouragement and technical expertise without which I could not have accomplished the task. I am also grateful to the copy-editor, Fran Brown, for her excellent work and good advice, and to Jeremy Worth for help in creating the pdf to send to press.

In terms of institutional support, the Mycenaean Epigraphy Group, Cambridge Faculty of Classics, deserves special mention. The Mycenaean Epigraphy Room possesses resources which are unparalleled in the world for Linear B studies, including a library based on Chadwick's personal collection, important and unique photographic collections and archives including the Ventris-Chadwick correspondence relating to the decipherment of Linear B. It was a luxury being so close to these resources when I was in Cambridge, and the present work would not have been possible without access to them. I am grateful to the Mycenaean Epigraphy Group and the Faculty of Classics for permission to consult them as a visitor now I am in Oxford.

I would also like to thank the British School at Athens, whose research facilities and collections are one of the most important in the world for study of the Aegean Bronze Age and more. The School has contributed substantially to my work both in Greece and in the UK over many many years, not only through its outstanding resources but through providing crucial practical support and by means of the opportunities it offers to meet and learn from other scholars. I will be lastingly grateful.

I would also like particularly to thank the librarians and staff of the Sackler Library, especially Graham Piddock. Libraries are key to research in the humanities and this book would not have been possible without the kindness, generosity and patience of those who make them work 'on the ground'.

Many funding bodies supported this research, and I am grateful to both those who funded the original thesis and those who provided support during preparation of the book. I was honoured to be elected to a Michael Ventris Award in 1997, and a British Federation of Women Graduates Award in 1996. The thesis was made possible a British Academy (subsequently AHRB, now AHRC) Studentship. The Faculty of Classics, Cambridge, provided support at crucial times and, in addition to my gratitude for the generally outstanding library and other facilities they offer to graduate students, I am particularly thankful for a grant from the Graduate Studies Fund in my final year which contributed substantially to my completing the writing-up. I was honoured to have been elected to a Sir P.M. Laurence Studentship (1999, 2000), the Craven Studentship (1998) and the Sir Isaac Newton Award (1998–2000), and am grateful for awards from the Henry Arthur Thomas Fund, which contributed to travel in connection with research. My family also provided important support for which I am very grateful. Jesus College, Cambridge, provided outstanding support during my graduate studies, especially with regard to accommodation, and I will be lastingly grateful to the Governing Body of Fitzwilliam College, for election to a Research Fellowship in 2000–2004. The importance of such fellowships for young researchers cannot be overestimated. Publication of the book was supported by the School of Archaeology and the Faculty of Classics, Oxford.

Τέλος, θα ήθελα να ευχαριστήσω ολούς τους `Ελληνες τραγουδιστές, ιδιαίτερα τον Γίαννη Κότσιρα και Αλκίνοο Ιοαννίδη, για την μουσικί τους που βοήθησε πολή τους τελεφταίους μήνες.

Lisa Maria Bendall
Oxford, 2007

CHAPTER 1
ECONOMICS AND MYCENAEAN RELIGION

1.1 RELIGION, ECONOMY AND LINEAR B

The decipherment of Linear B by Michael Ventris in 1952 gave rise to many important discoveries, not least of which was that numerous deities of the classical pantheon were known to speakers of the Mycenaean Greek dialect already during the Aegean Late Bronze Age. Whether Mycenaean and classical deities had the same attributes or were associated with similar mythological cycles is unknown, but many of the theonyms were the same. This revelation was of great significance for the study of early Greek religion, but it was also immediately apparent that the nature of the texts imposed limitations. Even before the decipherment it was recognised that the Linear B documents were exclusively economic and administrative records. There are no 'religious texts' of the type available for many societies of the ancient Near East – no hymns, ritual texts or prescriptions, accounts of myths or belief systems, instructions for appointing cult personnel or for carrying out activities such as divination. In Linear B, deities and religious personnel are mentioned only in instances when the scribes needed to record economic transactions or juridical situations involving them. These included the making of offerings, the gathering of provisions for religious festivals, and the collection and monitoring of taxes and obligations (for instance in the case of land tenure) with which religious figures happened, along with many 'non-religious' figures, to be associated. The difficulty of understanding Mycenaean religion from such exclusively economic and administrative sources has long been recognised,[1] but relatively few attempts have been made to analyse the purely economic information about religion which we do have in the Linear B documents.[2] Such an analysis is essential to establishing a framework for understanding the place of religion in Mycenaean palace society.

The present work addresses just one of the many questions that can be asked about economics of religion in the Mycenaean world, but it is a fundamental one:

> What proportion of the Mycenaean palatial economy was directed towards or invested in support for religion?

This question is essential to understanding the significance of religion in Mycenaean elite society and the extent of palatial involvement in the religious sphere. It also provides a basis for addressing issues such as how many cult personnel and shrines may have been supported and the nature of and mechanisms for such support. Perhaps most importantly, it allows critical insight into the context(s) within which religious matters were recorded by the Linear B scribes. It will emerge that this issue has implications not only for religion but for Mycenaean bureaucratic activity more generally, particularly in terms of what sorts of transactions were normally recorded in Linear B and why.

---

[1] E.g. Chadwick 1976, 85; 1985, 191–2; see also Carlier 1987, 258. One immediate positive effect of the decipherment, however, despite the difficulties, was to challenge the view that 'Mycenaean' and Cretan religious systems could be viewed as a unity (cf. Nilsson 1950).

[2] Two shorter studies which take this approach are Hiller 1982; Lupack 1999. See also Morris 1986, esp. 12–14; Hiller 1981; Carlier 1987; Hägg 1992; Antonelli 1995; Lupack 1997; 1998; Bendall 2001a; 2001b; Bendall 2003, 226. Lupack's unpublished doctoral dissertation (University of Austin, 2002; *non vidi*) also takes this approach.

Our study proceeds by means of a systematic examination of the Linear B documentation for all commodities used for religious purposes of any nature. For each commodity, disbursements for religious purposes are compared with (1) disbursements for other purposes, and (2) overall palatial resources, insofar as these can be estimated.

Chapter 1 addresses three methodological issues that must be dealt with at the outset. The first is how references to 'religion' can be identified in the Linear B records. The second is the problem of 'temple economies', an idea introduced into the literature at an early stage and which has given rise to some confusion. Third, the dates of the Linear B tablets and the degree of comparability within and between sites are considered. Chapter 2 provides a general survey of documents relating to religion; such an overview is necessary because there has been a significant increase in data since publication of the last reviews of the evidence, particularly in relation to feasting and festivals.[3] Chapter 3 sets out the methodology for the study and initiates the investigation with an examination of evidence for perfumed and unperfumed olive oil. The oil records are some of the most complex and extensive in the Linear B corpus and provide the opportunity to define and elaborate categories of document functions referred to in subsequent chapters. Chapters 4, 5 and 6 examine the remaining commodities, grouped mainly by type of product and method of measurement. Chapter 4 deals with two commodities which, like oil, were measured as liquids: honey and wine. Chapter 5 deals with commodities quantified in dry measures: wheat, barley, flour, figs, olives and cyperus. Chapter 6 deals with animals (cattle, sheep, goats and pigs), animal products (cheese, skins, wool), textiles, and commodity ideograms not securely identified. One omission from the list of 'commodities' dealt with may be noted here: men and women. Humans do sometimes appear in contexts, including religious ones, in which whatever their exact juridical status they appear to be 'at the disposal' of the palaces.[4] But, apart from the opacity of these situations, they are complex in ways that differ from palatial treatment of other 'commodities' and, while analysis along the lines set out here would be interesting, it would also risk introducing confusion and is best left aside for present. Finally, Chapter 7 attempts to synthesise the data presented in Chapters 3–6 and to draw conclusions.

The remainder of the present chapter is divided into three sections, each addressing one of the issues noted above: religion in Linear B, 'temple economies', and tablet chronology and comparability.

1.2 'RELIGION' AND 'RELIGION IN LINEAR B'

It is necessary at the outset to consider briefly how evidence for religion can be identified in the Linear B documents.[5] In view of the persistent difficulty of forming a workable cross-

[3] General surveys of Linear B evidence for religion include: Gérard-Rousseau 1968; Adrados 1972; Chadwick 1976, 84–101; 1985; Baumbach 1979b. Murray's fine 1979 dissertation remains the only complete survey, but it is unpublished and now dated, particularly with regard to festivals and feasting and in light of new tablet joins. Killen's section on religion in the forthcoming revised edition of *Documents* will be an essential reference when it appears, and Weilhartner's (2005) new book on offerings now well covers much of the material. Other key studies include: Lejeune 1958c; Olivier 1960; de Fidio 1977; Hiller 1981; 1997; Carlier 1987; Killen 1987b; Hooker 1990. See also Stella 1958; Gérard-Rousseau 1973; Palmer 1983a; 1983b; Szemerenyi 1987. See also Constantinidou 1989. For recent literature on feasting and festivals see Chapter 2, esp. n 57 and n 60.

[4] Lejeune 1958b; *Documents*, 123–4; Killen 1979a; Hooker 1987b; Hiller 1988. Finley (1964) offers some valuable comparative material on the difficulties of applying modern definitions of 'slavery' to various situations in the classical world; see also Gelb 1979.

[5] Similar problems exist with identifying religion in the archaeological record; see e.g. Renfrew 1979; 1981a; 1985; Hägg 1981a; 1985; 1995; 1996; 1998; Wright 1994; 1995a. More generally see Rutkowski 1968; Taylour 1969; 1970; Vermeule 1974; Mylonas 1972; 1977; Van Leuven 1975; 1978; Hägg & Marinatos 1981; Kilian 1988a, 145–9; Rehak 1992; Whittaker 1997; Shelmerdine 2001b, 362–72; Laffineur & Hägg 2001; Hägg 2002.

cultural definition of 'religion' and, indeed, recent doubts over whether the concept of religion as a cross-cultural essence is valid at all,[6] the approach taken here is what might broadly be termed phenomenological. We are concerned with things, places and times. The Linear B documents deal with movements of goods for particular purposes, to particular places or individuals, for specialised use, in the context of specific activities. These phenomena can be identified in the records, and studied, with or without a working definition of 'religion'. In a sense, what we are really addressing here is the economics of offerings, festivals, shrines and cult personnel.

Taking the term as broadly understood in modern contexts, the identification of data relating to 'religion' follows the same methods of procedure laid down for the study of Linear B in general. There are two essential elements to such studies, one linguistic and the other contextual. Linguistic interpretation relies on the etymological method and on the reconstruction of the morphology and phonology of Mycenaean on the basis of Proto-Indo-European and later Greek. Contextual interpretation considers the setting in which a (loosely defined) word is embedded and, crucially, what other words it is associated with. Neither of these elements can be used in isolation. For example, similarity of form (that is phonetic and morphological plausibility within the Linear B spelling rules) would not alone ensure the identification of a Mycenaean word with a word conjectured for or actually attested in later Greek; contextual analysis must also demonstrate a plausibility of meaning arising from the way in which a word is used and the sorts of statements and information with which it is associated. Thus, the interpretation of a particular sign-group as a deity's name requires not only confirmation that the sign-group is a proper noun rather than some other part of speech, such as verb or adjective, but also corroboration from its particular context and associations. Examples of corroborative contexts could be, for instance, where an association with offerings is likely, or where a word appears alongside other sign-groups suggestively similar to names belonging to divinities in later Greek.[7]

The degree and kind of evidence needed to identify a particular sign-group as the name of a divinity is thus no different in principle from that needed to identify any other sign-group in Linear B with a more mundane vocabulary, but the peculiar nature of deities and religious associations can give rise to confusion. In identifying a word such as, for instance, *ka-ko* as /*khalkos*/ 'bronze/copper', all that is meant is that 'bronze/copper' was indicated by the same word in Mycenaean as in Classical Greek. Nothing is necessarily implied about the social, practical or symbolic functions of bronze in the Mycenaean world. Such things may be investigated, but that is a separate venture from the primary identification of the word. With religious terms, however, social function, meaning and significance are so tied up with the words themselves that they may be thought to be implied merely in the primary identification. However, to claim that the sign group *po-se-da-o-ne* (for example) is to be interpreted as the dative of the god's name Poseidon does not entail that the mythical and symbolic associations of the classical deity of the same name need have applied in the Mycenaean setting. What is being stated is rather that, in the barest sense, *po-se-da-o-ne* was used by speakers of Mycenaean Greek to refer to a deity. What exactly they conceived of as 'Poseidon', what his attributes and associations were, are separate questions and ones which lie beyond the scope of the present study.

---

[6] E.g. Asad 1993; Bremmer 1998; Herva 2006; Anderson forthcoming. On 'division into modern epistomological categories' see e.g. Goody & Watt 1968, 54.

[7] A good illustration of the latter is provided by Chadwick (1958a, 70–1), discussing his correspondence with Ventris in the early days of the decipherment: 'One of my early suggestions was the value *nu* for sign no. 55. I had noted that it gave some good words, and in particular the divine name *Enualios* in company with Athena and Poseidon. Ventris wrote back: "I've a rooted objection to finding gods' names on the tablets … but *Athana potnia* [mistress Athena] certainly looks too good to be true."' On the issue in general see also e.g. Carlier 1987, 259–61.

While the Mycenaean religious 'belief system(s)' may remain obscure, the Linear B data offer the opportunity to probe the place of religion in Mycenaean society in purely social, economic and, to some extent, symbolic terms. The present work attempts to do just that.

1.3 'TEMPLE ECONOMIES' AND 'REDISTRIBUTION'

It was observed soon after the decipherment of Linear B that the closest parallels for the Mycenaean economy are not to be found in the modern world or in classical Greece or Rome, but in the economies of the ancient Near East and others which were similarly structured.[8] The validity or otherwise of this claim will be touched on further below but, assuming it to be correct in essence, an initial question to ask would be whether the similarity extended to the structure of and relationship between religious, social and political institutions.[9] Some Near Eastern societies were characterised by the presence of economically powerful temples existing alongside the 'state' sector and interacting with it in various ways. Thus, for the Mycenaean world, we may ask whether there were independently wealthy religious institutions and, if so, what their relationship was to the palaces.[10]

Various pieces of evidence suggest that the Mycenaean religious sphere was not independently constituted. The power of Near Eastern temples is often reflected in their material culture: their large and spatially well-defined architectural complexes, situated in prominent central locations, associated with luxury goods and with independent administrative and storage facilities.[11] In comparison, Mycenaean shrines are small and relatively simple, are often located in marginal areas, and lack evidence for independent administration; Linear B archives are found only in palaces.[12] The primary monumental structures known from the Mycenaean world are the palaces themselves (plus associated structures such as tholos tombs and fortifications), which has led in some cases to the suggestion that, in addition to their administrative and political roles, they were the main cult centres.[13]

Certain aspects of the Linear B evidence may seem to support this idea. References to religion are relatively frequent in the Linear B records, suggesting that religious affairs were of considerable interest to the palatial elite. The extensive documentation of commodities invested in religion and land associated with religious personnel may convey the impression that cult consumed a large proportion of palatial resources. Moreover, some aspects of political structure (such as kingship) and economy (especially industrial manufacture) appear to have been specially associated with religion,[14] leading some scholars to speak in terms of a sacral-political syncretism or even a 'temple economy'.[15] An important aim of the present study is the

---

[8] Finley 1957; also Killen 1985, 273 n 2; Chadwick 1987b; de Fidio 1987; 1992; 2001; Foster 1987. *Documents*[1] drew extensively on Near Eastern parallels although without specifically addressing the overall nature of the economy. For a good summary of various models suggested for the Mycenaean economy see Morris 1986, 8–26.
[9] See Killen 1985, 288–90 n 50.
[10] Carlier 1987; Hägg 1995; Lupack 1999.
[11] E.g. Postgate 1994, 109–36 for early Mesopotamia. However, one cannot generalise this statement to all periods and areas of the ancient Near East; MBA temples in Syria for instance were small and thus more comparable to the Mycenaean examples. I am grateful to S. Dalley for discussion on this point.
[12] E.g. Carlier 1987, 256 (but note his caveat that the absence of major built structures need not preclude the possible existence of a religious organisation); Wright 1991 (noting a special association of religion with palaces); 1994, 61–2; Bendall 2004, 128; Hamilakis & Konsolaki 2004, 146. The significance of archives being found only in palaces was early emphasised by Finley (1957, 134).
[13] E.g. Thomas 1976, 110; cf. Wright 1994, 59–60, 76; also 1991.
[14] Carlier 1984; 1990; Killen 1985, 289; Palaima 1995a.
[15] The main proponent of the idea was L.R. Palmer, who suggested that 'temple economy' might be a more apt description for the Mycenaean situation than 'palace' or 'state economy' (Palmer 1963, 95, 137, 221, 230, 278, 280, 482). The idea is mentioned on the pages cited, but nowhere in the book is there a development of the argument or any substantive discussion of the issue. For a good short summary of Palmer's views see Morris 1986,

investigation of such claims. In the absence of a comprehensive review of the evidence it has been difficult to evaluate suggestions and to develop adequate frameworks for discussion. It will be argued here that such models are of questionable applicability to the Aegean Late Bronze Age and that it may be misleading to speak of the Mycenaean situation in terms of a syncretism between the political and religious spheres, much less a 'temple economy'. Rather, the Mycenaean case may represent an altogether different type of situation which should be understood in its own terms.

In order to clear the ground for a different perspective, it is useful to revisit the issue of 'temple economies' as it arose in its original context in scholarship dealing with southern Mesopotamia. The idea that an entire economy might have been driven by religious institutions who owned all or the majority of the land and resources has long since been discarded in its source area, yet still appears from time to time in Aegean studies, partly because the relationship between political and religious institutions remains a valid subject of inquiry, and partly because the issue is sometimes conflated with the concept of 'redistribution', to which we return below. The need to revisit the matter may seem odd to scholars of ancient Near Eastern civilisations but the debate is less well known in literature on the prehistoric Aegean and it is important to be absolutely clear.

The concept of a 'temple economy' was based on an initial confusion, the essence of which was that a single archive from the temple bureaucracy of the deity *Bau* of Lagash in Sumer dating to ca 2500 BC had been elevated to the status of a template for the whole of the pre-Sargonic economy. A useful discussion of critiques of the idea and the related concept of 'state economy' was provided by Gelb.[16] As he noted, the *Bau* archive was itself inherently complex and its interpretation was complicated by the fact that it was not retrieved through proper excavation but was reconstructed through the examination of over 1800 published and unpublished texts scattered throughout various museums. The difficulty was not so much with the basic analysis of the 'Household of *Bau*', but with the idea that this one archive described everything happening in Lagash, or – worse – in the whole of Sumer, at the time.[17]

Gelb also challenged the concept of 'state economy', the idea that states owned and controlled all land and sources of economic production. The problem here was rooted in questions about land tenure and ownership. On the basis primarily of the absence of sale contracts for private land in the Ur III period, it was held that the supposed 'temple economy' gave way to a 'state economy' at that time. As Gelb describes the argument: 'since there are no contracts ... land could not be sold; and since land could not be sold, ergo, it must have belonged to the state'.[18] Again, a particular instance was taken to describe an entire economy. In dissent, Gelb pointed both to the dangers of arguing *ex silentio* and to finds from Nippur which suggested that privately owned land did exist. He suggested that the absence of sale contracts might be explained by a prohibition on the sale of land at the time, rather than by exclusive state ownership.[19]

Gelb summarised his view and concluded with a number of questions, as follows.[20]

12–14. Tegyey (1984) also argued for a 'temple economy'. Note that even if this idea is rejected one may still speak of an 'economy of the sacred' (e.g. Bintliff 1977, 145–70; Horden & Purcell 2000, 423–38).

[16] Gelb 1969; see Snell 1997, 148–9, for a short, recent summary. Important earlier discussions include Diakonoff 1954; 1959; Kramer 1963, 75–7.

[17] Gelb 1969, 140.

[18] Gelb 1969, 147.

[19] Gelb 1969, 148. Note that in the suggestion of a prohibition on land sale there could be an implication of state economic *power*, even without straightforward ownership. Yet reasons could also have been social (Postgate 1994, 183) or – importantly – due to biases in the surviving records (e.g. Van de Mieroop 1997; 2000, 42), a point we return to in Chapter 7.

[20] Gelb 1969, 154.

> As I see it, three types of land-tenure economies co-existed side by side from the beginning of Mesopotamian history to the end of the Ur III period, as they doubtless existed throughout all subsequent periods. They are: state economy, temple economy, and private economy. There is no longer any question of one type of economy being exclusively dominant in one given period ...
>
> The questions which remain to be answered are:
> 1) The relative size of the holdings by the state, temple, and private owners in different periods and areas.
> 2) The relation between the state and the temple in respect to their holdings.
> 3) The relation between the state (crown) holdings and the private holdings of the king and his family.
> 4) The private-family as against the private-individual ownership of land.
> 5) The degree of control of the state and/or temple over the privately owned land.

Although couched in terms of land ownership and tenure, questions of this nature can be (and have been) usefully generalised to other areas of the economy. It may be loosely stated that something along the lines of co-existing state, temple and private 'economies' or spheres of economic activity is now the general consensus in Near Eastern scholarship, although issues such as the relative extent and nature of the interactions between the various sectors in different times and at different places remain debated.[21]

The general question is bound up – and sometimes conflated – with Polanyi's analysis of ancient economies which differentiated them in key ways from modern economies, especially 'capitalist' and 'market' economies.[22] Polanyi proposed 'reciprocity' and 'redistribution' as alternative models to 'markets', and argued that, applied to the ancient world, such models can better explain matters such as movement of goods through long-distance trade and the generation of surplus sufficient to support specialised craft-workers. Polanyi's arguments against the very *existence* of ancient markets have been successfully challenged on various grounds,[23] but his models in general (especially in their revised versions) remain useful in many ways.[24] Not least, they highlight a differentiation observed also by Finley that there was not one single model for 'the ancient economy', but a multiplicity of different forms operating at different times in different places.[25] It was Finley who first, building on Ventris and Chadwick's publication of *Documents* in 1956, articulated the idea that the Mycenaean economy is best characterised as 'redistributive'.[26] To paraphrase Polanyi, in 'redistributive' or 'command' economies goods and commodities circulated (were 'redistributed') through the authority (at the 'command') of a central body which was normally the dominant political power.[27] An important modification to the model was later made by Earle, who noted that by the time of his writing the term 'redistributive economy' had come to be used of so many different types of situations that it was in danger of losing its usefulness.[28] He suggested a number of sub-groupings for 'redistributive economies', including one of particular relevance here, 'mobilisation', which he defined as 'the recruitment of goods and services for the benefit of a group not coterminous with the contributing members'.[29] He noted that while some forms

---

[21] E.g. Diakonoff 1959; 1974; Kramer 1963, 74–8 esp. 75; Foster 1987; Maisels 1990, 269; Postgate 1994, 109, 125, 191; Baines & Yoffee 1998, 225–33 (see 227 for further references); Van de Mieroop 2000, 42; 2004.
[22] Polanyi 1957.
[23] See e.g. Snell 1997, 150–1 for summary and bibliography.
[24] See e.g. Liverani 2001, 5–9; de Fidio 2001, esp. 16–17; Chase-Dunn & Hall 1997, 23–4, 29–35. It is agreed that the models must not be 'applied too rigidly' (de Fidio 2001, 17), and that such analytical tools may be used 'without necessarily accepting many presuppositions and implications of Polanyi's own views' (Liverani 2001, 5).
[25] Finley 1985, 27–9, esp. 28.
[26] Finley 1957; 1985, 28–9; see also Killen 1985, 241–2, 274 n 4. De Fidio (1992; 2001, esp. 15 n 3) makes some useful comments about the extent of Polanyi's influence on Finley's work which, as she notes, should not be over-exaggerated.
[27] Polanyi 1957, 250.
[28] Earle 1977, esp. 214–17; see also Morris 1986, 29–30.
[29] Earle 1977, 215.

of 'redistribution' may be 'widely represented at all levels of social complexity', 'mobilisation' is 'more limited in its function and in its distribution' and is associated with ranked and stratified societies.[30] His citation of a passage by Dalton helps further to define the notion and is worth reproducing here:[31]

> the channelling upwards [mobilization] of goods or services to socially determined allocative centres (usually king, chief, or priest), who then redistribute to either their subordinates at large by providing community services, or in specific allotments to individuals in accordance with their political, religious, or military status.

It is this form of 'redistribution' which best characterises the Mycenaean palace economy, a convenient description being, to paraphrase Killen, 'the mobilisation of resources upwards for the benefit of a dominant elite'.[32] The mechanism was extractive and biased towards the palaces, benefits for other areas of society being incidental to elite interests which centred on the enhancement of power and prestige through political, military and economic control and manipulation.[33]

In Aegean studies, discussions sometimes suffer from lack of clarity about which models are used and how they are to be understood. For instance, in a recent article by Parkinson, there is a conflation of 'redistributive' with 'state' or 'temple economies' as originally debated for the Near East.[34] He cites the following passage by Postgate, speaking of ancient Mesopotamian temples.[35]

> Until the 1950's the government of the early [Near Eastern] city was almost universally characterized as a 'theocracy', and cuneiform scholars wrote of the 'temple-city'. Claims were even made that at Lagas the temple owned all the land and employed the entire population … This extreme view is now discredited. We cannot any longer maintain that because the temples collected commodities and distributed them to its dependents the entire economy operated through 'redistribution', or that the priests controlled all agricultural and commercial activity.

Parkinson concludes from this that:[36]

> Hence, it is misleading to characterize even ancient Near Eastern economies as being based upon the ill-defined concept of 'redistribution', much less to base the interpretation of Mycenaean economics upon their possible similarities to these much larger and structurally different institutions.

Yet it is important to recognise that Postgate refers specifically to the debate concerning the House of *Bau* archive (note his mention of Lagash) and the understanding that the economic order witnessed in that archive (i.e. 'redistribution') cannot be generalised to the *whole* of the economy. This is not the same as maintaining that 'redistribution' does not remain a useful concept. As Gelb and others argued, the temples and states were major players but they were not exclusive wielders of economic control and they did not own everything. However, the concept of 'redistribution' *per se* may still be usefully applied to the administrative mechanisms of *some* temples, states and other public bodies. As emphasised above, the issue is not whether 'command economies' existed, but their nature, extent and relationship with other elements.

---

[30] Earle 1977, 216.
[31] Earle 1977, 216, citing Dalton 1967, 153.
[32] Killen 1985, 251–5, 283–4. On 'mobilisation' in regard to the Mycenaean economy see also e.g. de Fidio 1982; 1987; 1992; 2001; Halstead 1992a; 1999c; Palaima 2001; 2003a.
[33] For the Incan Empire as similarly non-benevolent see Earle & D'Altroy 1982, 271; D'Altroy & Earle 1985, 188–90; see also LeVine & Earle 1992. But also note Halstead & O'Shea 1982 on famine relief.
[34] Parkinson 1999, 74–5. For criticism of Parkinson's views see Killen 1999d.
[35] Parkinson 1999, 74, citing Postgate 1992, 109.
[36] Parkinson 1999, 74.

It is crucial that, in speaking of an 'Asiatic economy', as Killen does in his classic account of the Mycenaean economy,[37] the reference is to a Gelb-type understanding, not to the single-player models which Gelb and other scholars rejected (although it is agreed that the term 'Asiatic economy' is out-moded and should be abandoned[38]). One factor that has contributed to the polarisation of debate in the Aegean is that it does seem that the Mycenaean 'palaces' *were* the 'major players' at the time(s) of the Linear B administrations, so that the situation lay near one end of the possible spectrum of extent of economic power. This is thought to be the case not because of an unthinking reliance on monolithic views of 'state economies', nor *via* an argument from silence based on the lack of evidence for 'private' ownership[39] (although such evidence is indeed virtually absent). Rather, positive evidence suggests that palatial activity in some areas of the economy was so extensive that there was little room for significant activity originating in areas of society unconnected with the palaces. For example, the Linear B documentation at Knossos relating to flocks of sheep kept for wool records some 80,000–100,000 animals in central Crete.[40] Since historical figures for the sheep population of the island are around 500,000,[41] the numbers for central Crete in Linear B are likely to represent a substantial proportion of all the sheep in the region.[42] This is to argue not that the palace controlled all sheep on the island, but that it was likely to have been the most prominent and important holder at the time.

The issue relates of course to the long-standing divide between 'formalist' and 'substantivist' views of ancient economies.[43] It would be pointless to provide here yet another review of this drawn-out and rather stale debate; the intention is only to achieve improved clarity about what 'temple economy' might mean (or not mean) and to distinguish this notion from 'redistribution', which is commonly agreed to remain a useful model for the internal workings of the Mycenaean palace economies as witnessed in the Linear B documents. A classic example of Linear B redistribution is seen in the textile industry as elucidated by Killen. The records indicate that the palace at Knossos held the means of production of raw materials (wool),[44] supervised the movement of these materials to weaving workshops and sometimes to further specialised 'finishing' workshops under the so-called *ta-ra-si-ja* system (in which equal weights of raw materials were issued and finished products were received back),[45] and oversaw the subsistence of craft-workers (some, but not all, full-time) through the issue of monthly rations.[46] The word *internal* should probably be emphasised. It may be accepted that 'external' movements of goods, such as long-distance trade, were differently organised,[47] and that, as is recognised in scholarship on the Near East, there is no need to believe that the palaces

[37] Killen 1985, 242; but note also his caveats e.g. 255, 283–4, 288–9.

[38] As Killen does in his revised version of the article (Killen forthcoming[c]); I am grateful for access to a copy before publication. On abandoning the term see also e.g. Maisels 1990, 268–9; Trigger 2003, 51–2, 377; for the origin of the term see e.g. Gelb 1979; Morris 1986, 25–6.

[39] As suggested by e.g. Sjöberg 1995, 26.

[40] For derivation of the figures and references see Section 6.2.2.1.

[41] Killen 1964, 5 n 23.

[42] Note, however, Halstead's argument (1999a), elaborating a suggestion by Killen (1993), that the shepherds were required to make good losses from palace flocks at the expense of their own, which would imply the existence of large non-palatial flocks. However, the historical figures for the sheep population should be kept in mind unless one wishes to argue (which could be done) that the Mycenaean sheep population was larger than in subsequent periods.

[43] The literature is extensive; see e.g. Earle 2002, 1–8 for a brief overview and further references in n 48 below. It might be suggested that the introduction of the terms 'primitive' or 'primitivist' in association with the 'substantivist' view was particularly unfortunate since it imposed an unnecessary evolutionist framework which obscures some of the more useful aspects of the theories. Economies may be unlike 'modern' economies, but still be highly complex: being *different* should not imply being 'primitive'.

[44] Killen 1964; 1993.

[45] Esp. Killen 1979b; 1984a; 1985; 2001a.

[46] Chadwick 1988.

[47] E.g. Sherratt & Sherratt 1991; Halstead 1999c.

controlled and managed *all* means of production nor that they 'owned' everything.[48]

In connection with this final point, the extent to which the Linear B documentation is biased towards the palatial perspective may be reiterated, but this issue of visibility should not be conflated with the issue of socio-political control. While it is likely that the majority of the population in a Mycenaean 'polity' (however loosely defined) lived through subsistence agriculture,[49] the social, political and economic subordination of this sector to the palaces is indicated by factors such as its subjection to interference and taxation, including a very onerous form of 'taxation', corvée labour.[50] Since the wider populations constituted the majority elements in terms of numbers, it might be said that the main economic activity in the polities was *not* redistributive (whatever its character), but again an argument that the *dominant* model was state-organised redistribution need not be understood in an extreme way as holding that the palaces owned, controlled and managed *all* production.[51]

The Mycenaean economy is one of the areas of study that Gelb may have had in mind when he commented as follows:[52]

> The temple and/or state economy theories have in the past few years spread beyond narrow Assyriological circles into secondary and tertiary sources to the extent that it is impossible to find a book on ancient history, scholarly or popular, which does not subscribe to these theories.

As discussed above, questions about the interaction between the economic and religious spheres cannot be properly framed in light of such notions and a comprehensive investigation of the material is needed from a different perspective, but without discarding the useful concept of 'redistribution' as applied to the internal workings of the Mycenaean palace economy. Such an undertaking is attempted in the present study.

---

[48] Aspects of non-palatial organisation of the economy have become a focus in recent years, particularly with regard to the extent to which 'markets' were important. For the Near East see e.g. Monroe 2000; Goddeeris 2002; Bell 2005. For the Aegean specifically see e.g. Morris 1986; 1987; Halstead 1992a; and, less successfully, Sjöberg 1995, 19–20, 27 (attempting to interject modern concepts of 'rational economic behaviour' into the debate; the idea that utility theory is an accurate and adequate tool for explaining human behaviour has been fundamentally challenged even in modern economic contexts; see e.g. Kahneman & Tversky 1979; McCabe *et al.* 2001); Galaty & Parkinson 1999. It may be noted that the search for 'markets' is as much bound up with 'modern' concerns as were (as is often pointed out) Polanyi's own (e.g. Mann 1986, 60–2; Sherratt & Sherratt 1991, 352; Snell 1997, 150; Earle 2002, 7–8; Van de Mieroop, 2004, 56–7), and can tend to be overstated as well as making questionable assumptions such as that 'private' may be equated with 'market' (see e.g. Van de Mieroop's review [2005] of Goddeeris 2002). The bibliography on 'redistribution' vs. 'markets' is very extensive; for a recent bibliographical essay see Horden & Purcell 2000, 606–7 (see also above, n 43).

[49] But without assuming a 'timeless Mediterranean subsistence economy'; see e.g. Halstead 1987; 1989; 2005; Horden & Purcell 2000, 270–8, with 590–2 (another useful bibliographical essay); Forbes 2002; Kristiansen & Larsson 2005, 32–3.

[50] Although this need not mean that control in all cases was territorially homogeneous nor tightly bureaucratically structured in every region of a given polity (Driessen 2001a, esp. 111–12). On corvée in Linear B see e.g. Hiller, 1988; Bendall 2003, 206; Killen 2006b; Deger-Jalkotzy forthcoming.

[51] Killen 1985, 255–6. Note Morris's relevant observation (1986, 26) that 'the economic activities carried out and administered by the palace were only those necessary to maintain political control of the kingdom, and that the production and distribution of goods consumed by the majority of the people in the kingdom took place at local and regional levels'. A good example of production outside the palaces is the simple textile **146*, which was made in regional settlements and obtained by the palaces through taxation (see Section 6.4.1).

[52] Gelb 1969, 137.

1.4 COMPARABILITY AND CHRONOLOGY OF THE LINEAR B RECORDS

Finally, we should consider the comparability and dates of the Linear B records. All sites which have yielded Linear B tablets so far – Knossos, Pylos, Mycenae, Tiryns, Thebes and Chania – have documents which in one way or another deal with the religious sphere, with the possible exception of Tiryns, probably due merely to the paucity of tablets from this site.[53] The majority of evidence comes from Knossos and Pylos, which thus inevitably form the focus of our study. Data from other sites are included where available; in particular, there is important new evidence relating to religion at Thebes.

A well-known difficulty in comparing Linear B records from different sites is that the documents (1) were created in different political, historical and/or administrative circumstances, and (2) belong to different periods.[54] To some extent, these circumstances do not present significant difficulties for the present study because data from each site are analysed separately in the first instance. The next step, bringing the evidence together, is done in an explicitly comparative framework which makes no *assumptions* about potential similarities or differences.[55]

The major difficulty faced here is where records may come from different chronological periods at the *same* site. As is well known, the clay documents come from destruction layers, their preservation due to their being baked hard by the fires; they were intended as temporary records and were kept only for short periods of time, normally less than a year, often much less.[56]

At Pylos, the situation is relatively unproblematic because the tablets are almost all from the same destruction horizon, dated to the LH III B/III C transition.[57] A very few may be earlier, but none of these happens to be involved in the present study.[58] Documents at Thebes and Mycenae are not all of the same dates, but those which concern us belong to single deposits and are either contemporary with each other or do not involve commodities also found in non-contemporary deposits. At Thebes, the tablets from the Arsenal and the new tablets from Odos Pelopidou belong to the end of LH III B2,[59] as do the Of tablets.[60] The sixty sealings (fifty-six inscribed) from Odos Oidipodos, near one of the city gates, date to LH III B1.[61] At Mycenae, the tablets from the West House Group date to mid-LH III B,[62] while those from the Citadel

---

[53] There are just twenty-seven tablets from Tiryns, all fairly fragmentary. TI Uh 12 may conceivably be a festival rations record (see Section 2.3.3.5).

[54] E.g. *Scribes RCT*, 217–32; Driessen 2001b; Palaima 2001, 153.

[55] Comparing and contrasting data from different sites has a healthy tradition in Linear B studies, although similarities in general seem to be stronger than differences. The extent to which documents from different sites are similar is not an assumption (as Galaty and Parkinson [1999, 4] seem to imply) but rather came as a great surprise when the Pylos tablets were discovered. Explicitly comparative studies include Olivier 1984; Hooker 1987a; Tegyey 1987; Shelmerdine 1988; Killen 1993; Halstead 1990–1991. See *Documents*, 75 for comments on the surprising uniformity of the dialect; also Thompson 1996–1997; 1997. For a fascinating diachronic study comparing administration at Knossos from ancient to modern times see Bennet 1990.

[56] E.g. *Documents*, 114; Chadwick 1976, 18, 28; Killen 1984b; Bennet 1988b.

[57] *PoN* I, 419, 421. Popham (1991) proposed an earlier destruction with later reoccupation, but for a refutation of this view see Mountjoy 1997; Shelmerdine 2001b, 373 with n 277, 381 with n 325.

[58] *Scribes Pylos*, 165. The proposed earlier tablets were Ae 995, Ua [now La] 994, Xa 1419, Xa 1420, Xn 1449. However 1449 now joins Vn 1339, a tablet from the main group (Melena 1996–1997a, 166). Note Xa 1419 includes the sign-group *di-wo-nu-so*[, but the context is insufficient to determine whether it is here a theonym or a man's name (for a clear attestation of Dionysos as a theonym see Section 4.2.2).

[59] *Thèbes* I, 14; *Thèbes* III, 12–13.

[60] *Thèbes* III, 11.

[61] *Thèbes* III, 11–12.

[62] *MT* II, 5; *MT* III, 32

House come from the end of LH III B.[63] New excavations at Petsas's house have yielded tablets from LH III A2, the earliest so far found on the Greek mainland, but these do not relate to religion.[64] The single relevant tablet from Chania came from destruction debris probably dating to the end of LM III B1.[65]

The main problem is Knossos, where the question of the date(s) of the tablets has been the subject of a long-standing and well-known debate.[66] J.-P. Olivier's classic study of the Linear B scribal hands in the 1960s made a central contribution to resolving the related issue of the 'unity of the archives', the idea that all Linear B tablet deposits were contemporary. As Olivier demonstrated, some are and some are not. He identified a number of deposits which must have been contemporary with each other since they include tablets written by scribes who also wrote tablets found in other areas.[67] These he summarised as follows:[68]

1. Tablets from the West Magazines and Long Corridor [F], the Corridor of the House Tablets [E5] and the Gallery of Jewel Fresco [G1] are contemporary.
2. This group has connections with the Area of the Bull Relief [I1–I2–I3] (the North Entrance Passage area) and the East-West Corridor [J1] in the East Wing.
3. The East Wing [J] deposits as a whole have no direct connection with the tablets from the Area of the Bull Relief [I1–I2–I3], but are linked through the West Magazines [F] and the South-West Area [B].
4. The South-West Area [B] is connected with the East Wing [J], the West Magazines [F] and the Area of the Bull Relief [I1–I2–I3].

In effect, what this argues is that the *main* tablet deposits at the palace are contemporary.[69] Olivier also listed a number of deposits which *may* be contemporary, plus some which are probably or certainly not.[70] Among those about which there is some doubt are three deposits of particular relevance here, the Room of the Chariot Tablets [C], the Room of the Column Bases [E1], and the Clay Chest [A]. These require a brief further discussion.

The Room of the Chariot Tablets [C] (RCT hereafter) was connected with other deposits only through a single tablet, Fp 48, and Olivier rightly noted that evidence for a link with the main groups was thus not strong.[71] The room has now been the focus of two comprehensive studies by Driessen.[72] It had always been apparent that the RCT tablets differed palaeographically from those in all other areas,[73] leading Chadwick to question even whether they were proper

---

[63] *MT* III, 38.
[64] Iakovides 2000, 65–6; Shelton 2002–2003; see also Bartoněk 2003, 531–2.
[65] Hallager *et al.* 1992, 61–70, esp. 67.
[66] Boardman & Palmer 1963. See Driessen 1990, 5–6 for a summary of the argument with references.
[67] The necessary conditions for Olivier to reach his conclusions were rigorously applied. For instance, a single tablet by a single scribe would be considered insufficient evidence to link deposits; rather groups of tablets and multiple linkages were sought (*Scribes Cnossos*, esp. 111–14).
[68] *Scribes Cnossos*, 115–16. The letters in brackets refer to Olivier's findspot references (*Scribes Cnossos*, 21–4). The text given here is a translation and paraphrase of Olivier's summary with the findspot names added for clarity; it is not a direct quote. Note some important modifications to Olivier's findspots (but not altering the substance of the present passage) have been made by Firth in recent years (1996–1997; 2000–2001a).
[69] Which is not the same as arguing that *all* are contemporary, on which see e.g. Driessen 1990, 7. It should be mentioned that Driessen (1999, 214–20) casts some doubt on the contemporaneity of the NEP in a preliminary study, but also notes (pp. 220–3) that features of administrative processing may be responsible for the phenomena he observes. It is regarded here as unlikely that the NEP tablets will turn out to be earlier. See also Firth 2000–2001a, 220–6.
[70] *Scribes Cnossos*, 116–17 (for possible contemporary deposits), 117–21 (for deposits probably not contemporary).
[71] *Scribes Cnossos*, 116–17.
[72] Driessen 1990; *Scribes RCT*; see also Driessen 1997.
[73] *Scribes Cnossos*, 66–8.

records at all rather than, for instance, practice exercises for a scribal school.[74] However, as Driessen has shown, the most plausible explanation for the peculiarities and isolation of the RCT documents is that they belong to an earlier period than the other tablets.[75] His proposed LM II date is not universally agreed,[76] but the view that the records are not contemporary with other deposits is widely accepted,[77] and is followed here. The implication of this for the present study is that the RCT tablets should be treated separately from the other Knossos tablets, and this is done throughout.[78]

On the other hand, it is not accepted here that the tablets from the Room of the Column Bases [E1] (RCB hereafter) are not contemporary, a possibility also raised by Driessen.[79] Olivier rightly left a question mark over their contemporaneity with other deposits since the only link was a possible find of a tablet by h. 141, the scribe of the Fh tablets, in Magazine IV [F3].[80] However, the Fh tablets fit in well with the organisation of the 'Department of Perfumery and Offerings' (see Section 3.2.3.1), which was located in this part of the palace, and their findspot may make sense in the context of likely circulation patterns in this department.[81] Fuller study of the area would be desirable, but for the time being there is sufficient reason to take these tablets as contemporary and we proceed on this basis.

The Clay Chest [A] is more problematic. Links with hands of other areas are tenuous. Hand 138 *may* have written a tablet (X 453) coming from Magazine IV [F3]; and h. 139, who wrote the Fs series, *may* be the same scribe as h. 140 who was active with regard to tablets found in the north end of the Long Corridor [F18] and the Gallery of Jewel Fresco [G1].[82] Certainty is impossible, but for present purposes we assume contemporaneity rather than further over-complicating the analysis. The Clay Chest documents are listed in separate tables in any case, so the calculations could easily be redone taking them apart; the overall conclusions of the present study would not be affected.

Finally, while the date of the main deposits of Knossos tablets is still debated, most scholars

---

[74] Chadwick 1968a, 19–21.

[75] See *Scribes RCT*, 15–17 for discussion, with n 36–8 for further references. The one tablet linking the RCT with other deposits, Fp 48, almost certainly came instead from the Clay Chest [A] and was mixed up with the RCT records during excavation and storage (both deposits were excavated on the same day); see Section 3.2.3.3, notes to Table 3-4, *s.v.* Fp(1) 48 for further discussion and references.

[76] Driessen 1990, 117, 130; *Scribes RCT*, 10, 12–13 (with n 15 addressing dissenting views), 218–19. *Contra* see e.g. Popham 1993, esp. 177.

[77] E.g. Godart 1992, 257; Firth 2000–2001a, 154–5.

[78] For lists of tablets from the RCT see *Scribes RCT*, 270–87 and Firth 2000–2001a, 190–1.

[79] Driessen 1990, esp. 70; 1997, 120; 1999, 214; 2001a, 97–8. With regard to the last study, note that Driessen's observations (pp. 102–3) about the TN distribution of the RCB tablets would be consistent with, but need not compel, an earlier date. See also Firth 2000–2001a, esp. 204–5.

[80] *Scribes Cnossos*, 116.

[81] As argued by Foster 1977a. Note that the same man, *ku-pi-ri-jo*, appears in tablets from both areas (Fh, Ga, Gg); see Section 3.2.3.5. I am undertaking a new study of the area, incorporating architectural considerations, Linear B, and Firth's and Driessen's work on findspots. In all likelihood, the Fh tablets fill an important niche in the operations of this part of the palace. As suggested by E. Hallager (1977, 71), they were probably found where they were because the RCB is where the entrance to the West Magazines, one place where oil was kept, was located. It would be undesirable to work on (or store tablets in) the dark magazines, so a writing place with more light just outside the entrance would make sense. At the same time, scribes working in the same department (i.e. the Department of Perfumery and Offerings) but with commodities better stored on a (less damp?) upper floor, such as spices and textiles, seem to have been operating in a nearby 'entrance area' to such storerooms, at the top of the staircase leading from the Central Court, so that many of their tablets fell from the upper floor into the Gallery of Jewel Fresco [G1]. See also recently Duermeijer (2006) who discusses part of the same conclusion, but without reference to the wider context of this department.

[82] See *Scribes Cnossos*, 116, also 83–5. But note Fs 3, which is from the Clay Chest but not by h. 139, has some 'graphic affinities' with the Fh tablets of h. 141 (*Scribes Cnossos*, 86).

accept an ascription to early LM III A2, ca 1375 BC.[83] It is worth noting that the methodology followed here means that the central argument would not be affected whatever the correct date since the essential issue is contemporaneity.

1.5 CONCLUSION

The present chapter has set out the central aims of the study – assessment of the extent of resources dedicated to religion by the Mycenaean palaces – and addressed three methodological issues.

First, the difficulty of offering a workable cross-cultural definition of 'religion' was noted, and it was maintained that despite the interpretative difficulties deities' names, cult personnel and other such relevant references can be identified in the Linear B records through following the same procedures set out for the interpretation of more 'mundane' vocabulary. Second, the concept of 'temple economies' was discussed as it arose in Near Eastern scholarship, and an effort was made to distinguish 'temple economy' from the broader concept of 'redistribution' as well as to note some nuancing of Polanyi's original model in subsequent critiques and modifications.

Finally, it was observed that references to religion occur at nearly all sites which have yielded Linear B tablets and the dates of the various deposits of tablets was discussed. It was emphasised that in the present study tablets from a single site are evaluated separately in the first instance and data from different sites are brought together within an explicitly comparative framework. With regard to intra-site analysis, only the Knossos tablets pose a significant problem, dealt with here through considering the RCT tablets separately. Other deposits are taken in tandem, even though it is recognised that a few of these *may* be non-contemporary, a procedure justified on the grounds that so few documents are involved that the overall analysis is unlikely to be affected.

The next chapter undertakes the necessary task of setting out the main categories of Linear B records relating to religion. Following this data survey, Chapter 3 initiates the central analysis.

[83] Recently, see Preston 2004, 323, with background references to the debate; also Driessen 1990, 121; *Scribes RCT*, 10, 220–1; Hatzaki 2004.

CHAPTER 2
LINEAR B DOCUMENTS RELATING TO RELIGION

2.1 ECONOMIC SUPPORT FOR RELIGION IN LINEAR B

The Linear B documents indicate that Mycenaean palaces provided economic support for cult in a variety of ways, which can be summarised as follows:

1. Presentations of offerings, including:
   - regular monthly gifts
   - occasional gifts of exceptional value
   - offerings on the occasions of festivals
2. Organisation of banquets and festivals, including:
   - contributions of foodstuffs and other supplies
   - secondment of slaves and support personnel
   - provision of rations to personnel and participants during the festivities
3. Regular support for deities and cult personnel through 'ordinary' palatial maintenance systems, such as:
   - disbursement of rations (not well attested)
   - allocation of plots of tenured land
   - dedication of produce from specially allocated flocks and workshops

This chapter presents an overview of the various types of documents involved. It is not intended as a comprehensive survey of Linear B documents relating to religion, but is needed both because until recently no up-to-date account existed in print,[1] and because a framework is needed for the categorisation of tablets in subsequent chapters. The documents can be grouped into four main categories: (1) offerings records, (2) banqueting records, (3) land tenure records, and (4) records dealing with 'Collectors' (the last two being subsumed under 'palatial maintenance systems' above). The categories are intended as heuristic rather than absolute; they are a useful guide so long as they are not over-rigidly applied. There are numerous cases where a tablet may belong to more than one category; for example, Un 718 is classed here as both a 'land tenure' and a 'banqueting' record (see below). There are also cases where categories shade into one another conceptually. Many of the 'offerings records', for instance, deal with offerings made on the occasions of banquets or festivals,[2] so might in a sense be called 'banqueting records'. Similarly, animals to be sacrificed at festivals, recorded on what are here called 'banqueting records', were in a very real sense 'offerings', especially where associated with particular divinities.[3] However, a clearer sense is gained of the nature of, for example, PY Fr 343, which records an offering of perfumed oil to Poseidon on the occasion of a festival, by referring to it an 'offering record' than as a 'banqueting' or 'festival record'. In the same way, while lists of foodstuffs for feasts may include 'offerings', the central purpose of such lists was to record goods for human consumption, including sacrificial victims, at state-organised banquets.[4]

---

[1] See Chapter 1 n 3 for references.

[2] Bendall 1998–1999.

[3] E.g. Carlier (1987, 261) lists as 'offerings': libations, animals or humans for sacrifice, and objects consecrated to divinities.

[4] Weilhartner (2005) instead separates blood and bloodless offerings, a distinction with an eminent scholarly pedigree, but not amenable to the aims of the present study (nor necessarily reflecting Mycenaean attitudes).

It should be noted that 'banqueting' is used throughout as a shorthand for 'banqueting and festivals'. Most festivals would likely have included banquets (although we cannot be certain), but it is improbable that banquets took place only on the occasions of festivals. In this connection, it should also be noted that not all banquets were necessarily 'religious' in nature (whether or not associated with a festival), although it may well be that every killing of an animal involved ritual activity. The question is at issue even for the much better documented classical Greek world,[5] and the data are insufficient to determine what Mycenaean attitudes would have been (although we can take as virtually certain that they would not have drawn distinctions along the modern lines of 'religious' vs. 'secular').[6] For present purposes, we treat all records that fall into the 'banqueting' category as relating to the religious sphere, despite an awareness that this is problematic and might be inappropriate for a different sort of study. This approach is adopted here because many of the 'banqueting' records clearly *do* relate to religious sacrifice (for instance, where theonyms appear; see Section 2.3.2.1 below) and separating out those which are uncertain (there are none clearly *non*-religious) would create small sub-categories of data with limited usefulness for the present project.[7] At each stage, what is done should be sufficiently transparent that if one or another of the particular determinations is not agreed, the relevant tablet(s) might be extracted and the figures recalculated. It will be appreciated that no changes to the *overall* patterns and conclusions would thereby be produced.

The four categories of documents are discussed in turn. The primary focus in each case is the identification of which tablets may be so described (but in light of caveats above); the overall aim is to give a general sense of what Linear B documents of each category look like. More coverage is given where better clarity is achieved through discussing tablets as a group rather than spread out over a number of chapters, given the arrangement of our study by commodity types. Offerings records rarely include more than one type of commodity and are best understood set alongside other non-offerings records dealing with the same commodity. Treatment of such records in the present chapter is therefore brief. Banqueting records, on the other hand, almost invariably record more than one type of commodity, often many more. Rather than introducing such tablets haphazardly, according to the first commodity they happen to record that is encountered in our study, it is best to deal with them here as a group. Land tenure records are also discussed as a group, but our treatment is deliberately brief. The subject is of great importance for 'economics of religion' but, apart from the fact that the majority of evidence derives from a single site (Pylos) and cannot necessarily be extended to the rest of the Mycenaean world, the documents have been well covered elsewhere and a summary of some main conclusions is all that is required. The main issue which concerns us for present purposes is whether or not a document does relate to land tenure involving a religious aspect. The same is the case for documents involving 'Collectors'.

It will be clear that much more could be said about all of the categories of records than is done in this book; in general, our discussion is confined to identification of the type of record. Other aspects of these documents are important and the issues raised highly interesting, but the purpose of this study is not to cover every aspect of the Linear B data relating to religion (for which, in particular, more reference to the archaeological material would be needed[8]). It is

[5] As Jameson (1988, 87) noted: 'The [classical] Greeks derived virtually all their meat (aside from game) from the ritual of sacrifice.' But see also his caveats pp. 87–8 and 114 n 1, e.g. meat from sacrificial animals could be bought and sold in the 'ordinary' way. Note too that while libations of wine apparently were poured whenever wine was drunk in classical Greece (Parke 1977, 20–1; Burkert 1985, 70), this does not make every occasion on which wine was consumed a 'religious' one. For classical dining and sacrifice in general see Van Straten 1995. Note that a former argument that evidence for Mycenaean sacrificial ritual was not strong (Bergquist 1988), is now superseded by data for sacrificial victims at Pylos (Isaakidou *et al*. 2002; see n 60 below for further references).

[6] A recent distinction even in modernity (e.g. Bremmer 1998). Killen (2006a, 100–1 n 62) comments helpfully on the distinction (or not) with regard to Mycenaean banqueting.

[7] In the context of a different inquiry, however, such distinctions would indeed be worth exploring.

[8] See Bennet 1984; 1988b and references in Chapter 1 n 5.

hoped that an answer to the central question of the present study may contribute to the overall project of developing more integrated approaches: an improved understanding of the extent of palatial resources involved and the nature of the Linear B evidence relating to Mycenaean religion is essential to that goal.

2.2 OFFERINGS RECORDS

2.2.1 INTRODUCTION TO OFFERINGS RECORDS

As noted above, for the purposes of this study offerings records are best discussed in the context of other documents recording the same commodities, and the account here is thus intentionally brief. To put the documents in context, however, it may be useful to begin with a few notes on offerings in classical Greece and the ancient Near East. This is not to impose later (or earlier) models on the Mycenaean world; the intent is purely heuristic. While specific features of ritual and belief would have been different in other settings, it is useful to be aware of what types of things might be seen as religious offerings in cultural contexts where the making of offerings was an integral part of religious activity.

Certain types of offerings appear in a wide range of societies – for instance, votive offerings, libations, 'sacral meals', ritualised dining including animal sacrifice and other dedications on the occasions of festivals are known both in classical Greek and in many ancient Near Eastern religions. In classical Greece, the most common form of votive offering was the setting up or deposition of artefacts (especially spoils of war) in sanctuaries.[9] Other common forms included dedications of first fruits, the erection of an altar or even the foundation of a new sanctuary.[10] Slaves might be committed to temple service, or gifts made of valuable goods such as cloth and garments, animals to supplement temple flocks (as distinct from sacrificial victims), or tracts of land. Personal items might be dedicated at times of life passage – for instance, hair on various occasions, girdles or toys on marriage, or tools of trade on retirement.[11]

Similar sorts of commodities were offered in both ancient Near Eastern and classical contexts, with some variations. Libations in the classical world were above all of wine, oil, honey and water,[12] as seems to have been the case also for the Mycenaeans (water of course being uncertain as it would be invisible both archaeologically and in Linear B). In Mesopotamia, water, beer and (later) wine were used for libations,[13] as were various aromatics.[14] Honey appears to have been less commonly used than in the Aegean, and is correspondingly less often found as offerings.[15] Oil (possibly sesame rather than olive) together with water was used in lecanomancy, which had a cultic status.[16] Hittite records mention both honey and oil in an invocation for 'wayward' gods;[17] oil was used for dipping bones in funeral rites, and beer and wine to extinguish the pyre.[18] Sacral, token meals for deities were sometimes eaten by priests

---

[9] Burkert 1985, 69.
[10] Burkert 1985, 66–9.
[11] Burkert 1985, 70. For gifts of land and people in Mesopotamia see e.g. Postgate 1972, 815–6.
[12] Burkert 1985, 70–3.
[13] Postgate 1994, 90–100, 120. Kramer (1963, 140) lists water, beer and wine as used by the Sumerians.
[14] Postgate 1994, 120.
[15] Oppenheim 1977, 44; see also Redford 1992, 212. Zettler (1996, 97, citing an unpublished paper by M.A. Powell) notes that the Sumerian word translated as 'honey' is probably rather date, fig or grape syrup.
[16] Oppenheim 1977, 208, 212. Oil and water appear also in the oath ceremony by which the gods bound themselves to Marduk (Jacobsen 1976, 182) and featured in ritual cleansing ceremonies (Jacobsen 1976, 124).
[17] Gurney 1990, 136.
[18] Gurney 1990, 137–9.

after dedication, a practice known also in Mesopotamian and classical settings.[19]

In Linear B, the major commodity issued as offerings at both Pylos and Knossos was perfumed olive oil. At Knossos, honey was next in importance (in terms of scale), while wine appears in offerings and banqueting records from many sites. Other commodities offered include unguent, barley, cyperus, wool, textiles and metal vessels. One basic distinction which may be drawn is between 'consumables', such as oil and honey, which would probably have been destroyed through ritual action or distributed to cult personnel, and items which might constitute or contribute to 'standing wealth', such as metal vessels, textiles and humans. Flocks of animals dedicated to specific deities also come in some sense under this rubric, and are dealt with in the section on 'Collectors' (Section 2.5). Again, the categories are heuristic, not absolute, but an important difference between consumables and 'durable' dedications in the Linear B records is that animals in standing flocks would in a sense have already been dedicated and appear in the documents in the context of censuses or inventories, while most offerings records deal with more immediate transactions.[20]

Our main aim in what follows is to establish a basic sense of what a Linear B 'offerings record' looks like and some criteria for identifying such records. We will also briefly examine evidence for 'durable' offerings which may have contributed to the 'standing wealth' of shrines.

2.2.2 IDENTIFYING OFFERINGS RECORDS

The present section focuses on how 'offerings records' may be identified in the Linear B records. We begin with two non-controversial examples, one from Pylos, one from Knossos. The texts are as follows (further discussion and references for both are in Section 3.2).

PY Fr 1224 (S1202-H2)

.a pa-ko-we , e-ti-we
.b pa-ki-ja-ni-jo-jo me-no , po-se-da-o-ne OLE+*PA* Z 2

KN Fp(1) 1 + 31 (138)

.1 de-u-ki-jo-jo 'me-no'
.2 di-ka-ta-jo / di-we OLE S 1
.3 da-da-re-jo-de OLE S 2
.4 pa-de OLE S 1
.5 pa-si-te-o-i OLE 1
.6 qe-ra-si-ja OLE S 1[
.7 a-mi-ni-so , / pa-si-te-o-i S 1[
.8 e-ri-nu , OLE V 3
.9 **47*-da-de OLE V 1
.10 a-ne-mo , / i-je-re-ja V 4
.11 *vacat*
.12 to-so OLE 3 S 2 V 2

.2 *-ka-* perhaps over ⟦ ⟧.
.6-7 The numeral on one of these lines must be restored as 2 to produce the total.
.9 **47-* perhaps over ⟦ ⟧.

PY Fr 1224 records a disbursement of a small amount of sage-scented oil (*/sphakowen/* 'sage') to the god Poseidon in the 'month of *pa-ki-ja-ne*'. *pa-ki-ja-ne* was one of the major towns of the Hither Province and an important religious site. KN Fp(1) 1 also records a month name, followed by various recipients, including deities (e.g. */Diktaiōi Diwei/* 'to Zeus of Dikte',

[19] Burkert 1985, 68; 1987, 46; Postgate 1972, 815. Wright (2004b, 28 n 59) mentions a similar practice in modern Buddhism. One might also compare the *deipna* left for Hekate at her shrines at crossroads in classical Greece; Burkert 1985, 171 (I am grateful to R.T. Anderson for this point).
[20] On this now see Weilhartner's (2005) distinction between 'direct' and 'indirect' offerings.

/pansi theoi(h)i/ 'to all the gods'), shrines (e.g. Amnisos,[21] **47-da-de*) and religious personnel (e.g. */anemōn hiereiāi/* 'to the priestess of winds'), perhaps receiving the offerings as an intermediary.

An example of a similar record involving a different commodity is as follows (see Section 4.2.1.2 for further discussion and references).

KN Gg(1) 702 (103)
.1 pa-si-te-o-i / me-ri **209*^{VAS} 1
.2 da-pu$_2$-ri-to-jo , / po-ti-ni-ja 'me-ri' **209*^{VAS} 1

Here we again have *pa-si-te-o-i* 'all the gods', this time in receipt of */meli/* 'honey', along with a further offering of honey to 'the Lady of the Labyrinth'.[22] *po-ti-ni-ja /potnia/* 'Lady/Mistress' is an honorific title applied in Homer and later Greek to both goddesses and human women, but the contexts and the great number of epithets with which the word is found in the Linear B tablets (as here, for example) suggest that *Potnia* is divine. (This is not to imply that the term could not also have applied to human women in Mycenaean Greek, simply that we do not seem to have such usage attested in the preserved records.) Whether a single goddess or many different ones are indicated by the epithets is not crucially important here.[23] The reference to 'all the gods' makes clear the force of Gg(1) 702 as a record of offerings, supported by the religious overtones of the second designation.

The three tablets seen so far share a number of features. First, the recipients of the goods have clear cultic connections, being either deities, shrines (usually with the allative suffix *-de*) or religious personnel. The presence of theonyms and shrines is strongly suggestive of offerings records. However, other contextual support is needed as deities can appear in other contexts, such as banqueting and land tenure, while places such as *pa-ki-ja-ne* and Amnisos were not only important shrines, but major settlements which appear in contexts such as taxation. Similarly, the appearance of religious personnel may be consistent with an offerings context, but such personnel also appear in other contexts, for instance land tenure and personnel records (e.g. PY An 1281[24]). Even where religious personnel are in direct receipt of goods, the context need not be 'religious' *per se* – in the PY Qa series, for instance, various religious officials receive a commodity **189*, but many officials without cult connections do as well.[25]

Another feature, shared by the first two examples above, is the appearance of month names. Curiously, month names do appear to be diagnostic of offerings records. Offerings are not always accompanied by month names, but *all* tablets which have month names are records of offerings, where the function of the record can be determined.[26] This is significant, and we will return to the issue in the final chapter. The following month names, festival names and other time designations have been identified at Knossos and Pylos.

---

[21] Amnisos was an important settlement and one of the harbour-towns of Knossos. It is frequent in offerings records but also appears in other contexts, such as taxation and industry. See Hiller 1981; 1992; 1997; Schäfer 1991.

[22] No transcription is given for the word interpreted as 'Labyrinth' as the form is disputed (although it is clearly genitive). The bibliography is extensive; see e.g. *Documents*, 310, 475, 538; Godart 1975; *DMic*. I, 156–7; for a recent discussion see Thompson 2005.

[23] See Chadwick 1957; 1985, 195. The general bibliography on *Potnia* is very extensive; most recently see Boëlle 2001; Kopaka 2001; Morris 2001; Thomas & Wedde 2001; Trümpy 2001; Palaima 2004, 113. See also Van Leuven 1979; Ruijgh 1996.

[24] Although this particular example may have to do with banqueting since the document is connected with Fn 50, a festival rations record (Section 2.3.3.1); see Bendall 2003, 207–10.

[25] Bendall 2003, 212–13, with further references.

[26] See e.g. *Documents*, 407. Other records do refer to months – particularly rations records, e.g. the recently joined An/Fn 7 with *o-pi-me-ne*, probably */opi mēn(n)ei/* 'per month' (Chadwick 1988, 73; Melena 1996–1997b, 171–6, esp. 173), and KN E 777 with the ideogram LUNA indicating 'month' – but these records do not include month *names*. See also Palaima 2004a, 286.

Knossos[27]

month names

a-ka-[. . *ṛị*?]*-jo-jo me-ṇọ*[(Oa 745)

a-ma-ko-to me-no (Fp(1) 14)

de-u-ki-jo-jo me-no (Fp(1) 1)

di-wi-jo-jo me-no (Fp(1) 5, F 726)

ka-ra-e-ri-jo me-no (Fp(1) 6, –7, –15, –18; Gg(1) 7569; M(1) 1645)

ra-pa-to me-no (Fp(1) 13)

sa-pa-nu-wo me-no (X 949)

wo-de-wi-jo me-no (Fp(1) 16, –48; Ga 953; V(2) 280)

festival name

te-o-po-ri-ja (Ga 1058; Od(1) 696??)

tablets with *me-no*, but month name not preserved

Ga 5672; Gg(1) 704, –5552, –8053; M 724

Pylos

month name

pa-ki-ja-ni-jo-jo me-no (Fr 1224)

festival names

re-ke-to-ro-te-ri-jo (Fr 343, –1217)

to-no-e-ke-te-ri-jo (Fr 1222)

month, festival or other time designations?

me-tu-wo ne-wo (Fr 1202)

po-ro-wi-to (Fr 1218, –1221, –1232; Tn 316)

Although caution should be maintained, the apparent connection between month names and offerings suggests a number of further identifications of offerings records, even where useful text such as theonyms is lacking. An example is Gg(1) 7369; the text is as follows.[28]

KN Gg(1) 7369 (103)

.1 ka-]ra-e-ri-jo-jo me-no[

.2] LANA 1 M 1 me-ri ṣ[

This tablet deals with honey and wool (see Sections 4.2.1.1 and 6.3.3.1). That it is an offerings record is suggested not only by the appearance of a month name, but by its being a member of the Gg(1) set of h. 103, a prolific scribe who dealt mainly with aspects of the textile industry,[29] but who also wrote a few offerings records (primarily of textiles). Most tablets of the Gg(1) set are too broken for their functions to be determined with certainty, but at least one is clearly an offerings record (Gg(1) 702 above) and the same is probably true for the entire set since 'sets' tend to deal with single subjects (virtually by definition; see Conventions 4). Other aspects of the tablets are consistent with such an interpretation.

As just seen, palaeography and/or pinacology can sometimes be contributory factors to identifying a tablet as an offerings record. Findspots are also relevant. Gg 10 is an example:

KN Gg 10 (138)

.1]**209*^{VAS} 2 [

.2]ṭẹ-o *ME+RI* **209*^{VAS} 1[

.3] *vacat* [

.2 Over ⟦ ⟧.

There is nothing in the text of this tablet which would justify identification as an offering record without other evidence (]*ṭẹ-o* need not be */theos/*; it could be the ending of some other

[27] See Weilhartner 2005, 98–9 for those at Knossos.

[28] There is a misprint in *KT*[5]: *ka-*]*ra-e-ri-jo-jo* is correct; see *CoMIK* III, *s.v.* 7369.

[29] *Scribes Cnossos*, 44–50; Killen 1984a, 52; Shelmerdine 1988, 348–9; Landenius-Enegrin 1995.

word[30]). But that Gg 10 *is* an offering record is suggested by a combination of scribal hand and findspot. The scribe of Gg 10, h. 138, also wrote the Fp(1) set, an example of which was seen above, and all tablets of which are securely identified as offerings records. Of the other documents ascribed to h. 138, not one can be securely identified as *not* being an offering record. Furthermore, Gg 10 was found alongside the Fp(1) tablets in the Clay Chest.[31] The other documents from this findspot were the tablets of the Fs set, which are related to religion (see Section 3.2.3.4), and C 33, a possible banqueting record (Section 2.3.2.3). In short, documents of the Clay Chest deposit seem to be exclusively religious in content. These considerations make it highly likely that Gg 10 is an offering record.[32]

A further feature shared by all the tablets examined so far is that they record relatively small amounts of the commodities in question. PY Fr 1224 records a mere Z 2 (about 0.8 litres on the VC values); KN Fp(1) 1 has relatively small amounts (e.g. V 1, S 1) in all but one instance (which, probably significantly, is intended for '*all* the gods'); and honey offerings tend to be of one or at most two jars. Small numbers are common for offerings records in general, and the same is usually true also for banqueting records.[33] However, there are exceptions. For instance KN F(2) 866 records 10 units of figs going to the shrine of Dikte (on the VC values some 960 litres[34]), and there are on the other hand documents without religious connections which also record small numbers. So this feature may be regarded as suggestive of, but not necessarily diagnostic of, offerings records.

In every instance, a combination of factors must be considered, with attention to circumstances which may be distinctive to the individual case. For example, it was noted above that members of a set normally deal with the same subject. However, the picture is not always clear and we should discuss here at least one difficult case.

KN M(1) 1645 ASHM (1938.711) (103)
.1 ka-]ra-e-ri-jo-jo , me-no
.2]-wi-jo-do *pe *146* 1

This tablet belongs to the M(1) set of h. 103, one of the scribes encountered above. The appearance of a month name here is highly suggestive of an offering record and the small number would be consistent with such an identification. As we saw, h. 103 does write offerings records, so this too would be consistent, although by no means definitive proof since the majority of h. 103's output is not related to offerings. The real difficulty here is the character of the M(1) set which as currently defined has three members: M(1) 559, –720 and –1645. M(1) 559 is clearly not related to offerings and –720 need not be.[35] Thus the month name in M(1) 1645 points towards offerings, and other features are consistent, but the character of the set is neutral or points away. Which factor(s) should take precedence in our judgement about this tablet? Individual circumstances are key. The M(1) set is not as clearly defined as most sets are, and it is uncertain that the three tablets really were filed and intended to be read together. M(1) 559 is from F10 (Magazine XI), while –720 is from G1 (the Gallery

---

[30] E.g. *qe-te-o*.
[31] *Scribes Cnossos*, 104, cf. 21–2.
[32] See also Weilhartner 2005, 47, with n 83.
[33] This feature of offerings records has often been noted. See for instance Foster's observations that 'small quantities are typical of cult offerings' (1977a, 23) and that in the Knossos Department of Perfumery and Offerings (see Section 3.2.3.1), offerings are smaller than issues for other purposes (1977a, 32–3). For similar observations with regard to banqueting records see n 79 and n 230 below.
[34] Perhaps the issue was for staff maintenance? But the basic structure of the document is not dissimilar to other tablets discussed here as 'offerings records'; see Section 5.5.1 for the text.
[35] Weilhartner (2005, 60) affirms M(1) 720 as an offering record, but based only on the findspot. This would on its own in any case be insufficient and in this case there are specific problems with taking the findspot as an indicator (see next note). The two words on the tablet are both *hapax legomena*. *DMic.* takes *ze-ne-si-wi-jo* as an AN and *o-re-o-po* with several question marks as a possible adjective describing the textile(s). Nothing here need point in the direction of an offering record.

of Jewel Fresco[36]). These findspots are near enough to one another that a common original location on the upper floor is not inconceivable, but neither is it inevitable. The findspot of M(1) 1645 is unknown,[37] so it is impossible to surmise whether it was filed with the others or not. The uncertainties surrounding the M(1) set suggest that set membership should not here outweigh other factors. The likelihood is that M(1) 1645 is an offerings record.

Finally, we give two examples where offerings are counter-indicated.

KN Fh 5451 + 5496 + *frr.* (4) (141)

.a za-we-te [
.b a-mi-ni-si-ja / a-pu-do-ṣị OLE 30[

This tablet mentions Amnisos, site of an important shrine as seen above, but here the word appears as an ethnic adjective and without the allative suffix. The vocabulary is related to taxation (the word *a-pu-do-si /apudosis/* is the standard term for tax payments[38]), not offerings, and this is certainly a taxation rather than an offerings record. Note also the very large number involved.

Another example is as follows.

KN Fp(2) 5472 + 5476 + *frr.* (5) (222?)

.1 ku-pi-ri-jo / su-ko-ne ỌḶẸ [
.2 si-ja-ṃạ[ ] OLE 1 S [
.3]*vest.*[ ]de ỌḶẸ 2 [
.4] *vacat* [

.1 Traces at right of ỌḶẸ, too faint to be numerals (erasure? accident?).

The relatively large amounts of oil would be unusual (although not impossible) for an offerings record, but the decisive factor here is the appearance of the word *ku-pi-ri-jo*, the name of a well-known individual involved in the perfume industry at Knossos (see Section 3.2.3.5). There can be no doubt this tablet is related to perfumery, not offerings.

We conclude with a table summarising common features of offerings records with an indication of the degree of importance of various factors in their identification.[39]

---

[36] Weilhartner (2005) takes all tablets from [G1] as offerings records but see Chapter 4, n 4.

[37] Weilhartner (2005, 60) gives '[G1]?', based on the observation that the other offerings records of h. 103 come from this findspot. It may well be that M(1) 1645 does too, but this is guesswork. *Scribes Cnossos* and *CoMIK* give no findspot. The impossibility of ascribing one was recently reaffirmed by Firth (1996–1997, 41), although he later (2000–2001a, 236, Table II1.12) also includes M(1) 1645 as possibly coming from [G1].

[38] *DMic.* I, 88–9.

[39] A similar account is given by Palaima (2003b, 115) although not all his points are universally accepted. He mentions that type of goods may be relevant to identifying offerings records, but this is a weak indicator. As we shall see, most goods can appear in offerings contexts, even if very rarely, while almost all of them appear also in non-offerings contexts. However, Palaima may have had banqueting records in mind and with regard to these, types of commodities in tandem is indeed supportive evidence (see next section).

Table 2-1. Identifying offerings records

type of feature	specific instances	degree of importance in identification
recipients of religious character	deities	consistent with; diagnostic of religious context, but not found only in offerings records
	sanctuaries (usually with *-de*)	usually diagnostic of (but there are a couple banqueting records mentioning shrines)
	religious personnel	consistent with; diagnostic of religious context, but not found only in offerings records
	dative plural groups	frequent in offerings records, but also seen in other contexts (see Sections 2.3.3 and 3.2.3.5)
sacred terminology	*i-je-ro*	diagnostic of religious context, but can appear on banqueting records
	qe-te-jo and variant forms	appears to have religious connotations (usually? always?); common also on banqueting records
time references	month names	apparently diagnostic
	festival names	diagnostic
membership of set with religious character		strongly suggestive, but set membership and coherency must be firm
small amounts		normative but not invariable for offering tablets, so highly suggestive, but not necessary proof
findspot		depends upon individual circumstances
scribal hand		depends upon individual circumstances
type of good		not diagnostic of offerings records, but cf. banqueting

2.2.3 EVIDENCE FOR STANDING WEALTH IN THE FORM OF VOTIVES

While the majority of offerings in the Linear B records are of consumable items such as oil or honey, there are occasional records of offerings of durable goods which may have contributed to the standing wealth of the sanctuaries. Textiles, for instance, might have contributed to goods in store, although other uses such as handouts to temple staff (cf. PY Un 6?) or for distribution at feasts are attested.[40] An example of a textile offering to a specified deity is as follows:

KN Oa 745 [+] 7374 (—)

.1 a-ka-[ ]-jo-jo , me-ṇọ[

.2 da-pu$_2$-ṛị[-to-jo]po-ti-ni-jạ *ri *166+WE* 2̣2̣[

.1 Traces of two or three signs before *]-jo-jo*, the last perhaps a *-ṛị-* badly drawn and incomplete.
.2 Possible divider before *ri*.

Oa 745 records a number of textiles going to the 'Lady of the Labyrinth' (see previous section). The disbursement is sufficiently large (22 units if the reading is correct) to have contributed to the standing wealth of the shrine. However, the reading is uncertain and, even if correct, other possibilities for the use of the items may be suggested, as just noted.

More positive evidence for standing wealth comes from records involving metal vessels, such as the well-known offerings record PY Tn 316. It is not necessary to review here the very extensive literature on this tablet.[41] For present purposes a brief look at the text will suffice.[42]

---

[40] Killen (1994, 70) draws a parallel with Incan festivals. On textile offerings in Linear B generally see Nosch 2000b; Nosch & Perna 2001.

[41] See e.g. *Documents*, 284–9, 458–64; Ruijgh 1967c; Chadwick 1985, 200; 1976, 89–92; Carlier 1987, 265–6; Willi 1994–1995; Nagy 1994–1995; Palaima 1995b; 1996–1997; 1999a; del Freo 1996–1997; Weilhartner 2005.

[42] Text as in *PTT*; for very minor modifications (not shown here) see Bennett 1992, 110.

PY Tn 316 (H44)

Recto

.1	po-ro-wi-to-jo ,	
.2		i-je-to-qe , pa-ki-ja-si , do-ra-qe , pe-re , po-re-na-qe
.3	pu-ro	a-ke , po-ti-ni-ja AUR *215*^{VAS} 1 MUL 1
.4	ma-na-sa , AUR *213*^{VAS} 1 MUL 1 po-si-da-e-ja AUR *213*^{VAS} 1 MUL 1	
.5	ti-ri-se-ro-e , AUR *216*^{VAS} 1 do-po-ta AUR *215*^{VAS} 1	
.6		*vacat*
.7		*vacat*
.8		*vacat*
.9		*vacat*
.10	pu-ro	*vacat*
		reliqua pars sine regulis

Verso

.1		i-je-to-qe , po-si-da-i-jo , a-ke-qe , wa-tu
.2		do-ra-qe , pe-re , po-re-na-qe , a-ke
.3a		-ja
.3	pu-ro	AUR *215*^{VAS} 1 MUL 2 qo-wi-ja , na-[ ] , ko-ma-we-te-
.4		i-je-to-qe , pe-ṛẹ-*82-jo , i-pe-me-de-ja-qe di-u-ja-jo-qe
.5		do-ra-qe , pe-re-po-re-na-qe , a , pe-re-*82 AUR *213*^{VAS} 1 MUL 1
.6		i-pe-me-ḍẹ-ja AUR *213*^{VAS} 1 di-u-ja AUR *213*^{VAS} 1 MUL 1
.7	pu-ro	e-ma-a$_2$, a-re-ja AUR *216*^{VAS} 1 VIR 1
.8		i-je-to-qe , di-u-jo , do-ra-qe , pe-re , po-re-na-qe a-ḳẹ
.9		di-we AUR *213*^{VAS} 1 VIR 1 e-ra AUR *213*^{VAS} 1 MUL 1
.10		di-ri-mi-jo⌞ ⌟di-wo , i-je-we , AUR *213*^{VAS} 1 MUL 1 [ ] *vacat*
.11	pu-ro	*vacat*
.12		*vacat*

The document lists thirteen gold vessels, eight women and two men going to thirteen deities (one merely implied) at six shrines (taking *pa-ki-ja-si* as 'one'). There are numerous problems of interpretation, but at least it is clear that the deities are the recipients (see e.g. *v*.9 *di-we* /*Diwei*/ 'to Zeus', a clear dative), and that the goods are coming from Pylos (*pu-ro*). The vessels may well have contributed to standing wealth of the shrines, although other possibilities, such as ritual destruction, cannot be entirely discounted. The purpose of the humans is unclear and has been much discussed; they probably either were dedicated as temple servants or were intended for sacrifice.

Yet more positive evidence for shrines possessing metal as standing wealth is provided by PY Jn 829,[43] the heading of which reads: 'thus they [various officials] will provide *na-wi-jo* bronze as points for spears and javelins'. A central issue in discussions of this tablet was whether *na-wi-jo* indicates 'ship' bronze or 'temple' bronze.[44] Either interpretation is possible given the Linear B spelling rules, but it is not clear what 'ship bronze' would mean. It might be bronze incorporated into the fabric of ships, or bronze brought by ship. But Aegean Bronze Age ships probably did not use bronze as part of their building materials, being constructed using wooden mortise-and-tenons,[45] and bronze brought by ship would presumably be collected from harbours, not from the inland Pylian towns listed in Jn 829. An interpretation as temple bronze is thus now generally accepted. The implication is that various shrines around the polity generally had such resources in their possession.[46]

The heading of Jn 829 provides a clue to the political climate in which the collection was made. Although assessment was made with reference to the standard Pylian taxation districts, Jn 829 is not an ordinary tax record. The heading is explicit about the purpose for which the bronze was extracted, and it is difficult to connect 'points for spears and javelins' with

43 See e.g. Carlier 1987, 272–3.

44 See *Documents*, 511–14; Chadwick 1976, 141; Hiller 1979; Leukart 1979.

45 See Hocker & Palaima 1990–1991, 304–5, 312; Palaima 1991; Leukart 1979, 183–4; Hiller 1979, 190.

46 E.g. Chadwick 1976, 141–2.

anything but a military context. Appropriation of temple wealth for military purposes in times of crisis was of course known in the ancient world.[47] A number of other Pylos texts have also been proposed as relating to an emergency, although the issue remains controversial.[48]

It is possible that PY Ae 303 should also be seen in this context. The text is as follows:

PY Ae 303 (S8-H42)

.a i-je-ro-jo

pu-ro , i-je-re-ja , do-e-ra , e-ne-ka , ku-ru-so-jo MUL 14[

Ventris and Chadwick interpret the text: 'At Pylos: 14+ female slaves of the priestess on account of [*e-ne-ka*] sacred gold.'[49] What 'sacred gold' may be is unclear: possibly gold in temple stores or ritual paraphernalia (perhaps acquired through mechanisms such as seen in Tn 316). Also unclear is how the women 'account' for it, or how it 'accounts' for them: *e-ne-ka* must represent classical /*heneka*/, but what was its meaning in Mycenaean Greek?

L.R. Palmer attempted to explain the document by reading *e-ne-ka* as 'on behalf of, in the service of', but this unusual interpretation and his association of the term with religion have not gained general acceptance.[50] As Killen points out, *e-ne-ka* is not exclusively associated with religion (witness, for instance, its occurrences with *o-pa*) and there is no reason to assume a different meaning for the word without strong contextual support.[51] The normal classical sense of 'because of, on account of' gives acceptable readings in all cases where *e-ne-ka* is attested in Mycenaean, and the implication of Ae 303 need only be, as he notes, 'that the slaves are present in the household of the priestess because of the sacred gold (i.e. because it needs guarding) or (as *Documents* suggests) because they have been acquired by the priestess as a result of a payment in sacred gold'.[52] Killen's further discussion of PY Ea 805, where a man holds a plot of land *e-ne-ka a-no-qa-si-ja*, which he reads as 'by way of *compensation for* manslaughter' (my emphasis),[53] may suggest a parallel for the situation in Ae 303: that the women were provided *in compensation* for sacred gold, perhaps in circumstances similar to those of Jn 829. Chadwick proposed that a demand for gold, like bronze, is witnessed in the Pylos documents, interpreting a further tablet, Jo 438, where gold is contributed by various officials, as an attempt to raise funds, perhaps to pay for mercenaries.[54] In such a context, the female slaves of Ae 303 would have made an ideal recompense for 'sacred gold' appropriated by the palace. Slaves would in themselves be valuable, their ownership prestigious and thus appropriate to the priestess's standing, but in a military sense they would be among the more 'dispensable' items from a calculating point of view.[55]

However that may be, the implication of at least Jn 829 recording an appropriation of temple goods (whether or not in time of crisis) is that some shrines normally had such things in their

[47] For instance, in Thucydides (I.121.3 & 143.1) there is talk of seizing the funds at Olympia and Delphi to pay mercenaries; see also Dillon 2002, 192. For an archaeological example of scrap metal intended for recycling from the Mycenaean world (although not in a religious context), see Catling & Catling 1984, 206–7.

[48] See Hooker 1982; Baumbach 1983; Lang 1990; Shelmerdine 1987a; 1999c; Smith 1992–1993, 206–7; Palaima 1995b; 1999a; 1999b.

[49] *Documents*, 166.

[50] Palmer 1963, 277–8. Palmer's account undergoes a transformation as one proceeds through *Interpretation*. His earlier translation 'Pylos: slaves of the priestess in charge of the sacred gold' is preferable to later developments, although still not satisfactory. Doubts about which of *ku-ru-so-jo* or *i-je-ro-jo* is a noun or adjective led to an eventual reading: 'in the service of the golden shrine' (Palmer 1963, 127; and see *Documents*, 166) as slightly less eyebrow-raising than 'in the service of the sacred gold'.

[51] Killen 1992b, 378–80.

[52] Killen 1992b, 378, citing *Documents*, 166.

[53] Killen 1992b, 379–80.

[54] Chadwick 1998–1999. Note some rowers in the Pylian fleet received *o-no* 'payments' (An 724): perhaps of gold? (Cf. Godart 1999, 252.)

[55] Ae 110 dealing with the *klāwiphoros* might also be explained in such a way. For the Ae tablets in general see Pluta forthcoming.

possession, as noted above. We should further note, however, that this would not necessarily be evidence for major independent wealth – the individual contributions in Jn 829 are fairly small (e.g. about 3 kg of bronze from each of the Hither Province districts).

2.3 BANQUETING AND FESTIVAL RECORDS

2.3.1 INTRODUCTION TO BANQUETING RECORDS

It had long been known that some Linear B documents listed animals intended as sacrificial offerings,[56] but only relatively recently was it recognised that several of the 'mixed commodity' records (U- Class, by definition), often previously referred to as 'inventory' records, were in actuality lists of foodstuffs drawn together on specific occasions for large-scale, state-organised festivals and feasts.[57] This understanding led to further types of records being recognised as relating to banqueting and festivals, particularly the PY Fn tablets which are now understood as records of rations for religious personnel and other support staff on such occasions,[58] and the PY Ta tablets which record a set of furniture, vessels and instruments of sacrifice (chains, swords and hammer-mallets) probably also for use on the occasion of a particular feast.[59]

The Linear B evidence can be brought together with archaeological evidence for banqueting,[60] and informed by anthropological perspectives which draw attention to the importance of consumption and commensality relevant to economy, labour mobilisation, status, politics and identity across a wide range of societies.[61] For the Mycenaean world, banqueting is now understood as one of the central arenas for the representation, negotiation and manipulation of social and political identity. All sites which have yielded more than a few Linear B documents have records now recognised as relating to banqueting. The majority of evidence comes from Pylos and Knossos, but there are also numerous documents from Thebes and Mycenae and one tablet from Tiryns may be a festival rations record. The appearance of banqueting records throughout the Mycenaean world, coming from sites with different histories and whose Linear B documents are not contemporary, suggests that banqueting was a standard feature of Mycenaean palace society and remained so over a relatively long period of time.

The main types of Linear B documents relating to banqueting can be summarised as follows:

1. lists of banqueting foodstuffs and sacrificial animals
2. lists of rations for support staff at banquets and festivals
3. lists of furniture, equipment for sacrifice, vessels and other paraphernalia

---

[56] E.g. *Documents* 436, 440–1, 484, 581 (note in the first edition of *Documents*, VC, with understandable caution, simply note that the reason for the impost [they were taking them as collections] of goods on tablets such as Un 2 and -138 is unclear; see pp. 219–21); Killen 1964, 1; Gérard-Rousseau 1971; Chadwick 1976, 95–6, 132.

[57] In an important early paper, Palaima (1989, see esp. 108–10) noted the curious fact that all records of oxen at Pylos happen to deal with animals for sacrifice. The crucial starting point for recognising feasting as a major phenomenon was the publication of the Thebes sealings by Piteros, Olivier and Melena (1990) and Killen's observations on and extension of their work presented in conference papers in 1990 (Killen 1992b) and 1991 (Killen 1996b); the key article is Killen 1994; see also Godart 1999.

[58] Killen 2001b.

[59] Killen 1998b; Speciale 1999; 2000.

[60] A key paper is Bennet & Davis 1999; two recent important collections of articles are Halstead & Barrett 2004 and Wright 2004a. See also Nikoloudis 2001; Bendall 2004. On the zooarchaeological material see Halstead 1998–1999; Isaakidou *et al.* 2002; Halstead & Isaakidou 2004; Stocker & Davis 2004; Hamilakis & Konsolaki 2004. Earlier discussions include Säflund 1980 (a paper with important insights although not all of its conclusions are acceptable) and McCallum 1987a; 1987b.

[61] E.g. Douglas 1987; Sherratt 1995; Dietler & Hayden 2001. In a specifically Aegean context see Hamilakis 1996; 1999a; 1999b.

These three types of documents are referred to as 'banqueting records' in the present study. As noted above, some of the 'offerings records' also relate to banqueting, especially where offerings are made on the occasions of banquets and/or festivals,[62] but it is useful to keep the distinction.

We will examine in turn each of the types of banqueting record listed above, beginning with banqueting foodlists and proceeding to festival rations records and texts dealing with banqueting paraphernalia. It is useful to begin with a brief discussion of how such records generally came to be recognised, with some notes on the extent to which banquets may have had a religious, or at least a 'ceremonial', dimension. Documents recording banqueting 'foodlists' from each site (Pylos, Knossos, Mycenae, Thebes) are examined in turn. Our discussion of the Pylos tablets will focus particularly on criteria for identifying banqueting foodlists. The overall focus for the purposes of the study here is on the identification of the records; it is recognised that the tablets are significant from many other perspectives which cannot be pursued in the present analysis.

2.3.2 LISTS OF BANQUETING FOODSTUFFS

2.3.2.1 INTRODUCTION TO BANQUETING FOODLISTS

It is appropriate to begin a discussion of banqueting 'foodlists' with an account of the 1990 publication by Piteros, Olivier and Melena (POM hereafter) of the sealings found in 1982 at Thebes, many of which recorded animals such as goats, pigs and sheep. A few examples of the texts are as follows.

Wu 60		**Wu 65**	
.α	SUS^{m}	.α	OVIS^{f}
.β	pa-ro , sa-me-we	.β	te-qa-de
.γ	*vacat*	.γ	qe-te-a$_2$
Wu 50		**Wu 52**	
.α	CAP^{f}	.α	SUS+*SI*
.β	qe-te-o	.β	a-ko-ra-jo
.γ	a-ko-ra	.γ	*vacat*

POM observed that the inscriptions share a number of similarities with Un 138 from Pylos, the text of which is as follows.[63]

PY Un 138 (S138-H42)

.1	pu-ro , qe-te-a$_2$, pa-ro , du-ni-jo
.2	HORD 18 T 5 po-qa OLIV 4 T 3 V 5
.3	VIN 13 OVIS^{m} 15 *WE* 8 OVIS^{f} 1 CAP^{m} 13 SUS 12
.4	SUS+*SI* 1 BOS^{f} 1 BOS^{m} 2
.5	me-za-wo-ni HORD 4 T 8 V 1 ka-pa OLIV 7

Palimpsest; four lines ruled, with numerals visible in .4.

Both the Thebes sealings and PY Un 138 include the word *qe-te-a$_2$*, a transaction term probably having the general sense 'to be paid',[64] and the phrase '*pa-ro* + MN in dative', with the sense of *chez* or 'from', 'at the hands of'.[65] Further, as POM observe, the total numbers of

[62] Bendall 1998–1999.

[63] Piteros, Olivier & Melena 1990, 171–84, esp. 172–4. On Un 138 as a banqueting record see also Palaima 1989, 109–10, 116; 2004b; Killen 1994; 1996b; Halstead 1998–1999, 163–5; Bendall 2004, 106; Weilhartner 2005, 164. Text transcription from *PTT*.

[64] Piteros, Olivier & Melena 1990, 152–3; Hutton 1990–1991; *DMic*. II, 201–2 *s.v. qe-te-jo*. It may have a sense of payments 'resulting from fines' perhaps in respect of religious obligations (Hutton 1990–1991, 130; Palaima 2004b, 108), but this need not be so in every instance (e.g. the L(5) cloth tablets).

[65] Piteros, Olivier & Melena 1990, 152.

different sorts of animals appearing in the sealings are nearly identical to those in Un 138; the figures are shown in Table 2-2.[66]

Table 2-2. Correspondence of TH sealings and PY Un 138

TH Wu		
OVIS^{m}	13	
OVIS^{f}	2	
OVIS^{x}	1	**= 16**
CAP^{m}	6	
CAP^{f}	7	
CAP^{x}	1	**= 14**
SUS^{m}	6	
SUS^{f}	2	
SUS	1	
SUS^{x}	1	**= 10**
SUS+*SI*		**2**
BOS^{m}		**1**
BOS^{f}		**1**
we/*WE*	3	
**190*	5	**= 8**
[ ]^{m}		**1**
TOTAL		**53**

PY Un 138		
OVIS^{m}	15	
OVIS^{f}	1	
		= 16
CAP^{m}		**13**
SUS		**12**
SUS+*SI*		**1**
BOS^{m}		**2**
BOS^{f}		**1**
WE		**8**
TOTAL		**53**

As POM argue, the similarities imply that the sealings were brought together, and Un 138 was written, for a single coherent purpose, the nature of which is suggested by PY Un 2.[67]

Un 2 (S2-H1)

.1 pa-ki-ja-si , mu-jo-me-no , e-pi , wa-na-ka-te ,
.2 a-pi-e-ke , o-pi-te-ke-e-u
.3 HORD 16 T 4 CYP+*PA* T 1 V 3 *O* V 5
.4 FAR 1 T 2 OLIV 3 T 2 **132* S 2 *ME* S 1
.5 *NI* 1 BOS 1 OVIS^{m} 26 OVIS^{f} 6 CAP^{m} 2 CAP^{f} 2
.6 SUS + *SI* 1̣ SUS^{f} 6 VIN 20 S 1 **146* 2

.3 HORD over erasure; or *O* ideogram?
.4 FAR over erasure; **132* over erasure.
.5 Bottom rule, originally lower, was erased, probably together with original text, and redrawn; traces of erasure from *NI* to OVIS^{m}.
.6 Over traces of erasure of original rule of .5, probably not actual erasure.

The most probable interpretation of the heading is /*muiomenōi epi wanaktei*/ 'on the initiation of the king',[68] and the tablet is understood as a list of foodstuffs for consumption at a banquet on the occasion of an important ritual event. Killen notes a parallel for ceremonial feasting on such occasions in Incan society: food and cloth would be distributed to the populace upon 'the death of a king or the inauguration of a new one'.[69] The parallel would not of course extend to specific religious practice, but there might be similarities in the social function of state-organised banqueting, relating for instance to prestige and social cohesion.

While Un 138 and the Thebes sealings do not specify an event, as Un 2 does, they are, as POM indicate, similar types of records and thus likely to deal with similar types of occasions. In

[66] Piteros, Olivier & Melena 1990, 173–4. For the complete data from the Thebes sealings see Section 2.3.2.5, Table 2-7.
[67] Piteros, Olivier & Melena 1990, esp. 278–80. For Un 2 as a banqueting record see also Killen 1994; 1996b; Godart 1999, 251; Palaima 2004b; Weilhartner 2005, 159–61. For earlier references as an 'offerings record' (which of course it is) see Carlier 1987, 159, 261; Palaima 1989, 108. The text follows *PTT* (unchanged in *PoN* IV except slight modification to apparatus) but shows *o* in line .3 as an ideogram (see Section 5.7).
[68] *Documents*, 221, 440–1; *Mémoires* III, 32–3; Carlier 1987, 259; Killen 1994, 72. For the tablet in general also see e.g. Carlier 1984, 91–4; Palaima 1989, 108, 110, 116.
[69] Killen 1994, 70.

support of the idea that ritual sacrifice was involved is the fact that some of the animals are described in the sealings as *i-je-ra*/*i-je-ro* (e.g. Wu 44, –86), /*hiera*/ and /*hieron*/ 'sacred', indicating sacrificial victims.[70] The other commodities listed on Un 2 and Un 138 include barley, olives and wine, all appropriate goods for consumption at a feast. Killen has argued that other items recorded on the Thebes sealings, such as the unidentified commodity **134* (=**190*), were also for human consumption.[71]

While it is not necessary that banquets would always have a primarily 'religious' focus, as in Un 2, that some were at least connected to ceremony is indicated by records such as Cn 418, which describes animals *chez*, or provided by, one **we-u-da-ne-u*. The text is as follows.[72]

Cn 418 (Ciii)

.1 pa-ro , we-u-da-ne-we
.2 ṛẹ-ụ-ko , a-ko-ro-we-e BOS+*SI* 2
.3 re[-u-]ḳọ , ma-ra-p̣ị , pe-ko , a-ko-ro-we BOS+*SI* 1
.4 OVIS^{m}?]3 CAP^{m} 3̣ *ẈẸ* 3 CAP+*Ẹ* 3
.5]*vest*.[ ]2 [ ] 3 ⟦ ⟧
.6] *vestigia* [
.7 re-u-ko[ ]ṃạ-ra-[pi]pe-ko , a-ko-ro-we[BOS+*SI*
.8 OVIS^{m} 1 CAP^{m} 3 *WE*[ ]CAP+*Ẹ* [ ] ṢỤṢ^{x}[
.9 *vacat*
mutila

.1 *-u-* over erasure, possibly ⟦*da*⟧.
.3 OVIS^{m}]3 possible, but difficult; traces of erasure.
.4 CAP+*E*: CAP^{m} apparently over ⟦CAP^{f}⟧ not excluded.
.5 Possibly]C̣ẠP̣^{f}[ ]2 [ ]ḄỌṢ^{x} 3.

As Killen notes, 'the careful descriptions of the oxen on ll. .2 and .3, which include the colour term *re-u-ko*, "white", and the qualification of these animals as *SI*, which may abbreviate *si-a$_2$-ro*, σίαλος (cf. the SUS+*SI* entry on 138), is consistent with the view that the animals listed here are intended for sacrifice'.[73] The reference to colour is significant because if the purpose were purely 'utilitarian' consumption the outer appearance of the animals would be irrelevant. (The animals may also be selected for age – *WE* probably abbreviates /*wetelon*/ or /*wetalon*/ 'yearling'.[74]) A religious dimension to feasting is further indicated by banqueting foodlists which mention theonyms (e.g. Un 6, -718, -853) or religious personnel (Un 6). Linguistic support is seen in the use of words such as *i-je-ra* and *i-je-ro* noted above and possibly *sphaktēria* (see the KN C(2) set below), although this need not always have had a religious intention.[75] In sum, indications of sacral ceremonies, concern with physical attributes of the animals, use of vocabulary relating to sacrifice, and references to deities and cult personnel suggest a religious or at least ceremonial dimension to Mycenaean feasting in general, even if this is not so in every instance.

In the following sections we survey the evidence for banqueting foodlists from Pylos, Knossos, Mycenae and Thebes. We conclude with a brief note on evidence for wild animals and hunting relevant to banqueting.

---

[70] Piteros, Olivier & Melena 1990, 157.
[71] Killen 1992b, esp. 375.
[72] Cn 418: New joins have changed the text (Melena 1994–1995a, 95–6; 1996–1997b, 176). See also Melena 1992–1993b, 313; 1994–1995b, 277. The text here follows *PoN* IV. Note this tablet is classified Cn rather than U- as it deals exclusively with livestock (rather than mixed commodities). The Cn tablets are page-shaped documents recording mainly sheep, goats and pigs; most are flock census records; see Lang 1966b; Godard 1970; Killen 1993.
[73] Killen 1994, 77. For discussion of the terms see Palaima 1989, 104–8, 110, 114–15; Killen 1992–1993a, 102, 104–5; 1994, 77, 79; Godart 1999, 249. Other references to Cn 418 as a banqueting record include Halstead 1998–1999, 163–5; Bendall 2004, 105–6; Weilhartner 2005, 151–2.
[74] Documents, 590; Killen 1987a, 327–8.
[75] Piteros, Olivier & Melena 1990, 157.

2.3.2.2 BANQUETING FOODLISTS AT PYLOS

The present section surveys banqueting 'foodlists' at Pylos with particular attention to how such records may be identified. For reference, Table 2-3, at the end of the section, sets out the documents identified here as banqueting foodlists. We may begin with Un 2 and Un 138, encountered above.

Un 2 (S2-H1)

.1	pa-ki-ja-si , mu-jo-me-no , e-pi , wa-na-ka-te ,
.2	a-pi-e-ke , o-pi-te-ke-e-u
.3	HORD 16 T 4 CYP+*PA* T 1 V 3 *O* V 5
.4	FAR 1 T 2 OLIV 3 T 2 **132* S 2 *ME* S 1
.5	*NI* 1 BOS 1 OVIS^{m} 26 OVIS^{f} 6 CAP^{m} 2 CAP^{f} 2
.6	SUS + *SI* 1 SUS^{f} 6 VIN 20 S 1 **146* 2

PY Un 138 (S138-H42)

.1	pu-ro , qe-te-a$_2$, pa-ro , du-ni-jo
.2	HORD 18 T 5 po-qa OLIV 4 T 3 V 5
.3	VIN 13 OVIS^{m} 15 *WE* 8 OVIS^{f} 1 CAP^{m} 13 SUS 12
.4	SUS+*SI* 1 BOS^{f} 1 BOS^{m} 2
.5	me-za-wo-ni HORD 4 T 8 V 1 ka-pa OLIV 7

Ignoring the headings for the time being, these tablets share a number of features. First, both record a variety of goods, many of which are the same (HORD, OLIV, VIN, OVIS, CAP, SUS, SUS+*SI*, BOS). As noted above, Un 2 and Un 138 belong to a Class of documents (U-) usually termed 'mixed commodity records' (a range of ideograms being the defining criterion for U-Class documents).[76] Not all mixed commodity records have to do with banqueting (Un 267 for instance is a list of raw materials for perfume manufacture[77]), but where the character of the lists is similar to those of Un 2 and –138 a banqueting context is often indicated. The context is sometimes confirmed by other considerations – the range of commodities (including animals) on Un 138, for example, makes it impossible that this should be a perfumery record. Neither can it be a flock census record, the most common context in which animals appear. The combination of different sorts of animals and their appearance together with wine and foodstuffs suggest consumption rather than herd management.[78]

A further feature both tablets share is that they record relatively small numbers of animals. This is a common feature of banqueting records (as it is of offerings records, as noted above),[79] so can be a useful indicator. However, some livestock management records also have small numbers (e.g. the KN Ch tablets), and some banqueting foodlists have relatively large numbers (e.g. the KN C(2) set and Uc 161), so the criterion should be used with caution.

Another suggestive identifying feature is the appearance of theonyms. Un 6 offers an example.[80]

[76] On the Un tablets in general see Palmer 1994, published before much of the work on banqueting had developed. She identifies the records as inventories, taxation or harvest records, or rations lists, but does note that the foodstuffs of Un 1185 may have been 'destined for religious use' (Palmer 1994, 113–17, esp. 114; also see Palmer 1999). For Ua 9, –17, –25 and –434 as probable banqueting records see Killen 1994–1995b.
[77] Shelmerdine 1985, 17.
[78] See Palmer 1994, 190 for the observation that wine does not appear on ordinary rations records.
[79] Chadwick 1985, 200; Palaima 1992b, 65; Killen 1993, 216 n 5; 1994, 77 (and cf. n 33 above and n 230 below). For numbers on the banqueting foodlists in general see Bendall forthcoming(a); forthcoming(c).
[80] Un 6: Text from *PoN* IV but without the new unpublished non-joining fragment; see Bennet 1992, 105.

Un 6 (S6-H6)

Recto

.0 *supra mutila*
.1 po-se-ḍạ[-o-ne] BOS^{f} [ ]OVIS^{f} [ ]SUS+*KA* 1 SUS^{f} 2
.2 *vacat*
.3 pe-re-**82* BOS^{f} 1 OVIS^{f} 1 SUS + *KA* 1 SUS^{f} 2
.4 pe-re-**82* BOS^{f} 1 OVIS^{f} 1 SUS + *KA* 1 SUS^{f} 2
.5 *vacat*
.6 **146* 37 **1̣6̣6̣*+*ẈẸ*[
.7 *AREPA* S 1 V 2̣[
.8 BOS^{m} 2 BOS^{f} 2 ọṿịṣ^{x}[

Verso

prior pars sine regulis
.1]i-je-re-ja TELA+*ṬẸ*[
.2 ka-]ra-wi-po-ro TELA+*TE*[
reliqua pars sine regulis

Like Un 138 and Un 2, Un 6 involves a range of commodities and the numbers are relatively small. Although the list of goods is not as varied as in the other two records, a variety of commodities appears and some of the same commodities are involved (e.g. the animals and the textile **146*). A religious association is confirmed by the allocation of the animals to specific deities (Poseidon and the female deity *pe-re-*82*),[81] and by the appearance on the *verso* of a priestess and another religious official, registered against a type of textile. A 'banqueting' rather than 'offerings' context as defined in the present study is indicated by the range of commodities recorded, including animals for sacrifice which implies feasting. The tablet is generally agreed to be a banqueting record.[82]

Sometimes religious associations are not apparent in the first instance but can be inferred through comparison with other documents. Un 47 offers an example; the text is as follows.[83]

Un 47 (S138-H42)

.1 ro-u-so , ro-u-si-jo , a-ko-ṛọ[
.2 *NI* T 9 V 3 i[
.3 CYP+*O* 3 T 4 V 1 VIN [
.4 HORD 41 T 1 V 4 ka[
.5 OVIS^{m} 13 OVIS^{f} 8 *WE*[

The variety and types of commodities on this document again resemble those in Un 2 and –138 and the small amounts recorded are suggestive of banqueting. A religious context is implied by the designation *ro-u-si-jo a-ko-ro*, known as the location of a shrine on two of the oil offerings tablets, Fr 1220 and Fr 1226 (the latter includes the word *te-o-i* /*theoi*(*h*)*i*/ 'to the gods'). *ro-u-so* is well known as one of the major towns of the Hither Province, but the formation with *a-ko-ro* never occurs outside religious contexts (cf. *pa-ki-ja-ni-jo a-ko-ro*, which appears in offerings records). Again, the tablet is commonly agreed to be a banqueting record.[84]

As with the offerings records, scribal hand may aid identification.[85] For instance, Un 47 is by H42, the scribe who wrote Un 138. Two further tablets by this scribe are as follows.[86]

---

[81] The double entry for *pe-re-*82* may be intended to earmark sacrifices for different days of a festival; Palaima 2004b, 108–9; Bendall forthcoming(a). *pe-re-*82* is securely attested as a theonym by its appearance in Tn 316.*v*.4.5 where the goddess receives an offering of a golden bowl and a woman.

[82] Palaima 1989, 108–10; Godart 1999, 251; Palaima 2004b; Weilhartner 2005, 161–3.

[83] Un 47: Text unchanged since *PTT*. Apparatus not given here.

[84] Palaima 1989, 109; 2004b; Killen 1992b, 369; 2004, 159; Halstead 1998–1999, 163–5; Weilhartner 2005, 164.

[85] At Pylos, findspot is less of a factor than at Knossos, because most of the records come from the AC and work on the exact locations of tablets in this room is still ongoing (see Pluta 1996–1997). It will be interesting to see how the filing system dealt with banqueting records when the data become available. Some relevant work along these lines has already been done (e.g. Palaima 1995a).

[86] Texts from *PTT*, but the Ua 17.1 apparatus is from *PoN* IV. The Ua 25 apparatus is in progress so not given here.

Ua 17 (S138-H42)

Recto

.1]1 T 7 VIN 47 S 1 V 5

.2]7 OVIS^{f} 7 *WE* 17 CAP^{m} 31 SUS^{f} 20

lat.inf.]14 [

Verso

]3̣0[ ]Ṭ 7 [ ] Ṭ 4̣ V 2̣

Probably palimpsest, but probably also with traces of actual erasure.
.1 Space available and break favour HORD].
.2]7: only 7 units, with a trace at left possibly]ỌVỊṢ^{m}.
v. Palimpsest, its text often to be distinguished from the actual text with difficulty.

Ua 25 (S138-H42)

Recto

.1 SUS + *SI* 3 BOS^{f} 2 BOS^{m} 8

.2 OVIS^{m} 67

Verso

v. HORD 2̣9̣ T 8 V 2̣

The mix and types of commodities on these records are consistent with banqueting.[87] Neither tablet has a heading so no further help is provided by the texts, but as noted by Palaima, in addition to Un 47 and Un 138, H42 also wrote the Ae tablets, which mention cult officials and refer to a man named *du-ni-jo*, possibly the same person who contributes goods for banqueting on Un 138.[88] The interests of this scribe thus lie in areas associated with religion and ceremonial feasting. Further, the pig ideogram SUS on Ua 25 is ligatured with *SI*, which as noted above appears to abbreviate /*sialos*/, 'fattened', presumably for slaughter. This ligature does not appear outside the context of banqueting records as far as is known. The inclusion of wine on Ua 17 is also significant. Wine is never issued as ordinary rations,[89] and while it does appear in perfumery records, the presence of animals makes clear that Ua 17 is not a perfumery record. These factors in combination strongly suggest that Ua 17 and –25 are banqueting foodlists.[90]

Three more difficult tablets by H42 are as follows.[91]

Fa 16 (S138-H42)

i-qo CYP+*O* 8 T 2 V 1̣ ⟦ ⟧

PUNCT *dextra*.

Ua 9 (S138-H42)

.1 HORD 100 T 1 V 2 ka-p̣ạ[

.2 OLIV 88 T 7[

Palimpsest.

Ua 434 (S138-H42)

.1]G̣ṚẠ 80[

.2]CYP+*O* 13 [

.2 Trace at left, perhaps unit or divider.

While the general interests of H42 concern banqueting, that need not mean that *every* tablet he wrote was a banqueting list. The full dossier of this scribe is: the Ae series, An 128, Fa 16, Ua 9, –17, –25, –434, Un 47, –138, Va 482.[92] Va 482 deals with ivory and has no apparent connection with religion.[93] The Ae series does have a religious connection, as just noted, An

[87] Killen 1994, 80; 1994–1995b, 373.
[88] Palaima 1989, 109–10.
[89] Palmer 1994, 190.
[90] Killen 1994, 80; Halstead 1998–1999, 163–4. Weilhartner (2005, 157–8) reserves judgement; he discusses the records together with Ua 9 and –434.
[91] Texts from *PTT*.
[92] *Scribes Pylos*, 103–5.
[93] Killen 2003.

128 may be a festival rations list (Section 5.2.3), and the other records examined so far are banqueting foodlists. Are Fa 16, Ua 9 and Ua 434 also connected with religion or banqueting?

L.R. Palmer suggested that Fa 16 is a record of an offering to a horse or 'horses' (*i-qo*),[94] but the word could also be a man's name and the document could even record a collection rather than a disbursement.[95] It is true that CYP+*O* is frequent in banqueting and offerings records and HORD, OLIV and GRA are all attested in such records (although wheat is rare),[96] but the large amounts in Fa 16, Ua 9 and Ua 434 far exceed those found in any of those securely identified. A better parallel for such amounts is seen in 'harvest' records and Killen notes that GRA and CYP+*O* regularly occur together in such records at Knossos (for instance the KN F(2) tablets). Thus it may be, as he suggests, that H42 was involved in food collection more generally.[97]

Taking these tablets as harvesting records need not be at odds with our identification of the general interests of H42. The goods might, for instance, have been collected with the ultimate intention of securing provisions for banquets rather than for general consumption. Or the situation could be similar to that seen in the Department of Perfumery and Offerings at Knossos, which dealt with particular types of commodities often used as offerings (see Section 3.2.3.1). Scribes of this department wrote the majority of the Knossos offerings records, but they also recorded collections of the commodities with which they were concerned as well as disbursements of the goods for other purposes. It is conceivable that H42 would have been involved in the collection of the materials needed for banqueting as well as the monitoring of their disbursal for feasting and for other uses.

Three final 'mixed commodities' (U- Class) records which may deal with banqueting can be discussed together. The texts are as follows.[98]

Un 612 + Xn 1122 (S2-H1)

.1]*KO*[*qs*
.2]-ẉạ-[ ] VIN 5
.3] CAP^f 1

.1 Perhaps]*KO* 1[, but]*ko*[and/or]*ko*-[not impossible.
.2 Possibly]-*ẉạ-ṭọ*[.

Un 1177 + *fr.* (Cii)

supra mutila
.1 OVIS 6 [
.2 BOS 1 [
.3 *ME* V 4 ⟦ ⟧ *AREPA* V 1̣[
.4] 1̣ tu-ṛọ$_2$[
.5 *deest*

.1 OVIS over ⟦ ⟧.

Un 1185 [+] Xn 1460 (S2-H1)

.1]ṭị[
.2 tu-ro$_2$, *ṬỤṚỌ$_2$*[ ]o , *vest.*[ ]*vest.* [
.3 *O* T 1 V 1 Z 1[ ] *vacat*
.4 OVIS 3 *WE* 20 [ ]ṣụṣ^x 10
.5 a$_3$-ka-na-jo *A$_3$* S 1 V 1 Z 2

Probably palimpsest and margin *infra*. Cut *infra* along the rule.
.2 Trace of sign at right of]*o* ,.

---

[94] Palmer 1963, e.g. 220, 277–8, 422.
[95] Killen 1992b, 368; Rousioti 2001, 307.
[96] Killen 2004, 157.
[97] Killen 2004, 157; see Rousioti 2001, 307 for a similar suggestion for Fa 16. Weilhartner (2005, 114–15) takes Fa 16 as a probable offerings record.
[98] Un 612: For new readings see Melena 2000–2001b, 373–4; Xn 1129 may be part of same tablet (Melena 2000–2001a, 365); see also Melena 1994–1995, 282; 1995–1996, 162. Un 1177: Text from Melena 2000–2001b, 376; the tablet was joined to a newly-found fragment. Melena notes (*loc. cit.*) that Un 1177 could actually be by H6. Un 1185: For the text see Bennett 1992, 120; Melena 1994–1995b, 286.

Un 612 is said to resemble Un 616, a perfumery record by the same scribe,[99] but the appearance of a goat makes it unlikely that it was a perfumery record. The combination of an animal with wine make a banqueting context more probable. In Un 1177 and –1185, the mix and type of commodities plus relatively small numbers are consistent with banqueting. No help comes from headings or other text (both tablets are fragmentary) nor scribal hand (H1 was the most prolific scribe at Pylos and wrote records of many types; Cii is non-specific), wine does not appear and none of the animals are described as being 'fattened'. But one clue which does point further towards a banqueting context is the appearance of cheese in both tablets. This commodity appears only in banqueting records (see Section 6.3.1) and, given that its only use would have been as a foodstuff, along with the similarity between the lists here and those in other banqueting records, the probability is that these are banqueting records.[100]

So far we have dealt with mixed commodity records. Several single commodity records also relate to banqueting. Two well-known examples are as follows.

Vn 20		(H25)	**Cn 608**		(S608-H1)
.1	o-a$_2$, e-pi-de-da-to		.1	jo-a-se-so-si , si-a$_2$-ro	
.2	pa-ra-we-wo , wo-no		.2	o-pi-da-mi-jo	
.3	pi-**82*-de	50	.3	pi-**82*	SUS+*SI* 3
.4	me-ta-pa-de	50	.4	me-ta-pa	SUS+*SI* 3
.5	pe-to-no-de	100	.5	pe-to-no	SUS+*SI* 6
.6	pa-ki-ja-na-de	35	.6	pa-ki-ja-si	SUS+*SI* 2
.7	a-pu$_2$-de	35	.7	a-pu$_2$-we	SUS+*SI* 2
.8	a-ke-re-wa-de	30	.8	a-ke-re-wa	SUS+*SI* 2
.9	e-ra-to-de	50	.9	e-ra-te-i	SUS+*SI* 3
.10	ka-ra-do-ro-de	40	.10	ka-ra-do-ro	SUS+*SI* 2
.11	ri-jo-de	20	.11	ri-jo	SUS+*SI* 2
.12	*vacat*				

Vn 20 records wine being sent to each of the nine towns of the Hither Province and Cn 608 records pigs being fattened at the same places, presumably in preparation for slaughter. It is not clear that the pigs would be consumed at these places (rather than, for instance, being sent to the palace), but the wine at least is clearly being distributed (note the allative *-de*), presumably in connection with feasting. These tablets are generally accepted as banqueting records, and are taken as evidence for banquets at regional settlements.[101]

Cn 3 is probably also a record of sacrifice away from the palace; the text is as follows.

Cn 3		(S608-H1)
.1	jo-i-je-si , me-za-na ,	
.2	e-re-u-te-re , di-wi-je-we , qo-o ,	
.3	a$_2$-ra-tu-a , o-ka-ra$_3$,	BOS 1
.4	pi-ru-te , ku-re-we	BOS 1
.5	e-na-po-ro , i-wa-si-jo-ta ,	BOS 1
.6	o-ru-ma-to , u-ru-pi-ja-jo ,	BOS 1
.7	a$_2$-ka-a$_2$-ki-ri-ja-jo , u-ru-pi-ja-jo-jo ,	BOS 1
.8-9	*vacant*	

The interpretation of the heading is disputed, but Cn 3 is closely connected with the *o-ka* tablets, and may refer to animals destined for feasting by troops detailed on those records.[102]

---

[99] Shelmerdine 1985, 20–1.

[100] Palaima (1989, 109) reasonably enough takes Un 1177 as not clear, as does Weilhartner (2005, 168). On Un 1185 see Palaima 1992b, 65 (as a banqueting record); Weilhartner 2005, 160–1. Palaima (1992b, 65–7) relates *A*$_3$ to the ideogram *A* on Un 1320, suggesting it is some sort of animal product; see also Melena 1987b; Bendall 2003, 223.

[101] Palaima 1989, 117–18; Palmer 1994, 75–8; Godart 1999, 253–4; Bendall 2004, 109–10; Weilhartner 2005, 152–3.

[102] See the useful discussion by Palaima 1989, 104, 107–8, 110, 114–17; also *Documents*, 207, 435–6; Palmer 1956, 141; 1963, 175–6; Godart 1999, 250–2; Weilhartner 2005, 149–50. Killen (forthcoming[a]) suggests that *me-za-na* may be a female deity connected with Messenia (cf. Palmer 1963, 434).

Another single commodity tablet registers female goats against various named individuals.

Cn 1287					(H31)
.1	a-*64-jo ,	a-ke-ro	CAP^{f} 1	/*angelos*/?	'herald'?
.2	te-re-do	ka-na-pe-u	CAP^{f} 1	/*knapheus*/	'fuller'
.3	na-ma-ru-ko		CAP^{f} 1		
.4	qe-ta-ko	ke-ra-me-u	CAP^{f} 1	/*kerameus*/	'potter'
.5	da-u-da-ro ,	pe-re-ke-u	CAP^{f} 1	/*plekeus*/?	'weaver'?
.6	mu-ti-ri-ko ,	di-u-ja , do-e-ro	CAP^{f} 1	slave of *di-u-ja*	
.7	a$_2$-ra-ka-wo	ke-re-ta-o do-e-ro	CAP^{f} 1	slave of MN	
.8	a-sa-ma-o		CAP^{f} 1		
.9	mo-ri-wo		CAP^{f} 2		
.10	ma-ni-ko		CAP^{f} 1		
.11–12	*vacant*				
Verso					
	drawing of a labyrinth				

Most of the Cn tablets are herd management records dealing with shepherds and their flocks (see Section 2.5.1 for an example), but Cn 1287 records single animals registered against people who are notably not goatherds. Herd management is thus counter-indicated, and it is probable that this is a record of minor contributions for banquets by various craftsmen and temple servants (the slave of the female deity *di-u-ja*).[103] A parallel for contributions by a slave is provided by one of the Knossos banqueting records, C(2) 915, discussed below. Cn 1287 is accepted by various scholars as a probable banqueting record.[104]

Various sealings may also relate to banqueting. The texts are as follows.[105]

banqueting

Wr 1325			(S1331-Ci)
.α	CAP^{m}	*supra sigillum*	(*CMS* I, no. 319)
.β	*vacat*		
.γ	o-pa		
Wr 1331			(S1331-Ci)
.α	OVIS^{m}	*supra sigillum*	(*CMS* I, no. 329)
.β	*vacat*		
.γ	o-pa		
Wr 1334			(S1331-Ci)
.α	CAP^{m}	*supra sigillum*	(*CMS* I, no. 329)
.β	*vacat*		
.γ	*vacat*		
Wr 1416			(—)
.α	ṢỤṢ^{m}	*supra sigillum*	(*CMS* I, no. 180)
.β	*vacat*		
.γ	*vacat*		
	Reading very doubtful, BOS^{f} not excluded.		

other/unclear

Wp 1327			(Ci)
.α	*sigillum*		(*CMS* I, no. 324)
.β	]ṢỤṢ^{x} 3̣5̣0		
.γ	pe-re-i-to		
Wr 1329			(S1331-Ci)
.α	*sigillum*		(*CMS* I, no. 317)
.β	20		
.γ	*vacat*		
Wr 1330			(S1331-Ci)
.α	*sigillum*		(*CMS* I, no. 312)
.β	*vacat*		
.γ	ọ-pa		
Wr 1332			(S1331-Ci)
.α	*WI*	*supra sigillum*	(*CMS* I, no. 329)
.β	o-pa		
.γ	*vacat*		
Wr 1333			(S1331-Ci)
.α	*sigillum*		(*CMS* I, no. 329)
.β	*deest*		
.γ	o-pa		

[103] Killen 1999a, 334; Bendall 2003, 216–17; 2004, 108–9.

[104] A possible banqueting context for Cn 1287 is argued for also by Killen 1999a, 334; Godart 1999, 251; Halstead 1998–1999, 164; Weilhartner 2005, 154–6. Palaima (1992b, 64–5) notes the labyrinth on the *verso* may suggest a religious context.

[105] Texts are as in *PTT*, except Wr 1416 is as in *PoN* IV (reading ṢỤṢ rather than ÇẠP – either way the reading is very doubtful as noted in the apparatus of both volumes – and adding the seal number which is absent in *PTT*). Wr 1327 is now reclassified Wp. Wr 1458 is read differently in *PoN* IV; see n 110 below.

Wr 1458

	supra mutila	
.α	.]f [	*supra sigillum* (*CMS* I, no. 329)
.β	*vacat*	
.γ	*deest*	

Wr 1325, –1331, –1334 and –1416 closely resemble the Thebes Wu sealings and are likely to have had a similar purpose.[106] Particularly significant is the appearance of animal ideograms together with *o-pa*, which represents /*hopā*/ 'finishing', the general sense of which, as Killen has established, is: '"preparing" finished objects or livestock, either by refurbishing them or by bringing them up to a required condition', in the case of livestock by fattening them for slaughter.[107]

The purpose of the other sealings is unclear. The reading on Wp 1327 is uncertain – it could also be ẸQỤ – and even if it did refer to pigs the large number would be unprecedented for a banqueting record (see further discussion in Section 4.2.4.2). *WI* on Wr 1332 might be oxhide,[108] but could also refer to an animal.[109] Two further sealings deal with *o-pa* 'finishing' but no ideograms are written so it is unclear what was being 'finished'. What the number '20' on Wr 1329 refers to is similarly unknown. Finally, Wr 1458 may record an animal, in which case it would presumably be a banqueting document, but the reading is uncertain.[110]

Finally, we consider a few documents which are inconclusive or are certainly not banqueting records. They are discussed in numerical order.

Cn 440

Cn 440 (Ci)

	supra mutila
.1	] *vest.*
.2	] *vacat*
.3	] *vacat*
.4	] 5
.5	]*vest.*[ ]*vest.*[ ] *vacat*
.6	] 5
.7	]SUS^x 3̣1[ ] *vacat*
.8	]SUS^x 14 [ ]ṢỤṢ^f[*qs*] *vac.*
.9	]*vacat* [
	infra mutila

.3 Less space between rules, but not exactly an *angustum*.
.4]5 corrected possibly from 6?
.5 Traces of two signs on the left: the first could be]*nọ*[, the second]ÇẠP̣^{f}[*qs*. Over erasure.
.6 Probably [SUS^f; traces at right edge of lacuna indicate that 36 (or 38) is possible.
.8 ṢỤṢ^x+*SI* possible.
.9 Rather broad, but no bottom edge.

If SUS+*SI* were securely read in line .8 (see apparatus) a banqueting context would be indicated, but the reading is uncertain.[111] The tablet structure and relatively large numbers of pigs suggest rather a herd management record.

---

[106] Killen 1999a, 336; Bendall 2003, 214–15 with further bibliography; see also now Weilhartner 2005, 169–70, 227. For the Pylos sealings in general see Pini 1997; Olivier 1997.
[107] Killen 1999a, esp. 332–6, 338. The word 'finished' is used in the same way in modern English to refer to animals fattened for slaughter (*loc. cit.* 332).
[108] Killen 1999a, 335; Bendall 2003, 214.
[109] Killen 1999a, 336.
[110] Wr 1458: *PoN* IV now reads]*Ẹ*[(which could also be an animal; see Palaima 2000, 265).
[111] Cn 440: Text from *PoN* IV, but with underdotting as in *Minos*. It is substantially unchanged from earlier published transcriptions (Melena 1994–1995b, 279; also Melena 1992–1993a, 78–9; 1992–1993b, 315; 1994–1995a, 97; 1996–1997, 177), but the apparatus to lines .8 and .9 is new. Weilhartner (2005) does not address Cn 440 so presumably does not consider it a banqueting record. Halstead (1998–1999, 164–5) takes it as a possible herd management record.

Cn 1069

Cn 1069

.1	]ko[
.2	]wo-to ⟦ÇẠP̣ᵐ 6⟧
.3	]-wo CAP^{f} 10
.4	] *vacat*

Cn 1069 might have been thought of as a banqueting record on account of the small numbers, but it now joins Cn 441 and turns out to be part of a herd management record[112] (a good reminder that small numbers are not in themselves a sufficient criterion to identify banqueting records).

Cn 1075

Cn 1075

.0		*supra mutila*
.1		] OVIS^{f} X 15 [
.2	]	*vacat* [

Cn 1075 is, probably, like 1069, a herd management rather than a banqueting record. Cross-marks (line .1) are not found in banqueting records, but do appear in flock census records (e.g. Cn 131).[113]

Cn 1116

Cn 1116 (Ci)

.0	*supra mutila*
.1	]ṢỤṢ^{f} 26
.2	]ṢỤṢ^{x} 12
.3	]*vacat*

The arrangement of the text would make this likely to be a herd management record, now confirmed by its being found to join Cn 491.[114] It should be noted that the ideogram was not securely read in any case and the join now shows ÇẠP̣ to be the more probable reading.

Cn 1197

Cn 1197 (S131-H1)

.1	a-si-ja-ti-ja [	
.2	wa-e-ro	OVIS^{m} 1[
.3	ti-ko-ro	OVIS^{m} 1 [
.4	e-sa-re-we	OVIS 3[
.5	e-re-e-we	OVIS^{m} [
.6	*vacat* [	

Cn 1197 may be a banqueting record (note the small numbers), but there is no corroborative support. The words in lines .4–5 are official titles of some sort,[115] but it is unclear whether they are nominative plural or dative singular. If the latter (more likely), one might draw a parallel with records such as Cn 1287 and Un 138. However, the document must remain 'Unclear'.[116]

---

[112] Cn 1069: Text as in *PTT*; for the join and new text see Melena 1994–1995a, 97 (also 1992–1993a, 80; 1992–1993b, 322).

[113] This is now confirmed by a join to Cn 485, reported in *PoN* IV.

[114] Cn 1116: Text given here is from *PTT*. The join changes the reading of both documents significantly (and they are of course reclassified to the lower number, Cn 491); Melena 1994–1995b, 280.

[115] Killen 1992–1993b, esp. 113–14. Cn 1197 text as in *PTT* (unchanged in *PoN* IV).

[116] Halstead (1998–1999, 163–5) takes Cn 1197 as a possible consumption record; Weilhartner (2005, 153–4, 227) too accepts it as a banqueting/offerings record.

Cn 1286

Cn 1286 (Cii)

.1 o-pi-ra-i-ja OVIS 3 CAP 1
.2 *vacat*
.3 *vacat*
.4 *vacat*
.5 *vacat*
reliqua pars sine regulis

Cn 1286 is regarded as 'Unclear' but may be a banqueting record. Small numbers of animals are recorded, and the scribe had ruled out several lines as if more text had been expected. If these had been filled in, Cn 1286 would resemble Cn 1287. The tablet also somewhat resembles the Cc records, next.[117]

The Cc tablets

Cc 660 (S4-H21)

.a a-ke-o , a-ke-re
me-ta-pa , pa-ro ka-ra-su-no CAP^{m} 30
Palimpsest, perhaps with actual erasure before CAP^{m}; cf. in hand and formula the set of Cn 40 &c.

Cc 665 (S4-H21)

ne-wo-pe-o , po-ti-ni-ja OVIS^{m} 100 SUS 190

Cc 1258 (S4-H21)

] CAP^{f} 30
cut at right

Cc 1283 (S4-H21)

]OVIS^{m} 1 [

Cc 1284 (S4-H21)

]ụ , pe-re CAP 8 [

Cc 1285 (S4-H21)

ma-se-de , OVIS^{m} 6[

Cc 660 and Cc 665 are herd management records. The scribe who wrote them, H21, also wrote a great many of the Cn stock management records (see Section 2.5.1).[118] Cc 660 in particular resembles many of the single entries on such records with the formula: TN (*me-ta-pa* in this case) + *pa-ro* 'chez' + MN (the shepherd, here *ka-ra-su-no*). Cc 665 is unusual in that it does not record a shepherd name (*ne-wo-pe-o* is a TN, attested elsewhere as the location of a female work-group[119]), and that the flock is designated to the deity *Potnia*, presumably in her role as 'Collector'; we will return to this tablet below (Section 2.5.2).

The next four Cc tablets could be banqueting records on account of the relatively small numbers recorded,[120] but they may also be flock management records. It may be significant that they were found in a different find-spot from the first two. Cc 660 and 665 were found, as were the Cn herd management records, in the Archives Complex. The other four Cc tablets on the other hand come from the Northeastern Building, a redistribution complex or 'clearing

[117] Bendall 2003, 216. Halstead (1998–1999, 163–5) takes Cn 1286 as a possible consumption record; Weilhartner (2005, 154–5, 227) accepts it as a banqueting/offering record. Cc tablets: Texts as in *PTT* (there are very minor changes to the apparatus in *PoN* IV).
[118] *Scribes Pylos*, 80–5.
[119] See Chadwick 1988.
[120] Bendall 2003, 216.

house' for goods and personnel entering the palace.[121] Many of the sealings discussed above as similar to the Thebes sealings and probably, like them, related to animals assembled for a feast, come from this building. It could be that these four tablets relate to animals being moved ('assembled') rather than to the ordinary flock management activities of H21 (there is no reason of course that a scribe who dealt with ordinary flocks should not be involved on occasion with supplying animals for feasting – and note he manages at least one 'deity' herd). A possible hint towards religious associations is that *ma-se-de* on Cc 1285 appears elsewhere as a recipient in a possible offerings context (Mn 1411; see Section 6.4.1.1). These records are best left for the time being as 'Unclear', but a possibility that they record animals intended for sacrifice is open.[122]

Finally, we have a tablet recording wheat and figs.

Un 1426

Un 1426 (S1426-Ci)

.0 *supra mutila*
.1]e-we ,
.2 wa-]na-ka-te
.3]a_3-sa GRA 12
desunt e.g. 2 versus
.6]ki-ri-te-wi-ja-pi ,
.7] *NI* 5
.8] *vacat*

Un 1426 may be a rations record, since wheat and figs appear commonly together on rations records at Pylos.[123] A 'religious' connection may be indicated by the appearance of the words *wa-na-ka-te* (see Section 3.2.2) and *ki-ri-te-wi-ja-pi*, a feminine appellative which most scholars consider to have cult connections.[124] If this is so, festival rations may be involved (see Section 2.3.3.1), although the word also occurs on what seem to be 'ordinary' rations records (e.g. KN E 777). In any case, Un 1426 does not appear to record a banqueting 'menu'.

A summary of the banqueting foodlists at Pylos along with other texts discussed here is given in Table 2-3. (Note that tablets Un 718 and –853 are discussed below; Section 2.4.4.)

Table 2-3. Banqueting foodlists at Pylos

securely identified banqueting records		probable/ possible	unclear, but possibility open	unclear, but possibly related	unclear	herd management records
Un 2	Cn 418	Un 612	Cn 1197	*Harvesting records?*	Wp 1327	Cn 440
Cn 3	Cn 608	Un 1177	Cc 1258	Ua 9	Wr 1329	Cc 660
Un 6	Un 718	Un 1185	Cc 1283	Fa 16		Cc 665
Ua 17	Un 853	Cn 1287	Cc 1284	Ua 434		Cn 1069 [+441]
Vn 20	Wr 1325		Cc 1285	*Festival rations??*		Cn 1075
Ua 25	Wr 1331		Cn 1286	Un 1426		Cn 1116 [+491]
Un 47	Wr 1334		Wr 1330			
Un 138	Wr 1416		Wr 1332			
			Wr 1333			
			Wr 1458			

[121] Bendall 2003, esp. 224–5.
[122] Halstead (1998–1999, 164–5) also takes Cc 660, –665 and –1258 as possible herd management records, and Cc 1283, –1284 and –1285 as possible consumption records. Weilhartner (2005, 148, 227) accepts the Cc tablets as possibly recording animals for banqueting.
[123] Un 1426: text from *PTT*. Weilhartner (2005, 168) also takes this tablet as some sort of a rations record with possible religious connections.
[124] *DMic.* I, 363 (*s.v. ki-ri-te-wi-ja*); but the connection is not unanimously accepted (see *DMic. loc.cit.* n 6). The term appears again below in Section 2.5.2.

2.3.2.3 BANQUETING FOODLISTS AT KNOSSOS

An account of banqueting records at Knossos should begin with Killen's discussion of the C(2) tablets.[125] The texts are as follows.

C(2) 908 (112)
]pa-ro , / de-ki-si-wo CAP^{f} 1 [

C(2) 913 (112?)
.1 pa-ro , e-te-wa-no , *a*$_{3}$ CAP^{m} 1[
.2 pa-ro ko-ma-we-te CAP^{m} 1 pa[
.2 CAP^{m} over ⟦CAP^{f}⟧.

C(2) 914 (112)
.A pa-ra-ti-jo OVIS^{m} 50
.B a-ka-wi-ja-de / pa-ro , CAP^{m} 50
Left end and central division (under *pa-ra-ti-jo*) erased.

C(2) 915 (112)
.A] OVIS^{f} 10 [
.B] pa-ro , a-pi-qo-ta / pa-ro , do-e-ro CAP^{f} 10 [

C(2) 922 + 5764 (112)
]te-ru-wo-te CAP^{f} 1 [

C(2) 941 + 1016 + *fr.* (112)
Recto
.A OVIS^{m} 8̣[
.B pa-ro / a-pi-qo-ta , sa-pa-ka-te-ri-ja OVIS^{f} 10 [
Verso
.A ⟦ ⟧ [
.B ⟦wi-jạ[⟧ [
r.B Traces at right.

C(2) 5765 + *fr.* (112)
] CAP^{f} [

C(2) 7064 + 7543 + 8226 (112?)
.1 a-ki-ri-ja CAP^{m} 2̣6 CAP^{f} [
.2 *vac.* [ ]ḳẹ 3[
.2 3[probably over ⟦ ⟧.

C(2) 8225 + *fr.* (112)
] CAP^{f} 1[
Perhaps 2̣[.

C(2) 8578 (112)
]pa-ro , [
Possible trace at right.

Killen begins by asking whether, given the evidence for state-organised banquets at Pylos and Thebes, we have similar evidence for Knossos. He draws attention to the similar pattern of entry in some of the C(2) tablets (908, –913, –922, –8225) to some of the Thebes sealings, in that in each case the formula '*pa-ro* + MN(dat.)' is followed by small numbers of animals. The specific examples of the Thebes sealings he draws attention to are as follows.

[125] Killen 1994; 1996b. C(2) set: Texts from *KT*^{5}.

Wu 47
.α SUS^{m}
.β pa-ro te-qa-jo
.γ ro-we-wi-ja

Wu 59
.αa *171* 36
.αb [ ]SUS^{x}
.β pa-ro , sa-me-
.γa -we
.γb ro-we-wi-jạ[

Wu 60
.α ṢỤṢ^{m}
.β pạ-ṛọ , sa-me-we
.γ *vacat*

As Killen points out, although 'the *pa-ro* plus personal name plus single animal entry formula on both the sealings and the tablets is certainly not a complex one, it is not one common on the tablets as a whole, where records of animals much more often relate to a whole flock.' Further, where the formula does appear in herd management records 'the numbers in the animal entries which follow are invariably large, and evidently relate to entire flocks'[126] (note also that herd management records almost invariably include toponyms referring to the locations of the flocks). Killen asks 'whether this similarity is not significant: whether, in fact, the purpose of the C(2) tablets is not identical to that of the sealings, i.e. to record the receipt (whether actual or intended) by the palace of animals that are destined for consumption at some kind of ceremonial banquet'. He observes that one tablet of the set, C(2) 941, includes the word *sa-pa-ka-te-ri-ja*, and revives Lejeune's suggestion that this may be */sphaktēria/*, referring to animals intended for slaughter. He notes that other interpretations of the word are difficult, and parallels for the unusual spelling can be provided.[127] He concludes that the tablets may record individual contributions to feasts by important officials (e.g. *a-pi-qo-ta*, one of the main Knossian 'Collectors'; see Section 2.5), similar to those of *du-ni-jo* in PY Un 138 and **we-u-da-ne-u* in PY Cn 418.[128]

In what follows, we examine the remaining probable or possible banqueting records from Knossos. For present purposes, discussion is limited to the issue of identification. The documents are examined in order of Class mark and number to facilitate referencing. Most of the records are C- Class; the rest are D-, U- and W- Class, plus there is one X fragment.

We begin with the C- Class tablets, starting with the C(3) set.[129]

C(3) 905 (109)
] SUS 1 [

C(3) 967 (109?)
pu-na-so , [
Trace at right.

C(3) 979 + 1032 + 7051 + 7052 + 7657 (109)
do-ti-ja , / ra-ja , pu-na-so-qe , 'ra-su-to-qe' a-to-mo SUS 1

C(3) 1030 + 7055 (109)
e-ko-so , / du-ma SUS 1
Cut at right.

C(3) 1039 (109)
.a] e-ra-wo , du-ma [
.b **56*-]ko-we-qe ṢỤṢ^{x}[

[126] Killen 1994, 74.
[127] Killen 1994, 75–6, referring to *Mémoires* II, 203 n.18.
[128] A connection with banqueting for the C(2) set is widely accepted, e.g. Godart 1999, 249; Halstead 1998–1999, 152, 160; Bendall 2004, 107–8; Palaima 2004b, 105–6, 123.
[129] C(3) set: Texts from *KT*^{5}. C(3) 9666 was formerly regarded as part of the C(1) set by h. 107 (see *KT*^{5}); for the new classification see Godart *et al.* 1992–1993, 64; *CoMIK* IV, 181, *s.v.* 9666.

C(3) 7057 (109)

]ma SUS 1̣[

Cut and smoothed at bottom.

C(3) 7058 + 7922 + *fr.* (109)

]ḍạ-mo-ko-ro SUS 1

C(3) 7793 + 9287 (109)

da-]mọ-ko-ro ṢỤṢ^{x} 1̣[

C(3) 9666 + *fr.* (109)

]ṢỤṢ^{x} 1 [

inf. mut.

The tablets register pigs against toponyms (e.g. *e-ko-so*) and individuals identified by official titles (e.g. *du-ma*). A few factors point in the direction of banqueting.[130] First, pigs are kept primarily for consumption, and appear only in banqueting and herd management records. Toponyms are common on herd management records, but the appearance of single animals rules out the possibility that these are flock records, as does the fact that the officials are fairly high-status: these are not records of shepherds.[131] A probable explanation is that these records supply another instance of important officials making individual contributions for a feast as in the KN C(2) set, Thebes sealings and PY Un 138.[132] The *pa-ro* formula is lacking, but it need not be that the formula was used systematically in every instance.

The remaining C- Class records are discussed in numerical order.[133]

C 33

C 33 (—)

sup. mut.

.1]^{f} 2[

.2]OVIS^{f} 6[

.3] OVIS^{f} 1 [

.4] *vac.* [

.3 Trace to right perhaps *ṇi*[, but more likely X̣[.

The small numbers recorded suggest a banqueting context and support for this interpretation comes from the findspot. C 33 was found in the Clay Chest [A], along with important sets of offerings records (the Fp(1) and Fs sets), and there are *no* tablets from this deposit which are clearly related to any other purpose. The tablet is thus likely to be a banqueting record. It was argued above that findspot is not necessarily a conclusive indicator, but in this case the special character of the Clay Chest deposit makes it highly likely that C 33 was related in function to the other tablets with which it was found (cf. discussion of Gg 10 in Section 2.2.2).

C 394

C 394 (—)

Recto

.1 *vac.*[

.2 qe-[

.3 BOS^{m} 1 *sa* OVIS^{m}[

.4 pạ-ja-ọ-ne / pa-ḍẹ[

.5]*vest.*[

inf. mut.

---

[130] Scholars who accept the C(3) set as relating to banqueting/consumption include Halstead (1998–1999, 152, 160) and Godart (1999, 254).

[131] On the status of titles such as *du-ma* and *da-mo-ko-ro* see Lindgren 1973 II, 32, 40–1.

[132] Godart 1999, 254; cf. Bendall 2004.

[133] All texts from *KT*^{5}.

Verso

.1]no
.2]*sa* OVIS^{m} 1 *sa* CAP^{m} 1[
.3]we *p̣ạ* OVIS^{m} 1 [
.4] *vest.* [
.5 *inf. mut.*

r.4 -*ọ*- of *p̣ạ-ja-ọ-ne* virtually certain: traces very difficult to reconcile with *p̣ạ-ja-ẉọ-ne*.

As argued by Killen, the small number and heterogeneous mix of animals in C 394 would be consistent with a banqueting interpretation, and sacrifice is suggested by the probable appearance of two deity names, *pa-ja-o-ne* and *pa-de*.[134] As he remarks, given this context, it is tempting to interpret the adjunct *sa* found on this document as an abbreviation of *sa-pa-ka-te-ri-ja*.[135]

C 902

C 902 (201)

.0 *sup. mut.*
.1 mi-ru-ro / si-pe-we BOS *ne* **170* 12
.2 o-du-ru-wi-jo / ko-re-te BOS *ne* **170* 12
.3 wa-to / ḳọ-re-te BOS *ne* **170* 12 // wa-to / da-nu-wo 'BOS' **170* 12
.4 si-ra-ro / ko-re-te BOS 1 *ne* **170* 12
.5 **56*-ko-we / e-ra-ne BOS 1 *ne* **170* 12
.6 o-du-ru-we / u-wo-qe-we BOS 1 *ne* **170* 12
.7 ri-jo-no / ko-re-te BOS 1 *ne* **170* 12
.8 ru-ki-ti-jo BOS 1 *ne* **170* 12
.9 a-pa-ta-wa / ko-re-te BOS 1 *ne* **170* 12
.10 ku-ta-i-to / ko-re-te BOS 1 *ne* **170* 12
.11 re-ri-jo / e-re-ta BOS 1 *ne* **170* 12
.12] wa-to / we-re-ẉẹ BOS 1 *ne* **170* 12
.13 *inf. mut.*

.12 Text probably complete at left.
.13 Bottom line probably uninscribed.
v. (→) ruled (10 lines) but not inscribed.

C 902 lists officials (*ko-re-te*) and men's names (e.g. *si-pe-we*) associated with various towns (e.g. *wa-to*, *a-pa-ta-wa*).[136] Against each entry is registered a bovine and 12 units of **170* with the adjunct *ne*. The commodity **170* is unidentified, but one possibility is that it was fodder and Palaima, taking it in this sense, suggests a possible connection with fattening for slaughter.[137] Godart too takes the tablet as a banqueting record, suggesting the officials were making contributions to the palace along the lines of the Thebes sealings and other documents, a proposal followed also by Killen.[138] However, as Killen further points out, **170* need not necessarily be directly associated with the animals – it could simply represent a further commodity being offered or contributed. Without a better understanding of what **170* represents it is difficult to be certain but in either case an association with sacrifice is likely.

C 954

C 954 + <1632> + 5016 (—)

Recto

.1] OVIS^{f} 1 mo-ro-qa OVIS^{f} 1 ke-to-ro OVIS^{f} 1 we-wo-ni-jo C̣ẠP̣^{f} [
.2]ḳụ-no-o CAP^{f} 1 pe-ri-te-u OVIS^{f} 1 me-tu-ro CAP^{f} 1 si-[
.3] CAP^{f} 1 di[-pte-ra-]po-ro-i C̣ẠP̣^{x} 1̣[

---

[134] Killen 1996b, 79–80. *pa-ja-o-ne*, in a variant spelling *pa-ja-wo-ne*, is attested in V 52, a list of deities; *pa-de* in e.g. offerings record Fp(1) 1.

[135] Killen 1996b, 80. Other discussions of C 394 as a sacrifice/banqueting record include Palaima 1992a, 473; Halstead 1998–1999, 152, 158–9, 161; Weilhartner 2005, 79–80.

[136] For the TNs and official titles see e.g. Driessen 2001a, 104–8; Killen forthcoming(a).

[137] Palaima 1989, 91, 101–2.

[138] Godart 1999, 251–4, esp. 252; Godart & Tzedakis 2003, 75; Killen forthcoming(a). Halstead (1998–1999, 153, 160) gives the tablet with a question mark.

Verso

.1	]-ne-wa CAP^{f} 1	[
	reliqua pars sine regulis	

<1632>: missing; text from *Scripta Minoa* II, pl. 62.
.3 Restore as *di*[-*pte-ra-*]*po-ro-i* (cf. PY Fn 50.6, etc.)?

The small numbers and range of animals in C 954 point towards banqueting, and the mixture of official titles (e.g. *mo-ro-qa*) and men's names (e.g. *pe-ri-te-u*) recalls other banqueting 'contribution' records. The word in line .3, which is almost certainly to be restored as *di*[-*pte-ra-*]*po-ro-i*, is further suggestive since this is an occupational title associated with religious festivals (Section 2.3.3). C 954 is thus likely to be a banqueting record.[139]

C 1561

C 1561 (—)

.a	]ka-te-ri-ja [
.b	]wo OVIS^{f} [

.a Oblique stroke inside *-ja* not accidental.

If, as Killen suggests, the word in the first line of C 1561 is to be restored *sa-pa-ka-te-ri-ja*, this is probably a banqueting record.[140]

C 1902

C <1902> (—)

.1	]68 C̣ẠP̣^{f} 2
.2	] C̣ẠP̣^{f} 45
.3	] *vac.*

Missing; text from Evans' *Notebook* 1905, p. 9a.

The text of C 1902 is too damaged to be certain, but this is more likely a herd management than a banqueting record. Note 2 + 68 = 70 (line .1), a typical round number for a flock record.[141]

C 5669

C 5669 (—)

.0	*sup. mut.*
.1	]**2̣5̣8̣* 12 CAP^{f} 3̣[
.2	]**2̣5̣8̣* 12 CAP^{f} 2̣[
.3	]*vest.*[
.4	*inf. mut.*

.1 **258* better than **150*.

C 5669 is regarded as 'Unclear' but a possible banqueting record. Ideogram **258* is a more elaborate version of **152*, which represents oxhide. Skins do appear in banqueting contexts,[142] but there is no further evidence from which to judge the function of this document.[143]

C 6021

C 6021 (—)

.1	]no-re CAP^{m} 1̣[
.2	]ra-zo[

.2 Trace at right.

[139] Halstead (1998–1999, 158–9) also considers this a possible consumption record.
[140] Killen 1994, 75; also Halstead 1998–1999, 153, 160; Godart *et al.* 1990–1991, 388 *s.v.* X 9191.
[141] Halstead (1998–1999, 158–9) gives it as a possible consumption record.
[142] E.g. PY Un 719; see Killen 1999a.
[143] Although Killen forthcoming(a) draws attention to the possible significance of the number 12, found in other ritual contexts. Halstead (1998–1999, 158–9) classes the tablet as a possible consumption record.

The small number in line .1 may suggest banqueting, but the text is too fragmentary to tell.[144]

C 7048

C 7048 (—)

sup. mut.
.1]*vest*.[
.2]-je-re-u OVIS [
.3] $OVIS^x$[
inf. mut.

.3 Trace at left, perhaps]*ta*.

]-*je-re-u* in C 7048.2 might be restored as *i-je-re-u*, the only word attested with this ending, and a priest together with sheep may suggest a banqueting context (cf. Am(2) 821?; Section 2.5.2), although caution must be maintained as the text is so incomplete. The tablet is best regarded as 'Unclear', while leaving the possibility open.

The remaining C tablets

The final few C- Class documents may be treated as a group.

C 7054 (—)

]24 CAP^m 20

CAP^m roughly corrected from CAP^f. At least one erased ten below 20.

C 7059 + 7877 (—)

.A]ka-ma-o [$]^f$ 1̣0̣[
.B]-no , CAP^f 20[

.B Perhaps]*o-ṇọ*.

C 7060 + *fr*. **[+] 8791** (—)

Recto
.1 $]^f$ [ ]3 *WE* 1
.2]*vac*.[ ] *vac*.
Verso
ri[

Cut at bottom.
r.1 Upright before]3 could be the base of OVIS, $OVIS^m$, CAP or CAP^m.
v. Perhaps ⟦*ri*⟧ and further traces of ⟦ ⟧ to right of it.

C 7062 + 8348 (—)

] 1̣ OVIS 2 'e-u-[·]-ṃạ-ẉị-jo OVIS 1'

Traces at left (looks like a big]ṣọ). *e-u-*[·]-*ṃạ-ẉị-jo*: third sign possibly -*sụ*-.

C 7515 (—)

]BOS 1 [

Possibly]*mu* 1. Traces at right.

These tablets may be banqueting records on account of the small numbers,[145] but for the purposes of the present study it is preferable to regard them as 'Unclear'. Very little text is preserved on any of these documents and the single word in C 7062 is obscure.

The Ce tablets

We next have a number of records from the RCT classified as Ce. This is a series, not a set, and the records need not be related in function (indeed, some are certainly not). Halstead's recent categorisation of the tablets, as set out in Table 2-4, provides a useful starting point.[146]

---

[144] Halstead (1998–1999, 158–9) considers it a possible consumption record.
[145] Halstead 1998–1999, 158–9.
[146] Halstead 1998–1999, 152–3, Table 1, 158–9, Table 2. (Note Ce 144 is only given in Table 1 since the numbers are lost.) On these documents see also *Scribes RCT*, 205–6.

Table 2-4. Halstead's classifications for the Ce tablets

herd management records	consumption record	unclear
A. *securely identified*	A. *securely identified*	Ce 163
Ce 50*	Ce 50*	
Ce 59	B. *possible*	
Ce 144	Ce 61	
Ce 7061	Ce 113	
B. *possible*	Ce 139	
Ce 50*	Ce 152	
Ce 162	Ce 156	
	Ce 283	
	Ce 8345	
	Ce 8346	
	Ce 9109	

Note
* = Document appears more than once in the table.

Halstead takes Ce 59, –144 and –7061 as 'herd management' texts, Ce 162 as a 'possible herd management' text (the first three deal with working oxen; note Ce 162 lists 10,000 sheep[147]) and Ce 163 as 'Unclear'. These identifications are straightforward and the tablets require no discussion here (but see Section 6.2.1.1); our focus is on the 'consumption records'. Note Halstead omits Ce 76, –7516 and –8279; the first is 'Unclear' but the other two may be banqueting records and are discussed below.[148]

Ce 50

Ce 50 (124)

Recto

.1a a-qi-ru OVIS^{m} 134 qa-ra$_2$-wo OVIS^{f} 43

.1b te-pa-ra , pe-re-qo-ta

.2 a-nu-ko OVIS^{f} 51 ro-ru OVIS^{f} 32

Verso

.1a a-qi-ru OVIS^{m} 190 q̣ạ-ra^{2}-wo OVIS^{f} 144

.1b o-pa

.2 a-nu-ko OVIS^{f} 133[ ] ro-ru OVIS^{f} 150

lat. sup. we-ka-ta BOS^{m} 4

.1b On both *r.* and *v.* this register written in minuscule between the first signs of l. 1a.
*r.*1b *te-pa-ra* over ⟦ ⟧ (*-pa-* over ⟦*si*⟧).
l.s. (in fact, the *lat. inf.* of the *v.*) 4 from ⟦6⟧ (written as 4 + ⟦2⟧).

Ce 50 is clearly concerned with herd management, but an association with banqueting is suggested by the word *o-pa* in line .1b, which, as noted above, indicates beasts being fattened for slaughter.[149] Killen observes that the large numbers of animals on the record 'are much larger than those found in sacrifice/banquet contexts' but, pointing to the example of C(2) 914 which records 100 animals, concludes that a similar purpose is 'not inconceivable'. However, as he also points out, the appearance of the word *we-ka-ta* 'working' in association with oxen on the edge of the tablet indicates that not all the animals here were intended for consumption (for *we-ka-ta* see Section 6.2.1.1), but it may be that the document is 'recording animals of different types' (there is no reason in principle that a document might not deal with a mix of subjects, although more usually they do not).[150] Halstead puts the document in both the 'herd

[147] It also has on the *verso* an erasure of SUS^{f} followed by a number 500 (not given in transcription, but seen in the photo in *CoMIK* I, *s.v.* 162; see also *Scribes RCT*, 205). The *KT*^{5} apparatus notes: 'Many traces of ⟦ ⟧ on both sides…Tablet possibly used for rough working.'
[148] Ce tablets: All texts are from *KT*^{5}, except the apparatus to Ce 152, from *KT*^{6}.
[149] Killen 1999a, esp. 333, 335–8; Halstead 1998–1999, 160–1; see also Melena 1983a, 259–63; *Scribes RCT*, 205.
[150] Killen 1999a, 333.

management' and 'consumption' categories,[151] a reasonable compromise. What is important for present purposes is that the sheep being fattened do not form part of a banqueting 'menu', such as PY Un 138 or Un 2, where goods had been brought together for *specific* occasions. It seems more likely that the Ce 50 animals were being earmarked for *future* consumption. One possibility is that the animals had been separated out from other flocks in order to be fattened.[152] Halstead's neutral term 'consumption text' covers both possibilities, and if we wish to make a distinction (which is useful here) we might speak of 'fattening records' (which in a real sense are still 'herd management records') as distinct from banqueting 'menus' or 'foodlists'. The distinction helps make sense of the large numbers on Ce 50 since we need not envisage animals drawn together for a particular occasion, but ones which have been earmarked as a group for 'fattening' but which might be culled over a period of time and for different events.

Ce 61

Ce 61 + *fr.* (124)
.1 o-ro-ke-u[
.2 me-*86-ta BOS 1[
.3 ra-wo-ti-jo BOS 1 [
.4 re-u-ka-ta BOS 1 [
.5 ti-ri-sa-ta[
.6 *inf. mut.*

.1 Possibly *o-ro-ke-u-*[or *o-ro-ke-u* BOS[.
.5 Possible trace of the 'ear' of BOS at right.

Ce 61 could be a banqueting record, but there is nothing to confirm this. Small numbers alone are insufficient indicators, and only one type of animal is represented. Cattle are found also in flock management and ploughing records, and this tablet could just as well record an issue of single animals to various named ploughmen (see Section 6.2.1.1).

Ce 113

Ce 113 ('124')
]o SUS 7 *KO*[

]*o* perhaps adjunct.

Ce 113 should be considered together with Ce 8279 and Ce 8346 (texts below); the first may, and the second certainly does, also record SUS plus *KO*. *KO* sometimes indicates *ko-ri-ja-do-no* 'coriander' (see Section 6.6.2.5), but being associated with pigs here might abbreviate *ko-ro* /*khoiros*/ 'piglet' (cf. *WE*).[153] These documents could be herd or breeding records, or may record pigs and piglets for sacrifice. They are considered here 'Unclear' but possible banqueting records.[154]

Ce 139

Ce 139 + *fr.* ('124')
.1 a-ku-ṇạ-i OVIS 2̣1[
.2 do-ti-ja OVIS 30[
.3 *vacat* [

Ce 139 is more likely to be a herd management than a 'banqueting' record. *a-ku-ṇạ-i* is *hapax*, but is probably a toponym in parallel with the well-attested toponym *do-ti-ja*. The numbers of

[151] Halstead 1998–1999, 158–9; note he takes the *o-pa* entry as applying also to the 144 ewes in line .1a, but the layout suggests it more likely applied only to the 190 rams.
[152] For instance, enclosure restricting movement would encourage weight-gain (Halstead 1998–1999, 157).
[153] Bennett *et al.* 1989, 235 *s.v.* Ce 8346; *Scribes RCT*, 206.
[154] Halstead (1998–1999, 158–9) classes them similarly.

animals involved (both of which are broken) fall within the range of both banqueting and herd management records, but toponyms, particularly set out in list form, are more common on the latter type of record.

Ce 152

Ce 152 + 8256 ('124')
Recto
.1 je-[
.2 ja-sa-[ ]BỌṢ 1 OVIS 1 C̣ẠP [
.3 ta-ta-ta BOS 1 OVIS 1 [
.4 da-na OVIS 1 CAP 1 [
.5 *vacat* [
Verso
.1 ạ-re-ko-to-re BOS 1 OVIS 1 CAP 1
.2]ọ-ne BOS 12 OVIS 12 CAP 12
.3]-na-i BOS 12 OVIS 12 CAP [
.4 *inf. mut.*

r.1 *je-ḍạ*[possible.
.2 Perhaps *ja-sa-ṛọ*[; BOS and end of line over ⟦ ⟧.
.4 Trace at right.
v.3 BOS^f or BOS$^{[f]}$? Possible trace of 1ọ[after CAP.

Ce 152 was long ago identified by Killen as a banqueting record,[155] but the structure and precise function of the document remain unclear. It is unfortunate that the words in lines .2 and .3 of the *verso* are lost since they look like datives, with a plural in line .3 (*ạ-re-ko-to-re* in *v*.1 is almost certainly the dative of the MN *Alektōr*[156]), and dative plurals are often found in offerings contexts (see e.g. Sections 3.2.2 and 3.2.3.5), although by no means exclusively so.[157] The repeated entries recall the structure of Un 6 which may record offerings on successive days of a festival. None of the individuals here is attested as a divinity, however, and they may rather be persons responsible for the dedications. In any case, it is probable the record has something to do with banqueting.

Ce 156

Ce 156 ('124')
.0 *sup. mut.*
.1]-na-zo BOS 1̣[
.2 te-wa-jo BOS 3[

.1 One or two signs missing before]-*na-zo*.

Ce 156 is similar to Ce 61 and is considered 'Unclear' for the same reasons.

Ce 283

Ce 283 [+] 7250 ('124')
Recto
]200 e-po 60[ ] 10 OVIS 40
Verso
⟦i-wẹ⟧[ ]⟦-jạ⟧ [

283 *r*.: *-po* 60[over ⟦ ⟧.
7250 *r*.: Over ⟦ ⟧.
v. ⟦*i-qẹ*⟧[also possible, but less likely.

Ce 283 is 'Unclear'. *e-po* may be /*eriphos*/ 'kid',[158] and kids (and yearlings) are found on

[155] Killen 1964, 1. See also *Scribes RCT*, 205 with n 19; Halstead 1998–1999, 158–9; Weilhartner 2005, 84–5; and Killen forthcoming(a).
[156] *DMic*. I, *s.v. a-re-ko-to-re*.
[157] Killen forthcoming(a).
[158] Scafa 1977; *Scribes RCT*, 206

banqueting records – but they are found on other sorts of records too, particularly breeding records. The round numbers point in the direction of a flock management record; also the figure '200' would be unique for a banqueting record.

Ce 7516

Ce 7516 ('124')
.1]57 *PO* 7 CAP[
.2]3 SUS^x[
.3]*vest*.[
inf. mut.

Whole tablet probably palimpsest.
.1 ⟦ ⟧ between the row of 4 tens and *PO*: hence the abnormal arrangement of tens and units.
.2 Trace before]3.
.3 Not incompatible with]100[, but]*ko*[*vel sim.* would also fit.

Ce 7516 is 'Unclear', although the small numbers and mix of commodities may suggest banqueting. The meaning of *PO* here is unknown (for *po*/*PO* in general see Section 6.6.3.2). In the oil tablets *po* used as an adjunct abbreviates *po-ni-ki-jo*,[159] but here it could represent for instance /*poloi*/ 'foals',[160] an unusual, but by no means inconceivable, subject for sacrifice. Since so much text is lost, all possibilities remain open.

Ce 8279

Ce 8279 ('124')
]1 *KO* 130[

Trace at left and above]1. Traces of ⟦ ⟧.

See discussion of Ce 113.

Ce 8345

Ce 8345 + *fr.* ('124')
]BOS^m 6 [
inf. mut.

Nothing whatsoever can be determined about the purpose of Ce 8345.

Ce 8346

Ce 8346 + 8644 + 9111 ('124')
]SUS^x 4 *KO* 80[

See discussion of Ce 113.

Ce 9109

Ce 9109 ('124')
.0 *sup. mut.*
.1]OVIS^m 1 CAP^m [
inf. mut
↓
v. *sup. mut*
] CAP^m [
inf. mut

r. Palimpsest. 'Second' unit probably palimpsest. ⟦*su*⟧ visible between OVIS^m and CAP^m, ⟦*jo*⟧ after CAP^m.
v. Possibly]⟦CAP^m⟧[; if not, over ⟦ ⟧.

---

[159] Foster 1977b, esp. 61–4.
[160] Bennett *et al.* 1989, 235 *s.v.* Ce 8346.

The small numbers and mix of animals in Ce 9109 might suggest banqueting, but confirmation is impossible since the document is so fragmentary and it is best considered 'Unclear'.

Summary of the Ce tablets

Table 2-5 summarises the Ce tablet classifications followed in the present study. It should be noted that where a tablet is listed here as possible, all that is indicated is that a banqueting context cannot actually be excluded.

Table 2-5. Ce tablet classifications in the present study

banqueting records	'fattening' record	herd management records	unclear
A. *probable*	Ce 50*	A. *securely identified*	Ce 61
Ce 152		Ce 50*	Ce 139
B. *possible*		Ce 59	Ce 156
Ce 113		Ce 144	Ce 163
Ce 7516?		Ce 7061	Ce 8345
Ce 8279		B. *possible*	Ce 9109
Ce 8346		Ce 162	
		Ce 283?	

Note: * = Document appears more than once in the table.

We now turn to the D- Class tablets.[161]

D 1024 and –5954

D 1024 + 7130 (—)

.1]ṛạ-jo , ma-ti-jo OVIS 1̣1̣0̣[

.2]e-ra-ja , qi-ni-te-we OVIS 100 sa[

.1 If 1̣1̣0̣[is correct, probably 1̣3̣0̣[or 1̣4̣0̣[, since the 10 is placed low.
.2 *sa*[perhaps adjunct (cf. C 394.3, etc.).

D 5954 (—)

sup. mut.
]ḳẹ-mo / *sa* Ọ̣ṾỊṢ^{m} [

Halstead discusses these as possible banqueting records,[162] based on the appearance of the adjunct *sa*, which, as Killen has argued, may abbreviate *sa-pa-ka-te-ri-ja*. This is likely for the second record, D 5954, where the adjunct appears before the ideogram as it does in C 394.3, but D 1024 is suspect (despite the apparatus). The *sa* follows the ideogram (which adjuncts almost never do) and the tablet is broken so *sa* could simply be the start of another word (possibly *sa-pa-ka-te-ri-ja*, but maybe something else). D 5954 is regarded here as probable and D 1024 as simply 'unclear'.

The Dm set

Dm 1175 + 1456 (117)

.a a_3-mi-re-we OVIS^{m} 4

.b ra-su-to , / e-ka-ra-e-we OVIS^{m} 10

Dm 1179 + 5364 (117)

.A] a_3-mi-re-we OVIS^{m} 5

.B ku-]ta-to , / e-ka-ra-e-we OVIS^{m} 67

[161] D 1024, –5954 and the Dm set: All texts from KT^5.
[162] Halstead 1998–1999, 161.

Dm 1180 + 5048 (117)
.A a_3-mi-re-we , OVIS^{m} 4
.B pa-i-to / e-ka-ra-e-we OVIS^{m} 20

Dm 1182 (117)
to-u-na-ta , / e-ka-ra-e-we OVIS^{m} 21

Dm 1184 + 8408 **[+] 5176** (117)
.a e-ka-ra-e-we
.b pa-i[-]ṭọ , / o-we-to , o-pa , OVIS^{m} 15

The Dm set, by the major sheep scribe h. 117, comprises fifteen documents; the five examples here show the main variations. The texts are fairly uniform and the majority of the set has the form of the first three shown, with town name (e.g. *pa-i-to*) followed by two groups of OVIS^{m}, described by different terms. *a_3-mi-re-we* may represent */aimilēwes/* 'enclosed animals' and *e-ka-ra-e-we* may be */engraēwes/* 'for fattening'. Note also the appearance of *o-pa* on Dm 1184 (its sole appearance in the set). Halstead gives the Dm tablets as 'consumption' texts,[163] and we follow his suggestion that these are records of animals at various locations being fattened for sacrifice. The comments made above with regard to Ce 50 apply here. These are probably not banqueting 'menus', but may be described as 'fattening' records.[164]

We now turn to the U- Class documents, beginning with the Uc tablets.

Uc 160 [+] Uc 8032

Uc 8032 [+] Uc 160 ('124')
sup. mut.
.1 *vest.*[
.2 me-ri[
.3 qi[
inf. mut.
↓
v. *sup. mut.*
.1] *vac.*
.2]6̣
.3] *vest.*
inf. mut.

Part of the left hand edge of the same tablet as 160, but exact position relative to the main fragment cannot be established.
*v.*1 Possible traces of ⟦ ⟧.
.2]6̣ over ⟦ ⟧.

Uc 160 ('124'd)
sup. mut.
.1]*vest.*[
.2] Z 3 ⟦ Ẓ ⟧
.3]V 1 Z 1 VIN S 1 V 3 Z 2
.4] V 5 Z 3 de-ṛẹ-ụ-ḳọ VIN S 4̣
.5]Ṿ 5 Z 2 CYP 1[
.6 *inf. mut.*
↓
v. .1 *sup. mut.*
.2 a-pi-po-re-we *$*209$*^{VAS} 6̣[
.3 i-po-no *$*213$*^{VAS} 14 [
.4]-ṛọ *$*212$*^{VAS} 17 [
.5 *inf. mut.*

Uc 8032 is part of the left hand edge of the same tablet as 160, but its exact position relative to the main fragment cannot be established.
*r.*3 S over ⟦ ⟧.
.4 *de-ṛẹ-ụ-ḳọ*: three of these signs precede VIN and one follows it.
.5 CYP[+?] possible.
*v.*3 14 perhaps over ⟦ ⟧.

These two documents from the RCT are part of the same tablet, with Uc 160 being on the right.[165] The many entries and small amounts recorded have parallels in Knossian and Pylian offerings records, but a connection with banqueting rather than offerings *per se* may be suggested by the list of vessels on the *verso*, which includes bowls and kraters, perhaps for use in banqueting. *me-ri*[on Uc 8032 *may* represent *me-ri-du-ma-te*, a title which appears among cult personnel at Pylos (Section 2.3.3.1). The tablet also resembles some festival rations/'sacred meal' records (Section 2.3.3); in any case a connection with feasting is probable.[166]

---

[163] Halstead 1998–1999, 152, 156–9 with Table 2; see also 1996–1997, 187.
[164] Killen (1999a, 333) also discusses these as consumption texts.
[165] Texts as in *KT*[5]; some minor amendments to the apparatus of Uc 160 (not shown here) are made in *KT*[6].
[166] Palmer 1994, 176.

Uc 161

Uc 161 ('124')

.1]OVIS 197 SUS 1 [

.2] 3 OLIV 30 *NI* 10 VIN 60[

.2 Trace before 3 possibly]T.

v. Graffito (cf. Xd 9125 *v.*).

Uc 161, also from the RCT, is probably a banqueting record.[167] The number of sheep is unusually large for a foodlist, but the single pig and the appearance of olives, figs and wine together suggest banqueting. This may simply have been a very large feast: 197 sheep would yield some 4000–5000 kg of meat, which would be in keeping with the some 2800 litres of olives recorded, and 1700 litres of wine.[168]

U 5717

U 5717 (—)

]^{f} 90 *E* 40

Cut at right.

U 5717 records ninety units, probably of female animals, along with forty units of something represented by the syllabogram *E* used as an ideogram. Since the other ideogram on the tablet (probably) represents some type of animal, *E* here may abbreviate *e-po* 'kid' (see above, *s.v.* Ce 283), but there are any number of other things it might instead represent (see Section 6.6.2.2). The tablet is 'Unclear', and the large numbers on the whole make it unlikely to be a banqueting record although large figures do sometimes appear on such records.

U 7063

U 7063 + fr. (—)

.1] *vac.*

.2]*sạ* OVIS^{m} 2 OVIS^{f} 1 **134* 6 VIN [

.3]OVIS^{f} 1 *pa* OVIS^{f} 1 **134* 4

.4]OVIS^{x} 2[ ]ọṿịṣ^{x}[

inf. mut.

.1 Cut and smoothed at top in middle of register (.1 is lower half of original register).

.2 1 **134* on right edge, 6 VIN on *v.* (→).

.3 4 on right edge.

U 7063 is a record which, given the parallels for the type of list from Pylos, one would immediately suspect might concern banqueting. The numbers of animals are small, and they appear together with wine. Further, the ideogram **134* appears on the Thebes sealings in a variant form **190* (**134* and **190* are equivalent),[169] thus all three commodities on U 7063 are paralleled in banqueting records.[170] Finally, the tablet may, like C 394, abbreviate *sa-pa-ka-te-ri-ja* as *sa*.[171]

Wb sealings

Some of the Wb sealings may be relevant to banqueting. The texts are as follows.[172]

---

[167] It is so interpreted by e.g. Halstead (1998–1999, 161) and Driessen (*Scribes RCT*, 208–9). See also Palmer 1994, 176. Uc 161, –5717 and –7063: All texts from *KT*^{5}.

[168] Bendall forthcoming(c). For the method of calculation used here see Bendall forthcoming(a).

[169] Piteros, Olivier & Melena 1990, 163–6. For **134* as a kind of foodstuff see Killen 1992b, 366–7.

[170] For U 7063 as a banqueting/offerings record see Killen 1992b, 367; 1994, 73; 2006a, 89; Palmer 1994, 173–4, 176 (as 'offerings'; but she takes it once as a possible 'collection' record, p. 189); Weilhartner 2005, 93–4.

[171] Killen 1996b, 79–80; Halstead 1998–1999, 161.

[172] Wb sealings: Texts from *KT*^{5}.

Wb 5283 (—)

sup. mut.

.1]-ṭị-[

.2] OVIS^{m}[

.1 Traces of ⟦ ⟧.

Wb 5527 (—)

sup. mut.

.1] ọṿịṣ^{f} LANA[

.2]*vac.*[

inf. mut.

Wb 5664 + *frr.* (—)

sup. mut.

] OVIS^{m}

inf. mut.

Wb 5697 (—)

sup. mut.

?OVIS]^{m} [

Possibly CAP]^{m}, BOS]^{m}, etc.

Wb 6058 (—)

.1]ṣị-we OVIS^{m} [

.2]ra-ze[

.1 OVIS^{m} over ⟦OVIS^{f}⟧.

Wb 8491 (117?)

sup. mut.

] , ọṿịṣ^{m} [

Perhaps traces at left.

Wb 9844 (—)

sup. mut.

.1] ḳị[

.2 *inf. mut.*

.1 Trace at right, not incompatible with ọṿịṣ^{x}[.

Those Wb sealings which record livestock resemble the Thebes and Pylos sealings, discussed above as related to banqueting. Wb 5527, however, records a further ideogram, LANA. Wool is attested in banqueting contexts (e.g. PY Un 6), but a possible connection with deliveries of wool from flocks should be kept in mind (note that one of the sealings, Wb 8491, may be by the major sheep scribe, h. 117).

Finally, we have an X fragment which may be relevant.

X 9191

X 9191 + *fr.* + *frr.* (—)

.a] sa-pa-ka-[

.b]ḍẹ , / u-ta-no , [

.a *sa-pa-ka-ṭẹ*[possible.

.b Or]*ḳẹ*. Possible traces at right.

The text is very damaged, but the appearance of what is probably to be restored as *sa-pa-ka-*[*te-ri-ja* in line .a should make this a banqueting record.[173] The mention of *u-ta-no* in this context is of interest because this is known as the location of a shrine (see e.g. Fp(1) 13.3).[174]

Table 2-6 summarises the categories to which tablets were assigned above. Note that a few further suggested instances, rejected in this study, are discussed in Chapter 6.

[173] Killen 1994, 75; Halstead 1998–1999, 153, 160. X 9191: Text from *KT*[6]. It is published in Killen 1994, 75 and Godart *et al.* 1990–1991, 388. All give the same reading except for the first sign in line .b which is read as *ḳẹ* by Godart *et al.* and *ṭị* by Killen.

[174] As noted also by Palaima 2004b, 106.

Table 2-6. Banqueting foodlists at Knossos

banqueting records	probable banqueting records	possible banqueting records	'consumption'/ 'fattening' records	unclear, but possible	unclear	probably/definitely not banqueting records
C(2) set	C(3) set	Wb 5283	Dm set	Ce 113	Ce 61	*herd management?*
Uc 160 [+] 8032	C 33	Wb 5527	Ce 50	C 5669	Ce 156	Ce 139
Uc 161	Ce 152	Wb 5664		C 6021	D 1024	Ce 283
C 394	C 902	Wb 5697		C 7048	C 7054	C <1902>
U 7063	C 954	Wb 6058		Ce 7516	C 7059	*unlikely*
X 9191	C 1561	Wb 8491		Ce 8279	C 7060	U 5157
	D 5954	Wb 9844		Ce 8346	C 7062	
				Ce 9109	C 7515	
					Ce 8345	

2.3.2.4 BANQUETING FOODLISTS AT MYCENAE

A number of documents from Mycenae may deal with banqueting. We begin with the most probable one.

Ue 661

Ue 661 NMA 7709 (*60*)
.1 jo-po-ro-te-ke **134* 100 *NI* +**155*^{VAS} 15
.2 *NI*+CIRCULUS 5 [Note: *NI*+CIRCULUS = **248*]
.3 *vacat*

Chadwick long ago suggested that Ue 661 may relate to dining and that *jo-po-ro-te-ke* might be /*hō prothēke*/ 'thus he set out', but the proposal received relatively little attention until revived recently by Killen.[175] As Killen points out, the tablet comes from the West House and many of the records from this location evidently deal with food and rationing.[176] Given the new evidence from Thebes, he argues that 'it is immediately attractive to suggest that the context on Ue 661 is similar and that *jo-po-ro-te-ke* does indeed mean "thus he set out" in the technical sense of "thus he served (as food)".' He further draws attention to a possible parallel with PY Un 2, proposing that the *o-pi-te-<u>-ke-e-u* of Un 2.2 might be the palace official in charge of the palace 'chest' or 'vessels' (standard meanings of τεῦχος in Classical Greek), perhaps in the sense of dining services or other provisions for banqueting.[177] As he notes, it is not clear whether the 'dining' in this instance would have related to a ceremonial banquet or an ordinary domestic one.

Weilhartner's more recent objections to seeing the tablet as related to dining should be considered in light of improved understanding of the function(s) of buildings such as the West House group.[178] He rightly notes (as does Killen) that many of the records deal with rations for clearly 'ordinary' workers and proposes the goods may simply be in store, in keeping with Shelmerdine's identification of the group as 'clearing houses'.[179] However, we now have at least one further example of a 'clearing house' in the Northeastern Building at Pylos, and a common feature of such places is that they deal with a great variety of goods and different types of circumstances.[180] Thus, the presence of 'ordinary' rations records in such an

[175] *MT* III, 62; Killen 1992b, 375–6. See also Varias Garcia forthcoming. The text here is as given by Killen with Museum number and scribe as in *TITHEMY*; the transcriptions are identical except *TITHEMY* transcribes *NI*+CIRCULUS as **248*. The sign is basically *NI* with a circle drawn above it. All other texts here are from *TITHEMY*.
[176] Killen 1992b, 367.
[177] Killen 2004, 162. See Piteros, Olivier & Melena 1990, 179 for the spelling error.
[178] Weilhartner 2005, 218–20.
[179] Shelmerdine 1997.
[180] Bendall 2003, esp. 224.

establishment has no specific bearing on whether or not any other individual record in the building had a related function. The Northeastern Building did yield what seem to be 'banqueting records',[181] alongside other documents with clearly religious associations.[182] Scribes in the building were dealing with movements of goods in general, both for religious and for other purposes.[183] To be clear, this argument does not lend *support* to interpretation of Ue 661 as related to dining, it simply suggests that the presence of 'ordinary' rations records in the same context is no obstacle.

As pointed out by Shelmerdine, in addition to Ue 661, tablets such as Ue 652, Ue 663 and Ui 651 also resemble the banqueting records of the type discussed by Killen.[184] We examine these three briefly, beginning with Ue 652.

Ue 652

Ue 652	Nauplio M. 13844 + 13847		(—)
Recto			
.1	o-ku-su-wa-si , ko-na ,	GRA[	
.2	pe-ru-si-nwa	GRA[	
.3	OLIV 5 CYP+*KU* 5 CYP+*O* 7 *ḳọ* ẠRỌṂ[		
.4A		po-ro[	
.4B	pe-ru-si-nwa *Ṇ Ị* 36	ni[	
Verso			
.1	] VIN 22		
.2	] GRA 3 T 3		
	reliqua pars sine regulis		

.4B Less probably *NI*[.
v.2 Trace at left.

Ue 652 includes several of the types of commodities which appear on banqueting records. However, the appearance of the word *pe-ru-si-nwa /perusinwa/* 'last year's' would be unique for a banqueting record, whereas it is common on 'collection' or 'delivery' records (especially taxation records). It is thus more probable that Ue 652 is some sort of delivery or collection record, possibly for a harvest[185] (cf. e.g. the KN F(2) 'harvest records', which list many of the same commodities[186]), as Varias Garcia also suggests.[187]

Ui 651

Ui 651	Nauplio M. 13842	(—)
Recto		
.1	ka-ra-[	
.2	ko-ra	
.3	ke-ko-jo	
.4	a_3-so-ni-jo *RE*[	
.5	o-pe-ra-no-ro *RE* ̣70[	
.6	*inf. mut.*	

[181] Bendall 2003, 215–17.
[182] E.g. the Qa tablets and An 1281.
[183] Weilhartner draws a clear distinction between cultic and profane, a separation which there is reason to doubt existed in the society with which we are dealing. While it is important to note that not every occasion on which food was consumed represented an instance of 'ceremonial banqueting' (as Killen, cited above, is careful to observe), it need not be that the degree of importance of the occasion was rooted in a cult/other distinction.
[184] Shelmerdine 1997, 392.
[185] Palmer 1994, 181–3, drawing on Varias Garcia's 1993 doctoral thesis, *non vidi*. Varias Garcia (forthcoming) points out that incoming foodstuffs might of course end up being used for a banquet, although this would still make Ue 652 a collection record. Killen (2004, 162) takes it as 'Unclear'; Weilhartner (2005, 219–20) discusses it in passing.
[186] Killen observes, in a personal communication cited by Varias Garcia (forthcoming), that the order of commodities is the same as on KN F(1) 17, which resembles the *a-ma* harvest records (on which see e.g. Killen 1994–1995a).
[187] Varias Garcia forthcoming.

Verso
.1] *RE* 100 *A* 1
.2] *RE* 92
.3] *RE* 100 *A* 1[
.4]-sa-wo *RE* 100 *A*[ ]*vac.*
.5]ḍọ-jo[ ]100 *A*[ ]*vac.*
.6]*vest.*
inf. mut.

r. Palimpsest.
*v.*3 Trace of sign at left.
.5]*ṛẹ-do-jo* not impossible.
.6 *vest.* not incompatible with]*A* 1[.

Two commodities appear on this document but both are unidentified and they are not types common in banqueting records. The regular lists of entries resemble more those found on rations or collection (e.g. taxation) records.

Ue 663

Ue 663 Nauplio M. 13854 (—)

.1]to-so
.2]67 VIN 5

Possibly cut at right.
.1 Trace at left, possibly divider.

Ue 663 seems a better candidate for being a banqueting record (the totalling word /*tos*(*s*)*os*/ 'so much' does appear on banqueting tablets; cf. Er 312). However the text is so fragmentary that the function of the record must be considered 'Unclear'.[188]

Ue 611

Ue 611 NMA 7709 (*60*)
Recto
.1 ku-]pe-ra 4 a-po-re-we 2 pe-ri-ke 3
.2]ka-ra-te-ra 1 po-ro-ko-wo 4 a-ta-ra 10
.3]pa-ke-te-re 30 ka-na-to 5 qe-ti-ja 10
.4]qẹ-to 2 ti-ri-po-di-ko 8 ka-ra-ti-ri-jo 7
.5]*vac.*[
Verso (—)
.1 [.]pi-ro-qe-mo , a-ke
.2 OLIV+*TI* 3 OLIV 1 *NI* 2 VIN S 2[
.3 *vacat*
inf. mut.

r. Probably less than one cm of clay missing at left.
.4 Perhaps only 5.
v. Palimpsest.
.1 No satisfactory explanation for what, in the «Wingspread Convention», is transcribed as **188* (corresponding to Linear A *188*); in fact, the upper left-hand part of the «sign» could be part of the original text, e.g. *jạ*.
.3 Perhaps trace of an erased S below the S in l. 2.

Our final document, Ue 611, may have something to do with banqueting. Chadwick discussed the *verso* of this tablet as a rations record,[189] but it is now understood that wine is not normally issued as ordinary rations.[190] As Killen points out, a parallel for Ue 611 may be KN Uc 160, which also lists vases and mixed commodities, and was discussed above as a banqueting record.[191] Ue 611 could have had a related function.[192] Discussions of the document tend to

---

[188] Palmer 1994, 183; Varias Garcia (forthcoming) sees it as possible banqueting record.
[189] *MT* II, 112.
[190] Palmer 1994, 190–1, 195.
[191] Killen 1992b, 376. See also Palmer 1994, 180; Varias Garcia forthcoming. Killen (2004, 162) regards the document as 'Unclear'.

revolve around the interpretation of the word *a-ke* on line .1 of the *verso*.[193] At least three different verbs might be possible, all of which happen to yield interpretations consistent with this being a banqueting record, but the complications of the interpretation of the word mean that it is neutral as evidence. Whatever the case, a banqueting context is suggested, even if it cannot be proven, the vessels recorded on the *recto* perhaps serving as tableware for the feast (as Varias Garcia also suggests, noting again the parallel with KN Uc 160).[194]

2.3.2.5 BANQUETING FOODLISTS AT THEBES

As discussed above (Section 2.3.2.1), the Thebes sealings found in 1982 record animals and other foodstuffs intended for a feast. The complete data for the sealings are set out in Table 2-7 below.[195]

One of the new tablets from Odos Pelopidou is also probably a list of banqueting foodstuffs. The text is as follows.[196]

Uo 121 (—)

.a **153* 1 VIN S 1[

.b OVIS 1 CAP 1 **190*[

Uo 121 presents a fairly typical list of banqueting foodstuffs, including animals, wine (some 9.6+ litres), **190* (= **134*, found only in religious contexts; see Section 6.6.3.4), and a sheepskin (**153*).[197] A parallel for the last is Un 718.4.8 where one sheepskin each is contributed by *e-ke-*ra_2*-wo* and the *dāmos* in a land tenure/banqueting context.

Some further series of the new Thebes tablets may also be related to banqueting, or at least consumption of foodstuffs in a sacral context; these are discussed below as 'festival rations' in Section 2.3.3.3.

Table 2-7. The Thebes sealings

hand	*sigillum*	Wu	BOS	CAP	OVIS	SUS	**171*	**190*	other ideo-gram	other text .β	other text .γ
—	A [1]	44		CAP^{m}						*i-je-ra*	*vacat*
—	B [1]	45							none	**56-pu-so*	*ro-we-wi-ja*
α	C [5]	46		CAP^{f}			**171* 30			*pa-ra-wo , o-pa*	[**171* 30]
γ?	D [7]	47				SUS^{m}				*pa-ro te-qa-jo*	*ro-we-wi-ja*
—	D [7]	48						**190*		*vac.*[ ]*vac.*	*vac.*[ ]*vac.*
β	E [3]	49			OVIS^{m}					*qe-te-o*	*a-ko-ra*
β	E [3]	50		CAP^{f}						*qe-te-o*	*a-ko-ra*
γ	D [7]	51				SUS^{m}				*te-qa-de*	*qe-te-*a_2
δ	F [5]	52				SUS+*SI*				*a-ko-ra-jo*	*vacat*
—	F [5]	53	ḄỌṢ^{m}							*qẹ-ṭẹ-ọ*	*i-ri-ja*
ε	G [3]	54		CAP^{m}						*vacat*	*vac.*[ ]*vac.*

[192] Although it should be noted that the two sides seem to have been written by different scribes: the *recto* by scribe 60, the *verso* by an unknown hand.

[193] Palmer 1994, 179–80; Varias Garcia forthcoming; *DMic*. I, 36.

[194] Varias Garcia forthcoming. Weilhartner (2005, 220) rejects Ue 611 as a banqueting record, due to the philological difficulties. The issue should remain open, but there is a possibility that further support may be forthcoming if it is correct that the word *po-ro-ko-wo* in Ue 611.2 was the word for 'rhyton' in Mycenaean Greek, as suggested elsewhere (Bendall forthcoming[b]).

[195] The data in Table 2-7 are from the transcriptions in *TITHEMY*, 41–50.

[196] *Thèbes* I, 40, 306; *Thèbes* III, 91. For the findspot see *Thèbes* I, 9–13; *Thèbes* III, 12, 18.

[197] The editors rightly note that the list particularly recalls PY Ua 25 (*Thèbes* I, 306, 371). See also Palaima 2003b, 114; 2004b, 98, 108, 120; Weilhartner 2005, 204–5; Killen 2006a, 90.

hand	*sigillum*	Wu	BOS	CAP	OVIS	SUS	**171*	**190*	other ideo-gram	other text .β	other text .γ
—	H [2]	55				SUS^{m}				*ka-ru-to*	*vacat*
α	C [5]	56		CAP^{m}			**171* 30			[*o-*]*pe-re-ta o-pa*	[**171* 30]
—	I [1]	57			OVIS^{x}					*vacat*	*deest*
α	C [5]	58				SUS				*qe-ri-jo-jo o-pa*	*a-ma-ru-to*
ζ	J [2]	59				[ ]SUS^{x}	**171* 36			*pa-ro , sa-me-we*	*ro-we-wi-jạ*[
ζ	J [2]	60				ṣụṣ^{m}				*pạ-ṛọ , sa-me-we*	*vacat*
—	K [2]	61			ọṿịṣ^{f}					*deest*	*vacat*
ε	G [3]	62		CAP^{m}						*vacat*	*vacat*
β	E [3]	63				SUS^{f}				*qe-te-o*	*a-ko-ra*
—	M [1]	64							*WE*	*o-pa*	*vacat*
γ	D [7]	65			OVIS^{f}					*te-qa-de*	*qe-te-a*$_2$
—	H [2]	66				SUS^{m}[				[.]-[.]-*ẹ*	*i-je-ro*
η	O [5]	67			OVIS^{m}					*po-ro-e-ko-*	*-to*
δ	F [5]	68				SUS+*SI*				*a-ko-ra-jo*	*vacat*
—	P [1]	69		CAP^{f}						*vacat*	*vacat*
—	F [5]	70			OVIS^{m}					*a-e-ri-qo*	*vacat*
—	L [3]	71							PYC+*O*	[PYC+*O*]	*vacat*
—	F [5]	72			OVIS^{m}					*vacat*	*vacat*
—	Q [1]	73			ọṿịṣ^{m}					*vacat*	*vacat*
—	O [5]	74		*we* CAP^{m}						*ạụ*-[.]-*ẹ*	*vest.*[
—	G [3]	75				SUS^{m}				*e-qi-ti-*	*-wo-e*
α	C [5]	76	BOS^{f}				**171* 30			*a-e-ri-qo*	*o-pa*
—	O [5]	77							[ ]^{m}	*vest.*[	*-ta*
—	K [2]	78			OVIS^{m}				*W̱Ẹ*	[*W̱Ẹ*] see app.	*vacat*
θ	R [5]	79			OVIS^{m}					*vacat*	*vacat*
—	S [3]	80						**190*		*vacat*	*vacat*
—	L [3]	81							see app.	]*vest.*[	*vacat*[
—	T [1]	82			OVIS^{m}					*vacat*[	*deest*
θ	R [5]	83			OVIS^{m}					*vacat*	*vacat*
θ	R [5]	84			OVIS^{m}					*vacat*	*vacat*
θ	R [5]	85			OVIS^{m}					*vacat*	*vacat*
ι	U [2]	86			OVIS^{m}					*i-je-ro*	*vacat*
ι	U [2]	87		CAP^{m}						*i-je-ro*	*vacat*
α?	C [5]	88		CAP^{x}						*ra-mi-jo , o-pa*	*deest*
—	D [7]	89						**190*		*a-pu-do-ke*	*vacat*
κ	V [2]	90		CAP^{f}						]*de*	*vacat*
θ	R [5]	91			OVIS^{m}					*vacat*	*vacat*
η	O [5]	92		CAP^{m}						*po-ro-e-ko-*	*-to*
—	S [3]	93			OVIS^{m}					*vacat*	*vacat*
γ	D [7]	94		CAP^{f}						*a*$_2$*-pa-a*$_2$*-de*	*vacat*
—	S [3]	95						**190*[		*vacat*	]*vacat*
γ	D [7]	96				SUS^{f}				*te-qa-de*	*qe-te-a*$_2$
—	W [1]	97		CAP^{f}						*vacat*	*vacat*
—	O [5]	98						**190*		*deest*	*vacat*
κ	V [2]	99		CAP^{f}						*a-dwe-ẹ*	*deest*
	TOTAL		**2**	**15**	**17**	**12**	**126**	**5**	—	—	—

Notes
Wu 78: App.: *WE* could be adjunct to OVIS^{m} (cf. Wu 74).
Wu 81: App. .β: Very probably the base of P̣Ỵ Ç+*Ọ* (cf. Wu 71).

2.3.2.6 BANQUETING AND WILD ANIMALS

Before we conclude our survey of banqueting foodlists, it is worth considering briefly a few instances where wild animals may appear in the Linear B records in connection with banqueting. Hunting was of major importance in the Mycenaean world and the pursuit of and feasting upon wild animals had implications for the negotiation of social, political, and gendered identities.[198] There is potential for bringing together zooarchaeological and Linear B data in this connection since bones of boar, deer and lions are attested in Mycenaean palatial contexts. For example, at Pylos two of the deposits of specially selected and curated cattle bones retained from burnt offerings included deer,[199] and Wright notes a possible parallel in curated boar mandibles at Thebes.[200] It has already been recognised that the following two documents from Pylos may be relevant in this context.[201]

Cr 591 (Cii)

.1	]-wa CERV 3
.2	]e-[ ] CERV 3
.3	]ne-wi CERV 2[ ]*vacat*
.4	]-wa CERV 1[ ]*vacat*
.5	]-ti-ro[ ] CERV[ ]2
.6	]ja-[CERV]2
.7	CERV] 3

Cr 868 (S868-Ci)

.1	a_3-se-we [
.2	ne-se-e-we CERV[
.3	te-re-ne-wi-ja CERV[
.4	na-pe-re-wa CERV[
.5	te-ko-]to-na-pe CERV[
.6	]na-wo CERV 1
.7	qe-re-me-ti-wo CERV 1
.8	*vacat*
.9	*vacat*

Both tablets record small numbers of CERV(us), deer. The words in the first tablet are too poorly preserved to identify, but the second tablet, Cr 868, registers deer against various minor toponyms.[202] The purpose of the documents is not clear, but at least one possibility is that the animals were being supplied for banqueting.[203] It is not implausible that they were, as Bennet speculates, 'the elite's contributions to feasts from their own special activities',[204] although contributions by (hunters at?) the TNs themselves is also possible.

This is not the place to explore the issue of hunting further, but two other possible instances of 'wild' animals in the Linear B records may be briefly noted.

1. Boar may appear in PY Un 6, a banqueting foodlist discussed above (Sections 2.3.2.1 and 2.3.2.2). The animals offered to Poseidon and *pe-re-*82* on this tablet include pigs qualified with a ligature, SUS+*KA*, which may well abbreviate /*kapros*/ 'boar'.[205]
2. On KN C(2) 7064 (see Section 2.3.2.3), *a-ki-ri-ja* applied to a list of male and female goats may represent /*agria*/ 'wild (creatures)'.[206]

---

[198] Morris 1990; Hamilakis 2003.

[199] Halstead & Isaakidou 2004, 144, 148; see also Isaakidou *et al.* 2002; Stocker & Davis 2004. For deer as burnt offerings in the classical world see Jameson 1988, 115 n 5; also Barringer 2001 for general comparative material. For discrepancies between Linear B textual evidence and zooarchaeological evidence for deer see also Halstead 1998–1999, 185; 2003, 257, 260. For lions see e.g. Thomas 1999.

[200] Wright 2004b, 33 n 78; see also 38–41, 49, 51 for hunting in connection with feasting more generally.

[201] Hamilakis 2003, 244; and see n 203 below. Cr 868 is now joined to Cr 875, with new text (Melena 1996–1997a, 163; see also Melena 1994–1995b, 284).

[202] See Killen 1996–1997b, esp. 182–5.

[203] Palmer (1999, 469) suggests the animals may have been captured live, perhaps for ritual use, rather than delivered as carcases; Weilhartner (2005, 156–7) sees a possible connection with 'offerings'; Halstead (1998–1999, 163–4, 170, 185–6) takes the tablets as 'consumption' records. See also Hamilakis 2003, 244. For a different, less likely, scenario (deer killed in the process of land clearance) see Palaima 1992b, 72–3.

[204] Bennet 2001, 35. For hunters in Linear B see also Hiller 1998–1999; forthcoming.

[205] *Documents*, 484; Bendall forthcoming(a).

[206] Killen 1976, 122 n 9: *DMic.* I, 44 *s.v. a-ki-ri-ja*. See also Hiller forthcoming.

2.3.3 FESTIVAL RATIONS RECORDS

2.3.3.1 FESTIVAL RATIONS AT PYLOS

In 1960, Olivier identified what he called a *liste-type* of tablet dealing with what he interpreted as *desservants du sanctuaire*, 'temple servants': An 39, –207, –424, –427, –594 and Fn 50.[207] Killen recently related these documents to the remainder of the Fn series, with the exception of Fn 1427 (now An/Fn 7[208]), which refers not to temple servants, but to other types of workers in the employ of the palace.[209] He suggests that the Fn documents list rations for support staff at state-organised festivals. Fn 187 provides an example of the type of document.[210]

Fn 187			(H2)
.1	a-pi-te-ja	ḤỌṚḌ[ ]	*NI* 2
.2	po-si-da-i-jo-de	HORD[ ]	*NI* T 1
.3	ka-ru-ke	HORD [ ]	F̣ẠṚ
.4	pạ-ki-ja-na-de	HORD T 1[ ]	*NI* T 1
.5	ka-ru-ke	HORD T 1 V 3	*ṆỊ* T 1 V 3
.6	de-do-wa-re-we	HORD T 1	
.7	ḳụ-ṛị-na-ze-ja	HORD T 2	*NI* T 2
.8	u-po-jo-po-ti-ni-ja	HORD T 5̣	*NI* T 4
.9	o-pi-tu-ra-jo	HORD T 3	
.10	au-to-**34*-ta-ra	HORD T 1	
.11	a-ma-tu-na	HORD T 1	
.12	te-qi-ri-jo-ne	HORD V 3	
.13	u-do-no-o-i	HORD Ṭ 3	
.14	po-te-re-we	HORD Ṭ 4	*NI* T 4
.15	a-ke-ti-ri-ja-i	HORD T 1 V 3	
.16	ka-ru-ke	HORD T 1 V 3	
.17	i-so-e-ko	HORD T 2 ⟦Ṿ 3⟧	
.18	po-si-da-i-je-u-si	HORD T 1 V 3	
.19	**34*-ke-ja	HORD T 1 V 3	*NI* T 1 V[
.20	a-ro-ja	[HORD] V 3	
.21	ka-ru-ke	ḤỌṚḌ Ṭ 1̣ Ṿ 3̣	
.22–23	*vacant*		

The list in Fn 187 comprises named persons (e.g. *a-pi-te-ja*, line .1), a deity (*u-po-jo-po-ti-ni-ja*, line .8), shrines (e.g. *po-si-da-i-jo*, line .2), and persons designated by craft or religious titles (e.g. *a-ke-ti-ri-ja-i /askētriāhi/* 'to the decorators', specialist textile workers in line .15; *po-si-da-i-je-u-si*, a group based on the name of Poseidon in line .18).

In suggesting that Fn 187 and related documents record festival rations, Killen drew on Chadwick's observation that the figures on Fn 79, if expressed in the unit V, are all divisible by a common factor of five. Since V 1 is near in quantity to Z 3, a man's standard daily ration, Chadwick proposed that the document recorded rations for a period of five days.[211] Killen pointed out that along this line of thought Fn 187 may be a three-day ration and Fn 50 may be a daily ration on the basis that one person, *a_3-ki-a_2-ri-jo*, who appears on both Fn 79 (the five-day ration tablet) and Fn 50, receives exactly one fifth of his Fn 79 allotment on Fn 50. He then asks under what circumstances rations would be given for periods of one, three or five days, and draws on classical parallels to suggest that the lengths of time might correspond to

207 Olivier 1960, 137–8, 160.
208 For join with An 7 and discussion see Melena 1996–1997b, 171–6. The issue of whether this tablet should now be classified Fn or An is not entirely resolved (see Killen 2004, 159, Table 8.2 n i).
209 Killen 1999c, 218–19; 2001b; and now 2006a, esp. 90–7. For a similar view, differing in some details, see *Thèbes* I, 368. Also see Perpillou 1976.
210 Fn 187: Text as in *PTT* except line .19 as later read by Bennett (1992, 108).
211 Chadwick 1976, 118–19.

the periods for which festivals were commonly held.[212] The *desservants de sanctuaire* and other persons would then be support staff comprised of both religious and ‘ordinary’ personnel (the latter probably on ‘temporary secondment’) at state-organised festivals.

Since festivals may or may not have included banquets, as discussed above, the Fn tablets are not properly speaking ‘banqueting records’. However, they are connected with religion and concern occasions on which feasting would have been a likely activity. As noted previously, it is counter-productive to insist on over-classification. For instance, foodstuffs registered directly against shrine and deities, as in Fn 187.2.8, might be described as straightforward ‘offerings’, and there does seem to be evidence in the records for offerings being made in tandem with festivals – there are several correlations for instance between the Fr series and the Fn series and other banqueting records.[213] However, many of the allocations cannot be described as offerings (e.g. the issue ‘to the decorators’), and it is better to describe these tablets as a group as ‘festival rations records’.

2.3.3.2 TEMPLE SERVANTS AT KNOSSOS

Several of the Pylos ‘temple servant’ occupational titles appear also at Knossos. *di-pte-ra-po-ro-i* is probably to be restored in the banqueting record C 954, discussed above (Section 2.3.2.3), and *e-to-wo-ko* appears in an offering record, Fh 462 (cf. the small amounts and the shrine name, **47-so-de*), the text of which is as follows.

Fh 462 + 2008 + 5470 (141?)

Recto

.1]-si-ja V 1 a-ri-ja-wo-ne [ ] *vac.*

.2]si-ja / e-to-wo-ko V 3 *47-so-de S 1

Verso

.1]de V 3

.2] *vac.*

r.1 Perhaps]-*p̣ạ-si-ja*; possibly]*ḳụ-p̣ạ-si-ja*. -*si*- over ⟦ ⟧. Sign in damaged area after *a-ri-ja-wo-ne* perhaps Ṿ.

e-to-wo-ko follows a sign-group which is partially lost, but might be restored as *qe-ra-si-ja*, a deity frequently attested as a recipient of offerings at Knossos (although other restorations are possible). If that were the case, we may have an instance here of two recipients which, where it occurs elsewhere (e.g. in the Fr series; see Section 3.2.2), is attractively interpreted as receipt by the one on behalf of the other.[214] However that may be, the appearance of *e-to-wo-ko* in a religious context is in keeping with the associations identified for it by Olivier at Pylos.

The Pylian title *o-pi-te<-u->ke-e-u* (Un 2, An 39) also appears (in the plural) in the following tablet from Knossos.[215]

B 798 (107)

sup. mut.

.1	]-ḳọ [	
.2	ḳẹ-sa-do-ro	VỊR[
.3	a-ke-ta	VIR[
.4	ạ-na-qo-ta	VIR 6
.5	ko-ma-we-ta	VIR 2
.6	pe-qo-no	VIR 1
.7	ra-wo-qo-no	VIR 1
.8	ko-a-ta	VIR 2
.9	ku-ni-ta	VIR 3
.10	o-pi-te-u-ke-we	VIR 2
.11	i-se-we-ri-jo	VIR 3

.9 -*ni*- over ⟦ ⟧.

[212] Killen 2001b, 440–1.

[213] Bendall 1998–1999.

[214] See Killen forthcoming(a).

[215] Text from *KT*^{5}; there are minor changes to the apparatus (not shown here) in *KT*^{6}.

B 798 is a list of Knossian 'Collectors', with numbers of men registered against them. It is unclear why this *o-pi-te-u-ke-e-u* would belong in such a list as the record has no clear association with religion, but if the word is correctly interpreted as 'official in charge of */teukheha/*' in the sense of vessels or chests (see Section 2.3.2.4 above) such a person might have exercised his duties in a variety of contexts.

Other 'temple servant' titles include *me-ri-du*[*-ma-te* (a probable restoration in X 1045),[216] and *mi-ka-ta* in the following tablet.

Vc(1) 64 ('124'r)

mi-ka-ta 1

Cut at both ends. ⊕ Vc 170 ⊕ Vc 7540.

The Vc(1) set is from the RCT and appears to record men who have full sets of the type of equipment issued in other tablets from the room (including the eponymous chariots).[217] There is no guarantee that *mi-ka-ta* is a title here, rather than a name, although other titles do appear in the Vc(1) set (e.g. *wa-na-ka* on Vc(1) 73).

Finally, it may be noted that the KN Fs tablets have sometimes been suggested as records of rations (or perhaps 'sacred meals') for temple personnel, as discussed below (Section 3.2.3.4).

2.3.3.3 FESTIVAL RATIONS AND SACRED MEALS AT THEBES

Some of the new Thebes tablets have parallels with the PY Fn tablets and may be related in function.[218] The series concerned are classified Av, Fq, Ft, Gf and Gp. All except the Gf series are discussed elsewhere and only an overview is required in the present section.

The Av series is made up of eight tablets dealing with wheat and men (Section 5.2.5).[219] The three Gf tablets record some unknown commodity measured (mostly) in units of weight.[220] The Gp series comprises fifty-four palm-leaf shaped tablets, mostly written by scribe 306 and dealing primarily with wine (Section 4.3.5, Table 4-7). The Fq series includes some 124 page-shaped tablets, written primarily by scribe 305 and dealing with barley (Section 5.3.4, Table 5-5).[221] The Ft tablets are divided into three 'lots': Ft 140, Ft 182, and the remainder.[222] Ft 140 is a measure of land capacity in terms of olives and wheat (see Sections 5.2.5 and 5.6.3) and Ft 182 is a fragmentary text recording olives (Section 5.6.3). The remaining fourteen Ft tablets (Section 5.6.3, Table 5-11) are palm-leaf shaped tablets recording olives, written by scribe 311, and having connections with the Fq and Gp series. A few examples from the series are as follows.

Av 100 (304)

.1	] *vestigia*	
.2	], po-te-we , si-to , ku-na-ki-si GRA 2 V 2 Z 2	
.3	]so , / si-to GRA 3	
a	] VIR 1	MUL 1
.4 b	]no pa-ro , zo-wa , e-re-u-te-ri	
.5	]	wi-ri-ne-u VIR 1

216 Also, *me-ri-*[appears in B 799 *v*.3, a list of men by name; it may be the start of a name rather than a title.
217 Chadwick 1976, 168–9; *Scribes RCT*, 202.
218 For the new *Odos Pelopidou* tablets in general see *Thèbes* I; *Thèbes* III; *Thèbes* IV. Preliminary reports on the tablets included: Aravantinos *et al.* 1995; Aravantinos 1996; 1999. See also Chadwick 1996–1997; Lejeune 1997b; 1997c; 1997d; Killen 1999c; Weilhartner 2005; papers in Deger-Jalkotzy & Panagl 2006.
219 *Thèbes* I, 166–80, 406.
220 *Thèbes* I, 274–6. The commodity *may* be saffron, based on a *possible* restoration in Gf 108.2.
221 *Thèbes* I, 157. They are probably fragments of some eighty documents (Sacconi 2001, 467). Two tablets ascribed to the series are attributed to scribe 307, five to scribe 310 and one possibly to scribe 306 (*Thèbes* I, 159).
222 *Thèbes* I, 157, 370. Ft 140 was found in the Arsenal, not with the other Ft tablets.

Av 101 (304)
.1]*vest.*[
.2]ḍạ-ṛọ VIR 1 *vest.*[
.3]pọ-me-ne VIR 2 ḍạ[
.4] a-ko-da-mo VIR 2 T 6 Ṿ[
.5]Ṿ 2 ma-di-je T 6 V 4 ko-ru-we T 2[
a] ku-su-to-ro-qa
.6 b]-ṭẹ / ṣị-ṭọ⌞ ⌟to-pa-po-ṛọ-ị[

Fq 258 (305)
.1 ma-ka HORD T 1 V 3 Z 1 a-ko[da-mo
.2 ma-di-je V 3̣ Z 2 ko-wa Ẓ[
.3 to-jo V 3 ra-ke-da-mi-ni-jo FAR[
.4 qẹ-ṛẹ-ma-o Ṿ 1 Z 2̣ we-re-ṇạ[-ko
.5 zo-wa V 1 ka-wi-jo FAR V 1[
.6 o-]ụ-ḳọ-we-ị Ṿ 1̣ ḍọ-ṛọ-jo Z[
.7]-ḍẹ Z 2 ạ-ḳạ-de[
inf. mut.

Ft 217 (311)
.1 ka-pa OLIV T 2 V 4 a-ko-da-mo V 4
.2 ka-no V 4

Gf 134 (305? / —)
sup. mut.
.1]*vestigia*[
.2 a-me-ro⟦M⟧ te[
.3 ṃị-ṭọ-qa-do M [
.4 *inf. mut.*

Gp 110 (306)
.1]qe , VIN S 1 na-ne-mo V 2 [
.2]FAR , V 2 mo-ne-we S 1 **56*-ru[-we

Gp 201 (306)
.a] ma-ka V 1̣[
.b]1̣ e-pe-to[-i

The editors of the new corpus, Aravantinos, Godart and Sacconi (AGS hereafter), observe that the Av, Fq, Ft, Gf and Gp series are closely related and share similarities with some of the PY Fn tablets.[223] A central point is that the types of recipients are similar in both the Fn and Thebes tablets,[224] being made up of:

- named individuals
- groups of persons indicated by ethnicons
- craftworkers
- religious personnel or 'temple servants'
- deities
- sacred animals (at Thebes only).[225]

AGS discuss the Fn tablets in terms of foodstuffs 'destinée à une sorte de repas sacré consommée à l'occasion de fêtes organisées en l'honneur de divinités',[226] which makes one think of offerings or 'sacred meals'. But whatever precise terms used to describe the situation

[223] *Thèbes* I, 363–71; Killen 1999c, 218–19; Sacconi 2001, 467, 469. AGS divide the Fn series into groups, not all of which they see as relating to the same function, but as Killen has shown they are all related except An/Fn 7 (see Section 2.3.3.1).
[224] *Thèbes* I, 364; Sacconi 2001, 467–8; Killen 2006a.
[225] The appearance of words interpreted as deities at Thebes is much disputed, as is the status of the animals; see e.g. papers in Deger-Jalkotzy & Panagl 2006 (on the animals see also the balanced account of Rousioti 2001 and Killen 2006a, 100 with n 61).
[226] *Thèbes* I, 368.

(again, it may not be helpful to over-categorise, especially where the evidence is so unclear), something along the lines of rations or handouts at festivals may be envisaged. As AGS note, some of the issues at Thebes are so small as to relate possibly to individual meals rather than to provisions intended for a period of days.[227]

The religious character of the Av–Gf–Gp–Fq–Ft series is not universally accepted, and the issue remains controversial,[228] but it is unnecessary here to review these debates in detail. No consensus is likely to be achieved in the near future, and the main conclusions of the present study will not be greatly affected, however the Thebes tablets are understood.

For present purposes we accept the editors' view that the Fq–Ft–Gp series and probably the Av series do have religious connections along the lines of the Fn series (the Gf series is of no further relevance here since the commodity is unknown). No commitment is made here to the interpretation of individual words, it is merely agreed that the disbursements on the particular occasion(s) concerned were made for purposes connected in some way with religious activity, whether 'sacred meals', 'festival rations' or something else. The reasons for adopting this position may be briefly stated; some of the points are stronger than others.[229]

1. The amounts mentioned on the records are usually very small, a feature in general of records recording religious handouts (e.g. the PY Fn series, the KN Fs series).[230]
2. The commodities concerned are frequent in documents of this sort, especially HORD and FAR, also VIN and CYP+*O*.[231] As Killen points out, HORD is extremely rare in ordinary rations records but is frequent in religious contexts, while FAR appears *only* in religious contexts.[232]
3. The vocabulary is consistent with that found on records relating to religious contexts.
    - The word *qe-te-jo* appears (e.g. TH Gp 109), which is frequent on banqueting/offerings records (cf. PY Un 138).[233]
    - Allative suffixes are frequent (e.g. **63-te-ra-de* on Gp 109+), as they are on offerings records.[234]
    - Dative plural groups appear, e.g. *te-ka-ta-si* /*tektasi*/ 'carpenters' (Gp 112+). Dative plural groups appear too of course in other contexts, but they are particularly common in offerings records and the Fn series.[235]
    - Figures appear who are attested in offerings records elsewhere (e.g. *ke-re-na*/*-i* on Gp 176; cf. KN M 719).[236]
4. There are parallels with the PY Fn tablets (excluding An/Fn 7); compare especially Fn 187 (Section 2.3.3.1).[237]

Whether the Av records are of quite the same type is more uncertain. Killen notes that:[238]

- The amounts on these are much greater than on the other records

---

[227] See Sacconi 2001, 469.
[228] Most polemically Palaima 2003b, also 2000–2001. But a religious association is accepted by numerous scholars; see e.g. papers in Deger-Jalkotzy & Panagl 2006. Killen (2006a, 100–2) specifically addresses some of Palaima's objections.
[229] Killen 1999c, 218–19; 2006a.
[230] Killen 2006a, 82–4; see also n 33 and n 79 above.
[231] Killen 2006a, 84–6.
[232] Killen 2004, 156–7, 160–1; and see Section 5.4.1.
[233] Killen 2006a, 88. The word *i-je-ro* may also appear (Fq 200), but the reading is very uncertain.
[234] Killen 2006a, 87–8.
[235] Killen 2006a, 88–90, 108; Killen forthcoming(a).
[236] Del Freo 1999; Killen 2006a, 86–7.
[237] Killen 2006a, 90–8.
[238] Killen 1999c, 218–9. For GRA as rations see Killen 2004, 156–7.

- There is no specific reference to divinities (unless *si-to* is so interpreted)
- Some of the entries deal with the persons themselves (MUL, VIR) rather than issues to them
- The commodity is not HORD but rather GRA, which is the primary commodity used at both Pylos and Knossos for 'ordinary' rations.

There is still a possibility that the Av tablets did have some connection with cult activity – some of the recipients, as AGS observe, appear also in the Fq–Ft–Gp series – and it may be that these too are records of religious handouts, with the larger amounts indicating provisions for longer periods of time.[239] The question remains open.

2.3.3.4 FESTIVAL RATIONS/SACRED MEALS AT MYCENAE

Fu 711 from Mycenae may be another record of the 'festival rations' type.[240]

Fu 711 Nauplio M. 26703 (—)

Recto

sup. mut.

.1] Ṿ[

.2]ḤỌṚḌ V 2

.3]5̣ HORD T 7 V 3

.4] HORD V 2

.5-6] *vacant*

.7] Z 2 ku-ne , FAR Z 2

.8]1̣ ka-ra-u-ja FAR Z 1̣ *NI* Z 1

.9]Ṿ 3 a-re-ke-se-[.] [.] T 2̣[

.10]3 Z 1 CYP+*O* T 1 [[5]]

.11] Z 2

Verso

.1 ṣẹ-wọ-[

.2 to-wo-ṇạ[

.3 a-re-ke-ṣẹ[

.4 qo-we [

reliqua pars sine regulis

An early suggestion by Palmer that Fu 711 may give evidence for a dog deity (*/kunei/* 'to the dog' in line .7) and a bull deity (*/g^{u}owei/* 'to the bull' in line *v*.4) was rightly treated with scepticism.[241] However, since the appearance of sacred animals at Thebes and the recognition of festival rations records (or sacred meals or, more neutrally, religious handouts), a religious context for Fu 711 seems more acceptable. The document has similarities with the new Thebes material, for instance small amounts (e.g. Z 1, Z 2), and the presence of FAR, HORD and CYP+*O* (note also *NI* from the PY Fn tablets). A religious association for Fu 711 need not compel us to accept theriomorphic divinities in the Mycenaean world – 'sacred animals' need not have been worshipped as actual gods[242] (cf. e.g. the house-snake of the Erechthion at classical Athens).

2.3.3.5 FESTIVAL RATIONS AT TIRYNS?

Uh 12 from Tiryns may be a record of similar type to those discussed above, if *di-pte-ra-po-ro* is correctly restored in line .2 (see apparatus), but little more can be said about this very fragmentary tablet. The text is as follows.

---

[239] Killen 2004, 159, n vii; see also 2001, 441–3. Killen (2006a, 97–100) more recently suggests that the Av records are after all related and that the main difference is in the period of time, with the Fq tablets being provisions for single meals (which would account for the many repetitions in the series) and the Av tablets for longer periods.

[240] Palmer 1983, 283–7; Godart & Sacconi 1996, 110–11; Killen 1999c; 2004, 159–60, with n iv (as an 'offering record'), see also 161–2; Rousioti 2001, 307.

[241] Palmer 1983, 283–7; see Rousioti 2001, 307.

[242] Rousioti (2001) gives a balanced account.

Uh 12 (—)

.1] *vacat* [

.2]ḍị-p̣ṭẹ-[ ] *NI*[

Perhaps part of same tablet as X 17.

.2]*ḍị-pṭẹ-ṛạ*[possible; traces before *NI*[*not* accidental and compatible with]*ṛọ*, so]*ḍị-pṭẹ-ṛạ*[*-po-*]*ro* not impossible.

2.3.4 BANQUETING PARAPHERNALIA

A final type of record related to banqueting concerns furniture and other equipment for feasting and sacrifice. The Pylos Ta series (actually a set), whose function had remained obscure since the decipherment, was recently identified by both Killen and Speciale independently as recording paraphernalia intended for use in ceremonial dining and sacrifice.[243] The series lists metal drinking and serving vessels, tables and chairs, and sacrificial equipment such as swords, hammer-axes and golden chains for binding the victims.

The Ta set is unique in its detail, but several other documents include lists of vessels, some of which may relate to disbursements on the occasions of feasts. PY Tn 996, for instance, comes from a pantry in which many clay vessels were also found and probably records a temporary release from the storeroom for banqueting or related activities (see Section 6.5.1.1 for text and references). At Mycenae, Ue 611, discussed above (Section 2.3.2.4) and like PY Tn 996 found in a 'pantry', records vessels on the *recto* and banqueting foodstuffs on the *verso*. At Knossos, the K(1) set records vessels, some of which might have been appropriate for use at banquets (e.g. the *di-pa* on K(1) 740 and –875) or for religious purposes (e.g. the bull's head rhyta on K(1) 872); see Section 6.5.1.2. The evidence relating to vessels is of particular interest because it is highly conducive to being linked with the archaeological data, as has recently been done in a useful survey by Wright.[244]

2.4 RELIGION AND LAND TENURE

2.4.1 LAND TENURE AT PYLOS

The majority of documentation relating to Mycenaean land tenure comes from Pylos, but terminology and structural features of documents from Knossos, Tiryns and Thebes suggest that similar systems existed elsewhere. The Pylian land tenure records are numerous and detailed, but our discussion here is deliberately brief. Land tenure is important to the question of economy and religion in the Mycenaean world since a great many of the holdings were in the hands of religious personnel or entailed religious obligations, but the present work is not intended as a study of land tenure specifically and the subject has in any case already been extensively treated elsewhere.[245] In terms of our central aim here, a general survey of the documents will suffice along with an indication of the degree to which deities and cult personnel are represented and the types of holdings in which they are involved.

Land tenure records are distinguished by a standard set of terms and phrases plus the presence (usually) of the ideogram GRA (wheat), which in this context indicates a measure of land, rather than the grain itself (see Section 5.2.1). The purpose of the records was probably to supply the palace with the information it needed on which to assess the holdings (a) for taxes and (b) for service obligations of various types. The Pylos records relate to several different

---

[243] Killen 1998b; Speciale 1999; 2000.

[244] Wright 2004b; see also 1995b. The classic study of Linear B ideograms and their archaeological correlates more widely is Vandenabeele & Olivier 1979.

[245] Including very recently in a book by del Freo (2005 [2006]) *non vidi*; see also Palmer 1998–1999 [2002].

estates, which Lejeune grouped as follows (with minor additions).[246]

1. domaine de *pa-ki-ja-na* (H41 and H1: Eb, Ed, En, Eo, Ep; Aq)
2. domaine X (H43: Ea)
3. domaine Y (H1: Eq, except for –213)
4. domaine de *sa-ra-pe-da* (H24: Er 312, Er 880, Un 718)
5. domaine de *ki-ri-ti-jo* (?) (H11 and H1: Es)
6. *a-ke-re-wa* (H1: Eq 213)

The ways in which deities and cult officials were involved in land tenure can be summarised as follows.

1. Tenures might be held by religious servants and officials.
2. Land could be owned or held by deities and exemptions might apply to such holdings.
3. Contributions of grain and foodstuffs might be owed to deities by lease-holders in connection with obligations related to their holdings.

These types of involvement are discussed in turn. In the case of the third, it is not clear whether the obligations were due because the deity was an 'owner' of the land or because the land happened to be of a type to which religious obligations for some reason applied. It may also be noted that it is not clear what it means for a deity to 'own' a plot of land. Presumably it would have been the sanctuary that benefited from the holding.[247] We will return to the matter briefly in the conclusions.

2.4.2 HOLDINGS BY RELIGIOUS PERSONNEL

In numerous cases, religious servants and officials held plots of land in which the palace evidently had some interest, since the records relating to these holdings were kept at the palace, even if it was not the actual 'owner'. The holdings appear to have been grouped on particular estates, the major one being at *pa-ki-ja-ne*, one of the nine major towns of the Hither Province and known from multiple offerings records as an important cult centre (see Sections 2.2.2 and 3.2.2).[248] Five series of tablets relate to this estate, four of which form two redactions of a single coherent document. The Eo and Eb series make up one copy, the En and Ep series the other. The Eo and Eb tablets are palm-leaf shaped, with one entry or a small, related group of entries per tablet. The corresponding En and Ep records are page-shaped tablets constituting a 'fair copy' onto which the Eo and Eb entries have been grouped together, more or less according to type of landholding.[249] In the fifth series, the Ed tablets give totals for various sub-groupings of the landholdings.

Two examples from the 'fair copy' are as follows. The first record, En 609, gives the heading for the 'full document'.

---

[246] Lejeune 1976, 81.
[247] For comparative material from classical Greece see Isager 1992.
[248] The literature on the *pa-ki-ja-ne* land tenure records is extensive. See e.g. *Documents*, 232–74, 443–56; Bennett 1956; Lejeune 1958b; 1958c; 1965; 1966; 1974; 1975; de Fidio 1977; 1987; Chadwick 1979; 1987a; Ruijgh 1987; Carlier 1987, 269–70; del Freo 2005 *non vidi*.
[249] Most scholars take the Eb/Eo records as the first copy and the Ep/En as the second. For the possibility these might be reversed see Carpenter 1983; 1984. However, our current understanding points generally towards shorter documents being drawn up into larger documents rather than the other way around (Killen 1984b; 1994; Piteros, Olivier & Melena 1990).

En 609		(S74-H1)
.1	pa-ki-ja-ni-ja , to-sa , da-ma-te ,	*DA* 40
.2	to-so-de , te-re-ta , e-ne-e-si	VIR 14
.3	wa-na-ta-jo-jo , ko-to-na , ki-ti-me-na , to-so-de⌞ ⌟p̣ẹ-mo	GRA 2 V 1
.4	o-da-a_2 , o-na-te[-re] , e-ko-si , ẉạ-na-ṭạ-jo-jo , ko-to-na ,	
.5a		GRA V 1
	a-tu-ko , e-te-do-mo , wa-na-ka-te-ro , o-na-to , e-ke , de , pe-mo	
.6	i-ni-ja , te-o-jo , do-e-ra , o-na-to , e-ke , to-so-de , pe-mo	GRA T 2 V 4
.7	e-**65*-to , te-o-jo , do-e-ro , o-na-to⌞ ⌟e-ke , to-so-de , pe-mo	GRA T 2
.8	si-ma , te-o-jo , do-e-ra , o-na-to , e-ke , to-so-de , pe-mo	GRA T 1
.9	*vacat*	
.10	a-ma-ru-ta-o , ko-to-na , ki-ti-me-na , ṭọ-so-de , pe-mo	GRA 2 T 3
.11	o-da-a_2 e-ko-si a-]ma-ru-ta-o , ko-to-na , o-na-te-re	
.12	so-u-ro te-o-jo do-]e-ro , o-na-to , e-ke , to-so-de , pe-mo	GRA V 3
.13	e-do-mo-ne-u te-o-]jo , do-e-ro , o-na-to , e-ke , to-so-de , pe-mo	G̣ṚẠ Ṭ 1
.14	e-sa-ro te-o-jo do-]e-ro , ọ[-na-to]ẹ-ḳẹ[to-so-de]p̣ẹ-ṃọ	GRA V 3
.15	wa-na-ta-jo te-re-ta o-]ṇạ-ṭọ , e-ke , to-so-de , pe-mo	GRA T 1
.16	e-ra-ta-ra i-je-re-ja do-e-ra]pa-ki-ja-na , o-na-to , e-ke , to-so-de , pe-mo	GRA T 1
.17	po-so-re-ja te-o-jo do-e-ra]ọ-na-to , e-ke , to-so-de , pe-mo	GRA T 1 V 3
.18	i-je-re-ja pa-ki-ja-na o-na-]to , e-ke , to-so-de , pe-mo	GRA T 3

The word *pa-ki-ja-ni-ja* is either a variant form of the toponym,[250] or an ethnic adjective referring to *da-ma-te*. *da-ma-te* is apparently a plural noun, but what it refers to is unclear. A proposed interpretation as /*damartes*/ 'wives' is problematic, since the meaning would be inappropriate to the present situation, although Carratelli's suggestion of an original sense of 'family units', 'households' is more appealing.[251] Ruijgh on the other hand proposed that the word is a pre-Hellenic loan-word related to a variant form in the Linear B texts, *du-ma* (with plural *du-ma-te*), with the semantic value of 'chief, master'.[252] Whatever the word means, there seem to be forty of them (taking *DA* as a syllabogram used as an ideogram abbreviating the same word).

Line .2 states that within (/*en-ehensi*/ 'they are in') the *da-ma-te* are fourteen *te-re-ta*, interpreted as /*telestai*/, plural of /*telestās*/, an official title with religious associations in later Greek, although such a connotation should not necessarily be assumed for the Mycenaean era. The original meaning may have been something like 'he who owes service'.[253]

Following the heading, the tablet is divided into two paragraphs, each dealing with the lessees of a different *ko-to-na* /*ktoina*/ 'plot' belonging to an individual whose name appears in the genitive (e.g. in line .4 *wa-na-ta-jo-jo*). Many of the persons have cult connections, for instance those described as 'slave/servant of the god' (*te-o-jo* /*theoio*/ *do-e-ro*/*-ra* /*doelos*/ or /*doela*/) and the 'Priestess of *Pa-ki-ja-na*' (/*hiereia*/; lines .16.18), but some appear to be 'ordinary' craftsmen, for instance *au-tu-ko* (line .5), described as the /*wanakteros*/ 'royal' *e-te-do-mo*.[254] What exactly the expression 'slave of the god' meant is uncertain, partly because the precise meaning of /*doelos*/ in Mycenaean is unclear. In later Greek it meant 'slave', but some of the persons so described in Mycenaean seem to be relatively high-status individuals.[255]

En 609 is followed by En 74, –659 and –467, together forming the 'first part' of the document. This first part is divided into a total of thirteen paragraphs, each dealing with the leases attached to a different man. Next, the six Ep tablets form the 'second part' of the document. One example is given here.

---

250 *Documents*, 568.

251 Carratelli 1954, 225; *Documents*, 242, 447, 538. I am grateful to J.T. Killen for reminding me of this.

252 Ruijgh 1987. A difficulty with this idea is that one has to assume that *to-sa* is a scribal error for *to-so*. I am grateful to J.T. Killen for bringing this to my attention.

253 *Documents*, 234.

254 The meaning of *e-te-do-mo* is uncertain, but it need not be a title specifically connected with religion as elsewhere in this group of records a 'royal' fuller and potter appear (see e.g. Palaima 1997).

255 See e.g. Lejeune 1958b. At least some, however, do seem to have been of lower status and could be bought and sold – e.g. in KN B 8224 – so were probably chattel slaves. See Chapter 1 n 4 for further references.

Ep 704 (S74-H1)

.1 o-pe-to-re-u , qe-ja-me-no , e-ke , ke-ke-me-na , ko-to-na , to-so , pe-mo[ ]G̣ṚẠ 2 T 5
.2 u-wa-mi-ja , te-o-jo , do-e-ra , o-na-to , e-ke-qe , i-je-re-ja , ḳẹ-ra , to-so pe-mo GRA T 1 V 3
.3 e-ri-ta , i-je-re-ja , o-na-to , e-ke , ke-ke-me-na , ko-to-na , pa-ro , da-mo , to-so , pe-mo GRA T 4
.4 ki-ti-te-wi-ja , o-na-to , e-ko-si , ke-ke-me-na , ko-to-na⌞ ⌟pa-ro , da-mo , to-so , pe-mo GRA 1 T 9
.5 e-ri-ta , i-je-re-ja , e-ke , e-u-ke-to-qe , e-to-ni-jo , e-ke-e , te-o ̦, da-mo-de-mi , pa-si , ko-to-na-o ,
.6 ke-ke-me-na-o , o-na-to , e-ke-e , to-so pe-mo GRA 3 T 9̣
.7 ka-pa-ti-ja , ka-ra-wi-po-ro , e-ke , ke-ke-me-no , o-pe-ro-sa , du-wo-u-pi , wo-ze-e , o-u-wo-ze , ⟦to-ṣọ⟧
.8 to- ṣọ[pe-mo GRA]4

An essential difference between the En and Ep tablets is that the former record what is described as *ki-ti-me-na* land and the latter *ke-ke-me-na* land. The precise meaning of these terms is still disputed, but Chadwick expressed what is surely the essential point when he remarked that that *ki-ti-me-na* 'does not refer to any physical difference in the type of land, but to a juridical distinction, possibly to its ultimate ownership as opposed to present occupation'.[256] As he demonstrated, *ki-ti-me-na* and other land tenure terms are related to vocabulary appearing on the Pylos rowing tablets and it is possible to draw a connection between various categories of tenure and obligations to provide men for military service, an evidently important aspect of Mycenaean land-holding.

Another example of records belonging to a single estate are the Ea tablets of H43 (Lejeune's 'domaine X'). A few examples are as follows.[257]

Ea 754 (S28-H43)

.a { ra-pte
{ ti-ri-da-ro e-ke , o-na-to , ko-do-jo , ko-to-na GRA T 6[ ]*vacat*

Ea 756 (S28-H43)

.a { ki-ti-me-na
{ sa-ke-re-wo , i-je-re-wo , ko-ṭọ-ṇạ GRA 6 [

Ea 782 (S28-H43)

.a { ra-wa-ke-si-jo
{ ru-ko-ro , e-ke , o-na-to , pa-ro , mo-ro-qo-ro-jo , ko-to-na po-me-no GRA T 1

The Ea tablets share much of the juridical terminology of the En–Ep documents, but include fewer religious figures (although they do appear – note the priest in Ea 756 above). A sense of the difference between the holders at *pa-ki-ja-na* and in the Ea series may be gained by comparing the persons concerned by occupation (where known), as in Table 2-8.

Table 2-8. Land-holders at *pa-ki-ja-na* and in the Ea tablets

A. Land-holders at *pa-ki-ja-na*	B. Land-holders in the Ea tablets
A1. *With religious connections*	**B1. *With religious connections***
23 (+1?) male 'slaves of the deity'	1 Dionysos (deity)
22 (+1?) female 'slaves of the deity'	1 priest
1 priestess (by name, *e-ri-ta*)	1 *di-<pte>-ra-po-ro* (if restoration correct)
1 priest (by name, *we-te-re-u*)	
2 *i-je-ro-wo-ko* (sacrificing priest) (one a *telestās*)	
1 *klāwiphoros* ('Key-bearer', a cult title, by name *ka-pa-ti-ja*)	
3 priestess's slaves	
1 Key-bearer's slave	
1 *ki-ri-te-wi-ja* (female group, cult related?)	
1 man called *po-ti-ni-ja-we-jo* (see Section 2.5)	
1 *mi-ka-ta* (from 'temple servants' lists)	
Sub-total A1: 57 (+2?)	**Sub-total B1: 3**

[256] Chadwick 1987a, 82. On the rowing tablets see also Killen 1983a.

[257] On the Ea tablets see esp. Lejeune 1976. The texts here are from *PTT*.

A. Land-holders at *pa-ki-ja-na*	**B. Land-holders in the Ea tablets**
A2. *Without religious connections or uncertain*	**B2. *Without religious connections or uncertain***
1 *a-pi-me-de* (an *e-qe-ta*, 'Follower') by name	1 *a-pi-a*$_2$*-ro* (MN)
3 *a-pi-me-de do-e-ro* (the Follower's slaves)	1 *du-ni-jo* (MN)
1 king's *e-te-do-mo*	3 tailors
1 king's fuller	1 *e-pi-we-ti-ri-jo* (connection with textiles?)
1 king's potter (also a *telestās*)	1 unguent boiler
1 fuller (also a *telestās*)	1 *e-te-do-mo* (cf. also in En/Ep)
1 *a-si-to-po-qo* (cook?; see Chapter 7 n 34)	1 wheelwright *ra-wa-ke-si-jo* (belonging to the *lāwāgetās*)
1 shepherd (also a *telestās*)	1 *ru-ko-ro* (MN) *ra-wa-ke-si-jo*
1 *po-ro-du[-ma*? (by name *su-ko*, also a *telestās*)	1 *su-qo-ta* (MN) *ra-wa-ke-si-jo*
1 obscure (*qe-ja-me-no*, Ep 704.1)	2 shepherds
9 *telestai* with *ki-ti-me-na* land, occupations unknown	1 *me-ri-te-wo* (/*melitēwos*/? 'bee-keeper'?)
5 *ko-to-no-o-ko*, occupations unknown	1 *a-ke-ro* (herald?)
2 *ka-ma-e-we*, occupations unknown	9 unidentified
Sub-total A2: 28	**Sub-total B2: 24**
TOTAL A: 85 (or 87?)	**TOTAL B: 27**

Fifty-seven individuals of the *pa-ki-ja-ne* group have clear or likely religious associations, as opposed to just three in the Ea series. (It is true that the *pa-ki-ja-ne* group has more holders overall, but the proportions are still markedly different.) An overall similarity in both series, however, is the appearance of craftworkers, officials and religious personnel. Examples of craftworkers are the 'royal' fuller and potter of the *pa-ki-ja-ne* group and the tailors and unguent-boiler of the Ea tablets. Examples of officials are the *po-ro-du-ma* and *a-pi-me-de* (probably an *e-qe-ta*[258]) from the *pa-ki-ja-ne* group and *du-ni-jo* from the Ea tablets. The way in which secular and religious figures are mixed both at *pa-ki-ja-ne* and in the Ea tablets suggests that the religious standing of the land-holders was not the essential administrative concern. What seems to have been more important was the juridical status of the plots.

Finally we may note records relating to Lejeune's 'domaine Y'. The texts are as follows.[259]

Eq 36 (S74-H1)

.1]-we-jo , wa-tu ,
.2] , a-de-te
.3 to-]ṣọ-de , pe-mo GRA 2
.4 o-da-a$_2$]ạ-de-te , ⟦e-ke ⟧
.5 to-so-]ḍẹ˪ ˩pe-mo GRA 2
.6 o-da-a$_2$]ṇị-jạ-de ,
.7 *mutila*
.8 *mutila vel non extabat*
.9 *mutila*
.10 to-so-de pe-mo]GRA 1 o-ḍạ-ạ$_2$[
.11]ḳẹ-me , to-so-de , ⟦ ⟧
.12 pe-mo GRA *qs* o-]da-a$_2$, a-ta-wo-ne-jo ,
.13]pạ-ra-jo , po-ṇẹ-to-qe-ṃị ,
.14]•-• ,. to-so-de , pe-mo , GRA 4
.15 o-da-]a$_2$, po-se-da-o-no[ ]do-e-ro , pa-[
.16 to-]so-de[pe-mo GRA]T ˪4[

[258] Lindgren 1973 I, 141; II, 186. She rightly notes he need not have religious connections (suggested on the basis of his appearance on this tablet).
[259] Eq 36: text from Melena 1992–1993b, 308–9, but with underdotting as in *PTT* and line .15 from *PoN* IV; see also Bennett 1992, 122; Killen 1999b, 343–4 (for the reading and the suggestion that *po-ne-to-qe-mi* in line .13 means 'and he is working it'). Eq 146: text from PTT, with new reading in line .11 (Bennett 1992, 107); joins reported in Melena 1992–1993b, 310 and 1994–1995a, 95, but no change to text.

Eq 146 (S74-H1)

.1 o-da-a_{2}⌞ ⌟te-re-ta , e-[
.2 ko-ro , to-so-de , pe-mo ⟦GRA ⟧ GRA [
.3 o-da-a_2 , po-ro-te-u , e-ke , to-so-de , pe-mo GRA 1
.4 o-da-a_2 , re-pi-ri-jo , e-ke , to-so-de , pe-mo GRA 1
.5 o-da-a_2 , a-de-me-we , e-ke , to-so-de pe-mo GRA 1 V 3
.6–8 *vacant*
.9 o-da-]a_2 , [ ]-me-no , i-ja-te , o-na-to ,
.10 e-]ḳẹ , to-so-de⌞ ⌟pe-mo GRA 1
.11 o-da-a_2 , a-si-wi-jo , ị-q̣ọ-na-to-mo ,
.12 o-ṇạ-ṭọ , ẹ-ḳẹ[to-]so-de pe-mo GRA T 7
.13–15 *vacant*
.16 to-so-de pe-]mo GRA T 3

No detailed discussion is needed here, but we may note these tablets also record at least one person related to religion, the man described as *po-se-da-o-no do-e-ro /Poseidāōnos doelos/* 'servant/slave of Poseidon' in Eq 36.15.

2.4.3 HOLDINGS BY DEITIES

An example of a holding by a deity, Dionysos, was encountered above in the Ea series. In the present section we briefly survey general evidence for such holdings. We begin with the tablet already referred to.

Ea 102 + 107 (S28-H43)

di-wo-nu-so-jo , e-ka-ra GRA 2 T 6 [

The text of Ea 102 results from a new join by Melena.[260] Two important discoveries arising from this join were that (1) *di-wo-nu-so* at Pylos does refer to a deity,[261] and (2) a holding by a deity was recorded in the Ea series. Melena interprets *e-ka-ra* as */eskharā/* 'hearth, fireplace', and observes that the tablet documents 'an allocation of a piece of land to a sanctuary itself'.[262]

Another instance of a holding by a deity may be inferred through an exemption applying to one of the holdings in former Xn 1357, now identified by Killen as a member of the Na series,[263] a set of some 100 palm-leaf shaped tablets which deal with land tenure holdings involving flax (*SA*) at various toponyms.[264] The text of Na 1357 is as follows, along with a few examples of some more typical Na tablets.[265]

Na 543 (S106-H1)

.a , e-ko-si
ka-ra-do-ro , ko-ro-ku-ra-i-jo *SA* 30

Na 1013 (S106-H1)

.A] , wa-na-ka[
.B] , e-re-u-te[ ] *SA* [

[260] Melena 2000–2001a, 357–60. Xa 102 was recognised as an Ea tablet by Bennett (1992, 107).

[261] The word is attested twice at Pylos, but in both cases interpretation as an MN was at least possible so identification as a deity could not be certain. In fact, Dionysos was nowhere attested with certainty as a deity in the Mycenaean world until the discovery of a tablet from Chania in which the religious context was clear (see Section 4.2.2). The subsequent Pylos join affirms Dionysos as an established member of the Mycenaean pantheon already in the Late Bronze Age.

[262] Melena 2000–2001a, 360. The sense of *e-ka-ra* as 'portable hearth, brazier' was already established with regard to PY Ta 709.2; see *Documents*, 499, 542; Chadwick 1986, 521.

[263] Killen 1996a, 147. The tablet is also now discussed by Perna 2004, 214–18.

[264] Foster 1981; Killen 1992–1993b.

[265] The text of Na 1013 is from Melena 2000–2001a, 369; the tablet now joins Na 1356. Texts of Na 543 and –1027 are as in *PTT*.

Na 1027 (S106-H1)
e-na-po-ro , *SA* 70

Na 1357 (S106-H1)
.1 to-]sa-de , e-ma-a$_2$, e-re[
.2 to-]sa-de , e-po-me-ne-we , [
.3 to-]sa-de , ka-ke-we , e-re-u-te[
.4]ṭọ-sa-de , ko-re-te-re , e-re-u[

The Na tablets always record a toponym (e.g. *ka-ra-do-ro*, *e-na-po-ro*) and an assessment (e.g. *SA* 70), with sometimes a note of the holders (e.g. in Na 543) or of an exemption (e.g. Na 1013, where the exemption appears to be in respect of the *wanax*). Na 1357 records a number of holders, including in line .1 *e-ma-a$_2$* 'Hermes', securely attested elsewhere as a deity. Killen notes that although 1357 is taller than most other Na tablets, it had actually been pinched out along the bottom to expand the writing area. He draws attention to the fact that three of the contributors on the tablet appear also on Nn 831, the text of which is as follows; the shared words are underlined.[266]

Nn 831 (S106-H1)

.1	ko-ri[si-jo? ri-]no , ⟦do-so-ṃọ⟧		
.2	u-re[ ]	*SA*	4
.3	a-mo-ke-re[ ]	*SA*	1
.4	e-re-e-u	*SA*	2
.5	qo-u-ko-ro [ ]	*SA*	2
.6	a-ro-je-u [ ]	*SA*	1 [
.7	a-mu-ta-wo [ ]	*SA*	4
.8	e-po-me-ne-ụ[ ]	*SA*	4
.9	ko-re-te[ ]	*SA*	24
.10	po-me-ne [ ]	*SA*	2
.11	ka-ke-u[ ]	*SA*	1
.12-15	*vacant*		

Killen suggests that the surface area of Na 1357 was expanded because the holding involved an unusual number of exemptions and that the complexity of the situation led the scribe to draw up an additional, more detailed record, Nn 831, showing what was to be paid by whom after the exemptions were accounted for. He proposes that Hermes does not appear on Nn 831 because the deity received a complete exemption.[267]

The possibility of land being held by deities and exemptions applying to such holdings may shed light on the well-known dispute between the priestess of *pa-ki-ja-na* and the *dāmos* in Ep 704.5.6, in which the priestess claimed that the god held a plot and that it was *e-to-ni-jo*. The precise meaning of *e-to-ni-jo* is not known, but it indicates a juridical distinction and apparently described a particularly desirable type of holding, possibly one to which exemptions applied.[268]

We may conclude with a note of a holding in connection with the deity *Potnia*.

Eq 213 (S74-H1)
.1 o-wi-de , a-ko-so-ta , to-ro-qe-jo-me-no , a-ro-u-ra , a$_2$-ri-sa ,
.2 a-ke-re-wa , o-ro-jo , to-so-de , pe-mo GRA 8
.3 o-da-a$_2$, e-ri-no-wo-to , o-ro-jo , to-so-de , pe-mo GRA 20
.4 o-da-a$_2$, ko-tu-wo , o-ro-jo , to-so-de , pe-mo GRA 2̣0
.5 o-da-a$_2$, po-ti-ni-ja-we-jo-jo , o-te-pe-o-jo , o-ro-jo , to-so-de , pe-mo GRA 6
.6 o-da-a$_2$, ko-no , o-ro-jo , to-so , pe-mo GRA 40

---

[266] Nn 831: Text from *PTT*.
[267] Killen 1996a, 147; see also Killen (1983d, 218–19) for the observation that Nn 831 is an *assessment* (see *do-so-mo*) rather than an actual payment record (as he points out, the figures add up neatly to 45, suggesting a top-down approach common in other Pylian taxation records, e.g. the Ma series).
[268] Chadwick 1987a, 81. For a similar point see Shelmerdine 1998b, 93.

Eq 213 records a tour of inspection by the important official *Alxoitās* of various land-holdings, one of which (line .5) is described as somehow pertaining to or belonging to the deity *Potnia* (on the form of the word see Section 2.5). The word *o-te-pe-o-jo* here is probably a toponym, in parallel with well-attested toponyms such as *a-ke-re-wa* and *e-ri-no-wo-to* (lines .2 and .3). The repeated word *o-ro-jo* is obscure,[269] and the purpose of the tour of inspection is unclear, but might possibly involve assessments for military service. As noted above, land tenure was associated in some instances with obligations to provide rowers for the Pylian fleet, and, as Chadwick observed, *ko-ni-jo* on the rowing tablet An 610 might be an ethnic of the TN *ko-no* in Eq 213.6.[270] If so, there may be a connection between the fact that a 1 : 5 ratio pertains on both records between the amounts recorded for *a-ke-re-wa* and *ko-no*, i.e. GRA 8 : GRA 40 on Eq 213 and VIR 25 : VIR 126 on An 610. Possibly, Eq 213 formed part of the basis on which the numbers of men in An 610 were calculated (note both tablets are by H1),[271] raising the further possibility that *Potnian* land was also subject to such obligations. Or would the deity, like Hermes, have received an exemption?

2.4.4 HOLDINGS WHICH ENTAILED RELIGIOUS OBLIGATIONS

Some holdings entailed obligations to provide banqueting foodstuffs or other types of payments to deities. As noted above, it is not clear whether these arose as a result of the deities actually owning the land or whether the land simply happened to be of a type subject to such obligations.[272]

The main example is seen in a group of related documents: Er 312, Er 880, Un 718 and Un 853 (Lejeune's 'domaine de *sa-ra-pe-da*').[273] We begin with Un 718.

Un 718 (S312-H42)

.1 sa-ra-pe-da , po-se-da-o-ni , do-so-mo
.2 o-wi-de-ta-i , do-so-mo , to-so , e-ke-ra_2-wo
.3 do-se , GRA 4 VIN 3 BOS^m 1
.4 tu-ro_2 , *$TURO_2$* 10 ko-wo , **153* 1
.5 me-ri-to , V 3
.6 *vacat*
.7 o-da-a_2 , da-mo , GRA 2 VIN 2
.8 OVIS^m 2 *$TURO_2$* 5 a-re-ro , *AREPA* V 2 **153* 1
.9 to-so-de , ra-wa-ke-ta , do-se ,
.10 OVIS^m 2 me-re-u-ro , FAR T 6
a -ma
.11 VIN S 2 o-da-a_2 , wo-ro-ki-jo-ne-jo , ka-
.12 GRA T 6 VIN S 1 *$TURO_2$* 5 me-ri[
.13 [me-]ṛị-to V 1

Palimpsest.
.4 10 possibly over erasure, if not trace of previous text.
.8 *a-re-<pa>*; cf. *AREPA*.
.11 *-jo* , *ka-'ma'* over erasure.
.12 *me-ri*[over erasure.
.13 Perhaps]1̣1 or]2̣1.

The heading of Un 718.1 reads: *sa-ra-pe-da* (an obscure toponym) /*dosmos*/ 'payment, assessment' /*Poseidāōni*/ 'to Poseidon', followed by (line .2) a word probably in dative plural,

[269] *DMic*. II, *s.v. o-ro-jo*.
[270] Chadwick 1987a, 78 with n 5.
[271] Killen (2006b, 75) makes the same suggestion.
[272] See Killen (2004, 158 n iv) for a concise statement.
[273] Discussions include *Documents*, 280–4; Lejeune 1975; de Fidio 1977; Carlier 1984, 54–63; 1987, 269–70; Palaima 1989, 109; 2004b, 110–11. Note the sealing Wa 731 is also related. Transcriptions are taken from the following sources. Er 312: *PTT* I, 135–6. Er 880: *PTT* I, 135–6 (with restorations as suggested in Chadwick 1987a); a join is reported in Melena 1994–1995b, 284, but no change to text. Un 718: *PTT* I, 244, 249, except for line .13 (Bennett 1992, 116). Un 853: Melena 1992–1993b, 319–20, but with reference to *PTT* I, 244–5, 249 and *PoN* IV. I am grateful to C.W. Shelmerdine for her comments on the transcriptions; any remaining errors are my own.

perhaps /*owidertāhi*/ 'sheep-flayers' (possibly a cult title of some sort[274]), and again 'payment, assessment'.

The subsequent text can be construed as four paragraphs, each listing the assessment for a different individual or group. The first contributor is *e-ke-ra$_2$-wo*, an important person known from other tablets (possibly the *wanax* himself[275]), who is said to 'give/contribute' 'so much' /*tos(s)os…dōsei*/. The next contributors are the /*dāmos*/ (in later Greek 'people', but evidently with a specific juridical meaning in this context[276]), and the *lāwāgetās*, another important individual, thought to be second in command after the *wanax*.[277] Finally, an assessment is made for *wo-ro-ki-jo-ne-jo ka-ma*. The second word refers to a type of holding (it is common in other land tenure records and there is a related noun *ka-ma-e-u*, which apparently refers to one who possesses such a holding). The first word could be a possessive adjective of the *-e-jo* type (see Section 2.5.1) formed from a man's name, *Wroikiōn*.[278]

The contributions include wheat, wine, cheese, animals and sheepskins. The types of commodities involved look very much like those found in typical lists of banqueting foodstuffs, and it may be that the goods were brought together for a similar purpose. On the other hand, caution is recommended because, as Killen has pointed out, there are differences with the banqueting 'menu' lists (for instance, wheat and sheepskins do not appear on the other records; also, we are dealing with assessments here, rather than actual deliveries).[279]

As was brilliantly demonstrated by de Fidio, the 'assessments' on Un 718 arise in connection with land-holdings on Er 312 and Er 880, the texts of which are as follows.[280]

Er 312		(S312-H42)
.1	wa-na-ka-te-ro , te-me-no [	
.2	to-so-jo pe-ma GRA 30	
.3	ra-wa-ke-si-jo , te-me-no GRA 10	
.4	*vacat*	
.5	te-re-ta-o[ ]ṭọ-ṣọ p̣ẹ-ma GRA 30	
.6	to-so-de , te-re-ta VIR 3	
.7	wo-ro-ki-jo-ne-jo , e-re-mo	
.8	to-so-jo , pe-ma GRA ˛6[	
.9	*vacat*	

Palimpsest (*p̣ẹ-ṃạ* visible in .2, *ṛạ*[in .8, ҀṚẠ in .9).
.8 ˛6[: probably complete, 5 units preserved, maximum 7.

Er 880		(S312-H42)
.1	e-]ke-ra$_2$[-wo ki-]ti-me-no , e-ke	
.2	sa-ra-pe-do[ ]pu$_2$-te-me-no	
.3	to-so [ki-ti-ta]GRA 30[+20] *vacat*	
.4	to-so-de , [a-ki-ti-]to , pe-ma GRA 4̣2[	
.5	to-sa , we-je[-we]1100[	
.6	to-sa-de , su-ẓạ[ ]1̣1̣00[	
.7	*vacat*	
.8	ku-su-to-ro-qa , to-ṣọ , pe-ma 94	
.9-10	*vacant*	

.4 4̣2[: complete at right but broken below, possibly 5̣4̣.
.5 Possibly *we-je*[*-we* may be conjectured, cf KN Gv 863.
.7 Probably whole line erased.
.8 Probably whole line erased and rewritten.

---

[274] *Documents*, 485, 566; Lejeune 1975, 60.
[275] His identity is disputed and the literature is extensive; see e.g. Chadwick 1975; Lindgren 1973 II, 153–5; Palaima 1995a; Killen 1999b, 352–3.
[276] Lejeune 1965; Palaima 2004b, 111. It may be that the correct sense is not 'village community' as in *Documents*; the word seems rather to refer to bodies of land-holders. I. Morris (2000, 100–1) makes some relevant comments.
[277] Lindgren 1973 II, 134–6.
[278] Killen 1983c, 83–4.
[279] Killen 2004, 158–9 n v; see also Killen 1983d, 218; Godart 1999, 251.
[280] De Fidio 1977.

Er 312, like Un 718, is divided into four 'paragraphs' or entries. The first deals with the /*wanakteros temenos*/, the 'enclosure' of the *wanax*. The size of the holding is given in terms of wheat used as a measure of land (see Sections 2.4.1 and 5.2.1). The second entry deals with the *temenos* of the *lāwāgetās*, and the third with the holding of three men described as /*telestai*/, a title connected with land-holdings in the En–Ep records. Finally, we have a holding described by the word *wo-ro-ki-jo-ne-jo*, seen in Un 718.

A correspondence between the four paragraphs was already recognised in *Documents*[1], where VC set it out as follows:[281]

Un 718	=	**Er 312**
E-ke-ra₂-wo	=	*wa-na-ka-te-ro te-me-no*
lāwāgetās	=	*lāwāgesios temenos*
dāmos	=	*telestāōn temenos*
wo-ro-ki-jo-ne-jo ka-ma	=	*wo-ro-ki-jo-ne-jo e-re-mo*

Subsequently, however, de Fidio demonstrated that the first correspondence does not hold. Rather, the Un 718 assessment was made on the basis of Er 312 plus Er 880, where the *ki-ti-me-no* holding of the same man *e-ke-ra₂-wo* appears,[282] again at *sa-ra-pe-da/do*.[283]

That the assessments in Un 718 were due with respect to the land-holdings on Er 312 plus 880 is indicated by the close relationship which exists between the percentages of the contributions and the size of the holdings, if it is assumed that the holding of the *wanax* and the *a-ki-ti-to* (with *a*-privative, 'not' *ki-ti-to*) holding of *e-ke-ra₂-wo* are exempt.[284] Killen recently gives an updated version of the figures which we reproduce as Table 2-9 here.[285]

Table 2-9. Land-holdings at *sa-ra-pe-da*

Er 312 + 880	**GRA**	**% of taxed land (GRA 96[)**	**% of dosmos (Un 718)**
(*) *wanax*	30	0	0
lāwāgetās	10	10.5	11
telestai = dāmos	30	31.5	33
Wroikiōn	6[	6	6
e-ke-ra₂-wo (pe-pu₂-te-me-no)	50[	52	50
(*) *e-ke-ra₂-wo (a-ki-ti-to)*	42[	0	0

(*) exempt

As the table shows, the correspondence is nearly exact. The reference to Poseidon in Un 718.1 suggests that the plots according which the assessments were made, if not actually owned by the deity, were linked to obligations concerning him. As already seen, juridical obligations were a standard feature of Mycenaean land tenure,[286] and it is unsurprising to find that in addition to military and service obligations some of them related to provisions for religion.[287]

A further example of obligations involving Poseidon is seen in Un 853, the text of which is as follows.

[281] *Documents*[1], 264–5.
[282] The restoration in line .1 was much debated but the equation now seems secure; see Killen 1999b.
[283] De Fidio 1977; Killen 1999b. See also Palmer 1994, 48–9, 66–72.
[284] De Fidio 1977, esp. 114–26.
[285] Killen 1999b, 352.
[286] See p. 68 with n 256 above.
[287] See Chadwick 1976, 113.

Un 853 (S6-H6)

Recto

.1]-ḳẹ-ra$_2$-u-na , e-ṛạ-[•] ⟦ ⟧ [
.2 po-se-da-o-ne⌞ ⌟re-[•]-no 6 [
.3 **146* 18̣[ ] LANA 2 M 2[
.4 *AREPA* V 4 [ ] 1 OVIS^{m} 1 OVIS^{f} 1 C̣ẠP̣^{f}[
.5 SUS+*KA* 2 SUS^{f} 4[ ] Ṭ 1̣ FAR T 1 V [
.6 VIN 5 ṬẸḶẠ [ ]1 TELA+*PA* 1
.7 *vacat*
.8 *vacat* [ ] *vacat*
.9 *vacat* [ ] *vac.* [
.10]3[ ]*vac.*[
.11]-we-e-a$_2$[

Verso

.1]e-[•]-me-de , ḍọ[ ]ḍụ-ru-wo-qo
.2 *deest*
.3-7 *vacant*

Recto palimpsest, with vestiges of ruling and text.
.1 *e-ṛạ*[over erasure; *e-ṭạ*[not impossible; e-ra-ja not excluded.
.2 *re-ḳọ-no* possible.
.5 Whole line over erasure; T 1 probably corrected from T 2.
.6 ṬẸḶẠ[+^{x}] possible, interior of sign missing; following number not more than 1.
v. Broad margin at top to accommodate the irregular surface.
*v.*1]*e-ḳẹ-me-de* not impossible; *ḍọ*[possibly *ụ*[; end of line over ⟦*ro-wi-jo*⟧.

The tablet again deals with contributions or assessments of the man *e-ke-ra$_2$-wo* (line .1) in connection with Poseidon (line .2). As Killen has now demonstrated, Un 853 is linked to Un 6, which records animals for sacrifice to Poseidon and the deity *pe-re-*82* (Section 2.3.2.2 above).[288] The amounts in Un 6.6–8 are twice those on Un 853.3–4, as shown in Table 2-10.[289]

Table 2-10. Correspondence of Un 6 and Un 853

commodity	Un 6	Un 853
**146*	37	18̣[
**166+WE*	?	?
LANA	5 (= M 15)	2 M 2 (= M 8)
AREPA	S 1 V 2[(= V 8[)	V 4 [
BOS^{m}	2	?
BOS^{f}	2	?
OVIS^{m}	?	1
OVIS^{f}	?	1
CAP^{f}	?	?

Finally, a further set of tablets, the Es series, also deals with contributions to Poseidon with respect to land tenure.[290] Briefly, Es 650 lists the holdings of thirteen men, while Es 644 gives the amount for each man of his *do-so-mo we-te-i-we-te-i*, /*dosmos wete*(*h*)*i wete*(*h*)*i*/, 'yearly payment'. Each of the remaining Es tablets records one man with his *do-so-mo* to Poseidon and three other figures. The payments to Poseidon are always greater than the 'yearly payments' on Es 644, so these may be amounts payable in addition to the yearly payments.

2.4.5 CONCLUSION TO LAND TENURE

In the above we saw examples of land tenure holdings by religious personnel and deities, and observed that exemptions sometimes applied to such holdings. We also saw instances of religious obligations consequent on land-holdings, whether because the land 'belonged' to a

[288] Killen 1999b, 350–3.
[289] Killen 1999b, 351. As he notes (p. 352) Un 6 and Un 853 may refer to the *same* items.
[290] Bibliography includes: *Documents*, 275–82, 456–8; Ilievsky 1966; de Fidio 1977, 13–75.

deity or because it happened to be land to which religious obligations for some reason applied.

The difficulty in understanding precisely what it meant for a deity to 'own' a plot of land was touched on. Presumably it would have been the sanctuary that benefited from the holding. It should be noted, however, that this need not constitute evidence for independent temple wealth. Deity land is recorded by the palace in the same way as other holdings are and it may be significant that exemptions needed to be specially recorded, rather than being assumed.[291] It would be interesting to know whether deities held land traditionally and in their own right, or in consequence of some special dispensation (whether for set periods or in perpetuity).

A point worth noting here is that, in contrast with the situation we will see below with regard to 'Collectors' (Section 2.5), there is some evidence that cult officials were sometimes involved in the actual management of the holdings, or at least were deeply concerned in their affairs (which would be unsurprising since they were direct beneficiaries). The well-known dispute between *Eritha* and the *dāmos* mentioned above indicates that the priestess had an immediate and active interest in defining the status of the plot which, according to her, belonged to the deity. A further suggestion of active involvement is seen in the next lines of the same tablet, Ep 704.7.8, where it is stated that the woman *Karpathia*, the 'Key-bearer' (a cult title), was obliged to 'work with two', but does not do so. Despite the obscurity of the situation, it at least seems that *Karpathia* was able to make choices about whether the 'work' (whatever it was) was carried out, suggesting a degree of active engagement on her part. It should also be noted, however, that the situation with regard to *Karpathia* is all the more opaque because it is not apparent whether her holding belonged ultimately to a deity, to the palace, or to some individual, so it is uncertain to whom the 'obligation' was due. That such distinctions were important is shown by the fact that deity land is in at least some instances specified separately.

In general, the impression might be conveyed that, apart from the Ea series, land tenure at Pylos is frequently associated with cult figures. Religious personnel are heavily represented in the *pa-ki-ja-ne* group, while the Er and Es series are mainly concerned with payments to Poseidon. Even in the Ea series a few religious figures appear. This might seem to suggest a strong connection between religion and land-holding in general. It should be remembered, however, that the tablets document very small percentages of the overall land in the polity and that they probably relate to places near the palace.[292] Further, they may be unusual even for local estates, perhaps involving special circumstances that required more detailed record-keeping. With regard to the *pa-ki-ja-ne* records, another possibility is that they were drawn up because it was at the time of the annual festival at the cult place *pa-ki-ja-ne* that land tenure holdings associated with this place (or sanctuary) were assessed. That such a festival did take place, that it was annual and that it took place during the period covered by the records is indicated by Fr 1224, which records an offering to Poseidon (the subject of several of the records discussed above) in 'the Month of *pa-ki-ja-ne*'.[293] The text is as follows.

Fr 1224 (S1202-H2)

.a pa-ko-we , e-ti-we

pa-ki-ja-ni-jo-jo me-no , po-se-da-o-ne OLE+*PA* Z 2

Cut at right; Z over V.

---

[291] Note that classical shrines owned their own land, but such lands were normally administered by the state. They were inalienable in the sense that cities could not sell them: they belonged to the temples, but this does not mean that temples operated as independent economic units. See papers in Linders & Nordquist 1987 and Linders & Alroth 1992.

[292] For the argument that land-holdings at Pylos were near the palace see Killen 1987b. Both *pa-ki-ja-ne* and *a-ke-re-wa* are known through the reconstruction of Pylian political geography to lie near the centre of the Hither Province, thus in the general region of Pylos itself (see e.g. Chadwick 1976).

[293] Cf. *Documents*, 478, 568: '"Month of P.", i.e., when the great festival takes place at P.'

The naming of months after important festivals was a standard feature of later Greek language, and it would not be surprising to find the same was true in Mycenaean. Whatever the case, we cannot assume that the records we have seen are necessarily typical even for Pylos, much less for the whole of the Mycenaean world.

In general, despite the caveat just noted, it is probable that service obligations of some type *were* a standard feature of Mycenaean land tenure. Some of the obligations were clearly military in nature, others related to industrial production (e.g. the perfumers, the 'royal' fuller, and other craft-workers may have been obliged to provide their specialist work), and some, as we have seen, had to do with religion. It is important to observe that holdings by religious individuals are identical in juridical character to those held by others, but nevertheless such holdings were important and were meticulously recorded. Religious matters are not singled out as economically distinct, but they do appear to have been of special concern to the palace.

2.5 DEITIES AS 'COLLECTORS'

2.5.1 INTRODUCTION TO 'COLLECTORS'

In addition to land tenure, religious figures received support through dedicated beneficiary allocations of raw materials and industrial produce. This view depends on a particular interpretation of the figures known variously in Linear B scholarship as 'Collectors', 'Owners', 'Bénéficiaires' or 'Overseers'.[294] For convenience and because it is now more or less agreed practice, we will use here the term 'Collector', although it is acknowledged that this is not the best description of these individuals.[295] The term was proposed in *Documents*[1] in connection with two of the sheep tablets of Pylos, Cn 655 and Cc 660, which provide a good starting point for our discussion.[296] The texts are as follows.

Cn 655 (S719-H1/S4-H21)

.1	ma-ro-pi , qe-re-wa-o pa-ra-jo	OVIS^{m}	136
.2	ma-ro-pi , to-ro-wi-ko , pa-ra-jo	OVIS^{m}	133[
.3	ma-ro-pi , ke-ro-wo-jo	OVIS^{m}	85
.4	ma-ro-pi ra-pa-sa-ko-jo	OVIS^{m}	69
.5	ma-ro-pi , pu-wi-no , a-pi-me-de-o , a-ko-ra	OVIS^{m}	190
.6	ma-ro-pi , i-wa-so , we-da-ne-wo , a-ko-ra	OVIS^{m}	70
.7	ma-ro-pi , ti-re-wo , pa-ra-jo	OVIS^{m}	70
.8	ma-ro-pi , o-ka-ri-jo , pa-ra-jo	OVIS^{m}	95
.9	ma-ro-pi , e-ti-ra-wo , pa-ra-jo	OVIS^{m}	70
.10	ma-ro-pi , a-ta-ma-ne-u , pa-ra-jo	OVIS^{m}	60
.11	ma-ro-pi , qi-ri-ta-ko , a-ke-o-jo , a-ko-ra	OVIS^{m}	90[
.12	ma-ro-pi , a-ri-wo , a-ke-o-jo , a-ko-ra	[	]14
.13	ma-ro-pi , ro-ko-jo , we-da-ne-wo , a-ko-ra	[	]80
.14	ma-ro-pi , o-pe-re-ta , we-da-ne-wo	OVIS^{f}	86
.15	ma-ro-pi , po-ro-qa-ta-jo , we-da-ne-wo	OVIS^{f}	63
.16	ma-ro-pi , to-ru-ko-ro , we-da-ne-wo	OVIS^{f}	88
.17	ma-ro-pi , ma-ma-ro , we-da-ne-wo	OVIS^{m}	90
.18	ma-]ro-pi , ma-du-ro we-da-ne-wo	OVIS^{m}	100
.19	ma-ro-]pi , se-no , we-da-ne-wo	OVIS^{f}	40
.20	ma-ro-]pi , ta-ta-ke-u , [we-]da-ne-wo	OVIS^{f}	30

[294] See Bennet 1992, 65. A general bibliography on 'Collectors' includes: *Documents*, 200–3, 434, 437; Palmer 1957; 1963; Olivier 1967b; 1972; 1988; 2001; Lindgren 1973 II, 185–7; Killen 1976; 1979b, 176–9; 1983c; 1985; 1992–1993b; 1995 (see esp. 214, 222); 2001a; Bennet 1985; 1992; Carlier 1992; Driessen 1992; Godart 1992; Ruijgh 1998–1999; Nosch 2001b; Rougemont 2001a.

[295] See Killen 1976, 119; Bennet 1992, 66, 101. Olivier's (1967b, 84) 'bénéficiaires' would be more accurate, but 'Collector' has come to have a 'technical' sense apart from its strict meaning and is now widely used (e.g. Olivier 2001). As J.T. Killen once pointed out to me, the term is so inappropriate that it loses all meaning, except to indicate in a terminological sense those who stand in this particular economic relationship with the palace.

[296] *Documents*[1], 200–1, 387.

Cc 660 (S4-H21)

.a a-ke-o , a-ke-re

me-ta-pa , pa-ro ka-ra-su-no CAP^m 30

Palimpsest, perhaps with actual erasure before CAP^m ; cf. in hand and formula the set of Cn 40 &c.

Cn 655 records flocks of sheep at the place *ma-ro-pi* along with the names of the shepherds responsible for them (the second word in each entry). In some instances (lines .5–6, .11–20) a further man's name appears in the genitive (*a-pi-me-de-o*, *we-da-ne-wo*, *a-ke-o-jo*) along with the word *a-ko-ra*. Cc 660 involves one of the same men, *a-ke-o*, in connection with the apparently related word *a-ke-re*. VC proposed interpreting this as */agērei/* 'he collects (sheep)', with an action noun */agorā/* in Cn 655, and suggested that the persons were officials involved in collecting tribute for the palace, hence the term 'Collector'.

Some features of the above tablets are seen also in the documents of Knossos, where again in some cases a man's name in genitive or as a possessive adjective in *-e-jo*[297] appears in addition to shepherds' names on flock management records. Some examples are as follows.

De 1152 (117)

.A we-we-si-jo-jo OVIS^m 46 OVIS^f 22

.B ko-ro , / da-*22-to , *o* OVIS^m 12

Da 1323 + 5243 + 5325 + *fr*. (117)

.A a-no-qo[ ]OVIS^m 100[ ] *vac.*

.B ke-ti-ro , / e-ra[ ] *vac.*

.B *vest.* at end?

De 1371 + 1480 + 7115 + 8741 (117)

.A te-ra-po-si-jo , OVIS^m 80 OVIS^f 8

.B o-to-ro-qa , / da-wo *o* OVIS^m 12

Da 1392 + 1619 + 7112 + *fr*. (117)

.A a-te-jo OVIS^m 100

.B ku-ke-to , / se-to-i-ja , ạụ-to ,

.B *ạụ-to* , written very faintly.

In these tablets, the shepherd's name is always given first (e.g. *ko-ro*, *ku-ke-to*) followed by a toponym (e.g. *da-*22-to*, *se-to-i-ja*). In each case, a further man's name appears in the top line. As at Pylos, there are tablets both with and without these extra names. An example of a tablet without the extra name is as follows.

Da 1495 + 5175 + 5563 (117)

.A OVIS^m 200

.B qo-te-ro / pa-i-to

In the barest sense, the 'extra' names in cases such as those cited above are what Linear B scholars mean by 'Collector'.[298] There are four such individuals at Pylos and about thirty-five at Knossos.[299] The 'Collectors' appear also in connection with workshops producing textiles, for instance in the following tablet.

Lc(2) 7377 + 7385 + 8016 (113)

.A] 'pa-we-a' TELA^3 12 3

.B]ẉẹ-ri-jo-jo , / ku-do-ni-ja LANA 18

↓ (115)

v.]to-u-ka LANA 4

.A For the isolated 3 at the end of the line, cf. Lc 483, Lc 7433, Lc 7438.

---

297 *Documents*, 201–3; Killen 1983c.

298 Although a connection with the word *a-ko-ra* is now regarded by some scholars as dubious (Driessen 1992; Godart 1992; but see also Killen 1976).

299 E.g. Driessen 1992, 206–7.

As Killen explains, the document records 'stints' for the production of cloth by a workgroup 'belonging' to a 'Collector', probably to be restored as *i-se-we-ri-jo-jo*, at the place Kydonia.[300] One of the several difficulties encountered by VC's early suggestion of 'tribute collectors' above is that, as has now long been understood, the Knossos and Pylos sheep tablets are not taxation records but pertain to palace-owned sheep producing wool for the textile industry.[301] 'Collectors' appear at all levels of this process, from the collection of wool, to supply of the raw materials to workgroups, and receipt back of the finished products.

The status and significance of the 'Collectors' has been debated at length. Palmer initiated the discussion in his review of *Documents*[1] with the suggestion that 'Collectors' were not in fact palace officials collecting tribute, but were rather themselves the owners of the flocks (and workshops).[302] Other suggestions have included middle-men, beneficiaries,[303] overseers,[304] members of local elites (as owners but acting in some administrative capacity),[305] tax-farmers[306] and tamkars.[307] Various observations have been made about the 'Collectors' that are relevant to elucidation of their function(s). A few of the key points are as follows.

1. 'Collector' flocks and deliveries are totalled separately from those of 'non-Collectors' (which are totalled instead by toponym), and the ratio of 'Collector' items to 'non-Collector' items tends to be 30 : 70.[308]
2. 'Collector' records were kept in the central palaces and were managed by the same scribes, and in the same way, as other flock and workgroup records.[309]
3. 'Collectors' do not appear in connection with particular sites (probably indicating an association with the palaces themselves[310]).
4. Deities can appear as 'Collectors' (see below).
5. At least one of the 'Collectors' at Pylos is an important palace official (*a-ko-so-ta*).[311]
6. Many of the same 'Collector' names appear on tablets from different sites, but there is no question of the same persons being involved (particularly given the chronological differences).[312]

This is not the place for detailed discussion of the function of 'Collectors', partly because it is not essential for the purpose of the present study to determine what this was (if a consensus were even possible). Our central question here concerns commodities used in connection with religion in any capacity whatsoever, but the focus is on the *amounts* of commodities, not on precisely what they were used for. (The uses are of course both important and highly interesting, but the issue belongs to a different study.) Without further ado, the view followed here is that the most probable explanation of 'Collectors' is that they were something along the lines of 'owners' but in the sense of 'beneficiaries'. As articulated by Killen, 'Collectors' were:[313]

---

[300] Killen 1976, 119–20.
[301] Killen 1964; 1993.
[302] Palmer 1957.
[303] Olivier 1967b, 84.
[304] Bennet 1985, 240.
[305] Bennet 1992, 96–7.
[306] Carlier 1992.
[307] Landenius-Enegrin 1995, 119.
[308] Olivier 1967b; 1972.
[309] Killen 1995, 213.
[310] Driessen 1992, 212–13.
[311] Lindgren 1973 II, 185–7; Bennet 2001.
[312] Killen 1979b, esp. 177; Olivier 2001 – note his comment (p. 151) that this important point is all too often overlooked.
[313] Killen 1979b, 177. See also *Documents*, 434; Olivier 1967b, 84; 1972; 2001; Driessen 1992; Killen 1992–1993b, 121; 1995, 213. Killen (1964, 15) entertained the idea very early: 'it may be that the place was responsible for their [the flocks] management, but made over their produce to others'.

> members of the nobility, the royal family, or the like who were allocated part of the productive capacity of the kingdom for their own benefit (hence their appearance as 'owners' of flocks, weaving workgroups, etc.), and whose names appear at more than one site because, as members of this class, perhaps as members of the same dynasty, they tended to be given names from a certain limited stock.

This view explains many of the anomalies associated with 'Collectors', is consistent with everything known about 'Collectors', and avoids difficulties which can be raised with regard to other suggestions.[314]

One point that does need to be stressed within this perspective is that the proposed interpretation does not involve seeing 'Collectors' as engaged in any sort of administrative, productive or bureaucratic activities. The records were kept centrally at the palaces and the persons managing the business were evidently the scribes who wrote the records on which 'Collectors' appear, precisely as they administrated 'non-Collector' flocks and workgroups. It is common still to hear of 'Collectors' being somehow 'active' in management or production,[315] but it need not be that 'Collectors' necessarily ever saw their flocks and workers or even knew where they were (although as there is a prestige issue here, they may well have known the locations and something about the numbers involved), since these aspects were managed in the ordinary way by the palace scribes. What was crucial was that the 'Collectors' received in some way the benefit of the output of the flocks and workshops associated with them. This point about management requires emphasis. It so happens that some of the persons identified as 'Collectors' are indeed known to be officials, but such persons were 'Collectors' not by virtue of their administrative roles but rather by virtue of a particular economic relationship to the palaces (although it may indeed have been that they were rewarded with the status of 'Collector' owing to the value of their work). This point is important because it is relevant to the position of deities as 'Collectors'.

Deities appear as 'Collectors' in documents from at least three sites: Knossos, Pylos and Thebes. The Knossos texts are the most straightforward; some examples are as follows.

Dl(1) 916 (118)
.A OVIS^{f} 50 ⟦ ⟧ *WE*[
.B di-ta-ka-so / e-ko-so *ki* OVIS^{m} 10 *o ki* OVIS^{m} 40[
.A Perhaps ⟦*ọ* Ọ̣VỊṢ̃ [ ] ⟧.

Dl(1) 949 + 7145 + 7660 (118)
.A e-se-re-e-jo OVIS^{f} 40 LANA 2 [
.B i-pe-ta / su-ri-mo *o* OVIS^{f} 20 *o ki* OVIS^{m} 60 [
.A Trace at right, perhaps *ọ*[LANA.

Dl(1) 7503 + 7638 + 7847 (118)
.A po-ti-ni-ja-we-jo OVIS [^{f}
.B te-wa-jo , / si-ja-du-we *o*[

Dl(1) 7771 (118?)
.A] po-ti-ṇị[-ja-we-jo
.B]qo-ta , / ra-ja [
.B Perhaps trace at left.

The Dl(1) series records breeding flocks producing lambs and wool. Dl(1) 916 illustrates the basic formula: shepherd's name, place, number of ewes, number of lambs born (*ki* OVIS^{m}) and number expected. Dl(1) 949 adds a reference to a 'Collector', *e-se-re-e-jo*. In Dl(1) 7503 and

---

[314] Note that the objection that the affairs of 'private' individuals should not be recorded in palace records (Carlier 1992, 160) does not apply here because the persons envisaged are uniquely connected with the palaces. It may not be helpful to think in terms of a 'public/private' distinction in this context.

[315] E.g. Bennet 1992, 96–7, 101; Nosch 2001b, 131.

7771, instead of a man's name in the 'Collector' position, the word *po-ti-ni-ja-we-jo* appears. This is an adjectival formation from *Potnia*, indicating some connection with the deity. The position of the word is exactly parallel to that of the men's names, as is the adjectival formation in *-e-jo*,[316] so that *Potnia* is indicated as a 'Collector' in precisely the same way that the various men are 'Collectors'. The understanding of 'Collectors' accepted here thus applies to the deity *Potnia* in this situation, that is, the deity is the beneficiary of the produce of the flocks. As has long been suggested, what this probably translates into 'in reality' is that support was being provided for *Potnia's* shrines and cult personnel.[317] It is important to notice, however, that in line with what was stressed above there is no necessity for the personnel and shrines actually to have been engaged in any economic *activity* as a result of the status of *Potnia* as 'Collector'.[318] All that is implied is that they would have received the goods.[319]

Deities appear as 'Collectors' in connection with three industries: textile production, bronzeworking and perfumery. The evidence is reviewed below. In addition, this is an appropriate place to consider the old problem of whether the 'Collector' **ma-ri-ne-u* should be regarded as a deity.

2.5.2 DEITIES AS 'COLLECTORS' IN THE TEXTILE INDUSTRY

Potnia appears as a 'Collector' in connection with flocks and textile workshops at Knossos, Pylos and Thebes. We begin with Knossos.

Examples of records of *Potnian* flocks at Knossos were given above. The deity Hermes, too, is found in connection with flocks. The relevant text is as follows.[320]

D 411 + 511 (—)

di-ko-to / e-ma-a_2-o OVIS^f 60 *WE* 30[

-*ma*- and perhaps *e*- over ⟦ ⟧. Perhaps to be read as *e-ma-a*$_2$ *o* OVIS^f. Perhaps traces after 30[.

Hermes appears here in the genitive (probably – the suggested alternative reading in the apparatus is less likely), in parallel with the ordinary 'Collectors' documented in Linear B. A full list of the tablets on which deities appear in connection with flocks at Knossos is given in Section 6.2.2.1, Table 6-7.

We also have evidence for the existence of workgroups belonging to *Potnia* at Knossos, in G 820. The text is as follows.

G 820 + *fr*. ASHM (1910.215)/HM (—)

.1] ,. [·]-ṇạ , e-ko-si , a-pi , ku-do-ni-ja / pa-sa 'ki-ri-ta' LUNA 1

.2 ja-]pu_2-wi-ja-qe , **56*-ko-we-i-ja-qe LUNA 4

.3 da-]**22*-ti-ja , ku-ta-ti-ja-qe , po-ti-ni-ja-we-ja , a-pu , ke-u-po-de-ja

.4] LUNA 4

820: Oxford; *fr*.: Iraklio.

.1 Trace of ⟦ ⟧ after *pa-sa*.

.3 Text down to *po*- probably over ⟦ ⟧; -*pu* , *ke-u*- also over ⟦ ⟧.

---

316 Though the digamma remains a puzzle; see Ruijgh 1967b; Risch 1972; Killen 1983c, 73–4. See also Killen 1964, 15; and recently Weilhartner 2005, 95 with n 208 for further bibliography. On *Potnia* as a 'Collector' in general see Hiller 1981; Nosch 2000a; 2001b; Weilhartner 2005, 94–8, 229.

317 *Documents*, 434; *Scribes Cnossos*, 133; Carlier 1987; Hiller 1981; 1982; Lupack 1999, 26.

318 *Contra* Lupack (1999, 27) it need not be that 'the personnel of these sanctuaries engaged in economic activities, like agriculture and shepherding'.

319 Consistent with this view is that it is not specified *which* shrines are associated with the Knossian *Potnia* – it seems unlikely that there was only one.

320 Killen 1976, 123; 1983c, 73–5; Carlier 1987, 271; Antonelli 1995; Nosch 2000a; Weilhartner 2005, 95–6. Also, *Scribes Cnossos*, 133: 'plutôt que d'offrandes à *e-ma-a*$_2$, il pourrait s'agir d'un troupeau appartenant au sanctuaire de ce dernier'.

The tablet records monthly rations (indicated by the ideogram LUNA), apparently of barley if *ki-ri-ta* is */krithā/*, for female workgroups associated with various toponyms (e.g. **56-ko-we*, *da-*22-to*), including in line .3 some designated as *Potnian*. The further word *ke-u-po-de-ja* probably refers to the attested Knossian 'Collector' *ke-u-po-da*, and a likely explanation of the document is that one or two groups of women (if the *da-*22-to* group is distinct from the *ku-ta-to* group) who were previously workers 'of' *ke-u-po-da* are now allocated to *Potnia*.[321]

Another possible example of rations for a workgroup with a religious connection is seen in the following text.

E 777 ASHM (1910.214) (—)
.1 ko-no-si-ja / ki-ri-te-wi-ja-i LUNA 1 GRA 100[
.2 a-mi-ni-si-ja LUNA 1 GRA 100 [
.3 pa-i-ti-ja LUNA 1 GRA 100[
↓
v. .1 a-ze-ti-ri-ja GRA 1̣0̣[
reliqua pars sine regulis
Cut at left.
r. Whole text probably palimpsest: ⟦*jo*⟧ visible in .2.

E 777 records monthly wheat rations for women of Knossos, Amnisos and Phaistos. On the standard ration of T 2 per woman monthly,[322] the provisions would be sufficient for 500 women at each place. The women of Knossos are described as *ki-ri-te-wi-ja-i*, which seems to be a derivative of */krithā/*, and which is taken by most scholars as indicating some sort of connection with cult (although there are some grounds for doubting such a connection, the large number of women so designated in the present instance being one).[323] Whatever the case about a possible cult connection, the disbursements seem to be global rather than to designated groups so we are probably not dealing here specifically with 'Collectors'.

A final Knossos tablet of possible relevance is Am(2) 821. The text is as follows.

Am(2) 821 + *frr.* (—)
.1]ra-jo , / e-qe-ta-e , e-ne-ka , ẹ-mi-to VIR 2 // ki-ta-ne-to , / su-ri-mo , e-ne-ka , 'o-pa' VIR 1̣
.2 si-ja-du-we , ṭạ-ṛạ , / i-je[-re-]u , po-me , e-ne-ka , 'o-pa' X VIR 1 // ko-pe-re-u , / e-qe-ta , e-ki-'si-jo' VIR 1
.3] *vacat*
.1 Many traces of ⟦ ⟧; *-ka* of *e-ne-ka* over ⟦ṾỊṚ⟧.

The text deals with personnel, several of whom are *e-qe-ta* /$heq^u etai$/ 'Followers'. A man *ta-ra* in line .2 is described apparently as a priest-shepherd (*i-je-re-u po-me*) *e-ne-ka* */heneka/* 'on account of' *o-pa*. He is located at *si-ja-du-we* and it is suggested that there may be some connection with the flocks of sheep of *Potnia*, several of which were located at this TN.[324] As Killen suggests, in light of his interpretation of *o-pa* as indicating 'finishing' in the sense of 'fattening' in the case of animals (see Section 2.3.2.3), it might be that the 'fattening' in Am(2) 821 was undertaken with relation to flocks (or some elements of flocks) associated with the deity.[325] (The man *ki-ta-ne-to* at *su-ri-mo* in line .1 is known from Da 1108 as a shepherd at this TN; he too is apparently involved in 'fattening'.)

If there is some connection between flocks of *Potnia* and banqueting, a parallel situation might

[321] Killen 1983c, esp. 72, following Ruijgh 1967a, 263. Ruijgh's suggestion was that the women work for a 'priest of *Potnia'*, but Killen (1983c, 74) argues that the form may be derived from the divine name itself. Weilhartner (2005, 98) also discusses the text.
[322] Chadwick 1988.
[323] For references see Section 2.3.2.2 above, under PY Un 1426.
[324] Deger-Jalkotzy 1978, 88–92, esp. 89. For the appellatives see Lindgren 1973 II, 55. On the tablet in general see Sourvinou 1968 (she interprets the term parallel to *o-pa* in line .1, *e-mi-to*, as */emmisthos/* 'salary'; cf. *DMic.*).
[325] Killen 1999a, 332–3, also 326. See also Weilhartner 2005, 96.

possibly obtain at Pylos. Cc 665 was discussed above (Section 2.3.2.2), and was judged 'Unclear' with regard to whether it was a banqueting record, although it is certainly related to religion. We give the text again here.

Cc 665 (S4-H21)
ne-wo-pe-o , po-ti-ni-ja OVIS^{m} 100 SUS 190

At this point in the discussion further possibilities can be proposed for this tablet. It is clearly a 'flock management record' as defined by Halstead (see above Section 2.3.2.3), and although it is unlikely to be a banqueting 'menu' it may well relate to flocks kept specifically to supply animals for sacrifice. A connection with feasting is particularly suggested by the presence of pigs, since pigs primarily supply meat. Sheep on the other hand might be kept for consumption or for secondary products such as wool. There may be a slight hint in this of a situation similar to that contemplated for Am(2) 821, where the same flocks might supply both secondary products and animals for slaughter. But the evidence is unclear and this speculation must remain tentative.

Finally, there is evidence for deities in connection with textile workgroups at Thebes. The tablets of the Of series record issues of wool to workers, workshops and workgroups, in three cases involving deities: Hera (Of 28.2), Hermes (Of 31.3) and *Potnia* (Of 36.2).[326] Texts of these and a few other documents useful for the elucidation of the series are given below; texts for the remainder of the series are set out in Section 6.3.3.3, Table 6-17.

Of 25 (*303*)
.1 ma-ri-ne-we-ja-i , / a_3-ki-a_2-ri-ja LANA 4[ ]*vest.*[
.2 a-ma-ru-to-de , / pa-pa-ra-ki LANA 6
.3-5] *vacant*

Of 27 (*303*)
.1 [. .]-ri-ta-de *ku* LANA 1
.2 a-ka-i-je-ja , du-qo-te-ja LANA 2
.3 a-ka-i-je-ja , pu_2-ke-qi-ri-ne-ja LANA 2
.4 *vacat*

Of 28 (*303*)
.1 pi-ṛọ-pe-se-wa , *ku* LANA 2
.2 i-da-i-jo *ku* LANA *PA* 2 e-ra , ke-o-te-ja *ku* LANA 1
.3 *vacat*

Of 31 (*303*)
.1 do-]de *ku* LANA *PA*[
.2]ḍọ-de *ku* LANA *P̣Ạ*[
.3 e-ma-a_2 , re-[

Of 33 (*303*)
.1 ku-ru-me-no *ku* ḶẠṆẠ *PA* 1 ọ-**34*-ta-o , do-de *ku* LANA *PA* 1
.2 qi-wo , / di-u-ja-wo *ku*[LANA]*PA* 2

Of 35 (*303*)
.1 ko-ma-we-te-ja , te-pe-ja , *ku* LANA 1
.2]ma-ri-ne-we-ja-i , a-ki-a_2-ri-ja-de *ku* LANA 3

Of 36 (*303*)
.1 no-ri-wo-wi-de *ku* LANA 1 a-ke-ti-ra_2 , wa-na-ka[
.2 po-ti-ni-ja , wo-ko-de , a-ke-ti-ra_2 *ku* LANA 1 [

[326] *TT* II, 91. As Chadwick (*loc. cit.*) remarks, these are the only three clearly identified divine names in the series. However, a number of other possible divine connections have been proposed (*TT* II, 92–5); see Section 2.5.5.

As Chadwick explained in his publication of the series, the Of tablets deal with multiple entries of wool and the basic formula consists of two elements: a 'personal name or occupational description in the dative case' (or, as he adds, sometimes in the nominative) and/or 'an indication of address'.[327] Examples of personal names are *ku-ru-me-no* (Of 33.1), *di-u-ja-wo* (Of 33.2); for occupational terms we have *te-pe-ja* (Of 35.1) and *a-ke-ti-ra*$_2$ (Of 36.1.2). Addresses are, for instance, *a-ma-ru-to-de /Amarunthon-de/* (Of 25.2) and *a-ka-a*$_2$*-ri-ja-de /Aigialiān-de/* (Of 35.2). It was Killen who first noted that there might be a connection with 'Collectors'. He observed the many parallels between occupational terms on these tablets with those found at other sites (as noted by Chadwick), and commented:[328]

> Once given these parallels between Thebes and the other sites, it is tempting to wonder whether the Of descriptions of the type *ko-ma-we-te-ja* (Of 35) may have, not merely the same formation, but also the same function as the adjectives of the type *pe-ri-qo-te-jo* on the KN SHEEP and CLOTH records: i.e., whether they may not denote workgroups 'owned' by 'collectors'.

Thus, the disbursement of wool in, for instance, Of 35.1 would be to a female workgroup belonging to the man *ko-ma-we* as a 'Collector'. Issues in connection with deities must be seen in this context. That they are not 'offerings' *per se* but rather issues to workgroups is indicated by the word *a-ke-ti-ra*$_2$ in connection with *Potnia* in Of 36.2, which is attested at other sites as a description of female workgroups */askētriai/* 'finishers'.[329] That some of the products manufactured by these workgroups might end up as offerings eventually is not unlikely,[330] but the essential point for present purposes is that the deities stand here in the position of 'Collectors' and the concern of the tablets is with allocations of wool for industrial processing not with the disbursement of offerings. Note again, as argued above, that this does not indicate involvement of cult personnel *per se* in production and manufacture; all that is needed is that the sanctuaries would receive the results of the processing, in the same way as any other 'Collector'.

Much has been made of the fact that the wool for *Potnia* is being sent to her 'house': *wo-ko-de /woikon-de/*.[331] This might indicate that the work is being carried out at a shrine associated with the goddess. However, although this suggestion cannot be dismissed, neither is it necessary: the disbursement might simply be going to a workshop belonging to the deity. The point is discussed further below (Section 2.5.5) where we consider the matter of whether **ma-ri-ne-u*, the name underlying the forms in Of 25 and –35 above, is to be regarded as a deity.

Finally, it may be noted here that AGS suggest TH Av 104 as a possible list of workers connected with deities and festivals.[332] Pending further work on the Thebes material, we reserve judgement for the time being.

2.5.3 DEITIES AS 'COLLECTORS' IN THE PERFUME INDUSTRY

Four unguent-boilers are mentioned by name in the Pylos archives: *ko-ka-ro* (Fg 374), *tu-we-ta* (Un 267), *pi-ra-jo* (Un 249) and *e-u-me-de* (Ea 773, –821, –822). Each is described in at least one attestation as an *a-re-pa-zo-o /aleiphazoos/* 'unguent-boiler', and the man *pi-ra-jo* is further designated as *po-ti-ni-ja-we-jo*. These 'unguent-boilers' or 'perfumers' receive raw materials from the palace and, in two instances at least, are recipients of rations (Fg 374; see Section 5.5.2) and land tenure grants (Ea 773, –821, –822). The man *e-u-me-de* may have been

[327] *TT* II, 87.
[328] Killen 1979b, 176.
[329] *TT* II, 87. There are various references at Pylos (see Chadwick 1988, 78) and in a variant spelling the word appears also at Mycenae and Knossos.
[330] *TT* II, 91.
[331] *TT* II, 89; Hiller 1981; Lupack 1999, 28.
[332] *Thèbes* I, 175.

the head of the industry. He is seen receiving oil (presumably treated) from *ko-ka-ro* in the following tablet.

Fr 1184 (S1202-H2)
.1 ko-ka-ro , a-pe-do-ke , e-ra$_3$-wo , to-so
.2 e-u-me-de-i OLE+*WE* 18
.3 pa-ro , i-pe-se-wa , ka-ra-re-we 38
Possibly entire tablet palimpsest.
.1 , *e-ra$_3$-wo* , *to-so* over actual erasure.

The text in lines .1–2 is interpreted as '*K*. gave olive oil, so much, to *E*.: 18 units'. The text in the final line refers to a transfer of stirrup-jars /*khlārēwes*/, the standard vessel in which oil was stored and transported. In other texts *ko-ka-ro* is associated with rations and *e-u-me-de* with land tenure, suggesting a higher status for the latter.[333]

Our central concern here is with the four texts in which raw materials are issued to the perfumers. The texts are as follows.[334]

Un 267 (S2-H1)
.1 o-do-ke , a-ko-so-ta
.2 tu-we-ta , a-re-pa-zo-o
.3 tu-we-a , a-re-pa-te ⟦ , ze-so-me ⟧
.4 ze-so-me-no ⟦ ko ⟧
.5 ko-ri-a$_2$-da-na AROM 6
.6 ku-pa-ro$_2$ AROM 6 **157* 16
.7 *KAPO* 2 T 5 VIN[a] 20 *ME* 2
.8 LANA 2 VIN[b] 2
.9 *vacat*
.10 *vacat*
.11 *vacat*

Un 249 (Cii)
.a po-ti-ni-ja-we-jo
.1 pi-ra-jo , a-re-pạ-ẓọ[-o] ku-pa-ro$_2$ AROM 2 T 5
.2 wi-ri-za LANA 2 [ ] **157* 10
.3 *vacat* [ ] *ḲẠP̣Ọ* T 6
.4–5 *vacant*
.1 *a-re-pa-zo*[*-o*: cf. Un 267.2.

Un 592 (S2-H1)
.1]*kọ* AROM 8 T 8
.2]6⌟ M 2 *KAPO* 3 T 4
.3]Ṣ 1 V 4 *ko* AROM 4 T 4
.4]S 1 V 3 LANA 6
.5]Ṭ 5 ra-ka , **1̣5̣4* 2̣1
.2]6 : 5 units preserved.

Un 616 (S615-H1)
Recto
.1 ku-ru-ro$_2$ AROM 13 T 5
.2 *KAPO* 4
.3 **157* 28
.4 LANA 5 *ME po* 6 S 1 V 4
.5 ko-ṛị-jọ-ḍạ-na
.6 AROM 21
.7 ị-ṛẹ-ẉẹ[ ]*ṆỊ* T 2

---

[333] Killen 2001a, 80.
[334] Un 267: text as in *PTT* I with VIN distinguished as in Bennett 1992, 109 and PoN IV; apparatus not given (as nothing relevant to reading for present purposes). Un 249: text as in *PTT* I; *PoN* IV reads 10 rather than 21 in line .5, regarding the extra marks as accidental. Un 616: Formerly An and with new text (Bennett 1992, 114–15); for apparatus and fuller references for text sources see Section 5.5.2.

Verso

.1 ta-we-si-jo-jo , ke-ro-si-ja VIR 20[
.2 a-pi-qo-o , ke-ro-si-ja VIR 17̣ [
.3 a-pi-o-to , ke-ro-si-ja VIR 18
.4 o-to-wo-o , ke-ro-si-ja VIR 13̣

Latus sinistrum

ka-ma-e-we VIR 10

That the four mixed commodity tablets above are issues of raw materials to perfumers is well established.[335] Un 267 is usually understood as reading: 'Thus *Alxoitās* gave to *Thuestās* the unguent-boiler aromatics for unguent which is to be boiled: coriander, six units; cyperus, six units; etc.'[336] The commodities in the other three tablets are similar. It is not necessary to discuss these documents at length; the purpose is to give the texts for reference (since the commodities here are counted in subsequent chapters) and to note the presence of *po-ti-ni-ja-we-jo* in Un 249.1a, suggesting that at least one of the unguent-boilers belonged to *Potnia* as a 'Collector'. The possibility that 'Collectors' appear in relation to the perfume industry as well as to the textile industry was first argued by Killen.[337] Again, what this means in terms of actual production is uncertain, but it should be noted that the disbursement in Un 249 looks very much like those to perfumers who are not associated with 'Collectors' and from the industrial point of view there may have been no distinction in the type of work undertaken.

2.5.4 DEITIES AND BRONZEWORKING

The Jn series at Pylos lists groups of bronzesmiths located at various places who receive distributions of raw material from the palace for manufacture.[338] Appearances of bronze in general in the Pylos tablets are discussed below (Section 6.5.2.1; see also Section 2.2.3 above); our focus in the present section is on appearances of 'Collectors'.

Chadwick recognised early on that references to groups of smiths described as *po-ti-ni-ja-we-jo* (Jn 310, –431) must indicate that they were somehow 'in the service of *Potnia*'.[339] He suggested that archaeological evidence for bronzeworking associated with cult caves in Crete might suggest a context for interpreting such mentions, perhaps along the lines of a religious craft guild. However, the matter depends on how '*Potnian*' is to be understood here. In the context of other appearances of the term as designating 'Collector' flocks and workgroups, it is tempting to take the word in the same way in the Jn series. The texts of the two tablets involved are as follows.[340]

Jn 310 (S310-H2)

.1]a-ke-re-wa , ka-ke-we , ta-ra-si-ja , e-ko-te ,
.2 ti-qa-jo AES M 1 N 2 qe-ta-wo AES M 1 N 2
.3 a_3-so-ni-jo AES M 1 N 2 ta-mi-je-u AES M 1 N 2
.4 e-u-ru-wo-ta AES M 1 N 2 e-u-do-no AES M 1 N 2
.5 po-ro-u-te-u AES M 1 N 2 wi-du-wa-ko AES M 1 N 2
.6 *vacat*
.7 to-so-de , a-ta-ra-si-jo , ka-ke-we[ ] *vacat*
.8 pa-qo-si-jo 1 ke-we-to 1 wa-[ ]re-u[1] *vacat*
.9 pe-ta-ro 1

[335] The classic discussion is Shelmerdine 1985. See also Foster 1974; 1977a; Beck & Beck 1978; Palmer 1994.

[336] Killen 1995, 215; Shelmerdine 1985, 17.

[337] Killen 1995, esp. 215–21. The suggestion with regard to the man *ku-pi-ri-jo* at Knossos is discussed below (Section 3.2.3.5).

[338] For the Jn series in general see Lejeune 1958e; *Documents*, 352–9, 508–10; Lang 1966a; Smith 1991; 1992–1993.

[339] *Documents*, 509; see also 413; also e.g. Carlier 1987, 270; Weilhartner 176–9.

[340] Jn 310: Text unchanged from *PTT*; minor join reported in Melena 1992–1993b, 312. Jn 431: The text has been affected by a series of joins and is drawn here from *PoN* IV. Publications include: Melena 1992–1993a, 78 (text unchanged); 1992–1993b, 314 (text unchanged); 1994–1995b, 278; Smith 1992–1993, 228 (citing an unpublished manuscript of E.L. Bennett's); Bennett 1992, 111 (change to reading in line .3); 1996-1997, 138.

.10 *vacat*
.11 to-so-de , do-e-ro , ke-we-to-jo 1 i-wa-ka-o 1
.12 pa-qo-si-jo-jo 1 po-ro-u-te-wo 1
.13 *vacat*
.14 po-ti-ni-ja-we-jo , ka-ke-we , ta-ra-si-ja , e-ko-te ,
.15 i-ma-di-jo AES M 3 tu-ke-ne-u AES M 3
.16] AES M 3 i-wa-ka AES M 3
.17 a-]ta-ra-si-jo , pu$_2$-si-ja-ko 1

Jn 431 (S310-H2)
.1 a-pe-ke-i-jo , ka-ke-we , ta-ra-si[-ja e-ko-te
.2 wi-ja-ni-jo AES M 5 ka-ra-**82*[ ] AES M 5[ ] ko-tu-ro$_2$ AES M 5
.3 ma-na-si-we-ko AES M 5 da-ṃạ-so AES M 5 qe-ta-ko AES M 4
.4 a-ko-to-wo AES M 7 u[ ]i-jo AES M 6
.5 ma-wa-si-jo AES M 5 qe-to-ro-no AES M 7
.6 qa-si-re-u , a-pi-qo-ta 1 [ ]i-**65*-qe 1
.7 to-so-de , ka-ko , AES [L 1] M 24
.8 *vacat* [ ] *vacat*
.9 to-so-de , a-ta-ra-si-jo , ka-ke[-we] *vacat*
.10 a-ta-tu-ro 1 i-ta-ra-jo 1 sa[1] *vacat*
.11 wi-ja-te-wo 1 no-e-u 1 tu-ri-ja-jo 1 qe-ta-ko-jo , do-e-ro 1
.12 a-ka-ma-wo 1 e-pe-ke-u 1 **82*-de 1 pu-te-u 1
.13 ko-ne-wa-ta 1 qe-to-ro-no 1 mo-re-u 1 a-e-ri-qo 1
.14 *vacat*
.15 *vacat*
.16 a-pe-ke-e , ka-ke-we , po-ti-ni-ja-we-jo , ta-ra-si-ja , e-ko-te
.17 ko-za-ro AES M 6 a-ke-wa-ta AES M 3 sa-ke-re-u AES M 6
.18 we-we-si-jo AES M 3 ko-ta-wo AES M 3 da-u-ta-ro AES M 6
.19 *vacat*
.20 to-so-de , ka-ko AES M 27 [
.21 *vacat* [
.22 to[-so-de]a[-ta-]ra-si-jo , ka-ke-we , ka-ri-se-u 1 du-ko-so[1
.23 ko[ ]1 e-u-wa-ko-ro 1 ke-we-no 1 a-ta-o 1 [
.24]wa-ti-ro 1 me-ri-wa-[•] 1 [
.25] i-je-re[-wo]VIR 10 to-sa-no-jo VIR 5
.26 VIR]1 a-mu-ta-wo-no VIR 31

The documents begin with the standard formula for the Jn series: /*khalkēwes tala*(*n*)*siā ekhontes*/ 'bronzesmiths having allotments'. Jn 310 records smiths at the town *a-ke-re-wa* (an important town, one of the district capitals and possibly the harbour town for Pylos), while Jn 431 records men at *a-pe-ke-e* (see line .16), expressed in the heading (line .1) as an ethnicon. Each tablet goes on to list men by their names along with the amounts of their allotments, followed by a group of men who are *a-ta-ra-si-jo* 'without allotments'. Jn 310 then lists men to whom slaves are allocated, and finally a group of smiths who have 'allotments' and are described as *po-ti-ni-ja-we-jo*. The third paragraph of Jn 431 similarly lists *Potnian* smiths with 'allotments' (line .16).

The idea that *po-ti-ni-ja-we-jo* here refers to *Potnia* as a 'Collector' in the same way as in other contexts where it appears receives support from Killen's recent argument for the existence of other 'Collectors' in the Jn series. He points out that]*nu-we-jo* in Jn 725.14 and *a-to-mo* in Jn 832.9 may be references to 'Collectors', rather than, as was sometimes suggested, toponyms.[341] The first may attractively be seen as a possessive adjective of the *-e-jo* type associated with 'Collectors' elsewhere, as discussed above. The second, *a-to-mo*, is attested in other records as an official title, and while Killen considers the possibility that it could be a homograph, he concludes it is more likely to be the same word and notes a possible parallel from Knossos for a 'Collector' described by his official title. The texts of the two documents are as follows.[342]

[341] Killen 1995, 214–15; and now see Olivier 2001.
[342] Jn 725: Text from *PoN* IV (but without the *Recto originalis* which is given there); see Bennett 1992, 117 (new readings); Smith 1992–1993, 245; Melena 1992–1993b, 318–9 (text unchanged); 2000–2001b, 374 (text unchanged). Jn 832: Text unchanged from *PTT*.

Jn 725 (S310-H2)

.1 e-ni-pa-te-we ka-ke-we , ta-ra-si-ja , e-ko-te
.2 te-pe 1 pa-qo-ta[1]e-ka-no 1 au-ta-mo 1
.3 we-we-si-jo 1 pe-re-qo-no 1 ti-ri-[•] 1[ ]ko-no 1
.4 ma-ka-ta 1 o-na-se-u 1 wi-jo-ro-jo 1
.5 wa-tu-ta 1 o-tu-wo-we 1 po-ro-ko 1 po-ro-u-jo 1
.6 pe-re-ta 1 o-wo-ta 1 o-pe-ra-no 1 o-ru-we-ro 1
.7 a-tu-ko 1 re-u-ka-ta 1 o-wa-ko 1 wo-wi-ja-ta 1
.8 ko-ma-do-ro 1 po-so-ra-ko 1 wa-ti-ko-ro 1 i-*65-qe 1
.9 *vacat*
.10 to-so-de] , ka-ko AES L 2 M 18
.11]*vacat*
.12 *vacat*
.13 *vacat*
.14]-nu-we-jo , a-pi-jo 1 AES M 5 ne-qe-u AES M 3
.15]ne-u AES M 1[ ]e-u-me-ne AES M 3
.16]e-ru-ta-jo AES M 4
.17 *vacat*
.18 *vacat*
.19 *vacat*
.20 *vacat*
.21 *vacat*
.22 *vacat* [ ] *vac.*
.23 a-ke-re-wa , ka-ke-we , e-u-ko-me-no 1[ ] *v.*
.24 di-nu-wa-ta 1 wa-du-ri-jo 1 o-wi-da 1 [
.25 to-so-de , ka-ko AES M 12 [
.26 *vacat* [

Jn 832 (S310-H2)

.1 ro-u-so , ka-ke-we , a-ke-te-re
.2 e-ke-ro 1 si-mu-ta 1 ra-u-ta 1
.3 *vacat*
.4 a-ta-ra-si-jo , ka-ke-we
.5]-ka-no 1 ma-ri-ta 1 ka-ra-u-ko 1 wo-ti-jo 1
.6 *vestigia* [
.7 wa-na-ta-jo 1 ka-u-ṣọ[1
.8 ḳạ-[ ] *vacat* [
.9 a-to-mo , ka-ke-we , a-ḳẹ-te [
.10 pa-qo-si-jo 1 pi-ro-ka-te 1 e-wi-ṭẹ[-u 1
.a -qe
.11 me-ra-to 1 a-*64-jo 1 a-e-ri- 1 pa-ra-ke-te-e-u AES M 3
.12 *vacat*
.13 ạ-ta-ra-si-jo , ka-ke-we
.14 a-ri-qa 1 o-na-jo 1 si-pa-ta-no 1
.15 a-da-ma-o 1 a-no-ra-ta 1 pu-wa-ne 1

The entries in each case (Jn 725.14–16; Jn 832.9–11) are similar structurally to the *Potnian* entries in Jn 310 and Jn 431 suggesting that *Potnia* was a 'Collector' in a similar way.[343] This would mean that it is not necessary to think in terms of a religious craft guild but merely of an ordinary workgroup dedicated to the goddess. A caveat should be added here that it would be unsurprising if certain aspects of manufacture – especially in transformative crafts such as bronzeworking – were imbued with magical and religious significance (note the classical deity Hephaistos). Also, it could well be that *Potnian* workshops were specialised in creating votives and so forth (compare bronze workshop production connected with classical sanctuaries[344]). But the point here is that the presence of *Potnian* workers in the Jn series does not constitute evidence for such things, at least not as far as can be determined from the present data.[345]

343 A number of further 'Collectors' in the Jn series has now been adduced by Olivier (2001, 149).
344 Risberg 1992. But archaeological evidence for the Bronze Age seems negative (e.g. Schallin 1997, esp. 160).
345 See Smith 1990–1991, 183–4 for comments along similar lines.

2.5.5 **MA-RI-NE-U*: HUMAN OR DIVINE?

A final matter which must be considered here is the long-standing question whether **ma-ri-ne-u* (not actually attested in the nominative) was a name belonging to a man or to an otherwise unknown deity. The answer one way or the other is not crucial to our conclusions as we go through the commodities survey because the amounts of the items associated with **ma-ri-ne-u* are not so substantial as drastically to alter our calculations, but a decision needs to be made for the sake of consistency and it is convenient to discuss the issue here since **ma-ri-ne-u* is attested as a 'Collector'.

The idea that **ma-ri-ne-u* might be a deity was first suggested by Chadwick in his publication of the Thebes Of tablets discussed above (Section 2.5.2). We repeat here the relevant texts.

Of 25
.1 ma-ri-ne-we-ja-i , / a_3-ki-a_2-ri-ja LANA 4[ ]*vest.*[
.2 a-ma-ru-to-de , / pa-pa-ra-ki LANA 6
.3-5] *vacant*

Of 35
.1 ko-ma-we-te-ja , te-pe-ja , *ku* LANA 1
.2]ma-ri-ne-we-ja-i , a-ki-a_2-ri-ja-de *ku* LANA 3

Chadwick (surely correctly) identifies *ma-ri-ne-we-ja-i* as a dative feminine plural possessive adjective of the *-e-jo* type based on the masculine name **ma-ri-ne-u*.[346] The name is attested at Knossos in a number of documents; some examples are as follows.

Ga(1) 674 (135)
.a] pe-ma
.b]ṃạ-ri-ne-we , / ko-ri-ja-do-no , AROM 10

Gg(2) 713 + 994 (135)
ma-ri-ne-we , / do-e-ra '*ME+RI*' **209*^{VAS}+*A* [
Perhaps **209*^{V}+*A* 1̣[.

As(2) 1519 + *fr.* (101)
.0 *sup. mut.*
.1] VIR 1
.2 i-we-ro VIR 1
.3 ne-o-to VIR 1
.4 qa-ti-ja VIR 1
.5 o-pi-si-jo VIR 1
.6 pa-ja-ro VIR 1
.7 ki-ke-ro VIR 1
.8 i-to VIR 1
.9.10 *vacant*
.11 ṃạ-ri-ne-wo , wo-i-ko-de
.12 to-so VIR 10
.13.14 *vacant*
.15 *inf. mut.*
.1 Traces of three or four signs at left.
.12 Over ⟦ ⟧.

Ga(1) 674 records a disbursement of coriander seed to **ma-ri-ne-u* (in the dative). Gg(2) records an issue of honey 'to **ma-ri-ne-u*, to his (female) slave' (this tablet is discussed again below, Section 4.2.1.2). As(2) 1519 lists men being sent 'to the house' /*woikon-de*/ of **ma-ri-ne-u*.

[346] *TT* II, 90–1; see also Killen 1983c, 75.

Chadwick begins his discussion of **ma-ri-ne-u* at Thebes with the observation that since at least three deities appear in the Of series it is worth enquiring whether some of the other recipients might also have a religious association.[347] He notes that the context of the Knossos Gg honey tablets is predominantly religious (but see below and Section 4.2.1.2) and draws attention to the parallel between the /*woikos*/ of **ma-ri-ne-u* in KN As(2) 1519.11 and the /*woikos*/ of *Potnia* in TH Of 36.2 (text above, Section 2.5.2). He further speculates that perhaps in Mycenaean Greek /*woikos*/ was used to refer to the 'house' of a deity while the alternative word for house /*dō*/, attested in e.g. Of 33.1 in association with a man's name (text above, Section 2.5.2), was used for human abodes. However, as he also notes, 'later usage gives no support to this conclusion and the idea must remain speculative'.[348] With regard to Ga(1) 674 Chadwick further observes that **ma-ri-ne-u* receives the same amount as the /*wanax*/ does in Ga(1) 675, and that this suggests rather a human recipient (unless /*wanax*/ be a divine title in this context in parallel with the PY Fr series, although this is less likely as the word is further qualified in that context; see Section 3.2.2). Finally, Chadwick remarks that it is 'a strange coincidence' that **ma-ri-ne-u* should be found with a /*woikos*/ and female slaves at Knossos and with female slaves at Thebes, which coincidence might be explained if the name referred to a deity.

Chadwick rightly reserved judgement on these reasonable speculations, but in the light of subsequent work on 'Collectors' further evidence is relevant to the matter. The issue has been discussed by various scholars, and opinion remains divided.[349] Killen raised many of the fundamental objections in an early paper, a primary one being that **ma-ri-ne-u* was not the only 'Collector' name found at more than one site and the phenomenon is thus not so surprising after all.[350] He further pointed out that in some cases the names appearing at multiple sites were in contexts which made clear that they were human rather than divine. As Olivier has now established, the 'international' character of 'Collector' names, very many of which appear at various sites, is to be expected rather than otherwise.[351] Killen further casts doubt on the idea that the issues of honey and coriander to **ma-ri-ne-u* at Knossos suggest offerings and proposes they instead relate to perfumery,[352] a point now widely accepted (see Sections 3.2.3.5 and 4.2.1.2). It might be possible to accept this last point and still see the manufacture as related to **ma-ri-ne-u* as a divine 'Collector',[353] but there is no need to do so and the tentative nature of Chadwick's original speculations must be emphasised. Let us review them again individually, with critiques in light of subsequent research.

1. **ma-ri-ne-u* appears in the Gg tablets, many of which do include references to deities, but the series is now divided into sets according to scribal hand and the tablets of the Gg(2) set, to which Gg(2) 713 with its reference to **ma-ri-ne-u* belongs, contain no other words which might be theonyms. The Gg(1) and Gg(2) offerings records are written by different scribes (see Section 4.2.1.1), and the Gg(2) set contains records clearly linked with the perfume industry (see Section 4.2.1.2). Gg(2) 713 is thus a perfumery, not an offerings, record.
2. The Ga(1) set, to which Ga(1) 674 belongs, was written by the same scribe as the Gg(2) set (h. 135) and likewise involves perfumery. As is the case with the

[347] *TT* II, 93.
[348] *TT* II, 93, see also 89.
[349] Weilhartner (2005, 48–50, 58) accepts the word as referring to a divinity; Carlier (1987, 257, 259, 267 with n 42) takes it as probable; AGS (*Thèbes* I, 281–2) reject it; Melena (1976a, 137–40) regards the matter as inconclusive. See also Foster 1977a, 31; plus *DMic.* II, 426 for further bibliography.
[350] Killen 1979b, 177.
[351] Olivier 2001, esp. 150, 156 for **ma-ri-ne-u*.
[352] Killen 1979b, 178. See also Killen 2001a.
[353] As does Weilhartner 2005, 49.

Gg(2) records, no other words in this set relate to divinities.[354]

3. The evidence for /*woikos*/ referring specifically to shrines in the Mycenaean period is inconclusive and there is no support for such usage in later Greek, as Chadwick noted.[355]
4. It is no longer to be considered remarkable that a 'Collector' name should appear at more than one site, as noted above.

In sum, not one of the reasons for taking **ma-ri-ne-u* as a deity is sustainable in the light of later scholarship. The equation is therefore rejected here, and **ma-ri-ne-u* is regarded as a man's name.

2.5.6 DEITIES AS 'COLLECTORS': CONCLUSION

The present section has reviewed some of the evidence for deities as 'Collectors', which on the understanding of 'Collectors' followed here means that they were beneficiary recipients of the output from certain dedicated flocks and workgroups. Deities as 'Collectors' appear in connection with bronzeworking, perfumery and the textile industry and are found at Knossos, Pylos and Thebes. At least three different deities are attested as 'Collectors': *Potnia*, Hera and Hermes. **ma-ri-ne-u* is not accepted here as a deity.

In reality, as noted above, the beneficiaries of the dedicated economic resources were probably the shrines and cult personnel serving the deities. As we observed, such persons received support from the palaces also through land tenure (at least at Pylos). There is evidence that both receiving palatial support through being a 'Collector' and receiving support through land tenure were associated with higher status and prestige than was the receiving of 'ordinary' rations, and there is some further evidence that being involved in the system associated with 'Collectors' was more prestigious than land tenure. The two may overlap in that some individuals are attested as recipients of support through both systems (for instance, *a-pi-me-de* at Pylos), but the 'Collector' groups on the whole are smaller and more 'exclusive' than the land tenure groups. In this connection, it is interesting that only deities, and not cult personnel in their own right, are attested as 'Collectors' (although we cannot exclude the possibility that some of the 'Collectors' known only by name, of whose place and role in the palatial societies we are ignorant, were in fact cult personnel).

It was noted above that the view of 'Collectors' as beneficial recipients of dedicated workshop output need not mean they had any involvement in actual production, or administration of production. It seems clear from the similarity of the documents on which 'Collectors' are recorded to those which do not include a 'Collector', plus the fact that these documents were kept all together in the palaces, that administration relating to 'Collector' items was carried out by palace scribes in the usual way. 'Collectors' may well have had a personal interest in knowing something about their dedicated flocks and workgroups since there was a prestige factor involved, and such knowledge might have been of considerable value for the advertising of one's status in elite society. But such knowledge need not imply managerial activity. If this is true of 'Collectors' in general, it applies also to deities, and to the shrines and cult personnel who were the 'real' beneficiaries. There is sometimes a tendency to regard divine 'Collectors' as a special case, implying a special connection between religion and the industries with which deities are associated as 'Collectors'. It is not clear this view is justified. Deities in an *economic* sense stand in the same relation to the various industries with which they are

[354] H. 135 is listed as dealing with perfumery and offerings by Shelmerdine (1988, 352–3), but the single tablet she notes as related to offerings (Ga 1058) is only tentatively ascribed to this hand (135?) and probably comes from a different findspot than the records securely attributed – the findspot is uncertain (K1?; *Scribes Cnossos*, 82); the others are from I4.

[355] See also *Thèbes* I, 281–2.

associated as do 'ordinary' 'Collectors', and separating them out purely because of the religious connection takes a step beyond what the data give evidence for. (One could equally take the view that there was a special connection between for instance the textile industry and men named *ko-ma-we*.)[356] Whatever the case, we may conclude by reiterating the point that our conclusions about the extent of resources in the present study would not be affected, whatever view one takes of 'Collectors'.

2.6 CONCLUSION

The present chapter has presented a general survey of documents related to religion in Linear B according to the main categories of types of economic support documented in the records: offerings, banqueting and 'elite maintenance', the last including both land tenure and deities as 'Collectors'.

The discussion of offerings focused on the question of how offerings tablets are identified in the Linear B corpus; the majority of individual instances will be seen in subsequent chapters. Banqueting records, on the other hand, were discussed as a group both because opinions relating to them have substantially changed in recent years so that a summary was needed and because banqueting 'menu' lists involve (many by their very definition as 'mixed commodity records') a variety of commodities, so could not be conveniently placed within the discussions of individual commodities to follow in the next chapters.

Land tenure was surveyed very briefly. The issues it raises are of great importance, but have been treated in detail in other works (including, as noted, some very recent), and it should be emphasised that the majority of evidence comes from one site only and that the findings from Pylos are not necessarily extendable to other parts of the Mycenaean world. Finally, evidence for deities as 'Collectors' was surveyed. A particular view of 'Collectors' was endorsed here, but it is acknowledged that there is still no consensus on the matter and the thoughts expressed here may be regarded as provisional only. As noted above, whatever the truth about the 'Collectors', the conclusions of the present work would not be affected, since the central question here is not so much about the *nature* of the economic resources allocated for religious purposes as about the *extent*. It is enough to know that deities did appear as 'Collectors', which is not disputed, and to have identified the relevant records.

Chapter 3 initiates the central investigation of our study. It begins with a summary of the commodities to be examined and some introductory remarks on the types of records involved and potential complicating factors. The remainder of the chapter examines documents recording olive oil and products made from it. Further commodities are discussed in Chapters 4, 5 and 6; conclusions are drawn in Chapter 7.

[356] Although not germane to the present study, it may be noted that the view adopted here of the *type* of connection between deities and workshops goes counter to the long-held notion that there may have been a special relationship between religion and industry in the Mycenaean world (see Bendall 2003, 184–5 with n 17 for references, 226). The idea arose from supposed archaeological attestations of shrines connected with workshops plus the fact of workshops 'belonging' to deities in the Linear B tablets. However, on the view of 'Collectors' here, no *special* association between industry and religion is suggested by the Linear B evidence. With regard to the archaeological data, it has been argued elsewhere that the Northeastern Building at Pylos (one of the main proposed examples of a shrine associated with a workshop) was after all not a workshop and that evidence for a shrine in the building is dubious (Bendall 2003, esp. 185–6, 226). Other proposed workshop/shrine connections remain to be (re)considered, but my suspicion is that the connection will turn out to be untenable (see Kryzyszkowska 1997; Schallin 1997, esp. 161). Note such a finding would have no impact on whether such a connection existed in other cultural contexts, for instance in Crete and Cyprus, where in both cases the evidence is much stronger (e.g. Poursat 1983; Knapp 1986).

CHAPTER 3
INTRODUCTION TO THE COMMODITIES SURVEY AND ANALYSIS OF OLIVE OIL

3.1 INTRODUCTION TO THE COMMODITIES SURVEY: AIMS AND METHODS

We now come to the central task. The remainder of this book considers the Linear B evidence for the extent of palatial resources committed to support for the religious sphere. In the following chapters, amounts of commodities disbursed for religious purposes or allocated to deities and religious personnel through mechanisms of elite maintenance are compared with the overall amounts of such commodities likely to have been available to the palaces. The central question is: How substantial a proportion of the Mycenaean palatial economy was directed towards support for religion?

As we proceed, it will become apparent that the Linear B documents provide a problematic record for the types of assessments desired. Various complicating factors, such as hazards of preservation, seasonality, or sheer obscurity of the texts, skew the dataset in various ways. In some cases, the difficulties are so extreme that the entire enterprise may seem hopeless. Yet it is not. In the first place, it is possible in many cases to achieve reasonable assessments, and this is worthwhile. In the second place, it will be seen that the omissions and lacunae in the data are more strongly patterned than has hitherto been appreciated. This is of interest in itself and may contribute to our understanding of how Mycenaean scribal administration operated. It has long been observed that the Linear B documents give a biased view of the Mycenaean economy because only 'palatial concerns' are recorded, but even with regard to the palatial economy there is more bias than is often recognised. A heightened awareness of the pattern allows an improved understanding of documentation relating to religion.

Table 3-1 lists all commodities recorded in connection with the religious sphere in the extant Linear B corpus. They are listed either by type (e.g. 'textiles') or by the sort of measure involved.

Table 3-1. Linear B commodities used for purposes connected with religion

liquids	solids	animals and animal products	textiles	metals	not securely identified	
olive oil	wheat	bovines	*146	gold	_E_	_PO_
unguent	barley	sheep	*166	bronze	_KA_	_RA_
honey	flour	goats	*166+_WE_		_KAPO_	_TE_
wine	figs	pigs	TELA		_KE_	_U_
	olives	sheepskins	TELA+_PA_		_KO_	_WI_
	cyperus	cheese	TELA+_TE_		_MA_	*132
		wool			_ME_	*134/*190
					_O_	*150
					_PE_	*157

Two types of information are of primary interest here. First, what proportion of the total quantity recorded for of all palatial disbursements of a given commodity did amounts disbursed for religious purposes represent? Second, what proportion of overall palatial resources in a given commodity – insofar as this can be estimated from existing records – did disbursements related to religion represent? The first figure relates to how the commodity was used, the second tells how much of the total resources were invested in such uses. The two figures together should allow judgement about the proportion of the palatial economy invested in religion.

A word is required about what is meant by palatial 'disbursements'. Items were disbursed by the palaces for various purposes and in differing circumstances. A particularly important distinction for present purposes is between items issued for 'final use' and issues for industrial processing. Items issued for 'final use' would be consumed by those to whom they were issued. They thus represent real expenditure on the part of the palaces. Examples are religious disbursements such as offerings, and issues of rations (whether for 'ordinary' workgroups or support staff at festivals). The palaces might receive further benefit from such issues – with rations, for instance, in the form of labour – but there would be no direct return of the commodity itself. This differs from issues of raw materials to workers for industrial processing (for instance through the *ta-ra-si-ja* system[1]) where the commodities would be returned from the workshops to the palaces in altered form; for example, wool might be returned as textiles, bronze as vessels or arrowheads, and untreated oil as perfumed oil. Such issues do not represent real expenditure, since the finished items would remain available to the palaces for future disbursement. Our calculations must take account of this distinction.

A related complication is that in a few cases commodities issued for industrial purposes would be consumed in the manufacturing process and thus not after all returned. Examples are issues of wool to perfumers (PY Un 267) or oil to tanners (KN Fh 5428). Wool and oil are used in perfumery and tanning but, unlike the primary raw materials required for such industries, would not return to the palace in material form. Such issues will be counted for present purposes as 'final disbursements', that is, actual expenditure.

We must also note differences in types of receipts, particularly between primary 'income' and receipts of final products from workshops where skilled labour value has been added, but where the raw materials had already 'entered' into the system at a previous stage. Examples of actual 'income' would be commodities on taxation and harvest records, both of which concern primary collections of resources. Here too, however, a further distinction can be drawn. In the case of taxation, commodities normally 'enter' the palatial system from the 'non-palatial' sector, while in the case of harvests, the origins of the goods are unclear because the basis of Mycenaean agricultural systems remains poorly understood.[2] It may be that the palaces ran agricultural estates (perhaps along the lines of the Turkish *çiftlik*), possibly farmed by slaves, peasants (perhaps under a tithing or share-cropping system), tenured officials or craftsmen, or some combination of these. Or harvests might represent something more like taxes, levies on 'non-palatial' lands (whatever 'non-palatial' would mean here – perhaps land held in common by villages).[3] Fortunately, resolution of the question is not essential for present purposes. What is important is that the resources became available to the palaces for final use, whatever their ultimate source. When a tablet says something such as *e-pi-ke-re /epi khērei/* 'in hand', for instance at the TN *da-wo* in KN F(2) 852, this can be taken at face value: the commodities so

[1] On *ta-ra-si-ja* see e.g. Killen 1985, 273–5; 2001a.
[2] For discussions see e.g. Chadwick 1976; Killen 1985, 244–5; 1994–1995a; 1998a; Halstead 1992b; 1995a; 1995b; 1999b; 1999c; 2001.
[3] Killen 1998a, 20–3.

described are 'in the hand' of – that is, in stores controlled by – the palace.[4] Note this need not necessarily mean inside the palace building – goods may have been stored in outlying buildings in the surrounding settlements or in other places where the palaces had storerooms (e.g. at *da-wo*). In either case, what is crucial is the availability of the resources to the palaces for use. Receipts of this type should be distinguished globally from receipts of finished goods from the various industries. Receipts of workshop output also of course represent 'resources', since the items are now available for final use, but in industrial manufacture the *same* commodities and materials may be represented at various stages of their progress through the system and we must avoid counting them twice.

A final complicating factor is that in a few cases disbursements are recorded which are not made by the palaces as corporate bodies, but by individuals, as is the case, for instance, with some of the records of banqueting foodlists (e.g. PY Un 138), as noted in Chapter 2.[5] It is difficult to separate out such documents as it is not always clear what is going on. For present purposes, such instances are noted but not counted separately. In general, the amounts involved are small and would not affect the overall general picture.

The study proceeds by examining each commodity in turn.[6] As noted previously (Section 1.4), data from each site are considered separately in the first instance to avoid chronological and other complications. Further, at Knossos, tablets from the RCT are considered separately from those of the main destruction horizon. The majority of our documentation comes from Knossos and Pylos, and our focus is thus on these two sites; evidence from other sites is included where available.

The remainder of the present chapter initiates our investigation with an examination of the Linear B evidence for olive oil and products made from it, perfume and unguent.

3.2 OLIVE OIL (**130* = OLE)

3.2.1 OLIVE OIL IN LINEAR B

Olive oil, both untreated and perfumed, was the major commodity appearing in offerings records at Pylos and Knossos; other sites have not yet yielded evidence for oil offerings.[7] At both places there is evidence for important perfume industries, and it seems that a significant amount of the oil collected by the palaces was used in perfumery.[8] The series in which oil was documented (PY Fr; KN Fh, Fp, Fs) represent some of the most extensive and comprehensive

---

[4] Killen 1994–1995a, 331–3, esp. 332.

[5] E.g. Bendall 2004, 105–11.

[6] Another approach would be to examine types of transactions in which the commodities were involved. Thus, wheat for example might fall in different sections, dealing with banqueting, land tenure and so forth. However, it is more straightforward to examine individual commodities, whatever purpose they were put to, because in each instance the question is what proportion of palatial resources of a given commodity were intended for religious purposes as compared with other purposes. This primary focus does not preclude a subsequent study approaching the material from the point of view of different *types* of religious (or other) activities.

[7] Outside Knossos and Pylos, the oil ideogram **130* appears only on MY Fo 101, which does not concern offerings (see *Documents*, 218; Killen 1981, 37–45; Shelmerdine 1997, 390).

[8] On the perfume industry see particularly Wylock 1970; Foster 1977a; 1977b; Shelmerdine 1984; 1985; also 1987b. Other studies of oil in Linear B include: *Documents*, 217–18, 303–8, 439, 475–83; Bennett 1958a (= *OOT*); Lejeune 1958d (= *Mémoires* II, 141–65, see esp. 157–62); Adrados 1965; Chadwick 1966; Gérard-Rousseau 1966; Doria 1968; Godart 1968a; 1968c; 1969; 1987; Duhoux 1976a, 134–49; Baumbach 1979a; Jasink 1983; Melena 1983b (replacing Melena 1980; see 1983b, 89); Tegyey 1989; Palmer 1994, 125–42; Boulotis 1996; Speciale 2001; Weilhartner 2003. For archaeologically oriented studies of Aegean LBA oil see e.g. Blitzer 1993; Hamilakis 1996; 1999a; Capita 1997; Riley 1999, 36–55; 2002. For a useful bibliographical essay referring also to later periods see Horden & Purcell 2000, 581–2.

evidence for religious offerings in the Mycenaean archives. They also include other types of records, such as taxation and industrial records, and thus provide the opportunity to elaborate on the various categories of receipts and disbursements noted above. We begin with Pylos.

3.2.2 OLIVE OIL AT PYLOS

The oil ideogram at Pylos appears primarily in the Fr series,[9] a group of fifty-one tablets[10] recording transactions involving perfumed oil, the production of which was a major Pylian industry. The only (possible) appearance of OLE outside the Fr series is on a label, Wa 1248, the reading for which is now regarded as uncertain.[11] Tablets of the Fr series are set out in Table 3-2.

Table 3-2. The Pylos Fr tablets

A. Disbursement records

A.1 Clearly religious

Rm	scribe	Fr	recipient	plural group	'address'	time designation	amount	= V	other text
38	S1202-H2	1206	po-ti-ni-ja a-si-wi-				ỌḶẸ+*PA* 5 V 4	94	to-so qe-te-jo
23	S1202-H2	1236	u-po-jo po-ti-ni-ja		pa-ki-ja-ni-jo a-ko-ro		OLE+*PA* S 1 V 1	7	
23	S1217-Cii	1225	u-po-jo po-ti-ni-ja				OLE+*A* S 1	6	e-ra$_3$-wo . . . we-a$_2$-no-i a-ro-pa
23	S1202-H2	1231.1*	po-ti-ni-ja	di-pị[-si-]jo-i			*lost*	0.25+	
23	S1202-H2	1235.2	po-ti-ni-ja	]wạ-na-so-i			OLE+*PA* V 3	3	pa-ko-we
23	S1219-Cii	1219	po-se-da-o-ne	wa-no-so-i			OLE+*A* V 2	2	
38*	S343-H4	343	po-]se-da-o-ne			re-ke-to-ro-te-ri-jo	OLE[	0.25+	e-ti-we
23	S1202-H2	1224	po-se-da-o-ne			pa-ki-ja-ni-jo-jo me-no	OLE+*PA* Z 2	0.5	pa-ko-we e-ti-we
38	S1202-H2	1202	ma-te-re te-i-ja			me-tu-wo ne-wo	OLE+*PA* 5 S 1 V 4	100	pa-ko-we
23	S1202-H2	1226	te-o-i		ro-u-si-jo a-ko-ro		OLE+*PA* V 3	3	pa-ko-we
103*	Cii	1355	te-o-i				*lost*	0.25+	a-ro-pa pu-[
38	S343-H4	1204	ti-ri-se-ṛọ-e				OLE Z 1	0.25	wo-do-we
23	S1202-H2	1220.1			ro-u-si-jo a-ko-ro		OLE+*PA* V 4̣	4	pa-ko-we
23	Cii	1230			di-wi-jo-de		OLE+*A* V 1	1	
23	S1217-Cii	1217			pa-ki-ja-na-de	re-ke-e-to-ro-te-ri-jo	OLE+*A* V 1	1	e-ra$_3$-wo pa-ko-we we-ja-re-pe[
23	S1202-H2	1233	]so *?*		pa-ki-ja-na-de		OLE+*PA* V 1	1	
38?*	S343-H4	1209*			pa-ki-ja[-na-de		*lost*	0.25+	
41?*	S343-H4	1211*			pa-ki-]jạ-na-de		OLE V[	1+	e-ti-we
23	S1202-H2	1216		pa-ki-ja-ni-jo-i			OLE+*PA* 1 V 2	20	pa-ko<-we>
23	S1202-H2	1222		wa-na-so-i		to-no-e-ke-te-ri-jo	OLE+*PA* V 1	1	
							TOTAL	**245.75+**	

[9] See *OOT* (= Bennett 1958a) for original publication of the Fr tablets and Shelmerdine 1985 for a detailed discussion of the Pylian perfume industry. *Documents*, 476–83 sets out some important interpretative points. See also Jasink 1983; Carlier 1987, 262–5; Trümpy 1989; Stavrianopoulou 1995; plus (now dated) Gallavotti 1959; Gérard-Rousseau 1966; Doria 1968. A version of Section 3.2.2 has appeared in print previously (Bendall 2001b).

[10] Excluding 1255 (see notes to Table 3-2). *PTT* I also happens to have 51 Fr tablets (including 1255), but the membership of the series has now been modified as detailed in notes to the table.

[11] For Wa 1248 *PTT* (I, 260) reads:] OLE[, but *PoN* IV now transcribes]*jọ ko*[. Bennett had originally read]-*re* OLE[(*OOT*, 67, pls. XVIII–XIX). That two signs are present is agreed, as noted in the apparatus to *PTT* (I, 261): 'trace of sign at left;]*ṛẹ* is difficult, perhaps even]*jọ*, but no satisfactory reading is possible'. (From the photograph in *OOT*, *re* appears more likely than *jo*, but autopsy is more reliable.) More important for present purposes is the issue of whether the oil ideogram appears. OLE was regarded by both *OOT* and *PTT* as secure (note the reading in *PTT* is undotted) and appears from the *OOT* photograph to be more satisfactory than *ko* (it seems difficult to reconcile the traces in the photograph with *ko*), but *PoN* IV regards *ko* as secure. The issue is not crucial here since the number (if it had one – labels usually do not) is lost, but it would have been of interest to have an example of a label recording oil. Labels such as Wa 1248 often accompanied tablets written in other rooms of the palace then moved to Rm 7 of the Archives Complex for processing, with some ending up stored with tablets in Rm 8 (Palaima & Wright 1985, 257–8, 260–1; *Scribes Pylos*, 183; see Chadwick 1958b for initial observations linking labels to tablet series). Wa 1248 was found in Rm 8 (*Scribes Pylos*, 217), but it is not certain what tablets it was associated with (Pluta's new study of the AC may eventually shed some light on this matter; see Pluta 1996–1997). Presumably a label recording oil would have related either to disbursement tablets written in outlying rooms and moved to the AC for processing or storage, or to allotments to (or deliveries from) perfumers, which were normally kept in the AC.

A.2 Probably religious

Rm	scribe	Fr	recipient	plural group	'address'	time designation	amount	= v	other text
23	S1202-H2	1234	wa-na[*?*				*lost*	0.25+	
23	S1219-Cii	1221		wa-na-se-wi-ja		po-ro-wi-to	OLE+*A* S 1	6	
23	S1202-H2	1228	e-re-de *?*	wa-na-so-i			OḶẸ +*PA* V 1	1	
63*	S1202-H2	1251*		wa-na-so-ị[			OḶẸ [	0.25+	
23	S1219-Cii	1215*	wa-na-ke-te	wa-na-se-wi-jo			–	–	we-a-re-pe sa-pe-ra ⟦1⟧ *RA*
23	S1202-H2	1227	wa-na-ka-te	wa-na-so-i			[OLE]+*A*? S 1 V 1	7+	
23	S1202-H2	1235.1	wa-na-ka-te	wa-]na-so-i			OLE+*PA* 1	18	pa-ḳọ[-we]
23	S1202-H2	1220.2	wa-na-ka-te	di-pi-si-jo-i			OLE+*PA* S 1	6	
23	Cii	1232		di-pi-si-jo-i		po-ro-wi-to	OḶẸ+*P̣A* S 1	6	pa-ko-we
23	S1217-Cii	1218		di-pi-si-je-wi-jo		po-ṛọ[-wi-to	OLE+*A* S 1	6	we-ja-re-pe e-ra$_3$-wo
103*	Cii	1338	e-qo-me-ne-[*?*	di-pi-si-jo-i[			*lost*	0.25+	
23	S1217-Cii	1240	e-qo-[*?*	di-pi-si-jo			OLE+*A* V 1 [	1+	e-ra$_3$-wo pa-ḳọ[-we
23	—	1245	e[*?*	]jo-i			*lost*	0.25+	pa[
							TOTAL	**52+**	

A.3 Connections unclear

Rm	scribe	Fr	recipient	plural group	'address'	time designation	amount	= v	other text
23	S1202-H2	1231.2	ke-se-ni-wi-jo[				]OLE S 1[	6+	
38	S1202-H2	1205		a-pi-qo-ro-i			OLE+*PA* S 2 V 4	16	we-ja-re-pe
23	Cii	1244			me-ki-to-de[		*lost*	0.25+	
23	Ciii?	1223.1			]ti-no-de		OLE+*A* S 2	12	we-a-re-pe pa-ko-we e-ra-wo
23	Ciii?	1223.2			Probably ti-no-de?		OLE+*A* S 2	12	]wo-do-we-qe we-a-re-pe
							TOTAL	**46.25+**	

B. Industrial transaction and inventory records

Rm	scribe	Fr	purpose	main text	amount	= v	other text
AC	S1202-H2	1184.1-2	INDUSTRIAL	ko-ka-ro a-pe-do-ke e-ra$_3$-wo to-so e-u-me-de-i	OLE+ *WE* 18	324	
	S1202-H2	1184.3	INDUSTRIAL	pa-ro i-pe-se-wa ka-ra-re-we 38	—	—	
32	S1203-Cii	1200	INVENTORY?		*lost*	0.25+	pa-ko-we a-e-ti-to[
38	S1203-Cii	1201	INVENTORY	ku-su-p̣a ṭọ-so	OḶẸ+ *P̣O* 1̣4 V 2[	254+	
38	S1203-Cii	1203	INVENTORY		OLE 1 S 1 V 2	26	ku-pa-ro-we wo-do-we
38	S1203-Cii	1208	INVENTORY?		OLE 3 S 2 V 4	70	wo-]ḍọ-we
x	—	1214*	INVENTORY?		OḶẸ+ *P̣O* 2̣ [	43+	
					TOTAL	**717.25+**	

C. Type of record unclear

Rm	scribe	Fr	recipient	plural group	'address'	time designation	amount	= v	other text
C.1 OLE ideogram									
		1207.1	]so-de				OLE+*A* V 3	3	
38	H41	1207.1	]so-de understood?				V 1[	1+	wo-do-we
		1207.2	]so-de understood?				[OLE]V 1	1+	
23	Cii	1237*	]to-no[*?*				OLE+*A*	1	
23	S1202-H2	1238	]so-de				OLE	6	wo-do-we
32	—	1194	]de				OLE+*Ạ* V 1	1	OḶẸ[
38*	S343-H4	1212					OLE S 1	6	
23	S1202-H2	1241					[OLE] 1 [	24+	qe-te-jo jo[
23	S1217-Cii	1242					*lost*	0.25+	a-ro-pa e-ra$_3$-wo e-pị[
23	—	1243					[OLE]^x V 1	1	
23	S1202-H2	1246					OLE+*PA* [	6+	]-we
23	—	1229					OLE+*PA* V 1	1	]ṛọ
							TOTAL	**51.25+**	
C.2 *AREPA* ideogram									
32	S1202-H2	1198					]*ẠṚẸP̣Ạ* 2 S 1 V 5	47	

Notes

General

All tablet texts are given in full, but the word order is not exact since text is arranged according to category of information. Linear B word dividers are omitted.

The table takes into account new tablet joins and readings since the publication of *PTT* I, and the transcriptions have been checked against *PoN* IV. Tablets particularly affected are designated with an asterisk in the 'Fr' column.

Where an asterisk appears in the 'Rm' column, a note appears below under 'Findspots'.

? indicates category of text uncertain. Such text is usually placed in the 'recipients' column for convenience, but may refer to a recipient or something else.

Note that in Fr 1201, –1203, –1208 and –1214, *PoN* IV transcribes *po* rather than *PO* (*PTT*), reflecting that the sign is an adjunct rather than an ideogram (for *po*/*PO* see Section 6.6.3.2).

The table excludes Fr 1255, which is probably wrongly classified (see Shelmerdine 1985, 65–6; Bennett 1992, 125). This tablet was found in Rms 71–72, away from the other Fr tablets (*Scribes Pylos*, 126, 206) and the oil ideogram does not appear on it in any case.

Individual tablets

1194: The apparatuses to *PTT* and *PoN* IV note 'OLE+*ṢỊ* not impossible', but *Ạ* is (surely rightly) given as the preferred reading (see also Shelmerdine 1985, 32–3). Traces to the right seem to be another OLE (both corpora read ỌḶẸ[): *PTT* (I, 159) notes 'second OLE perhaps over erasure', while *PoN* IV has 'a second OLE possibly erased'. This doubtful second OLE is not counted here.

1209 and 1211: These tablets, quasi-joined in *PTT* I, are now dissociated (Bennett 1992, 125), although they are still ascribed to the same hand and stylus (S343-H4).

1214: This tablet is a new addition to the series, found by Bennett (1992, 104, 127) among some 1955 fragments, with joins and new texts by Melena (1994–1995a, 100; 2000–2001b, 379) (all *s.v.* Fr 1479). Melena suggests this may be the piece numbered 1249 in *OOT*, 68. *PoN* IV renumbers it as 1214.

1215: The appearance of OLE on Fr 1215 is conjectural and the latter part of the second line of the tablet has a complex history of readings. The first line is non-problematic, as is the start of the second line which begins with the sign-group *sa-pe-ra*. It is agreed that this is to be read as a single word, although the syllabograms are spaced unusually far apart from one another and the interpretation of the word is uncertain. The real difficulty is how the rest of the line, which involves some erasures, is to be read. A further single sign *ra* appears, with some strokes to the left either attached to it or belonging to an erased sign under or next to it. In the original publication, Bennett (*OOT*, 47, pls. X–XI) read it provisionally as an ideogram *ṚẠ*, but commented that 'it is best to wait for autopsy to see what is really there'. *PTT* (I, 156, 159) emended the transcription to *ra*, and removed the underlying dots, which was preferable since the sign itself is clear enough, the doubt being whether it was intended as an ideogram or a phonogram. (The *PTT* apparatus comments that there is an 'erasure beginning after -*ra* and extending under *ra*', suggesting the possibility that the second *ra* may originally have been part of a word.) Another possibility is that the sign is to be read as a ligature, as suggested by Palmer (1963, 242, 245) and later Bennett (1992, 120), who further sees an erased numeral: '⟦1⟧ just before OLE+*RA*'. *PoN* IV, on the other hand, reads the sign simply as *RA* and notes in the apparatus that it is immediately preceded by ⟦1⟧. The published photo (*OOT*, pl. X) shows traces that would be compatible with an erased OLE either under or (originally?) ligatured to *ra*, although it seems that whatever the final version was meant to represent it was not OLE+*RA* since the supposed OLE element appears so very faintly (see also Shelmerdine 1985, 33, who notes Chadwick's observation that the marks are probably erasures). The two vertical strokes lying one above the other immediately to the left are presumably the traces of the supposed ⟦1⟧. The safest conclusion is that the reading remains unclear. In any case, the wording of the tablet and its findspot are in line with other Fr tablets and there is no reason to doubt it is connected to this series. For the purposes of the table, *RA* is given in the column for 'other text' and no numbers have been counted.

1223: The scribe of 1223 is now held to be uncertain. Palaima (*Scribes Pylos*, 108–10) attributed the tablet to H44, who wrote just one other surviving document, the offering tablet Tn 316. He makes a good case for the similarities but, given the limited material, certainty is difficult. *PoN* IV still considers the document to be Ciii (see index), but without ascription to a particular scribe.

1227: '[OLE]+*Ạ* possible' according to *PoN* IV. *PTT* (I, 159) notes the tablet is palimpsest.

1231: *PoN* IV shows an extra sign *ṭẹ*[, not previously published. (The tablet appears in Melena 1996–1997a, 165, but text unchanged there.)

1237[+]1239: The quasi-join suspected by Melena (1992–1993a, 81) is now confirmed (Melena 2000–2001b, 377).

1249: See 1214.

1251: New reading (Melena 2000–2001b, 377).

1479: See 1214.

<u>*Findspots*</u>

For Fr findspots in general see primarily Shelmerdine 1985, 64–6 and *Scribes Pylos*, 141–51, 166–9, 205–6. A few remaining anomalies are noted below, along with some further information noted in *Scribes Pylos*.

343: According to *Scribes Pylos*, 151, this was found in two parts, one discovered in the initial 1939 excavations in Trench VI (see *PoN* I, 6, with Fig. 401) in the area later labelled Rm 41, and one found in 1955 in the surface above the wall between Rms 37 and 41. The origin thus appears to have been the room above Rm 38 (see also Shelmerdine 1985, 64–5, with n 119 for further references).

1184: 'Chasm Rooms 7–8' (*Scribes Pylos*, 205). Confusion over the findspot arose from the tablet originally being ascribed to Rm 32 by Bennett (*OOT*, 11, 40; note Bennett refers to the old room numbering system in which 32 was 48), followed by *PTT* (II, 54), but this was corrected to the chasm (Bennett 1964b, 251; see also *PoN* I, 100) as noted by Shelmerdine (1985, 23 n 42, see also 68 and 110) who comments that the excavation notebooks make the findspot clear. (The correction is noted also by Sacconi 1967, 97 n 14 and Jasink 1983, 46, citing Bennett.)

1209 and 1211: *PoN* IV gives the findspots as '38?' and '41?' respectively (cf. *Scribes Pylos*, 206, where the findspots are given as secure). But *PTT* (II, 54) gives findspots for both as Rm 38 (Shelmerdine 1985, 64 has no separate listing for 1211). *Scribes Pylos*, 151 notes that the *fr*. of 1209 (*1955*/77) was found in sifting, and that of 1211 was found in Rm 41. The origin of both should be the room above Rm 38 since this is where the others were stored; the table gives the locations as in *PoN* IV.

1212: 'Room 38 or 43' (*Scribes Pylos*, 206). Found in stone pile in doorway between the two rooms, probably originating from the spill from above Rm 38 (*Scribes Pylos*, 151).

1251: 'Court 63 E(2)' (*Scribes Pylos*, 206; see 169 for discussion and references).

1338: 'Area 103 by larnax' (*Scribes Pylos*, 206). 1338 is reported in *PTT* II to have come from Rm 43, but this is probably due to a confusion having arisen over its reported proximity to a larnax and which larnax was meant. The likelihood is that it was found near the larnax of Area 103, where 1355 was found in the following year (Shelmerdine 1985, 65; Jasink 1983, 50).

1355: 'W of Room 103' (*Scribes Pylos*, 206). See note to 1338.

The majority of Fr tablets record disbursements of perfumed oil to deities, shrines and persons, but a few seem to be inventory records, and at least one deals with an industrial transaction (Fr 1184, recording a transfer from one perfumer to another). In the table, Group A (with three sub-groups) comprises non-industrial disbursement tablets. Group B has inventory and transaction records.[12] Group C contains tablets where so much text is lost that the category cannot be accurately determined.[13]

Each row corresponds to one tablet, except in the few cases where two entries appear on a single tablet – these are labelled by line number and put in their appropriate places according to the schema, such that parts of one tablet may appear in different groups. Our focus here is on Group A, the non-industrial disbursement records. In addition to ideograms and numbers, the main types of information on these tablets are: (1) recipients, (2) 'addresses' of some kind

[12] Shelmerdine 1985, 23–4 (for Fr 1184), 99 (for inventory records; the new tablet 1214 is taken to be an inventory record here on analogy with others identified by Shelmerdine); for 1184 see also Carlier 1987, 262; Killen 2001a, 179–80. Although I have followed Shelmerdine in taking tablets of S1203-Cii as inventory records, an unresolved puzzle remains the question of why only *PO* oil (and not other types) is ever inventoried, while *PO* oil is never disbursed. We return to this issue in Chapter 7. Shelmerdine also takes the three tablets of Rm 32 as possible inventory records, which is not followed here except for Fr 1200, by S1203-Cii (this last, however, without any great conviction). The other two are Fr 1194 and 1198. For Fr 1194, Shelmerdine (1985, 93, see also 102, 120) argues in favour of its identification as an inventory record that more than one type of oil may appear and that]*de* might be restored *to-so-*]*de*. But the restoration is conjectural and the second oil ideogram is not securely read. The tablet is here regarded as simply 'Unclear'. Fr 1198 records a large amount of *AREPA*, but the text is entirely lost and so is also regarded here as 'Unclear'. I also regard as 'Unclear' two further documents suggested as possible inventories, Fr 1207 and 1238 (Shelmerdine 1985, 102). Although Bennett (*OOT*, 46, 62) does suggest the possibility of restoring *to-*]*so-de* on these documents, he regards an alternative of e.g. *ro-u-*]*so-de* as good or better, which would make them disbursement records. We cannot tell.

[13] Most of these seem to be disbursement tablets, judging from their general form and layout. In the case of Fr 1241 this must be the case because it records *qe-te-jo*, a sort of payment (cf. Fr 1206) – but the recipient is lost entirely, so it is not clear whether the connections would have been religious or otherwise.

and (3) time designations.[14] Each data type appears in a separate column; the remaining columns show other notes made by the scribe (primarily descriptions of the oil: sage-scented, rose-scented, 'for anointing', and so forth). The tablets are grouped according to the recipient or, where there is none, by toponym or other type of information. The texts given are complete, but the order of sign-groups is not exact. To the right of the number column, the figures are shown reduced to the unit V to facilitate comparison.

The three sub-groups of Group A are: A.1 'Clearly religious'; A.2 'Probably religious'; A.3 'Unclear'. The 'Clearly religious' entries refer to well-attested theonyms such as Poseidon and *Potnia*, well-known shrines such as *pa-ki-ja-na*, and words commonly agreed to be festival names such as *to-no-e-ke-te-ri-jo*.[15]

The 'Probably religious' section is used for entries involving the words *wa-na-so-i* and *di-pi-si-jo-i* and the related *wa-na-se-wi-ja/jo* and *di-pi-si-je-wi-jo*, except where these appear in conjunction with 'Clearly religious' words. The meaning of *wa-na-so-i* and *di-pi-si-jo-i* is disputed,[16] but the insight that they *function* as 'addresses' is crucial, whatever their semantic significance.[17] They are probably best explained as plural datives of advantage.[18] A religious association is indicated for *wa-na-so-i* by its appearance with Poseidon on Fr 1219 and with a festival name on Fr 1222 (both in the 'Clearly religious' group). Parallel usage suggests a similar association for *di-pi-si-jo-i*. Thus, although the terms need not indicate figures who are in themselves divine, it is probable that they relate somehow to religion. The terms are separated out here not to imply particular doubt about their connection with cult, but in order not to prejudice the central argument about the amounts of oil related to religion in the Pylos disbursement tablets. By isolating these more controversial terms at the outset (except where they are connected with words judged 'Clearly religious') the calculations can be done both with and without them. It will be seen that the main conclusions are unaffected whether or not the 'Probably religious' group is included.[19]

The 'Unclear' section (A.3) includes sign-groups which may or may not be associated with religion. Placement in this group should not be taken to imply that these references are necessarily 'non-religious', simply that they are unclear. Arguments on both sides have been made for most of the terms here and it is worthwhile reviewing these briefly.

---

[14] *Documents*, 477–8; Shelmerdine 1985, 69.

[15] In a previous version of this table (Bendall 2001b, 451) Fr 1222, recording *to-no-e-ke-te-ri-jo*, was placed in the 'Probably Religious' group. This was done so as to be as conservative as possible with regard to the main argument presented. However, the placement has been understood as an expression of doubt about whether or not this really is a festival name and since I fully agree with the broad scholarly consensus that it is (although the exact interpretation remains elusive; see *DMic*. II, 362; and now Petrakis 2002–2003) it seemed appropriate to move it.

[16] See Shelmerdine 1985, 73–9 for an excellent discussion.

[17] See *Documents,* 478–9; Shelmerdine 1985, 74. A structural analysis of the Fr series reveals two important elements in the designations: recipient and address. Either of these may be omitted, but there are no clear examples of double recipients, so *wa-na-so-i* and *di-pi-si-jo-i* are likely to function as 'addresses'. 'Addresses' may be either toponyms or groups of persons, who presumably would be charged with passing the offering on to the recipient. The terms might be either toponyms in the dative-locative or groups, parallel in form with *pa-ki-ja-ni-jo-i* (Fr 1216) and *de-u-jo-i* (KN Fh 352). I am grateful to J.T. Killen for discussions clarifying this point. See Killen forthcoming(a).

[18] Shelmerdine 1985, 77.

[19] A note should be added on a sign-group in the 'recipients' column, *wa-na-ka-te /wanaktei/* 'to the ϝάναξ'. *Wanax* is the title used for Mycenaean kingship, and elsewhere in the tablets he is certainly human (e.g. Ta 711), but the use of the term for both divine and human kings is attested in Homeric Greek and the Mycenaean usage may have been similar. Chadwick (1985, 196–7) takes the term as divine in the Fr series; Shelmerdine (1985, 78; 1998b, 92) puts the probability more on the side of a human recipient. If human, the king might be functioning as a dignitary in a ritual context, or perhaps might receive offerings in the same way as a deity, a practice which would have contemporary Near Eastern parallels. See also Gérard-Rousseau 1968, 232–6, esp. 235; Hooker 1979; Carlier 1984; Kilian 1988b; Palaima 1995a; Ruijgh 1999; Maran & Stavrianopoulou 2007. It is worth noting that in the Fr tablets, *wa-na-ka-te* never appears alone, but always in association with *wa-na-so-i* and *di-pi-si-jo-i*. *Potnia*, which in some ways may be structurally similar to *wanax*, also appears either with these terms or with an epithet.

The term *ke-se-ni-wi-jo* in Fr 1231.2 is interpreted as */xenwion/*, probably meaning here 'as a guest gift' or 'for guests'.[20] There is nothing in particular to associate oil so designated with religion, although it may be significant that *Potnia di-pi-si-jo-i* appears in the first line of the tablet. However, there seems no reason in principle that the same tablet should not record both an offering and an issue for more mundane use (although it should also be noted that the entire text of the tablet may belong to a single entry).[21] The evidence is insufficient to decide one way or the other, but the possibility that the context here might be religious is open.

On Fr 1205, *a-pi-qo-ro-i* is agreed to represent */amphik^{w}oloihi/* 'to the attendants', but it is not clear whether or not these 'attendants' may have had a religious association (for instance, in the sense of temple servants). The term is used both of ordinary servants and of women priests in Classical Greek,[22] and the same could have been true in Mycenaean. The word appears elsewhere at Pylos in contexts where there is no reason to believe there was any connection with religion,[23] but opinion is divided with regard to the appearance in the Fr series. Some consider the Fr 'attendants' as religious in parallel with the predominantly divine association of other Fr recipients;[24] while others stress that the series need not deal exclusively with religious figures.[25] Both possibilities remain open.

The sign-group *me-ki-to-de*[on Fr 1244 is obscure.[26] It appears nowhere else in the corpus and there is no context on the tablet to elucidate its meaning. It may be a toponym with *-de*, but the word may be incomplete at right and, even if it is complete, not every word ending in *-de* is a TN plus allative. Either way, it is unclear whether or not it had religious associations.

The next sign-group,]*ti-no-de* on Fr 1223, probably is a TN with allative, because *ti-no* is attested elsewhere as a Pylian location (An 18.9). There is suggestive evidence pointing towards a religious association for this term in at least some instances,[27] but certainty is impossible and since the sign-group is broken at left we cannot even be fully confident that we are dealing here with *ti-no* rather than with some other word ending in the same way. Again, the associations of this tablet are unclear.

To sum up, tablets in the 'Unclear' group may have religious associations or may not, but this cannot be determined on present evidence. An initial point to note here is that none of the disbursement tablets in the Fr series record *clearly* non-religious disbursements. A simple count of the entries highlights this observation. Of the thirty-eight entries in Group A, twenty are 'Clearly religious' and thirteen are 'Probably religious', while five entries are 'Unclear'. The 'Clearly religious' entries form 53% of the overall total. The 'Clearly' and 'Probably religious' entries taken together form 87% of the whole. Indeed, since the 'Unclear' group is simply 'unclear', it is possible that 100% of the non-industrial disbursements preserved in the Fr series were intended for religious purposes. Shelmerdine noted that 'the *principal* function of the series was not to record offerings, but to monitor the palace's supply of perfumed oil'.[28]

---

[20] Shelmerdine 1985, 79–80; see *DMic.* I, 353–4 for the term in general.

[21] Bennett (*OOT*, 59–60) followed by Chadwick (*Documents*, 477–8) considered *xenwia* here to be subsumed under the entry to *Potnia*, with the sense of *Potnia* receiving the oil 'by way of a guest-gift'. There is no way to resolve the issue since the end of the tablet is lost and this is where a separate entry of oil for *Potnia* would have appeared had there been one.

[22] See Dillon (2002, 74): 'Greek women priests were generally referred to as *hiereiai* (sacred women), and a general word *amphipolos* ('attendant') was also used.' While we cannot assume that the Mycenaean term had the same semantic possibilities of the classical word, we also cannot assume the contrary.

[23] Aa 804, Ad 690 (Chadwick 1988, 78).

[24] E.g. Chadwick 1985, 197.

[25] E.g. Shelmerdine 1985, 78, 97–8, 121.

[26] See *DMic.* I, 466.

[27] See discussion in Bendall 1998–1999, 7, with references.

[28] Shelmerdine 1985, 78.

Quite so, but at least 53%, probably 87% and possibly 100% of the disbursements do relate to offerings. This calls for explanation and we will return to the matter in the final chapter.

We may now turn to the amounts of oil disbursed. Totals recorded for the three sub-groups of Group A are summarised in Table 3-3.

Table 3-3. Oil in Pylian disbursement records

	V
A.1 Clearly religious	245.75+
A.2 Probably religious	52+
Sub-total A.1 + A.2	**297.75+**
A.3 Unclear	46.25+
TOTAL A	**344+**

The V 245.75+ which is 'Clearly religious' constitutes 71% of the overall total (V 344). In other words, a *minimum* of 71% of oil in the disbursement records is allocated for offerings. If the 'Probably religious' group is included (V 297.75), the proportion is 87%. This is a large amount, no matter how it is calculated and, as just noted, the figure could actually be 100%. This may seem to suggest that a majority of perfumed oil at Pylos was intended for religious offerings, but some further calculations are needed before reaching such a conclusion.

The disbursement records do not reveal how much oil was available to the palace overall. Including the inventory and industrial records, some V 1061.25 units of oil are recorded in the Fr series.[29] The 'Clearly religious' disbursements are 23% of this. Including the 'Probably religious' disbursements gives 28%, while including all of Group A gives 32%. However, the amounts considered here are not strictly comparable because the final destination(s) of oil in store or involved in industrial transactions is unknown – it could end up as offerings, or as any number of other things. Nevertheless, the calculation is useful in beginning to hint at the scale of the industry.

Shelmerdine's discussion of trade is further useful in this regard. She attempts to determine just what we want to know: how much oil was present in the overall industry.[30] An important clue is provided by amounts of coriander present on lists of ingredients issued to perfumers, totalling AROM 40 T 2.[31] On the Ventris & Chadwick values for dry measures this is some 3859.2 litres, or 1157.76 kg.[32] Classical parallels suggest that 1 kg of astringent (which is what the coriander was probably used as) would treat 2.5 kg of oil. Shelmerdine thus calculates that 1157.76 kg would be sufficient to treat 2894.4 kg, or 3183.84 litres, of oil.[33]

The amount of oil which could be treated with the coriander might be added to the other amounts already in store and being disbursed, since this would give the total amount of oil present, expected and recently disbursed. Even if some of the Fr oil had been treated in the previous year, it was available and on hand at the time the tablets were written, and thus represents 'available resources'. The V 344+ of the disbursement tablets of Group A would on

[29] Excluding Fr 1255 (see notes to Table 3-2, *s.v.* 'General') and –1198 (which does not record OLE, but probably *AREPA*). Shelmerdine (1985, 152 with n 272), gives a figure of V 742 Z 3. This excludes (for reasons I appreciate) Fr 1184, the transaction record (V 324). Fr 1214, unrecognised at the time of her writing (see notes to Table 3-2), adds another V 43+.

[30] Shelmerdine 1985, 151–2.

[31] The tablets are Un 267, Un [formerly An] 616, Un 592. See Shelmerdine 1985, 21 for a tabular breakdown and Section 2.5.3 for the texts.

[32] Shelmerdine 1985, 152. Her conversion factor (drawn from Melena 1976a, 134) is 100 litres = 30–32 kg of coriander seed.

[33] Shelmerdine 1985, 152. Her conversion factor is 1 kg = 1.1 litres of oil.

the VC values amount to some 550.4 litres. The Group B tablets record 1147.6 litres, which added to the other values equals 4881.84 litres (1147.6 + 3183.84 + 550.4), of which the Group A disbursements are 11%.

So many variables are involved that it would be hazardous to take the above series of calculations as absolute, but they may have some value as indications of orders of magnitude. Roundly stated, the tablets suggest that something on the order of 11–34% of oil at Pylos was disbursed for religious purposes, as calculated from the surviving documentation.

One difficulty with our calculations touched on above is that the ultimate use of the oil awaiting treatment or being inventoried is unknown: it might after all eventually be disbursed as offerings. But there are reasons for doubting this. First, classical and other ancient parallels suggest a wide range of uses for perfumed oil, especially personal hygiene.[34] It seems unlikely that the Mycenaeans made no use of their resources for such a purpose, but rather sent it *all* to shrines and deities. Indeed, as we shall see, there is evidence for non-religious uses in the documents from Knossos; the single tablet recording oil from Mycenae is also not related to religion (see n 7 above). Second, the amounts recorded for issues of oil are all very small, with two exceptions, the issues of V 100 (Fr 1202) and V 94 (Fr 1206) to two goddesses. This is not the place to discuss reasons for these large disbursements,[35] but it is important to note here how *very* unusual they are and how much they contribute to the overall totals. Without these issues, the total for Group A is a bare V 150. Also, apart from the two large issues, the range of individual Group A disbursements is between V 0.25 and V 20 – relatively small amounts. Indeed, only seven out of thirty-eight disbursements are larger than V 7, so those at the top of the range somewhat distort the general picture. In general, individual disbursements were very small.

Industrial transactions, however, are much larger. The amount of oil involved in the single industrial transaction seen in Fr 1184 (V 324) nearly equals the full total of all the disbursement records (V 344+) put together. The disbursement records concern many different recipients and cover at least two festivals and two or three different time periods. Thus, a single industrial transaction may account for some two or more months of supplies used for offerings. Unless offerings were given *only* in the months that happen to be recorded and not during the rest of the year (which seems unlikely), there must have been other transactions of the type seen in Fr 1184 at other points during the year, simply to maintain the supply required for offerings. In other words, a number of additional records of the type of Fr 1184 are likely to have once existed.[36]

The care with which even small disbursements for offerings are recorded suggests that records for this activity may be more or less complete (over the given period of the administrative cycle), in contrast to the incomplete documentation for overall resources. This in turn may suggest that, whereas totals for amounts disbursed for offerings might be roughly accurate, resources used for other purposes may have been underestimated. As seen above, as more evidence is taken into account, the percentage for offerings becomes lower. If a full range of evidence for total resources were available, the offerings percentage might be even smaller. Shelmerdine's coriander calculation above was undertaken by her in an attempt to determine whether enough surplus existed beyond the attested disbursements to make it possible that some of the commodity was being traded. Her conclusion that this was likely is supported by extensive archaeological evidence for oil trade more generally, although the specific role of

[34] See Shelmerdine 1985, 123–30; also Adrados 1964, esp. 141–2; Hamilakis 1996, 20.
[35] As J.T. Killen points out to me, *to-so* on Fr 1206 suggests a total, so the tablet may refer to more than one offering. However, the disbursement on Fr 1202 is made in connection with a time designation suggesting a single offering (albeit perhaps an annual one). See also Morris 2001, 423.
[36] This is also likely since the transaction comes from just one of the four perfumers mentioned in the Pylos records.

Pylos in such trade remains obscure.[37] Similarly, relevant to present purposes, even without being certain of the ultimate uses of the oil, it is apparent that a great deal more was available to the palace than is attested in the Fr series.

That being the case, it is curious that for the most part only disbursements relating to offerings should be preserved. If it is reasonable to suspect that perfumed oil was also being used for trade and domestic purposes, why are the records silent with regard to these? And why are there no records of the other crucial aspect of the operation, the acquisition of oil by the palace in the first place? In contrast to Knossos (see below), there are no records of harvests or taxes. How did oil come into the palace's available stores and why was this not recorded? We will return to this issue.

We might finally speculate how much oil may have been involved in religious offerings annually. On the VC figures, the 'Clearly religious' disbursements amount to some 393.2 litres. As noted above, the administrative period of the Fr tablets is unlikely to have covered more than one to two months, or three at most. We might thus speculate that the palace was sending out some (4 x 393.2=) 1572.8 litres of oil per year (assuming a twelve-month year).[38] Unless the months for which records exist happened to have been very unusual, this provides a general order of magnitude which, if it errs, probably errs on the side of being too low. In conclusion, although the use of perfumed oil for offerings was unlikely to account for a large part of the palace's resources, the amount involved still reflects a considerable investment in labour and raw materials, and suggests that its ritual use was not insignificant to the Pylian palatial elite.

3.2.3 OLIVE OIL AT KNOSSOS

3.2.3.1 INTRODUCTION TO OIL AT KNOSSOS

Oil at Knossos is recorded in the Fh, Fp and Fs series, plus a few other, mostly F- Class, tablets.[39] The Knossos records differ in several respects from those at Pylos. Most importantly, Knossos has records of disbursements to non-religious figures and of oil coming into the system from various settlements. These documents provide a stronger basis for calculation than was available at Pylos. On the other hand, a complication not encountered at Pylos is that perfumed and raw oils are not distinguished.[40] The oil of the Fp series is likely to have been perfumed, on analogy with Pylos,[41] whereas the Fs series records oil together with foodstuffs, perhaps implying that it was for culinary purposes.[42] The Fh series probably records a mixture of perfumed and non-perfumed oils: for instance, where the oil represents a major tax payment it is most likely not perfumed, but where it is going to a shrine it could be either. For present purposes, no distinction between perfumed and raw oil will be made. This is not as problematic as might appear: perfumed oil did after all have to start as unperfumed oil, so both may be taken into account in terms of total resources.

---

[37] Shelmerdine 1985, 141–51; 2001, 347–8. Also e.g. Catling *et al.* 1980; Haskell 1984; 1997; Tournavitou 1990; Cline 1994; Dickinson 1994, 251–2; Day & Haskell 1995; Van Wijngaarden 2002.

[38] Not an unreasonable assumption. The ideogram LUNA, representing the moon, is used to designate monthly rations at Knossos (see Section 2.2.1), suggesting the Mycenaean month was based on (or at least linked to) lunar cycles, which demands a 12–13 month year. An/Fn 7 provides new evidence in support of this (Melena 1996–1997b, 173); see also Chadwick 1988, 73.

[39] On Knossos oil see esp. *Documents*, 217–18, 303–8, 439, 475; Chadwick 1966; Godart 1968a; 1968c; 1969; 1987; Duhoux 1976a, 134–49; Foster 1977a; 1977b; Baumbach 1979a; Tegyey 1989; Palmer 1994, 125–42; Speciale 2001.

[40] The sole clear appearance of OLE with a ligature (*+A*) is on F 726, an offerings record. The ideogram on Fh 386 appears also have been ligatured, *possibly* with *O*; see Godart 1987, 202. An adjunct *te* is recorded on Fh 340, but it is not clear whether this pertains to the type of oil or something else.

[41] See *OOT*, 37 for a comment on the general comparability of Fp to Fr; also Adrados 1964, 138–41.

[42] Palmer 1994, 128; but the culinary use of oil should not necessarily be assumed (see n 154 below).

The Fh, Fp and Fs series were written and kept within a single scribal department, generally known as 'the Department of Perfumery and Offerings', which was the subject of an extensive study by E. Foster.[43] It was based in the West Wing of the palace and dealt with materials such as olive oil, honey and various spices. Foster lists the functions of the department as follows:[44]

> (a) the supervision of all collection and distribution of raw materials for perfume manufacture;
> (b) most of the palace's disbursements for cult offerings, involving both commodities collected by this department and those collected in other offices;
> (c) other distributions of the goods collected by this department (notably payments of olive oil to individuals).

It is interesting that cult offerings should be primarily managed by a particular department. This suggests a coherency of purpose with regard to this function, which we will see further reflected in the structure of some of the series. At the same time, this was not a 'cult department' *per se*; it seems rather that the focus was on particular sorts of commodities and the management of these for whatever purpose.[45]

We will examine the series individually and then bring all the data together. Before we begin, we will consider separately the documents from the RCT since these are probably earlier than the other records, as discussed in Section 1.4.

3.2.3.2 OIL IN THE ROOM OF THE CHARIOT TABLETS

Three documents from the RCT record oil; the texts are as follows.

Fp 7707 + 8014 + *frr.* ('124'?)
.1]ỌḶẸ 121 S 2
.2]ỌḶẸ 16̣7 [
.3] *vac.*
.2 Could be 17̣7.

F(1) 9110 ('124')
]2̣0̣ OLE 2̣ [
Trace of upright, in the break, at bottom right.

Xd 7259 ('124')
] ỌḶẸ 4 [
Trace of ⟦ ⟧ below 4.

None of these records preserves sufficient text to allow its function to be determined, so they would be marginal to our study in any case; there is nothing to suggest that any of them is an offerings record. It is worth noting, however, that large amounts of oil were obtained by the palace even at the time of the RCT administration.[46] Fp 7707 alone records a total of V 5196, some 8313.6 litres on the VC values. In general, figures on these tablets are similar in scale to those seen on the better-understood later records, to which we now turn.

---

[43] Foster 1974 *non vidi*; 1977a; 1977b; cf. *Scribes Cnossos*, 125–6.
[44] Foster 1977a, 41.
[45] As Foster (1977a, 41) notes: 'The two primary concerns of this office, perfumery and cult offerings, were perhaps felt by the Mycenaeans to be closely related, since both perfumed oil and the raw materials used in its manufacture were much used in cult observances.' A parallel for keeping separate records for commodities used in perfumery may exist in accounts for the Akkadian empire, as described by B.R. Foster: 'Records of oils, fats and aromatics were often separate from those of other materials, as if they were sometimes a specialty within administration. Their use as food, cosmetics, offerings, and for industrial purposes was documented' (Foster 1993, 33).
[46] As noted by Driessen (*Scribes RCT*, 208).

3.2.3.3 THE FP(1) SET

The Fp series comprises two groups of tablets which although both classed as Fp are not closely related to one another. We begin here with the Fp(1) set; the Fp(2) records will be dealt with below. The Fp(1) tablets form a coherent set,[47] dealing with religious offerings. A few examples are as follows.

Fp(1) 1 + 31 (138)

.1 de-u-ki-jo-jo 'me-no'
.2 di-ka-ta-jo / di-we OLE S 1
.3 da-da-re-jo-de OLE S 2
.4 pa-de OLE S 1
.5 pa-si-te-o-i OLE 1
.6 qe-ra-si-ja OLE S 1[
.7 a-mi-ni-so , / pa-si-te-o-i S 1[
.8 e-ri-nu , OLE V 3
.9 *47-da-de OLE V 1
.10 a-ne-mo , / i-je-re-ja V 4
.11 *vacat*
.12 to-so OLE 3 S 2 V 2

.2 *-ka-* perhaps over ⟦ ⟧.
.6-7 The numeral on one of these lines must be restored as 2 to produce the total.
.9 **47-* perhaps over ⟦ ⟧.

Fp(1) 6 (138)

.1 ka-ra-e-ri-jo / pa-si-te-o-i S 1
.2 qe-ra-si-ja OLE S 1

.1 *-e-* over ⟦ ⟧.

Fp(1) 13 BM (GR 1910.4-23.1) (138)

.1 ra-pa-to 'me-no' , *47-ku-to-de OLE V 1 pi-pi-tu-na V 1
.2 au-ri-mo-de OLE V 4 pa-si-te-o-i S 1 qe-ra-si-ja S 1
.3 a-ne-mo-i-je-re-ja OLE 1 u-ta-no , 'a-ne-mo-i-je-re-ja' S 1 V̩ 3

.1 *ra-* over ⟦ ⟧.
.2 *pa-* probably over ⟦ ⟧.
.3 OLE 1 to end over ⟦ ⟧.

Fp(1) 14 + 27 + 28 + *frr.* (138)

.1a me-no OLE
.1b a-ma-ko-to , / jo-te-re-pa-to // e-ke-se-si V 1
.2 qe-ra-si-ja S 1 a-mi-ni-so-de , / pa-si-te-o-i S 2 a-re V̩[

.1b *e-ke-* over ⟦ ⟧.

Fp(1) 16 (138)

.1 wo-de-wi-jo , 'me-no' , pa-si-te-o-i S 1
.2 qe-ra-si-jo OLE S 1

Cut at left.
.1 *pa-si-te-o-i* over ⟦ ⟧.

[47] The Fp(1) tablets were written by the same scribe and were filed together in the Clay Chest (*Scribes Cnossos*, 104); for problems with the findspot of Fp 48 see Notes to Table 3-5.

The Fp(1) set has been much studied, and there is no need to discuss it at length here.[48] The tablets record small amounts of oil issued to various deities, shrines and religious personnel over a number of months. The data are set out schematically in Table 3-4.

Table 3-4. The Knossos Fp(1) set

month names:	**de-u-ki-jo-jo**	**wo-de-wi-jo**		**ka-ra-e-ri-jo**		**ra-pa-to**	**di-wi-jo-jo**	**a-ma-ko-to**
recipient	**Fp 1**	**Fp 16 & 48**		**Fp 6, 7, 15, 18**		**Fp 13**	**Fp 5**	**Fp 14**
di-ka-ta-jo di-we	s 1							
di-ka-ta-de				**Fp 7**	s 1̣[			
da-da-re-jo-de	s 2			**Fp 18**	—?			
pa-de	s 1	**Fp 48**	s 1					
si-ja-ma-to		**Fp 48**	s 2					
**56*-ti				**Fp 15**	s 2			
**47*-ku-to-de						v 1		
pi-pi-tu-na						v 1		
au-ri-mo-de						v 4		
e-ke-se-si								v 1
pa-si-te-o-i	OLE 1	**Fp 16**	s 1	**Fp 6**	s 1	s 1	s 1	
pa-si-te-o-i		**Fp 48**	s 1̣	**Fp 15**	s 1			
pa-si-te-o-i				**Fp 18**	s 1[			
qe-ra-si-ja	s 1[	**Fp 48**	s 1	**Fp 6**	s 1	s 1	s 1	s 1
qe-ra-si-jo		**Fp 16**	s 1					
pa-si-te-o-i (Amnisos)	s 1[	**Fp 48**	s 1					s 2
e-ri-nu	v 3							
**47*-da-de	v 1							
a-ne-mo-i-je-re-ja	v 4					OLE 1		
a-ne-mo-i-je-re-ja (u-ta-no)						s 1 ṿ 3		
a-re								v[
]-jo				**Fp 18**	s 1			
Monthly sub-totals in v	**[68]**	**48**		**48+**		**45**	**12**	**20+**
Fp(1) set TOTAL	v 241+							

<u>**Notes**</u>

Fp(1) 1: The sub-total for Fp(1) 1 is taken from the total recorded by the scribe in line .12 (OLE 3 s 2 v 2). To achieve this total, s 2 must be restored in either line .6 or .7.

Fp(1) 7: There was probably only one entry on this tablet, despite the fact that this would be unusual for an Fp(1) record. The tablet is broken, but the upper right corner curves in such a way as to suggest the end of the document. (The tablet appears similar in dimensions and shape to Fp(1) 6, which does record two entries, but lays them out differently.)

Fp(1) 18: I accept here Alice Kober's suggestion, recently discussed by Firth (2000–2001b, 307, citing an unpublished extract from T.G. Palaima), that the missing tablet Fs <32> was part of Fp (1) 18, yielding a new text given by Firth as follows.

Fp(1) 18 + 32 (138)
.1 da-da-re-jo-de , / ka-ra-e-ri-jo , me[-no
.2]-jo s 1 pa-si-te-o-i s 1[

No changes would be made to the numbers in any case. Note that there *may* have been a further lost entry in line .1, but the curvature of the tablet at right suggests the end of the document so there would not have been room for this (note we do have the right end of this tablet: <32> would have joined on the left). If this is correct, the disbursements to 'all the gods' and the figure whose name is lost in line .2 were probably both made at the shrine 'Daidaleion'. The lost figure may

[48] The principal studies include *Documents*, 303–8, 475; Chadwick 1966; Melena 1974a; 1983b; Foster 1977a; 1977b; Baumbach 1979a; and now Weilhartner 2005, 21–8 (Weilhartner's table, pp. 25–6, is clearer than mine for some purposes, but less useful for the numbers, which he gives in litres).

have been *qe-ra-si-jo*, which appears on Fp 48. This is often taken as a scribal error for *qe-ra-si-ja*, but since the word is in any case poorly understood, a variant cannot be excluded. In the Fp series *qe-ra-si-ja/jo* invariably appears along with issues to 'all the gods', so would be appropriate here, but certainty is impossible.

Fp(1) 30 is omitted from the table as the numbers are lost and the function of the surviving fragmentary words is unclear. The word *to-so-*[*de*? is preserved on the *recto* (possibly suggesting a totalling tablet), and *ko-no*[*-so*? appears on the *verso*.

Fp(1) 48 is included, since it probably belongs to this set despite having been originally ascribed to the RCT; the RCT and Clay Chest tablets were excavated concurrently and it is suspected that Fp 48 became accidentally associated with the wrong deposit (*Scribes Cnossos*, 117; Chadwick 1968a, 17; Driessen 1990, 96 with n 333; 1997, 120; *Scribes RCT*, 20 n 8). Popham (1993, 179) rightly points out that the point is difficult to prove, but there are good epigraphical reasons for believing that Fp 48 really does belong to the Fp(1) set as well as pinacological reasons, e.g. that the clay of Fp(1) 48 is different from that of the other RCT tablets (see Driessen 1988, 126 n 12). The ascription is accepted by Firth (2000–2001a, 183) in his important review of Knossos findspots.

The table is organised according to the order of the longest document, Fp(1) 1, which lists a number of deities and shrines with amounts of oil designated to them, under the heading of a month name, *de-u-ki-jo-jo me-no*.[49] The remaining Fp(1) tablets have a similar structure, though all are shorter and Fp(1) 1 is the only one that provides a totalling figure (*to-so* /*tos*(*s*)*os*/ 'so much').[50] Six different months appear, affording a rare glimpse at the period of time over which a Linear B dossier was kept. The recipients vary somewhat from month to month, but 'all the gods' (*pa-si-te-o-i* /*pansi theoi*(*h*)*i*/ dat.pl.) and *qe-ra-si-ja* always receive some offering. As Fp(1) 1 is a totalling tablet, it may be that the records for *de-u-ki-jo-jo me-no* are complete. There is some suggestion here of standard monthly offerings, although the data are too meagre to allow a firm conclusion.[51] The extant numbers total V 241+ (a few numbers are lost, but probably would not have added substantially to the total). It might be noted that if it were true that the amount issued in Fp(1) 1 was intended to be issued monthly, the expenditure would have been V 408 for six months or V 816 for a year (assuming a year of twelve to thirteen months[52]). Converted into modern units this would be about 109 litres per month, or some 653 litres per six months and 1300 litres per year. Such amounts may seem substantial (though the inflation of the figures in this way may not be justified), but, as we shall see, they are well within the resources of the palace for this period.

3.2.3.4 THE FS SET

The Fs series forms a set of seventeen documents,[53] which were found together with the Fp(1) set in the Clay Chest.[54] Examples of the texts are as follows.

[49] An attempt was made to give other entries also in the order they appeared on the tablet. This was possible for all but Fp(1) 5, –18 and –48, which register *qe-ra-si-ja* and 'all the gods' in the opposite order to that in the table.

[50] With the possible exception of Fp(1) 30; see notes to Table 3-4.

[51] It has been observed that in the *de-u-ki-jo-jo me-no* the *pa-si-te-o-i* receive OLE 1 and *qe-ra-si-ja* receives S 1[. Similarly, in the *ka-ra-e-ri-jo me-no* the *pa-si-te-o-i* receive S 1 + S 1 + S 1 = OLE 1, while *qe-ra-si-ja* again receives S 1, perhaps suggesting that the same amounts were issued every month. Records for *ka-ra-e-ri-jo me-no* are probably incomplete, however, so this must remain speculative. Melena has further suggested that since disbursements to 'all the gods' seem to be made in three lots in *ka-ra-e-ri-jo me-no*, it may be that the Mycenaean month was divided into three ten-day periods (Melena 1974a, 95; Palmer 1994, 130–4).

[52] See n 38 above.

[53] Fs <32> is probably not a member of the set; see notes to Tables 3-4 and 3-5. Also, Fs 3 is by a different scribe (unattributed to a scribal hand), but is included in the set by Chadwick (1968b, 492, see also 490) on the grounds of format, content and findspot (see also Chadwick 1966, 30; 1968a, 16; Palmer 1994, 127).

[54] *Scribes Cnossos*, 84, 104. For a recent study of the series see Palmer 1994, 125–42 plus now Weilhartner 2003; 2005, 28–34; see also Chadwick 1966, 30–2; de Fidio 1977, 108–14.

Fs 2 (139)
.A HORD T 1 *NI* V 3 OLE Z 2
.B sa-na-to-de , FAR V 1 VIN V 1
↓
v. *ME+RI* Z 1
Possible traces of ⟦ ⟧.
.1 Erased sign after T (perhaps F̣ẠR?).

Fs 4 (139)
.A HORD T 1 *NI* V 3 FAR V 2 VIN V 2
.B a-ro-do-ro-o , / wa-ḳẹ-ta , HORD T 1 *NI* V 3 OLE V 1
.B *wa-ḍẹ-ta* also possible.
↓
v. *ME+RI* Z 2

Fs 8 (139)
.A HORD T 1 *NI* T 1[
.B pa-de , FAR V 2 [
↓
v. *ME+RI* **211*^VAS^*+PO* 1[

Fs 11 (139)
.A] HORD T 1 *NI* T 1 FAR V 2 VIN V 2
.B]qe-sa-ma-qa , / ta-mi-te-mo , HORD T 1 OLE V 1
↓
v. *ME+ṚỊ* Z 2

Fs 23 (139)
.1 ja-pe-re-so , HORD T 2 *NI* V 3 VIN V 2
.2 FAR V 1 OLE V 1
.2 V after OLE over ⟦ ⟧.
↓
v. *ME+RI* Z 1

Each recipient in the Fs series is allotted small amounts of HORD (barley), *NI* (figs), OLE (oil), FAR (flour), VIN (wine) and *ME+RI* (honey). The amounts received are more or less standard, though in some cases they are doubled (e.g. Fs 23), or two allotments are made (e.g. Fs 4, 11). R. Palmer has argued that the standard amounts are consistent with a ten-day ration for an active adult,[55] and points out that the repetition of two of the names (*a-*65-ma-na-ke* on Fs 3 and Fs 20; *sa-na-to-de* on Fs 2 and possibly Fs 22) may suggest that the disbursements were regular. This is entirely possible, but the evidence is insufficient to be certain. Also unclear is the use to which the goods were put. They could for instance have been intended to support personnel at the sanctuaries, or have been meant as token meals for the deities (or both).[56] Whatever the purpose, what most concerns us here is the amounts of the various commodities expended. The data are set out in Table 3-5. The table gives data for all commodities attested in the Fs series and will be referred to in subsequent sections dealing with those commodities.

It may be noted that only two of the Fs recipients, *pa-de* and *me-na*, are certainly attested elsewhere, both in religious contexts.[57] The rest are *hapax legomena* (with the possible exceptions of the entries on Fs 19[58] and Fs 26[59]), so their identification as 'religious' is not

---

[55] Palmer 1994, 130–4.
[56] See Palmer 1994, 128–42, for a recent discussion, plus now Weilhartner 2003, esp. 49–50.
[57] *pa-de*: Fp(1) 1, –48, Ga(3) 456. *me-na*: Killen forthcoming(a) argues persuasively for a recipient */Mēn(n)ā(i)/* 'to the Moon' on E 842, and the Fs figure may be the same, but as he notes the graph on Gg(3) 717 represents a different word (probably */mēns/* or */mens/* nominative of 'month').
[58] A Pylos sealing, Wr 1539, records the ideogram VIN along with the sign-group *e-ti-wa-*[, but this need not refer to the same word, particularly as it is incomplete. *e-ti-wa-ja-qe* at Knossos (Od 681) appears to be an ethnicon referring to *e-ti-wa*. See also *e-ti-wa-ja*, a woman's name proceeding from an ethnicon in KN Ap 639.8, and a possible MN in PY Va 15 (*DMic.* I, 258). Even if *e-ti-wa* was a Knossian TN, however, we are not necessarily dealing with the same word in the Fs series. The evidence is inconclusive.

certain. In general, because 'religious' figures appear in the Linear B tablets in economic contexts, there is no reason in principle why certain tablets may not involve a mixture of secular and religious figures. However, single tablets and sets do usually deal with related subjects, as a function of administrative convenience. The common opinion that the Fs tablets are associated with religion is accepted here.[60] The total recorded for oil (V 9.75, or 15.6 litres) is in any case so small that our final calculations will not be much affected.

Table 3-5. The Knossos Fs tablets

Fs	recipient	HORD		*NI*		OLE		FAR		VIN		*ME+RI*	*ME+RI*
		amt.	= V	**amt.**	= V	**amt.**	= V	**amt.**	= V	**amt.**	= V	**amt.**	= V
2	sa-na-to-de	T 1	6	V 3	3	Z 2	0.50	V 1	1	V 1	1	Z 1	0.25
3	a-**65*-ma-na-ke / me-na	T 1	6	V 3	3	Z 1	0.25	V 1	1	—	—	—	—
4	a-ro-do-ro-o , / wa-ḳẹ-ta	T 1+1	12	V 3+3	6	V 1	1	V 2	2	V 2	2	Z 2	0.50
8	pa-de	T 1	6	T 1[	6	*lost?*	***0.50***	V 2	2	*lost?*	***1***	**211+PO* 1[*	??
9	]ki-to , o-ja-de , [	*lost**	***6***	*lost?*	***3***	*lost?*	***0.50***	*lost?*	***1***	*lost**	***1***	]Z 1	0.25
11	qe-sa-ma-qa , / ta-mi-te-mo	T 1+1	12	T 1	6	V 1	1	V 2	2	V 2	2	Z 2	0.50
12	*lost*	]1	***6***	V 3	3	Z 2	0.50	]2̣	***2***	V 1	1	*lost?*	***0.25***
17	]i	T 1	6	V 3	3	Z 2	0.50	V 1	1	V 1	1	Z 1	0.25
19	e-ti-wa	T 1	6	V 3	3	Z 2	0.50	V 1	1	V 1	1	Z 1	0.25
20	ạ-**65*-ma[-na-ke	*lost?*	***6***	*lost?*	***3***	*lost?*	***0.50***	*lost?*	***1***	*lost?*	***1***	Z 1̣[	0.25
21	ka-u-da	T 1	6	*lost?*	***3***	*lost?*	***0.50***	V 1	1	V 1[	1	—?	?
22	]ṇạ-to-de	T 1	6	V 3	3	*lost?*	***0.50***	V 1	1	V 1	1	*lost?*	***0.25***
23	ja-pe-re-so	T 2	12	V 3	3	V 1	1	V 1	1	V 2	2	Z 1	0.25
24	lost	T 1	6	V 3	3	Z 2	0.50	V 1	1	V 1	1	*lost?*	0.25
25	]de	T 1	6	V 3	3	Z 2	0.50	V 1	1	V 1	1	*lost?*	***0.25***
26	]ki-ri-jo-de[	*lost?*	***6***	*lost?*	***3***	*lost?*	***0.50***	V 1	1	*lost?*	***1***	Z [	***0.25***
29	]de	*lost?*	***6***	*lost?*	***3***	*lost?*	***0.50***	*lost?*	***1***	*lost?*	***1***	]1̣	0.25(+?)
	TOTALS		**120**		**60**		**9.75**		**21**		**19**		**4 + 1 pot**

Notes

General

A dash ındicates the tablet is complete and has no entry for the given commodity. Where it is uncertain whether the commodity was represented or not the table gives '*lost?*' and the figures have been restored in the V column. Such restoration is a departure from the usual practice for other tables, but is done here because the structure of the series makes it extremely likely (although not certain – see Fs 3) that most of commodities were originally present on most Fs tablets. The numbers restored are in any case so small that no real difference is made. Assumed values for the restored figures are shown in bold italic.

Individual tablets

8: This tablet instead of recording a measure of honey registers it in terms of a vessel, **211+PO*. This is unique for the Fs series, although using vessels to measure honey is standard in the Knossos Gg tablets (where the vessel, however, is an amphora; see Section 4.2.1.1). On **211+PO* see Vandenabeele & Olivier 1979, 205–7, 265–6, Pl. CXXXIII; Palmer 1994, 127 n 4; Bendall forthcoming(b).

9: The ideogram for HORD is attested, but the measure and number are lost. The apparatus notes that a trace at right is probably VIN. The ideogram on the *verso* is lost but only honey ever appears in this place and the measure is preserved, so the number can be given with reasonable confidence.

11: *KT*[5] gives V 22 for VIN, but this is a misprint; cf. the photo in *CoMIK* I, 8.

12: *NI*, OLE and VIN are attested and two other numbers appear on the *recto*, the ideograms for which are lost. These are probably HORD and FAR, since the other missing commodity *ME+RI* appears only on the *verso* (although a double occurrence of HORD cannot be excluded). We cannot know if the ideogram for honey was originally present as this would have occurred in the broken left edge of the tablet.

[59] Weilhartner (2003, 48; 2005, 31, 52) suggests restoring *ki-]ri-jo-de* in Ga 953 [+] 955 (the context is offerings), which is possible, but by no means necessary.

[60] E.g. de Fidio 1977, 108; Palmer 1963, 237.

21: The space on the tablet where honey would normally have appeared is preserved so it was probably not present.
22: We cannot tell whether honey was present or not. The tablet is broken at left and depending on the length of the word to be restored on the *recto*, there may have been enough room on the *verso* for *ME+RI* to have appeared.
<**32**> has traditionally been thought to belong to the Fs set but there is reasonable support for an old suggestion of Alice Kober's that really it was part of Fp(1) 18 and this is followed here (see notes to Table 3-4 *s.v.* Fp(1) 18).

3.2.3.5 THE FH SERIES

The Fh series is a group of some 155 records written for a variety of purposes.[61] The tablets are set out in Table 3-6, arranged into eleven groups. The grouping is in the first instance by basic function where it is clear what this is, and in the second instance (especially where the function is less clear) by type of information present (e.g. man's name, toponym+*de*, and so forth). The groups are similar to those set out by Godart,[62] but have been somewhat rearranged and expanded to suit present purposes, and various new joins and other information have been incorporated. An attempt has been made to confine the majority of commentary to the notes to the table, so as to remain focused on our central inquiry, but where necessary it is given in the text. Throughout, our central concerns are (1) whether we are dealing with disbursements, receipts, or oil in store, (2) whether the transaction is connected with religion, and (3) what the numbers relevant to the various types of records are. Unfortunately, it is now difficult to use the figures helpfully supplied by Godart because numbers in his earlier articles were superseded by the discovery of some sixty-one new Fh fragments in the Iraklion Museum in 1984,[63] and his later figures are given in terms of litres whereas we need them here in Mycenaean units for comparison with the other series.

We will discuss each of the groups in Table 3-6 in turn, then attempt to summarise the data and consider the numbers.

1. Totalling tablets

The two tablets in Group 1 are totalling records.[64] Fh 367 records *to-so-ku-su-pa /tos(s)on xumpan/* 'so much altogether'.[65] Fh 366 also includes the totalling word *to-so*, plus the taxation term *a-pu-do-si* (see next), so is probably a totalling record for taxation payments.[66] The amount recorded in Fh 366 exceeds the amount recorded in Fh 367,[67] so evidently was not meant to be subsumed under that entry despite the latter reading 'so much altogether'. Godart

---

[61] Note that the Fh series is not a 'set', although the tablets do share scribal hand (141) and findspot (most were found in the NE corner of the Room of the Column Bases; see Firth 2000–2001a, 203–5, with references, also Section 1.4 above). However, the content and formulas are not standardised (except insofar as they all deal with oil), and in terms of filing it may be that they were grouped in separate containers according to the diverse subjects treated. For the few Fh tablets reportedly found outside the RCB, see Notes to Table 3-6, *s.v.v.* 462, 1056. A number of tablets are not securely ascribed to h. 141, mostly because the texts are too damaged to be sure, but given the findspots and subject matter the ascription is likely in most cases.
[62] Godart 1968a; 1969; 1987.
[63] Godart 1987, 201.
[64] Fh 5434 has not been included in this group because the suggestion that *to-*]*ṣọ* should be restored at the start of the document (*KT*[5], 182) is very tenuous; see Notes to Table 3-6, *s.v.* 5434. The tablet is instead in Group 2.
[65] *Documents,* 587; *DMic.* I, 411; *DMic.* II, 370.
[66] Godart 1968a, 599; 1987, 202.
[67] Assuming the quasi-join with –5503 is correct; see Notes to Table 3-6.

Table 3-6. The Knossos Fh series

Fh	category and tablet text	OLE	= V	epigraphic notes	interpretation notes
	1. Totalling tablets				
366[+]	to-so / a-pu-do[-si	339 V 5	6107	App.: Prob. [+] Fh 5503*	See chapter text
367	to-so-ku-su-pa	330 S 1	5946		*/tos(s)on xumpan/* 'so much altogether'
	2. *a-pu-do-si* records				
	2a. Clearly a-pu-do-si *records*				
340	ka-ro / a-pu-do-si 'te' OLE	23 S 2	426		*ka*.: prob. TN, *hapax* at KN*
349	ru-ki-to / a-pu-do-si	53 V 3	957		TN, well attested
<374>	a-pu-ḍọ[-si	*lost*	1+	May be same tablet as 5444 below*	
<379>	a-]pu-do-si	17 S 2[	318+	May join <381> (Group 10a)*	
5434	to-]ṣọ / a-pu-do-si	*lost*	1+	App. suggests restoration, but doubtful* May join <388> (Group 11)*	]*ṣọ* could be ending of TN.*
5444	]*vest.* / a-pu-do[	*lost*	1+	May be same tablet as <374> above*	
5451.a 5451.b	za-we-te a-mi-ni-si-ja / a-pu-do-ṣị	 30[	 540+		*za*.: 'this year' prob. */tsāwetes/* or similar *a*.: TN, Amnisos, well attested
5459	a-]p̣ụ-ḍọ-ṣị	3̣7̣ S 1	672		
	Sub-total 2a		**2916+**		
	2b. Possible a-pu-do-si *record*				
377	]ṣị	152 V 2	2738		Possibly *a-pu-do-si*, but unclear*
	TOTAL 2		**5654+**		
	3. Perfumery records				
	3a. Texts without o-no				
371	]o-se-ko-do / ku-pi-ri-jo	13 S 1	240	Also records *MU* 10	*ku*.: see chapter text *o*.: prob. MN, dat., *hapax*
5246	ku-pi-ri-jo / ma-ro-ne	100	1800		*ma*.: MN, dat. of *ma-ro*?*
5446.1 5446.2	ku-pi-ri-jo / u-ne[to-ro-qa / a-nu-[	*lost* *lost*	1+ 1+	App.: perhaps *a-nu-wẹ*[	*u*.: prob. start of AN* *a*.: prob. start of AN* *to*.: see chapter text
	Sub-total 3a		**2042+**		
	3b. Texts with o-no				
361.a 361.b	[*ku-pi-ri-jo* understood] ku-pi-ri-jo / o-no zo-a	21 S 2 [3̣ V 3̣	391 57	*ku*. written large at left, covering both lines*; Judging from the spacing, the number in .a is probably complete, so no + shown.	See chapter text
372	ku-pi-ri-jo / o-no	150	2700	Note on number*	
5447	]-ki-ro / ku-pi-ri-jo o-no	9̣ S[	168+	+Fh 5452 now rejected*	]-*ki-ro*: prob. ending of a MN*
	Sub-total 3b		**3316+**		
	3c. Mixed record and unclear				
347.1 347.2 347.2	ma-ro-ne / ku-pi-ri-jo we-we-ṛọ , / o-no a-ri-to-[.]jọ	6 S 2 1 V 2	120 18 2	Also records *MU* 5 2 entries on same line 2 entries on same line Now joins 5 *frr*. of 9093 from which 9093bis now dissociated	*ma*.: MN, also on 5246 (Group 3a)* *we*.: MN, dat. (prob. nom. in V(2) 147.1) *a*.: MN dat. or type of oil, *hapax**
5490	]ku-pi-ṛị[-jo	*lost*	1+		
	Sub-total 3c		**141**		
	TOTAL 3		**5499+**		
	4. Miscellaneous transaction records				
	4a. Other o-no *payments*				
348.1 348.2	o-no , i-su-ku-wo-do-to , qe-te-o , ⟦te-o⟧	1 S 1 1	24 18	*i*. apparently covers both lines*	*i*.: MN, dat., *hapax*
5431	o-na , de-ṃị-ṇị-jo	2 S 2	48		Prob. 'payments' for beds*
	Sub-total 4a		**90**		
	4b. A disbursement record?				
364.a 364.b	do?]-ke , a-ku-tu-ru-wo[ ]u-te-si	— *lost*	— 1+	App.: poss.]ḍọ-ke Only one entry*	*a*.: MN, prob. nom., *hapax* *u*.: dat.pl. prob. of occ. title, ending *hapax*
	4c. A receipt record?				
370.a 370.b	ko-no-so[ ]*vac.*]mu-to / de-ka-sa-to	— 7̣0	— 1̣2̣6̣0̣	Only one entry* Figure prob. correct*	*ko*.: TN, Knossos; *mu*.: MN, nom., possibly complete; *de*.: */dexato/* 'received'
	5. Men's names (rations?)				
341	pe-da-i-ra / du-ni-ja	4 S 2 V 1	85		*pe*.: MN, dat.; *du*.: eth. adj.?
342	a-ne-ra-to do-re-we	2 2	36 36	Two entries on same line	*a*.: MN, dat., *hapax* *do*.: MN, dat., *hapax*
344	ka-pa-ri-jo-ne	1	18		MN, dat. of *ka-pa-ri-jo*, well attested*
345	du-ru-po	V 1	1		MN, dat. (nom. in As 1516.17)*; also in 368 below
346	a_3-ki-pa-ta	2[	36+		MN, dat., deriv. from occ. title 'goatherd'
360.a 360.b	[ma-si-dwo] ki-ra-*56-so , u[ma-si-dwo / me-[	— *lost*	— 1+	*ma*. probably covers both entries App.: Perhaps *me-ṣạ-ṭọ*[	*ki*.: poss. AN* *ma*.: prob. MN, dat., prob. *hapax**
368	o-pi , du-ru-po	S 1	6		*o*.: 'at workshop/house of'; *du*.: MN, also in 345 above
<378>	]ma-qa-to	*lost*	1+	Reading uncertain*	Prob. MN, dat., *hapax*

Fh	category and tablet text	OLE	= V	epigraphic notes	interpretation notes
<382>	ko-ro-ja-ne	*lost*	1+		MN, dat., *hapax*
<384>	]re-pi-ru-nu-we[	*lost*	1+	Reading uncertain*	MN or title, dat., *hapax**
<392>	u-ru-pi-ja[	*lost*	1+		MN?, *hapax*?*
1057	**56*-i-ti	S 1	6	Hand and findspot uncertain*	Prob. MN, dat. (see chapter text, Group 9); cf. 5487 below
1059	wi-na-jo / e-ra-jo	V 1	1	Hand and findspot uncertain*	*wi.*: MN (well attested)*; *e.*: ethnic of *e-ra*
5429	wa-po	*lost*	1+	App.: Perhaps 1̣[	MN, dat., *hapax**
5463	qa-to-no-ṛọ[	*lost*	1+		MN, dat. (nom. in As 1516.7)
5465	ko-ki-de-jo / qa[	*lost*	1+		Prob. possv.adj. from MN *ko-ki-da*, attested*
5486	]kọ-pe-re-we	*lost*	1+		MN, dat. of *ko-pe-re-u* (attst. Am(2) 821.2)
5487	**56*-ị-ti-jẹ[	*lost*	1+		Prob. MN, or possv.adj.?*; cf. 1057 above
5502	ku-ru-me-ne-jo / de-u-ḳị-jọ[	V 2̣[	2+		*ku.*: prob. possv.adj. based on MN*; *de.*: MN*
	TOTAL 5		**237+**		
	6. Rations or industrial?				
	6a. Occupational titles				
386	ka-ke-we	S 1 V 1	7	App.: OLE+[ ]; poss. OLE+*Q̣*	Occ.title, dat.sg. /*khalkēwei*/ 'to the bronzesmith' [but could be nom.pl.]
1056	ra-pte-re	V 3	3	Hand and findspot uncertain*	Occ.title, dat.sg. /*rhaptērei*/ 'to the tailor' or 'leather-sewer' [but could be nom.pl.]
5428	wi-ri-ne-we	12 S 1	222		Occ.title dat.sg. /*wrīnēwei*/ 'to the tanner' [but could be nom.pl.]
5435	wi-ri-ne-we [	*lost*	1+		See 5428 above
	Sub-total 6a		**233+**		
	6b. with de-ma-si				
353	ra-ma-na-de / de-ma-si	S 1	6		*ra.*: TN+*de*, attst. in Ai 762*; *de.*: poss. /*dermasi*/? 'for skins'? or a dat.pl. appellative*
5432r 5432v	]-pte-si / [.]-u-pi-ri-[.]-ị]de-ma-si	S 1 2	6 36	App.: Poss. *ṇạ-u-pi-ri-jọ-ị*	?*ra*]-*pte.*: perhaps /*rhaptērsi*/?;]-*u.*: dat.pl.masc. ethnic?*; *de.*: see 353 above
	Sub-total 6b		**48**		
	TOTAL 6		**281+**		
	7. Dative plural groups				
352	de-u-jo-i	S 1	6		Pers.apel.masc.dat.pl.*, *hapax*
356	o-mi-ri-jo-i	1[	18+	App.: Probably only one unit	Pers.apel.masc.dat.pl.*, *hapax*
5498	*entry lost* ru-do-ro-ị	S 1 S 1[	6 6+	Both entries on line .b, number for second on line .a; text of *ru-di-ro-i* much smaller	Prob. pers.apel.dat.pl., *hapax*
	TOTAL 7		**36+**		
	8. Toponym + *-de*				
	*8a. With *47-so-de*				
462.1	]-si-ja	V 1	1	App.: .1 Perhaps]*p̣ạ-si-ja*; poss.]*ḳụ-p̣ạ-si-ja*; App.: .2 Sign in damaged area after *a.* perhaps Ṿ. [Reading looks good to me] .2 Two entries on same line; different findspot, poss. diff. hand*	*ḳụ-p̣ạ-si-ja*: if reading correct, prob. ethnicon* *a.*: MN dat.; nom. attst. in KN Uf(2) 990]*si.*: numerous words with this ending – perhaps an ethnicon, or deity name *qe-ra-si-ja*?? *e.*: prob. a type of temple servant (see chapter text) **47.*: TN+*de* (a shrine; see chapter text)
462.1	a-ri-ja-wo-ne [	Ṿ [1?	1+		
462.2	]si-ja / e-to-wo-ko	V 3	3		
462.2	**47*-so-de	S 1	6		
462 *v*.1	]de	V 3	3		
351	**47*-so-de	V 3	3		
357.1 357.2	**47*-so-de e-ra-de	2 S 1 2 V 1	42 37		**47.*: see chapter text.; *e.*: TN+*de*, well attested, but not frequent on offering records
393	**47*-so-de[	*lost*	1+		
5430	**47*-so-ḍẹ[	*lost*	1+		
5479	]**47*-so-de / wa-u-so[	*lost*	1+		*wa.*: title or MN? *hapax*
5501	**47*-so-de	1	18	Tablet complete	
9064	]**4̣7̣*-so-de [	*lost*	1+	App.: Perhaps trace at right.*	
	Sub-total 8a		**118+**		
	8b. Other, prob. or def. religious				
365.a 365.b	da-]**83*-ja-de]ḍạ-so-de	V 1 V 1	1 1		]**83.*: TN+*de* (see chapter text), also on 9067 below]*ḍạ.*: TN+*de* (see chapter text)
9067	da-]**83*-ja-de [	*lost*	1+	App.: Traces at right.	See 365 above
5467.a 5467.b	] di-ka-ta-de[ ]de / i-je-[	S 1̣? 1 V 1̣[	6+ 19+	App: Perhaps Ṣ 1̣ App.: Perhaps *i-je-ṛọ*[	*di.*: TN+-*de*, a shrine, well attested (e.g. Fp 7) *i.*: Prob. shrine (esp. if app. reading correct)
	Sub-total 8b		**28+**		
	TOTAL 8a + 8b		**146+**		
	8c. Other/unclear				
373	tu-ni-ja-ḍẹ , / te-[	*lost*	1+		TN+*de*, well attested (see chapter text)
5505	me-ra-de	S 1	6		Prob. TN+*de*, prob. *hapax**
	Sub-total 8c		**7+**		
	9. Offerings records				
	9a. Fairly certain				
<390>	e-ri-nu[	*lost*	1+		Theonym, well attested (see chapter text)
5475	qe-ra-si-[ja?	*lost*	1+	App.: Trace on right edge, would fit *ja*[	Theonym, well attested (see chapter text)
	Sub-total 9a		**2+**		

Fh	category and tablet text	OLE	= V	epigraphic notes	interpretation notes
	9b. Possible/probable				
2013	]jạ-[.]-jo / pe-da i-je-[ro?	*lost*	1+	App.: Perh.]*jạ-mị-jo*. Poss. *pe-da i-je-rọ*[.	'toward the sanctuary'?? see chapter text
9077	**56*-ti[	]1 S 1	24+		Prob. theonym (Fp 15.2) (see chapter text)
	Sub-total 9b		**25+**		
	TOTAL 9		**27+**		
	10. Descriptions of oil				
	10a. zo-a *and* e-pi-ko-wa				
343	du-pu$_2$-so / zo-a	15	270	2 entries on same line	*du.*: MN, prob. dat. [but see chapter text], *hapax*; *zo.*: see chapter text e.: see chapter text
343	[*du.* understood] e-pi-ko-wa	1̣ S 1 V 3	27		
355	qa-ti-ja / zo-a	30	540		MN, dat. [but see chapter text], attst. As(2) 1519 *zo.*: see chapter text
359.a	zo-a[		—	But may have had entry in first line too?*	*zo.*: see chapter text *ku.*: TN, well attested; *e.*: obscure*
359.b	ku-do-ni-ja / e-te-jạ[	*lost*	1+		
369	zo-a / a-ra-si-jo	*lost*	1+		Prob. MN., nom. in Df 1229.B (cf. X 1463)
380	]jo-te / zo-a	33 S 1	600	2 entries on same line	]*jo.*: no plausible word with same ending* *zo.*: see chapter text *e.*: see chapter text
380	[*jo.* understood] e-pi-ko-wa[	*lost*	1+		
5436	]-de , / zo-a	23 S 1	420		-*de* is 'unclear'*; *zo.*: see chapter text
5453.a	ko-[				*ko.*: Knossos?? (cf. 370) *zo.*: see chapter text
5453.b	zo-a / a-[	*lost*	1+		
	Sub-total 10a		**1861+**		
	10b. po-ro-ko-wa				
350	po-ro-ko-wa	2	36	Tablet text complete	See chapter text
<381>	]po-ro-ko-wa , a[	*lost*	1+	May join <379> (Group 2)*	See chapter text
	Sub-total 10b		**37+**		
	10c. to-qa *and* to-ro-qa				
339	o-pa-wo-ne-ja / to-qa	24	432		*o.*: prob. possv.adj. based on MN*
358	] , to-ro-qa	10	180		See chapter text
<376>	?to-]ro-qa	1[	18+		See chapter text
<391>	]ro-to-qa	20[	360+	App.:]*ro to-qa*[? cf. 339 and 8299*	See chapter text
5497	to-ro-qa	5	90	Tablet text complete	See chapter text
8299	]qọ-ta / to-qa	*lost*	1+		See chapter text
	Sub-total 10c		**1081+**		
	10d. ne-wo				
362.1	⟦ne-wo	8̣3⟧.	⟦1̣4̣9̣4̣⟧	.1: Entry erased; smaller units may be present* .2: *tu-ni-ja*?* number: see notes* No ascription to hand.*	
362.2	tu-[	7 Ṿ 2[?	128+		
<375>	]ne-wo	10[	180+		Needn't be *ne-wo*, as could be the ending of a different word
5506.a	] *vest.*			Note traces of another word at top; App. gives poss. readings* Number probably complete.	]*ra-de*: could, but needn't be, TN+*de*
5506.b	[. . .]-ra-de / ne-wo-jo	4[ ]	72+		
	Sub-total 10d		**380+**	and perhaps ⟦1̣4̣9̣4̣⟧ erased	
	11. Unclear				
<383>	ku-do[	*lost*	1+		Restore *ku-do*[-*ni-ja*?
<385>	do-ni-ja[	*lost*	1+		Obscure, *hapax**
<387>	]te-o[	*lost*	1+		
<388>	tu-ri[	*lost*	1+	May join 5434 (Group 2)*	Restore *tu-ri*[-*so*?*
<389>	]qa-nu-we[	*lost*	1+		MN? [but unclear], *hapax**
2014 *r*	]de	S 2	12		Needn't be allative]*ra-i*: dat.pl.??
2014 *v*	]ra-i / ko[ ]	S 1	6		
5437	*lost*	] S 2	12+		
5442	a-]mi-ni-ṣị[	*lost*	1+		TN if reading (and restoration) correct
5443 *r*	ro-ru[	*lost*	1+		*ro.*: prob. MN dat.*, attst. in sheep tablets *u.*: TN or MN (both attested)
5443 *v*	ụ-ta-no , [	*lost*	1+		
5450	]me-no	2 S 2	48		
5452	] *MU*	*lost*	1+	Join with 5447 now rejected*	
5455	]no	V 1	1		
5456	ta-nu-[	*lost*	1+		
5457	*lost*	70	1260		*ta-nu-ko* attst. at PY
5458	*lost*	V 3̣	3̣	App: trace at left, perhaps]wẹ ?	
5471.1	]ṣị-na-jo	*lost*	1+		Both *hapax*, prob. MNs (Bennett 1989, 218)
5471.2	]-ni-ja-mo	*lost*	1+		
5477	]rạ-u-to[	*lost*	1+		
5481	*lost*	S 1	6		
5483	*lost*	S 1	6		
5493	]no	*lost*	1+		
5494	zẹ-[	*lost*	1+		
6001	]wa-ja , / qa-ṣạ[	*lost*	1+		
7336	*lost*	2 S 2	48		
8436	*lost*	] V 4̣[	4+	Joins 9087 [*KT*[6]]	

Fh	category and tablet text	OLE	= V	epigraphic notes	interpretation notes
8740	*lost*	2̣[ ]1̣	37+	Unit before 1̣ lost: either 37+ or 42+	
8802	]*vest.*[ ]o[	*lost*	1+		
9008	*lost*	?]32[?	32+	Unit of measure lost	
9017	]ẹ-ṛạ-[	*lost*	1+		
9021	*lost*	]S 1[	6+		
9030	]*vest.*[	*lost*	1+		
9042	]ḍọ[	*lost*	1+	Unascribed to hand*	
9043	*lost*	*lost*	1+		
9058	]*vest.*[	*lost*	1+		
9062	*lost*	3[	54+	App.: Perhaps 4̣[	
9063	]ni-ja	1̣[	18+		
9065	*lost*	] Ṣ[	6+		
9066	*lost*	?]2 V 3	15+	Unit of measure lost: either 15+ or 39+	
9068	]ṇẹ-[ ]*vest.*[	*lost*	1+		
9070	]ạ-p̣ạ-to-re[	*lost*	1+	App.: or Ṣ[and traces	*Hapax*?; theonym?;* cf. Gg(3) 5185?
9071	]2 ṛụ[	*lost*	2+		
9072	] ru-ki[	*lost*	1+	*vestigia* on *verso*	
9073.1 9073.2	*vest.*[*vest.* [	*lost* *lost*	1+ 1+	4 lines in all, .3-4 are *vacant*	
9074	]ẉạ-ṭẹ[	*lost*	1+		
9076	]jẹ-ẉẹ[	*lost*	1+		
9078	*vest.*[	*lost*	1+		
9079	ạ[	*lost*	1+	App.: ṃẹ[or other signs also possible.	
9080	*lost*	]S 2	12+	*KT*[6] app. notes]1̣ preserved on *verso*	
9081	*lost*	?]3̣[?	3+	Unit of measure lost	
9084	*lost*	?]5	5+	Unit of measure lost	
9085.1 9085.2	]*vest.*[ ]*vest.*[	*lost*	1+		
9088	*lost*	*lost*	1+		
9089	]*deest.*[	*lost*	1+		
9090	]*deest.*[	*lost*	1+		
9091	]*vest.*[	*lost*	1+	App.: Perhaps]ṛụ[	
9094	]ḍẹ	*lost*	1+		
9097	]ạ$_3$-ṃị[	*lost*	1+		
9098	]ṛạ[	*lost*	1+		
9099	]q̣ạ[	*lost*	1+		
9100	]j̣ạ-[	*lost*	1+		
9101	ẉị[	*lost*	1+		
9102.1 9102.2	]*vest.*[ ]*vac.*[	*lost*	1+		
9103	*lost*	?]1̣[?	1+	Unit of measure lost App.: Reading extremely doubtful.	
9104.1 9104.2	]*vest.*[ ]*vac.*[	*lost*	1+		
9107	]*vest.*[	*lost*	1+		
9108	]*vest.*[	*lost*	1+		
9149	] *vacat*	*lost*	1+	App.: Probable trace at left. Not certainly Fh tablet*	
	TOTAL 11		**1644+**		

Notes

General

Throughout the table, an asterisk indicates that there is a note below on the epigraphy or interpretation. Notes are given in order of the tablet numbers.

Interpretations follow *DMic*,. unless otherwise noted. Note that most of the forms given by *DMic.* as dative cannot be securely identified as such within the Linear B spelling rules and the determinations have been made on the basis of the assumption that most of the Fh records deal with disbursements. That this is true of *most* of the Fh documents is almost certainly correct, but we should bear in mind possible exceptions.

App. = Apparatus to *KT*[5] or *KT*[6].

The following are no longer considered Fh tablets: 988 (see note); 5337; 5727; 5970; 7571 (for all see note *s.v.* 5337); 8297 (see note); 8646 (may be Fh; see note).

Epigraphic notes

348: *i-su-ko-wo-do-to* is presumably understood for both lines, one entry referring to an *o-no* type disbursement, the other to a *qe-te-jo* type (but see Hutton 1990–1991, 111–12, 118–20).

359: Unclear whether or not there were originally two entries, as we do not know what *e-te-ja*[means (see Interpretation notes).

361: *ku-pi-ri-jo* covers both lines, but the reason for two entries is unclear. In some Fh tablets where two entries refer to the same recipient (or contributor) two different types of oil are recorded (e.g. 343 and 380). Here, however, no second descriptive term appears. From the layout, it is evidently not the case that one number was covered by *zo-a* and the other by *o-no*. *o-no* appears in the second line and it is not clear whether it is meant to cover the upper entry at all (*zo-a* clearly only refers to the second). Possibly, *o-no* was meant to cover both lines and the upper entry was meant to refer to 'ordinary' oil, while the lower one refers to this *zo-a* type. This is supported by an erasure at the end of the lower line of OLE 20. The upper line records OLE 21, so perhaps this number had first been written below, then when the scribe saw that that it would not fit well, he moved the number to the upper line?

362: *KT*^{5} apparatus notes 'text badly damaged'. Line .1: number followed by smaller unit, perhaps S 2 (Bennett) or V 4 (Ventris). Line .2: Some earlier readings (Ventris, Bennett) had seen *tu-ni-ja*. Ventris and Bennett differ on whether the unit of measure accompanying the 7 was OLE (Bennett) or S (Ventris); the former is to be preferred as S 7 should not (normally) appear (I am grateful to I. Image for drawing this to my attention). The figure in the table is given on the basis of this conclusion. Due to the poor preservation of the text, the scribal hand is regarded as uncertain (unascribed in *KT*^{5}), but the tablet was found with the other Fh tablets in the RCB (Firth 2000–2001a, 205) so was probably written by 141.

364: The oil ideogram at right is large, indicating there was only one entry, to which all text belongs.

366: The numbers come from Fh 5503, so although we assume here the quasi-join is correct (also accepted by Godart 1987, 202), we should note with some caution.

370: The number was almost certainly 70, judging from layout of the signs. The tablet comprises one entry only – Knossos in first line is not a separate entry and OLE is written large at right.

372: The number is 150, not 100 as in *CoMIK* I, 142. A new join (+5440) subsequent to *CoMIK* I supplies the further digits (Bennett *et al.* 1989, 203–4; *KT*^{5} 178; *CoMIK* IV, 220).

374: This tablet, recorded as missing, may in fact be the same tablet as Fh 5444, also in Group 2 (Firth 2000–2001b, 303).

378: It has been suggested that the reading may be wrong and that the correct reading is instead *ma to-qa* OLE (Firth 2000–2001b, 305, citing a personal communication from J.L. Melena). I have left the entry for the moment with 'MNs', but if the suggestion were confirmed (if that ever be possible since the tablet is missing), it should be moved to the *to-qa* group. Since the figure is lost in any case, it hardly matters for present purposes either way.

379: May join Fh <381> (Firth 2000–2001b, 305).

381: See 379 above.

384: The initial sign may have been *o* rather than *re* (Firth 2000–2001b, 306, citing a pers. comm. from J.L. Melena). Melena (1985, 481) notes there may have been a divider between *pi* and *ru*.

388: See 5434.

391: This suggestion is supported by Firth's reading of Evans' *Original Handlist* (Firth 2000–2001b, 306–7).

462: Different findspot (*probably* F3 – West Magazine IV; *Scribes Cnossos*, 23, 86, 106, 115; supported by Firth 2000–2001a, 175), and ascription to scribe doubtful (141?). See also Weilhartner 2005, 36.

998: Fh 998 has now been reclassified as X 998 and the reading changed from *e-ru-sa* OLE 1[to *e-ru-sa-mo*[. The apparatus comments that the former reading is 'much less likely' (*CoMIK* I, 412). Also, the findspot is given as I3, so there remains no reason to associate this with the Fh series (it had not been ascribed to h. 141 in any case).

1056: Fh 1056, 1057 and 1059 are apparently from a different findspot from the other Fh tablets, and are not securely identified as belonging to h. 141. (This does not mean they need be reclassified, however, since Fh is a series, not a set.) The scribal ascription is given with a question mark by Olivier (*Scribes Cnossos*, 85) and *KT*^{5} gives no ascription. (*CoMIK* I, 431–2 gives '141?', but the corrigenda in *CoMIK* IV, 295, corrects this to no ascription ('suppress «141»'), while still classifying the tablets as Fh.) However, it may be noted that every sign is formed in precisely the way that 141 forms his signs, with the possible exception of *na* on 1059. Thus, while it is rightly regarded as uncertain whether the tablets were written by 141, they could possibly be. (On the other hand, Olivier comments that pinacologically these tablets 'forment un lot à part (cf. la provenance) du point de vue de l'aspect' [*Scribes Cnossos*, 87].) The findspot appears to be K1, the Room of the Clay Signet (*Scribes Cnossos*, 86, 110; Firth 2000–2001a, 238) and there is a chance that these tablets are not contemporary (Firth 2000–2001a, 238–9), although the evidence is inconclusive. Given the various doubts, these tablets should arguably be considered separately, but the amounts involved are fairly small (V 6, 3 and 1), and do not greatly affect the calculations here in any case, so have been included in the table. See also Weilhartner 2005, 36.

1057: See 1056.

1059: See 1056.

5337: 5337, 5723, 5970, 7571 are taken as Fh in Godart 1987, 203–4, but are all classed as X in *CoMIK* and *KT*[6], and are not listed by Firth (2000–2001a, 205) as coming from the RCB. Nothing suggests any of the three 5000–series tablets here are likely to come from the RCB, on which see Firth & Melena 2000–2001. X 5337 is from 'Batch A', fragments mostly coming from the East–West Corridor (Firth & Melena 2000–2001, 321–2); X 5723 is 'Batch G', fragments mostly from the North Entrance Passage plus a few from Mag. XV (*loc. cit.* p. 323); X 5970 is from 'Batch J', fragments mostly from North Entrance Passage and East–West Corridor (*loc. cit.* p. 324).
5434: See Interpretation notes.
5444: See 347 above.
5447: The join with Fh 5452 was rejected post *KT*[5] (Bennett *et al.* 1989, 216–17), so *MU* 7 is no longer read on this tablet. For possible reading see Interpretation notes.
5452: Join with Fh 5447 (Group 2) now rejected; see 5447 for references. This leaves the tablet without an apparent oil ideogram (*MU* 7 is read), although it is still considered an Fh tablet (on analogy with Fh 347 and –371).
5503: See 366 above.
5506: The apparatus notes that the vestigia in line .a perhaps reads *te*-[.]-*ro* or *te*-[.]-*i*; that in line .b perhaps reads *wo*-[.]-*ja-ra-de* or *wo*-[.]-*wo-ra-de*.
8297: This is taken as Fh by Godart (1987, 205) with the possible theonym *qe-ra*[-*si-ja*, but the tablet is now classified as X (*KT*[5], *KT*[6]) and unascribed to a hand, so is excluded from the table.
8646: Classified as X in *KT*[5] and *CoMIK*, but *KT*[6] queries whether it may be an Fh tablet. Unascribed to hand.
9042: Unascribed to hand and not in Firth's RCB list (2000–2001a, 205), but given as Fh by *KT*[6] (but not *KT*[5]).
9064: Reading and apparatus comment from *KT*[6] (*KT*[5] had noted this as a possible reading).
9149: Not in *KT*[5] as Fh or X but *CoMIK* IV and *KT*[6] have as Fh with hand uncertain ('141?').

Interpretation notes
339: *DMic.* notes probably AN fem. **opāwon-eia*, better than an adj. in *-eia* (Killen 1983c, 82), but I see no grounds for choosing. Killen suggests a possessive adjective in *-eiā* derived from an (unattested) MN *o-pa-wo*, in parallel with other possible adjectives of this type elsewhere in the series: *ko-ki-de-jo* from the MN *ko-ki-da* (see –5465), *ku-ru-me-ne-jo* from the MN *ku-ru-me-no* (see –5502). These may qualify OLE, while *o-pa-wo-ne-ja* may qualify *to-qa*. I am grateful to J.T. Killen for discussion on this point.
340: *ka-ro* is *hapax* at KN and the sign-group in PY Ub 1318.6 represents a different word.
344: *ka-pa-ri-jo* attested U 4478.14, Vc 72, V 60, V 77.
345: A man *du-ru-po* appears in the *qa-si-re-wi-ja* of *a-nu-to* in As 1516.17; he needn't be the same man.
347: *ma-ro-ne* is securely attested at KN only in Fh 347 (Group 3c) and –5246 (Group 3a). It is probably the dative of *ma-ro*, attested as a MN at Pylos in Cn 328.2 (note that the other appearance of this sign-group at Pylos, in Cn 40.10.12, must be a TN not MN, probably a nom.pl. of rubric replacing the more usual dat.-loc. *ma-ro-pi*). There may be a few other attestations of the MN at Knossos, but in each case the sign-group is broken at left and *-ma-ro* could be the ending of a different name (KN Dc 1148.B, V 7513.1, B 1055.8, and perhaps X 7947). In any case, the word certainly does not refer to the same person in the different instances. The word in 347.2, *a-ri-to*-[.]-*jo*, is unattested elsewhere and may be either a MN or perhaps an adjective describing a type of oil (*DMic.* I, 104). Godart (1987, 203) takes it as a MN, but given that the letter size is the same as that of the word *o-no*, whereas the letter size for the MN *we-we-ro* is larger, it may be that both issues pertain to *we-we-ro*. (If the second entry, which does seem 'subsidiary', did refer to a MN, perhaps it was meant to be subsumed under the payment to the first man, perhaps as a sub-worker? But this is mere guessing.)
352: The word is rightly noted with question marks in *DMic.* (I, 168) as '¿quiza relacinado con el culto?', but the guess is tenuous, based on a supposed link with a form of Zeus questionable in Mycenaean (Gérard-Rousseau 1968, 60 n 5). The word is *hapax* (it was formerly read in Fh 5502, but no longer – see note to 5502). For similar doubts see Godart 1969, 60–1.
353: *ra-ma-na-de*: *DMic.* (II, 210) notes 'prob. designación de un santuario', but the TN+*de* formula is not exclusively used in offerings situations (cf. PY An 35) and the Fh series does not deal primarily with offerings so there is no support from either form or context. Godart (1969, 57) does take this as a sanctuary. The only other possible occurrence of the word (without the final -*de*) is in Ai(2) 762 (broken at left) with MUL and the term *e-ne-ra* (obscure, something to do with textiles). *de-ma-si*: *DMic.* (I, 165–6) has this as probably dative plural, possibly of a personal appellative, but it could also be a reference to skins (see *DMic. loc. cit.* for references to previous suggestions along these lines) and Shelmerdine has made a case for taking this, together with the references to 'tanners', as evidence for industrial disbursements in the Fh series (Shelmerdine

1995, 103). However, it may after all be a dative plural group receiving offerings at a shrine; see chapter text, Group 6 and n 94 below).

356: *o-mi-ri-jo-i* is probably a dative plural appellative of some sort (*DMic.* II, 23–4). Proposed interpretations are based on etymological guesses and cannot be confirmed. Mühlestein (1958, 223) suggested /*omrioihi*/ cf. classical ὄμβριος 'rainy', attested as an epithet of Zeus; possibly rain-demons or rain-priests in parallel with the 'Priestess of Winds' of the Fp tablets. Various morphological criticisms have been made of the suggestion (Gérard-Rousseau 1968, 152; *Documents*, 564; Ruijgh 1967a, 189, 452), but the issue remains unresolved (see Thompson forthcoming). (Although it doesn't impact on the philological arguments either way, it is worth noting here in passing that the archaeological support Mühlestein adduces for rain-gods (*PM* IV, 450) is based on the Thisbe treasure, now known to be a forgery, so does not stand; a parallel with the 'Priestess of Winds' would still of course be acceptable.) Another possibility would be /*homilioihi*/, perhaps with the sense of 'those who preside over the ὅμιλος' 'crowd, throng' (Carratelli 1955, 228). The one factor not reliant on etymological guesses which might support a religious connection is the parallel of (apparently) dative plural groups in the Fr series (e.g. *di-pi-si-jo-i*). However, not all dative plural groups had religious connections and in the end all that is really clear is that the word refers to recipients of oil (Godart 1969, 60–1; also *DMic. loc. cit.* with further references). Note the sign-group is *hapax*: a possible appearance elsewhere (in C 911 as an MN) cited by Mühlestein is now read differently.

359: *e-te-ja*: cf. the obscure term *e-te-jo* (Gg 521)? Even if it is the same term, we do not know what it refers to. (Gg 521 is a totalling tablet – see Section 4.2.1.5.)

360: Godart originally included this tablet in his anthroponym group (1969, 41), but later specifically excludes it on the (reasonable) grounds that it is difficult to classify (1987, 208 n. 14). I have left it with the anthroponyms, but without any real conviction. Since the numbers are in any case lost, it hardly matters for present purposes. *ma-si-dwo* is written large at left and was apparently meant to cover both entries. *DMic.* (I, 428) has it as an MN in the dative, which is followed by most scholars, but since the word is (probably) *hapax* certainty is impossible. Risch (1957, 32 n. 14) suggests a TN and a possible comparison with]-*si-du-wo*[on X 1000 (the apparatus to KT^5 notes '*ma-si-du-wo* possible'), but this tablet is now classified as Np(2) and other tablets in that set have an MN rather than a TN in the parallel place on the tablet, so the likelihood (but again without much conviction) is on the side of an MN. *ki-ra-*56-so* may also be a MN, but it is likewise *hapax*; as noted by *DMic.*, it may possibly be compared with the MN *ka-ra-*56-so* (note different vowel) attested at Pylos (En 659.19; Eo 269).

377: Godart (1987, 203) puts this with the *a-pu-do-si* tablets but see chapter text (Group 2).

380: No plausible word with the same ending: *i-jo-te* is a verb (numerous attestations), *ki-ri-jo-te* a description of sheep,]-*re-wi-jo-te* (PY Aq 64.1) a participle (*DMic.* II, 248).

384: If Melena's suggestion is correct (see Epigraphical notes) this could be *o-pi ru-nu-we* (perhaps dative of the attested AN *ru-nu* in Ln 1568.4b).

385: Godart (1987, 204) includes this with the MNs, but the word is *hapax* and it is impossible to be sure. *DMic.* (I, 188) simply notes the term is obscure.

388: See 5434 below.

389: Godart (1987, 204) includes this with the MNs, and this is followed by *DMic.* (I, 184), but reasons for taking it as 'Unclear' are that (1) the term is (probably) *hapax*, (2) the word is incomplete, possibly at both ends, and (3) the tablet is missing so that no verification of the reading is possible. If an early suggestion by Melena that **83* = *nwe* is correct, the word could possibly be compared with *qa-*83-to*, attested as a MN on KN Sc 257, but this is speculative and the suggestion remains unconfirmed (see Melena forthcoming).

392: Godart (1987, 204) has this as a MN, and this is preferred by *DMic.* (II, 390 *s.v. u-ru-pi-ja*[), but noting that it could instead be a TN or ethnicon (cf. PY *u-ru-pi-ja-jo*?) (*loc. cit.* with references).

462: If the reading is correct (see KN V(5) 1043.B where the same reading is also possible), this will probably be an ethnic of *ku-pa-sa* (attested on KN V(2) 145.3).

1059: *wi-na-jo* is attested in Da 1197, Db 1225, –1282, –5198, Dv 1330, K(1) 875. Most of these must be different individuals, but the *wi-na-jo* of Dv 1330 has some chance of being the same person as in Fh 1059 since he is located at *e-ra* (although this could just as well be coincidence – given that the name was obviously popular, there is no reason that two men in the same place might not have had the same name). The word also appears on stirrup-jars at Midea and Knossos.

5246: See 347.

5429: *hapax*: *wa-pa-no* (nom.) in PY Jn 601.4 is a different name.

5431: Probably, as Killen (1995, 219) suggests, the tablet refers to payments for beds: *o-na*, neut.pl. of *o-no* 'benefits'/ 'payments'; *de-mi-ni-jo* gen.pl. /*demniōn*/ 'bed/bedding' gen. of reason explaining why the payments had been made (the plural *de-mi-ni-ja* is attested elsewhere in Linear B, e.g. PY Vn 851; *de-mi-ni-jo* on the Pylos sealing Wr 1326 is probably neut.sg.nom.).

5432: If the reading *na-u-pi-ri-jo-i* is correct, perhaps 'to the Nauplians'? But even if this were so, the reference needn't be to the Argolid, since another place with the same name could exist in Knossian territory (*Documents*, 562; Bennett *et al.* 1989, 215–16).

5434: The apparatus of *KT* restores *to-*]*so*, but *so* could also be the end of a toponym, giving a tablet similar in structure to e.g. Fh 340 or 349 (TN + *a-pu-do-si*), as noted recently by Firth who further suggests that possibly 5434 joined with 388 giving the contribution for *tu-ri-so* (Firth 2000–2001b, 306). Godart originally also (1968a, 598–9) took 5434 as a standard TN + *a-pu-do-si* tablet. He subsequently suggested (1969, 39–40) that it could be a totalling tablet for *zo-a* oil, but later (1987, 203 with n 10) abandoned this view, rightly noting that the restoration *to-*] was 'purement arbitraire'.

5436: Godart (1968a, 604) first takes the ending *-de* as an allative, but later (1987, 207) lists it as an AN. I take it here as 'unclear'.

5443: Assumed on basis of other tablets, but of course it doesn't *have* to be dative.

5446: No other word starts with *u-ne*. *a-nu* is the beginning of a number of ANs (*a-nu-ko, a-nu-mo, a-nu-to, a-nu-wa, a-nu-wa-to, a-nu-wi-ko*), and there is no means of choosing between them. Godart (1987, 205) withdraws his earlier comments (1969, 53) about a particular association of *a-nu-* with *to-ro-qa*, in light of new evidence.

5447: *KT*[6] app.: ']*wị-ki-ro* possible.' *-ki-ro* is attested as ending of *o-ki-ro* (MN, Dv 1509, a shepherd at Phaistos), *si-ki-ro* (obsc. in U 8210, something to do with hides, if this is the value of *DI+PTE*), and *wo-ki-ro*, attested at Pylos. (*po-ki-ro*[which appears on a couple textile tablets is not an MN but probably the start of *po-ki-ro-nu-ka*.) *wi-ki-ro* is not otherwise attested.

5465: *ko-ki-de-jo* is probably a possessive adjective based on a man's name *ko-ki-da*, attested in Sd 4403.a, So 4430.a (Killen 1983, 73). For the function of this type of possessive adjective see note to 5502. One might speculate that *qa*[was the beginning of *qa-si-re-wi-ja*, but it could just as well have been a man's name.

5487: See chapter text (Group 9) and note to 5502 (for a possible parallel for the form of the word).

5502: *ku.* is probably a possessive adjective based on the attested MN *ku-ru-me-no* (KN Sc 236; also at Pylos and Thebes) (Killen 1983, 81–2). As Killen (1983, 84–8, esp. 88) has elucidated, the function of the *e-ja*/*-jo* suffix was to express not a patronymic 'son of Klumenos' (the form of which would be *ku-ru-me-ni-jo*, attested in Da 1173), but 'belonging to, or connected with, Klumenos'. The next word, *de-u-ki-jo*[, recalls the month name at KN attested in the Fp(1) set, *de-u-ki-jo-jo*, in which case the tablet might record a religious offering since month names are invariably (or almost invariably) found only on offerings records. However, *de-u-ki-jo* is attested as a man's name in MY Au 102.7, so this may be the correct explanation. (A little support for this alternative interpretation comes from the observation that while the end of the tablet is broken it appears that not very much has been lost and, while there might have been room in missing area for a further *jo*, there would not have been room for this plus *me-no* which is usually – but not invariably – written in the case of month names.) Note that the earlier reading of the word as *de-u-jo-i* (Godart 1969, 42; 1987, 204; followed in *DMic.* I, 408) is now abandoned (*KT*[5] 185; *CoMIK* III, 87).

5505: *me-ra-de* may be a TN+*de* (*DMic.* I, 437 takes it as 'probably' this, but also notes the possibility it is an AN). Melena (1974b, 316) takes it as a TN, citing it as a possible parallel for the word *me-a-de* on E 842.1b (an offering record) which he suggests may be a scribal error for *me-ra-de*. This of course cannot be confirmed, nor can the existence of a TN *me-ra*. The only attestation of *me-ra* (noted by Melena) is on Uf(2) 839, but this is in a position not encouraging interpretation at a TN (*da-*22-to* already appears on this tablet in the standard place for Uf(2) TNs, and two TNs on one of these tablets would be unusual). Godart (1987, 205) has *me-ra-de* in the group of 'allatifs, desservants de sanctuaire et divinités'. It is grouped for present purposes with the TNs, but could just as well be something else.

9070: Killen (1992, 361–2) suggests]*a-pa-to-re*[might be a theonym if it can be related to Gg(3) 5185, but as he notes, we cannot be certain the word is complete. It is left here as 'Unclear'.

---

suggests that Fh 367 was a totalling tablet for disbursements,[68] but this was based primarily on similarities in various figures which are no longer tenable. We return to the function of this record below.

[68] Godart 1968a, 604, see also 606; 1987, 202, 209–10. He calls it 'le total des sorties d'huile' as opposed to the *a-pu-so-si* 'entrée' document Fh 366. Note this terminology is sometimes translated in English by referring to 'exit' and 'entry' records.

2. Taxation records

Group 2 tablets include the word *a-pu-do-si* /*apudosis*/, the standard term for tax payments; it is understood to refer to actual payments/deliveries rather than assessments.[69] (It can also refer to goods being returned to the palace from workshops to which raw materials had been allocated,[70] but the appearance of town names here suggests taxation.) The members are identical to those in Godart's 'Groupe *a-pu-do-si*',[71] except that the totalling tablet Fh 366 is with the totalling tablets in Group 1, and a doubtful member of the group, Fh 377, is listed separately under 2b.[72] Where we can tell, the payments are from towns,[73] as is common for taxation records. Fh 5451, recording the contribution from Amnisos, further notes that the payment is for 'this year', another rubric commonly found on such records.[74]

The extant figures in 2a total V 2913, but three figures are lost. In the table they are restored as 1+ each, following our standard practice and giving a total of V 2916+, but the real amounts would likely have been much higher since figures for this type of record are typically large – extant figures on the documents here range from V 318+ to V 957. Adding three times the smaller amount would give a total of V 3858 (318 x 3 = 945; 945 + 2913 = 3858) and adding three times the larger would give V 5784 (957 x 3 = 2871; 2871 + 2913 = 5784). Or one might prefer to take the average of the extant figures (V 582.6), which would yield V 4660.8. These restorations are of course hypothetical, but help gain a sense of how much may have been lost.

An important question for us to consider here is whether the figures on the individual *a-pu-do-si* records would have, in the original state of the dossier, added up to the figure on the *a-pu-do-si* totalling record, Fh 366 (V 6107). Godart has made various attempts to determine this, but as he rightly remarks, it is difficult to find a convincing formula.[75] One possibility he explores is that Fh 377, the tablet relegated to 2b in our table, should be included in the *a-pu-do-si* total.[76] Using our figures (i.e. unconverted to litres), this would give an overall total of V 5651 (= 2913 + 2738), but there remain the three 'missing' figures to be added in. If this is done according to the average calculated above we have V 7398.8, which is much more than the figure on the totalling tablet. The problem is exacerbated if the average for the missing figures is calculated with Fh 377 included, which is what Godart rightly does since if this tablet is to be included in the sum it should also contribute to the average. The resulting average on our figures would be V 941.8,[77] and adding three times this amount (for the lost figures) to the total we have: (941.8 x 3) + 5651 = 2825.5 + 5651 = V 8476.5, which as Godart notes is far too high. He subsequently subtracts V 2738 (the figure on Fh 377) obtaining V 5738.5, which is again too low, although perhaps closer to the right order of magnitude, but

[69] See *Documents*, 217, 439, 533; Killen 1984b, esp. 183–4; 1985, 270; Duhoux 1968, esp. 85–6; 1976a, 160; *Mémoires* IV, esp. 107; Foster 1977a, 25; 1977b, 54; *DMic*. I, 88–9.

[70] E.g. Killen 1992b, 367.

[71] Godart 1987, 203.

[72] There are several reasons for doubting that Fh 377 should be included in the group. The evidence for its being an *a-pu-do-si* + TN tablet is not strong. Only a single sign is preserved and the reading is not secure so it is not certain that the sign is *si*. Yet even if it were *si*, there are a great many words attested in Linear B (nearly 60) which have this ending. Also, the number on the tablet is very much higher than those on any of the securely identified *a-pu-do-si* + TN tablets – nearly three times even the highest one (V 957 on Fh 349). Figures of this magnitude are attested in the extant Fh documents, but not in Group 2. Rather, they are seen in Group 3, the tablets having to do with perfumery and it could be that Fh 377 was this type of tablet. However, we cannot be certain and the tablet should simply be regarded as 'unclear'.

[73] Definitely so for Fh 349 (*ru-ki-to*) and –5451 (Amnisos); probably also for –340 but *ka-ro* is *hapax* so we cannot be certain it is a TN; the others are too broken to tell. See Godart 1968a, 599.

[74] See e.g. Killen 1984b, 176.

[75] Godart 1987, 210.

[76] Godart 1987, 203.

[77] 426 + 957 + 318 + 540 + 672 + 2738 = 5651; 5651 ÷ 6 = 941.8.

rightly concludes that the procedure is unconvincing.[78] A particular difficulty is that this figure was obtained using the number on Fh 377 to calculate the average, and if it is decided that Fh 377 should *not* be added to the total, then it should not be used to calculate the average either. If we do not include Fh 377 we again have V 4660.8, the original figure above.

On the whole, it is probably best simply to accept that too much is uncertain for us to be able to bring the total for amounts on individual records in line with the totalling tablet.[79] Since, on the other hand, we do have a totalling record, it would be wrong to *add* the individual payments to the figure since the possibility exists that they were subsumed under it. Hence, for present purposes, it is probably best to take note of the figures for individual payments, but to use the figure from the totalling record (V 6107) in estimating overall resources.

3. Perfumery records

Group 3 tablets have to do with the perfume industry, and probably concern oil for production and related matters. They all include the sign-group *ku-pi-ri-jo*. The meaning of this word has been long disputed but Killen has recently drawn together convincing support for a long-standing suggestion that the word is here should be interpreted as a man's name, *Kuprios*, rather than an adjective /*kuprios*/ 'of Cypriot origin or type', and argues that this man was an important official within the perfume industry and was probably also a 'Collector'.[80] As Killen points out, *Kuprios* is seen making issues to other men, probably perfume manufacturers, in tablets such as Fh 347 and –5246 (and probably Fh 5446 and –371), in parallel with the issue to a perfumer on PY Un 267 by *Alxoitas*, one of the 'Collectors' at Pylos.[81] He also draws on an observation by Olivier that the amount associated with *Kuprios* on Fh 372 (V 2700) stands in the ratio of 31:69 with the amount recorded in the totalling tablet Fh 367, which is very similar to the 30:70 ratio of 'Collector' to 'non-Collector' flocks seen in the sheep tablets and probably in the Lc(1) cloth and wool records.[82] It is further important that *Kuprios* is associated with the transaction term *o-no*. Killen supports the suggestion that this word derives from the same root as the Classical Greek verb ὀνίνημι, and has the sense of 'benefit' or 'payment', suggesting that 'it is used for "benefits" of various kinds, including "benefits" given to "collectors" by virtue of their position and "benefits" (or "payments") given in return for commodities or service'.[83] Hence the *o-no* given to *Kuprios* on Fh 372 would be a 'benefit' by virtue of his status as 'Collector' and the *o-no* issued to other men would be in line with 'benefits' or 'payments' for services such as seems to be the case with the issues to a net-

---

[78] Godart 1987, 210.

[79] In addition to the (likely) possibility that some tablets have been lost, it may also be that some towns had not yet made their payments, or that these had not yet been incorporated into the totalling tablet figures, as Godart (1987, 210) suggests.

[80] See Killen 1995, 215–21; Olivier 1996–1997, 287–91; also Killen 1979b, 178; Bennett *et al.* 1989, 216–17; Olivier 2001, 151, 154, 156. For a view to the contrary see e.g. Palaima 1991, 293–5. The word does seem to be an adjective meaning 'Cypriot' on Od 667, as suggested by Melena (Bennett *et al.* 1989, 204–5) and accepted by e.g. Killen (1995, 215) and Olivier (1996–1997, 287–8). However, it is clearly a man's name at Pylos in Cn 131.3, Cn 719.7, Jn 320.3, and most likely also Un 443 (see Section 5.2.3). A connection between *ku-pi-ri-jo* and perfume manufacture has long been noted (e.g. Melena 1976a; Foster 1977a, 30, 32), and Godart (1968c, 68; 1987, 209–10) saw the term as a professional designation referring to unguent-boilers, in parallel to the term *a-re-pa-zo-o* attested at Pylos. However, Killen's elucidation is more consistent with the evidence. (Also note, there is no longer any reason to speculate that *Kuprios* was a god, as in Foster 1977a, 31.) See Killen 2001a for a discussion of the management of the perfume industry at Pylos, which has parallels with the Knossian situation. See also Speciale 2001, 156–7, for some important observations on the organisation of oil production at Knossos. While appreciating most of her points, I do not however understand her objection to *Kuprios* being both a palace official *and* a 'Collector'.

[81] Killen 1979b, 178; 1995, 217.

[82] Killen 1995, 216–17; Olivier 1996–1997, 290.

[83] Killen 1995, 219. On *o-no* see also Chadwick 1964, 21, 23; *Documents*, 506; Killen 1995, 218, 223–4; *DMic*. II, 27–8.

maker and a weaver (or weavers) on PY Un 1322 (Sections 5.5.2 and 6.4.1.1).[84] In sum, *Kuprios* is likely to have been an important official in the perfume industry who received a beneficial proportion of the resources for his own use and who was in charge of issuing both oil for manufacture and 'payments' to perfumers for their work.

The documents have been divided into three sub-groups: 3a includes texts without the word *o-no*, 3b has texts with *o-no*, and 3c has a document with both types of entries plus a very broken document which clearly contains the word *ku-pi-ri-jo* but about which nothing further can be said. Records in 3a are probably issues to perfumers for manufacture, although we cannot be certain of this in the case of the broken texts since the word *o-no* may have appeared in the missing areas. In 3b, the first two tablets appear to record *o-no* 'payments' to *Kuprios* (for the word *zo-a* in Fh 361 see Group 10 below), and the third tablet, Fh 5447, perhaps involved an *o-no* 'payment' to another man most of whose name is lost. In sub-group 3c, Fh 347.1 records a small issue to *ma-ro-ne*, who received a substantial amount in Fh 5246 (sub-group 3a). Line .2 records an *o-no* payment to a man *we-we-ro*, perhaps a beneficial 'payment' for himself, and adds a further entry the status of which is unclear (see notes to the table). It is conceivable that *ma-ro-ne* was also receiving a payment here with respect to *o-no*, but this is uncertain.

The issues to perfumers for manufacture amount to V 2042+, and the *o-no* disbursements amount to V 3316+ (or V 3457+ with Fh 347). In light of the interpretation of the function of *o-no* discussed above it might be thought surprising that the *o-no* payments would collectively amount to *more* than the issues for manufacture, but the records are too incomplete to read very much into this. Some figures are certainly lost (e.g. Fh 5446 and 5490), and it is likely enough that some whole tablets are lost altogether.[85] Further, we cannot be certain that the tablets are dealing with oil which is all at the same stage of manufacture. For instance, did *o-no* 'payments' consist of already perfumed oil? Or were they being issued for the purpose of being treated in 'Collector' owned workshops? These questions are difficult to answer, but the important thing to notice for our purposes here is that a very large amount of oil is moving about in the perfume industry: at least some V 5499, perhaps some 8798.4 litres. This is of the same order of magnitude as amounts recorded on the totalling records, and if Olivier's observation about the ratio between the amount of oil issued to *Kuprios* as an *o-no* and the amount on the totalling tablet Fh 367 is correct it may be that Fh 367 was a totalling tablet for the perfume industry. This would help explain why it registers *less* oil than is found in the totalling record for the *a-pu-do-si* payments. However, it is difficult to be sure, and for present purposes it is probably better to take our figures from the Group 3 records, which do clearly deal with the perfume industry.

4. Miscellaneous transaction records

Group 4 has records which contain miscellaneous transaction terms but which do not belong in the groups already discussed. In sub-group 4a, Fh 348 and –5431, with the payment terms *o-no*, *o-na* and *qe-te-jo*, record disbursements although, unlike Group 3, there is no necessary connection here with the perfume industry. In sub-group 4b, Fh 364 may record a disbursement if the possible reading]*ḍọ-ke* noted in the apparatus is correct,[86] but this is uncertain and the record should be omitted from our final calculations since its function is unclear (the number is lost in any case[87]). In sub-group 4c, Fh 370 is a record of oil 'received' (*de-ka-sa-to* /*dexato*/) at Knossos, but the nature and beneficiary of the receipt are unclear.

[84] Killen *loc. cit.*; see also Bendall 2003, 211, with further references.

[85] Or are too damaged to be recognised as members of this group – note the very large number of 'Unclear' tablets of Group 11.

[86] Possibly end of *a-pu-do-ke* or *o-do-ke*, with the man *a-ku-tu-ru-wo* the authorising official and]*u-te-si* perhaps a recipient group in dative plural (*pace* Godart; see next footnote).

[87] Godart (1987, 208 n 14) similarly omits it. He comments that the record is parallel to Fh 370, but the verbs here have the opposite force so this remains unclear.

Godart takes the tablet as a disbursement record with *]mu-to*, against whom the oil is registered, being a 'Collector'.[88] But we could also take this as a delivery record of oil being received *by* the palace, with *]mu-to* perhaps the official responsible for the transaction. The word *a-pu-do-si* does not appear (there does not seem to be space for it in the missing parts of the tablet), but this does not preclude the possibility that this was a record of incoming goods of some sort.[89] However this may be, since the purpose of the document is obscure we should take note of the large number, but be cautious about adding it to anything else.

5. Anthroponyms

Group 5 tablets are characterised by MNs, probably most or all in the dative although it usually is not possible to tell from the spellings.[90] Interpretations in the table follow *DMic.* unless otherwise noted. Despite some uncertainties, these are probably all disbursements (even where they are nominatives they could be nominatives of rubric). None of the tablets here has any necessary connection with religion (on **56-i-ti*, see below under Group 9). They are probably issues for rations, although some may have been to named craftsmen for industrial use as discussed in connection with Group 6.

6. Industrial disbursements

Group 6 tablets probably record either rations or disbursements of oil for industrial purposes (or both).[91] Tablets in 6a record disbursements to craftsmen identified by their occupational titles. Fh 5428 records an unusually large disbursement (V 222) to the tanner(s) (either */wrīnēwei/* dat.sg. 'to the tanner' or */wrīnēwes/* 'tanners', nominative of rubric).[92] This could have been intended as rations for the worker(s), but in light of the high number is more likely to have been intended for use in industrial processing.[93] Shelmerdine suggests that the two tablets in sub-group 6b recording *de-ma-si*, possibly */dermasi/* 'for skins', may relate to a similar function.[94] An issue to a tailor(s) or leather-worker(s) in Fh 1056 may also have been for industrial use,[95] possibly, if the first, as a treatment to give a particular sheen to the

---

[88] Godart (1987, 207 n 13, 208). Note he takes 'Collector' however not in the sense suggested by Killen, but as a person receiving the allotment 'pour le traiter industriellement ou pour la rédistribuer à d'autres groupes de personnels'.

[89] Note that *de-ka-sa-to* and *de-ko-to* appear on the KN Le cloth receipt records, where *a-pu-do-si* is also found. I am grateful to J.T. Killen for bringing this to my attention. One wonders whether Fh 370 might not be a record of receipts from estates immediately surrounding Knossos itself. The palace might well manage its own local estates in a slightly different manner than those of the outlying areas.

[90] The group is smaller than the one given by Godart (1987, 203–4), partly because we here list separately occupational terms (Group 6) and dative plural groups (Group 7), plus have regarded numerous entries as 'unclear' (Group 11). Differences are as follows. Entries on –347.2 are in Group 3 with the rest of the tablet; –348 is in Group 4; –350 and –381 are in Group 10 (neither records an AN); –352, –356 and –5498 are in Group 7; –5337, –5723, –5970, and –7571 are no longer regarded as Fh tablets so are omitted from the table altogether (see Notes to Table 3-6 *s.v.* 5337); –5449 is now joined to –5431 (Group 4); –1056, –5432 and –5443 are in Group 6; and the following tablets are regarded as 'unclear': –385, –387, –389, –5450, –5455, –5456, –5471, –5477, –5493, –5494, and –6001. I include one tablet, –360, excluded by Godart (see Notes to table, *s.v.* 360).

[91] Godart (1968a, 599–602; 1987, 203–4) discusses most of the tablets here with his AN group; see Godart 1969, 48–51 for a separate discussion of some of the occupational terms. On *ka-ke-u* see also Shelmerdine 1988, 355; Speciale 2001, 152 n 26. It does not matter greatly for present purposes whether one considers the disbursement to be for industrial processing or for rations.

[92] Godart takes the term as an AN referring to a 'Collector' (Godart 1968a, 600; 1987, 208; see also *Thèbes* I, 168).

[93] Foster 1977a, 34 with n 57; Melena 1983b, 117–18; see also Shelmerdine 1985, 130; 1995, 103.

[94] Shelmerdine 1995, 103. However, as J.T. Killen kindly points out to me, Fh 353 with *ra-ma-na-de de-ma-si* would be odd if an 'industrial' record since a name of a recipient would be expected. It is more likely that the tablet records a religious offering 'to' a shrine (+ *de*) with *de-ma-si* the name of a cult group (cf. *ru-do-ro-i*, etc.). I have left the tablet in Group 6, but agree this explanation is the more likely (see also note to Table 3-6 s.v. 353).

[95] For the suggestion that *ra-pte-re* may refer to persons sewing leather rather than cloth see *Documents*, 578 *s.v. ra-pte-ri-ja*.

textiles.[96] In her discussion of evidence for disbursements of this type, Shelmerdine suggests that a number of further Fh tablets may record issues for textile industrial processing, on the grounds that the TNs involved are well-known textile centres: Fh 373 with *tu-ni-ja*, –5443 with *u-ta-no*, –9067 with *da-*83-ja*, and –357 and –1059 with *e-ra* and a man described by the ethnicon *e-ra-jo* respectively.[97] This may well be right, but it is difficult to be certain since most of the texts are rather fragmentary, and these documents have been left for the time being with the TN group (Group 8) or, in the case of Fh 1059, with the MN group (Group 5). Fh 5443 appears in the 'Unclear' group (Group 11), for reasons discussed there. Our total figures would not be greatly affected in any case since the numbers on three of these tablets are lost. The two which survive (on –357 and –1059) would add V 80 to the present group.

7. Dative plural groups

Group 7 has tablets with occupation titles in dative plural. These are sometimes suggested as having religious connections (see Notes to Table 3-6, *s.v.* 352, 356, 5498), although on the whole all are quite obscure. *DMic.* rightly refrains from making a judgement beyond that they are personal appellatives of some type and refer to recipients of oil; Godart likewise recommends caution.[98] They are separated out here because it is essentially unclear whether they are rations for individuals, disbursements for religious purposes or disbursements for some other purpose (and not all need have the same explanation). For present purposes they are taken as relating to religion based on parallels with the Fr series.

8. Toponyms

Group 8 has tablets where the main information supplied (or surviving) is one or more toponym with the allative or forms that appear to be this. Particularly frequent is the sign-group **47-so-de*, instances of which have been gathered together in sub-group 8a. This word appears only in the Fh series, and most of the tablets here are broken so there is little contextual evidence for the meaning. That it is indeed a TN+allative is supported by its appearance in parallel with the well attested TN *e-ra+de* on Fh 357. It is normally taken as the name of a shrine,[99] and this is followed here, although it is difficult to be sure. Some supporting evidence comes from Fh 462, where the word appears along with the occupational title *e-to-wo-ko*, which occurs elsewhere only in religious or quasi-religious contexts (a list of temple servants and two festival rations records at Pylos: An 39, Fn 50, Fn 79; see Section 2.3.3.1), and probably refers to a temple servant of some sort.[100] A further supporting argument, though not a very strong one, is that all other TNs which begin with the sign **47* certainly *are* shrines: **47-da-de* (Fp(1) 1.9), and **47-ku-to-de* (Fp(1) 13.1); see also **47-ta-qo*[on KN Xd 140.2b, probably an AN (or theonym?) rather than a TN, but with an apparent religious connection since it is associated with *da-pu-ri-ṭọ*[. Melena in a recent discussion has pointed out that in view of the absence of syllabogram **47* altogether in the writing of some of the most prolific scribes (writing about non-religious affairs), it is likely that 'the trait rendered

---

96 Shelmerdine 1985, 129–30; 1995, 103–4; see Robkin 1981 for experiments on treatment with oils; also Melena 1975a, 92–3; 1983b, 117. There is a possible parallel for issues of oil to textile workers in MY Fo 101 (Shelmerdine 1997, 390–1); although it could also be that rations were involved (Killen 1981).

97 Shelmerdine 1995, 103, 106 n 29. She also notes that there may be a further mention of tailors(?) if *ra*]-*pte-si* can be restored on Fh 5432 (Group 6b). But see n 95 above.

98 *DMic. s.v.*; Godart 1969, 60–1.

99 E.g. Killen 1987b, 163; *DMic.* II, 467; Gérard-Rousseau (1968) however omits it from her index of 'religious mentions', and see Shelmerdine's suggestion in the discussion of Group 6 above that Fh 357 which also records the TN *e-ra* dealt with an issue for industrial processing.

100 Olivier 1960, 62–8; Godart 1969, 49; Killen 2001b, 437–9. Note the Pylos lists of this type do sometimes include 'secular' staff who have been seconded for work at festivals, but the balance of probability is on the side of *e-to-wo-ko* referring to religious personnel. The other word on Fh 462, *a-ri-ja-wo-ne*, is a man's name in dative (the nominative appears on Uf(2) 990, referring to a *telestās* at the TN *qa-ra*; there is nothing to suggest he is the same man).

by means of the syllabogram was no longer considered necessary, but only a traditional "flavour" associated with certain peculiarly Cretan names.[101] This would be consistent with usage in religious contexts, although it certainly does not compel such a conclusion. We should also note, however, that the very large amount of oil with which **47-so-de* is associated in Fh 357 would be unusual for a religious offering and would be more in keeping with industrial disbursements such as in Group 6, as suggested by Shelmerdine who sees this tablet as recording industrial disbursements for the treatment of textiles. For present purposes the tablets in 8a will be taken as relating to religious offerings, but the uncertainties should be kept in mind.

In sub-group 8b,]**83-ja-de* is probably to be restored as *da-*]**83-ja-de*, which is explicitly linked with a shrine on Fp 363.2 (*da-*83-ja-de i-je-ro*). However, the TN also appears in non-religious contexts, in connection with shepherding (Dv 1086.B), and agriculture (E(2) 670). There is also an obscure reference to it in connection with the *wanax* and *po-pu-ri-jo* 'purple' in X 976.[102] The other TN with which *da-*83-ja* appears on Fh 365,]*ḍạ-so-de*, is no help in determining the context here since it is *hapax*.[103] It is generally taken as a shrine name, based on its appearance in the present tablet.[104] Although certainty is impossible, the small numbers on Fh 365 would be consistent with an offering, and it is taken here as a probable offering record. Finally, Fh 5467 is certainly an offering record, with the well attested shrine *di-ka-ta* in line .a, along with further probable reference to a shrine in line .b.[105]

In sub-group 8c we have two other apparent TN+*de* formations, but the connections here are unclear. In Fh 373, *tu-ni-ja* is a well-known TN, attested in sheep tablets (e.g. Db 1246) and in connection with textile production (e.g. Ak(1) 630, Lc(1) 547, Le 641). It does not appear in any securely identified offering record however, so the existence of a shrine at *tu-ni-ja* remains uncertain.[106] Fh 5505 contains a single word *me-ra-de* which might be a TN+*de* formation, but is again (probably) *hapax*.[107]

To sum up, we will for present purposes consider entries in sub-groups 8a and 8b as religious and leave 8c as 'unclear'. The amounts from 8a and 8b total V 146+, over half of it (V 79) notably derived from the questionable tablet in 8a, Fh 357.

9. Offerings records

Group 9 contains certain or probable offerings records. In sub-group 9a, Fh <390> and –5475 have words securely attested as recipients of offerings: *e-ri-nu* (Fp(1) 1.8) and *qe-ra-si-*[*ja* (Fp(1) 1.6 +)[108]. In 9b, **56-ti*[on Fh 9077, if complete, may be a theonym: **56-ti* is attested as a recipient of offerings on Fp(1) 15.2 (where the word is complete). However,]**5̣6̣-ti* is also found written on the edge of As 8342 where, whether complete or not, it refers to a man since the ideogram VIR is recorded. There is a further possible connection with two words which were placed among the MNs: **56-i-ti* (Fh 1057) and **56-ị-ti-jẹ*[(Fh 5487). The latter may

[101] Melena, forthcoming. But we should also note here Melena's observation that for h. 141 the syllabogram **47* is indistinguishable from *je*, so possibly we are not dealing with the specialist sign here.
[102] The only other possible occurrence is in X 7592, context lost. A man's name based on the TN, *da-*83-jo*, is also attested (Vc(2) 7517) .
[103] Assuming the reading is correct. Quite a few Knossian TNs end in *-so*, but no others in *-da-so* (the few words which have this ending are MNs).
[104] *DMic*. I, 158; Godart 1969, 57.
[105] Godart 1969, 57.
[106] Killen (1987b, 163–4), for instance, does not include it in his list of places in receipt of religious offerings.
[107] See Notes to Table 3–6.
[108] Godart (1969, 41) originally included *qe-ra-si-ja* among the MNs, but *qe-ra-si-* does not begin any attested MN whereas the theonym is attested in numerous documents. In a later article (Godart 1987, 205) Fh 5475 is omitted, while *qe-ṛạ*[*-si-ja* on –8297 is included under religious offerings. However, this tablet is now reclassified X (see Notes to Table 3-6).

possibly be a formation with the *-e-jo* suffix of the type discussed by Killen, other examples of which are found in the Fh series.[109] However, the word is not certainly complete so we cannot be sure, and in any case, since the suffix can apply to both MNs and theonyms, this does not help us determine what the word is here. Melena takes **56-ti* and **56-i-ti* as variants, probably referring to a theonym.[110] Godart notes that we cannot be certain whether they are variants or not[111] and takes **56-i-ti* as a MN.[112] *DMic.* takes **56-ti* as a probable theonym and **56-i-ti* as a probable MN,[113] which is followed here but without any strong conviction. Finally, Fh 2013 should be an offering record if *i-je-ro* is correctly read.[114]

10. Special descriptions

Group 10 has tablets which contain the terms *zo-a* (10a), *e-pi-ko-wa* (10a), *po-ro-ko-wa* (10b), *to-ro-qa* or *to-qa* (10c) or *ne-wo* (10d).[115] With the exception of *ne-wo*, which must be */newos/* 'new', none of these words is well understood. They are generally thought to refer to various different types, treatments or uses of oil. A full discussion is unnecessary for present purposes, but we may examine them briefly.

The word *zo-a* is commonly thought to represent */dzohā/*, derived from ζέω, perhaps indicating oil intended for boiling. Although other possibilities exist, the most likely explanation is that the oil so designated was somehow involved in perfume manufacture.[116]

The words *e-pi-ko-wa* and *po-ro-ko-wa* look as if they might have something to do with χέω 'I pour'. *e-pi-ko-wa* is generally accepted as **epikhowāi*, possibly 'for anointing' or 'for libations',[117] while *po-ro-ko-wa* is generally taken as nom. or dat.sg. of **prokhowā* (> προχοή) 'outpouring',[118] perhaps with the sense 'for libation'.[119] Whatever the case, neither word need

---

[109] Killen 1983c (see notes to Table 3-6 *s.v.* Fh 5502 for discussion). The reading comes from a join made after Killen wrote and so is not mentioned in his article, but for a suggestion that this is the same type of ending on Fh 5487 see Melena 1987a, 213. As J.T. Killen kindly points out to me, now that we know that dat.sg. of *-i* stems, at Thebes at least, is in *-je* (*ma-di-je*, etc.), another attractive possibility is that it is dat.sg. of **56-i-ti* (nom.); see Morpurgo Davies 1999, 396 n 18.

[110] Melena 1987a, 210, 213–14; also Killen 1992a, 356–8. J.T. Killen kindly points out to me that this is the likeliest explanation given the regular fluctuation in spelling of the *-i* diphthong and the possibility that the difference in spelling of this word corresponds to different hands: **56-ti* is written by h. 141, while **56-i-ti*/*-je* is written by a scribe who may, but need not be, h. 141 (h. 141??).

[111] Godart 1969, 58–9.

[112] Godart 1968a, 600; 1987, 204; but once as a theonym: 1969, 58. A former reading on tablet Fh 5487 (**56-ro*-[) is in his AN group (1969, 41, 44; see also 1987, 204). Fh 9077 is not included in his study as it came to light later (it is in *KT*[5], but not in *KT*[4]).

[113] *DMic.* II, 470–1, 473.

[114] *pe-da* is probably */peda/* 'towards, about' (*DMic.* II, 94).

[115] The list here differs from those of Godart in minor ways. The lists for *zo-a* are identical (cf. Godart 1987, 207), except that Fh 361 is here given in Group 3 since it mentions *ku-pi-ri-jo*. Godart (1987, 204) lists *po-ro-ko-wa* under the MNs (not claiming that they are MNs, however, but giving them as technical terms). For *to-ro-qa* (Godart 1987, 206) the list here adds Fh 376 and puts Fh 5446 in Group 3 since it mentions *ku-pi-ri-jo*.

[116] *DMic.* II, 459, with references. Godart (1968a, 605; 1987, 202) suggests oil from a second pressing, but this is not commonly accepted (e.g. Melena 1983b, 110). The possible connection with perfumery is underlined by the appearance of *zo-a* on Fh 361, one of the *ku-pi-ri-jo* perfumery records, although this does not resolve the matter since it is not being issued to a perfumer but seems to be part of *Kyprios*'s *o-no*. However, there are reasons for linking the word with the term *ze-so-me-no*, middle participle of ζέω, which is certainly attested in the context of perfume manufacture (PY Un 267). Note that Godart (1987, 209) now rejects his earlier suggestion (1968a, 604–8) that all the *zo-a* oil in the palace was accounted for and totalled separately.

[117] *Documents*[1], 392: 'A kind of olive oil, perhaps that used for anointing: *epikhowā* [Cf. ἐπιχόα · κατάχυσις Hesych.].' See *DMic.* I, 225, with full references. *DMic.* takes it as fem.dat.sg. noun, but of course we cannot tell from the Linear B spelling (e.g. Melena [1975a, 41] suggests this and *po-ro-ko-wa* are neut.nom.pl.adjs. of *elaion*, though this suggestion has not found much support).

[118] *Documents*, 477, 573: 'A technical term describing oil' possibly 'to describe runny oil as contrasted with unguent' (although most of the oil in the Fh tablets must be 'runny' so the reason for specifying such an attribute

have any religious connotation, even if the proposed interpretations are correct, since 'pouring' could relate also to non-religious activities.[120] Although not crucial for present purposes, a point worth noting is that, whatever the underlying etymological connection between the words *e-pi-ko-wa* and *po-ro-ko-wa* (which from the forms does indeed appear likely), from a structural point of view they *function* differently within the Fh series. The texts involved are as follows.

Fh 343 (141)

du-pu$_2$-so / zo-a OLE 15 e-pi-ko-wa ỌḶẸ 1̣ S 1 V 3

Fh 380 + 2006 + 5445 + *frr.* (141)

]jo-te / zo-a OLE 33 S 1 e-pi-ko-ẉạ[

Fh <381> (141??)

]po-ro-ko-wa , a[

Missing; text from *Scripta Minoa* II.

Fh 350 (141)

po-ro-ko-wa OLE 2

Cut at right.

For Fh 343 and –380, the layout of the tablets suggests not that *e-pi-ko-wa* is a separate recipient (or contributor), but rather that the main named individuals (*du-pu$_2$-so* and *]jo-te*) are receiving/contributing two types of oil: *zo-a* and *e-pi-ko-wa*. In each case the AN is written in majuscule at left, covering the whole tablet, while the *zo-a* and *e-pi-ko-wa* entries follow in smaller script, clearly subordinate to the main entry.[121] This would accord well with interpretation of *e-pi-ko-wa* as some sort of technical term describing a type (or use) of oil in parallel with *zo-a*, whatever the precise meanings of the words.

The structure of the two tablets on which *po-ro-ko-wa* appears, however, is entirely different. While Fh <381> is lost, so that no weight can be put on arguments from this document,[122] it is clear that *po-ro-ko-wa* is the sole entry on Fh 350, the text of which is complete. This is noted also by Godart who sees the oil as 'destinée à *po-ro-ko-wa*' while still in the end taking the word as a technical term.[123] But need it be? Such an entry would be unique (with one possible exception, see *to-ro-qa*, next) for the Fh series, and indeed for the Linear B records more generally. As a single entry, the word really should refer to a recipient or contributor, rather than a type of oil or a specified use – 'for libations' for instance does not really count as a 'destination': one would expect a shrine name, a deity name, or an intervening person or group to be indicated. This would be the crucial information, along with the numbers. Is it possible, despite the reasonable temptation to compare the word with *e-pi-ko-wa*, that we have here an otherwise unattested occupational term or MN? (Perhaps cf. Dv <1416> and Dv 5049, with readings *po-ro-ko-*[in a place on the tablet where we should find an MN referring to a shepherd?) This would leave unaffected the suggestion that *e-pi-ko-wa* is indeed a technical term describing oil, which is very likely given the structure of the tablets on which it appears,

here alone would be unclear). See *DMic.* II, 148, with further references. On the related term *po-ro-ko-wo* see Bendall forthcoming(b).

[119] E.g. *Mémoires* II, 157 (Lejeune 1958d); Duhoux 1976a, 137.

[120] As noted by Gérard-Rousseau 1968, 91.

[121] Melena (1983b, 111–12) points out that the *e-pi-ko-wa* entry on Fh 343 is one-tenth of the *zo-a* entry and suggests that the *e-pi-ko-wa* amount is thus determined by the *zo-a* amount, although he rightly notes that this cannot be confirmed since the number is missing on the other relevant document. He further suggests the *e-pi-ko-wa* amount may have been intended to compensate for reduction through boiling, but even if the ratio is significant, other explanations are possible.

[122] If Firth is right about Fh <381> possibly joining with <379> (see Notes to Table 3-6, *s.v.* 379) this would be an *a-pu-do-si* record, but since both tablets are lost no confirmation is possible.

[123] Godart 1969, 54–5; 1987, 204.

and it would not stop the words from being etymologically connected, albeit with a different function.

A somewhat similar situation arises with regard to *to-ro-qa*. It is generally taken as a technical term describing oil,[124] perhaps */trokʷhā(i)/* (cf. τρέφω) 'for alimentary consumption' or, as Ruijgh suggests, */trokʷā/* (cf. τρέπω) 'to be turned/stirred' (in the sense of processing),[125] although again there is little consensus. All these suggestions are based on etymological guesses and cannot be confirmed from the tablet contexts. However, it may be significant that, like *po-ro-ko-wa*, *to-ro-qa* can appear as the sole entry on a tablet, as it does in Fh 5497, the text of which is complete.[126] This is noted also by Godart, who argues that various other features suggest that *to-ro-qa* may be an MN, possibly referring to a person similar in position to *Kuprios*.[127] While it is not necessary to accept that *to-ro-qa* was actually a 'Collector' as is now argued for *Kuprios*, the idea that he is a man involved in the perfume industry would better explain the entry on Fh 5497 than interpretation as a technical term, and would be consistent with the large amounts of oil with which the word is associated. It would also be consistent with the appearance of the word in a parallel position to *Kuprios* on Fh 5446 (Group 2). Whether such an explanation might apply also to *to-qa* depends on whether or not they are variant graphs for the same word, which remains uncertain.[128]

However the words are interpreted, a central question here is whether the tablets record collections or disbursements of some sort (or a mix of different types of records). The few secure MNs which appear could be nominatives or datives so do not help.[129] Godart regards the *zo-a* tablets (10a) as disbursements,[130] but if it is correct that they relate to perfumery (which is likely) they should not be taken as 'disbursements for final use' but rather as referring to oil moving about within the industry. The possibility of collections also cannot be entirely dismissed.[131] Either way, the large numbers recorded on the *zo-a* tablets would accord well with either collections/deliveries (Group 2) or perfumery (Group 3), and it should be noted that none of the certainly identified disbursements for final use involves such large numbers.

The more modest amount recorded in association with *po-ro-ko-wa* in 10b, on the other hand, would be consistent with a disbursement for final use, whether as rations, offerings, *o-no* 'payments', or for use in industry.

---

[124] *DMic*. II, 366, with references.

[125] Ruijgh 1968, 705–7. It is seen as contrasted with some process involving 'boiling' described by *zo-a*, but note that the two terms never appear together (cf. Godart 1969, 55) – *zo-a* is rather contrasted with *e-pi-ko-wa*. Also with the sense of processing, Melena (1975a, 58) suggests */tr̥kʷā/* denoting an 'oil press', although he later (1983b, 107–8) notes difficulties with the idea.

[126] It may also be the sole entry in Fh 358 and <376>, but the texts are broken so we cannot be certain.

[127] Godart 1968a, 603, 609 (but *contra* in the same volume see Ruijgh 1968, 707 n 49); 1969, 53–6. The features he cites (not all of which are necessarily accepted here as significant) are: both *to-ro-qa* and *Kuprios* (1) are mentioned numerous times in the series (but so are some other words), (2) are associated with large quantities of oil, (3) appear together on Fh 5446 (our Group 3), (4) are associated with ANs (but only if *to-qa* and *to-ro-qa* are variants of the same word, which can be questioned), (5) can figure as sole entries on tablets (although *Kuprios* does not actually appear as sole entry, but does appear once with no other word but *o-no*).

[128] *to-qa* was once thought to be a scribal error for *to-ro-qa* (e.g. Ruijgh 1968, 705 n 33, 706 n 43) but it is now attested more than once, which makes this less likely (Godart 1987, 205; *DMic*. II, 363); it could still be a variant (although it would be odd for the same scribe to use both forms). Both *to-qa* and *to-ro-qa* appear only in the Fh series, with the possible exception of X 9734 (]*ṭọ-ro-qa*[). It might be noted that in the two cases for *to-qa* and once also for *to-ro-qa* (Fh 358) the word is written smaller than the main entry, which may suggest it is somehow 'subordinate', but for an appearance of *ku-pi-ri-jo* in an exactly parallel position see Fh 371 (Group 2).

[129] *DMic*. gives them all as dative, but this is based on the assumption that they are disbursements, which need not be so.

[130] Godart 1968a, 604; 1969, 55; 1987, 208. Note there are no clear datives or allatives (only]-*de* is preserved on Fh 5436, which could be anything).

[131] The layout of Fh 359 with the TN *ku-do-ni-ja* is not dissimilar to the layout of the taxation record Fh 5451 with *a-mi-ni-si-ja* although the crucial word *a-pu-do-si* is absent.

The numbers in 10c, associated with *to-ro-qa*/*to-qa*, are again very large.[132] Godart takes them as disbursements but if he is correct that *to-ro-qa* is connected with perfumery they could be issues for manufacture or some related purpose. They could also be collections/deliveries.

Finally, Godart takes the *ne-wo* records (10d) also as disbursements, but very little text is preserved on any of these documents (]-*ra-de* on Fh 5506 needn't be a TN + *de*), and 'new' could just as well refer to receipts, rather than issues, of newly collected (or harvested and processed) oil.[133]

On the whole, there are too many uncertainties to feel secure about the significance of any of these tablets, and for present purposes they have been kept separate to avoid adding the figures to one or more of our other categories without being certain they belong there. Since they are conveniently assembled here, they can at least be taken account of, even if what precisely should be done with them remains unclear.

11. Unclear

Group 11 contains tablets where the text is so broken that little or nothing can be determined about the function, or where they are simply 'unclear' for other reasons. Fh 5442 gives an example of both aspects. It may relate to the TN Amnisos, but the reading is uncertain, and even if Amnisos is correctly read the function of the record is unclear because this TN is frequently mentioned and appears in a variety of types of records including taxation and offerings. There is no way to tell which was intended here. Another example is Fh 5443, the text of which is as follows.

Fh 5443 + 5454 (141)
ro-ru[
↓
v. ụ-ta-no , [
r. Perhaps erased.
v. Trace of sign at right.

This document was mentioned above (Group 6) as a possible industrial disbursement tablet, as suggested by Shelmerdine on the basis that *u-ta-no* is well attested in the sheep tablets (e.g. Db 1097, Dl 7075). However, *u-ta-no* is also attested in religious contexts (Fp(1) 1, –13), so this could be an offerings record, and theoretically at least it could even be a taxation record (although the appearance of the contributing TN on the *verso* would be unusual). Moreover, *u-ta-no* is not attested *only* as a TN – there is an example of a man of this name in the sheep records (Dd 1592), located at *ra-to*, and this is the sense in which *DMic.* takes the word in Fh 5443.[134] Given the number and the nature of the uncertainties, the tablet should simply be regarded as 'Unclear' for present purposes.

---

[132] Melena (1983b, 109-10) notes that generally *zo-a* and *to-ro-qa* are associated with large numbers whereas *e-pi-ko-wa* and *po-ro-ko-wa* are associated with (relatively) smaller ones.

[133] For the 'huile nouvelle' amongst the 'sorties' records see Godart 1987, 208; 1968a, 603–4. He notes (1987, 206) that the amount of 'new' oil may compare with the amount collected 'this year' from Amnisos (Fh 5451), suggesting (1968a, 603) that newly collected oil might be described as 'new' when it was disbursed. However, the numbers do not match up very well (V 540 on Fh 5451 vs. V 380 on Fh 362.2, –375 and –5506), and it is in any case not clear why the *apudosis* from Amnisos alone should be relevant. I cannot see any satisfactory evidence either way for taking 'new' oil as relating to disbursements rather than collections.

[134] *DMic.* II, 393; presumably in parallel with the probable MN (if the word is complete) *ro-ru* on the *recto*, which is attested in Ce 50.2 (where he is probably a shepherd), and Dq 1234 (where the person certainly is a shepherd, although the word in that tablet too may be incomplete); but Godart (1969, 203 n 9) takes *u-ta-no* in the Fh tablet as a TN.

Summary of the Fh series

We must now attempt to summarise Table 3-6 and bring the data together in some more manageable form. Essentially, the records fall into the following groups:

1. Records of tax receipts
   - totalling tablet (Fh 366)
   - taxation records (2a)
2. Perfumery records
   - transfers for manufacture (3a and 3c[135])
   - *o-no* payments to perfumers (3b)
   - possibly one totalling tablet (Fh 367)
3. Disbursements for final use
   - various sorts of *o-no* and *qe-te-jo* payments (some to perfumers)
   - to workers and other persons as rations
   - to craftworkers for use in industrial processing
   - offerings to religious personnel or establishments
4. Miscellaneous records whose purpose is uncertain
5. Records too damaged to speculate on, so 'Unclear'

Figures for these various categories are set out in Table 3-7. The first thing apparent from the table is that the palace had access to very large amounts of oil. The totalling tablet for *a-pu-do-si* receipts, Fh 366, records V 6107, perhaps some 9771.2 litres, and we cannot be certain whether this represents the full total for the year or whether it was a running total with amounts still coming in. In any case, it is clear that some places were capable of making substantial contributions – Amnisos alone, for example, contributes at least V 540 (the figure is broken so this is a minimum), perhaps some 864 litres, and *ru-ki-to* is responsible for even more, V 957, perhaps some 1531.2 litres.[136]

That a substantial quantity of the oil was intended for perfume manufacture is indicated by the large amount (V 5499+, perhaps some 8798.4 litres) recorded in connection with the tablets of Group 3. What is less clear is whether these numbers are 'additive': that is, does the amount moving around in the perfume industry represent a quantity *in addition* to the amount recorded on a tablet such as Fh 366, or is it subsumed under it? If subsumed under it, the implication would be that the vast majority of Knossian oil was earmarked for perfumery, but this was not necessarily the case and we will return to the issue below.

[135] 3c is a mixed record but is included under transfers because the largest figure on it is subsumed under an entry closely similar to one of the transfer records. It may of course be that the whole tablet rather refers to *o-no* payments, but the figures are not greatly affected either way.

[136] These amounts, while seeming large from one perspective, are by no means beyond plausible outputs for traditional agriculture and do not necessarily even approach the entire productive capacity of the villages. For comparison, a heavy pre-industrial harvest for Karpofora in Messenia was 12,000 kg (13,200 litres) (Aschenbrenner 1972, 54), although we do not know of course if conditions were strictly comparable (see Forbes 1993 for a discussion of some difficulties with using ethnoarchaeological evidence for oil production; also Halstead 1987, 78–9) nor the size of the region envisaged by the scribes when speaking of 'Amnisos' or '*ru-ki-to*'. Also, 'large' is of course a relative term; fluctuations in scale of production probably centred not so much in productive *capacities*, but in social, political and economic *choices* about extent of exploitation (see n 161 below).

Table 3-7. Summary of oil in the Knossos Fh series

	V
1. Taxation records	
Totalling tablet (Fh 366)	6107
Individual taxation records (Table 3-6.2a)	2916+
2. Perfumery records	
Transfer records (Table 3-6.3a+3c)	2183+
o-no payments (Table 3-6.3b)	3316+
TOTAL 2	**5499+**
Totalling record for perfume industry?? (Fh 367)	5946
3. Disbursements for final use	
3a. Non-religious purposes	
o-no 'payments' (expect perfumery) (Table 3-6.4a)	90
To MNs, prob. rations (Table 3-6.5)	237+
Rations and/or industrial (Table 3-6.6)	281+
Sub-total 3a	**608+**
3b. Religious purposes	
Dat.pl. groups (Table 3-6.7)	36+
TN+*de* (Table 3-6.8a+8b)	146+
Offerings records (Table 3-6.9)	27+
Sub-total 3b	**209+**
TOTAL 3	**817+**
4. Miscellaneous	
A possible receipt record (Table 3-6.4c [Fh 370])	1260
zo-a and *e-pi-ko-wa* oil (Table 3-6.10a)	1861+
po-ro-ko-wa oil (Table 3-6.10b [disbursements?])	37+
to-qa/*to-ro-qa* oil (Table 3-6.10c)	1081+
'New' oil (Table 3-6.10d)	380+ ⟦1494⟧
5. Unclear	**1644+**

It may be noted that totals are supplied in Tables 3-6 and 3-7 only where it is clear that the amounts should be added. For instance, in 3-7.1 'taxation records' it is likely that amounts derived from the individual towns are subsumed under the amount in the totalling tablet Fh 366, so should not be added to it. Also, the 'miscellaneous' tablets (Table 3-7.4) should not be added to anything in the first instance because their interpretation is uncertain – they may be collections or disbursements or other sorts of transfers. Yet they should be taken note of since they record large amounts of oil and reflect some sorts of important transactions, even if we cannot discern their nature.[137] We should also note the amount of oil recorded for the Unclear documents. Giving a total here is of course spurious since it is virtually certain that these documents must belong to a variety of types, but it is important to be aware of the large amount of oil (some V 1644+) for which the data are lost.[138]

We should also note in general that a distinction must be made between disbursements in association with perfumery and all other sorts of disbursements. Oil issued for perfume manufacture does not represent 'disbursement' in the sense of real 'out-go' since it remains a palatial resource and will be returned as perfumed oil. On the other hand, industrial disbursements *not* related to perfumery are treated as final disbursements since, even though the palace will retain (or gain) some benefit from them in terms of the finished products which they contributed towards the manufacture of, the oil itself is consumed in the process. Such disbursements thus represent actual expenditures of oil. It will be noted that some

[137] However, a few clearly important tablets are omitted from the summary where the numbers are lost, e.g. 3-6.4b, Fh 346.

[138] It should also be noted however that over half of this amount comes from just one record (V 1260 on Fh 5457). Also note that although we have ascribed a nominal V 1+ to each fragment where the number is lost, some of these fragments may of course be bits of other tablets.

awkwardness results from separating *o-no* payments to perfumers (included under perfumery transactions) and *o-no* payments for others which are considered a 'final use'. Whether these should in fact be brought together is considered below.

Another issue is what was done with the majority of the oil, treated or untreated. It is not unlikely that significant amounts of it were intended for trade, as was argued by Shelmerdine to have been the case at Pylos, although the lack of documentation to that effect is notorious. Be that as it may, it is important that, unlike Pylos, we have numerous records dealing with disbursements for purposes other than for offerings, somewhat correcting the probably misleading impression that offerings may have consumed a majority of palatial resources. Before proceeding further, however, we should examine the remaining documents recording oil at Knossos.

3.2.3.6 THE FP(2) TABLETS

Although designated a 'set', in fact the Fp(2) tablets are not definitely by the same scribe (the ascriptions to hand are in all but one case doubtful), nor were they necessarily filed together,[139] and they seem to be a rather heterogeneous bunch. The texts are as follows.

Fp(2) 354 (222?)
.1]ka-ra-e-i-jo OLE 1 S 2
.2]jo OLE V 1 pa-ja-ni-jo OLE V 1
Cut at right.

Fp(2) 363 (222)
.1 qe-te-a , te-re-no OLE [
.2 da-*83-ja-de / i-je-ro S 2 ki-ri-te-wi-ja , [
.3 di-wo-pu-ka-ta S 2 [
.4] *vacat* [

Fp(2) 5472 + 5476 + *frr.*(5) (222?)
.1 ku-pi-ri-jo / su-ko-ne OLE [
.2 si-ja-ma[ ] OLE 1 S [
.3]*vest.*[ ]de OLE 2 [
.4] *vacat* [
.1 Traces at right of OLE, too faint to be numerals (erasure? accident?).

Fp(2) 5504 (222?)
a-ka-ta-ra-te-so-de OLE 10
Cut at right. *a-ka-ta-ra-te-so-de* over [[ ]].

Taking these in order, Fp 354 is probably an offering record, as suggested by the appearance of the month name *ka-ra-e-ri-jo* (albeit misspelled by the scribe[140]) and the small amounts involved. Fp(2) 363 is also an offering record, as indicated by the word *i-je-ro /hieron/* 'shrine' in line .2. Fp(2) 5504 may record an offering, since the allative *-de* is common on offerings records. However, we cannot be certain that *-de* here is an allative, since we cannot be sure that *a-ka-ta-ra-te-so*, unattested elsewhere, is a toponym. This tablet should be considered 'Unclear'. Fp(2) 5472 is not an offering record. As discussed in the previous section, the man *ku-pi-ri-jo* is involved in the perfume industry, so this is probably an industrial disbursement. Figures for the Fp(2) tablets are summarised in Table 3-8.

[139] Although they do all come from the same general findspot (see Firth 2000–2001a, 205). However, they were not with the other Fp tablets, but were found together with the Fh tablets in the RCB and in some ways (e.g. simply by being so heterogeneous; see also use of *ku-pi-ri-jo*) more resemble the Fh series than the tightly coherent Fp(1) set.
[140] See *DMic*. I, 319, with references.

Table 3-8. The Knossos Fp(2) tablets

Fp(2)	type and text	OLE	=V
	1. Offerings		
354.1	ka-ra-e-<ri>-jo	OLE 1 S 2	30
354.2	]jo	V 1	1
354.2	pa-ja-ni-jo	V 1	1
363.1	qe-te-a , te-re-no	OLE [	1+
363.2	da-*83-ja-de / i-je-ro	S 2	12
363.2	ki-ri-te-wi-ja	*lost*	1+
363.3	di-wo-pu-ka-ta	S 2	12
	TOTAL 1		**58+**
	2. *Perfumery*		
5472.1	ku-pi-ri-jo / su-ko-ne	ỌḶẸ [	1+
5472.2	si-ja-ṃạ[	OLE 1 S [	24+
5472.3	[ ]*vest*.[ ]de	ỌḶẸ 2	36
	TOTAL 2		**61+**
	3. *Unclear*		
5504	a-ka-ta-ra-te-so-de	OLE 1̣0̣	1̣8̣0̣

3.2.3.7 THE REMAINING OIL TABLETS

Finally, there are four tablets recording oil which do not belong to the series so far discussed. The texts are as follows.

F 726 (—)

.1]wi-jo-jo e-ra[

.2]ẉọ OLE+*A* V 1 [

.1 Trace at right, perhaps ẉọ[.

F 452 (—)

.1]ka-da-ra-so ỌḶẸ 2 [

.2]qa-ka OLE 1 pu-ri OLE S 2[

.3]-jo OLE S 3 o[

Widespread traces of ⟦ ⟧.

.3 Traces after *o*[consistent either with *o*-[or with *o*[(adjunct) or *O*[(ideogram).

F 7337 (—)

]24 S[

Trace before]24:]ỌḶẸ ?

F 7542 (—)

.1]31 *KO* 25

.2]6 Ṣ 1 OLE 9

.2 Traces at left.

F 726 is probably an offering record on account of the presence of a month name, the small amount recorded, and the indication that the oil has been treated.[141]

F 452 is 'Unclear'; nothing obviously connects it with offerings or religion. The sign-groups do not aid interpretation. Words ending *]ka-da-ra-so* and *]qa-ka* are not elsewhere attested; *pu-ri* (line .2) is a common man's name, but none of the attestations (B(5) 799.7; Ch 1029; Dv 5696.B; F 452.2; V(3) 479.2) need refer to the same man. It is also unclear whether the tablet deals with collections or disbursements. The relatively small amounts would be consistent with

[141] It is from the Gallery of Jewel Fresco [G1], which is consistent with its being an offering record, although not all tablets from this findspot can be so identified (see Chapter 4 n 4).

disbursements, but there is a possibility *o-pe-ro* may be restored in line .3,[142] in which case the tablet would record a collection (and the amount in line .1 is not so small). On the whole, however, disbursements are more likely since, as *pu-ri* is a man's name it is likely that the others are too, and there is a lack of evidence for receipts of oil from persons rather than places. The small amounts also suggest disbursements.[143] It is curious that the scribe has not 'rounded' up the figure in line .3 (i.e. from S 3 to OLE 1), possibly suggesting the transaction was not complete. Whatever the case, the tablet records V 84 of oil in total.

The remaining tablets are also 'Unclear', as none has sufficient text for its function to be determined (and note OLE is not securely read on F 7337).[144] To sum up, we have V 1+ disbursed for offerings and various amounts which are 'Unclear' (V 246 without F 7337; V 684 with it).

3.2.3.8 ADDING UP OIL AT KNOSSOS

All the figures from the various records are brought together in Table 3-9. Our central questions here are:

1. What proportion of all palatial disbursements of oil did amounts disbursed for religious purposes represent?
2. What proportion of overall palatial resources in oil did amounts disbursed for religious purposes represent?

With regard to the first question, the table gives V 1126.75+ total disbursements for final use, 46% of which (V 518.75+) was for offerings. The figure is surprisingly high, although significantly less than the 71–100% seen at Pylos. Also, as at Pylos, the number of tablets on which offerings appear is high. Twenty-seven tablets record 'secular' disbursements, while some fifty record offerings (65%). In other words, more tablets survive recording offerings than any other type of disbursement.

We might also, however, consider the figures with the *o-no* disbursements relating to perfumery added in, which gives us V 4442.75 (3316+1126.75), of which offerings are just 12%. Whether or not the figure is meaningful depends on whether *o-no* payments to perfumers represent 'final use' in the same way that *o-no* payments to other persons do. In one sense they probably do represent real expenditure, in the sense that the palace as a corporate entity will no longer have access to the oil so designated. But there are some oddities about these figures which make one suspect that a straightforward summation is misleading. We return to this shortly, but for the moment may simply note the figures with and without the *o-no* for perfumers: thus, roughly 12–46% of disbursements recorded at Knossos were for offerings.

Turning to the second question, we have at Knossos some more directly useful documents for estimating overall resources than we had at Pylos. Particularly helpful is Fh 366[+]5503, the totalling record for tax payments (assuming the quasi-join is correct). It records V 6107, of which our total disbursed for offerings represents about 8%. This compares with some 11–34% estimated for Pylos. At Pylos, overall resources could only be estimated from calculations of how much oil might have been treated by amounts of coriander in lists of perfume ingredients (which in any case only relates to perfumed oil and leaves raw oil unaccounted for); it may be significant that where we have more directly relevant records the figures are smaller – and possibly more realistic.

---

[142] *KT*[6] notes *o-pe*[-*ro* a possibility. On the other hand, if *O* stands here as an ideogram, this might be an offering record; see Section 5.7. But a collection/delivery is more likely. On *o-pe-ro* see Section 4.2.1.4, with references.

[143] I am grateful to J.T. Killen for bringing these points to my attention.

[144] If *KO* on F 7542 stands for coriander, the tablet may have to do with perfumery, but this is mere speculation.

Table 3-9. Oil at Knossos

	V
1. Taxation records	
Totalling tablet (Table 3-6.1 [Fh 366])	6107
Individual taxation records (Table 3-6.2a)	2916+
2. Perfumery	
2a. Transfer records	
Fh tablets (Table 3-6.3a+3c)	2183+
Fp(2) 5472	61+
Sub-total 2a	**2244+**
2b. o-no *payments*	
Table 3-6.3b	3316+
TOTAL 2a+2b	**5560+**
2c. Totalling record for perfumery?	
Table 3-6.1 [Fh 367]	5946
3. Disbursements for final use	
3a. Non-religious purposes	
o-no 'payments' (expect perfumery) (Table 3-6.4a)	90
to MNs, prob. rations (Table 3-6.5)	237+
rations or industrial? (Table 3-6.6)	281+
Sub-total 3a	**608+**
3b. Religious purposes	
Fp(1) (Table 3-4)	241+
Fs (Table 3-5)	9.75
Fh (Table 3-7.3b)	209+
Fp(2) (Table 3-8.1)	58+
F 726 (Section 3.2.3.7)	1+
Sub-total 3b	**518.75+**
TOTAL 3a+3b	**1126.75**
4. Miscellaneous	
A possible receipt record: Fh 370 (Table 3-6.4c)	1̣2̣6̣0̣
zo-a and *e-pi-ko-wa* oil (Table 3-6.10a) [related to perfumery?]	1861+
po-ro-ko-wa (Table 3-6.10b) [probably disbursements?]	37+
to-qa/to-ro-qa oil (Table 3-6.10c) [disbursements? perfumery?]	1081+
'New' oil (Table 3-6.10d) [receipts or disbursements?]	380+ ⟦1494⟧
5. Unclear	
Fh (Table 3-6.11)	1644+
Fp(2) (Table 3-8.3)	180
Other (F 452 + F 7542 [+ F 7337])	246 [684?]
TOTAL 5	**2070 [2754?]**

The perfumery records are also relevant here, particularly as the offerings may have been of perfumed oil (excepting perhaps in the Fs series). As at Pylos, a great deal of oil appears to be moving around within the perfume industry, some V 5560+, perhaps some 8896 litres, of which amounts for offerings are 9%. This figure is similar to that derived from a comparison with the taxation records, but we might also speculate whether some figures are 'additive': that is, does the amount moving around in the perfume industry represent a quantity *in addition* to the amount recorded on a tablet such as Fh 366, or is it subsumed under it? If added to it, then the amount for offerings would be smaller again. While it is difficult to be sure, there is something to suggest that some of the numbers at least *are* additive. In our discussion of *Kuprios* it was noted that the *o-no* paid to him stands in a 31:69 ratio to the amount of oil recorded on the totalling record Fh 367 which Olivier, followed by Killen, suggested may be a totalling record for perfumery. But it is important to note that the *o-no* is not subsumed under the totalling record, but is rather one third of the *overall* total, that is, the V 2700 of the *o-no* (Table 3-6.3b; Fh 372) and the V 5946 of the totalling record must be added, yielding V 8646. Our offerings records would be 6% of this larger amount. On the other hand, the amount going to *Kuprios* as an *o-no* would presumably no longer be available to the palace *per se*, so may be irrelevant. If we instead referred only to the totalling tablet (Fh 367) offerings would again be 9%. Be that as it may, a certain incompleteness in our documentation is highlighted. For instance, V 8646 is *more* than the V 6107 recorded for tax payments on Fh 366. In other words, the amount collected as taxes does not represent the total resources available to the palace for issuing to its perfumers. This is relevant to some of the other oddities in our records, referred to above. For instance, the *o-no* payments connected with perfumery are V 3316+ (Table 3-6.3b), whereas other transactions account for only V 2024+ (Table 3-6.3a), so it appears that *more* is going out as *o-no* payments in the preserved records than is being issued to work on, which seems unlikely to reflect the real situation. This is relevant to whether the *o-no* 'payments' connected with perfumery should be added or not to the other totals for 'final disbursements', as discussed above. In one sense they clearly should, but it is apparent that something is 'wrong' with the figures and it could further be the case be that *o-no* 'payments in kind' to persons working with the material might have a different status from other such disbursements.[145] Whatever is done, one senses that we are seeing something less than the entire picture here.

We should also take note of the Miscellaneous tablets. Fh 370, for instance, may record a receipt and does not appear to be an *a-pu-do-si* record (there are various lacunae on the tablet but none appears large enough for *a-pu-do-si* to have been written) so might not be subsumed under the totalling record Fh 366. It records V 1260, which is a substantial proportion (21%) of the total there (V 6107). It is not impossible that one town could have supplied so large an amount (see *ru-ki-to* with V 957), but it is also possible that this amount represents a further income from a different source[146] which should be added to Fh 366, giving V 7367. Our offerings records would be 7% of this. We should also note the large amounts described as *zo-a* and *to-qa/to-ro-qa*, some of which at least are likely to be collections or perfumery records rather than disbursements, as discussed above. A total of some V 2942 is described by these terms in the surviving records (Table 3-6.10a+10c+3b:36). If these are issues for processing, we may add them to other V 2244+ for transfer records (Table 3-9.2a). This gives V 5986 which is not far off the V 5946 in the supposed perfumery totalling tablet, so that one wonders if this might 'help' account for some of the missing transactions just noted. (On this calculation, the *o-no* 'payments' would be 36% or 39%,[147] a somewhat more reasonable proportion to expect going out as 'beneficiary payments'.)[148] Another substantial amount in the records is described as *ne-wo* (V 1494 on Fh 362, although this is of course an erasure so might not count, at least not in any straightforward way). It again is not clear whether these figures should be added – and if so, to what – but it is at least apparent that the palace had access to substantial resources very probably beyond what we see recorded in the extant tablets. While none of the procedures here can be verified, the central point is that the figure on Fh 366 should be taken as a *minimum* estimate so that offerings may have represented something *less* than 8% of overall resources.

Finally, we should note that amounts recorded for final disbursements of whatever sort do not tally with the large amounts indicating overall resources, however calculated.[149] Without the *o-*

[145] We may also note that the vast majority of the amount in this category is the payment to *Kuprios* (V 2700 of 3315), and the situation here may be unusual since he is probably himself an important palace official so disbursements to him might be somewhat different than those to persons who are not themselves a part of the 'corporate body'.

[146] Possibly, as suggested above, the amount from local Knossian estates which was totalled separately?

[147] It depends on whether one takes the total from the individual tablets (V 5186 + 3316 = 8502) or the totalling tablet (V 5946 + 3316 = 9262).

[148] It is in fact somewhat closer to the 30:70 ratio expected for 'Collectors', although probably most of the *o-no* issues are not to 'Collectors' and in any case the whole edifice may be illusory.

[149] Godart (1987, 210) calculated that *sorties* overall exceeded *entrées*, but this is questionable. His figures (Godart 1987, 208) depend on taking for instance Fh 370 (our Sub-group 4c) as a *sortie*, whereas it could be a delivery as discussed. He also includes as *sorties* the large amounts associated with *Kuprios*, but these figures include amounts which are not 'disbursements for final use' but rather transfers within the perfume industry, so better described as

no payments to perfumers included, disbursements represent 18% of the total recorded in Fh 366, and 20% of the total for the perfumery records (which figure is certainly on the low side since so many numbers are lost). Thus, some 80% of the resources of the palace are unaccounted for in terms of final disbursements. Including the *o-no* payments to perfumers would account for more of the overall resources – disbursements for final use would then be 73% of the amount on Fh 366, but this only helps if we can believe that three-quarters of Knossian oil was consumed by the perfumers themselves, which seems unlikely. The *o-no* 'payments' aside, it may be of course that our disbursements relate to only part of the year's record whereas the taxation records show instead the annual income (see e.g. 'this year's' on Fh 5451, the *a-pu-do-si* record for Amnisos). But even so, there seem to be gaps in the evidence. Although the Knossos tablets show more variety than Pylos, they are limited to just four types of disbursements. Did the Knossians do nothing with their oil beyond using it for offerings, rations, industrial processing and *o-no* payments? It was noted in our discussion of Pylos that classical and Near Eastern parallels suggest a number of other uses. To elaborate, for perfumed oil, Shelmerdine lists as ritual uses:[150] offerings, preservation of ivory and wood (in the case of cult statues, but this could have been done more generally too), treatment of textiles for cult statues or other ritual use, treatment of the dead, other consumption related to funerary practices[151] and grave gifts.[152] For secular uses she notes hygienic and cosmetic uses for both humans and animals (notably horses), especially application to skin and hair to prevent dryness and odours following or instead of bathing, plus treatment of cloth and leather (these last, as we have seen, probably reflected in the Linear B records).[153] Other possible uses of perfumed and unperfumed oil include alimentary consumption,[154] fuel for lamps,[155] soap, medicinal, lubrication, and preserving foodstuffs.[156] In short, there are more possible uses for oil – some attested archaeologically – than are accounted for in the Linear B records, even the more extensive ones of Knossos. We will not stop here to consider reasons for this, as we will return to the issue in the final chapter, but it is important to take note of the phenomenon, which we will see repeated in our examination of other commodities.

'issues for manufacture'. Such issues do not represent true expenditure since the oil would be returned as a treated product. The same is probably true for the *zo-a* records, also included in the total for *sorties*. In an earlier article, Godart had argued a point cited by others, e.g. Shelmerdine (1988, 355), that 'the amounts coming in and going out are likely to balance each other'. In light of his later work this is no longer tenable, but the fundamental difficulty is, as he himself (Godart 1987, 210) rightly concludes, that so many figures are lost that it is in any case rather difficult to come up with a convincing way to make the numbers tally.

150 Shelmerdine 1985, 123–8.

151 E.g. the numerous cooking vessels found outside the graves (or in dromoi) at Armenoi, some of which are reported as having contained olive oil (*Flavours*, 115–16).

152 Grave gifts of stirrup-jars are very common, although some may have contained wine rather than olive oil (Haskell 1984, 98; French 2002, 113; *Flavours*, 173); they would of course be highly suitable for either liquid. For an LM II example of fine vessels with strainers for use of perfumed oil products found in a grave at Chamalevri see Andreadaki-Vlazaki in *Flavours*, 48, 54–5; see also p. 113 for a III A2 small amphora from Armenoi which may have contained olive oil.

153 Shelmerdine 1985, 128–30; see also *Flavours*, 37.

154 Grieco (1993, 303–5), speaking of medieval Italy, makes two wider points, useful here, that the use of oil as a foodstuff has a tendency to be underestimated, but on the other hand neither should it be assumed that it was culturally preferred to animal oils, even where it was widely available; see also Forbes 1993, 216; Meeks 1993; Hamilakis 1999a, 45–6; Sherratt 2004, 187, 195. As Hamilakis and Sherratt (*loc. cit.*) both point out, there is no *unambiguous* evidence for culinary use of olive oil in the LBA Aegean. See also Jameson (1988, 99), noting for the classical world that 'one should not assume that olive oil was permanently and easily available'. It is not unlikely that both plant and animal fats formed part of the diet, as suggested by *Flavours*, 58 (animal only), 107–8, 112, 165 (both); Riley 2002, but the issue remains to be resolved and the data used by *Flavours* are not yet available.

155 Blitzer (1993, 168–9) suggests olive oil as a major fuel for lamps, while noting that some other plant oil or tallow could have been used as well. One of the braziers from the Mycenae cult centre may have traces of olive oil (*Flavours*, 134), but the data for this analysis are not yet available. A study of lamps at Mochlos found that beeswax was instead used (Evershed *et al.* 1997).

156 The list is by no means exhaustive. Uses of and attitudes to oil are highly interesting and it would be desirable further to bring such aspects together with the Linear B data, but the issue belongs to a separate study.

Although there are many uncertainties, we may tentatively conclude that, on the basis of the surviving records, some 12–46% of disbursements recorded at Knossos were for offerings, and that offerings constituted some 6–9% of overall resources. The findings are a useful corrective to those for Pylos where we had some 71–100% of disbursements going for offerings and some 11–34% as overall resources. Where we have the better documentation, the proportions allocated for offerings are smaller. In both cases, however, the picture appears incomplete. It would be hasty, for instance, to conclude that Pylos really did expend more of its resources on offerings. It seems more likely that at Pylos the types of records we have for Knossos were not preserved for some reason, or were unnecessary.

As a final note, the potential productive capacity of ancient oil industries should not be underestimated. While early modern sources are of course not necessarily relevant to the Bronze Age, it is interesting to note, as remarked by Rackham and Moody, that following the destruction of trees elsewhere in the Mediterranean during the Little Ice Age, Crete became a major supplier and '[b]y the 1730s ... was exporting an average of 1,600 *tons* of oil a year *to Marseilles alone*'[157] (my italics). It has been argued that ancient oil extraction methods did not produce lower-quality oil than today (on the contrary),[158] but the saving is in terms of man-hours expended on the process.[159] Modern Cretan olive trees are particularly productive,[160] and whether or not that feature extended into earlier periods, choices about the exploitation of the productive capacity would have been due to other factors than technological ability.[161] The documents from Knossos suggest that the productivity *was* exploited, perhaps to a greater extent even than might be guessed from the Linear B records.

3.3 UNGUENT(?) (**133 = AREPA*)

The substance indicated by ideogram **133* is some type of oil product. The ideogram is a ligature of *a*, *re* and *pa*, probably representing */aleiphar/* 'unguent', although, as Shelmerdine points out, it cannot have been completely solid since it is measured in liquid units.[162] It appears only at Pylos, on Un 6.7,[163] Un 718.8, Un 853.4, Un 1177.3, Wr 1437, and probably Fr 1198. The reading on Fr 1198 is uncertain (see Table 3-2), and the text is lost in any case so the purpose of this record is 'Unclear' – a pity particularly in light of the relatively large amount recorded. The sealing Wr 1437 may relate to a delivery (the amount is unspecified as is usual for this type of document), and the Un tablets are all banqueting records. The figures are set out in Table 3-10.

---

[157] Rackham & Moody 1996, 82.

[158] Riley (1999, 55; see also 2002, 67) reports on the relative productivity of Cretan trees in modern times: 'Before World War II Cretan olive trees averaged 2.2 kg of oil per tree, as compared to an average of 1.8 kg from Greece and 1.5 kg for Italy and Turkey ... In the district of Hierapetra on Crete in 1948–9, a particularly good season for olives, the crop averaged between 3.1 and 3.6 kg of oil per tree.'

[159] Mattingly 1993.

[160] Riley 2002, 66.

[161] See Hamilakis (1996, 25; 1999a, 47–9) for the suggestion that the beginning of systematic exploitation of olive oil in the Neopalatial Period and subsequent intensification was linked to an increase in trade, underlining oil as an elite item particularly as a base for perfumes and unguents. See e.g. Forbes 1993 *op. cit.* for discussion of when and why people might choose to produce for an export market. Of course 'large' is a relative term and no suggestion is intended that Bronze Age Crete was exporting on the scale mentioned above, but the Knossos Linear B administration does indeed seem to have been interested in export. For discussion of local Bronze Age scales of production see Warren 2004, esp. 164–5. The capacity of the storage pithoi in the West Magazines at Knossos was calculated by Graham (1987, 130–1) to be over 246,000 litres, much more than the amount noted in the Linear B records although of course not all of the pithoi would have contained olive oil (see e.g. Christakis 1999). See also Christakis 2004; 2005.

[162] Shelmerdine 1985, 34, 126.

[163] See Bennett (1992, 105) for the new reading.

Table 3-10. Unguent at Pylos

	AREPA	V
1. Banqueting		
Un 6	S 1 V 2̣[	8+
Un 718	V 2	2
Un 853	V 4	4
Un 1177	V 1̣[	1+
	TOTAL 1	**15+**
2. Delivery?		
Wr 1437	—	
3. Unclear		
Fr 1198	2 S 1 V 5	47

All the identifiable disbursement tablets are related to banqueting, and thus (in the cases here at least[164]) indirectly to religion. There is no way to calculate overall resources from these records, although the large amounts of oil being moved around in the perfume industry should be kept in mind. (If we did want to compare with the overall amount calculated in Section 3.2.2, the issues here would be just 0.8% – but it is far from clear that OLE is directly comparable with *AREPA*.) It is worth noting the curious circumstance that offerings of 'ordinary' perfumed oil (i.e. represented with the ideogram OLE) *never* appear on banqueting records, while by the same token amounts of *AREPA* never appear *except* in association with banqueting. Yet, as noted previously, it may be that many of the Pylos Fr tablets record offerings that were in fact made on the occasions of banquets.[165] If this is correct, why was it never the case that the offerings of oil and the banqueting foodstuffs should appear on the same record? Once again, one senses we are seeing something less than the entire picture.

[164] Un 6, –718 and –853 all mention deities names; –1177 is broken so uncertain.
[165] Bendall 1998–1999.

CHAPTER 4
WINE AND HONEY

4.1 INTRODUCTION

This chapter deals with wine and honey, two commodities which, like olive oil, were measured in liquid measures and happen to have been used in perfume manufacture. Due to constraints of space, the discussion is necessarily less detailed than for olive oil and is mainly confined to what is necessary for identification of the functions of the records concerned. Much more can be – and has been – said about these two interesting commodities than is done here; further references are given in the appropriate sections.

4.2 HONEY (*135 = ME+RI)

Honey was known and valued in the Aegean in the Bronze Age and there is both archaeological and Linear B evidence for it.[1] It is written in Linear B as *me-ri* = /meli/, commonly ligatured *ME+RI*. It was a major commodity used for offerings at Knossos, second only to olive oil, and appears also on an offerings record from Chania. Evidence for honey at Pylos is ambiguous. We discuss evidence from each of the sites in turn.

4.2.1 HONEY AT KNOSSOS

4.2.1.1 INTRODUCTION TO HONEY AT KNOSSOS

Honey appears at Knossos in the Fs set and the Gg series. The Fs set was discussed above (Section 3.2.2.3; Table 3-5); our focus here is on the Gg tablets. The series is characterised by the vessel ideogram **209*^{VAS}, often surcharged with *A*, abbreviating a word attested in the plural, *a-po-re-we /amphorēwe(s)/* 'amphorae'; it resembles the classical vessel of the same name.[2] The series comprises four sets plus several unconnected tablets. We first examine the sets, then the remaining records.

4.2.1.2 THE GG(1) AND GG (3) SETS: OFFERINGS RECORDS

The Gg(1) and Gg(3) sets both include offerings records, and come from the Gallery of Jewel Fresco (having fallen from above[3]), where numerous other offerings records were found.[4] We

---

[1] For archaeological evidence and honey in general see Ransome 1937; Crane 1975; 1983; 1999; Davaras 1984; Amouretti *et al.* 1993; Evershed *et al.* 1997; Melas 1999.

[2] Vandenabeele & Olivier 1979, 259–63; Anderson 1994–1995, 299, see also 296, 314, 319–21. As in Classical Greek, both short and full forms appear: *a-po-re-we /amphorēwe(s)/* (MY Ue 611; TH Ka 113), *a-pi-po-re-we /amphi-phorēwes/* (KN Uc 160 *v*.2). No distinction seems intended between vessels with and without the surcharge. See Uc 160 *v*.2, where *a-pi-po-re-we* is written so there is no doubt about vessel type, but the ideogram is not surcharged; also, in PY Tn 996.3]*ṛẹ-we* is preserved and again **209* is not surcharged. The ideogram appears both ways in the Gg series.

[3] Firth 2000–2001a, 233–7, esp. 234.

[4] See Weilhartner 2005, 45–51 for discussion of the honey records relating to offerings. Weilhartner (2005, e.g. 48, 106) takes all tablets from the Gallery of Jewel Fresco, findspot [G1], as offerings records. However, since they fell into this room from an upper storey, they should, as Firth (2000–2001a, 234) argues, be taken together with tablets

begin with the Gg(1) set, texts of which are as follows.

Gg(1) 702 (103)
.1 pa-si-te-o-i / me-ri $*209^{VAS}$ 1
.2 da-pu$_2$-ri-to-jo , / po-ti-ni-ja 'me-ri' $*209^{V}$ 1

Gg(1) 704 (103)
.1] me-no
.2]o-ne me-ri $*209^{VAS}+A$ 1

Gg(1) 7369 (103)
.1 ka-]ra-e-ri-jo-jo me-no[
.2] LANA 1 M 1 me-ri ṣ [

Gg(1) 5552 (103)
.1]ṃẹ-no
.2]2

Gg(1) 8053 (103)
.1]me-no
.2] *vac.*
.2 Possibly]1̣.

Gg(1) 702 and –7369 are most readily identified as offerings records. Both were discussed above in our examination of how offerings records may be identified (Section 2.2.2). The first records issues 'to all the gods' */pansi theoi*(*h*)*i*/ plus the 'Lady of the Labyrinth'.[5] The recipient in Gg(1) 7369 is lost, but the tablet mentions the month *ka-ra-e-ri-jo* (in the genitive[6]), which appears also on a large number of oil offerings records (e.g. Fp(1) 6, –7, –15, –18). As was noted above (Section 2.2.2), month names appear only in religious contexts, so this too is probably an offerings record. The remaining Gg(1) tablets are fragmentary, but the (probable) appearance of month designations plus shared hand and findspot suggest they too were offerings records.

Gg(1) 7369 is unusual for the Gg series in two ways. First, it records honey with a liquid measure rather than an amphora. This should be noted with regard to calculating total amounts, and we should further note that, since this scribe records honey both ways, we cannot be certain what the measure was in Gg(1) 5552 and –8053 where the relevant text is lost.

A second peculiarity of Gg(1) 7369 is that it records wool as well as honey. As we shall see (Section 6.3.3.1), wool offerings as such are rare. The Od(2) tablets form the only other sure example, and they may be connected to the present situation since they are also written by h. 103 and record offerings to Eileithyia (Od(2) 714) and Amnisos (Od(2) 718) which appear in a record of the Gg(3) set (below). In addition to writing the Od(2) and Gg(1) offerings tablets, h. 103 was an administrator in the textile industry,[7] thus precisely the person who would have had wool available for distribution. Why he involved himself in honey as well in this instance may have to do more with the matter at hand than with his ordinary activities. He was evidently working in close connection with h. 140, who wrote the Gg(3) tablets, which come from the same findspot,[8] and it is probably relevant that h. 140 was responsible for writing the following record of a textile offering (also involving Amnisos), even though, unlike h. 103, he was not normally involved with textiles.[9] The text is as follows (see also Section 6.4.1.3).[10]

---

from findspots [G2], [E3] and [H4] (for [H4] being adjacent to the Gallery of Jewel Fresco see Firth 1996–1997, 43; 2000–2001a, 199–200, 202, Fig. 4; Melena 1999, 382–3), and not all these are offerings records.

5 See Chapter 2 n 22.

6 There is a misprint in *KT*^{5}: *ka-*]*ra-e-ri-jo-jo* is correct; see *CoMIK* III, *s.v.* 7369.

7 *Scribes Cnossos*, 131–2, see 44–50 for the corpus by this hand; also Killen 1966; 1967; Foster 1977a, 33; Tegyey 1983; Shelmerdine 1988, 348; Landenius-Enegrin 1995; Weilhartner 2005, 45.

8 Firth 2000–2001a, 233–7, esp. 236.

9 So far as we know. The scribe wrote only five (known) documents: M 719, the three Gg(3) tablets and V 684, dealing with ivory.

10 The text is from *KT*^{5}, except the apparatus to line .2, from *KT*^{6}. On M 719 recently see Nosch & Perna 2001, 475; Weilhartner 2005, 61; Killen 2006a, 86–7.

M 719 (140)

.1 a-mi-ni-so ke-re-na , re-ne , [

.2 e-ne-si-da-o-ne , su-ja-to , **146* 1[

.1 *-na* over ⟦ ⟧ (which explains the wide spacing between *ke-re-* and *-na*). Sign at right possibly *pẹ*[, but this is very uncertain.

.2 **146* 1 over ⟦ ⟧ (perhaps ⟦*ME+RI*⟧ followed by VAS).

If a new reading by Killen is correct,[11] the scribe seems originally to have written honey, then erased it and written **146* (see line .2 apparatus). Whatever the reason for the change, there seems to be some connection between honey and wool/textiles,[12] at least in the sense that they were on certain occasions (e.g. as in the month of *ka-ra-e-ri-jo*) offered in conjunction.[13]

Texts of the Gg(3) set, are as follows.

Gg(3) 705 (140)

.1] a-mi-ni-so , / e-re-u-ti-ja '*ME+RI*' **209*VAS 1

.2]pa-si-te-o-i *ME+RI* **209*VAS 1

.3]o-ne *ME+RI* **209*VAS 1

.1 Traces at left.

Gg(3) 717 (140)

.1] , me-na , pa-si-te-ọ[-i

.2]ṣị-da-o-ne , *ME+RI* [

.1 Traces at left; -te- perhaps over ⟦ ⟧.

.2 Trace at right.

Gg(3) 5185 (140)

.1]-to , a-pa-ṭọ[

.2]o-ne *MẸ+RI*[

.1 Possibly]*ṛị-to*.

Gg(3) 705 records an amphora of honey for the deity Eileithyia at Amnisos,[14] one for 'all the gods', and one for a recipient whose name is partly lost. Gg(3) 717 records issues 'to all the gods' and to a recipient whose name again is partly lost[15] (the ending is the same as in Gg(3) 705.3, but there is no guarantee it was the same figure). In line .1 'to all the gods' is preceded by the word *me-na*. This might indicate a further recipient 'to the moon',[16] but, as Killen has pointed out, two recipients for a single offering would be unusual and this could instead be a scribal attempt to spell the mono-syllabic nominative of /*mēns*/ or /*mens*/ 'month'.[17] Finally, Gg(3) 5185 is fragmentary, but scribal hand and (probable) findspot[18] suggest it too is an offering record. Any proposed restorations of the preserved words must be speculative. Weilhartner follows a tentative suggestion by Killen that a possible parallel with the structure of Gg(3) 705 might suggest a TN, perhaps *ti-ri-to*, but the reading is uncertain and the suggestion impossible to verify.[19] Similarly, *a-pa-ṭọ*[might be an otherwise unattested deity's name,[20] but could be something else. Finally, the broken word in the second line,]*o-ne* might

---

[11] To appear in *KT*[6]. I am grateful for permission to mention this in advance of publication.

[12] Another possible connection is that another tablet by h. 103, M(1) 1645, recording an offering of **146*, also in the month *ka-ra-e-ri-jo*, and possibly found in G1 (Firth 2000–2001a, 236; but he earlier [1996–1997] gives the findspot as unknown), is actually grouped together with the Gg(1) set by Olivier on the basis of size (*Scribes Cnossos*, 50).

[13] Killen notes that fruit, honeycombs and wool were placed on the altar and doused in oil in the later cult of Demeter at Phigalea, Arcadia (Killen 1962, 61); see also Weilhartner 2005, 45–6.

[14] The Mycenaean form is *Eleuthía*, cf. the classical Cretan form Ἐλεύθυ(ι)α (*Documents*, 127, 310).

[15] It is usually restored as *e-ne-*]*ṣị-da-o-ne* on analogy with M 719, although other possibilities exist, and is interpreted as an epithet of Poseidon (*Documents*, 309, 543; *DMic.* I, 219; contra see Gérard-Rousseau 1968, 88–9).

[16] *Documents*, 309; cf. *DMic.* I, 434.

[17] Killen forthcoming(a).

[18] Firth 2000–2001a, 236.

[19] Killen 1992a, 362; Weilhartner 2005, 46–7.

[20] Killen 1992a, 361–3; Weilhartner 2005, 46.

refer to the same recipient as in Gg(3) 717 (see also Gg(1) 704), but again certainty is impossible.

The data on the Gg(1) and Gg(3) offerings records are summarised in Table 4-1.

Table 4-1. Offerings of honey in the Gg(1) and Gg(3) sets

tablet	h.	recipient	time	location	honey	amount **209*	amount liquid
Gg(1)							
702.1	103	pa-si-te-o-i			me-ri **209*	1	
702.2	103	da-pu$_2$-ri-to-jo po-ti-ni-ja			me-ri **209*	1	
704	103	?e-ne-si-da]-o-ne	] me-no		me-ri **209+A*	1	
5552	103	*lost*	]ṃẹ-no		*lost*	]2 ??	]2 ??
7369	103	*lost*	ka-ra-e-ri-jo		me-ri	—	ṣ[
8053	103	*lost*	]me-no		*lost*	1+??	1+?
		TOTAL Gg(1)				**3–6+?**	**V 6–9+?**
Gg(3)							
705.1	140	e-re-u-ti-ja		Amnisos	*ME+RI *209*^{VAS}	1	
705.2	140	]pa-si-te-o-i		Amnisos?	*ME+RI *209*^{VAS}	1	
705.3	140	?e-ne-si-da]-o-ne		Amnisos?	*ME+RI *209*^{VAS}	1	
717.1	140	pa-si-te-ọ[-i	me-na		*lost*	1+	
717.2	140	]ṣị-da-o-ne			*ME+RI*[	1+	
5185.1	140	]-to , a-pa-ṭọ[*			*lost* ?**	?	
5185.2	140	?e-ne-si-da]-o-ne			*ṂẸ+RI*[	1+	
		TOTAL Gg(3)				**6–7+**	

* May not be a recipient.
** May not have been separate entry.

The table leaves open the question of what the measure was on Gg(1) 5552 and –8053, where the indication of unit is lost, and gives totals for both alternatives. The two sets record some 9–13+ amphorae of honey plus some V 6–9+ in liquid measures.

4.2.1.3 THE GG(2) SET: PERFUMERY RECORDS

The Gg(2) tablets probably record industrial disbursements. They were found in the Long Corridor [F18] near the Gallery of Jewel Fresco (again having fallen from above), and were written by h. 135, who was active in the perfume industry.[21] The texts are as follows.

Gg(2) 713 + 994 (135)

ma-ri-ne-we , / do-e-ra ‘*ME+RI*’ **209*^{VAS}*+A* [

Perhaps **209*^{VAS}*+A* 1̣[.

Gg(2) 995 + 7370 + 7591 + 7764 (135)

ma-ki-ro-ne , / ku-pi-ri-jo ̦, ‘*ME+RI*’ **209*^{VAS}*+A* 6[

**209*^{VAS}*+A* over ⟦ ⟧. 6[perhaps over ⟦ ⟧.

v. Streaks, corresponding to fingermarks on *r*. (cf. Gg 5184).

Gg(2) 5184 (135?)

] **209*^{VAS}*+A* 4[

Basketry marks on *v*. (cf. Gg 995).

Gg(2) 7371 (135?)

] **209*^{VAS} 1[

Trace of an earlier ruling in the middle.

Traces at left certainly not]6̣:possibly]*i* or (more difficult)]*ṇọ*.

Gg(2) 7372 (135?)

]*209^{VAS}*+A* 24

Second ten probably added later.

[21] *Scribes Cnossos*, 81–2; Shelmerdine 1988, 353.

The two best-preserved records mention issues 'to **ma-ri-ne-u*, to his (female) slave' and to a man connected with *ku-pi-ri-jo*. This *ku-pi-ri-jo* is almost certainly the person encountered in the Fh tablets in connection with the perfume industry (Section 3.2.3.5). Honey is a known perfume ingredient,[22] and Gg(2) 995 is parallel in structure to issues of oil in tablets such as Fh 371 and 5246, so like them probably an industrial disbursement. Some of h. 135's other tablets also deal with *ku-pi-ri-jo*, in connection with perfume ingredients such as cyperus and coriander (e.g. Ga(1) 517, –676). **ma-ri-ne-u* was probably also involved in perfumery (like *Kuprios* he receives a large amount of coriander in Ga(1) 674, also by h. 135), so Gg(2) 713 too may relate to some industrial purpose.[23] Whatever the case, nothing connects the tablet with religion, unless one holds that **ma-ri-ne-u* is a theonym (see Section 2.5.5). A possible reading in that case would be that the materials are going to a perfume workshop 'owned' by the god, and Weilhartner, taking the disbursement in this sense, counts the record amongst his 'indirect offerings'.[24] There is nothing inherently implausible with this view – as we saw previously, there is a *Potnian* perfumer attested at Pylos – but, as argued above (Section 2.5.5), **ma-ri-ne-u* is unlikely to be a deity, so we take Gg(2) 713 here as an 'ordinary' issue for industrial processing. Since the figure on the record is lost, the quantitative conclusions would not be affected in any case.

The final three tablets are too fragmentary to judge their functions. The scribal hand would suggest they too are perfumery records, but since the identification is uncertain (135?) some doubt should remain. In any case, Gg(2) 7372 and –5184 at least are unlikely to record offerings since such large numbers (24 and 4+) would be unparalleled in honey offerings records (none of those securely identified gives more than two amphorae per recipient).

4.2.1.4 THE GG(4) SET: PROBABLE TAXATION RECORDS

The Gg(4) set probably records tax payments. They were found in Magazine VIII [F7] and were written by h. 220, who wrote no other surviving tablets.[25]

Gg(4) <706> (220)
]to / o-pe-ro **209*^{VAS} *'ME+RI'* 20
Missing; text from *Scripta Minoa* II, pl. 37.

Gg(4) 707 + 5022 (220)
]ra **209*^{VAS} *'ME+RI'* 2̣
↓
v.]180

Gg(4) 708 + 7718 + *fr.* (220)
]-to / o-pe-ro *'ME+RI'* **209*^{VAS} 20
↓
v.]780
r. Trace of ⟦ ⟧, especially at the end and perhaps under 20.

Gg(4) 7232 + *frr.* (4) (220)
]ọ-pe-ro **209*^{VAS} *'ME+<RI>'* 5 [
Perhaps traces at left.

Three tablets include the word *o-pe-ro /ophelos/* 'owing', indicating a deficit. The most common occurrences of this word are in connection with flock censuses (e.g. the sheep records) or where deliveries have been made but are incomplete in workshop and taxation contexts (e.g. the PY Ma tablets).[26] The Gg(4) tablets are probably of this last type, since honey would not be subject to census or produced in workshops. As tax records, these tablets would be relevant to overall resources. The figures for amounts actually received are lost, but the amounts recorded as 'owing' at least give a sense of what the palace expected to receive (some forty-seven amphorae). Note that the *versos* of two of the tablets give very high figures

[22] Foster 1977a, 30; Shelmerdine 1985, 19, 22, 23. It was used to make a paste of scenting materials in preparation for maceration and to coat vessels and hands when coming in contact with the oil, to prevent the transfer of undesirable scents following stypsis when the oil was particularly receptive.
[23] See Killen 1979b, 178.
[24] Weilhartner 2005, 48–50, see also 57–9.
[25] *Scribes Cnossos*, 94. A post-*KT*[5] join to Gg 7232 is reported by Godart *et al.* (1990–1991, 381); text unchanged.
[26] See e.g. Lejeune 1959; Killen 1993, 211; *DMic.* II, 33–4. For the Ma tablets see Lejeune 1956; 1979; Shelmerdine 1973; Killen 1984b.

(180+, 780+) but we cannot be certain these referred to the same commodity as on the *rectos* so they cannot be included in our calculations.

4.2.1.5 MISCELLANEOUS GG TABLETS

There remain twelve Gg tablets not ascribed to a set. We will discuss them in turn, beginning with one that may not be concerned with honey, but rather with the vessel **209* itself. The text is as follows.

Gg 5637 + 8243 (—)

.1]pẹ-ru-ṣị-[
.2]jọ ẓạ-we-ṭẹ-ṛọ **209*VAS[
lat. inf.]me-zo-e **209*VAS[

.1 Traces at left, very close to *pẹ-*, so could be part of the same word (or divider ?). Trace at right not incompatible with *ṇụ*[.

This document is probably a tax assessment, since standard taxation vocabulary appears (although the readings are not secure): the word in line .1 is probably to be restored *pe-ru-si-nu-wo /perusinwos, -oi/* 'last year's' and line .2 gives */tsāwesteros, -oi/* 'this year's'. No honey ideogram appears, although it could have followed the vessel ideogram (cf. the Gg(4) set). However, it may be significant that the vessel ideogram on the side of the tablet is associated with the comparative *me-zo-e /medzohes/* 'bigger', which is nowhere found in the context of honey, but does occur in lists of vessels (e.g. K(1) 829).[27] Gg 5637 is thus more likely to be a record of amphorae than of honey, and is excluded from our calculations.

Two further ambiguous cases are Gg 709 and –5548, the texts of which are as follows.

Gg 709 (—)

.a]-na [
.b] **209*VAS 2 [

.b Trace of a sign on right edge, probably an ideogram (perhaps AẸṢ[).

Gg 5548 (—)

⟦**209*VAS+*A* ⟧[
↓
v. ku[

Both tablets are too fragmentary to determine either their purpose or whether they pertain to honey or amphorae. AES, if correctly read in Gg 709.b (see apparatus), would point in the latter direction since bronze is a frequent adjunct on records of vessels (e.g. KN K(1) 740, Ws 8497; PY Tn 996).[28]

Another ambiguous, but more complex, case is Gg 521. The text is as follows.

Gg 521 + 712 (—)

to-so / e-te-jo **209*VAS 542 **1̣7̣2̣*[

**1̣7̣2̣*[very uncertain.

The tablet is clearly a totalling record (see *to-so /tos(s)os/* 'so much' and the high number, 542), but the total could refer either to the vessels or to honey. The word *e-te-jo* is unhelpful in elucidating the matter. It may possibly be connected with the word *e-te-jạ*[on Fh 359 (Table

[27] I am grateful to J.T. Killen for pointing this out to me.

[28] Weilhartner (2005, 47) takes Gg 709 as an offering record on the basis of the findspot being [G1] but, as noted above, not all texts from this area are offerings records (n 4 above). A reference to vessels rather than honey would not stop the document from being an offering record since vessel offerings are attested (e.g. PY Tn 316), but there is no way to judge in the present case.

3-6.10), which records oil described as *zo-a* in connection with the TN *ku-do-ni-ja*, in which case it might be an adjective of some sort, but its meaning is unknown.[29]

A slight hint that the tablet may after all record honey is given by the occurrence of the ideogram **172* (but note the reading is uncertain) which, although not securely identified, may represent honeycomb. The ideogram is elsewhere ligatured with *KE+RO₂*, possibly /*kērion*/ 'honeycomb' or 'wax', a suitable commodity to be associated with honey.[30] The texts of the relevant tablets are as follows.

U 746 (—)

]20 **172+KE+RO*$_2$ 10

Traces of [[ ]] and of an earlier division into two lines. *R̦O̦*$_2$ half-formed, but much more likely to be this sign than *R̦O̦*$_2$.

U 436 (—)

]1̦0̦ **172+KE*[

Trace at left.

**172* appears also in the Mc series,[31] and on another Gg tablet not yet discussed but which does certainly record honey. The text is as follows.

Gg 701 (—)

]i̦-to , / da-nwa *ME+RI* **209*^{V}*+A* 16 **172* 8

da-nwa, not attested elsewhere, is seen as 'quizá teónymo' in Aura Jorro's dictionary, 'parece designar al destinatario de una ofrenda'.[32] But there is no contextual support for this interpretation and the high number (sixteen) would be exceptional for an offering record – as noted above, no securely identified offering record for honey has more than two.[33] An alternative possibility is that this is a taxation record with the structure: toponym (?*pa-*]*i̦-to*) plus name of a man responsible for the payment (the Mc tablets for instance have this type of structure). If this were so, it might be significant that the tablet is similar to Gg 521 in having **209* followed by **172*. Could Gg 701 be the lone survivor of a set which was totalled in Gg 521? The two documents were found near enough to one another to make it at least possible that they were originally filed together.[34] If so, the implication would be that Gg 521 too was a

---

[29] Melena 1976a, 162; *DMic.* I, 255 (adj.masc.nom.pl.).

[30] *Documents*, 290, 302, also 51, 553. See also Vandenabeele & Olivier 1979, 293–4; Foster 1977a, 24.

[31] The Mc tablets may record commodities intended for making weapons, perhaps bows or chariot parts (*Documents*, 301–3, 474–5; see also Melena 1972; 1988; Perna 1996). Honeycomb would be useful in such a context for e.g. waxing thread; see Killen forthcoming(b). Note that the Mc ideogram is transcribed as **142*, but must be the same ideogram as **172*. **142* resembles the syllabogram *qe* with an 'ear'. **172* is identical to **142* except it lacks the four horizontal strokes which appear inside *qe*. As J.T. Killen points out (pers. comm.), this omission, however, is not significant, since in the Mc tablets, all written by a single scribe, the ideogram is written sometimes with and sometimes without the strokes. The structure of the Mc set is very rigid, and it is impossible that different commodities are indicated there by the different forms. Thus, **142* = **172*. Note that the commodity in the Mc series is measured in units of weight, making difficult Weilhartner's suggestion (2005, 51) that the same ideogram in Gg 701 could stand for a vessel analogous to **209*, since vessels are never weighed. Although not followed by Weilhartner, it is worth noting Evans had earlier made a similar suggestion based on a misunderstanding of the ligature on U 746 as showing the handles of a stirrup jar (*PM* IV.2, 733; see Vandenabeele & Olivier 1979, 294).

[32] *DMic.* I, 156.

[33] Weilhartner (2005, 50–1) takes the record as an 'indirect offerings' tablet on the basis of its being found with members of the Ga(1) set which list **ma-ri-ne-u* and *ku-pi-ri-jo*. He thus sees it as relating to perfumery in a religious context. For reasons noted previously (n 4 above), it is not necessary that this would have been so. In any case, it is by a different scribe.

[34] Gg 521 was found part in F7 and part in F8 (*Scribes Cnossos*, 158); Gg 701 was in F17. F7 and F8 are Mags. VIII and IX; F17 is the area of the Long Corridor 'Near Door of Mag. VIII' (*Scribes Cnossos*, 21–4). Given that the tablets fell from an upper storey (note Gg 521 fell into separate magazines), it is plausible that the documents came from the same original findspot although of course the point cannot be demonstrated. Just speculatively, the U tablets might also be related. They are similar in size and shape to Gg 701, each records a number for a lost

record of honey rather than amphorae. However, as this is speculative, we will keep the figures separate.

A final tablet where **209* appears without the honey ideogram is Gg 711.

Gg 711 (—)

] ⟦*209^VAS+A 27̣0⟧⟦

↓

v.]2̣9̣0 *KE* 200[

lat. inf.]ku-do-ni-jo , [

v. First numeral badly damaged and reading rather uncertain.
l.i. Probably traces at right.

It is possible that *KE* on the verso abbreviates *ke-ro₂*, but *ke* also appears as an adjunct to vessels so this could be a record of vessels instead (for *KE* see Section 6.2.2.4). In the former case it would be interesting that, if the lost ideogram for the figure 2̣9̣0 had been **209+A* (being perhaps a correction of the erased figure on the *recto*?), the structure would be similar to Gg 521 and –701 but indicating 'honeycomb' with an abbreviation *KE* rather than ideogram **172*. However, we cannot be certain and this tablet too must be considered 'Unclear'.

We finally have six Gg tablets which do record honey, but which are so fragmentary that little can be determined about them. The texts are as follows.[35]

Gg 10 (138)

.1]*209^V 2 [
.2]ṭẹ-o *ME+RI* *209^VAS 1[
.3] *vacat* [

.2 Over ⟦ ⟧.

Gg 703 (—)

]1̣ *ME+RI* *209^VAS+A 34[

↓

v.]8̣0̣[

r. Trace at right (after and above 34[).

Gg 710 (—)

]'*ME+RI*' *209^VAS 6 [

Gg 5007 (—)

] *ME+RI* *209^VAS+A 10[

Gg 7792 + *fr.* (—)

.a]-ko-ḍẹ
.b] *ME+RI* *209^VAS 1̣[

.a]*wọ-ko-de* or]*ṭọ-ko-de* possible.

Gg 9244 (—)

] '*ME+*[*RI*]' *209^VAS[
inf. mut.

The first tablet, Gg 10, as discussed in Section 2.2.2, is probably an offerings record because it was found in the 'Clay Chest' along with the Fp(1) set which was written by the same hand

---

ideogram followed by **172*, and one was found in the same area as the two Gg tablets. U 436 was found in E6, the Room of the Niche, on the other side of the Long Corridor wall from F17 although not immediately adjacent to it. U 746, however, came from farther afield, H5 near the Throne Room (on which see Firth 2000–2001a, 200–1).

[35] Texts from *KT*[5]; a proposed reading '*ṂẸ+ḌỊ*' in Gg 9244 (Melena *et al.* 1990–1991, 389) is not followed in *KT*[6].

(138). The small amounts recorded are consistent with this.[36] Gg 703 might be a taxation record on account of the relatively high number and possible parallel structure with the Gg(4) set (note the large number on the *verso*). Nothing can be said about Gg 710 and 5007 except that given the relatively large numbers they are unlikely to be offerings records. Gg 7792 may be an offering record if the final *-de* is an allative, but this would be uncertain even if the reading were secure and the tablet is considered here 'Unclear'.[37] Gg 9244 is also 'Unclear'.[38]

For the sake of completeness, a final occurrence of **209* may be mentioned, on Uc 160, a banqueting/offerings record. However, the sign for honey is missing and **209* is listed alongside other vessels, so probably amphorae rather than the contents were concerned.

4.2.1.6 DISCUSSION: HONEY AT KNOSSOS

Amounts of honey recorded in the Gg and Fs series are summarised in Table 4-2.

Table 4-2. Honey at Knossos

	*ME+RI *209*	= V		*ME+RI *209*	figure on *verso*
1. *Offerings*			**3. *Taxation***		
Gg(1) set	3–6+?	6–9+?	*3a. probable*		
Gg(3) set	6–7+		Gg(4) <706>	20	
Gg 10	3+		Gg(4) 707	2̣	]180
Fs set (Table 3-5)	1 [*211*^{V}]	4	Gg(4) 708	20	]780
TOTAL 1	**13–17+**	**10–13+**	Gg(4) 7232	5	
2. *Perfumery*			**Sub-total 3a**	**47̣**	
2a. definitely h. 135			*3b. possible*		
Gg(2) 713	1+		Gg 521	542	
Gg(2) 995	6+		Gg 701	16	
Sub-total 2a	**7+**		**Sub-total 3b**	**558**	
2b. probably h. 135			**TOTAL 3**	**605**	
Gg(2) 5184	4+		**4. *Unclear***		
Gg(2) 7371	1+		*4a. definitely honey*		
Gg(2) 7372	24		Gg 703	34+	8̣0̣
Sub-total 2b	**29+**		Gg 710	6	
TOTAL 2	**36+**		Gg 5007	10+	
			Gg 7792	1̣+	
			Gg 9244	1+	
			Sub-total 4a	**52+**	
			4b. need not be honey		
			Gg 709	2	
			Gg 711	⟦27̣0⟧	2̣9̣0
			Gg 5548	*lost*	
			Gg 5637	*lost*	

In assessing the figures, the first issue that must be dealt with is how to compare the approximately V 10–13+ measured in liquid units with the figures for amphorae. It is a reasonably large amount (some 16.0–20.8 litres), and must be accounted for. One approach would be to attempt to compare the amount with capacities of archaeologically attested amphorae, although these can vary widely. For the sake of argument, standard large amphorae at Pylos (Shape 45, a vessel which resembles ideogram **209*) had capacities varying from 10.5

[36] These points are noted also by Weilhartner (2005, 47). Note the number in the lower line although broken is unlikely to have been more than 3 because of the way the digits are laid out.
[37] Weilhartner (2005, 49) takes this as an 'indirect offerings' record on the basis of the possible reading]*wọ-ko-de*, which he takes as representing the workshop of a deity, but objections to this aside (see Section 2.5.5), note that]*ṭọ-ko-de* is also possible.
[38] It may join X 9235 (*KT*[6]), but this would not add much to the text.

to 15.1 litres.[39] The Gg liquid measures of 16–21 litres would fill one or at most two such vessels, so giving a total of 14–19+ amphorae for offerings. These figures are given provisionally and without suggesting that the procedure is not dubious on a number of levels – but the alternative of ignoring the liquid measures altogether would be yet more misleading. It should also be noted that vessel shape **211* from Fs 8 is here counted as an amphora although it was probably a smaller vessel.[40]

With these caveats in mind, let us examine the figures. The first two sections in the table, offerings and perfumery records, both count as 'disbursements for final use' since honey used in perfumery, unlike oil, would be entirely consumed in the manufacturing process. The figures should be considered both with and without the tablets not securely ascribed to h. 135, since scribal hand is the only reason for thinking these are perfumery records and they would otherwise be listed as 'Unclear'. If we include only those securely ascribed (2a), total disbursements come to 21–26 units; offerings account for 67–73% of these. Including all on the other hand (2a+2b) gives 28–35% (totals of 50–55). There is a large difference in the figures depending on what is included, but either way it can be said that a substantial proportion of disbursements of honey recorded in the surviving Knossos documents was for offerings.

Overall resources are (also) difficult to determine. The amount issued for offerings (including those counted in liquid measures) is about 30–40% of the total from the probable taxation records (3a). If it were correct, however, that Gg 521 records honey, the proportion issued for offerings would shrink to just 3–4%.[41] In this case it is not merely hazards of preservation that create difficulties, but our ignorance of the vocabulary and significance of this crucial document. We will encounter such difficulties throughout the study.

4.2.2 HONEY AT CHANIA

One of the five Linear B tablets so far found at Chania happens to be an offerings record.[42] The text is as follows.

Gq 5

.1	di-wi-jo-[de ,]di-ẉẹ	*ṂẸ+ṚỊ*	**2̣0̣9̣*^{vas}*+Ạ*	1̣	[
.2	di-wo-nu-so	*ṂẸ+ṚỊ*	[ ] 2̣		[

Two offerings are recorded: one amphora of honey for Zeus (*/Diwei/*) and two for Dionysos (*/Diwonusoi/*),[43] both at or going to the shrine of Zeus (*/Diwion*[*-de*]*/*).[44] The record is very

[39] *PoN* I, 382.
[40] It was possibly a piriform rhyton; see Bendall, forthcoming(b).
[41] Note the figure draws on Gg 521 alone rather than adding it to other tax records because, if it were a totalling tablet for the tax records, the other figures were presumably already subsumed. Of course it is possible that *e-te-jo* indicates a particular source and that Gg 521 was the totalling record for this source, but the figures are not much affected either way. Adding Gg 521 to the other records gives 605 units, of which the offerings are 2–3%
[42] Hallager, Vlasakis & Hallager 1992, 75–81.
[43] KH Gq 5 importantly established Dionysos with certainty as a member of the Mycenaean pantheon (Hallager, Vlasakis & Hallager 1992, 77). *di-wo-nu-so-jo* was already attested at Pylos (Xa 102, now Ea; Xa 1419), but the contexts were obscure (the tablets are fragmentary) and the word did not necessarily have to refer to a deity, despite the tantalising appearance on Xa 1419 *verso* of a possible compound containing the word for wine (Chadwick 1976, 99–100; *Documents*, 127, 411; cf. Puhvel 1964). Xa 1419 is still poorly understood, but subsequent to the publication of the Chania tablet, a new join shed light on PY Ea 102, which turns out to be a record of land connected to the *e-ka-ra /eskhara/* 'hearth (read: shrine)' of Dionysos (Melena 2000–2001a, 357–60); see Section 2.4.3.
[44] A shrine of Zeus is attested also at Pylos, both with and without the allative (Fr 1230, Tn 316.8, and probably Mb 1336). The allative in Gq 5 is restored (Hallager, Vlasakis & Hallager 1992, 76), but the identification is likely. E.g. if writing *di-wi-jo-jo*, attested as a month name (in gen.sg.) at Knossos (Fp(1) 5), the scribe would probably have written the word for 'month' as well.

similar to records of honey offerings at Knossos and, given the importance of honey for offerings there, it is of interest that one of the few tablets from Chania would turn out to concern honey offerings.

No other tablets from Chania record honey so we cannot comment on proportions of disbursements and overall resources, but it is worth noting that one of the Knossos records, Gg 711, records 2̣70 amphorae associated with this place (*ku-do-ni-jo*, ethnicon of Kydonia). This is one of the tablets which may rather deal with the vessels themselves than with honey (Section 4.2.1.5), but if it is a record of honey it would suggest western Crete was producing substantial amounts of the commodity.[45]

4.2.3 HONEY AT PYLOS

The ligature *ME+RI*, so common at Knossos, does not appear outside Crete, and the only direct mention of honey at Pylos is on Un 718, which contains the genitive *me-ri-to /melitos/* in line .5 (see also lines .12 and .13). In addition, one of the sealings from the Wine Magazine may record wine treated with honey,[46] and a man in the land tenure tablets (Ea 481, –711+) is called *me-ri-te-wo* (gen.), which if it means something like 'beekeeper' might attest to beekeeping on behalf of the palace.[47] Honey is probably represented in some cases by the syllabogram *ME* used as an ideogram on various tablets, but it is clear *ME* does not represent the same commodity in each instance where it appears and it is important to examine the contexts. The tablets involved are the Ma series plus Mn 11 (both in Section 6.4.1.2); three banqueting records, Un 2, –718, –1177[48] (Section 2.3.2.2); an offerings record, Un 219 (Section 6.6.2); and two perfumery records Un 267 and –616 [ex An] (Section 2.5.3). All of these records are discussed elsewhere as indicated. In the present section the question is only whether *ME* in a given instance represents honey.

The Ma tablets and Mn 11 can be dismissed at once. *ME* represents the same commodity in both cases (the tablets were written by the same scribe and share numerous ideograms), but it is unlikely to be honey. The Ma tablets are proportional taxation records dealing with six commodities. Two can be identified with confidence as a textile (**146*) and a skin (**152*), probably oxhide, but the other four are represented by syllabograms used as ideograms whose meaning is obscure. The most plausible interpretation of the series as a whole has been recently put forward by Killen, who argues that the commodities are being requisitioned for military preparations.[49] He suggests that *RI* is linen thread and *KE* may abbreviate *kērion*, beeswax, a substance (probably) already encountered at Knossos.[50] *ME*, however, is here unlikely to represent honey, because it is counted in whole units only and appears in very high numbers (in the hundreds).[51] It could possibly be something such as wood. If it is correct, however, that *KE* is beeswax, this would of course constitute evidence for a product *related* to honey, so would be worth noting in terms of overall resources. The commodity is measured in terms of weight in the Ma tablets (note the possible parallel with the KN Mc records where **172/*142* also is weighed) and an amount of M 149 is recorded, perhaps some 149 kg. If this

---

[45] As noted by Hallager, Vlasakis & Hallager 1992, 78–9. The balance of probability given the appearance of *KE* on this tablet is that it did indeed concern honey, but certainty is impossible.

[46] Wr 1360 recording VIN along with the word *me-ri-ti-jo*, possibly /*melitios*/ 'honeyed', but the word could also refer to e.g. a man's name. See Palmer (1994, 63; 1995, 275) for discussion and references; also Sherratt 2004, 203.

[47] Chadwick 1976, 125–6; *Documents*, 560. Also, the occupational title *me-ri-du-ma-te* seems to be a compound involving the word for honey; it appears in lists of temple servants so may refer to a religious functionary (e.g. An 39; Section 2.3.3).

[48] According to a new reading for Un 1177 (Melena 2000–2001b, 376).

[49] Killen forthcoming(b). On the series see also now Perna 2004.

[50] It has long been speculated that *KE* may indicate beeswax (see *Documents*, 465).

[51] *Documents*, 465.

was honeycomb, the palace apparently had access to substantial resources. But again the identification of the commodity is tentative.

The remaining cases are more positive. In the perfumery records, *ME* probably does record honey since the commodity was known as an ingredient in perfume manufacture (both record disbursements of raw materials to perfumers).[52] It is measured as a liquid in Un 616, which supports the identification.

One secure reference to honey in the context of foodstuffs commonly used for banqueting has already been mentioned (Un 718) and it is likely enough that *ME* represents honey in the other banqueting records too. A little support comes from the measures. In Un 1177 *ME* appears with the unit V, which could be liquid or solid, but in Un 2 *ME* is certainly recorded in liquid measures. In this tablet, the sign is preceded by another sign also suggested to indicate honey, **132*. The ideogram depicts a vessel similar to an amphora although more piriform in shape, surcharged with *ME*, and followed again by a liquid measure (S 2).[53] Perhaps two different honey-related products were intended, but the context provides no further clues. Both instances are included in the table, although it is not certain they do indeed related to honey.[54]

Finally, Un 219 (Section 6.6.2) is an offerings record of some sort which apparently deals with aromatics (cf. *tu-wo*, perhaps /*thuwos*/, in line 1). Honey would not be out of place on an offerings record, but there is no reason that it has to be present.[55] We include it in Table 4-3, but again without conviction.

Possible occurrences of honey at Pylos are summarised in Table 4-3.

Table 4-3. Honey at Pylos?

	honey??	= V		**honey??**	= V
1. ***Religious***			**2.** ***Perfumery***		
1a. Offering			Un 267	*ME* 2	36
Un 219	*ME* 1	18?	Un 616	*ME po* 6 S 1 V 4	118
1b. Banqueting			**TOTAL 2**		**154**
Un 718	*me-ri-to* V 4+*	4	**TOTAL 1b+2**		**180**
Un 2	*ME* S 1	6	**TOTAL 1+2**		**198??**
Un 2	**132* S 2	12	**3.** ***Deliveries of related products?***		
Un 1177	*ME* V 4	4	Wr 1360 (wine)	VIN *me-ri-ti-jo*	—
Sub-total 1b		**26**	Ma series (honeycomb?)	*KE* M 149	—
TOTAL 1		**44??**			

Notes
* Summed
Ma series and Mn 11: *ME* not honey.
Un 267: The figure follows Shelmerdine (1985, 17) in assuming two major liquid units are meant.

52 Foster 1977a, 30; 1977b, 62; Shelmerdine 1985, 17, 20–1.
53 Vandenabeele & Olivier 1979, 263–4.
54 For the sake of completeness we may also note in passing that Gérard-Rousseau (1968, 27) suggested the word *a*$_3$*-ka-na-jo* in the banqueting record Un 1185 may be an adjective /*hagnaios*/ referring to a 'pure' liquid of some sort, perhaps honey. However, as Palmer (1994, 114 n 135) rightly points out the word should be a substantive rather than an adjective (although I do not follow her further point that the amount recorded is unusually large to refer to honey; cf. Gg(1) 7369). Palaima (1992b, 65–6) suggests it is instead an animal product of some sort. In any case, nothing need connect the word with honey.
55 Note *PoN* IV now reads]*me* 1 rather than]*ME* 1, while noting that the latter reading is 'not impossible'.

Given the numerous uncertainties, the figures do not inspire much confidence. In particular, the question-marked figure given for Un 219 (1a) is probably best simply ignored since we do not know what the unit was or even if it was honey. Without this amount (and even with it), substantially more is disbursed for perfumery than in connection with religion – just 14% of final use disbursements are for banqueting. This is the first instance we have seen where use for religion does *not* account for surprisingly substantial amounts of a given commodity. We will return to this in the final chapter.

Finally, overall resources of honey at Pylos are impossible to estimate from the Linear B data, but if *KE* was honeycomb, the palace would appear to have had access to considerable resources.

4.3 WINE (**131* = VIN)

4.3.1 WINE IN LINEAR B

Wine appears primarily in banqueting contexts, and occasionally on offerings records and in non-religious contexts such as *o-no* 'payments' and perfumery. The majority of wine recorded in banqueting records will have been for human consumption at feasts. However, there is archaeological and iconographic evidence for libations,[56] and some of the wine may have been consumed in this way (so, as 'offerings').[57] Wine is securely attested in Linear B at four sites: Knossos, Pylos, Mycenae and Thebes. We will examine these in turn.

4.3.2 WINE AT KNOSSOS

Wine at Knossos appears in the Fs series (Section 3.2.2.3, Table 3-5), three banqueting records, Uc 160 and –161, both from the RCT, and U 7063 (texts for all in Section 2.3.2.3), and the following three Gm tablets.[58]

Gm 840 (—)

.1]ṇị-jo , / a-pu-da-se-we
.2]1 VIN 168̣
.3] VIN 100
.4]25 VIN 75[
.5 [ ]ṭọ [ ]125 VIN 155

reliqua pars sine regulis

Cut at bottom. Palimpsest.
.2 Trace of upright before]1.
.5 One sign (or, less probably, two signs) missing before] ṭọ. Trace of upright before]125.

Gm 5788 (—)

.1]si-jo , VIN[
.2] *vac.* [

[56] E.g. Hägg 1990.
[57] For a general discussion of wine in religious contexts see Palmer 1994, esp. 135–42; Wright 1995b. For wine in general (including later periods) see e.g. papers in Amouretti *et al.* 1993; McGovern *et al.* 1995; Horden & Purcell 2000, 582 (with further references); Mylopotamitaki 2002.
[58] All of these documents have been discussed by Palmer (1994, esp. 81–2, 172–7; 1995). Note with regard to the tablets identified here as banqueting records that Palmer's study predates some of the major work on banqueting and she sometimes endorses other explanations for these records. For instance, she takes Uc 160 as a 'collection or inventory' record (1995, 276) and U 7063 as a possible collection (1994, 189).

Gm 9878 (—)

sup. mut.

.1]VIN [

.2]VỊṆ [

inf. mut.

Perhaps .0 *sup. mut.*

.2 Perhaps ̣1[.

Gm 5788 and Gm 9878 are too fragmentary for their functions to be determined (and the numbers are lost), so our focus is on Gm 840.[59] The tablet is broken, but the right side preserves entries for very large amounts of wine plus part of the heading. The crucial question here is whether the document records receipts or disbursements, an issue discussed by Palmer.[60] The word *a-pu-da-se-we* in line .1 is probably dative singular or nominative plural of a functionary's title, possibly /*apudas*(*s*)*eus*/ 'distributor',[61] probably formed from ἀποδατέομαι.[62] While derivatives of δατέομαι should have a sense relating to 'distribution', Palmer argues for a scenario in which this sense could be compatible with Gm 840 being a record of collections:

> If *a-pu-da-se-we* is nom.pl., the *apudassēwes* are distributors, providing large amounts of wine to four recipients, cf. PY Vn 20, but if it is dative, the *a-pu-da-se-we* is understood to be the recipient of the wine listed in the next four lines, and so would act as an assessor or collector in this particular transaction.[63]
>
> … the internal structure of the tablet, and the irregular amounts listed suggest that *a-pu-da-se-we* is dative singular.
>
> … the lack of an obvious verb, the irregular quantities of each commodity and the similarity in format to tablets recording harvests point to *a-pu-da-se-we* who is (dat.sg.) collecting for later distribution rather than (nom.pl.) distributing at that moment.[64]

Gm 840 does in some ways resemble a harvest (or taxation) record, and the balance of probability is that it does record resources being collected by the palace (the irregular quantities being particularly suggestive).[65] On the other hand, if Gm 840 were a distribution, the suggested parallel with Vn 20 might suggest the wine was intended for banqueting (although it should be noted that the amounts recorded in Gm 840 are much larger than in any securely identified banqueting record except possibly Vn 20 itself).[66] The different ramifications in either instance plus other possibilities are discussed below.

---

[59] Palmer (1994, 176) takes them as collection records, which they may, but need not, be (see Killen 1994–1995b, 373).

[60] Palmer 1994, 81–2.

[61] *DMic.* I, 88 with references.

[62] Ruijgh 1967a, 355–6. He also mentions the possibility of an AN (*loc. cit.* 355 n.17), which is mentioned by Palmer (1994, 81), although she does not follow this interpretation (note Killen 1994–1995b, 373). See Palmer (1994, 73–85) for the various derivatives of δατέομαι. For a meaning more along the lines of 'to assess, measure' than to apportion (although the senses are of course similar) see Melena 1994–1995a, 97.

[63] Palmer 1994, 81.

[64] Palmer 1994, 82.

[65] See also Palmer 1994, 172–3, 189–90. 'Irregular amounts' are common on harvest records and 'tax records' relating to agricultural produce (see e.g. the Fh tablets, the Ga(2) set, etc.). There are other taxation records of course where assessments are made from the 'top-down' where the numbers tend to be more 'regular' (unless modified by factors such as e.g. exemptions); see Shelmerdine 1973; 1989; Olivier 1974; Lejeune 1979; de Fidio 1982; Killen 1996a.

[66] Palmer (1994, 76, 82, 115, 194, 196) directly compares the figures in Gm 840 with those in Vn 20, but caution is recommended. We do not actually know how wine was measured in Vn 20, since the ideogram for the major unit is not used. It may have been intended, but we cannot be certain. For amounts of wine in banqueting records at Pylos see Bendall forthcoming(a).

Table 4-4 sets out figures from all Knossos tablets recording wine. Uc 160 and –161 are from the RCT, so are listed separately.[67]

Table 4-4. Wine at Knossos

	VIN	= V
1. *Banqueting/offerings*		
1a. RCT		
Uc 160.3	S 1 V 3 Z 2	9.5
Uc 160.4	S 4̣	2̣4̣
Uc 161	60[	1080+
Sub-total 1a		**1113.5+**
1b. non-RCT		
Fs series	Table 3-5	19
U 7063	*lost*	1+
Sub-total 1b		**20+**
2. *Gm 840 (non-RCT)*		
Gm 840.2	168̣	3̣0̣2̣4̣
Gm 840.3	100	1800
Gm 840.4	75[	1350+
Gm 840.5	155	2790
TOTAL 2		**8964+**
3. *Unclear (non-RCT)*		
Gm 5788	*lost*	1+
Gm 9878	*lost*	2+

Note
Gm 9878: Note the VIN ideogram appears twice so we count '2'.

An initial point to observe is that the majority of wine in Section 1 is from RCT tablets: over V 1100 units, compared with just V 20+ from the non-RCT documents. The well-known problem of differential preservation of Linear B documents comes particularly sharply into focus here since this seems highly unlikely to reflect any real situation. Nevertheless, as biased as the figures evidently are, let us attempt to assess them. Apart from Gm 840 and the two 'Unclear' records, all disbursements are for religious (or semi-religious) purposes. We should consider the figures given different possible scenarios for Gm 840, which we reiterate:

1. Gm 840 records a collection
2. Gm 840 records a disbursement for banqueting
3. Gm 840 records a disbursement for other purposes.

We examine these in turn.

1. If Gm 840 is a record of collections, the amount collected is far larger than the amounts recorded as being disbursed, even including the RCT tablets: a mere 0.2% without the RCT tablets, and 12% with them. Including them is of course dubious since they are not contemporary, but this perspective on the figures again usefully underscores preservational factors. It is worth observing that even with the RCT tablets included, the majority of disbursements are simply 'missing', and there are no records of non-religious disbursements. Palmer also comments on this, noting that 'for the final year at Knossos, only the Fs series … and U 7063 tell us how the palace used the wine it collected.'[68]

[67] The findspot of U 7063 is unknown, but it is not from the RCT so could be contemporary with the other tablets. Since the numbers are lost it hardly matters for present purposes in any case.
[68] Palmer 1994, 176–7.

2. If Gm 840 is a disbursement for banqueting (which is considered here unlikely), these would be very large banquets indeed. (V 8964 would be some 14,342 litres – over 19,000 modern bottles.) In this case, there would be no disbursements for non-religious purposes, and no records of collections at all.

3. Although the primary use of wine is human consumption, that need not mean that every disbursement would be for banquets and offerings. As we shall see, at Pylos wine is sometimes issued as *o-no* payments and is used in perfumery. Also, it is conceivable that a palace might issue wine to workers or retainers, either as daily or monthly rations or in the form of larger allotments supplying households for extended periods. Such practices are known for the ancient Near East and the classical world, but there are no unambiguous Mycenaean examples of such usage, and without clear parallels one would hesitate to ascribe such a function to Gm 840. Palmer has made the important observation that while wine is given out as (temporary) maintenance e.g. during religious festivals, it is not disbursed as simple rations.[69]

In both scenarios (1) and (2), 100% of disbursement records would be for purposes related to religion. However, since the recorded disbursements, even with the RCT tablets included, do not account for a significant proportion even of Gm 840 alone, it should be noted that we simply do not have the documents for the majority of disbursements.

In terms of overall resources, whether the large amount of wine recorded in Gm 840 was being collected or disbursed it does give at least some sense of (at least part of) the scale of resources available to the palace. On the VC values the tablet deals with some 14,342 litres of wine. It is clear that the palace had access to substantial resources in the commodity, however obtained. Palatial involvement in viticulture is attested at Knossos, although, as Palmer notes, it was not monitored in the intensive way that, for instance, textile production was.[70] Gv 863, for instance, records 420 plants indicated by the word *we-je-we* and the ideogram **174*, which are probably vines trained up trees.[71] As noted above, the disbursements recorded in contemporary documents account for just 0.2% of the wine recorded at Knossos.

4.3.3 WINE AT PYLOS

Wine at Pylos, unlike Knossos, appears on numerous tablets and in a variety of contexts, including banqueting. The banqueting records were discussed above (Ua 17, Un 2, –47, –138 and –612 in Section 2.3.2.2; Un 718 and –853 in Section 2.4.4). Our focus here will be on the non-banqueting records, but a special feature noted above of some of the banqueting records should be mentioned here. In some cases the foodstuffs recorded were supplied not by the palace itself, but by important officials such as *e-ke$_2$-ra-wo*, **we-u-da-ne-u* and *du-ni-jo*.[72] Arguably, such contributions thus do not represent 'palatial resources' and should be counted separately. Yet to do this would in some ways itself be misleading. The persons involved are all high officials of various sorts – *e-ke$_2$-ra-wo* may even have been the *wanax* himself and **we-u-da-ne-u* the *lāwāgetās*.[73] However that may be, these are persons closely allied with the palace. Also, since the foodstuffs are intended for state-organised ceremonial banqueting, the resources were managed by and had become available to the palace as a corporate entity, whatever their origin. The tablets concerned in the present section are Un 138 (*du-ni-jo*) and Un 718 plus –853 (*e-ke$_2$-ra-wo*). It will be seen that our conclusions would remain unaltered whatever approach is taken to these records.

---

[69] Palmer 1994, 190; cf. Palmer 1995, 277.
[70] Palmer 1994, 188.
[71] Palmer 1994, 57–60, esp. 59; 1995, 276–7.
[72] For discussion and further bibliography see Bendall 2004, 105–7.
[73] Lindgren 1973 II, 134–6, 153; see Chapter 2 n 262 for further references. For *du-ni-jo* see Bendall 1998–1999, 7 n 25 with further references; Bendall 2004, 106.

We begin with a record of an issue of perfume ingredients to a perfumer, which was discussed above (see Section 2.5.3); we repeat the text here.

Un 267 (S2-H1)

.1 o-do-ke , a-ko-so-ta
.2 tu-we-ta , a-re-pa-zo-o
.3 tu-we-a , a-re-pa-te
.4 ze-so-me-no
.5 ko-ri-a$_2$-da-na AROM 6
.6 ku-pa-ro$_2$ AROM 6 **157* 16
.7 *KAPO* 2 T 5 VIN$_a$ 20 *ME* 2
.8 LANA 2 VIN$_b$ 2
.9 *vacat*
.10 *vacat*
.11 *vacat*

.3 , *ze-so-me.*
.4 Possibly damaged divider after *ze-so-me-no*; *ko-ri.*
.7-8 VIN in differing forms (a and b).
.9 *ri* at left.
Verso Large double mark possibly made with a small finger, not identifiable with a sign.

As noted previously, the heading is commonly read: 'Thus Alxoitas gave to Thyestes the perfume-boiler aromatics for perfume destined for boiling.'[74] The use of the ingredients has been elucidated by Foster and Shelmerdine;[75] wine was used for soaking aromatics to begin releasing their essential oils.[76] The ideogram here is – unusually – attested in two forms, the standard VIN and a truncated version, VIN$_b$. The variant has been proposed to represent either must,[77] wine of inferior quality,[78] or vinegar.[79] Since it is universally agreed to be a wine-related product, whatever exactly it is, it is counted for present purposes along with ordinary wine. Note that wine used in perfumery is considered as being disbursed for 'final use' because, like honey, and unlike oil, it is consumed in the manufacturing process.

Our next document records an *o-no* transaction. The text is as follows.

An 35 (H3/ —)

.1 to-ko-do-mo , de-me-o-te
.2 pu-ro VIR 2 me-te-to-de VIR 3
.3 sa-ma-ra-de VIR 3 re-u-ko-to-ro VIR 4
.4 *vacat*
.5 a-ta-ro , tu-ru-pte-ri-ja , o-no
.6 LANA 2 CAP^f 4 **146* 3 VIN 10 *NI* 4

Lines .5-6 (appropriate to class Un) possibly by a second hand.
.4 PUNCTS at top before *-ru-* and at bottom between *o-* and *-no*.
.6 **146* 3: corrected from 6 (stylus rub).

The tablet is divided into two paragraphs, written by different scribes and not necessarily directly related. The first refers to /*toikhodomoi*/ 'builders', the second to a transaction involving a man *a-ta-ro* who receives various commodities, including wine, in exchange for *tu-ru-pte-ri-ja*, probably /*struptēriās*/ 'alum'.[80] For the transaction term *o-no* see Section 3.2.3.5. The reasons for and circumstances of the exchange are not entirely understood,[81] but for present purposes it is enough to note the items were issued for final use.

[74] Shelmerdine 1985, 17; *Documents*, 223–4, 441–2.
[75] Foster 1977b, esp. 61–2; Shelmerdine 1985, esp. 17–20; see also Palmer 1994, esp. 88–91.
[76] Shelmerdine 1985, 19; Palmer 1994, 89.
[77] *Documents*, 223, 441.
[78] Stanley 1982; Shelmerdine 1985, 19.
[79] Palmer 1994, 89–91; see 35–6 for the form of the ideogram.
[80] *Documents*, 174, 422; Firth 2007.
[81] See Palmer 1994, 92–3 for a recent discussion with further references.

Next we have two Gn tablets, both discussed by Palmer.[82] The text of Gn 428 is as follows.

Gn 428 (Ciii)

.1]*vest*. , [ ] *vacat* [
.2]*vest*.[ ]me-jo , [
.3 ka-ra-te-mi-de VIN 1 S 2 [
.4 tu-ra-te-u-si VIN S 1
.5 o-ro-ke-we VIN S 1 i-do-me-ni-jo , S 1
.6 ki-jo-ne-u-si S 1
.7 *vacat*
.8 *vacat*

.1]*vest*.:]*mu*
.5-6 <VIN> S

The heading is lost, but *tu-ra-te-u-si* in line .4 must be the dative plural of *tu-ra-te-u*, attested in Ae 8 and 72. It is probably an occupational title, possibly related to cult since the Ae tablets have religious connections.[83] The other tablet in which the word appears, Vn 48, also has cult connections.[84] *ki-jo-ne-u-si* in line .6 is unattested elsewhere but also may be a dative plural title. The other words are probably men's names, presumably also dative. Gn 428 shares some formal features and (probably) vocabulary with Fn 324,[85] which deals with allocations to religious personnel and other workers at festivals (Section 2.3.3.1),[86] and Gn 428 may be a similar type of record.[87] In any case, the context is probably religious.

Gn 720 is less clear. The text is as follows.

Gn 720 (Ci)

.1 da-ka-ja-pi , pi-ke-te-i VIN 10
.2 i-ka-sa-ja , ru-ki-jo VIN 9
.3 *vacat*
.4 *vacat*
.5 *vacat*
.6 *vacat*
.7 *vacat*

.2 Erased and rewritten.

da-ka-ja-pi and *i-ka-sa-ja* are usually taken as TNs, and *pi-ke-te-i* and *ru-ki-jo* as MNs, possibly in the dative. Only one of the four words is attested elsewhere (at any site), *ru-ki-jo*, which is certainly a MN on Jn 415.11. Palmer takes the document as recording disbursements,[88] and notes that the amounts are similar to those on some of the mixed commodity records, identified after her study as banqueting foodlists.[89] Gn 720 could be related to such a context, although the format would be unusual in that most such records (a probable exception being Un 718) do not record TNs (although we cannot be certain that these are TNs since they are *hapax*).[90] An alternative possibility is that the tablet records a collection with a note of the location and the person responsible for the delivery. However, since doubt remains, the tablet is considered here 'Unclear'.

---

[82] Palmer 1994, 83–4, 189–90, 192.
[83] Palmer 1994, 83.
[84] *DMic*. II, 377; Palmer 1994, 83. A cautiously worded but strong case for the religious associations of *tu-ra-te-u* is now made by Killen (2006a, 106–7).
[85] Palmer 1994, 82–3. *o-ro-ke-we* and *i-do-me-ni-jo* in Gn 428.5 are likely restorations in Fn 324.5.7 respectively.
[86] Killen 2001b, esp. 441; note that these are not 'ordinary' rations but maintenance for the duration of festivals (see Section 2.3.3).
[87] Palmer (1994, 83, 119, 190), writing before Killen's article, agrees that these are religious 'handouts' of some sort.
[88] Palmer 1994, 84, 189.
[89] Palmer 1994, 192.
[90] Palmer (1994, 73) observed that this is one of just four records in the entire Linear B corpus that records wine alone. The new Thebes tablets have changed this picture but the relative rarity of documents dealing with wine alone is worth noting.

The next document, Un 1321, is also poorly understood. The text is as follows.[91]

Un 1321 (H34)

.1]-ta-ri-ja , a$_2$-to , o-ra-qe-ṭẹ[
.2]q̣ẹ-we , to-sa-ka-pa-ra VIN [
.3]ta-qe , a$_3$-te , to-o , GRA [
.4] , o-pa-ro-ze , ti-se , pa-ro[

.1 *-to-* perhaps over erasure.
.2 No spacing between *to-sa* and *ka-pa-ra*.
.3 Perhaps trace of sign after GRA, probably not a numeral; Ţ does not seem likely, and a syllabogram is not to be excluded.
.4 *-pa-ro-ze* over erasure, and the four signs *(o, pa, ro, ze)* are written with large intervals between them.

The tablet is broken and the surviving sign-groups are obscure.[92] As discussed elsewhere, the document is unlikely to relate to perfumery, land tenure or *o-no* transactions since none of the associated vocabulary appears (although this could have been present in the lacunae), and the appearance of VIN together with wheat (GRA, line .3) may suggest a banqueting context since the ideograms appear together only on such documents (including banqueting foodlists related to land tenure).[93] However, we cannot be certain and the tablet is considered here 'unclear'.

Finally, four sealings found in the Wine Magazine record wine (Wr 1358, –1359, –1360, and –1361).[94] These probably relate to deliveries to the palace,[95] but no numbers are recorded so it is not clear what we should 'count'.[96] The sealings are noted here, but not included in our totals.

Table 4-5 summarises the data for wine at Pylos. The amounts on Vn 20 are totalled separately since the unit of measure is unclear.

Table 4-5. Wine at Pylos

	VIN	= V		VIN	= V
1. *Banqueting*			**2. *Perfumery***		
1a. ordinary or unspecified			Un 267	22*	**396**
Un 2	20 S 1	366	**3. *o-no***		
Ua 17	47 S 1 V 5	857	An 35	10	**180**
Un 47	*lost*	1+	**TOTAL 2+3**		**576**
Un 138	13	234	**TOTAL 1+2+3**		2375 (or 9756)
Un 612	5	90	**4. *Unclear***		
1b. connected with land tenure			Gn 720	19*	342
Un 718	6*	108	Un 1321	*lost*	1+
Un 853	5	90	Wr 1358	—	—
1c. festival rations?			Wr 1359	—	—
Gn 428	3*	54	Wr 1360	—	—
TOTAL 1a+1b+1c		**1800+**	Wr 1361	—	—
1d. unit of measure unknown	*wo-no*				
Vn 20	410	**7380??****			

Notes: * Summed from various entries. ** If liquid measure used.

All except the 'Unclear' tablets concern disbursements for final use. Of these, the banqueting records account for the great majority of the whole: 76% without taking Vn 20 into account, 94% with it (assuming the units represented liquid measures). To an extent it is unsurprising that the majority of wine would be associated with banqueting since, although wine does have

[91] The text follows Bennett (1992, 120). The apparatus is from *PTT*, with points Bennett confirms deleted.
[92] See Palmer 1994, 115–16, for discussion with bibliography.
[93] Bendall 2003, 211.
[94] See Palmer 1994, 143–65 for extensive discussion of the sealings and Wine Magazine; Olivier 1997.
[95] For the function see e.g. Killen 1994.
[96] Possibly the ideograms are meant to represent single units; cf. the argument for the Thebes sealings recording e.g. sheep where each sealing = one animal (Piteros, Olivier & Melena 1990).

other uses, its main use would have been consumption. But Palmer's observation that wine does not seem to have been used for ordinary rations should be noted again here, as should the absence of records for 'everyday' consumption.

As at Knossos, calculating overall resources is difficult. Even if Gn 720 were a collection record, which is uncertain, it records a mere V 342, far less than the total disbursed.[97] One approach might be to look at archaeological evidence for storage capacities. The total amount of wine recorded on the banqueting records excluding Vn 20 is some 2880 litres, and Palmer calculates that the capacity of the pithoi in the Wine Magazine is some 4683 litres (although not all of the pithoi need have held wine),[98] so the documented amounts could certainly have been stored at the palace.[99] There is only one record at Pylos recording vines, Er 880, a record connected in some way to the contributions making up the *dosmos* to Poseidon of the man *e-ke-ra$_2$-wo* on Un 718 and –853 (Section 2.4.4).[100] The tablet records 1100 vines, but how much this would have produced is uncertain since there are many unknown variables such as how old the plants were. It is worth noting that Er 880 was drawn up for a specialised purpose (the *dosmos*), and it may not have been ordinary practice to survey estates in this way, which could explain the paucity of such records. Whatever the case, the palace clearly had access to considerable amounts of wine, and given the absence of collection records it is evident that the surviving documentation conveys something less than the entire picture.

4.3.4 WINE AT MYCENAE

Wine appears on three documents from Mycenae, Ue 611, –652 and –663, all of which were discussed in Section 3.2.4. As argued there, Ue 611 may record provisions for a banquet, although not necessarily of a religious nature. Ue 652 is a probable delivery record for a variety of foodstuffs, including VIN$_b$, perhaps vinegar (see above). Ue 663 is 'Unclear'. Table 4-6 summarises the data.

Table 4-6. Wine at Mycenae

tablet	VIN	= V
1. Dining		
Ue 611	VIN S 2[	12+
2. Delivery		
Ue 652	VIN$_b$ 22	396
	TOTAL 1+2	**408+**
3. Unclear		
Ue 663	VIN 5	90
	TOTAL 1+2+3	**498+**

Once again the picture is rather obscure. A relatively small amount, V 12+ (some 19.2 litres), may relate to banqueting, a large amount (some 633.6 litres) of some wine-related substance is (probably) being delivered, and a medium-sized amount (some 144.0 litres) of wine appears in an unknown context. There are no clear disbursements for non-religious purposes, so in a sense 100% of disbursements are 'religious', although it seems somewhat specious to make such a claim on the basis of one document. Taking Ue 652 as hinting at larger resources (even

[97] An ambiguity is introduced by the fact that some of the banqueting records deal with contributions made by others. Since, in the case of wine, these are all elites with connections to the palace, the distinction is a bit unclear.

[98] Palmer 1994, 193.

[99] Palmer suggests that there were other storerooms also in the area as well as ones at places such as the major centres to which wine is distributed in Vn 20 (Palmer 1994, 194). It is possible that some of the pithoi in the so-called Oil Magazines (Rms 23 and 24) may also have held other substances such as wine (e.g. Bendall 2004, 117–18).

[100] On the vines specifically see Palmer 1994, 48, 66–72.

though the precise commodity involved is a variant of wine) we may observe that the 'religious disbursements' were a mere 3% of these.

4.3.5 WINE AT THEBES

Wine at Thebes appears in Uo 121 and the Gp series. The ideogram may also appear on Ft 182 *lat.inf.* and X 180, but the readings are uncertain so these documents are left out of consideration here.[101] Uo 121 is probably a banqueting record (Section 2.3.2.5), and the Gp tablets may relate to festival rations or sacred meals (Section 2.3.3.3). In addition to wine, they seem to record FAR 'flour' (disputed[102]) and, once each, CYP+*O* and *KE*.

Table 4-7 gives data for the entire Gp series except Gp 161 (see next),[103] and will be referred to in sections dealing with the other commodities. It is important to note that owing to poor preservation it is often uncertain which commodity a given number refers to. In such cases, the numbers appear in a separate column labelled 'unknown'. Gp 161 may be a totalling tablet since it records much larger amounts of wine than any of the other records and no recipients are listed.[104] Amounts of wine on this tablet are thus omitted from the total in the table (in any case, they are erasures). For reference, the text is as follows.

Gp 161 (306?)
.1 ⟦ṾỊṆ 1̣ [ ]6̣ 7̣⟧
.2 ⟦VIN 6 S 2 ⟧

[101] On X 180 only a single line forming the left part of the sign is preserved (see photo in *Thèbes* I, 70). For Ft 182 the suggestion is confined to the apparatus: 'Traces à gauche, peut-être ṾỊṆ ???' (*Thèbes* I, 71; *Thèbes* III, 122).

[102] It has been suggested that the sign may in some cases instead be read as the (very similar) syllabic sign **65* (Palaima 2000–2001; 2003b, 115) but the issue is not crucial for present purposes. We here follow the view of the editors of the corpus (*Thèbes* I; *Thèbes* III; see also Killen 2006a, 103–6); see Section 5.4.5. Two particularly difficult readings in Gp 110 and 124 are noted in the table (see Killen 2006a, 103).

[103] The complete list is given in *Thèbes* I, 409–10. The Gp tablets are all by scribe 306 except as follows. 305?: Gp 150. 305?/306?: Gp 129, 144. 306?: Gp 146, 149, 154, 165, 168, 175, 186, 188, 197, 227, 230, 237. 309: Gp 157. Unascribed: Gp 153, 170, 179, 215, 235, 270, 290, 303, 313. Data for scribes is taken mainly from *Thèbes* I, 159.

[104] The text is given in *Thèbes* I, 281.

Table 4-7. The Thebes Gp tablets

Gp	text	VIN	VIN = V	FAR	FAR = V	unknown	unknown = V	*KE* and CYP
107.*l.s.*	to-so-wo[							
107.1	**63*-te-ṛạ[-de					*lost*	1+	
107.2	ẹ-p̣ẹ-[-to-i					*lost*	1+	
109.1.2	**63*-te-ra-de , di-wi-ja-me-ro , qe-te-jo ,	VIN 2 V 5	41					
110.1	]qe ,	VIN S 1	6					
110.1	na-ne-mo	V 2	2					
110.2	]**65* , ?*	V 2 ?*	2 ?*	]FAR , V 2 ?*	2 ?*			
110.2	mo-ne-we	S 1	6					
110.2	**56*-ru[-we					*lost*	1+	
111	]-ị					V 1 Z 3[	1.75	
111	*same?/lost?*	]VIN S 1 V 3̣ Z[	9.25+					
112.1	te-ka-ta-si ,	VIN V 6[	6+					
112.2	**56*-ru-we	V 2	2					
114.1	**56*-]ṛụ-we					V 3	3	
114.2	*same?/lost?*					?]2	??	
114.2	te-ka-ta-si					V 2	2	
119.1	pu$_2$-ke-qi-ri-ne	VIN[	1+					
119.2	**63*-te-ra-de	S 2	12					
119.2	**56*[-ru-we	*lost*	1+					
119.3	**63*-te-ra-de	S 2̣[	1̣2̣+					
122.1	**63*-te-ṛạ[-de					*lost*	1+	
122.2	a-ki-to ,					Ṿ[	1+	
124.1	]ko-**65*	VIN , FAR V 2[*	2+*	VIN , FAR V 2[*	2+*			
124.2				F̣ẠṚ V 1 Z 1 [	1.25			
127.1	i-si-wi-jo-i ,	VIN V 2 [	2					
127.2	**63*-te-ra-de	VIN 1[	1+					
129.1	we-ka-sa[					*lost*	1+	
129.2	e-mi-jo-no-i[					*lost*	1+	
144.1	]-we			FAR V 1[	1+			
144.2	a-ko-]da-mo					V 4̣	4	
144.2	a-ẉẹ[					*lost*	1+	
145.1	*lost*					]1 V 2	8+	
145.2	*lost*					]Ṿ 4	4	
146.1	*lost*	]Ṣ 1 V[	7+					
146.2	*inf. mut.*							
147.1	]q̣ẹ-te-jo ,							
147.2	]-si-qe , qe-te-jo	VIN 4̣[	72+					
149.1	*lost*					]T 3 V 1⟦1⟧	19+	
149.2	]*vacat*							
150.1	qe-da-do-ṛọ[					*lost*	1+	
150.2	ku-no					V 1 [	1	
150.*v*	to-jo					Ṿ[	1+	
153.1	]j̣ạ-de , ke-wa-to , [					*lost*	1+	
153.2	*lost*			]F̣ẠṚ 1 T 8 V 4	112			
153.2	ḍi[					*lost*	1+	
153.3	*inf. mut.*							
154.1	*lost*					]2 V 3 Z 2	15.5	
154.2	*lost*					]2	??	
157.1	**56*-ru-we[					*lost*	1+	
157.2	te-ri-a$_2$[					*lost*	1+	
158.1a	wo-ko							
158.1b	*lost*	]S 1	6					
158.1b	ka-sa[					*lost*	1+	
158.2	*lost*					]1	??	
158.2	**56*-ru-we					V 1[	1+	
164.1	]ḍẹ ,	VIN 2 S 2 V 2	50					
164.1	e-pe-to-i	S 1 V 1[	7+					
164.2	lost	]S 1	6					
164.2	a-ko-ro-da-mo	V 2	2					
164.2	**56*-ru-we	V 4	4					
164.2	to[					*lost*	1+	
164.*l.i.*	lost					]1	??	
164.*l.i.*	to-ro-wo	S 1 [	6					
165.0	*sup. mut.*							
165.1	*lost*	]ṾỊṆ 2	36					
165.1	**5̣6̣*[					*lost*	1+	
167.1	**63*-te-ra-de	ṾỊṆ[	1+					
167.2	a$_3$-ni-jo	S 1[	6+					

Gp	text	VIN	VIN = v	FAR	FAR = v	unknown	unknown = v	*KE* and CYP
168.1	**63*-te-ra-de ,	VIN S[	6+					
168.2	*vacat* [							
170.1	*lost*					]1	??	
170.2	*lost*					]1	??	
170.2	**56*-ru-we					V 2	2	
170.3	*lost*					]1̣	??	
175.1	]*vestigia*[							
175.2	]ta-si					V 3 Z 1̣[	3.25+	
175.3	] *vacat* [							
176.a	**56*-ru-we					V 3	3	
176.a	ke-re-na-i[					*lost*	1+	
176.b	**63*-te-ra-de ,	VIN S 1 V[	7+					
178.1	te-qa-jo-i[					*lost*	1+	
178.2	**63*-ṭẹ-ra-ḍẹ[					*lost*	1+	
179.1	u-re-we	VIN S 1	6					
179.1	ro-[	*lost*	1+					
179.2	a-ra-ki-to	Ṣ 1	6					
179.2	pi-ri[	*lost*	1+					
181.1	e-]pẹ-to-i	S 1	6					
181.2	*lost*					]1̣	??	
183.1	*lost*					]3̣	??	
183.2	]de	VIN S 1 V 3	9					
184.1	*lost*					]Ṿ 3	3	
184.1	to-pa-po-ro-i ,	VIN S 1	6					
184.2	]**5̣6*-ru-we	?	?			V 2	2	
184.2	e-pe-to-i	?	?			V 1	1	
186.1	*lost*	]S 1 Ṿ 1[	7+					
186.2	*lost*	]VỊṆ 3	54					
186.2	***5̣6* -ṛụ[-we					*lost*	1+	
188.a	*lost*					]Ṿ 1	1	
188.b	*lost*	]S 1	6					
188.b	**56*-ru-we	V 1	1					
195	]jo-i	S 1	6					
196.1	**63*-te-ra-de [	?	?			*lost*	1+	
196.2	e-pe-to-i	?	?			V 1̣[	1	
197.1	]**6̣3*-ṭẹ-ra-de	VỊṆ[	1+					
197.2	]ṣị					V 1	1	
197.2	a-ra-o					Ṿ[	1+	
199.a	*lost*					] 3	3?	
199.a	i-qo-po[					*lost*	1+	
199.b	*lost*	?	?			] 2̣	??	
199.b	pe-ṭạ[	?	?			*lost*	1+	
201.a	] ma-ka					V 1̣[	1+	
201.b	*lost*					]1̣	1+?	
201.b	e-pe-to[-i					*lost*	1+	
210.*l.s.*	*lost*							] *KE* [
210.1	*lost*	VIN 1 S 2[	30+					
210.2	*lost*					]1̣	1+?	
210.2	ko-ṭạ					Ṿ[	1+	
215.1	]a-me-ro , qe-da-do-ro			FAR V 3	3			
215.2	a-]ko-ro-da-mo			FAR V 1	1			
227.1	*lost*					]V 5	5	
227.1	a-ra-o					V 1[	1+	
227.2	ra-]ke-da-mo-ni-jo-u-jo					V 1[	1+	
230.1	**63*-te-]ṛạ-de	VIN 4̣[	72+					
230.2	]*vest.* [							
231.1	**63*-te-ra-de	VỊṆ[	1+					
231.2	a-ra-o [					*lost*	1+	
233.1	**63*-te-]ṛạ-de ,	VỊṆ[	1+					
233.2	e-pe]to-i[					*lost*	1+	
235.1	]ṭọ-jo					V 1	1	
235.1	a[					*lost*	1+	
235.2	] *vacat* [							
237.1	**63*-te-ṛạ[-de					*lost*	1+	
237.2	e-ṃị[-jo-no-i					*lost*	1+	
270.1	]qe-re-ṃạ[-o					*lost*	1+	
270.2	]*vacat*[							
290.1	]-ọ							CYP+*O* V 4
290.2	] *vacat*							
303.1	]te , i-je-re-wị-jọ			FAR Ṭ 1 Ṿ 2 [	8			
303.2	*lost*			]FAR[	1̣+			

Gp	text	VIN	VIN = V	FAR	FAR = V	unknown	unknown = V	*KE* and CYP
313.1				]FAR[	1+			
313.2	di-wi-ja[					*lost*	1+	
345	*lost*					]V 1	1	
345	**56*-ru-we					Z 2	0.5	
	TOTALS		**535.25+**		**130.25+**		**122**	

Notes

General

The 'unknown' column is used for cases (a) where the ideogram is lost, or (b) where a recipient is followed by a break such that it is unknown whether another ideogram would have been introduced (in which case the table reads '*lost*' in the 'unknown' column).

* = Amount shown in more than one column (see notes below).

l.s. = *lat. sup.*

l.i. = *lat. inf.*

Individual tablets

107: *l.s.* Perhaps 'so much wine'?

109: Either */Diwias meros/* 'portion of Diwia' (*Thèbes* I, 277) or 'two days' (*Mémoires* IV, 289).

110: The figure after *na-ne-mo* in line .1 must refer to wine. In the first entry of line .2 it is not clear if a FAR ideogram is introduced or not; both possibilities are shown. The second entry presumably refers to wine since a liquid measure is used.

112: Line .2 is probably but not certainly wine

119: Both figures after **63-te-ra-de* have liquid measures, so are wine.

124: Transcription reads: FAR , VIN V 2[; for references to discussions of this odd formulation see *supra* n 102.

129: Listed under both scribes with '?' (*Thèbes* I, 158–9).

144: Listed under both scribes with '?' (*Thèbes* I, 158–9).

164: The V entries following S in line .2 must still be wine.

179: All entries probably wine.

196: App. to line .1 notes: 'Trace à droite VIN[?'.

199: In line .a the measure is lost – V 3 is assumed, but it needn't be. Apparatus to line .b reads: 'Trace à gauche, peut-être VIN.'

201: Line .b unit of measure uncertain.

210: Line .2, first entry, unit of measure uncertain. *Lat. sup. KE*, See *Thèbes* I, 297 for comparanda for ideogram.

230: See line .2 apparatus: ']*ta-jo*[ou]*ta-na*[pas impossible'.

345: Only one line of text.

The Gp series overall records some V 535.25+ of wine (without the figure for Gp 161), and Uo 121 records V 6+, for a total of V 541.25+. 100% of disbursements relate to religion or banqueting. No disbursements for other purposes are recorded, nor is there any record of collections. It may be noted that if Gp 161 is a totalling tablet, as suggested above, it does not record totals for the entire series. The figure in line .1 is damaged but was less than VIN 2 (< V 36) and line .2 records VIN 6 S 2 = V 120, totalling not more than V 156. To conclude, the palace apparently had access to substantial supplies of wine (some 856.4 litres minimum are recorded), but there is nothing from which to attempt to assess overall resources.

4.4 CONCLUSION

Honey at both Knossos and Pylos seems to have been used both in offerings and in perfumery. Amounts disbursed for offerings at Knossos varied between 28 and 73% depending on how the figures were calculated. The amount at Pylos was only 14%, but there were uncertainties about whether the syllabogram *ME* really did represent honey. In both cases overall resources seemed to be much more substantial than the amounts disbursed, but there were again uncertainties over what should be counted and how (e.g. the issue over whether KN Gg 521 recorded honey). Whatever the case, given the importance of honey offerings at Knossos it is interesting that one of the few tablets from Chania would turn out also to record an offering of honey.

Wine appears at numerous sites and was used in connection with banqueting (unsurprisingly), as well as in perfumery and as *o-no* payments. Palmer makes the important point that while wine was handed out as temporary maintenance during religious festivals it was never used as 'ordinary' rations. At all sites, issues in connection with banqueting represent the majority of recorded disbursements, but there were considerable uncertainties over the interpretation of some documents (especially Gm 840 at Knossos). There are various hints at larger resources but it was difficult to gain any realistic sense of the true magnitude. To an extent, it would not be surprising if the primary use of wine really was for banqueting, although we should not assume the majority of consumption would have been at major state-organised festivals and feasts. MY Ue 611 may be a rare example of an issue of wine for 'ordinary' dining.

In general, calculations for wine and honey are more difficult and more subject to error than for oil, and in general the main impression that emerges is that the data are highly biased and are inadequate to supply the sort of figures we wish to obtain. It will be suggested in the final chapter that this point is itself of some significance.

CHAPTER 5
WHEAT, BARLEY, FLOUR, FIGS, OLIVES AND CYPERUS

5.1 INTRODUCTION

The present chapter deals with the major commodities measured in units for dry measures: wheat, barley, flour, figs, olives and cyperus. All of these except flour and cyperus happen to have been used for ordinary rations; flour was sometimes issued as festival rations and cyperus is common on banqueting foodlists. A new and thorough study by Killen deals with the majority of these commodities (all except cyperus),[1] obviating the need for detailed discussion in many cases. Killen identifies the following types of records:[2]

- rations records
- records of issues to participants in religious festivals
- records of religious offerings
- records of 'menus' for state-sponsored sacrificial banquets
- 'harvest' records
- 'benefit' or 'payment' records viz. texts which contain the term *o-no* (or its plural *o-na*), and which appear to refer to commodities given in exchange or compensation
- records of uncertain purpose.

Killen's identifications of category for individual tablets have in the main been followed here; exceptions are discussed below.

We will examine the commodities in turn. Before we begin, we should note in passing Palmer's suggestion that the values of ideograms **120* and **121*, interpreted as wheat and barley respectively, should perhaps be reversed.[3] The issue is not yet fully resolved, but difficulties with the suggestion have been raised and the traditional view is followed here.[4] We may note that our general conclusions would not be affected either way since each commodity is considered individually.

5.2 WHEAT (**120* = GRA)

5.2.1 INTRODUCTION TO WHEAT IN LINEAR B

The ideogram for wheat, GRA, can represent two different things in the Linear B records. On the one hand it indicates the grain itself; on the other it is used as a measure of land, indicating the amount of seed required to sow a particular plot.[5] This type of measure, known also from modern Greece, is particularly useful in a landscape where fertility varies radically, since an

[1] Killen 2004.
[2] Killen 2004, 155.
[3] Palmer 1989; 1992; forthcoming.
[4] Halstead 1995a; Killen 2004, 156, 163–8; see also Franceschetti 2001.
[5] *Documents*, 236–7; Killen 1987b, 175; 2004, 156.

acre of arid hillside is not comparable in terms of yield to an acre of rich valley sediment. In terms of production, what is important would be not the actual areas, but the yields.

The two cases are relatively easy to distinguish in Linear B. Grain when used as a land measure is normally accompanied by the word *pe-ma*, a variant *pe-mo*, */sperma/* = */spermo/* 'seed', or the abbreviation *pe*, sometimes ligatured to the ideogram: GRA+*PE*. Usually the context is land tenure, and the various formulaic structures and vocabulary of Mycenaean land tenure often provide further evidence for identifying which sense of GRA is indicated. As noted previously (Sections 1.1; 2.4), many of the land tenure records involved religious personnel, so would be of interest to the present study. However, our primary focus here is on assessing amounts of commodities where disbursed for religious purposes, and GRA in land tenure is not 'disbursed'. Further, since GRA in land tenure represents something different than when issued as ordinary rations, the amounts recorded in either case are not directly comparable and cannot be 'counted' together. Land tenure records are thus best left aside for the time being.

5.2.2 WHEAT AT KNOSSOS

Wheat at Knossos appears primarily in harvest and rations records. Only one document is related to religion; the text is as follows.

E 842 (—)

.1a	] di-wo[	
.1b	]ra , te-o-i / me-a-de [	
.2	]ọḷịṿ 24 T 4̣ PYC[ ] T 2 me-na GRA 2 T 4̣[	
.3	]pe-ro$_2$-[ ] 2 T 4 ki-da-ro GRA 2̣2̣[ ]ṭọ-so GRA[	

.3 Trace before 2 consistent with]GṚẠ.

The amounts here are high for an offerings record (minimum total GRA 24 T 4 = V 1464 = approx. 2342.4 litres), but the designation */theoihi/* 'to the gods' (line .1b) leaves no doubt about the nature of the connections. Possibly, the disbursements were made on the occasion of a festival or a banquet, which would account for the large figures. However that may be, the references to gods and (probably) to individual divine figures indicate that the allocations are, in at least some sense, offerings.[6] In any case, the tablet is clearly related to religion.

Land tenure apart, the remaining documents recording wheat are harvest records and ordinary rations records. Examples of harvest records are as follows.[7]

F(2) 852 + 8071 + 9919 + *frr*. (4) (—)

.1	da-wo / a-ma , e-pi-ke-re GRA 10300[
.2	OLIV+*A* 70 OLIV+*TI* 20 PYC+*O* 12[

Cut at left.
.1 10ọ00[quite possible.

E(2) 669 (103)

.1	]ṭị-jo GRA 195 OLIV+*A* 43 OLIV+*TI* 45
.2	]i-jo GRA 143 da-**22*-ti-jo GRA 70 OLIV 45

E(2) 670 (103)

.1	]ḍạ-**83*-ja-i GRA 302 OLIV 8ọ[
.2	ru-ki-ti-jo GRA 73 o-na-jo GRA[

[6] *Scribes RCT*, 208; Killen 2004, 157. For the recipients see Section 4.2.1.1 and Killen forthcoming(a). Killen supports early suggestions by VC (*Documents*, 309) of */Mēn(n)āi/* 'to the Moon' and possibly */Huperioni/* 'to the Sun' (which may find support in a possible reading in line .3 noted in *KT*[6].
[7] On harvest records see Killen 1994–1995a; 1998a; in general see Godart 1968b.

In records of this sort, large amounts of wheat, olives and sometimes cyperus are registered against various towns (*da-wo*, *da-*22-to*). F(2) 852 notes that the /*amā*/ 'harvest' is /*epi khērei*/ 'in hand' – that is, in store and presumably available for actual use.[8]

The rations records are of two types: records of monthly rations to workgroups and totalling records for these. Examples of the first type are as follows.

Ai(2) 752 + 753 (102?)

]re-ja MUL 3̣ ko-wa 1 ko-wo 1 GRA Ṭ[

Ai(2) 750 (102?)

]ko-wo 2 GRA 1 T 2̣[

Ai(2) 751 (102?)

ko-]ẉạ 1 GRA T 5

Cut at right.

The basic structure of these records – women, followed by female and male children, plus an amount of wheat – is very similar to the well-known monthly rations records at Pylos (see next section).[9] As at Pylos, these are probably monthly allocations, although this is not explicitly stated.

Two examples of the totalling tablets for rations are as follows.

E 777 (—)

.1	ko-no-si-ja / ki-ri-te-wi-ja-i	LUNA 1	GRA 100[
.2	a-mi-ni-si-ja	LUNA 1	GRA 100[
.3	pa-i-ti-ja	LUNA 1	GRA 100[
↓			
v. .1	a-ze-ti-ri-ja		GRA 1̣0̣[
	reliqua pars sine regulis		

Cut at left.

r. Whole text probably palimpsest: ⟦*jo*⟧ visible in .2.

E 847 + 5739 + 7341 + 9344 + *fr.* (—)

.1]no-so / a-no-qo-ta-o LUNA 1 GRA 10 T 2[

.2] LUNA 1 GRA 12 T 7̣ da-na-mo LUNA 1 GRA 1̣1̣[ ]Ṭ 7 [

.1 Traces of ⟦ ⟧ under *-no-qo-*.

.2 Traces of ⟦ ⟧ under first LUNA.

E 777 was discussed above (Section 2.5.2); it records wheat for female work-groups at Knossos, Amnisos and Phaistos. E 847 deals with a group possibly located at Knossos (cf.]*no-so*) and belonging to the well-attested 'Collector' *a-no-qo-ta*. That these are records of monthly rations is indicated by the ideogram LUNA.[10]

Amounts on the rations and harvesting records are summarised in Table 5-1; tablets where GRA is used as a measure of land are listed in Category 5 for reference. All tablets in Categories 1 and 2 are non-RCT records. Tablets in Categories 3 and 4 come from both the RCT and elsewhere, as indicated in the table.

[8] See Killen 1994–1995a; 1998a, 19; 2004, 156, 158 n ii.

[9] On which see Chadwick 1988 and Section 5.2.3 below.

[10] See e.g. Chadwick 1988, 73.

Table 5-1. Wheat in harvest and rations records at Knossos

	GRA	= V		GRA	
1. *Harvests*			**3. *Unclear***		**4. *Measure of land***
F(1) 157(?)	400[	24,000+	*4a. non-RCT*		*5a. non-RCT*
E(2) 668(?)	538 T 2*	32,292	E 36	10[	E 36(?)
E(2) 669(?)	408*	24,480	E 843	100[+*	E 749(?)
E(2) 670(?)	375+*	22,500+	F(2) 844	20 T 5	E 843(?)
E 749(?)	67 T 2 V 3+*	4035+	E 846	22[	E 846(?)
F(2) 845	]8	480+	E 849	130[	E 849
E 848 [+] 8040	6̣2[	3̣7̣2̣0+	F(2) 853	500[	E 1569
E 850	132 T 5	7950	F(2) 854	415*	E 7338(?)
F(2) 851	*lost*	1+	E 971	*lost*	E 9295
F(2) 852	10,300[	6̣1̣8,0̣0̣0+	E 1569	58 T 5*	E 9322
E 1035	100[	6000+	E 1574	4 T 2	F(2) 841
	TOTAL 1	**743,458+**	E 4466	45[*	F(2) 854.2.3(??)
2. *Rations*			E 5000	351+*	E 9295
2a. totalling records			F(2) 5001	3	E 9754
E 777	31̣0̣*	1̣8,6̣0̣0̣	E 5556	6[*	*5b. RCT*
E 847	3̣4 T 6̣+*	2076+	F(2) 7050	4̣5̣3	E(1) 71(?)
E 7350	1[	60+	E 7338	100[	E(1) 288(?)
E 9178	*lost*	1+	E 7339	*lost*	
	Sub-total 2a	**20,737+**	E 7340	200[	
2b. individual groups			E 8122	30[	
Ai(2) 750	1 T 2̣[	7̣2̣	Ws 8500	—	
Ai(2) 751	T 5	30	X 35	*lost*	
Ai(2) 752	Ṭ[	6+	*4b. RCT*		
Ai(2) 5543	6̣ T 7̣[*	4̣0̣2̣+	E(1) 71	]1 T 6	
Ai(2) 7026	1 T 7̣[	1̣0̣2̣+	E(1) 132	202̣[	
Ai 9502(?)	*lost*	1+	E(1) 165	9[T[*	
Ai 9503(?)	1̣0̣[	600+	E(1) 288	*lost*	
Ai 9504(?)	2̣[	120+	E(1) 8435	1̣0̣0̣ or 7̣	
Ai 9505(?)	T 5	30			
Ai 9514(?)	]1̣ T 6[	9̣6+			
	Sub-total 2b	**1459+**			

Notes

General

* = Summed.

The table draws on Killen 2004, 158, Table 8.1. The list in Category 5 follows Killen 2004, 169. Several tablets are listed here as 'Unclear' which Killen takes as *possible* harvest records: E 843, –4466, –5000, –7338, –7340; F(2) 844, –853, –854, –5001, –7050. They are taken here as 'Unclear' so as to err (if error it be) on the conservative side in terms of the argument. Other additions or differences are noted below.

Individual tablets

X 35: For this tablet as probably recording wheat see Killen 1996–1997, 131–2.

E(1) 71: Probably same tablet as F 7360; figures restored from latter.

E(1) 288: G̣ṚẠ.

E 749: Killen (2004, 158) takes this as a possible measure of land record. It is shown here in both columns; the amount of grain involved is in any case not large so the figures are not much affected.

E 849: A totalling tablet mentioning *pu-ta-ri-ja*.

F(2) 852: In addition to Killen 2004, see Killen 1985, 251; 1994, 67–8.

E 971: The additional text reads *se-to-i-ja o-pa*, so the tablet may record grain for fodder (Halstead 1998–1999, 167; see Section 2.3.2.3).

E 1569: Could be land tenure?

F(2) 7050: Reading uncertain; 4̣5̣3 is the minimum.

Ai 9502: Not noted by Killen since the GRA ideogram is not actually preserved, but presumably it would have been present since this is an Ai tablet.

Ai 9503: G̣ṚẠ; reading very doubtful.

Ai 9504: G̣ṚẠ.

Ai 9505: G̣ṚẠ.

E 9295: Not in Killen's list; see Godart *et al.* 1990–1991, 390.

E 9754: Not in Killen's list; see Godart *et al.* 1990–1991, 399.

We will first consider the disbursements. The amount of wheat on the offering record E 824 (V 1465+) is small compared to amounts disbursed for rations, being just 7% of issues on the rations totalling records alone (2a). Further, this figure may be on the high side since the Ai records are manifestly incomplete (although since we have – at least some of – the totalling records, perhaps this is not significant. Either way, it is evident that significant amounts of grain were being disbursed as rations and that offerings account for only a small proportion of this.

Turning to overall resources, some indications of the scale are provided by the harvest records. These document some V 743,458+, of which the amount issued on the offering record E 824 is a bare 0.2%. Clearly, the amount of wheat allocated for religion in the Knossos texts was negligible in comparison with the palace's overall resources.

A curious point worth observing here is that not only do religious allocations not account for a substantial proportion of overall resources, but neither do the amounts disbursed as rations. Offerings plus rations (totalling records only) taken together are some V 22,202+, which is only 3% of the amount collected in the harvest records. Of course, it must be noted that the rations are monthly whereas the harvests would presumably be annual. As mentioned previously, there are various reasons for thinking the Mycenaeans used a system of lunar months (the use of the ideogram LUNA being one), so there would have been some twelve or thirteen months per year. The amount issued for rations over a year then (on the basis of the preserved figures – note some are lost) would be some V 248,844, which is 33% of the amount in the harvest records. This is a more substantial proportion than the 3% just noted, but it still leaves some two thirds of the overall resources unaccounted for. It is clear that the palace had access to considerably more grain than we see being disbursed. This situation is in line with that observed for the other commodities so far examined (oil, wine, honey), but there is also a difference in that with wheat we do have at least some indication of what was being done with a significant proportion of the resources. In the cases of other commodities, including many still to come, disbursement records for the majority of resources are missing altogether. It is probably important that the wheat rations records were kept in connection with one of the central concerns reflected in the documents – the textile industry.[11] To return to our previous discussion of what constitutes disbursements for 'final use' as opposed to 'industrial' disbursements (Section 3.1), rations are in a sense both. They are counted here as 'final use' or 'real expenditure' because the commodity disbursed would be genuinely 'consumed' (in a very physical sense), rather than being returned in altered form to the palace as is the case with, for instance, wool issued for textile manufacture. However, the palace still received a 'return' on the expenditure since the underlying purpose of the consumption was maintenance of the workforce labouring towards the textile (and other industrial) production. These transactions therefore do not concern movements of goods *outside* the sphere of palatial industrial operations. The significance of this point will be discussed in the final chapter.

Finally, it is worthwhile simply noting the scale of agricultural activity in which the palace was involved.[12] On the VC values, the harvest records deal with some 1,189,532 litres of wheat.[13] Further, this is a minimum, since many of the 'Unclear' records could also be harvest records. Whatever was being done with the commodity, the resources were very substantial.

---

[11] This is to imply not that all the rations seen here were going to textile workers but that at least some of them were is indicated by the word 'decorators' on E 777.

[12] Cf. Killen 1998a; Godart 1977.

[13] Chadwick (1976, 117–18) noted that the amount recorded on F(2) 852 alone was some 775 tons. For a calculation of how much land would have been needed to grow the wheat recorded at *da-wo* on this tablet (1000 ha), see Halstead 1992a, 67; Bennet 1985, 237.

5.2.3 WHEAT AT PYLOS

At Pylos GRA appears primarily as a measure of land in land tenure records (Ea, Eb, Ed, En, Eo, Eq, Er, Es), and as grain in the standard rations records of the Ab series. It also appears in banqueting records, as *o-no* payments,[14] and in a document connected somehow with religion. The text of the last is as follows.

Un 443 (H6)
.1 ku-pi-ri-jo , tu-ru-pte-ri-ja , o-no LANA 10 **146* 10
.2 po-re-no-zo-te-ri-ja LANA 3
.3]do-ke , ka-pa-ti-ja , HORD 2 te-ri-ja GRA 1̣ LANA 5
reliqua pars sine regulis

The first line records an *o-no* payment connected with a man *ku-pi-ri-jo*, recalling the *o-no* payments to another man of the same name at Knossos.[15] The two commodities involved were also seen disbursed in connection with the an *o-no* payment for the same substance, alum, in An 35 above (Section 4.3.3). The word in the second line has been variously interpreted, but is apparently a compound of *po-re-na*, which probably refers to the persons offered as temple servants (or sacrificial victims) in Tn 316.[16] Line .3 may relate to cult personnel, if *ka-pa-ti-ja* is the same person named as the *ka-ra-wi-po-ro* in Ep 704. As Palaima points out, Un 443 is written by the scribe (H6) who wrote the banqueting foodlists Un 6 and Un 853, the former of which also refers to a (the?) *ka-ra-wi-po-ro*, so the identification is plausible.[17] The word *te-ri-ja* is obscure; it may be an anthroponym but this cannot be determined.[18] Given the various uncertainties, the entries in lines .3 and .4 are taken here as 'Unclear', although it is not unlikely that they relate to the religious sphere.[19]

A few of the rations records should also be discussed. The Ab tablets are relatively well understood since Chadwick's classic study.[20] A couple examples are as follows.

Ab 382 (S186-H21)
.A GRA 16 T 8 *DA TA*
.B ro-u-so , mi-ra-ti-ja MUL 54 ko-wa 31[ ] ko-wo 20 *NI* 16 T 8

Ab 578 (S186-H21)
.A GRA 2 T 4 *TA*
.B pu-ro , pe-ki-ti-ra$_2$ MUL 7 ko-wa 4 ko-wo 4 *NI* 2 T 4

The tablets list women work-groups at various toponyms (*ro-u-so*, Pylos), along with female and male children (*ko-wa/-wo*), the monthly rations for the group in wheat and figs,[21] and a note indicating whether supervisors are present (*DA*, *TA*; they receive extra rations[22]). The groups are usually given a descriptive term, normally an ethnic (e.g. *mi-ra-ti-ja*, from /*Milātos*/, in all probability Miletus in Asia Minor[23]) or occupational title (e.g. *pe-ki-ti-ra*$_2$

[14] Ua 158 and Un 1322, both discussed in Section 6.4.1.2.
[15] See Killen 1995, 219–21; drawing on Olivier 1996–1997, 290 with n 100; see also Palaima 1991, 280 with n 37. For the transaction see also e.g. Killen 1985, 265; Palmer 1994, 107–9.
[16] *DMic*. II, *s.v. po-re-no-zo-te-ri-ja*. See also Palmer 1994, 107–8; Palaima 1996–1997, 305–8; Nosch & Perna 2001, 474. For an alternative view, taking *po-re-na* as an infinitive, see Nagy 1994–1995; Willi 1994–1995; *contra* see Palaima 1996–1997.
[17] Palaima 1996–1997, 306–7; also Palmer 1994, 108; Weilhartner 2005, 163.
[18] *DMic*. II, *s.v. te-ri-ja*.
[19] Although, as Palmer (1994, 108) points out they are certainly not 'ordinary' offerings.
[20] Chadwick 1988.
[21] Chadwick 1988, 73–5.
[22] Chadwick 1988, 71–3; Killen 1983b.
[23] Chadwick 1988, 81, 91. Several other eastern Aegean toponyms appear as does (nearer to home) Kythera.

/pektriai/ 'carders [of wool]'[24]). The tablets resemble the Knossos Ai tablets discussed in the previous section. Fg 253 is probably a totalling tablet for the Ab series (it is by the scribe of the closely related Aa series). The text is as follows.

Fg 253 (S240-H1)

.1	]ra-so-ro	GRA 192 T 7
.2	]	GRA 192 T 7

Since this is a totalling record, we will use it for our sums rather than the figures from the Ab series.

The next three documents we will examine are all rations records but differ in various ways from the standard formula of the Ab series.

An 128 (H42)

Recto

.1	?mi-]ka-ta	VIR 41
.2	?mi-]ka-ta , po-ru-qo-to	VIR 6
.3	ke-re-te , ka-si-ko-no	VIR 5
.4	*vacat*	
.5	*vacat*	
.6	*vacat*	
.7	*vacat*	
.8	] *vacat*	
.9	] *vacat*	
.10	] *vacat*	
.11	GRA 2 T 6 V 5 Z 2	
.12	]2 T 6 V 5	
.13	] *vacat*	
.14	] *vacat* [ ] *v.*	

Verso

.a {		Z [2
{		HORD 5 T 3 V 4

An 128 is clearly a rations record, but it is not apparent whether these are 'ordinary' or festival rations. The scribe of this document, H42, wrote a great many banqueting 'menu' lists (Section 2.3.2.2), and ?*mi-*]*ka-ta*, if correctly restored in lines .1–2, is an occupation commonly attested in lists of temple staff.[25] However, since it is not possible to be certain we follow Killen here in taking this as an 'ordinary' rations record.[26]

The next two tablets may also relate to religion.

Fg 368 (S186-H21)

ke-sa-da-ra GRA 5 *NI* 5

Fg 828 (S240-H1)

ke-sa-da-ra GRA 5

These are clearly rations records (see GRA and *NI*, the standard rations commodities at Pylos in the Ab series), but both tablets record issues to a woman, *ke-sa-da-ra*, who may possibly have had a religious connection if she is the same woman who appears in Mn 1368 (see Section 6.4.1.2), so it is not clear whether these rations relate to religious purposes. (It is also not clear that the same person was involved, but the possibility remains open.) For this reason these disbursement are listed as 'Unclear', even though it is certain rations are involved. Note that

[24] Chadwick 1988, 82.
[25] Olivier 1960, esp. 47–8.
[26] Killen 2004, 158–60.

the amounts disbursed are greater than individual rations normally recorded in the Ab series. Possibly the issues were intended for longer periods of time, or the woman was of superior status (so received more[27]), or was receiving on behalf of larger groups.

The data are summarised in Table 5-2. We follow Killen's assessments here but list Ua 434 as 'Unclear' (See Section 2.3.2.2). Killen's view of this tablet as either a banqueting or a harvest record is agreed,[28] but it is taken here as 'Unclear' because it is impossible to decide. We also list Fg 368 and Fg 828 as 'Unclear', for the reasons above.

Table 5-2. Wheat at Pylos (except land tenure)

context	tablet	GRA	= V
1. *Religious*			
Land tenure/banqueting	Un 718	6 T 6*	396
Contributions to Poseidon	Es 644	*summed*	209
TOTAL 1			**605**
2. *Rations*			
To women workers	Ab series	—	—
To groups of men	An 128	2 T 6 V 5 Z 2	161.5
Totalling tablet for Ab series	Fg 253	192 T 7 [	11,562
To an unguent boiler	Fg 374	1	60
TOTAL 2			**11,783.5**
3. *o-no payments*			
To *ke-do-jo*	Ua 158	7	420
To craftsmen	Un 1322	4̣0̣+*	2̣4̣0̣0̣+
TOTAL 3			**2820+**
TOTAL 1 + 2 + 3			**15,208**
4. *Unclear*			
To *ke-sa-da-ra*	Fg 368	5̣	—
To *ke-sa-da-ra*	Fg 828	5	300
Banqueting or collection record	Ua 434	80[	4800+
Obscure	Un 443	1̣	6̣0̣
Harvest? collection?	Un 1319	—	—
Obscure (see Section 4.3.3)	Un 1321	*lost*	—
Land tenure???	Un 1426	12	720
TOTAL 4			**5880+**

Notes

* = Summed

Ab series: The Ab tablet figures are not included, since Fg 253 is probably the totalling tablet for this series. The preserved Ab total is V 7152 (adding figures from Chadwick's [1988, 69] table).

An 128: The figure in the table is from line .11. Line .12 gives a further amount which appears to be the same minus Z 2, but the ideogram is lost. It may have been figs, and the issue is discussed further in Section 5.5.2. A figure for barley appears on the *verso*.

Fg 368: Fg 368 and Fg 828 record identical amounts of GRA issued to the same woman, *ke-sa-da-ra* (Fg 368 adds figs). These may be duplicate records, so only one is added in (although they could be for successive months). (Note the figure for Fg 368 is secure even though the reading is uncertain since the number for *NI* appears.)

Ua 158: 7 over an erasure, but reading given as secure.

Ua 434: G̣Ṛ Ạ.

Fg 828: See Fg 368.

Un 1319: The representation is problematic (*PE* and A_2), so the figures are not given; for the function of the document being 'Unclear' see recently Killen 2004, 158; also Bendall 2003, 211.

Un 1322: At least one entry is entirely lost.

Disbursements related to religion are 4% or less of all disbursements. As at Knossos, some rations were issued monthly: this is certainly the case for the large amount (V 11,562) going to

[27] See Killen 2001a, 180.

[28] Killen 2004, 158.

the 'Women of Pylos'.[29] But it is unnecessary to multiply the figure to conclude that the amount of wheat issued for religious purposes was negligible.[30]

There are no harvest records for Pylos such as at Knossos (except possibly Ua 434 and Un 1319). There are, however, extensive land tenure records, which are all but absent at Knossos. One wonders if this complementary distribution is significant, or if hazards of preservation or other factors are responsible. If the distribution is significant, it may be that somewhat different cropping systems were in operation at the two sites. In any case, we are left rather in the dark about overall resources at Pylos.[31]

5.2.4 WHEAT AT MYCENAE

Wheat appears at Mycenae on just four tablets, none relating to religion. Au 658 is clearly a rations record; line .4 records GRA 4 allocated to twenty men at the standard monthly ration rate of T 2 per man. Eu 654 and –655 are 'Unclear'. The first is a fragment from a list of amounts registered against either donors or recipients, the designations being too broken to determine (it is probably a rations record although certainty is impossible). Eu 655 preserves only the word *to-so* plus the wheat ideogram; the number is lost. Finally, Ue 652 is a probable delivery record recording GRA 3 T 3 on the *verso* and two unknown amounts on the *recto* (Section 2.3.2.4).

5.2.5 WHEAT AT THEBES

The ideogram GRA appears at Thebes in only three tablets: Av 100, Ft 140 and Ev 212. The purpose of Ev 212 is 'Unclear'; it records GRA 6+. Ft 140 is probably a record of a measure of land capacity, where land is measured in terms both of wheat and of olives (probably the fruit rather than the trees).[32] The text is as follows, for reference.

Ft 140						(312)
.1	te-qa-i	GRA+*PE*	38	OLIV	44	
.2	e-u-te-re-u	GRA	14	OLIV	87	
.3	ku-te-we-so	GRA	20	OLIV	43	
.4	o-ke-u-ri-jo	GRA	3 T 5			
.5	e-re-o-ni	GRA	12 T 7	OLIV	20	
.6	*vacat*					
.7	*vacat*					
.8	to-ṣọ-pa	GRA	88	OLIV	194	
.9	*vacat*					

The Av tablets were discussed in Section 2.3.3.3. As noted there, the Av series has possible similarities with the Pylos Fn series recording festival rations, so should be related to religion.[33] Av 100 is the only tablet on which the ideogram GRA is actually found, but it is likely that the entire series dealt with the same commodity. The word *si-to /sītos/* 'grain' appears on Av 101 and where diagnostic fractions do appear in the series they refer to dry measures.

[29] Chadwick (1976, 118) noted that some 170 tons of wheat per annum (about 14 tons per month) were required to feed the 'Women of Pylos' alone.
[30] Although Ua 434 would change the picture if it were indeed related to banqueting. But it would still be more likely to record a collection than a delivery.
[31] Although the subject has been extensively discussed in the context of land tenure (see Section 2.4)
[32] Killen 1999c, 217; 2004, 156, 169; 2006a, 79–91. To avoid confusion, note that Killen 1999c refers to Ft 140 as 149, as this is the number the tablet had originally been published with (Aravantinos *et al.* 1995, 15).
[33] *Thèbes* I, 370; Killen 1999c, 218–19; 2001b, 441–3; 2004, 159 n vii.

Because of the various uncertainties both about the function of the Av tablets and about how counting should be done where the ideogram does not appear, no table is given here. Av 100 records a total of GRA 5 V 2 Z 2. In a sense, because Av 100 is the only (clear) disbursement tablet for wheat at Thebes, it could be said that religious activities account for 100% of disbursements in documents from this site (if we are correct in thinking Av 100 indeed has such a connection). In terms of overall resources, Ft 140.8 records a total of 88 units of wheat, which although not directly comparable since this is a land tenure record, starts to hint at larger resources. But the documentation is so incomplete that further speculation is pointless.

5.3 BARLEY (**121* = HORD)

5.3.1 BARLEY AT KNOSSOS

Apart from the Fs series (Section 3.2.3.4; Table 3-5), barley is recorded in only seven tablets, two from the RCT. Texts of the RCT records are as follows.

F(1) 51 ('124'd)

HORD T 7 V 5 Z 3̣[

→

v. .1 wa HORD T 1 V 3 po-ro-de-q̣ọ-no V 2 Z 2
.2 di-we HORD T 1 HORD T 4 Z 1 ma-q̣ẹ HORD V 6

F(1) 193 + 7361 + *fr.* ('124')

te-ra-po-ti HORD 9 T 8 V 3
HORD over ⟦G̣ṚẠ⟧.

F(1) 51 is an offerings record (see *di-we* /*Diwei*/ 'to Zeus' in line .2).[34] F(1) 193 is 'Unclear'. The single word is probably a masculine dative AN,[35] but it is *hapax* and the reason for the disbursement (or collection) is unknown.[36]

Texts of the remaining (non-RCT) documents are as follows. F(3) 741 and –8242 are listed together as they are probably both parts of the same tablet; the rest are in numerical order.

F(3) 741 (—)

sup. mut.
.1]-to[
.2] 'da-*22-to' HORD 2
.3]-ṛọ 'da-*22-to' HORD 2
.4]-ri 'da-*22-to' HORD 2
.5] *vac.*
inf. mut.
Probably same tablet as F 8242.
.1 Traces at right.
.2 Trace at left ?

F(3) 8242 (—)

.0 *sup. mut.*
.1]ḍạ-*22-to HORD [
.2 da-]*22-to ḤỌṚḌ[
inf. mut.
Probably same tablet as F 741.

[34] Shelmerdine & Bennet 1995, 131; *Scribes RCT*, 208; Gulizio *et al.* 2001, 454–5; Weilhartner 2005, 40–1.
[35] *DMic.* II, *s.v. te-ra-po-ti.*
[36] Killen (2004, 159) also lists this tablet as uncertain.

G 760 (—)

.a]no HORD 1 a[

.b po-ti]ni-ja-we-jo [

.a Upright after *a*[: *a*-[or *A*]̣[both possible.

Am(2) 819 (—)

.A .] we-ke-i-ja VIR 18 'ko-wo' 8

.B .]q̣ạ-ra / si-to LUNA 1 HORD 9 T 7 V 3

.A Traces of erased ruling

G 7525 (—)

.1]ko 1 HORD T 1 [

.2 *inf. mut.*

.1 Trace at left, perhaps]]̣ Possibly *KO*. Trace at right.

F(3) 741 and 8242 are 'unclear'; they may be rations or possibly harvest records.[37] G 760 may record an offering or rations in connection with *Potnia*.[38] Am(2) 819 records monthly rations to a male workgroup.[39] G 7525 probably records a disbursement, but the purpose is unclear (offerings? rations?).[40]

We may finally mention here G 820, discussed above (Section 2.5.2), which probably records barley, indicated by *ki-ri-ta /krithā/* rather than by the ideogram HORD. The tablet is a record of monthly rations to female workgroups located at various toponyms, and one or two of the groups are described as *Potnian*. The amounts of barley to be disbursed are not specified so there is nothing for us to 'count' here, but the record at least provides further evidence for barley as rations. It should be noted that the fact that the allocations are monthly and that the name of a known 'ordinary' 'Collector', *ke-u-po-da*, appears means these are not festival rations but rather have to do with 'ordinary' workgroups, one or two of which belong to *Potnia* as a 'Collector'.

Data from the other records are summarised in Table 5-3.

Table 5-3. Barley at Knossos

	HORD	= V
1. ***Religious***		
1a. non-RCT		
Fs series	Table 3-5	120
G 760	1	60
Sub-total 1a		**180**
1b. RCT		
F(1) 51	T 7 V 5 Z 3*	**47.75**
2. ***Rations*** *(non-RCT)*		
Am(2) 819	9 T 7 V 3	585
TOTAL 1a + 2		**765**
3. ***Unclear***		
1a. non-RCT		
F(3) 741	6	360
G 7525	T 1	6
F(3) 8242	*lost*	1+
1b. RCT		
F(1) 193	9 T 8 V 3	591

[37] Killen (2004, 159) takes both as uncertain.
[38] It is omitted from Killen's table (2004, 159).
[39] Killen 2004, 159.
[40] It is omitted from Killen's table (2004, 159).

Note
* **F(1) 51**: The figure in the HORD column is summed from figures on *verso*.

In the non-RCT records, disbursements for religious purposes account for 24% of all disbursements. In the RCT records, religious disbursements account for 100% of all (clear) disbursements. Obviously, this second figure might be significantly altered, depending on the interpretation of F(1) 193. It is important (not to say disturbing) that a single document might so affect the calculation, but rather than making the enterprise seem hopeless, what is interesting here is that the situation rather resembles that seen with the oil tablets: religious disbursements tend to be small, but they are spread over numerous tablets. In this case, counting the RCT and non-RCT tablets together, nineteen disbursements relate to religion (there are seventeen Fs tablets), but just one disbursement is clearly secular. Either barley at Knossos was not normally used for non-religious purposes (as seen above, the overwhelming majority of rations were issued in wheat), or this is another instance of religious disbursements being recorded with disproportional frequency, a phenomenon we shall encounter again.

Whatever the Knossians were doing with their barley, there are no records of how they obtained it, with the possible exception of F(3) 741, which, on the whole, is more likely to be a rations record.[41] This is another interesting lacuna in the data.

5.3.2 BARLEY AT PYLOS

HORD appears in An/Fn 7, An 128, Fa 1195, the Fn series and a few Ua and Un tablets. The An tablets record rations for male workgroups;[42] the Fn tablets are festival rations records, and the Ua and Un tablets are mostly banqueting foodlists. Ua 9 and Fa 1195 are 'Unclear'. Ua 9 was written by H42, a scribe who dealt primarily with banqueting records, although this need not have been his exclusive concern (see Section 2.3.2.2). Fa 1195, by an unidentified hand, is very unusual in that it preserves only the barley ideogram and the number (the tablet seems to be complete). The purpose of the disbursement is thus unknown. The disbursement in Un 443.3 is also 'Unclear' (see Section 5.2.3 for text and discussion). The data are summarised in Table 5-4 (next page).[43]

The figures in the table indicate that 89% of the disbursements of barley are for religious purposes; there are no unambiguous harvest or collection records. Ua 9 could conceivably be a harvest record in light of the large amount recorded, but, as just noted, even if this were a 'collection' it may somehow be connected with banqueting.[44] In any case, since total amounts disbursed exceed the amount in Ua 9, this tablet alone would still not account for 'overall resources'. The palace evidently had access to more resources than appear in the surviving records, however they were obtained.

[41] As Killen (2004, 157) observes, barley does not appear on any certainly identified harvest record.
[42] Killen 2004, 156.
[43] For differences between tablets in the table and those with HORD listed in *PTT* I see notes to Table 5-4. Also note that ḤỌṚḌ in Un 1177 (*PTT* I, 245) is now read ỌṾỊṢ (Melena 2000–2001b, 376), so this tablet is excluded; Killen (2004, 159) gives it in his table for barley as 'uncertain'. Killen (*loc. cit.*) also gives Ua 9 and –25 as possible banqueting records (see p. 160 n iii). We here take Ua 25 as a banqueting record and Ua 9 as 'Unclear', but it is agreed that the possibility of banqueting is open (see Section 2.3.2.2).
[44] Killen 2004, 160 n iii.

Table 5-4. Barley at Pylos

	HORD	= V		HORD	= V
1. *Banqueting*			**3. *Secular Rations***		
Un 2	16 T 4	984	An 128 *verso*	5 T 3 V 4 Z [2	322.5
Ua 25(?)	2̣9̣ T 8 V 2̣	1̣7̣9̣0̣	An/Fn 7 *verso*	9 T 9*	594+
Un 47	41 T 1 V 4	2470	**TOTAL 3**		**916.5**
Un 138	22 T 13 V 1*	1399	**TOTAL 1 + 2 + 3**		**8612+**
TOTAL 1		**6643**	**4. *Unclear***		
2. *Festival rations*			Ua 9	100 T 1 V 2	6008
Fn 41	*summed*	110+	Un 443	2	120
Fn 50	*summed*	63+	Fa 1195	13[ ]Ṭ 3	7̣9̣8̣+
Fn 79	*summed*	436+	Fn 918	*summed*	90+
Fn 187	*summed*	196+	Fn 965	*summed*	232+
Fn 324	*summed*	232.5+	Fn 966	*summed*	9+
Fn 837+867	*summed*	13+	Fn 972	*summed*	1+
Fn 970	*summed*	2+	Fn 973	*summed*	1+
TOTAL 2		**1052.5+**	Fn 974	*summed*	60+
TOTAL 1 + 2		**7695.5+**	Fn 975	*summed*	37+
			Fn 979	*summed*	1+
			Fn 989	*summed*	1+

<u>**Notes**</u>

* = Summed.

An/Fn 7: An 7 now joins Fn 1247 (Melena 1996–1997b, 171–6). Killen (2004, 159 n i) prefers to keep the An classification. Daily rations are given on the *recto* and monthly on the *verso*; only the latter are given here.

Ua 17: May originally have recorded HORD]1 T 7 (see apparatus to line .1, *KT*[6]), but this is uncertain, so not shown in table.

Fn 41: Figures partially restored from figures for OLIV.

An 128: Reading of ideogram uncertain (ḤỌṚḌ). Z 2 is restored due to a plausible correlation with the sum of quantities on the *recto* (Palmer 1992, 483; Killen 2004, 160 n ii; cf. *PTT* I, 57).

Fn 187: New reading in line .19 by Bennett (1992, 108).

Fn 324: Joins Fn 1454 and several *frr*. (Melena 1992–1993a, 75).

Fn 837: Now joins Fn 867 (*PoN* IV).

Fa 1195: The text apart from number and ideogram is lost (as autopsy of the photo in the Mycenaean Epigraphy Room, Cambridge, suggests).

5.3.3 BARLEY AT MYCENAE

Barley appears at Mycenae on Fu 711, which may record festival rations or sacred meals (Section 2.3.3.4). The amount preserved is V 49 – some 78 litres. There is nothing to compare it with.

5.3.4 BARLEY AT THEBES

Barley at Thebes appears only in the Fq series, which is probably connected with religion.[45] The series was discussed in Section 2.3.3.3 where an example of one of the texts given; two further examples are below.

Fq 125 (305)

.1]wị[

.2]wa V[ ]*vest*.[

.3]V 4 Z 2 qe-re-ṃạ-o V 1[

.4]Z 2 wa-do-ta Z 1 po-[

.5]1 ọ-ḳọ[-we-i

inf. mut.

[45] Aravantinos 1999, 71; Killen 2004, 159 n vii.

Fq 126 (305)

.1a		Z 1̣[
.1	o-te , tu-wo-te-to , ma-ka , HORD T 1 V[	
.2	o-po-re-i V 1 Z 2 ko-wa Z[	
.3	ko-ru Z 2 ke-re-ṇạ-ị V[	
.4	*inf. mut.*	

As seen in Fq 125, not all of the Fq tablets include the ideogram for barley. A few record flour (probably, but see Section 4.3.5 for doubts that have been expressed), two record commodities represented by the syllabograms *KE* (Fq 187) and *PO* (Fq 207), and on the majority no ideograms at all appear, in some cases because they are broken off but primarily because they were never originally written. Apparently a single ideogram was meant to cover numerous entries in this series, but without knowing how the documents were filed it is impossible to determine what the 'missing' ideogram(s) would have been. Most entries were in all probability dealing with barley, but since this is uncertain tablets without ideograms are excluded here.

Data for the tablets which do include the HORD ideogram are summarised in Table 5-5. Occasionally the ideogram for flour (FAR) seems to appear in the middle of a document (e.g. Fq 214), but that barley is still concerned is suggested by the inclusion of such entries in the totalling formulas headed HORD at the end. It is not clear whether all entries subsequent to the FAR entry would also be flour or whether the ideogram was meant to apply to that entry alone. The table has been laid out as if the latter were the case, but it need not be so. However, the general conclusions here are not much affected either way, since we take our figures from the totals (where these are given).

Table 5-5. The Thebes Fq tablets recording HORD

Fq	text	HORD	FAR	= V
126.1	o-te , tu-wo-te-to , ma-ka	HORD T 1 V[(. . .) Z 1[		7.25+
126.2	o-po-re-i	V 1 Z 2		1.5
126.2	ko-wa	Z[		0.25+
126.3	ko-ru	Z 2		0.5
126.3	ke-re-ṇạ-ị	Ṿ[		1+
130.1	o-te , o-je-ke-te-to ma-ka	HORD T 2[		12+
130.2	o-po-re-i	V 2		2
130.2	ko-wa	Z 2[		0.5+
130.3	ka-wi-jo		FAR V 1	1
130.3	re-wa-ko a-me[-ro	*lost*		0.25+
130.4	]ạ-ke-ne-u-si	V 2		2
130.4	ku-si	V 2[		2+
131.1	ma-]ka	HORD[		0.25+
213.1	ma-]ka	ḤOṚḌ[		—
213.2	o-po-re-i	Ṿ[		—
214.1	ma-ka	HORD T 1 Z[		—
214.2	o-po-re-i	V 1[		—
214.2	ma-di-jẹ[	*lost*		—
214.3	ko-ru-we	Z 1[		—
214.3	ṭọ-jọ[	*lost*		—
214.4	a-ke-ne-ụ-ṣị[	*lost*		—
214.5	a-me-ro	Ṿ 1̣[		—
214.6	i-qo-po-qo-i	V 1 [		—
214.7	o-to-ro-no		FAR V 2	—
214.7	me[	*lost*		—
214.8	o-ko-we-i	Z 2		—
214.8	do-ro-jo [	*lost*		—
214.9	wa-do-ta	Z[		—

Fq	text	HORD	FAR	= V
214.9	]ịa-so-ro[	*lost*		—
214.10	to-tu-no	Z 1		—
214.10	e-pi-qọ[-i	*lost*		—
214.11	pi-ra-ko-ro	Z 1		—
214.11	de-u-ke-we[	]Z[		—
214.11	[. .]ṃọ[	*lost*		—
214.12	ko-du-**22*-we	Z 1		—
214.12	sa-[.]-jo	V 3		—
214.12	ṃị-ṛạ[-ti-jo	*lost*		—
214.13	o-u-wa-ja-wo-ni	Z 2		—
214.13	a-ra-o		FAR Ṿ[	—
214.14	**ku-su-to-ro-qa**	**HỌṚḌ Ṭ 6̣ V 5[**		**41+**
229.1	ma-ḳạ[	*lost*		0.25+
229.2	o-po-re-i [	*lost*		0.25+
229.3	a-pu-wa	Z 2		2
229.3	ko-ẉạ[	*lost*		0.25+
229.4	ra-ke-da-mi-ni-jo		FAR [	0.25+
229.5	qe-re-ṃạ-o	V 1 Z 2		1.5
229.5	ṃạ[	*lost*		0.25+
229.6	a-me-ṛọ	V 1		1
229.6	ka-wi-jo	V 1[		1+
229.7	o-ti-ri-ja-i	V 1		1
229.7	me-to-re[-i	*lost*		0.25+
229.8	o-u-ko-we-i	Z 2		0.5
229.8	ḍọ-ro-jo	Z 1[		0.25+
229.9	ku-ne	Z 2		0.5
229.9	wa-ḍọ-ta	Z 1		0.25
229.9	po-[	*lost*		0.25+
229.10	to-tu-no	V 1		1
229.10	e-pi-qọ-i	Z[		0.25+
229.11	pi-ṛạ-ko-ro	Z 1		0.25
229.11	de-u-ke-we	Z 1 [		0.25
229.12	do-ra-ạ$_2$-ja	Z 1		0.25
229.12	e-pi-ṇị-ja	Z[		0.25+
229.13	*vacat*	—	—	—
229.14	**ku-su[-to-]ro-qa**	**HỌṚḌ[**	***lost***	**—**
254[+]255.1	de-qo-no	HỌṚḌ T 1 V 2 Z 3		8.75
254.1	o-te , a-pi-e-qe⌞ ⌟ke-ro-ṭạ	*none*		—
254.2	pa-ta , ma-ka	HORD Ṭ 1̣ V 2 Z 2		8.5
254.2	a-ko-da-mo	V 2		2
254.3	o-po-re-i[	*lost*		0.25+
254.3	]ṃạ-ḍị-je	V 1̣[Z?]1̣		1.25+
254.3	ḳạ-ne-jo	V 3		3
254.4	ko-wa	Z 2		0.5
254.4	a-pu-wa	Z 2		0.5
254.4	ko-ru	Z 2		0.5
254.5	qe-re-ma-o	V 1 Z 2		1.5
254.5	zo-wa	V 1		1
254.5	a-me-ro	V 1		1
254.6	ka-wi-jo		FAR V 1	1
254.6	**63*[ ]ka[ ]	*lost*		0.25+
254.6	i-qo-po-qo-i	V 1 Z 1		1.25
258.1	ma-ka	HORD T 1 V 3 Z 1		9.25
258.1	a-ko[-da-mo	*lost*		0.25+
258.2	ma-di-je	V 3̣ Z 2		3.5
258.2	ko-wa	Ẓ[		0.25+
258.3	to-jo	V 3		3
258.3	ra-ke-da-mi-ni-jo		FAR[	0.25+
258.4	qe-re-ma-o	V 1 Z 2		1.50

Fq	text	HORD	FAR	= V
258.4	we-re-na-[ko	*lost*		0.25+
258.5	zo-wa	V 1		1
258.5	ka-wi-jo		FAR V 1[	1+
258.6	o-]u-ko-we-i	Ṿ 1̣		1̣
258.6	do-ro-jo	Z[		0.25+
258.7	]-de	Z 2		0.5
258.7	a-ka-de[	*lost*		0.25+
263.1	ma-ka	HORD T[		6+
263.2	ma-di-je	V 1[		1+
263.3	ko-du[-**22*-je	*lost*		0.25+
269.1	]ku[	]Ṿ 2[		—
269.2	]-i	Ṿ 1̣		—
269.2	wa-do-ta	Z 1		—
269.3	*lost*	]Z 1		—
269.3	to-tu[-no	]1		—
269.3	mi-ra-ti-jo	V 1		—
269.4	*lost*	]Z 1		—
269.4	de-u-ke-we	Z 1		—
269.5	de-u-ti-jo	T 1		—
269.6	]o-ro-wa-ta	V 2		—
269.7	**ku-su-to-ro-]qa**	**HORD 1 V 2[ ]Z 3̣[**		**62.75+**
276.1	qe-]ṛẹ-ma-o[	*lost*		—
276.2	zo-wạ	Ṿ 1		—
276.2	a-ṃẹ-ro[	*lost*		—
276.3	o-u-ko-we-i	Z 2 [		—
276.4	ạ-ḳạ-ḍẹ-ị	Z 2[		—
276.5	jạ-ṣọ-ro	Z 1		—
276.5	a-ta-o[	*lost*		—
276.6	ẹ-p̣ị-do-ro-mo	Z 2		—
276.6	mi-ra-ti-jo	Ẓ 1[		—
276.7	ko-du-**22*-je	Z 1		—
276.7	do-ra-a_2-ja	Z 1		—
276.7	de[	*lost*		—
276.8	i-qo-po-qo-i	V 2 Z 1		—
276.8	o-ti-ṛị-ja-i	Ṿ 3[		—
276.9	ḳạ-ṭị-jọ	Z[		—
276.9	]ạ-ṇụ-to	Ẓ[		—
276.9	[me-]ṭọ-re-i	Z 2̣[		—
276.10	**ku-su-to-ro-qa**	**T 8 V 2[**		**50+**
285.1	ma-]ka	HORD T 1[		6+
285.2	*lost*	]V 1		1+
285.2	ma-di[-je	*lost*		0.25+
285.3	*lost*	]2̣		0.5+
285.3	ko-[	*lost*		0.25+
304.1	ma-ka ,	HORD Ṭ[		6+
304.2	ọ-po-re-ị[	*lost*		0.25+
357.1	ma-]ka	HORD Ṭ[		6+
357.2	ma-]di-je [	*lost*		0.25+
			TOTAL	**277.5+**

Notes

General

The totalling formula *ku-su-to-ro-qa* is given in bold.

Where a figure is lost altogether, Z 1 (= V 0.25) is restored rather than V 1 as is the usual convention, since many entries are not larger than Z 1.

Individual tablets

Fq 214: Line .14 gives the total for the whole document so only this figure is given.

Fq 229: A total is given in line .14 but the figure is lost so (unlike Fq 214) the individual entries are given.

Fq 254.1: Line .1 follows on to another line?

Fq 254.3: No room for another entry in line .3 so perhaps restore Z? (But reading difficult in any case.)

In total, some V 277.75+ is recorded, all in connection with religion. Thus, 100% of recorded disbursements of barley at Thebes were for religious purposes. There are no tablets from which to attempt to estimate overall resources.

We might here observe that a notable feature of the Fq tablets is how detailed they are and how small many of the issues are. What is interesting about this is that it is evident that the purpose of the records is not so much to track resources (since large amounts are not being expended), but to track specific allotments to specific individuals. This recalls the situation with the Knossos oil tablets, particularly the Fp(1) set, where small amounts are allotted over a series of months to the same individuals. In the Fq tablets too, many of the recipients from document to document are the same. Although month names do not appear in these records, one wonders if they might actually have been kept over a series of months, or at least might refer to a series of different offering occasions involving the same shrine(s?) or set of divine or religiously associated recipients.

5.4 FLOUR (**129* = FAR)

5.4.1 INTRODUCTION TO FLOUR

FAR appears at Pylos, Knossos, Mycenae and Thebes, exclusively in records of final disbursements for offerings, banqueting and festival rations.[46] There is thus a considerable bias in the recording of this commodity: flour as such was not normally recorded in Linear B. Palatial resources in flour cannot be calculated from the existing documentation but, given the large amounts of wheat and barley recorded (FAR might represent either[47]), considerable quantities must have been available.

5.4.2 FLOUR AT KNOSSOS

At Knossos, FAR appears only in the Fs series (Section 3.2.3.4). The total amount preserved or restored is V 21 (Table 3-5), perhaps about 33.6 litres.

5.4.3 FLOUR AT PYLOS

FAR appears in Un 2, –718, –853 (all banqueting records) and possibly Fn 187 (see note to table).[48] The data are summarised in Table 5-6.

Table 5-6. Flour at Pylos

tablet	FAR	= V
Fn 187	*no # written*	—
Un 2	1 T 2	72
Un 718	T 6	36
Un 853	T 1 V [	7+
	TOTAL	115+

Note

Fn 187: The reading of FAR in line .3 is very uncertain (Killen 2004, 161 n i). It does not appear to be followed by a number. Often where no number is written, the ideogram was intended to indicate a single unit 'one'. However, it is unclear whether this was the intention here and most

[46] Killen 1999c, 218; 2004, 160.

[47] Killen 2004, 167–8.

[48] It may originally also have appeared in Un 47⟦.4⟧, but the entry was emended to HORD.

issues on the tablet are of smaller amounts. On the other hand, *NI* 2 is issued in line .1, so a full unit of FAR is at least possible. But given the uncertain reading it is best simply to note the possibilities.

Altogether this is some 184 litres of flour, all issued for purposes connected with festivals or ceremonial banqueting. There is nothing from which to estimate overall resources.

5.4.4 FLOUR AT MYCENAE

At Mycenae flour appears only in Fu 711, which may record festival rations or sacred meals (Section 2.3.3.4). Some Z 3 (about 1.2 litres) is recorded.

5.4.5 FLOUR AT THEBES

Flour at Thebes appears in the Fq and Gp series, both connected with religion, and which were discussed in Sections 5.3.4 (Table 5-5) and 4.3.5 (Table 4-7) respectively. It was noted previously (Section 4.3.5) that some of the readings of FAR are contested. The issue remains to be resolved but in any case our overall conclusions are not affected by this particular problem (the commodities and sites are considered separately and one commodity at one site will not subvert the general pattern) and the view of the editors of the Thebes tablets is followed here.[49]

The Fq series, according to the counting system adopted for Table 5-5, records V 8+ of flour. The Gp series records some V 130.25+ of flour (Table 4-7). 100% of recorded disbursements are thus in religious contexts and there are no documents from which to estimate overall resources.

5.5 FIGS (**30* = *NI*)

5.5.1 FIGS AT KNOSSOS

Several land tenure documents at Knossos record fig trees (see below), but the fruit itself is rarely mentioned and appears almost exclusively in banqueting and offerings contexts. The banqueting foodlist Uc 161 from the RCT (Section 2.3.2.3) includes figs, as do the Fs tablets (Section 3.2.3.4, Table 3-5) plus F(2) 866, referring to the shrine of Dikte. The text of the last is as follows.

F(2) 866 (—)

]ṇị-jo / di-ka-ta-de *NI* 10 ma-ṣạ[

As Killen notes, the amount here is unusually large for an offerings record, but *di-ka-ta-de* is found elsewhere only in offerings contexts.[50] In any case, whether an offerings record or not, a connection with religion is indicated.

Figs also appear on the following three tablets.

[49] The one change which would occur if FAR were not read at all at Thebes would be the deletion of the present section. Yet even this would hardly affect the overall conclusions of the study, flour being just one of the many ideograms we deal with and evidence for its use at other sites being secure. In favour of reading FAR in at least some of the new Thebes tablets see Killen 2006a, 104–5.

[50] See Killen 1987b, 172–3 (and the same pages for *ma-sa*); also 2004, 161–2.

F(2) 5001 + *frr.* (4) (—)

.1 *sup. mut.*
.2]80 OLIV+*A* 3̣0[ ] *vac.* [
.3] *vac.* [
.4]GRA 3 OLIV+*A* 2 *NI* 1 T 3 Ṿ[ ]3[
.5–6] *vacant* [

F(2) 7343 (—)

.1]44̣[
.2]80 *NI*[

.1 Traces at left, perhaps not part of the numerals, though might be part of a further row of tens.
.2 Traces of ⟦ ⟧ (perhaps originally 5 tens in the second column of tens); right hand part of *NI* over ⟦ ⟧.

F(2) 7346 (—)

] *NI* 612̣[

F(2) 5001 may be a harvesting record (cf. OLIV+*A* in e.g. F(2) 852, –854), although the amounts in line .4 would be unusually small.[51] F(2) 7343 and 7346 are too damaged for their functions to be determined, but they too may have been harvest records.[52] It is in any case unlikely given the very large numbers (especially in F(2) 7346) that either was an offerings record. In all probability they were collection or inventory records and would have provided data regarding overall resources were the texts better preserved.[53] The data are summarised in Table 5-7.

Table 5-7. Figs at Knossos

	NI	= V
1. *Religious*		
1a. non-RCT		
Fs series	Table 3-5	60
F(2) 866	10	600
Sub-total 1a		660
1b. RCT		
Uc 161	10	600
2. *Harvests?*		
F(2) 5001	1 T 3 Ṿ[ ]3[	81+
F(2) 7343	*lost*	1+
F(2) 7346	612̣[	36,720+
TOTAL 2		**36,802+**

For both the RCT and non-RCT documents, there are no unambiguous instances of disbursements for any non-religious purpose, so 100% of recorded disbursements were for religious purposes. Yet it seems unlikely that the majority of figs at Knossos were consumed in cult. The single RCT record of figs cannot be 'compared' with anything, but regarding the non-RCT records, while it is not certain that the three F(2) tablets do record harvests, they at least indicate that a large amount of the commodity was available. The non-RCT religious disbursements are just 2% of the amounts preserved on these documents.

Furthermore, while references to figs as fruit are rare, fig trees are more common and may help to give a more realistic view of overall resources. They appear on the following tablets.

---

[51] Killen 2004, 161. A join by Melena completes the reading (Godart *et al.* 1992–1993, 57).
[52] Killen (2004, 161) notes it would be consistent with (although of course not proof of) such an interpretation that F(2) 7343 is a two-line tablet.
[53] Also note they are unlikely to be rations records, unless they were totalling tablets. On standard rations of T 2 per month, 3060 persons could be supported by the amount recorded in F(2) 7346.

Gv 863 (—)

.1]q̣ạ-ra , / jo-e-ke-to-qo , wo-na-si , ṣị[

.2] we-je-we *174 420 *su* ARB 104̣[

.1 *jo-e-ke-to-qo* , *wo-* over ⟦ ⟧.

Gv 864 (—)

.1] *174 69̣[

.2]su-za ARB 53[

.3] pu-ta *174 [

.1 Over ⟦ ⟧ involving 1st ruling and so present top of line .2.
.3 Over ⟦ ⟧. Trace at right.

Gv 862 (—)

.1]su-za ARB 1770

.2]jọ ARB 405

.3 ']ị-po-qa' ARB 10[ ] ARB 17 *174 20

.4]⟦ 4⟧

.5]365 *174 225

.6]⟦ *vest.* ⟧

→

v. Tallying

.1-3 Four varieties of the sign ARB are used, each associated with a different introductory word.
.3 Trace of sign before the second ARB (perhaps ']ṃẹ'). 20 over ⟦ ⟧?
.3-5 Over ⟦ ⟧ involving a process of reruling.
v. Ten or eleven tens.

F(2) 841 + 867 (—)

.1]-ti-ja , sa-pi-ti-ṇẹ-we-jo [

.2]ạ-di-*22-sa GRA+*PE* T 5̣ *NI* 8[

.3 .]nọ-di-mi-zo-jo[/] , GRA+*PE* 2 *NI* 34[

.4 pa-i-to , mi-sa-ra-jo , sa-pi-ti-ne-we-jo[

.5 su-za , *NI* 75 ka-po , e-[

.6]wa , OLIV 46 e-ra-wa[

.7.8] *vacant* [

.3 Traces after *-jo* probably minuscule sign (possibly *ḳọ*[or *ḍẉẹ*[).
.4 *pa-* over ⟦ ⟧.

These tablets record trees (ARB) designated as *su-za*, indicating fig trees (abbreviated to *su* in Gv 863).[54] F(2) 841 records *NI*, rather than ARB, but in the present case this represents trees rather than figs (the *NI* ideogram is in any case a simplified version of ARB).[55] Killen argues that this is a record of land-holdings (note GRA is ligatured with *PE* as in the Pylos land tenure tablets) by a man, *sa-pi-ti-nu-wo*,[56] at Phaistos (line .4) and another place, possibly *do-ti-ja* (line .1).[57] As a record of land, this document may not concern goods actually coming into the palace, but does reflect resources with which the palace was somehow concerned. They may be records of palatial estates or of land which was taxed or tithed in some way.

Altogether, 2044 fig trees are recorded in the documents. What might the potential yield of so many trees have been? Although fraught with uncertainties, we may gain some sense of the scale through considering yields from trees in pre-industrial Nichoria. These produced about 25 kg of dried figs per tree annually.[58] If Bronze Age yields were similar, 2044 trees would produce some 51,100 kg of dried figs. Even on a more conservative estimate – for instance, 15 kg per tree – the amounts are substantial, some 30,660 kg. To compare these figures with our offerings, given in V units, we would need to know (for instance) whether the fruit was fresh or

[54] Killen 1987b, 174.
[55] Killen 1987b, 174–7; 2004, 156; Palmer 1994, 47.
[56] The name appears in connection with a workgroup in As 1516.15, though this is probably not the same individual (Killen 1987b, 176 n 25).
[57] Killen 1987b, 176 n 24.
[58] Aschenbrenner 1972, 56, Table 4-4.

dried (the latter is perhaps more likely[59]) and how closely packed it was. Such information is altogether lacking, but a rough estimate may be worthwhile so long as it is emphasised that the calculation is highly speculative. The simplest procedure is to convert each type of data into litres. On the Nichoria yields, assuming 3 kg of figs = 1 litre, 2044 trees would yield some 10,220–17,033 litres. The non-RCT religious disbursements amount, on the VC values, to some 1056 litres, which is 10% of the lower figure and 6% of the higher one. Again, this line of reasoning is based on numerous uncertainties so little weight should be placed on these figures, but it seems at least likely that the palace had access to larger resources of figs than appear in the offerings records.

5.5.2 FIGS AT PYLOS

While figs are infrequently recorded at Knossos, at Pylos they appear on numerous records and in a variety of economic situations. Religious contexts include banqueting (Un 2, –47) and festival rations (Fn 187). The main non-religious use in the records is as rations for female workgroups (Ab series and Fg 253, a totalling tablet related to the series[60]). Fg 368 and –374 are also rations records.[61] Fg 368 was dealt with above (Section 5.2.3), where it was noted that although this is clearly a rations record it is listed as 'unclear' because the rations to the woman *ke-sa-da-ra* may have been for religious purposes. The text of Fg 374 is as follows.

Fg 374 (S240-H1)

a-re-po-zo-o , ko-ka-ro GRA 1 *NI* 1

Fg 374 records an issue to an unguent-boiler, *ko-ka-ro* (see Section 2.5.3).[62] The amount disbursed is greater than individual rations normally recorded in the Ab series (it is equivalent to monthly rations for five people). As was observed for *ke-sa-da-ra*, it may be that the issue was intended for longer periods of time, or that *ko-ka-ro* was of superior status so received more,[63] or was receiving on behalf of a larger group.

Three tablets record *o-no* 'payments'. An 35 was discussed above (Section 4.3.3); and Ua 158 and Un 1322 are discussed below (Section 6.4.1.2). For reference with regard to the numbers, the relevant parts of the texts are given here (in Un 1322 the ideograms and numbers are shown aligned to facilitate reading them).[64]

An 35

.5 a-ta-ro , tu-ru-pte-ri-ja , o-no
.6 LANA 2 CAP 4 **146* 3 VIN 10 *NI* 4

Ua 158 (Cii)

.1 ke-do-jo , o-na , e-qa-na-qẹ[
.2 **146* 20 GRA 7 *NI* 5̣ ⟦ ⟧ [
.3 *vacat* [

Palimpsest.
.2 *NI* 5̣ : *NI* 7̣ possible.

[59] In the case of rations (see Pylos), it is perhaps more likely they were dried because rations were issued monthly and fresh figs would not have been available for the whole year. But note, as Killen (2004, 161–2) suggests, the issue may have been a special supplement only for that month, perhaps on the occasion of a festival. In that case, it could well be that fresh fruit was involved. There is a general absence of fresh produce from the records (noted by e.g. Palmer 1999), but it does not seem possible to know either way.
[60] Chadwick 1988, 63–4; Killen 2004, 161.
[61] Killen 2004, 161–2.
[62] Shelmerdine 1985, 41; Killen 2001a, 179–80.
[63] See Killen 2001a, 180.
[64] Ua 158: Text as in Melena 1992–1993b, 310. Un 1322: Text as in Bennett 1992, 121. It takes into account a join suggested by Killen (*JHS* 96 [1976] 260), published in Melena 1992-1993b, 323. There is some minor further change to the text in *PoN* IV.

Un 1322 (Cii)

.1	] GRA [*qs*	
.2	]ṇọ-[ ]ọ-no[ ]	GRA 6 *ṆỊ* [*qs*
.3	de-ku-tu-wo-ḳọ[ ]o-no	GRA 2 *NI* 2
.4	ị-ṭẹ-wẹ , o-ṇọ[ ]	GRA 12
.5	we-a_2-no[ri]-no , re-po-to	**146* GRA 5
.6	we-[ ]no[	]**146* GṚẠ 1̣5
.7	*vestigia*	

Note that in Ua 158.2 the number '7' may be restored with relative security after *NI* since it is generally the case at Pylos that wheat and figs are issued in equal amounts.[65] In Un 1322.2, the same may be done, although it should be noted the reading for the number following GRA in line .2 is not secure.[66]

Lines .1–6 of Un 616 record allocations for perfumery.[67] The text was given in Section 2.5.3; we repeat it here along with the apparatus.

Un 616 (S615-H1)

Recto

.1	ku-ru-ro_2 AROM 13 T 5	
.2	*KAPO* 4	
.3	**157* 28	
.4	LANA 5 *ME po* 6 S 1 V 4	
.5	ko-ṛị-jọ-ḍạ-na	
.6	AROM 21	
.7	ị-ṛẹ-wẹ[ ]*ṆỊ* T 2	

Verso

.1	ta-we-si-jo-jo , ke-ro-si-ja	VIR 20[
.2	a-pi-qo-o , ke-ro-si-ja	VIR 17̣ [
.3	a-pi-o-to , ke-ro-si-ja	VIR 18
.4	o-to-wo-o , ke-ro-si-ja	VIR 13̣

Latus sinistrum

ka-ma-e-we VIR 10

.1 *ku-ro-ro₂*: *ku-<pa->ro₂*, cf. Un 249.1; 13: the 3 units (by their positions only) might have been added after
T, but were probably instead written high to accommodate the expected T and numbers; T minuscule; 5: the fifth stroke is odd, and might have been added to an original 4.
.2 *ka* (or probably *KAPO*) erased before *KAPO*.
.3 28: the last 5 strokes are irregular and might have been added, even one by one.
.4 *ME po* cf. OLE *po* in Fr 1201, 1203, 1208, 1214; 6: irregular disposition, 4 above and 2 below, possibly to
accommodate the expected S, but the last four are odd in appearance, and possibly added to original 2; S minuscule; 1 V 4̣ on *latus dextrum*; possibly V 5.
.5 Possibly over erasure of whole line.
.6 Probably over erasure of whole line.
.7 Possibly *i-ra₃-we*.
v.2 *a-pi-qo-<ta->o*.
Lat.sin. 10 over 10 units erased.
Lat.dex. *ṭạ* erased at left.

Why figs are included in such a list is unclear, since they are not known as a perfume ingredient. However, different subjects may be dealt with in this tablet. The *verso* lists male workgroups, and might be the foundation for a rations record (or at least an assessment of available manpower). The text sits oddly with lines .1–6 of the *recto* and could be unrelated to them if the scribe happened to be making notes about different things on the same tablet (unusual, but not impossible).[68] In *PTT*, *NI* was not read in line .7, so that it was supposed that

[65] '7' is possible; see apparatus (Melena 1992–1993b, 310).
[66] Un 1322: The text given here follows a new reading (Melena 1992–1993b, 323), with minor further amendments in *PoN* IV.
[67] Shelmerdine 1985, 20–1. Un 616: formerly classified An; new text and reclassification from Bennett 1992, 114–15, with reading of *ME po* rather than *me-po* in line .4 following *PoN* IV; apparatus as in *PoN* IV except note added line .4.
[68] Note the same list appears on An 261.

i-re-we[might be a commodity name (in parallel with plant names),[69] but in the light of the new transcription, *i-re-we* is perhaps more likely to be a recipient. Nevertheless, the entry remains 'Unclear'.

Un 1426 is also 'Unclear'; it may be a rations record, possibly with religious connections (see Section 2.3.2.2 for text and discussion). A final tablet which may have recorded figs is An 128 (Section 5.2.3).[70] The ideogram is lost for the commodity disbursed in line .12, but this is a rations record and supplementing the entry for wheat (line .11) with one for figs would be in parallel with other such records at Pylos. However, since this is uncertain, the tablet is not included here (the amount recorded against the lost ideogram is V 161+).

The data are summarised in Table 5-8.[71]

Table 5-8. Figs at Pylos

context	tablet	*NI*	= V
1. *Religious*			
Banqueting	Un 2	1	60
Banqueting	Un 47	T 9 V 3	57
Festival rations	Fn 187	*summed*	208
TOTAL 1			**325**
2. *Secular rations*			
For female workgroups	Ab series	—	—
Ab series totalling tablet	Fg 253	192 T 7	11,562
For an unguent boiler	Fg 374	1	60
TOTAL 2			**11,622**
3. o-no *payments*			
To a man *ke-do-jo*	Ua 158	7	420
For alum	An 35	4	240
To weaver, etc.	Un 1322	8̣	4̣8̣0̣
TOTAL 3			**1140**
TOTAL 1 + 2 + 3			**13,087**
4. *Unclear*			
Rations for *ke-sa-da-ra*	Fg 368	5	300
Perfumery?	Un 616	T 2	12
Rations??	Un 1426	5	300

<u>Notes</u>
Ab series: Figure not included, since Fg 253 is probably totalling tablet for series (see Section 5.2.3).
Ua 158: Figure restored (see chapter text).
Un 1322: Assumes that '6' should be restored in line .2 (see chapter text).

All tablets (including the 'Unclear' ones) record disbursements. Disbursements for banqueting and festival rations are a bare 2.5% of the total (excluding the 'Unclear' documents). The vast majority of recorded figs were for secular rations, particularly to female workgroups. There are no records of harvests or any indication of how resources were obtained, but it is again apparent that resources were substantial (some 20,939 litres appear in Categories 1–3 alone).

5.5.3 FIGS AT MYCENAE AND TIRYNS

Figs appear at Mycenae in four tablets: Fu 711, Ue 611, –652 and –661. The first was discussed in Section 2.3.3.4, the others in Section 2.3.2.4. Fu 711 may relate to festival rations

[69] *DMic.* I, 286.
[70] Palmer 1992, 483; Killen 2004, 160 n ii.
[71] The table corresponds with Killen's (2004, 162, Table 8.4) except that Fg 368 is taken as 'Unclear' for reasons given above.

or sacred meals; the recipient in line .8 receives figs (Z 1) and flour. Ue 661 records food 'set forth' for dining, possibly for a banquet although not necessarily with a religious nature. Two types of figs appear on this tablet, with different ligatures. Altogether twenty major units are recorded, but it is not clear that these are equivalent to 'standard' major units. Ue 611 is a probable banqueting foodlist; it records *NI* 2. Ue 652 may be a harvest or delivery record; the reading is *ṆỊ* 36 (note the reading is uncertain).

Given the various uncertainties (particularly the function and the nature of the unit in Ue 661), it is pointless attempting to produce calculations here. It may be noted, however, that the amount issued in the one offering record is very small, and that Ue 652 hints at access to more substantial resources.

A single tablet at Tiryns, Uh 12, records figs. It may be a festival rations record, if *di-pte-ra-po-ro* is correctly restored (see Section 2.3.3.5), but this is uncertain.[72]

5.6 OLIVES (**122* = OLIV)

5.6.1 OLIVES AT KNOSSOS

Olives at Knossos appear in two tablets related to religion, E 842 (Section 5.2.2) and Uc 161 from the RCT (Section 2.3.2.3). They also appear in various harvest records (often with wheat; see Section 5.2.2) and possibly in the following rations record, also from the RCT.[73]

Ap 5077 + *fr.*				('124'??)
.1		]e-ke		
.2		ko-]⟦wạ 1̣⟧ ko-wo 1		
.3	⟦	ỌḶỊṾ 1̣	⟧	
.4	⟦	?	⟧	

The appearance of olives in a Knossian rations record would add another dimension to contexts in which olives appear at the site and we include it in the table, but it should be noted that the ideogram appears in an erasure and the reading is not secure. The data are summarised in Table 5-9. The 'definite' and 'possible' harvest records are as identified recently by Killen.[74]

[72] Killen (2004, 162) also gives it as 'uncertain'.

[73] *Scribes RCT*, 201.

[74] Killen 2004, 162, Table 8.5. The table was printed omitting a line, which is restored here. After '854(?)', the next line should continue: '5001(?), 5043(??), 7050(?), 7345(?); F 8000(??)'. F 8000 preserves no text apart from the ideogram and number and is here considered 'Unclear'. Killen includes in the 'uncertain' category F 7337, but we exclude it here because the OLIV ideogram does not appear (the tablet records a liquid measure – the ideogram is lost, but the apparatus notes a trace of ỌḶẸ is possible; see *KT*[5], 200; *CoMIK* III, *s.v.* 7337). Killen omits F(1) 157 (presumably on grounds of the uncertain reading); it resembles a harvest record and is included as 'possible' here.

Table 5-9. Olives at Knossos

	OLIV	OLIV+*A*	OLIV+*TI*	= V
1. *Religious*				
1a. non-RCT				
E 842	]ỌḶỊṾ 24 T 4̣			146̣4̣
1b. RCT				
Uc 161	OLIV 30			1800
2. *Rations (RCT)*				
Ap 5077	⟦ỌḶỊṾ 1̣⟧			⟦6̣0̣⟧
3. *Harvests*				
3a. definite (non-RCT)				
F(2) 845		OLIV+*A* 12		720
F(2) 851		OLIV+*A* 46[		2760
F(2) 852		OLIV+*A* 70	OLIV+*TI* 20	5400*
Sub-total 3a				**8880**
3b. possible (non-RCT)				
E(2) 669	OLIV 45	OLIV+*A* 43	OLIV+*TI* 45	7980*
E(2) 670	OLIV 89̣[			5̣3̣4̣0̣+
F(2) 844	ỌḶỊṾ 10 T 2	OLIV+*A* 10 T 2		1224*
F(2) 853			OLIV+*TI* 3 T [	186+
F(2) 854		OLIV+*A* 52		3120
F(2) 5001		OLIV+*A* 3̣0[ ]OLIV+*A* 2		1̣8̣0̣0̣+ 120
F(2) 5043	OLIV 4[?T]2̣[OLIV 29 Ṭ 1			2̣5̣2̣ 1̣7̣4̣6̣
F(2) 7050	OLIV 120			7200
F(2) 7345		OLIV+*A* 53	OLIV+*TI* 6 T 7[	3582+*
Sub-total 3b				**32,550+**
TOTAL 3a+3b				**41,430+**
3c. possible (RCT)				
F(1) 157	ỌḶỊṾ 82 T 4			4944
4. *Unclear*				
4a. non-RCT				
F(2) 7357	OLIV 30[			1800+
F 8000		ỌḶỊṾ +*A* 8̣ Ṭ 5̣[		5̣1̣0̣+
4b. RCT				
F(1) 8437	]OLIV [			6+

Notes

General

* = Summed.

Individual tablets

F(2) 844: The ỌḶỊṾ 10 T 2 recorded on the *lat.inf.* is included in the table, but could possibly be a filing note(??).

F(2) 5043: The first figure is taken as if T 2 should be restored although this is of course uncertain – but not much is added in any case.

F(1) 8437: V 6+ is restored because no smaller amount than T 1 is attested in these records.

We may first consider the four RCT records. One is a banqueting record, one a rations record (but on which the ideogram OLIV is uncertain and appears in an erasure, as noted above), one a possible harvest record and one 'Unclear' (but probably also a harvest record). If we ignore the erasure on Ap 5077, 100% of disbursements of olives in the RCT records are for banqueting. If we take Ap 5077 into account, the percentage is still high, 97%. A suggestion of overall resources is supplied by the possible harvest record, which records V 4944. The amount on the banqueting record is 36% of this.

Turning to the non-RCT records, the only disbursement record, E 842, is connected with religion, so 100% of disbursements are for religious purposes. Whatever was being done with olives at Knossos, either it was not normally recorded in the Linear B archives, or the documents on which it was recorded were not normally preserved. Yet it is clear that the palace had access to very large amounts of olives, as witnessed in the harvest records – the 'certain' ones record V 8880, while the 'certain' and 'possible' ones together record V 41,430+, some 66,288 litres. (This circumstance of course relates also to the fact that it had access to very large amounts of olive oil, as seen in Chapter 3.) The amount recorded in E 842 is 16% of the amount in the 'definite' harvest records and 4% of the amount in the 'definite' plus 'possible' harvest records.

As observed for several other commodities, information about what was done with the majority of resources does not survive in the extant epigraphic record. It may be that the many harvest records are present because the tablets date from the time of year when olives were being harvested (December–January); presumably the entire yearly intake would be recorded around the same time. (But note that some of the commodities recorded on these records are gathered in at a different time in the year.) However that may be, disbursements should have been made throughout the year and, however short the administrative span of the documents, we might have expected to find more than three disbursement records, which are not even contemporary with one another. It is evident that the Linear B tablets give a very skewed account of uses of palatial resources in olives.

We may finally, for the sake of completeness, consider one further relevant document, F(2) 841, discussed above (Section 5.5.1) in connection with fig trees. As noted there, it is probably a land holdings record. Line .6 records forty-six olive trees, apparently at Phaistos (see line .4). A mere forty-six trees hardly accounts for all the of the olives and olive oil documented in other records (which in any case are coming from other places in addition to Phaistos), but this tablet adds another dimension to evidence for these commodities in the Linear B documents.

5.6.2 OLIVES AT PYLOS

Olives at Pylos appear in banqueting and festival rations records and, once, as rations to ordinary workers. An unusually large amount of olives appears on Ua 9, encountered above, which might be a banqueting or harvest record or perhaps a collection made on the occasion of a banquet (Section 2.3.2.2). The data are set out in Table 5-10.

Table 5-10. Olives at Pylos

	OLIV	= V
1. *Banqueting*		
Un 2	OLIV 3 T 2	192
Ua 25	*erased*	—
Un 138.2	*po-qa* OLIV 4 T 3 V 5	263
Un 138.5	*ka-pa* OLIV 7	420
TOTAL 1		**875**
2. *Festival rations*		
Fn 41.4	Ọ̣Ḷ̣Ị̣Ṿ T 3̣	1̣8̣
Fn 41.13	OLIV 1	60
Fn 79.1	OLIV 1[	60+
Fn 79.4	OLIV 1	60
Fn 79.5	OLIV 1	60
Fn 79.6	OLIV 1	60
Fn 79.7	⟦OLIV⟧	—
Fn 79.8	OLIV T 7	42

Fn 79.12	OLIV 1[	60+
Fn 79.14	OLIV 1	60
Fn 918.1	OLIV 1	60
Fn 918.2	OLIV T 5̣	3̣0
Fn 918.4	OLIV 1̣	6̣0
Fn 965.1	OLIV 1	60
Fn 975.3	OLIV [	6+
TOTAL 2		**696+**
TOTAL 1 + 2		**1571+**
3. *Secular rations*		
An/Fn 7	OLIV 9 (see note)	**540**
TOTAL 1 + 2 + 3		**2111+**
4. *Unclear*		
Ua 9	OLIV 88 T 7[	**5322+**

Notes

An/Fn 7: For the reading see Melena 1996–1997b, 171. The first paragraph records daily rations, the second monthly. OLIV appears in lines .1 and .2 for daily rations; the monthly rations are in lines .7 and .8. Only the monthly rations are given here (since they comprise the daily ones). The figure in line .8 is lost but would presumably have been half the number (6) in line .7, as line .2 gives half the number in line .1.

Ua 25: OLIV [was written then erased on the *verso* (*PTT* apparatus).

Un 138: Two sorts of olives are recorded.

Fn 975: T 1 is restored since no amount as small as V 1 (at least, as applied to olives) appears in the series.

74% of final disbursements are for purposes connected with religion, similar to the situation at Knossos, although not as extreme (there is at least one positive case at Pylos of olives used for secular rations). But Pylos has no harvest records, unless Ua 9 is one. The distributions are skewed in opposite ways: Knossos has collections, Pylos has disbursements. Yet even the Pylian disbursements must supply an incomplete account of palatial olive usage. Unless 74% (or some such figure) of Pylian olives really were intended for religious purposes, it must be supposed either that the majority of palatial uses were not recorded, or that such documentation is lost. Further, the Knossos harvest records indicate the palace possessed far greater quantities of goods than attested on the disbursement tablets, and there is every reason to expect this to be so for Pylos as well, despite the lack of documentation.

5.6.3 OLIVES AT THEBES

Olives at Thebes appear only in the Ft series. As discussed by AGS, the series is divided into three 'lots': Ft 140, Ft 182, and the rest (Section 2.3.3.3).[75] Ft 140, as noted above (Section 5.2.5, with text), is probably a record of a measure of land capacity. The text of Ft 182 is as follows.

Ft 182 (—)

.1] 100[

.2]1̣8 OLIV 71 ka-ṇẹ[

lat. inf.] 1 OLIV 5[

Ft 182 is probably a totalling record of some sort, given the large figures, but it is not clear what the totals were in reference to.[76]

[75] *Thèbes* I, 157, 370.

[76] Killen (2004, 162, Table 8.5) takes as religious offerings the Ft tablets other than Ft 140 and 'perhaps Ft 182'; see also *Thèbes* I, 268–9.

The remaining Ft tablets are probably offerings or sacred meal records, and are related to the Fq and Gp tablets (Section 2.3.3.3). The data they record are set out in Table 5-11.

Table 5-11. The Thebes Ft tablets

Ft	text	OLIV	= V
141.1	ka-pa	OLIV T 2 V 4	16
141.2	a-ko-da-mo	V 4	4
141.2	ka-si	Ṿ[	1+
142.1	*lost*	]Ṿ 4	4
143.1	ka-pa	OLIV Ṭ[	6+
143.2	ka-si[	*lost*	1+
148.1	*lost*	OLIV Ṭ[	6+
148.2	a-ko-]da-mo [	*lost*	1+
151.1	ka-pa	OLIV Ṭ[	6+
151.2	ka-[	*lost*	1+
193	a-]ko-da-mo	V 4	4
211.1	*lost*	]Ṿ 3	3
211.1	te[-de-ne-o	*lost*	1+
217.1	ka-po	OLIV T 2 V 4	16
217.1	a-ko-da-mo	V 4 [	4
217.2	ka-no	V 4 [	4
218.1	*lost*	]T 2 V 4 [	16
218.2	te-]de-ne-o [	*lost*	1+
219.1	ka-pa , ṣị-ṭọ , ko-ro-qe[	*lost*	1+
219.2	a-ko-da-mo	V 2	2
219.2	ka-si[	*lost*	1+
220.1	ka-pa / si-to	OLIV T 3 V 4	22
220.1	ko-ro	Ṭ[ ]Ṿ 2̣	8+
220.2	a-ko-da-mo	V 4	4
220.2	ka-si te-de-ne-o	OLIV T 1	6
234.1	ka-pa ko-ro	OLIV T 4 Ṿ[	25+
234.2	a-ko-da-mo	V 4	4
234.2	ka-si	Ṭ[	6+
246.1	a-ko-]ḍạ-mo	V 4 [	4
268.1	ka-pa	OLIV T 3 V 1	19
268.1	a-ko-da-mo[	*lost*	1+
268.2	ka-si	T 1 V 1̣	7
	TOTAL		**205+**

Note: Ft 220: 220[+]248

Some V 205+ is recorded in connection with religion. The function of Ft 182 is unclear but as it seems unlikely to be a disbursement record (since such large amounts are rarely disbursed), we can say that 100% of disbursements of olives in records at Thebes were (probably) for religious purposes. If Ft 182 did happen to record non-religious disbursements, the percentage would be drastically altered (the tablet records some V 4560+ of olives). In any case, the tablet suggests the existence of larger resources, as does Ft 140. Ft 140.8 gives a total of OLIV 194 (= V 11,640), of which the amount recorded in the remaining Ft series (without Ft 182) is 2%. Although Ft 140, as noted above, records olives as a measure of land so that the figures are not strictly comparable, the palace evidently had access to far more substantial resources than are reflected in the disbursement records.

5.6.4 OLIVES AT MYCENAE

Olives appear at Mycenae on Ue 611, which may relate to banqueting and which records OLIV+*TI* 3 and OLIV 1, and Ue 652, a probable delivery record, which records OLIV 5 (see Section 2.3.2.4 for both tablets). Thus, 100% of disbursements appear in connection (probably) with banqueting. In terms of overall resources, it is hardly likely that these are truly represented by the amount recorded on Ue 652, but for the sake of setting out the figures as they stand, the amount on Ue 611 is 80% of the amount on Ue 652, or 44% of their combined total.

5.7 CYPERUS (**125* = CYP = **124* = PYC)

5.7.1 CYPERUS IN LINEAR B

CYP and PYC represent cyperus; PYC is used by convention to indicate CYP written backwards, but no distinction in the commodity is indicated.[77] CYP/PYC is often ligatured, most commonly with *O*; also with *PA*, *KU*, *QA* and AROM. Sometimes the word is written out as *ku-pa-ro*/*-ro*$_2$, either alone or together with AROM, CYP/PYC or **171* (the word written before **171* in Ga(1) 519 allows identification of the ideogram as cyperus[78]); the adjective *ku-pa-ro-we* appears in the Pylos Fr series, designating oil treated with cyperus. In a few cases a syllabogram on its own may indicate cyperus. For example, in PY Un 2, *O* or *o* (the transcription depending on how the sign should be read) immediately follows an entry for CYP+*PA*. Usually *o* in Linear B abbreviates *o-pe-ro*, but here it almost certainly represents an intended ligature with CYP understood.[79] On the other hand, *O* in the PY Ma set plus Mn 11 almost certainly does not represent cyperus since it is measured there by weight, while cyperus is measured in dry units.[80] In each instance, the context is essential.

Opinion remains divided about what specific plants the various representations indicate.[81] The commodity most frequently intended is probably *Cyperus rotundus* L., used as a food flavouring and in perfumery (probably as a stymma rather than a scent[82]); some forms may represent *Cyperus esculentus* L.

Table 5-12 sets out the various forms at different sites. Cases where a syllabogram used alone may possibly represent cyperus are included in the table with a question-mark and discussed in the appropriate sections below; instances that can be immediately dismissed are indicated in the notes to the table. Two columns are given for Knossos: one for RCT tablets and one for non-RCT tablets.

---

[77] Sacconi 1979, 344–50.

[78] Killen 1992b, 371.

[79] *Documents*, 440, 563; Piteros, Olivier & Melena 1990, 178; Killen 1992b, 369; 1994, 73 n 26; Bendall forthcoming(a). An increased confidence that *O* is to be read as an ideogram in Un 2, rather than as *o* abbreviating *o-pe-ro*, results from our improved understanding of the function of the banqueting foodlists – they should not record deficits.

[80] For a new interpretation of *O* in the Ma series see Killen forthcoming(b).

[81] See Melena 1974b; 1976b; Foster 1977a; Piteros, Olivier & Melena 1990; Killen 1992b; 1999a, 337–8; Palmer 1999, 470–5; Sarpaki 2001, 217–9, 242, 252–3.

[82] Shelmerdine 1985, 13, 18, 21–2, 25–6.

Table 5-12. Possible representations of cyperus in the Linear B archives

ideogram	Knossos RCT	Knossos non-RCT	Pylos	Mycenae	Thebes
CYP/PYC	Uc 160*	Ga(3) 456 Ga 461 Ga(3) 464* E 842 Ga 1058 X 7776 Ga 7344 Ga 7347 G 7352 Ga(3) 8005* (+*QA*?) X 8812			
AROM+PYC		Ga(1) 517* Ga(1) 518			
CYP[+?]	F(1) 157* Uc 160*				
CYP/PYC+*O*	F(1) 5079	F(2) 852 F(2) 7050 G 7509	Fa 16 Un 47 Ua 434	Ue 652* Fu 711	Wu 71 Wu 81
O	Xd 149?? Xd 8034??		Un 2* Un 219? La 626??* Xa 639?? Un 1185		
CYP+*PA*			Un 2*		
CYP+*KU*	F(1) 157*	F(2) 5043		Ue 652*	
KU			La 626??*		
CYP+*QA*		Ga 5088 Ga 7358 Ga(3) 8005*??			
*171		Ga(3) 464* Ga(1) 519*	Aq 64 Un 1414	Ge 606	Wu 46 Wu 56 Wu 59 Wu 76
ku-pa-ro/-ro$_2$		Ga(3) [454] Ga(3) 465.2* Ga 517* Ga 519* Ga(3) [8005]*	Un 249 Un 267 Un 616		
ku-pa-ro-we			Fr 1203		

Notes

General

* Appears more than once in table.

Individual tablets

MY Ge 606: New reading (see Killen 1992b, 372).
PY Un 616: Formerly An (Bennett 1992, 114–15).
KN F(2) 852: Joins X 9919 (Godart *et al.* 1990–1991, 375).

Cases where cyperus is clearly not indicated

Knossos

C 394: *pa* (*v*.3) abbreviates some word (*pa-ja-o-ne*??).
D- Class tablets: *o* abbreviates *o-pe-ro*; *pa* abbreviates *pa-ra-jo*.
F 452: *o*[probably the start of *o-pe-ro* (see Section 3.2.3.7).
Ga 5672: *MA* now read (*KT*[5], 208), not *PA* (given as possible reading in Olivier *et al.* 1973).
L- Class tablets: *o* abbreviates *o-pe-ro*; *pa* abbreviates *pa-we-a ko-u-ra* or *pa-ra-ja*.
Nc 5100: *O* is used as an ideogram, but the tablet records PY Ma set types of commodities, so *O* here is unlikely to represent cyperus; see Killen forthcoming(b).
Uf series: *PA*, since together with *DA*, is not a commodity.

V(2) 337: *o*[in line .3 is probably the start of word.

Pylos

Ma series: Not cyperus since measured in units of weight, as noted above in the chapter text; see Killen forthcoming(b).

Mn 11: Same as Ma series.

Sh series: *KO*, O and *PA* are used as ideograms, but refer to armour not cyperus (*O* abbreviates *o-pa-wo-te*; Chadwick 1970, 122; Palaima 1996a, 380; *KO* abbreviates *ko-ru-to*; *Documents* 555; *PA* abbreviates *pa-ra-wa-jo*; *Documents* 567)

Un 1319: *PA* and *KU* here *may* represent cyperus, but the document is obscure in any case (for references see Section 5.2.3, Notes to Table 5-2). *o* in Un 1319.2 is probably not an ideogram (as rightly indicated by the *PTT* I transcription), but abbreviates *o-pe-ro*.

Un 1321: *PTT* (I, 249) suggested reading *O* in line .1 just as a possibility, but a new reading makes this less likely (Bennett 1992, 120; see text in Section 4.3.3). In any case the purpose of the document is obscure.

Mycenae

Ge 603: *KU* in the Mycenae spice tablets represents cumin (*ku-mi-no*) rather than cyperus; the word is actually written out on some tablets (e.g. Ge 602); see Killen 1983d.

Ge 604: See Ge 603.

Ge 606: See Ge 603.

Ui 709: This tablet concerns at least one of the same persons found on Ge tablets (*ke-po* on Ge 602, –603, –605), so probably *KU* here also abbreviates cumin.

Thebes

Of series: *PA* and *ku* qualify cloth/wool (see Section 6.3.3.3, Table 6-17).

Ug series: *O* is used ideogramatically (presumably abbreviating the start of a word) in the Ug series; see Chadwick 1970, 121–2. It could refer to cyperus or any number of other things. (But it is measured in whole units, so less likely to be cyperus.)

Whatever the differences underlying the various forms, they are here treated together, since the data are inadequate to allow distinction for present purposes. Only **171* is totalled separately, since it seems likely that a different unit of measure is used. The tables always indicate which form is involved.

5.7.2 CYPERUS AT KNOSSOS

Of the tablets listed in Table 5-12, three in particular (all from the RCT) require further discussion.[83] The first is Xd 149, the text of which is as follows.

Xd 149 + 8121 ('124')

sup. mut.
.1 *vacat*[
.2 e-ra [
.3 tu-ni-ja [
.4 ri-u-no [
.5]to [
.6 *inf. mut.*

→

v. *sup. mut.*
]o 70 [
inf. mut.

r. Traces of earlier ruling. Probable ⟦ ⟧ in l. 5.
v.]*o* possibly ideographic (i.e.]*O*).

On the *verso*, *o* may be used ideographically (see apparatus). This would be significant because the document records major towns on the *recto* and looks rather like a taxation record. However, certainty is impossible and this document is best classed as 'Unclear'. It should further be noted that even if *O* were being used ideogramatically, there would be no guarantee it represented cyperus here.

[83] For most of the documents discussed in this section see Melena 1974b; 1975b; 1980; Killen 1992b; Perna 2004; Weilhartner 2005.

A second tablet, Xd 8034, probably does use *O* ideogramatically. The text is as follows.

Xd 8034 ('124')

sup. mut.
.1]*vest.*
.2] *o* 8
.3]ṭạ-ra *o* 1
→
v. .0 *sup. mut.*
.1.2 *vacant* [

r.1 Possibly]1Ọ.
.2 Upright before *o*.

In line .3 the appearance of]*ṭạ-ra*, the end of a word, suggests that *o* should be an ideogram, thus transcribed *O*. However, nothing need indicate that it represents cyperus.

The third tablet, F(1) 5079, does probably record cyperus (although the readings are uncertain) and may be an offerings record; the text is as follows.

F(1) 5079 + 8259 ('124'd)

.1 ka-ma[
.2a di-pa-te[
.2b ka-[
.3a i-je-[
.3b [?]ka-ma[
.4a sa-i-[
.4b i-je-[
→
v. .1]30
.2a]ị CỴP+*Ọ* 6
.2b]da-jọ
.3]rọ , CỴP+*Ọ* 5
.3b]ṃọ 1̣
.4] , CỴP+*Ọ* 5
.4b]*vest.* 1̣
.5] 4

r. Signs in lines .b are small and alternate with large signs in lines .a (cf. Ce 50).
.1 *ka-* over ⟦ ⟧.
.2b Over ⟦ ⟧.
.3b Over ⟦ ⟧. Perhaps nothing lost before *ka*.
.4b *i-je-ṛẹ*[possible.
v.
.2b *-jọ* inside CYP+*O*.
.5 Possibly CYP+]*Ọ* 4.

The apparatus to line .4b notes '*i-je-ṛẹ*[possible', which might suggest a connection with religion since the only words attested with this beginning in the corpus are *i-je-re-ja* and *i-je-re-u* (plus a few related forms). Alternatively, this might be a record of land-holdings if line .1 originally read *ka-ma*[*-e-we*. But this is mere speculation and the document should be regarded as 'Unclear'.[84] Given that such large amounts appear, however, in the discussion below we consider the percentages both with and without this document.

Functions of the non-RCT tablets are fairly straightforward, but one document is worth a brief discussion since it is the only disbursement tablet certainly *not* for religious purposes.

Ga(1) 517 (135)

.a ku-pi-ri-jo
.b tu-wi-no , / ku-pa-ro AROM+PYC 1 [

[84] Driessen (*Scribes RCT*, 208) also regards the document as 'basically obscure'; he notes it may 'summarise quantities'.

Ga(1) 517 records a disbursement for the perfume industry involving the well-known person *ku-pi-ri-jo*, and a man *tu-wi-no* also known from perfumery records (Section 3.2.3.5). The disbursement here counts in a sense as 'final use' since the cyperus would be consumed in the manufacturing process; however, the palace presumably would receive back the treated oil so there is a difference between this and expenditures such as for offerings.

Table 5-13 summarises the data for cyperus at Knossos.

Table 5-13. Cyperus at Knossos

Disbursements				**Receipts**				
tablet	**ideogram**	**measure**	= V	**tablet**	**ideogram**	**measure**	**measure**	= V
1. *Religious*				3. ***Taxation*** (non-RCT)		*paid*	*owing*	
1a. non-RCT				*3a. non-**171				
E 842	P̣ỴC̣	]T 2	12+	Ga 461	CYP	10	*lost*	600
Ga 1058	PYC	T 1	6	Ga 7347	PYC	9*	3[*	720+
Ga(3) 456	PYC	T[	6+	Ga 5088	PYC+*QẠ*	9̣[		5̣4̣0̣+
Ga(3) 465	*ku-pa-ro*	T 2	12	Ga(3) 464◆	PYC	—	41 T 3*	2478
G 7509	PYC+*O*	6	360	Ga(1) 518	AROM+PYC	10[		600+
X 7776	*possibly* P̣ỴC̣	*lost*	—	**Sub-total 3a**				**4938+**
Sub-total 1a			**396+**	*3b.* *171				****171* (units)**
1b. RCT				Ga(1) 519	*ku-pa-ro* **171*	2[		2+
Uc 160	CYP	1[	60+	Ga(3) 464◆	**171*	8̣[		8̣+
2. *Perfumery*				**Sub-total 3b**				**10+**
Ga(1) 517	*ku-pa-ro* AROM+PYC	1	**60**	**4. *Harvests***				= V
5. *Unclear*				*4a. non-RCT*				
5a. non-RCT				F(2) 852	PYC+*O*	12		720
Ga 7344	PYC	4 T 2[	252+	F(2) 5043	P̣ỴC̣+*KU*	2̣ T 2		1̣3̣2̣
Ga 7358	PYC+*QẠ*	3	180	F(2) 7050	P̣ỴC̣+*O*[	*lost*		1+
Ga(3) 454	*ku-pa*[*-ro*	*lost*	1+	**Sub-total 4a**				**853+**
Ga(3) 8005	*ku-*]*pa-ro* PYC[	*lost*	1+	*4b. RCT*				
G 7352	P̣ỴC̣?	]3 T 2[	192	F(1) 157*	CYP+*KU*	5 T 3		318
X 8812	P̣ỴC̣[	*lost*	1+	F(1) 157*	CYP[+?	]1[		60+
5b. RCT				**Sub-total 4b**				**378+**
F(1) 5079	C̣ỴP+*Ọ*	16	960	**TOTAL 1a + 2**				**456+**
				TOTAL 3a + 4a				**5791+**

Notes

General

◆ = Tablet appears more than once in the table.

* = Summed.

Individual tablets

F(1) 157: Another]T 7 appears at the end of the line; it is unclear whether it belongs to CYP[+?] or to a further entry. For the tablet as a probable harvest record see *Scribes RCT*, 208.

Uc 160: Apparatus: 'CYP[+?] possible'.

Ga(3) 465: Line .1: no ideogram before T 1, but *ku-pa-ro* understood? Line .2: *ku-pa-ro* T 1.

F(2) 852: Reading of 12 confirmed by Godart *et al.* 1992–1993, 55–6; see also Godart *et al.* 1990–1991, 375.

G 7352: App.: 'Traces at left consistent with PYC'.

Ga(3) 8005: App.: 'PYC+*QẠ* not entirely impossible'.

Taking first the RCT tablets, 60+ units are disbursed in a banqueting context. There are no disbursements for other purposes, unless F(1) 5079 is one (as discussed above, either a disbursement for offerings or a collection[?] in connection with land tenure[??]). The probable harvest record F(1) 157 relates to overall resources. It records a minimum of V 378+, of which disbursements for offerings are 16%. The 'Unclear' record F(2) 5079 would change the picture radically if we knew its function. If it *were* an offerings record, it is notable that the amounts disbursed would far exceed the amounts recorded as coming in. Either way the incomplete nature of the database is underlined.

Turning to the non-RCT tablets, the majority of disbursements are for religious offerings (1a), but we do have one disbursement for industrial purposes (2). As noted above, the palace would have received back the finished product this commodity was used to treat, so this is not exactly a 'disbursement for final use', yet the stuff would have been consumed in the manufacturing process so for present purposes may be treated as real expenditure. Taking the offerings and industrial disbursements together (1a + 2), 87% of the non-RCT cyperus was disbursed for religious purposes.

Overall resources are indicated by the taxation (3a) and harvest (4a) records (taxation records for **171* are excluded here, as the final unit may be different). Religious disbursements form a small proportion, just 7%, of resources recorded on such records. It is worth noting that taking all the disbursement records, both religious and non-religious together (1a+2), yields a similar figure: just 8%. The use of the other 92% of the 'overall resources' is unattested in the surviving records.

5.7.3 CYPERUS AT PYLOS

Cyperus at Pylos appears primarily in banqueting and perfumery records. It is not clear in all cases whether *O* used as an ideogram does represent cyperus. In Un 2 it almost certainly does, as noted above. By analogy, it probably also does in the banqueting record Un 1185 (note the ligatured form is clearly attested in another banqueting record, Un 47). We first discuss three possible cases where *O* may represent cyperus, then examine the documents which do certainly represent cyperus.

The first 'possible' case is Un 219, an offerings record of some sort (see Section 6.6.2.1 for text and discussion). In this document, *O* is given in whole units, so measures do not provide a clue, but it may be significant that some of the other Un 219 ideograms can represent aromatics (e.g. *MA* = */marathwon/* 'fennel'; *KO* = */koriandnon/* 'coriander' or */skhoinos/* 'rush'). Belief that the tablet deals with aromatics and spices is supported by the word *tu-wo* in line .1 which might be interpreted as */thuwos/* 'aromatic substance'. Cyperus would be at home in such a context. It should be noted, however, that even if *O* does indicate cyperus here, the number is unusually large and it is uncertain whether the same measure was intended.

Texts of the next two tablets are as follows.

La 626 (S626-H13)

Recto

.a]**1̣6̣6̣* 2 a-**3̣5̣*-ṭọ 3̣[

.b]a-ro-ta TELA+*PA* 1 [

↓

Verso

]*ku* X 1 *o* 1 [

.a **166*: perhaps **1̣6̣6̣*[+*WE*]; -*35- identity uncertain, since stem is straight (perhaps neither **34* nor **35*, but a peculiar ro_2); -*ṭọ* 3̣: possibly -*ṃụ* 2̣, or -*ṭọ* 1 and trace of sign (e.g. *ṃẹ*[) at right. .b: ⟦**166*⟧ just above *a-ro-ta*.
Verso The X is written below the unit on on partially dry clay; the *o* might equally well be transcribed as an ideogram, *O*.

Xa 639 (Cii)

a-si-ja-ti-ja , e-te-wa-jo o[

o[on a larger scale, perhaps ideogrammatic; perhaps of class La.

In La 626 *O* is certainly used as an ideogram (see apparatus to the *verso*), but this tablet is a stint record for the textile industry and it seems unlikely that cyperus would appear on such a document even though it is paired with another sign which sometimes may represent cyperus, *KU*. Xa 639 records a TN followed by a MN, but the context is obscure (cf. the Sh series?) and it is not clear whether *O* here is used as an ideogram or is the start of some word.

The remaining documents do certainly record cyperus. Un 249, –267 and –616 are perfumery records (Section 2.5.3). The first records an issue to a *Potnian* perfumer so is taken here as connected with religion. Note, however, that the disbursement is not an 'offering' but for industrial processing. Fa 16 and Ua 434 are 'unclear'. As discussed above (Section 2.3.2.2), they may be related to banqueting and/or offerings (since they were written by a scribe whose dossier includes such records), but they may record collections rather than disbursements.

The final two documents record cyperus by means of ideogram *_171_. The text of the first is as follows.

Aq 64 (S64-H21)

.1	]-re-wi-jo-te	
.2	]-ja , mo-ro-qa , to-to , we-to , o-a-ke-re-se	_ZE_ 1 *_171_ 3
.3	ka-do-wo , mo-ro-qa , o-u-qe , a-ke-re-se	_ZE_ 1
.4	ru-ro , mo-ro-qa , o-u-qe , a-ke-re-se	_ZE_ 1
.5	ku-ru-me-no , mo-ro-qa , i-te-re-wa , ko-re-te , to-to , ẉẹ-ṭọ⌊ ⌋ọ-a-ke-re-se	*_171_ 6
.6	]pe-ri-mo , ti-mi-ti-ja , ko-re-te , to-to-we-to⌊ ⌋o-a-ke-re-se	_ZE_ 1 *_171_ 3
.a		o-a-ke-re-se
.7	pe-ri-me-de-o , i-*_65_ , po-so-ri-jo-no , te-ra-ni-ja , a-ke-re-se , to-to-we-to ,	*_171_ 12
.8	po-ki-ro-qo , e-qe-o , a-to-mo	_ZE_ 1
.9	_vacat_	
.10	_vacat_	
.11	_vacat_	
.12	o-da-a_2 , ko-to-na e-ko-te	
.13	e-ta-wo-ne-u , to-to-we-to , o-a-ke-re-se	_ZE_ 1 *_171_ 6
.14	a-qi-zo-we , to-to , to-to , we-to , o-a-ke-re-se	_ZE_ 1 [*_171_
.15	ne-qe-u , e-te-wo-ke-re-we-i-jo , to-to , we-to , o-a-ke-re-se	_ZE_ 1 [*_171_
.16	me-wi , e-ru-ta-ra , me-ta-pa , ki-e-wo , to-to-we-to , o-a-ke-re-se	_ZE_ 1 [*_171_
.17	_vacat_ [	
.18	_vacat_ [	
.19	_vacat_ [	
.20	_vacat_ [	
.21	_vacat_ [	
.22	_vacat_	

Aq 64, which forms a diptych with Aq 218, has something to do with land tenure (see line .12 'thus those having plots'), but the purpose of the record is obscure. As Killen argues, it probably relates at least partly to obligations to provide goods and services to the palace,[85] and is thus likely to be a collection record. The document is taken here as 'unclear', but will be referred to again below.

Finally, the text of Un 1414 is as follows.

Un 1414 (—)

.1	]20
.2	]*_1̣7̣1̣_ 4

The tablet is too fragmentary for anything about its nature to be determined and in any case the reading of *_171_ is not secure.[86]

Table 5-14 summarises data for cyperus at Pylos.

[85] Killen 1992b, 370–5, esp. 372.

[86] On this tablet see e.g. Killen 1992b, 371; Shelmerdine 1998–1999, 328–9.

Table 5-14. Cyperus at Pylos

tablet	ideogram	measure	= V
1. ***Banqueting***			
Un 2.3	CYP+*PA*	T 1 V 3	9
Un 2.3	[CYP+]*O*	V 5	5
Un 47	CYP+*O*	3 T 4 V 1	205
Un 1185	[CYP+]*O*	T 1 V 1 Z 1[	7.25+
TOTAL 1			**226.25+**
2. ***Offering***			
Un 219?	[CYP+?]*O*	15	900???
3. ***Perfumery***			
3a. Potnian			
Un 249	*ku-pa-ro₂* AROM	2̣ T 5	150
3b. other			
Un 267	*ku-pa-ro₂* AROM	6	360
Un 616	*ku<-pa->ro₂* AROM	13 T 5	810
sub-total 3b			**1170**
TOTAL 3			**1320**
TOTAL 1+3			**1546.25**
3. ***Unclear***			
Fa 16	CYP+*O*	8 T 2 V 1̣[	493+
Ua 434	CYP+*O*	13 [	780+
Aq 64	**171*	39+?*	n/a
Un 1414	**1̣7̣1̣*	4	n/a

<u>Notes</u>
<u>*General*</u>
* Summed.
n/a = Not applicable (**171* is counted in whole units, not fractional measures).
<u>*Individual documents*</u>
Aq 64: Assuming at least three units of **171* were present in each of lines .14–16 as parallels with the rest of the document would suggest.
Un 219: 900 assuming the unit is the same – which is very tenuous.
Un 616: Reading Bennett 1992, 114 15 (note the spelling mistake).
Un 1185: Reading Melena 1994–1995b, 286.

100% of 'final disbursements' apart from industrial issues are for banqueting and (possibly) offerings. However, the industrial disbursements also count in a sense as being for 'final use' since, although the palace would receive back the perfumed oil, the cyperus itself would be consumed in the manufacturing process, so represents 'real' expenditure. The amount issued for banqueting is thus 15% of all 'final use' disbursements. The offering record Un 219 is not taken into account here since it is not clear what the unit of measure is – the fact that the figure if converted into V is so large (V 900) suggests that *O*, if it really is cyperus in this document, is *not* being measured in the same units as elsewhere. We may finally compare the amount issued to the *Potnian* perfumer with amounts issued to other perfumers; it represents 11% of issues for manufacture.

In terms of overall resources, it may be noted that the amounts disbursed for perfume manufacture are quite large (V 1320). Some of the treated oil may eventually have been issued as offerings (although the one tablet recording oil treated with cyperus is not an offering tablet[87]), but in any case a substantial amount of the commodity was in circulation. As noted above, Fa 16 and Ua 434 may be collection records, as is probably Aq 64. The figure in Aq 64 cannot be compared with our other figures because not only is the type of cyperus different but it seems to be counted in different units. Fa 16 and Ua 434 record some 1273+ of cyperus, which is less than the total disbursed in the banqueting and perfumery records, so even if they

[87] Fr 1203 (Table 3-2.B) is unusual for the Fr series (Shelmerdine 1985, 38, 99).

are 'collections' they do not account for the total amounts disbursed. However one looks at the data, it seems apparent that economic transactions were being carried out for which we do not have the documentation.

5.7.4 CYPERUS AT MYCENAE

It was noted above (Section 5.7.1, see Notes to Table 5-12), that *KU* in the Mycenae spice tablets represents cumin not cyperus, but at least one, Ge 606, does record some form of cyperus, **171* (eleven units). The two remaining tablets on which cyperus appears are Fu 711 and Ue 652. Fu 711 is an offering tablet, recording CYP+*O* T 1. Ue 652 may be a taxation record on account of the appearance of the common taxation rubric *pe-ru-si-nwa*; it records CYP+*KU* 5 and CYP+*O* 7.

The situation is the opposite of that at Pylos: large amounts are recorded coming in and small amounts are disbursed. A scant 5% is disbursed as offerings compared with overall resources (not counting **171*). However, final uses of cyperus other than for religious purposes are not recorded in the surviving documents.

5.7.5 CYPERUS AT THEBES

Cyperus appears in the Wu sealings, recording foodstuffs for a banquet (Section 2.3.2.5, Table 2-7), and on one of the Gp tablets, probably also related to religion (Section 4.3.5, Table 4-7). The data are summarised in Table 5-15.

Table 5-15. Cyperus at Thebes

	CYP/PYC+*O*	
Wu 71	PYC+*O*	1?
Wu 81	PYC+*O*?	—
Gp 290	CYP+*O*	V 4
	171	
Wu 46	**171* 30	30
Wu 56	**171* 30	30
Wu 59	**171* 36	36
Wu 76	**171* 30	30
	TOTAL **171*	**126**

Notes
Wu 71: No number written.
Wu 81: The apparatus notes: 'Very probably the base of PYC+O'.

100% of resources are connected in some way with religion; there is nothing from which to calculate overall resources.

5.8 CONCLUSION

It seems evident in virtually all cases that the documentation is heavily biased. In many cases, religious disbursements form a significant proportion of all disbursements and often there is no useful documentation from which to estimate overall resources. However, where rations and harvest records exist, the picture looks very different and this deserves further comment. Wheat for instance was used for rations at both Knossos and Pylos, and at both sites disbursements for religious purposes form a relatively minor percentage of all disbursements (4–7%). Further, harvest records at Knossos make clear that substantial amounts of wheat were being obtained and that religious disbursements were negligible (0.2%). Similarly with figs, at Knossos all recorded disbursements were for religious purposes; if the commodity was used for ordinary rations, the records do not survive. Yet there are three probable harvest records, showing that (1) the palace had access to substantial resources and (2) the religious disbursements were but a small part of such resources. At Pylos, the situation is reversed. Figs were issued as rations to ordinary workers and amounts disbursed for religious purposes are correspondingly small (2.5%). There are no collection records at Pylos, but it is clear that here, as at Knossos, religious disbursements were not taking up substantial amounts of overall resources.

It may be significant that in all cases where relevant documentation is available, amounts disbursed for religious purposes turn out to be small or negligible. One suspects that this might be the case more generally and that if religious disbursements appear substantial this is due to bias(es) in the records. Moreover, there is a pattern to what is recorded. It is not merely that religious disbursements do not account for substantial portions of overall resources – disbursements *in general* do not do so, *except* where a commodity is used for rations. The only types of disbursements recorded apart from religious purposes and rations are *o-no* payments and issues for industrial manufacture, but the amounts registered for such purposes are usually negligible as compared with overall resources (with one or two exceptions, such as cyperus at Pylos). Whatever else may have been done with the bulk of these commodities and resources does not appear in the Linear B records.

CHAPTER 6
ANIMALS, ANIMAL PRODUCTS, TEXTILES, METALS AND OTHER COMMODITIES

6.1 INTRODUCTION

The present chapter deals with the remaining commodities which appear in connection with religion. The main groups are 'animals' (bovines, sheep, goats and pigs), 'animal products' (cheese, skins and wool), 'textiles', 'metals' and 'obscure commodities'. By the last what is meant is commodities either where the ideograms have not been securely identified or which are indicated by means of syllabograms used as ideograms and which can have different meanings in different cases. With regard to animals, numerical data have recently been provided in an important article by Halstead,[1] and reference is made to this throughout. It may be noted here that Halstead's counting conventions are slightly different from those used in the present study so the results do not always tally precisely.[2] The global figures, however, are unaffected, whatever system one employs; as noted at the outset, the essential point is internal consistency.

We will discuss each of the commodity groups in turn, beginning with animals.

6.2 ANIMALS

6.2.1 BOVINES (*109 = BOS)

6.2.1.1 BOVINES AT KNOSSOS

Some fifty-one tablets at Knossos record, or probably once recorded, bovines.[3] The relevant documents are the Ce tablets (from the RCT), the Ch, Co and C(1) sets and several other C-Class tablets. Most of the documents deal with working oxen and herds; three are banqueting records. We will survey the records briefly, then summarise the figures. The RCT tablets are discussed separately at the end.

The Ch tablets of h. 110 form a 'set' in the technical sense. Two examples are as follows.

Ch 896 (110)
ta-za-ro / a_3-wo-ro 'ke-ra-no-qe' *ne* , *we* BOS^m *ZE* 1

Ch 1029 + 5760 + 7625 + *frr.* (110)
pu-ri / a_3-zo-ro-qe , po-da-ko-qe BOS^m *ZE* 1[

---

[1] Halstead 1998–1999.

[2] Halstead (1998–1999, 154, 169) ignores 'animal ideograms without preserved numbers and preserved numbers without ideograms'. The present study counts ideograms without preserved numbers as 'one' (see Conventions).

[3] Palaima (1989, 98–9) gives the figure as forty-four tablets with another three possible. The higher figure given here includes tablets such as Co 903 which, given structural similarities with the other Co tablets, probably once recorded bovines although the ideogram is broken off and is thus (reasonably) omitted from Palaima's list (p. 99).

ta-za-ro and *pu-ri* are men's names and the remaining words are descriptions or descriptive names of the animals: /*aiwolos*/ 'variegated', /*kelainos-qe*/ 'and black', /*aiskhros*/ 'ugly, deformed', /*podargos-qe*/ 'and white-footed'.[4] As argued by Killen, the most likely explanation of the documents is that pairs (*ZE* = /*dzeugos*/) of working oxen are being allocated to ploughmen (the men named), the point of the descriptive terms being to identify the animals sufficiently well that it would be difficult for the ploughmen to return different, inferior beasts to the palace.[5] Godart's alternative hypothesis, that the Ch oxen are destined for sacrifice, is not accepted here.[6] It is true, as he points out, that colour terms are found in banqueting records (e.g. PY Cn 418), but it need not follow that animals were only described in such contexts. Godart further cites evidence for the importance of pairs of coloured animals in sarcophagal iconography, but it is difficult to link this with certainty to the Ch records, and it is important to note, as Killen observes, that *ZE* does appear in conjunction with the word *we-ka-ta* /*wergatās*/, indicating they are 'working' (e.g. C 1044, –5734, texts below), but never occurs in securely identified banqueting records.[7]

Complete data for the Ch set are given in Table 6-1.

Table 6-1. The Knossos Ch set

Ch	text	adjuncts	BOS *ZE*	no. of pairs	no. of oxen
896	ta-za-ro / a$_3$-wo-ro 'ke-ra-no-qe'	*ne* , *we*	BOS^m *ZE*	1	2
897	e-po-ro-jo / 'to-ma-ko' wo-no-qo-so-qe		BOS^m *ZE*	1	2
898	a$_3$-]wo-ro-qe , to-ma-ko-qe		BOS^m *ZE*	1	2
899	]ḳọ 'po-da-ko-qe'		BOS^m *ZE*	1̣[	2
900	']ḳọ-so-u-to-qe'		BOS^m *ZE*	1	2
972	au-to-a$_3$-ta [		*lost*	*lost*	2
1015	]no / wo-no-qo-so 'to-ma-ko-qe'		BOS^m *Ẓ Ẹ*[	*lost*	2
1029	pu-ri / a$_3$-zo-ro-qe , po-da-ko-qe		BOS^m *ZE*	1[	2
1034	] a$_3$-zo-ro-qe ẉọ[		*lost*	*lost*	2
5724	]qe , wa-no-qe		BOS^m *ZE*	1	2
5728	']pa-ko-qe'		BOS^m[	*lost*	2
5754	wi-du-ru-ta / a$_3$-wo-ro[		*lost*	*lost*	2
5938	a$_3$-]wo-ro-qe		BOS^m[	*lost*	2
7047	]ṇọ-q̣ẹ		BOS [	*lost*	2
7065	]-qe		BOS^m *ZE* [	*lost*	2
7066	]no-qe		BOS *ZE*	1[	2
7100	]a-ko-ro-we-i (*verso*:]a$_3$-ḳụ-ta [)		BOS *ZE*	1 [	2
7937	]ni-to[		⟦ḄỌṢ^m⟧	n/a	n/a
8222	]-qe		BOS^m [	*lost*	2
9765	*lost*		] *ZE*	1[	2
	TOTAL				**38**

Notes

General

The table departs from the usual rule of adding a plus to possibly incomplete numbers and counts lost figures as '1 pair' because the better-preserved tablets suggest each document recorded one pair and one only.

Individual tablets

Ch 7100 and –7937: These are probably part of the same tablet (*KT*[5], 51), therefore only the figure for one of them is given. The erased ideogram on 7937 was on the *verso*.

Ch 9765: This fragment could conceivably be part of e.g. 972 or 5754, but this is not suggested in *KT*[5], so the table gives it separately, with restored figures for each tablet; the total may thus be a bit high.

---

[4] Killen 1992–1993a, 101, 103, with further references. Note *DMic.* (I, 142) considers *a$_3$-zo-ro-qe* as without satisfactory interpretation.

[5] Killen 1992–1993a. See also Palaima 1989, 115 (with 106 for some of the terms); Halstead 1998–1999, 153, 161. With regard to concerns raised by Godart & Tzedakis (2003, 73–5), note the animal names were given by elites.

[6] Godart 1999, 249–50.

[7] Killen 1992–1993a, 101 n 2. Note that *ne* , *we* on Ch 896 may abbreviate *ne-wo we-ka-ta*(*-e*), rather than *ne-wo we-ta-ro* (*contra* Godart 1999, 150).

Altogether, some thirty-eight oxen are recorded in the Ch set, registered as working in pairs.[8]

Next we have the Co set of h. 107 which records 'Collector' flocks.[9] Some examples are as follows.

Co 904 + 8008 (107)
.1 ku-do-ni-ja / a-ko-ra-ja OVIS^{m} 117 OVIS^{f} 100[
.2 CAP^{m} 54 CAP^{f} 151 SUS^{f} 87 ḄỌṢ^{m}[

Co 909 + 7133 + 7835 + *fr.* (107)
.1 a-pa-ta-wa , / a[-ko-]ṛạ-ja OVIS^{m} [
.2 CAP^{f} 120 SUS^{m} 3 ṢỤṢ^{f} [
Possibly same tablet as Co 8347.

Co 8347 (107)
sup. mut.
] ḄỌṢ^{f} [
Possibly same tablet as Co 909.

The tablets record animals at Kydonia and *a-pa-ta-wa*; these are toponyms located in west Crete and the group as a whole has associations with west Cretan toponyms.[10] The word *a-ko-ra-ja* is probably, as argued by Killen, a neuter plural description of the animals (understanding 'creatures') conveying the sense of 'belonging to Collectors' (Section 2.5).[11]

Table 6-2 sets out data for all animals recorded in the set and will be referred to in subsequent sections.[12]

Table 6-2. The Knossos Co set

Co	town	other text	OVIS^{m}	OVIS^{f}	CAP^{m}	CAP^{f}	SUS/SUS^{m}	SUS^{f}	BOS^{m}	BOS^{f}
903	wa-to	a-ko-ra-ja	60	270	49	130	17	41	2	4
904	ku-do-ni-ja	a-ko-ra-ja	117	100[	54	151	—	87	*lost*	?
906	ka-ta-ra-i	a-ko-ra-ja	100	650	40[ ]	150	—	80	—	6
907	si-ra-ro	a-ko-ra-jo	202	750	125	240	21	60	2	10
909 & 8347	a-pa-ta-wa	a[-ko-]ṛạ-ja	*lost*	?	?	120	3	*lost*	?	*lost*
910 & 7056	o-]du-ru-wo	a-ko-ra-jạ[	?	600[	?	190	?	50	2	*lost*
	TOTALS		**480+**	**2370+**	**268+**	**981**	**41(+?)**	**319+**	**7+**	**22+**
	OVERALL TOTALS		**sheep: 2850+**		**goats: 1249+**		**pigs: 360+**		**cattle: 29+**	

<u>**Notes**</u>
<u>*General*</u>
— = The ideogram was definitely not present.
? = It is uncertain whether ideogram was originally present.
lost = Ideogram was probably or certainly present.
Where *lost* the total includes 1+, but '?' is ignored.
<u>*Individual tablets*</u>
906: BOS^{m} was erased. The layout of the horizontal strokes in the number for CAP^{m} suggests the

[8] Halstead (1998–1999, 158) counts just eighteen for the Ch series, based on different counting conventions (e.g. he omits Ch 9765 where the ideogram is lost).
[9] Discussions of the Co tablets include Godart 1972; Halstead 1998–1999, 152, 157; 1990–1991, 350–1; Palaima 1992a, 469–70.
[10] E.g. Killen 1976, 122–5; Driessen 1992, 211 (with a table similar to the one here).
[11] Killen 1976, 122–3.
[12] Figures in the table match Halstead's (1998–1999, 157–8), except that we add one for 'lost' animals. To avoid confusion, two misprints in his text are noted. A figure of 459 pigs (p. 157) is given elsewhere correctly (p. 158) as 359 (we add one for Co 909). The figure of 472 male sheep (p. 158) does not match the 480+ in our Table 6-2, but the total for both males and females is given as 2849 (p. 157), only attainable if the latter number of male sheep is added to the 2370 female sheep.

figure was at least 50 and may have been 60 but not more (see *CoMIK* I, 369; the possibility is noted in the KT^6 apparatus).

909 & 8347: Noted as 'possibly' from the same tablet (KT^5, 52–3).

910 & 7056: Noted as 'probably' from the same tablet (KT^5, 52–3). Note both parts preserve traces of SUS^f.

Next we have the C(1) set, also by h. 107. All except one tablet record bovines and two appear to deal with transfers of animals from one area to another: C(1) 5753 records *ko-no-so-de* 'to Knossos' and C(1) 901 has *e-wo-ta-de*.[13] The purpose of the transfers is unknown; the animals may have been working oxen, sacrificial victims or something else. The other two texts are similarly obscure, and the C(1) tablets are thus here considered 'Unclear'. Palaima suggests that one or two of the tablets may be 'preliminary records' for the Co series[14] and, if so, the group would not properly speaking form a 'set', but it is unnecessary to resolve this issue for present purposes since the records would in any case be 'Unclear'. The data are summarised in Table 6-3.

Table 6-3. The Knossos C(1) set

C(1)	text	BOS^f	BOS^m	BOS
901	e-wo-ta-de	20		*ta* 1
989	]-re-[.]-ja / ku-do-ni-ja	14[		
5544	lost		91[	
5753	ko-no-so-de	5	8	
	TOTALS	**39+**	**99+**	**1**
	TOTAL BOS	**139+**		

Note: The former C(1) 9666 is now reclassified as C(3) (Godart *et al.* 1992–1993, 64; *CoMIK* IV, 181).

It should be noted that C(1) 5544 may be a totalling tablet,[15] in which case the total for the entire set would be 91+, rather than 139+ (assuming animals from other tablets were subsumed under this figure). However, since it is clear neither that the C(1) tablets form a proper set, nor that 5544 is a totalling tablet, it is best to present the figures separately as done here.[16]

Texts of the remaining C tablets recording bovines are as follows, with the exception of C 394, a banqueting record, and C 902, a possible banqueting record (both in Section 2.3.2.3). Tablets which include the term *we-ka-ta*, or which record animals in pairs, deal with 'working' beasts, as noted above in the context of the Ch tablets. The others are 'Unclear'.[17]

'Working' oxen

C 1044 + 7053 (—)
.a] , we-ka-ta-e , [
.b] ke-u-po-da-o BOS^m *ZE* 1 [

C 1582 (—)
.a]ẉẹ-ka-ta [
.b]ṣạ / au-a_3-ta BOS^m[

[13] The transfer possibly was from *ku-do-ni-ja* (Killen & Olivier 1966, 83; see also Godart 1972, 420; but *contra* see Palaima 1992a, 470–1). On the C(1) set in general see also Palaima 1992a, 469–72; Halstead 1998–1999, 152, 157–60. Palaima (1992a, 470 n 29a) comments that J.T. Killen had in an unpublished paper suggested that *e-wo-ta-de* might refer to a festival rather than being a TN+-*de*.
[14] Palaima 1992a, 471, referring to C(1) 989 and -9666, but the latter is now reclassified (see Note to Table 6-3).
[15] Palaima 1992a, 471–2; *Scribes RCT*, 205.
[16] Halstead (1998–1999, 158) also considers them separately; his figures match those given here.
[17] For C 973 see Killen 1992–1993a, 103, 105. Texts are from KT^5.

C 5734 + 8224 (—)

we-]ka-ta BOS *ZE* 20

Cut at right.
Finger-nail mark on the *lat. inf.*

C 7698 + 7892 + 8223 + *frr.* (—)

tu-zo BOS *ZE* 1[

Palimpsest.
One oblique stroke on *v.*

'Unclear'

C 973 (—)

te-re-wa-ko / a_3-wa 1̣ tu-ma-ko ḄỌṢ[

C 5089 (—)

] BOS[f] [

Palimpsest: ⟦*u*- · - · ⟧ visible after ideogram.
Trace at top right (almost certainly not 1̣0̣).

C 5985 (—)

] BOS[m] [

C 7067 (—)

.1] *mo* BOS[m] [
.2] *vac.* [

C 7515 (—)

]BOS 1 [

Possibly]*mu* 1. Traces at right.

C 7566 + 8110 (—)

to-ro-wa-ko , ḄỌṢ[x][

ṢỤṢ[x][also possible.

C 9724 (—)

] BOS[m][
inf. mut.

C 9766 (—)

] ḄỌṢ[x][
inf. mut.

Left part of *ḳị*[not impossible.

Table 6-4 summarises the data from all tablets except those from the RCT.

Table 6-4. Bovines in non-RCT tablets

	BOS		BOS
1. Banqueting		***4. Unclear***	
C 394	1	C(1) set (Table 6-3)	139+
? C 902	13	C 973	1+?
2. Working oxen		C 5089	1+
Ch tablets (Table 6-1)	38	C 5985	1+
C 1044	2	C 7067	1+
C 1582	1+	C 7515	1
C 5734	40	C 7566	1+?
C 7698	2+	C 9724	1+
TOTAL 2	**83+**	C 9766	1+?
3. Collector herds		**TOTAL 4**	**147+(?)**
Co tablets (Table 6-2)	29+		
TOTAL 2+3	**112+**		
TOTAL 1+2+3	**126+**		

Notes
C 973: Reading of ideogram BOS not secure.
C 1044: *ZE* 1 = BOS 2.
C 5734: *ZE* 20 = BOS 40.
C 7566: Reading of ideogram not secure; may be SUS[.
C 7698: *ZE* 1[= BOS 2+.
C 9766: Reading of ideogram BOS not secure.

The only animals here being 'disbursed' in a sense for 'final use' (i.e. consumption) are those in the banqueting records. So all disbursements are for banqueting, but it is notable that there are so few consumption records referring to cattle at Knossos.[18] In terms of overall resources, altogether some 112+ animals belong to 'Collector' herds or are 'working'. The single beast recorded on C 394 represents a bare 0.8% of such resources; adding the possible banqueting record C 902, however, would bring the figure up to 13%, a significant difference, emphasising how a single tablet may affect the figures (the large number of animals on 'Unclear' tablets should also be noted).

We finally turn to the Ce tablets from the RCT. Most of these were discussed in Section 2.3.2.3, where the focus was on those which could be banqueting records. It was noted there that several of the Ce tablets deal with working oxen and two examples of this type are given here.[19]

Ce 59 ('124'c)
.1]ṃạ-sa / we-ka-ta BOS^m 6 , da-wo / we-ka-ta BOS^m 6
.2a ta-ra-me-to [·]-ṃọ
.2b ku-]ṭạ-to / we-ka-ta BOS^m 10 // da-*22-to / we-ka-ta BOS 6
.3a [·]-mo
.3b] tu-ri-so / we-ka-ta BOS^m 6 // ku-do-ni-ja / we-ka-ta BOS^m 50
.2b 10 over ⟦6⟧.
.3 Whole line over ⟦ ⟧.
.3a *ḍạ-mo* virtually impossible; perhaps *ṛẹ-mo*.

Ce 7061 ('124'?)
.0 *sup. mut.*
.1]BOS *ZE* 1
.2]BOS *ZE* 1
.3 *inf. mut.*

That these are 'working' oxen is indicated by appearances of the word *we-ka-ta* or the syllabogram *ZE*. Of the other tablets discussed in Section 2.3.2.3, Ce 152 was considered a probable banqueting record, but the others relevant here were judged 'Unclear'. Note that while some of the sheep recorded in Ce 50 are designated for consumption, the cattle listed on this tablet are specifically described as 'working'. The Ce data are summarised in Table 6-5.[20]

Table 6-5. Bovines in RCT tablets

	BOS		BOS
1. Banqueting		***3. Unclear***	
Ce 152	27*	Ce 61	3+*
2. Working oxen		Ce 156	4+*
Ce 50	4	Ce 8345	6
Ce 59	84*		
Ce 144	2+		
Ce 7061	4*		
TOTAL 2	**94+**		
TOTAL 1+2	**121+**		

[18] See Palaima 1992a, 473–4; Bendall forthcoming(c).
[19] Texts from KT^5.
[20] Og(1) 8038 (RCT) may record BOS, but the reading is unclear – *MU* is preferred in KT^6.

Notes
* = summed
Ce 144: *ZE*
Ce 7061: *ZE*

The only 'disbursement' is for banqueting. 22% of animals in the preserved records from the RCT, not counting 'Unclear' tablets, appear in a banqueting context.

In neither RCT nor non-RCT records do animals earmarked for sacrifice represent a majority of animals recorded (the figure of 22% for the RCT records may be regarded as 'significant' but it is worth noting it derives from a single tablet). Three points are worth highlighting here. First, the survival and interpretation of a single record can significantly affect the calculations: as observed above, without C 902 the proportion of bovines in banqueting records is 0.9%, with C 902 it is 13%. Second, it seems unlikely that the higher figures such as 13% or the RCT 22% accurately reflect realities. As Palaima comments in an important discussion, the surviving records are unlikely to indicate the real scale of traction animals available in Crete (or, as we shall see below, Messenia).[21] Third, the banqueting records are unlikely to represent the reality for numbers of animals sacrificed – it seems remarkable that there survive just two or three (with C 902) documents recording sacrifice of cattle at Knossos, and these are not even all from the same chronological period. The biases cut in both directions, making the numbers for the banqueting records both 'less' and 'more' than expected. The essential point is that the Linear B tablets do not provide adequate documentation for us to understand what was the actual situation. Overall, the oxen records of Knossos, both RCT and non-RCT, present a number of oddities and are very evidently considerably biased in their content. We will return to this point in our final discussion.

6.2.1.2 BOVINES AT PYLOS

Bovines appear at Pylos in eight tablets,[22] all of which happen to be banqueting records (Section 2.3.2.4). The data are set out in Table 6-6.

Table 6-6. Bovines at Pylos

tablet	BOS^f	BOS^m	BOS	BOS +*SI*	TOTALS
Un 2			1		**1**
Cn 3			5		**5**
Un 6	5+ [6]	2			**7–8+**
Ua 25	2	8			**10**
Un 138	1	2			**3**
Cn 418			3?*	3 [4+?*]	**6–7+**
Un 718		1			**1**
Un 1177			1		**1**
				TOTAL	**34–36+**

Notes
Un 6: Numbers in line .1 are restored. The figure in brackets is what would appear if the tablet started with two entries for Poseidon, as seems to be the case on the basis of a new fragment in *PoN* IV; for further discussion and references see Bendall forthcoming(a).
Cn 418: Three BOS+*SI* are recorded in lines .2 and .3; another may have appeared in line .7 (Melena 1994–1995a, 96). Also, an unjoined fragment probably bearing this ideogram may belong to Cn 418 (Melena 1992–1993b, 313; 1994–1995a, 96). The *PTT* apparatus for line .5 suggests: 'perhaps]ḄỌṢ^x 3'. Note proposed restorations by Palaima (1989, 104–5) should be read in the light of the new joins.

[21] Palaima 1992a, esp. 471–4.
[22] Palaima 1989, 99, 103. The appearance of *ZE* in Aq 64 should also be noted, which may (but need not) refer to oxen.

A total of some 34–36 animals is recorded.[23] In contrast with Knossos, there are no records of working oxen but, apart from the sheer improbability that cattle were used only for consumption at Pylian banquets, there is some evidence for other uses. In particular, large numbers of men called 'oxherds' (*qo-u-ko-ro* /g^u*oukolos*/ cf. βουκόλος) are recorded on some tablets. An 18 records ninety men at *ti-no*, while An 830 records 204 at various toponyms.[24] The large numbers of personnel involved have led to suggestions that *qo-u-ko-ro* in these documents might refer to herdsmen in general rather than oxherds[25] but, as Palaima points out, the men may have been ploughmen rather than herdsmen.[26] If this is correct, and we can take the men as associated with bovines rather than with herds more generally, the implication would be that a considerable number of oxen were available to the palace. If each man were assigned just one animal, those recorded in banqueting lists would form but 10% of the whole. If each man were assigned a pair, the figure would be 6%.

Further indirect evidence for bovines is supplied by references to oxhide, indicated by the ideogram **152* which represents a drawing of an animal skin surcharged with the syllabogram *WI*, probably abbreviating *wi-ri-no*, universally interpreted as /*wrīnos*/ 'oxhide'.[27] That the palace had access to oxhides implies that (at some point at least) it also had access to (or some claim on) the live animals. **152* appears in the Ma tablets, Mn 11 and in a sealing, Wr 1457. Over 200 units are recorded in the Ma tablets, implying an equal number of bovines, while Mn 11.6 records 105̣1 units, with a further 55 in line .10.[28] The Ma and Mn tablets are taxation records so it may be that the palace was drawing on resources which had originally been owned by the localities being taxed, but the force of the records is that the goods are being delivered to the palace (note particularly the sealing), and fact that the palace was able to draw on these resources implies at least some sort of control over them, even if simply the power to requisition them.[29] The supply of over 1000 hides suggests access to at least as many live animals. Taking the figures from Mn 11 alone, the number of animals supplied for banqueting is a bare 3% of 'available resources'.

On the whole, the evidence is suggestive that the situation at Pylos was not dissimilar to the situation at Knossos, and it is likely that hazards of preservation, its being the wrong time of year, or some variation in archival procedure account for the lack of records of working oxen at Pylos.[30] One may agree with Palaima in commenting, 'I think we must conclude that the Mycenaean administrations at both Pylos in Messenia and Knossos on Crete were dealing with much larger numbers of animals than our extant texts reflect.'[31]

6.2.1.3 BOVINES AT THEBES

Bovines appear at Thebes only in two sealings, Wu 53 and 76, both related to banqueting (Section 2.3.2.5; Table 2-7).[32] A total of two animals is recorded. There are no records of

[23] Note figures here differ from those in Halstead's (1998–1999, 164; he gives 30) because of different counting conventions.

[24] See the valuable discussion by Palaima (1989, 113–16; with 122–4 for a useful listing of Pylos *qo-u-ko-ro* records). A further minimum fifteen men fall under the heading of this occupational term on An 852. The word appears also in land tenure contexts (five Ea tablets referring to at least four different men; see Palaima 1989, 102–3), and taxation (Nn 831).

[25] Palmer 1963, 133, 451; Hiller 1988, 59–60.

[26] Palaima 1989, 115; 1992a, 465.

[27] *DMic.* II, *s.v. wi-ri-no*. **258* at Knossos is very similar and is probably a more elaborate version of **152*.

[28] The readings are due to a new join (Melena 1992–1993b, 308). Note that while the number of tens is uncertain (probably five) the 'thousand' is securely read.

[29] On the Ma tablets as requisitions of resources for military purposes see Killen forthcoming(b).

[30] Note also Palaima's pertinent comment (1989, 115) that the two sets of records belong to different administrative spheres.

[31] Palaima 1992a, 474.

[32] All occurrences of the ideogram are given in *Thebes* III, 313; cf. *TITHYMY*. For the sealings see Piteros, Olivier & Melena 1990; also Palaima 1992a, 465.

overall resources, but it seems not unlikely that, as at Knossos and Pylos, substantial numbers of animals would have been available to the palace at Thebes.

6.2.2 SHEEP (*106 = OVIS)

6.2.2.1 SHEEP AT KNOSSOS

The Knossos sheep records are some of the most numerous and complex documents in the entire Linear B corpus. Sheep appear in the Ce tablets, the Co set and C(4) sets, numerous other C- Class tablets, plus the many series and sets classified D, above all the 600 or so[33] tablets of the Da–Dg series. As brilliantly elucidated by Killen in the 1960s, the Da–Dg tablets are flock census records concerned with the management of sheep supplying wool for the textile industry and, as Olivier showed, many of these flocks are totalled in the Dn series.[34] It is unnecessary here to set out data from these documents, as this has been done elsewhere. Killen and Olivier calculate that a total of some 80,000–100,000 sheep were run in palace-owned flocks,[35] and this estimate is used here for 'overall resources'.[36]

Sheep appear in two contexts connected with religion: banqueting records and flock census records where the deities *Potnia* and Hermes feature as 'Collectors' (Sections 2.5.1; 2.5.2). We will examine first the flock census records since these are directly comparable with the 'overall resources' figure, itself derived from this type of record (or associated totalling tablets). Table 6-7 indicates numbers of sheep in the relevant flocks, together with numbers of lambs expected for breeding flocks (*ki* OVIS^{m}; replaced by *WE* in one instance) and amounts of wool.

Table 6-7. Sheep flocks dedicated to deities as 'Collectors' at Knossos

'Collector'	tablet	OVIS^{f}	*ki* OVIS^{m}	other	LANA supplied	LANA expected	LANA total
e-ma-a$_2$-o	D 411	60		*WE* 30[	—	—	—
po-ti-ni-ja-we-jo	Dl(1) 930	50	*o* 50		3 M [	6	9 M 1+
po-ti-ni-ja-we<-jo>	Dl(1) 933	40 *o* 20	*o* 60		3	9	12
po-ti-ni-ja-we-jo	Dl(1) 943	90	*o* 90		11	7̣	18
po-ti-ni-ja-we-jo	Dl(1) 946	70	*o* 70		7	7	14
po-ti-ni-]jạ-we-jo	Dl(1) 950	50	*o* 50		5	5	10
po-ti-ni-ja-we-ja	Dp 997	?	?		*lost*	—	—
po-ti-ni-]ja-we-jo	C 5730		?	OVIS^{x}[	?	—	—
po-ti-ni-jạ-we-jo	Dl(1) 7147	*lost*	*lost*		?	—	—
po-ti-ni-ja-we-jo	Dl(1) 7503	*lost*	*lost*		?	—	—
]po-ti-ni-ja-we-i-jo[	Dp 7742	?	?		?	—	—
po-ti-ṇị[-ja-we-jo	Dl(1) 7771	*lost*	?		?	—	—
po-ti-ni-]jạ-ẉẹ-jọ	Dl(1) 7905	*lost*	*lost*		*lost*		
po-]ṭị-ni-ja-ẉẹ-jọ	X 9716	*lost*	*lost*		?		
	TOTALS	**380+**	**320+**	—	**29 M 1+** **[= M 88+]**	**34**	**63 M 1+** **[= M 190+]**

[33] Olivier 1967b, 87; 1988, 219 n 3.

[34] Killen 1964; Olivier 1967b; 1972; 1988. See also Godart 1971; Killen 1993; Halstead 1996–1997; 1998–1999; 1999a; 2003, and further references in Sections 2.3.2.3 and 6.2.1.1.

[35] Killen 1964, 5 with n 23; 1993, 209. Some 62,000 sheep were recorded in the Da–Dg series (= most of Dn series) of h. 117 (Olivier 1967b, 80, 83, 89; cf. Olivier 1972, esp. 25–7; 1988, 264, 266–7). However, sheep recorded by other scribes must also be taken into account, as must the other h. 117 records which must be added since e.g. the 11,900 *ne* sheep (perhaps newborns) at Amnisos in Dn 1319 are not covered in the Da–Dg series, where the TN Amnisos does not appear (Olivier 1967b, 81). The raw total with such documents included is 92,900 (Olivier 1967b, 89). See also Halstead 1998–1999, 154 (p. 159 gives 155,821, but this counts the Da–Dg sheep twice as Dn is included in the totals); Halstead 1999a, 146 n 9.

[36] There are a few non-religious appearances of sheep which are not flock census records, but the numbers are relatively small and for present purposes the general figure is adequate.

Notes
Counting
The 'missing' twenty sheep in Dl(1) 933 are included in the total since it is implied that they will be supplied even if currently absent. Where an ideogram (or part) is preserved the table puts 'lost'; no lost values are restored (see text below). Where the ideogram itself is lost (or not originally present) the table puts '?'. It is assumed the (adult) Dl(1) sheep were all ewes since these are breeding records.
Individual tablets
Dl(1) 950: Joins X 7929 with new reading (but not affecting numbers); Godart *et al.* 1990–1991, 375.
C 5730: Also records CAP^f [. It is evidently a flock record of some sort, recording animals at *da-*22-to*. The restoration is speculative, but no other attested word ends in *-ja-we-jo*.
Dl(1) 7905: A new join with X 9328 gives the theonym (Godart *et al.* 1992–1993, 59).
X 9716: Joins Od 9775 with new text and is probably Dl (Godart *et al.* 1992–1993, 65).

Figures for about half the tablets are lost, and it would be reasonable to restore fifty animals in each case since this is the lowest figure on the records where the number is preserved,[37] giving some 630+ sheep. Even taking this higher figure, however, sheep in deity flocks account for less than 1% of the overall resources. It would perhaps be better to compare the records here only with other 'Collector' flocks. About a third of the flocks recorded at Knossos were associated with 'Collectors',[38] of which deity flocks are just 2%. It does not appear to be the case that deities were major 'Collectors'.[39]

We now turn to the banqueting records, considering first the RCT records, figures for which are shown in Table 6-8. We include here banqueting records judged only 'probable' or 'possible'. The animals recorded on the *recto* and *verso* of the 'fattening record' Ce 50 probably had a different status. This, plus the question of whether the word *o-pa* refers to all the sheep on the *verso* or only to some, is discussed below.

Table 6-8. Sheep in the Knossos RCT records

	OVIS^f	OVIS^m	OVIS/ OVIS^x	TOTAL
1. Banqueting records				
Ce 152			28	28
Uc 161			197	197
Ce 9109		1̣		1
TOTAL 1				**226**
2. Fattening record				
Ce 50 *verso*	427+	190		617+
TOTAL 1+2				**843+**
3. Herd management				
Ce 50 *recto*	126	134		260
Ce 139			51+	51+
Ce 283			40	40
TOTAL 3				**351+**
4. Herd management totalling record				
Ce 162			10,000	
TOTAL 4				**10,000**
5. Unclear				
Ce 76		1+		
Ce 163		7̣0+		
Ce 9109		1̣		

[37] Nosch (2000a, 215 n 25) does something similar.
[38] Olivier 1967b, 83; Bennet 1992, 85–6; also Bennet 1985, 239.
[39] Nosch (2000a, 211) similarly notes that the number of tablets recording *Potnia* sheep is insignificant compared to the some 1000 other sheep records.

Some 226 sheep are recorded as destined for sacrifice. In addition we should take into account the animals earmarked for fattening on Ce 50 (Section 2.3.2.3). Since our concern here is with numbers we must before proceeding consider a further difficulty presented by this document. It is useful to set out the text again.

Ce 50 (124)

Recto

.1a	a-qi-ru OVIS^m 134 qa-ra$_2$-wo OVIS^f 43
.1b	te-pa-ra , pe-re-qo-ta
.2	a-nu-ko OVIS^f 51 ro-ru OVIS^f 32

Verso

.1a	a-qi-ru OVIS^m 190 qạ-ra^2-wo OVIS^f 144
.1b	o-pa
.2	a-nu-ko OVIS^f 133[ ] ro-ru OVIS^f 150
lat. sup.	we-ka-ta BOS^m 4

.1b On both *r.* and *v.* this register written in minuscule between the first signs of l. 1a.
*r.*1b *te-pa-ra* over ⟦ ⟧ (*-pa-* over ⟦*si*⟧).
l.s. (in fact, the *lat. inf.* of the *v.*) 4 from ⟦6⟧ (written as 4 + ⟦2⟧).

It is not clear whether *o-pa* applies only to the first entry in line *v.*1a, the flocks of *a-qi-ru* (it is actually written 'within' the man's name[40]), or to all of the flocks on the *verso*. A definitive solution is not possible,[41] but the repetition of text on the *recto* and *verso* may point in the latter direction. As Melena has shown, features of the numbers rule out the idea that these are the same flocks at different stages and it is more likely a matter of flocks herded by the same shepherds having been separated out from one another for some reason.[42] In light of Halstead's observation that animals intended for 'fattening' might be kept separate (see Section 2.3.2.3), it may be that some animals are, and others are not, to be 'fattened'. It may also be significant that the animals on the *recto* are associated with the 'Collector' *pe-re-qo-ta* and 'Collector' flocks are often kept separate, whether they are being fattened or not. Epigraphically, it is apparent that the designations *o-pa* and *te-pa-ra* (obscure, possibly a TN) and *pe-re-qo-ta* were added as afterthoughts, perhaps to distinguish between otherwise nearly identical texts. Thus, while the short word *o-pa* looks as if it might apply to the *a-qi-ru* flock alone, taken together with the longer phrase on the *recto*, along with the other considerations, one is more inclined to believe that it was intended to mark all the entries on the *verso*. (Indeed, if it was the intention of the scribe to indicate all entries, there is nowhere else on the tablet he *could* have written the word.) We thus for present purposes will take all of these entries together as relating to *o-pa*.

All but one of the remaining tablets (Ce 76, –139, –163, –283) are 'unclear' (mostly due to their being very fragmentary). They record a total of 162 animals. The final tablet, Ce 162, was probably for rough working; [43] the text is as follows.

Ce 162 ('124')

OVIS 10000

↓

v. ⟦ SUS^f 500 ⟧

Many traces of ⟦ ⟧ on both sides. On *r.* OVIS 10000 is followed by a large number (9000+) partially erased. Tablet possibly used for rough working.

Although no words appear and the context of the 10,000 sheep is therefore obscure, it is clear enough that this is a totalling record, and thus of at least some relevance for 'overall resources'. (Driessen rightly comments on the interest of this tablet having been found in the RCT 'since it obviously suggests that some official was busy summarising quite substantial

[40] See the photo in *CoMIK* I.

[41] Melena (1983a, 259, 263) prefers the former; Driessen the latter (*Scribes RCT*, 205).

[42] Melena 1983a, 260–1. He noted that totals for the three ewe flocks are almost identical if the figures from *recto* and *verso* are added for each flock (the numbers are 187, 184 and 182).

[43] *KT*^{5} apparatus; *Scribes RCT*, 205–6. The text is from *KT*^{5}.

quantitative data'.[44]) The 'banqueting records' alone constitute just 2% of this figure; taking the *verso* of the 'fattening record' Ce 50 also into account gives 8%. Either way, the amounts consumed at specific banquets or earmarked for future consumption do not account for major proportions of the overall resources. In all likelihood the majority of sheep recorded in Ce 162 were being kept to produce wool for the textile industry, as is well documented by the later records. But it is important to note that only one, relatively small, much erased and roughly inscribed tablet with no fair-copy companion gives us even a hint at the scale of animals that may have been involved, again highlighting hazards of preservation.

We now turn to the non-RCT records. Data for those identified as banqueting records (Section 2.3.2.3) are summarised in Table 6-9.[45]

Table 6-9. Sheep in non-RCT banqueting records at Knossos

	OVIS^{f}	OVIS^{m}	OVIS/ OVIS^{x}	TOTALS
1. Banqueting records				
C 33	9			9
C 394		3+		3+
C 954	4			4
C 1561	1+			1+
C(2) 914		50		50
C(2) 915	10			10
C(2) 941	10	8+		18+
D 5954		1+		1+
U 7063	3	2	3+	8+
TOTAL 1				**104+**
2. Fattening records				
Dm (see Section 2.3.2.3)				417
TOTAL 1+2				**521+**

There are fewer animals for sacrifice, only some 104+, recorded on the non-RCT records than on the RCT records, but they are spread over a larger number of texts. In addition we have 417 sheep for 'fattening' on the Dm tablets, for a total of 521+. These animals account for a bare 0.5 % of the total recorded resources of the palace. Even if these figures are lower than what was actually consumed (which seems likely), consumption would not have been a major drain on resources.[46]

6.2.2.2 SHEEP AT PYLOS

Sheep at Pylos appear in banqueting and flock censuses records,[47] as at Knossos, but there are no examples of flocks dedicated to deities. Figures for the banqueting records are given in Table 6-10. The flock census records mostly belong to the Cn series.[48] Totals for the sheep in this series have been published elsewhere and there is no need for a re-count here. Halstead gives a figure of 10,218 sheep,[49] of which those allocated for banqueting represent less than

[44] *Scribes RCT*, 206.
[45] Halstead's (1998–1999, 158) figures differ slightly due to different counting conventions and because he includes as possible consumption records several documents considered here 'Unclear' (Section 2.3.2.3).
[46] Cf. Halstead 1998–1999, 171.
[47] Killen 1984a; 1993.
[48] Halstead (1998–1999, 165) gives a figure of 222 as he includes animals designated *WE* in the totals. This is reasonable since some (all?) of the 'yearlings' must have been sheep, but some of them might have been goats so *WE* is ignored here. For details of the figures see also Bendall forthcoming(a).
[49] E.g. Halstead 1990–1991, 355, Table 4. His later table (Halstead 1998–1999, 164–5, Table 4) gives a higher figure of 10,435, but this includes 'missing' sheep. On the Cn series in general see Lang 1966b; Godart 1977; Killen 1993; also 1984a.

2%. As at Knossos, animals designated for banqueting were a tiny fraction of overall resources.

Table 6-10. Sheep in Pylian banqueting records

	OVIS^f	OVIS^m	OVIS/ OVIS^x	TOTALS
Un 2	6	26		32
Un 6	3+*		1+*	4+
Ua 17	7	7?*		7 [14?]
Ua 25		67		67
Un 47	8	13		21
Un 138	1	15		16
Cn 418		1 [4?]		1 [4?]
Un 718		4		4
Un 853	1	1		2
Un 1177			6	6
Un 1185			3	3
TOTAL				**163+ [173+]**

Notes

Un 6: The figure '3' includes one female sheep restored in line .1. OVIS^x[in line .8 implies at least one animal (although note the reading is uncertain).

Ua 17: The ideogram for male sheep is missing but the structure of the tablet suggests that this is what the second surviving '7' would have referred to (see *PTT* app. to line .2), so '14' is restored in brackets.

Cn 418: For the suggested restored figure (in brackets) see Melena 1994–1995a, 95–6.

Un 1177: New join (to a tablet found in 1995) and reading (Melena 2000–2001b, 376).

6.2.2.3 SHEEP AT THEBES

Sheep at Thebes appear only in banqueting documents: Uo 121, recording one sheep, and eighteen Wu sealings (Section 2.3.2.5, Table 2-7), recording the same number of animals. There are no documents from which to calculate overall resources. It was noted above (Section 6.2.1.3) that it is unlikely that the palace at Thebes did not have access to more bovines than appeared in the records, and the same can be said for sheep. But here further evidence supports the statement: as we will see below (Section 6.3.3.3), the palace was receiving considerable amounts of wool. To obtain it, they must have had sheep, probably managed in similar ways to those documented at Knossos and Pylos although we do not have records to that effect.[50]

6.2.3 GOATS (**107* = CAP)

6.2.3.1 GOATS AT KNOSSOS

Goats appear at Knossos in banqueting, herd management and taxation records (the Mc series). Most of the tablets and series involved have already been discussed. The banqueting records were dealt with in Section 2.3.2.3. Herd management records include the Co series (Section 6.2.1.1, Table 6-2), and the three tablets of the C(4) set.[51] One of the herd management records, C 5730 (Section 6.2.1.1, Table 6-7), may record a flock of goats dedicated to the goddess *Potnia*, so is counted as 'related to religion' here.

The Mc tablets are proportional taxation records.[52] A typical example is as follows.

[50] Nosch 2001a; cf. Killen 1993.

[51] For C(4) see Halstead 1998–1999, 152, 157, 158; also 1990–1991, 351–2.

[52] Discussions of the Mc series include *Documents*, 301–3, 474–5; Baumbach 1971; Melena 1972; Olivier 1974; De Fidio 1982; Shelmerdine 1989; 1999a; Perna 1996; 2004; Rougemont 2001b. See also Killen forthcoming(b); Halstead 1998–1999, 153, 159, 162; and Section 6.4.1.2. Texts here are from *KT*^{5}.

Mc 4455 + 8449 + 8554 + *fr.* ASHM (1910.217)/HM (132)
.A 'a-pa-sa-ki-jo' **150* 28 CAP^{f} 17
.B ku-ta-to / **142* M 12 CORN 24
4455: Oxford; 8449 + 8554 + *fr.*: Iraklio.
.B M over ⟦12⟧.

The tablet records payments from the town of *ku-ta-to*; *a-pa-sa-ki-jo* is probably a man's name, referring to the person responsible for the collection or delivery. Alongside female goats, the town contributes horn (CORN), probably of the agrimi, **142*, probably honeycomb (Section 4.2.1.5), and **150* (unidentified). The purpose of the requisition is uncertain, but is probably military.[53] In any case, there is no reason to suppose a connection with feasting or religion, with the exception of a probable offering of **150* to Ares on one of the Mc tablets (see Section 6.6.3.5 below).

Estimating the number of goats recorded in the series is complicated (rather than simplified) by the existence of what appear to be two totalling tablets. The texts are as follows.

Mc 4457 + 5098 + 8264 + *fr.* (132)
.1 to-sa **150* 345 CAP^{f} 208[
.2 ḳẹ-[·] **142* L 5 M 4 CORN 345[
.1.2 Right end numerals probably complete.
.2 Trace before **142*, over ⟦ ⟧.

Mc 5107 + 5123 + 5693 (132)
**150* 354 CAP^{f} 200[

The totalling tablets record 408+ goats; the surviving records of the remainder of the series record 186.[54] It is not clear whether these are subsumed under the amounts on the totalling records or are in addition to them; the former is assumed here. It is also unclear whether one of the totalling records might not be a duplicate of the other (note the similarity of the figures) so that they should not be added together. We have done so here, but the possibility should be noted. The data are set out in Table 6-11.

Table 6-11. Goats at Knossos

A. Non-RCT records	CAP		CAP
1. *Banqueting*		**3. *Other flocks***	
C 394	1+	Co series	1249
C 954	6+	C(4) 911	700*
C(2) 908	1	C(4) 912	40
C(2) 913	2+	C(4) 917	500+
C(2) 914	50	**TOTAL 3**	**2489+**
C(2) 915	10	**4. *Tax***	
C(2) 922	1	Mc 4457	**208+**
C(2) 5765	1+	Mc 5107	**200+**
C(2) 7064	2̣7+	**TOTAL 4**	**408+**
C(2) 8225	1+	**TOTAL 3 + 4**	**2897+**
TOTAL 1	**100+**	**5. *Unclear***	
2. *Deity flock?*		C <1902>	47*
C 5730	**1+**	C 5669	5̣+*
TOTAL 2	**1+**	C 5730	1+
		C 6021	1̣+
		C 7054	20
		C 7059	20+
		C 7088	70*

B. RCT tablets	CAP
1. *Banqueting*	
Ce 152	16–27+
2. *Unclear*	
Ce 163	44+
Ce 7516?	1+
Ce 9109	2+

[53] Killen forthcoming(b).
[54] Halstead (1998–1999, 162) has 185, using his counting conventions.

Notes
General
* = summed
Individual tablets
Ce 152: The higher number results if 12 is restored in *v*.3 on analogy with *v*.2. The apparatus states: 'Possible trace of 1̣0̣[after CAP'.
C(4) 917: Reading of ideogram insecure. ṢỤṢ^f in *KT*^{5} is replaced with ÇẠP^x in *CoMIK* I, 378; a later join confirms CAP, perhaps fem., CAP$^{f.}$. (Godart *et al.* 1992–1993, 56). Other joins (not affecting previous reading) are reported in Godart *et al.* 1990–1991, 375.
C 7088: 'Unclear' here, but probably a herd management record (Halstead 1998–1999, 158).
Ce 7516: May be banqueting record.
Other: CAP may appear in C 7060, a possible banqueting record (Section 2.3.2.3), but the reading is uncertain (could be OVIS) so it is not included in the table.

In non-RCT tablets, some 2897+ animals are in the hands of the palace (3) or delivered as tax (4), of which animals in banqueting and deity flocks are about 3%. All 'disbursements' are for banqueting. The same is true for the RCT records, but here there are no documents relating to 'overall resources'.

6.2.3.2 GOATS AT PYLOS

Goats appear at Pylos in banqueting records (Sections 2.3.2.1, 2.3.2.2), in records of standing flocks and, once, as part of an *o-no* payment (An 35). Data for the banqueting records and the *o-no* payment are set out in Table 6-12. For standing flocks we use Halstead's figure of 1839.[55]

Table 6-12. Goats in contexts other than herd management at Pylos

tablet	m/f/x	CAP	tablet	m/f/x	CAP
1. *Banqueting*			2. o-no		
Cn 418	m	7	An 35	f	4
Cn 1287	m/f	11	**TOTAL 1 + 2**		**75**
Ua 17	m	31	3. *Unclear*		
Un 2	m/f	4	Cc 1258	f	30
Un 138	m	13	Cn 1286		1
Un 612	f	1	Cc 1284	x	8
Un 853	f	*lost*			
Wr 1325	m	1			
Wr 1334	m	1			
Wr 1416	f	1			
TOTAL 1		**71**			

Notes
m/f/x = male/female/gender unspecified
Cn 418: For joins see Melena 1992–1993b, 313; 1994–1995a, 95–7, with new text. For discussion of possible reading CAP+*E* in lines .4 and .8 with further references see Bendall forthcoming(a).

The banqueting and *o-no* records count as 'disbursements'; banqueting thus accounts for 95% of 'disbursements'. It does not, however, account for a significant proportion of overall resources. Animals designated for banqueting are just 4% of the number recorded in standing flocks. (And it may be noted that this figure is on the high side because the numbers in several flock records have been lost.)

6.2.3.3 GOATS AT THEBES

Goats at Thebes appear only in banqueting contexts: fourteen goats are recorded in the Wu sealings (Section 2.3.2.5, Table 2-7) and one goat in Uo 121 (Section 2.3.2.5). There are no records pertaining to overall resources.

[55] Halstead 1998–1999, 164–5. (On the counting conventions of the present study the figure would be 1854.)

6.2.4 PIGS (*108 = SUS)

6.2.4.1 PIGS AT KNOSSOS

Pigs appear at Knossos in banqueting contexts (Section 2.3.2.3) and in herd management records (most belonging to 'Collectors' in the Co series; see Section 6.2.1.1, Table 6-2). The data are set out in Table 6-13.[56]

Table 6-13. Pigs at Knossos

A. Non-RCT tablets	SUS
1. *Banqueting*	
C(3) 905	1
C(3) 967	***1***
C(3) 979	1
C(3) 1030	1
C(3) 1039	1+
C(3) 7057	1̣+
C(3) 7058	1
C(3) 7793	1̣+
C(3) 9666	1
TOTAL A1	**9**
2. Herd management	
Co series	359+
3. *Unclear*	
C 767	1+

B. RCT tablets	SUS
1. *Banqueting*	
Uc 161	1
Ce 113?	7
Ce 8346?	4
TOTAL B1	**12**
2. Herd management	
Ce 162	⟦500⟧

Notes

Ce 162: The number is not transcribed in *KT*[5] but is clear in the *CoMIK* I photo – however it need not *necessarily* go with the ideogram (see text below).

C 767: *CoMIK* I notes more of the tablet is preserved at right in *SM* II pl. 52; the number following SUS[f] may be 3̣.

C(3) 967: Ideogram and number both lost; '1' is restored on analogy with other set members (shown in bold italic).

C(3) 9666: Formerly C(1); see note to Table 6-3.

Other: **C 7516** may also record pigs, but the reading is uncertain (BOS preferred). **C(4) 917** ṢỤṢ[f] in *KT*[5] now CAP[f] (see notes to Table 6-11, *s.v.*).

For both the RCT and non-RCT tablets, banqueting accounts for 100% of recorded 'uses' for pigs, but the totals earmarked for specific feasts do not account for significant proportions of overall resources. For the non-RCT tablet the percentage is 3%; for the RCT tablets it would be 2% *if* the erased number in Ce 162 were used. It is not specious at least to take note of this figure because, although erased, it may reflect numbers of pigs the scribe was thinking in terms of. However, the tablet as a whole is a palimpsest (on both sides) and was 'possibly used for rough working' (as the apparatus notes; see text in Section 6.2.2.1), so the figure need not certainly pertain to the pig ideogram.

Another ambiguity is introduced by the fact that, as noted previously (Section 2.3.2.3), the C(3) set may record animals provided by individual contributors rather than by the 'palace' *per se*. Also, the Co records refer to 'Collector' flocks, so it is unclear in what sense these pigs belong to 'overall palatial resources', although the palace clearly had an interest in them. Probably the safest general observation would be that once again we witness considerable bias in the records. A mere nine or twelve pigs is unlikely to reflect real levels of palatial

[56] Halstead's (1998–1999, 158–9) figures differ from those here in that the new classification of C(3) 9666 puts it with 'banqueting' rather than 'herd management' records and 500 pigs are no longer seen on C(4) 917 where a new join shows the reading is 'goat' (see notes to Table 6-11); different counting conventions also result in a slightly different count for the C(3) set.

consumption in either period covered by the tablets, no matter who was providing them. Similarly, in terms of overall resources, it seems remarkable that only pig herds from western Crete are known (the Co toponyms refer to towns in west Crete; see Section 6.2.1.1) and no more local herds are recorded. For the RCT all we have is a *possible* reference to 500 pigs on a much erased tablet possibly used for rough work. This example once again highlights hazards of preservation, but it is less evident whether the situation with the Co records is also due to hazards of preservation or instead reflects other sorts of biases – or even the real case?

Finally it is worth noting that it may be assumed that all or most of the pigs would eventually have been consumed, whether at feasts or in 'ordinary' dining contexts, since pigs provide no secondary products and are raised primarily for meat[57] (once killed they do also yield skins and other items[58]).

6.2.4.2 PIGS AT PYLOS

Pigs at Pylos appear in banqueting foodlists (Section 2.3.2.3) and in herd management records. One of the herds – an exceptionally large one – is dedicated to the goddess *Potnia*, probably in the role of 'Collector' (Section 2.5.2). In addition, one sealing may possibly refer to pigs. We saw this document already in Section 2.5.2; the text is given again here. The only other possible appearance of pigs at Pylos is on a sealing, the text of which is as follows.[59]

Wp 1327 (Ci)

α. *sigillum*
β. pe-re-i-to
γ.]ṣụṣ^{f} 3̣50

Enclosed cord almost large enough to require 4 facets. SUS^{f}, but EQU not entirely impossible, the stem below on the extra semi-facet; the vertical strokes above head are difficult to explain.

The interpretation of *pe-re-i-to* is uncertain. As rightly noted by Aura Jorro, an interpretation as πλεῖστον/-ου, superlative of πολύς 'many', 'no pasa de ser una mera correspondencia formal'.[60] Being a sealing, this document should relate to deliveries to the palace,[61] but the reading of the ideogram is uncertain so it is not clear that pigs are the subject of the document – it could instead refer to, for instance, horses (see Section 2.3.2.2).[62] We may consider the figures both with and without this document. Figures from the remaining documents are set out in Table 6-14.[63]

[57] As is well known; see e.g. Leguilloux 2003, 256.
[58] Clinton (2005, 167–8) reports medicinal uses in classical antiquity; his article offers a useful survey of pig sacrifice in classical Greece; for pig sacrifice in a Mycenaean context see Hamilakis & Konsolaki 2004.
[59] For the reclassification see *PoN* IV.
[60] *DMic.* II, 104; also see Olivier 1997, 73.
[61] Palaima 1987; Killen 1994.
[62] I am grateful to J.-P. Olivier for strongly impressing upon me many years ago that an uncertain reading means just that: it is uncertain and no assumptions should be made. See Olivier 1997, 73 with n 23. On the sealing see also Bendall 2003, 215.
[63] The figures mostly tally with Halstead's (1998–1999, 164–5) except that he includes the 3̣50 Wp animals as pigs and uses different counting conventions.

Table 6-14. Pigs at Pylos

	ideogram	SUS		**m/f/x**	SUS	**location**
1. *Banqueting*			**2. *Deity flock***			
Cn 418	SUS^{x}	1+	Cc 665	SUS	**190**	ne-wo-pe-o
Cn 608	SUS+*SI*	25	**TOTAL 1+2**		**282+**	
Ua 17	SUS^{f}	20	**3. *Other flocks***			
Ua 25	SUS+*SI*	3	Cn 45.13	SUS^{f}	16	ra-wa-ra-ti-jo
Un 2.6	SUS+*SI*	1̣	Cn 45.13	SUS^{f}	8	ra-wa-ra-ti-jo
Un 2.6	SUS^{f}	6	Cn 45 *lat.inf.*	SUS^{m}	11	ra-wa-ra-ti-jo
Un 6.1	SUS+*KA*	1	Cn 272.3	SUS^{f}	4̣8	*lost*
Un 6.1.3.4	SUS^{f}	6 [8]	Cn 440.7	SUS^{x}	35	*lost*
Un 138.3	SUS	12	Cn 440.8	SUS^{x}	14	*lost*
Un 138.4	SUS+*SI*	1	Cn 440.8	SUS^{f}	1+	*lost*
Un 853.5	SUS+*KA*	2	Cn 599.7	SUS^{f}	30	a$_2$-pa-tu-wo-te
Un 853.5	SUS^{f}	4+	Cn 599.8	SUS^{f}	57	e-ko-me-no
Un 1185	ṢỤṢ	10	Cn 600.14	SUS^{m}	30	ti-mi-to a-ke-e
TOTAL 1		**92+**	Cn 600.15	SUS^{f}	12	ti-mi-to a-ke-e
			Cn 643.2	SUS^{f}	40	wi-ja-we-ra$_2$
			Cn 925.1	SUS^{m}	16	da-we-u-pi
			Cn 925.2	SUS^{f}	16	da-we-u-pi
			Cn 925.3	SUS^{f}	28	da-we-u-pi
			TOTAL 3		**362+**	
			TOTAL 2+3		**552+**	
			TOTAL 1+2+3		**644+ [646+]**	

Notes

Note that Cn 1116, which records a total of 36 ṢỤṢ is excluded from the table because it now joins Cn 491 (Melena 1994–1995b, 280) and the ideogram is now read as CAP (apparently secure in line .5).

Cn 45: Reading Bennett 1992, 106.

Cn 440: Reading Melena 1992–1993a, 79. Reading uncertain (ṢỤṢ^{f}) in line .8, but context makes likely.

Cn 418: The reading is uncertain (ṢỤṢ^{x}[) but inclusion in the table is justified (unlike the Wp record) by the fact that 418 is certainly a banqueting record (so EQU unlikely) and OVIS and CAP are already recorded on the same line and the reading is inconsistent with both them and with BOS. Hence, SUS is likeliest.

Un 1185: Reading uncertain (ṢỤṢ); see Melena 1994–1995b, 286.

Of animals in standing flocks (Categories 2 and 3), about 32% belong to a deity flock. Altogether, 41% of pigs are intended for banqueting or belong to *Potnia*. Without taking the *Potnia* herd into account, the pigs in banqueting records account for some 24% of pigs in standing herds. With the *Potnia* herd, the banqueting records account for 16% (but this is taking the *Potnia* flocks as non-religious, which cannot be right).

The documentation relating to banqueting – at least as far as pigs are concerned – is more extensive at Pylos than at Knossos, but some of the same observations apply. Wp 1327, for instance, introduces similar uncertainties and highlights hazards of preservation, with the added difficulty that, even if the reading were certainly SUS, we would remain unclear what all these pigs were being delivered to the palace for. Banqueting would be a likely reason, but the number would be without precedent for a banqueting record[64] (of any sort, but particularly a sealing). Might we imagine for instance a flock transfer? Further speculation is pointless in the light of the uncertain reading, but again the biases and difficulties are highlighted, while at the same time the overall picture appears less entirely implausible than what was seen at Knossos.

[64] See Bendall 2003, 215. Also, the amount of meat that so many pigs would yield seems somewhat implausibly large (some 24,500 kg; see Bendall forthcoming[a] for the method of calculation).

6.2.4.3 PIGS AT THEBES

Twelve pigs, including two 'fattened', are recorded in the Wu sealings, relating to banqueting (Section 2.3.2.5, Table 2-7). There are no records from which overall resources can be calculated.

6.3 ANIMAL PRODUCTS: CHEESE, SKINS, WOOL

6.3.1 CHEESE (**156 = TU+RO*$_2$)

Ideogram **156* is a ligature formed of *tu* and *ro*$_2$, spelling the name of the commodity /*turion*/ 'cheese'. It appears on just two tablets, both banqueting records from Pylos, Un 718 (twenty units) and Un 1185 (number lost). Whatever the figure for Un 1185, given the large number of female sheep and goats available to the palace (Sections 6.2.2.2 and 6.2.3.2), it is scarcely likely that the few items recorded constituted a substantial proportion of available resources. This is another instance of a palace having potential access to large quantities of a commodity which appears not normally to have been recorded in Linear B. Palmer, making a similar observation, comments that this 'points to a procurement system for cheese outside of the standard assessment collection systems',[65] which may be true at least for those systems where Linear B was used. We will return to this issue in the final chapter.

6.3.2 SHEEPSKIN (**153*)

Ideogram **153* is a drawing of an animal hide surcharged with the syllabogram *ko*, abbreviating *ko-wo* (written before the ideogram in PY Un 718.4), interpreted as /*kōwos*/ (cf. κῶας) 'sheepskin'.[66] **153* appears just three times in the entire Linear B corpus, twice on PY Un 718 and once on TH Uo 121; both tablets are banqueting foodlists. Un 718 records two units of **153*, one contributed by *e-ke-ra*$_2$*-wo* (line .4) and one by the *da-mo* (line .8). Uo 121 records one unit. There are no records from which to estimate overall resources at either site but, given the large numbers of sheep in palace herds at Pylos (Section 6.2.2.2), two units is a negligible proportion of what must have been available.

6.3.3 WOOL (**145* = LANA)

6.3.3.1 WOOL AT KNOSSOS

Wool appears in connection with religion at Knossos in two contexts: assessments for deity flocks (6.2.2.1, Table 6-7), and issues as offerings. It also appears as *o-no* payments, which we return to below. We will first examine the offerings records.

One of the offerings records, Gg(1) 7369, was discussed above in the context of honey (Section 4.2.1.2); it records offerings of wool and honey in the month *ka-ra-e-ri-jo*. It was noted that the scribe of this tablet, h. 103, was involved in the textile industry and may have been involved in wool offerings because this was a commodity he normally dealt with.[67] The remaining records of wool offerings are also by h. 103;[68] the texts are as follows.

---

[65] Palmer 1999, 467–8; see also 463–4, 482–3.
[66] *DMic.* I, 397 *s.v. ko-wo* (II).
[67] As noted earlier, he seems to have been working together with h. 140 who was also involved making in offerings of honey and textiles.
[68] But for the possibility that the Ga tablets of h. 219 may too record offerings of wool see Section 6.6.2.6.

Od(2) 714 (103)

.a a-*65-na [

.b e-re-u-ti-ja LANA 1 [

Od(2) 715 (103)

.a e-re-u-ti-ja

.b ta-wa-ko-to LANA 1

Od(2) 716 (103)

.a]e-re-u-ti-ja

.b] LANA 4

Od(2) 718 (103)

a-mi-ni-ṣọ[

Over ⟦ ⟧.

Od(2) 714, –715 and –716 record offerings to the goddess Eileithyia, encountered above on Gg(3) 705 (honey) where she was associated with Amnisos. That Od(2) 718 also mentions Amnisos suggests this too is an offering record, although the text is too broken to be certain.

One further tablet by h. 103 may also record wool offerings. The text is as follows, together with a fragment possibly from the same tablet.

Od(1) 696 (103)

.1]e-pi-ro-pa-ja , / o-du-we 'te-o-p̣ọ-ri-ja' M 2[

.2] LANA 2 M 1

.3] *vac.*

Possibly same tablet as L 698.

L 698 (103)

.1]ne-we , pe-ko-to *164[1][

.2]i-jo-te , 'ku-su-a-ta-o' 11[

.3]jọ-du-mi 'wo-ke' P 1̣[

Possibly same tablet as Od 696.

If *te-o-po-ri-ja* in Od(1) 696.1 were to be interpreted as a festival name /*theophoria*/, this tablet would presumably be an offering record.[69] However, the reading is uncertain, and if L 698, which shows no connection with cult, really is part of the same tablet, an offerings context would appear unlikely since it resembles more a workshop record.[70] Nor does any other record of the Od(1) set have a connection with religion.

Leaving Od(1) 696 aside, wool associated with religion at Knossos is set out in Table 6-15.

Table 6-15. Wool in religious contexts at Knossos

	LANA	= M
1. *Offerings*		
Gg(1) 7369	1 M 1	4
Od(2) 714	1	3
Od(2) 715	1	3
Od(2) 716	4	12
Od(2) 718	*lost*	1+
TOTAL 1		**23+**
2. *Deity flocks*		
Table 6-7		**190+**
TOTAL 1+2		**213+**

69 Hiller 1984; followed by Nosch & Perna 2001, 472; Weilhartner 2005, 64–5.

70 As argued in Section 2.5.5, *wo-ke* need not be taken referring solely to religious workshops.

A total of M 23 (about 23 kg) was issued as offerings and a further M 190+ (some 190+ kg) was collected from deity flocks. Neither of these amounts represents a significant proportion of overall resources. Useful figures in this regard are provided by J.-P. Olivier in his comparison of the amount of wool required to make the textiles recorded in the L series with the amount potentially produced by standing flocks. Olivier estimated that some 11,507 units of LANA (= M 34,521) would have been required for the textiles,[71] while around 10,000 units (M 30,000) could have been produced by the sheep[72] (his point was that adequate numbers of sheep existed to produce the wool required for the textiles). Note that the amounts are massive, with some 30–50 tons of wool per year being produced for the textile industry.[73] Taking the lower figure for the sake of argument, the amount issued as offerings is some 0.08% (of 10,000 units), while the amount collected from deity flocks is some 0.6%. The two together are 0.7%.

It might be more meaningful to take the deity flock wool only in comparison with wool from other 'Collector' flocks. The wool disbursements for textile manufacture in regard to 'Collector' and 'non-Collector' flocks follow the general 30:70 ratio observed by Olivier for the sheep.[74] The global figure is thus (very roughly[75]) 3333 units (= M 9999), of which the 190+ from deity flocks is 2%. Deities were apparently not major holders, even among 'Collectors'.

With regard to wool disbursements in general at Knossos, it should be noted that the vast majority of contexts in which wool appears relate to collections from flocks and disbursements to the textile industry. The series (and classes) involved are Dk, Dh, Dp, Dl, Lc, Ld, Ln, L-, M- (M 683 is an issue to 'decorators') and Od.[76] As discussed previously (Section 3.1.1), disbursements to textile workgroups do not represent an actual exit from the palatial system since the wool would eventually be returned as finished textiles. There is virtually no documentation directly relating to final uses of these textiles (see Section 6.4). The majority were probably traded; some were used as guest-gifts, special clothing and so forth.[77] Whatever the case, the majority of wool was intended for industrial production, while a small amount was issued as offerings. Apart from the offerings records, there are only two instances of issues of wool *not* in connection with the textile industry;[78] the texts are as follows.

M(1) 559 (103)

.1 ']ke' o-no , o-na LANA 2
.2]da-wi-jo *146 2̣

.2 Perhaps only 1.

Od 5558 (—)

sup. mut.
]ṇụ-we , o-na LANA[

These tablets record *o-no* (repeated in the plural *o-na*) payments, so should be taken into account for calculating 'disbursements for final use'. The figure in Od 5558 is lost, but restoring M 1+ (our usual practice) gives a total of M 7+ for both tablets. Offerings thus account for 77% of 'final use' disbursements in the surviving records. It seems remarkable that at Knossos (unlike, as we shall see, Pylos), wool scarcely appears in the documentation as it

[71] Olivier 1967b, 92.
[72] Olivier 1967b, 93.
[73] E.g. Killen 1984a, 50; 1994, 68.
[74] See Section 6.2.2.1 for the sheep, with references. For the wool/textiles see Olivier 1967b, 91; Killen & Olivier 1968, 137; Killen 1995, 216–17 with n 20; cf. also Killen 1979b, 155–6.
[75] The figure is anything but precise – it is only an indication of order of magnitude. Notice also that some of the figures from Table 6-7 are lost; but doubling or even tripling them would not significantly modify the picture.
[76] Wm 8493 and Ws 8152 are also probably related to such contexts, as are various rations and stint records on which LANA does not appear, e.g. the Ak series (see Killen 1972).
[77] See Killen 1964; 1985, 263–4.
[78] On L 758 and Og(2) 8150]*o-no* is almost certainly part of the end of a word.

stands apart from in direct relation with textile manufacture with the exception of these few offerings and *o-no* records. The situation appears similar to that encountered in other cases where the majority of final use disbursements was simply 'missing'.

6.3.3.2 WOOL AT PYLOS

Wool appears in the Linear B records of Pylos in the following contexts: (1) religious offerings and banqueting, (2) *o-no* payments, (3) perfumery and (4) probably textile production. Most of the documents have already been discussed. For (1) Un 6 and –853 see Section 2.3.2.2; for (2) An 35 and Un 443 see Sections 4.3.3 and 5.2.3 respectively; for (3) perfumery records see Section 2.5.3. The texts of (4), the probable textile production records, are as follows.

La 632 (S632-Ciii)
pa-wo-ko LANA[

La 635 (S632-Ciii)
mo-ro-ko-wo-wo-pi LANA[

The sign-group in La 632 is attested on Ad 691, where it is the genitive plural of a word attested in the matching document Aa 795 as *pa-wo-ke* probably /*pan-worges*/ 'maids of all work'.[79] It is not entirely clear that the sign-group in La 632 represents the same word.[80] If it does, this could conceivably be a rations record, although there are no other instances of wool issued as rations at Pylos. Another possibility would be that the 'maids of all work' were expected to undertake some sort of labour involving wool. *mo-ro-ko-wo-wo-pi* in La 635 is a TN with /*-phi*/ and involving a second element *wo-wo* /*worwos*/ 'frontier/border'.[81] Since the force of /*-phi*/ in Mycenaean in association with TNs is locative rather than ablatival,[82] the reference should be to wool *at* this place rather than from it. Hence, the tablet is more likely to deal with on-site production than with a delivery. Thompson observes that the document is similar to the KN Lc(1) stint records.[83] The evidence for taking the La tablets as textile production records is hardly conclusive, but it is the most likely explanation.

The data for all extant attestations of LANA are summarised in Table 6-16.[84]

Table 6-16. Wool at Pylos

	LANA	= M
1. *Banqueting/offerings*		
Un 6	5	15
Un 853	2 M 2[	8+
TOTAL 1		**23+**
2. o-no *payments*		
An 35	2	6
Un 443.1	10	30
TOTAL 2		**36**
TOTAL 1+2		**59+**
3. *Perfumery*		
3a. to a Potnian perfumer		
Un 249	2	**6**
3b. to 'ordinary' perfumers		

[79] The Aa, Ab and Ad series work as a unit (see Chadwick 1988 and Section 5.2.3 above).
[80] *DMic*. II, 92–3, *s.v. pa-wo-ke*.
[81] *DMic*. I, 458, *s.v. mo-ro-ko-wo-wo-pi*; II, 450, *s.v. wo-wo*.
[82] Thomson 1997, 84; 1998.
[83] Thomson 1997, 59.
[84] La 994 also records wool, but only the ideogram is preserved so the purpose of the record is unclear, and the tablet may belong to an earlier period than the others (see Section 1.4) so is excluded from the table.

Un 267	2	6
Un 592	6	18
Un 616	5	15
Sub-total 3b		**39**
TOTAL 3		**45**
TOTAL 1+3a		**29+**
TOTAL 1+2+3		**104+**
4. *Textile production*		
La 632	*lost*	1+
La 635	*lost*	1+
TOTAL 4		**2+**
5. *Unclear*		
Un 443.2	3	9
Un 443.3	5	15
TOTAL 5		**24**

Categories 1 and 2 concern 'non-industrial final disbursements', of which those for religious purposes account for 39%. It is not clear whether lines .2 and .3 of Un 443 given here as 'Unclear' relate to religion or not (they may well; see Section 5.2.3); if included with religious disbursements, the figure would be 57%. Categories 3 and 4 concern industrial disbursements, but there is a difference in that wool issued for the perfume industry would be consumed in manufacture, so should be counted as for 'final use', whereas wool issued in the textile industry would return to the palace in the form of finished textiles. As 'final use', category 3 can be taken together with categories 1 and 2. One of the disbursements is to an unguent-boiler described as '*Potnian*', so should therefore also be considered as 'relating to religion'. We thus have M 29+ 'related to religion' and M 104 overall, of which the first figure is 28%. Either with or without Category 3, disbursements for 'religious' purposes constitute significant proportions of all disbursements – 39% in the one case, 28% in the other – although the situation is not as extreme as at Knossos.

Turning to overall resources, we cannot call upon the sort of evidence used for Knossos since records of flock production targets and disbursements for the textile industry are missing, yet it is known that there was a similar industry at Pylos.[85] Remnants of related documentation survive in the fragmentary La tablets recording stints for cloth production by female workgroups. Only the two La tablets which actually preserve the ideogram LANA are listed in the table, but probably most (or all) of the others originally had this as well. It is worth mentioning that the cloth TELA+*TE* on La 1393 was almost certainly produced under the *ta-ra-si-ja* system (see *ta-ra-*[*si-ja* in line .1), an indication that the palace would have supplied the wool for making it.[86] The forty units of cloth on that tablet would have required some LANA 280.[87] Given that some fragments do exist, it may be that chance preservation is a factor here.

Despite the difficulties, some data do exist from which overall resources might be estimated. First, the Cn tablets record some 10,218 sheep in wool-producing flocks (Section 6.2.2.2). Although production targets are not recorded, the order of magnitude of the output can be estimated. At Knossos, each sheep was expected to yield approximately 1.6 kg of wool annually,[88] on which basis 10,218 sheep might produce some 16,349 kg of wool. Since M 1 is thought to weigh about a kilogram, this is the same number of M units. The 23+ units connected with banqueting are 0.14% of this; taking the *Potnian* perfumer into account as well

[85] Killen 1984a; 1993.
[86] I am grateful to J.T. Killen for drawing my attention to this point; see Killen 2001a.
[87] I am also grateful to C.W. Shelmerdine for pointing out that since LANA is not actually preserved in connection with TELA+*TE* at Pylos, we cannot be entirely certain that it was made of wool there. But it always is at Knossos, so the assumption is not unreasonable, although proper caution should be maintained.
[88] Killen 1964, 9. About 1.6 kg was expected for wethers and less for breeding ewes. This difference is not taken into account here since it is the order of magnitude in which we are interested.

gives 0.2%. Either way, the amounts are negligible.

A second piece of information corroborates this assessment. Although few records of disbursements of raw materials to textile workgroups survive, rations records help indicate the scale of the workforce. At least 214 women who were probably working with wool receive rations, and it must be stressed that this is a minimum.[89] (This may seem a small workforce to deal with some 16,000 kg of wool, but the figures are more comparable than may at first appear. Knossos wool/cloth ratios for various textiles range from three to ten units of wool per textile.[90] Taking an average of 6.5 LANA units of wool to one textile, about LANA 5333 might result in some 820 pieces of cloth. On this count, each of the 214 women need only be responsible for about four pieces of cloth per year.[91])

In sum, disbursements of wool for religious purposes appear to have consumed a negligible percentage of overall palatial resources. That being so, the question again arises of why such disbursements represent such a large proportion of total disbursements recorded. We are of course dealing with a very few records here, but that is in a sense the point: documentation of the ultimate use of the wool is 'missing'. Hazards of preservation are unlikely to supply a full explanation because a general pattern of such bias is becoming evident. Religious matters seem to have been recorded in Linear B with a frequency disproportional to the amount of resources they actually consumed. We will return to this.

6.3.3.3 WOOL AT THEBES

Wool appears at Thebes in the Of series and the new Oh tablets, both having to do with industrial processing. There are only three Oh tablets, recording a total of LANA 6 M 1.[92] None of them has anything to do with religion and they are from a different deposit so are best left aside; we focus here on the Of series.

The Of series records issues to workers, workshops and workgroups, in three cases involving deities: Hera (Of 28.2), Hermes (Of 31.3) and *Potnia* (Of 36.2).[93] The series was discussed above in Section 2.5.2 (see also 2.5.5). As noted there, we are probably dealing here with issues to workgroups belonging to deities as 'Collectors', rather than issues of offerings. Either scenario might be possible, but the issues connected with deities appear in exact parallel with issues to 'ordinary' workers (see especially Of 28) and it is likely that all disbursements in the series were made for similar purposes.

Data for the entire series are summarised in Table 6-17.[94] As noted by Chadwick, the essential elements in each entry (apart from the wool, adjuncts and numbers) are the 'personal name or occupational description in the dative case' and 'indication of address'.[95] Some of these 'addresses' are TNs, while others are forms that specify ownership by various men, such as *ḳọ-*

---

[89] Women specifically described as 'flax-workers' were not counted. Figures are calculated on the basis of Chadwick 1988.

[90] Killen 1979b, 157 n 13.

[91] It should be noted that not all of the women were weaving. Some were, for instance, carders or spinners. But these women will have shortened the time spent on a single piece of cloth by the actual weavers. The figures here are very rough, and nothing more than general order of magnitude is claimed for them. It will be extremely interesting to see how the new work of the Danish Centre for Textile Research may contribute to the picture (see Nosch & Andersson 2003).

[92] *Thèbes* I, 304–5.

[93] As Chadwick (*TT* II, 91) remarks, these are the only three clearly identified divine names in the series. For speculations on other see *TT* II, 92–5, but note the discussion above (Section 2.5.5) with regard to **ma-ri-ne-u*.

[94] The data are drawn from *TITHEMY*, 35–7. The series was first published by Chadwick (*TT* II, 86–107). Shelmerdine (1997, esp. 387–90) has made an important reassessment of the function of the room in which the series was found as being a place from which wool was issued *to* workshops, rather than itself being a workshop (cf. Bendall 2003). See also Nosch 2001a.

[95] *TT* II, 87.

ḍẹ-wa-o , do-de 'to the house of …*was*'.[96] The table is arranged so as to reflect this structure, which sometimes results in a reversal of word order.

Table 6-17. Wool at Thebes: the Of series

Of	MN (unless otherwise indicated)	workgroup/ workshop	toponym	occupation	adjunct	LANA	*PA*
25.1		ma-ri-ne-we-ja-i	a$_3$-ki-a$_2$-ri-ja			4[	
25.2	pa-pa-ra-ki		a-ma-ru-to-de			6	
26.1	pu$_2$-re-wa				*ku*		1
26.1	ka-ka[ ]?				*ku*		1
26.2	su-me-ra-we-jọ				*ku*		1
26.2		kọ-ḍẹ-wa-o , do-de			*ku*		1
26.3		di-u-ja-wo , do-de			*ku*		1
26.3				po-re-si?*	*ku*	1	
27.1			[. .]-ri-ta-de?		*ku*	1	
27.2	du-qo-te-ja (WN)	a-ka-i-je-ja				2	
27.3	pu$_2$-ke-qi-ri-ne-ja (WN)	a-ka-i-je-ja				2	
28.1	pi-rọ-pe-se-wa				*ku*	2	
28.2	i-da-i-jo				*ku*		2
28.2	**e-ra** , ke-o-te-ja (THN + appelative?)				*ku*	1	
29.1	o-pe-to-[.]		ne-we-to?		*ku*	*lost*	
29.2	erased				*ku*	*lost*	
29.3	pe-to-no-qa?		te-ru-sa?		*ku*	*lost*	
30.1	ko-[.]-re-u		ṭụ-ri-[?			*lost*	
30.2	qe-ṭạ-ṣẹ-u		po-[?			*lost*	
31.1		do-]de			*ku*		*lost*
31.2		]dọ-de			*ku*		*lost*
31.3	**e-ma-a$_2$** , re-[(THN)					*lost*	
32	erased (see note)						
33.1	ku-ru-me-no				*ku*		1
33.1		ọ-*34-ta-o , do-de			*ku*		1
33.2	di-u-ja-wo		qi-wo?		*ku*		2
34.1	ko-tu-ro$_2$ *DA*			a-pi-qo-ro , ne-wa		3	⟦1⟧
34.2	[ko-tu-ro$_2$ *DA* understood?]			a-ra-ka-te-ja , pa-ra-ja		1	
35.1		ko-ma-we-te-ja		te-pe-ja	*ku*	1	
35.2		ma-ri-ne-we-ja-i	a-ki-a$_2$-ri-ja-de		*ku*	3	
36.1				no-ri-wo-ki-de	*ku*	1	
36.1	wa-na-ka[			a-ke-ti-ra$_2$		*lost*	
36.2		**po-ti-ni-ja** , wo-ko-de		a-ke-ti-ra$_2$	*ku*	1	
37	a-re-i-ze-we-i	qa-ra$_2$-to-de			*ku*	10	
38.1	qa-ra$_2$-te				*ku*	10	
38.1	ḳạ[?		ra-mo-de?			*lost*	
38.2	ne-e-to?		u-de 'hither'?		*ku*	*lost*	
39.1	]vest.				*ku*	2	
39.2	vest. ṇẹ-a$_2$-ri-da , *DA*				*ku*	3[	1
40.1	]ḳẹ , *DA*				*ku*	6	
40.2	]vest.				*ku*	3	2
				TOTALS		**72+**	**17+**

Notes

General

? = Ascription of sign-group to assigned category not certain.

'*lost*' in the LANA column means everything after LANA is lost; thus, figures may have been lost in the *PA* column as well (although in most cases the entries seem to be exclusive of one another).

'*lost*' in the *PA* column means *PA* is attested but the number is lost.

Figures where '*lost*' appears are restored as '1'. The usual practice in the present study is to restore a smaller unit for lost figures, but since the lowest attested figure in the series is '1' it seems more reasonable to restore this than to complicate the table with fractional amounts. The overall totals are probably on the low side in any case.

Individual tablets

Of 26: **po-re-si* need not be an occupation. It has been suggested that it may be connected with *po-re-na* (PY Tn 316), so possibly has a religious connection.

Of 29: It may be that *te-ru-sa* is a MN (attested at KN) and *pe-to-no-qa* is a TN.

Of 32: Omitted from the table because the entire text is an erasure. (No complete words survive, only ']ṇọ' in line .2.)

A total of at least LANA 72+ and LANA *PA* 16+ (= 89+) is recorded in the series, of which one

[96] *TT* II, 88, 104.

unit is associated with each of Hera and *Potnia*, while the amount for Hermes is lost. Restoring '1' for Hermes on analogy with issues to the other deities would make religious disbursements some 3% of the whole. Restoring '10' on analogy with the highest figure in the series (Of 37, –38) (which seems a rather tenuous thing to do) would raise the figure to 12%.[97] An amount closer to the lower figure seems more likely.

Overall resources cannot be calculated from the surviving documentation. It was noted in our discussion of sheep (Section 6.2.2.3) that wool is attested (as we now see), but not the flocks that supplied it. The Of series indicates that Thebes, like Pylos and Knossos, was able to draw on resources of wool, but we do not at present have the documentation relating to the flocks.

6.3.3.4 WOOL AT MYCENAE AND TIRYNS

Wool appears at Mycenae in the Oe series and possibly X 508. Nothing in the Oe series obviously relates to religion,[98] but the presence of two *o-no* payments should be mentioned since this is a type of 'final use' disbursement in which we are interested. Oe 108 records LANA 4 connected with *o-no* (LANA 7 if the entry in the next line should also be understood under this rubric), and Oe 109 records the word but the ideogram and number are lost.

The text of MY X 508 is as follows.

MY X 508

.a] te-qa-de , *ta* [
]ze-ta , / pu-ka-ta-ri-ja⌊ ⌋ma-ri-ne[
Perhaps traces of ⟦ ⟧ (or palimpsest).
.a Traces at right, not incompatible with L̦Ạ̣Ṇ̣Ạ̣[(but *ta*-[remains theoretically possible).

X 508 records a shipment of *pu-ka-ta-ri-ja* cloth to Thebes (*te-qa-de* /*thēg*ʷ*ans-de*/).[99] LANA is not securely read (see apparatus to line .a), and in any case nothing connects the document with religion (since **ma-ri-ne-u* is not considered a deity in the present study; see Section 2.5.5). Mycenae thus differs from other cases we have seen in that religion does not here constitute a significant proportion of final use disbursements.

Finally, LANA is a *possible* reading on TI X 17, but the ideogram is more likely to be AUR (gold).[100] In any case, the wording is lost, along with any indication of the purpose of the document.

6.4 TEXTILES

6.4.1 **146*: A SIMPLE CLOTH

6.4.1.1 INTRODUCTION TO **146*

**146* appears only at Pylos and Knossos. It was some sort of simple cloth or robe, made not in the palatial workshops but in the districts and obtained by palaces through taxation.[101] The commodity appears in religious and banqueting contexts and was used in various sorts of

---

[97] Note this is 12 divided by 97 since 9 must be added to the overall total as previously calculated if we restore 10 for Hermes.
[98] See *MT* II, 110–11.
[99] Killen 1985, 269.
[100] *TITHYMY*, 31. Apparatus to line .2: ']M̦Ạ or]L̦ẠṆẠ difficult'.
[101] Chadwick 1964, 23–4; Lejeune 1956; 1964; 1979; Shelmerdine 1973; 1998–1999, esp. 327; Duhoux 1976b, esp. 116–20; Killen 1984a, 61–3; Nosch & Perna 2001.

transactions, particularly *o-no* 'payments'.[102]

6.4.1.2 ***146* AT PYLOS**

**146* appears in An 35 (Section 4.3.3), several Ua and Un tablets, and all Ma, Mb and Mn tablets except Mn 11. In some cases it is readily apparent whether the tablets concern receipts or disbursements. The Ma tablets record taxes; while An 35 and the Ua and Un tablets record disbursements, some for religious purposes, some as *o-no* payments. The Mb and Mn tablets are more problematic, but their functions have now been elucidated in a comprehensive study by Shelmerdine.[103] It is clear that they are somehow related to the Ma series, a well-known set of records dealing with tax payments from the districts into which the Pylian polity was divided for administrative purposes.[104] Six commodities appear in the series, all unidentified, except **146* and **152*, the latter probably oxhide.[105] With the exception of Mn 11,[106] which records a variety of the Ma tablet commodities but not **146*, the Mb and Mn tablets record only **146*. What function (or functions) did these tablets have in relation to the Ma series?

The Ma tablets were found in the Archives Complex, but the Mb tablets and all but three of the Mn tablets were found in the SW Area and were associated with a large number of sealings. It is likely that the SW Area, along with the Wine Magazine and the Northeastern Building, was an administrative 'entry area' for goods coming to the palace citadel.[107] Mycenaean sealings concern receipts of goods and it is probable that many of the tablets found along with them were associated in function. It may be that the Ma tablets represent a higher level of redaction, assessments, whereas the Mb and Mn tablets are records of individual receipts.[108] There is a difficulty, however, with taking *all* of the Mb and Mn tablets as receipts. Mn 1411, for instance, may be an offering record.[109] The text is as follows.

Mn 1411			(H14)
	supra mutila		
.1	*vest.*[		
.2	e-re-de , wa̩[	**146*	
.3	ma-se-de , ro-u-si[	**146*	
.4	*infra mutila*		

The evidence for taking this as an offering record is circumstantial, but there is sufficient reason to doubt that the document was a tax receipt. First, it is likely that the incomplete sign-group *ro-u-si-*[in line .2 should be restored as *ro-u-si-jo a-ko-ro*, which appears exclusively in banqueting and offerings records.[110] Second, the first word in line .2 *e-re-de* is a sign-group which appears elsewhere at Pylos only in an offering record, Fr 1228:

Fr 1228	(S1202-H2)
wa-na-so-i , e-re-de O̩L̩E̩+*PA* V 1	

e-re-de is often taken as a toponym with allative, but Shelmerdine argues convincingly that it

[102] Killen 1984a, 62; Shelmerdine 1998–1999, 332.
[103] Shelmerdine 1998–1999. I grateful for an early copy received with the kind permission of the author when writing the original version of this section.
[104] Shelmerdine 1973.
[105] But see Killen forthcoming(b) for new light on the identification of the Ma ideograms.
[106] This is to be reclassified Mm in *PoN* IV (see Shelmerdine 1998–1999, 337).
[107] Shelmerdine 1998–1999, 335–6; cf. Bendall 2003, 202–3 with further references.
[108] Shelmerdine 1998–1999, 331–2.
[109] As argued by Shelmerdine 1998–1999, 324–5, 334. The tablet is also now discussed by Perna 2004, 113–16.
[110] As suggested by Shelmerdine 1998–1999, 325. The only other sign-group at Pylos beginning with these three syllabograms is *ro-u-si-je-wi-ja*, a less likely restoration here. J.T. Killen kindly reminds me that caution is necessary because this could also the beginning of an ethnic adjective.

should rather be seen as a personal name, as is also the case for *ma-se-de*.[111] (Note too that *ma-se-de* appears elsewhere at Pylos only on Cc 1285, a tablet which *may*, in view of the small numbers of animals recorded, relate to banqueting.) There is no compelling reason that *e-re-de* might not be a recipient in the Fr record and a contributor in the Mn record, but the balance of likelihood is that he is a recipient in both cases. Shelmerdine, supporting the case for Mn 1411 being an offering record, further notes that *ẉạ*[in line .2 might be restored as *wa-na-so-i*, giving a tablet with 'recipient' and 'address' parallel to Fr 1228.

The function of Mn 1411 may have implications for two further tablets:

Mn 1367 (H14)

.1] **146* 26

.1 26 more probable than 25; possibly 20 corrected from 30, and 6 over erasure.

Mn 1368 (H14)

.1 ki-[ ]-to , ka[**146*
.2 ke-sa-da-ra , e-[**146*
.3 ke-sa-da-ra i-no[**146*

.2 Possibly *e-u*[.

These two fragments may, with Mn 1411, all belong to the same tablet.[112] If so, and if Mn 1411 has a religious connection, the woman *ke-sa-da-ra* may also have a religious connection, perhaps as a cult official of some sort. She was seen in two tablets previously (Section 5.2.3) receiving very large amounts of rations (monthly rations for twenty-five people), which would be consistent with such an interpretation. Persons who receive larger rations are often of elevated status or receiving on behalf of larger groups (although the possibility that she was for example an 'ordinary' workshop supervisor cannot be ruled out). The question hangs on the interpretation of Mn 1411 and on whether the fragments really belong to the same tablet. There are too many unknowns to be certain, but the possibility of a connection with religion must be at least kept open. Amounts on these two fragments are considered 'Unclear' here, but they should perhaps be added to the figure on Mn 1411.

Another tablet which is unlikely to be a tax record is Mb 1366, which registers two units of **146* against the sign-group *di-wi-jo*. This word appears elsewhere only in Tn 316 *v*.8 and the Fr series (with the allative *-de*) as a location where offerings are sent: /*Diwion-de*/ 'to the shrine of Zeus'. The possibility that this is a man's name here rather than the shrine cannot be excluded (men's names are recorded elsewhere in the Mb series), but, as Shelmerdine argues, it is more likely that this tablet too records an offering.[113]

Mb 1365 may also record a disbursement, though not for religious purposes. The text as now restored by Melena is as follows.[114]

Mb 1365 (H14)

]ke-do-jo-no[ ]i-jo **146* 4 [

As Melena and Shelmerdine both note, the wording is plausibly interpreted as the 'son of *ke-do-jo*', a man also known from Ua 158, which likewise records **146*.[115] The text is as follows.

[111] For *e-re-de* and *ma-se-de* as recipients rather than toponyms with allative see Shelmerdine 1985, 71–8, esp. 75–6; 1998–1999, 325.
[112] *PTT* I, 200; Shelmerdine 1998–1999, 315.
[113] Shelmerdine 1998–1999, 323.
[114] Melena 2000–2001b, 378. It joins Mb 1386 (ex-Xa), recognised as an Mb tablet by Bennett (1992, 127).
[115] Shelmerdine 1998–1999, 335 also connects these and supplies the reading given here (see also Melena 1992–1993b, 310).

Ua 158 (Cii)

.1	ke-do-jo , o-na , e-qa-na-q̣ẹ[	
.2	*146 20 GRA 7 *NI* 5̣ ⟦ ⟧ [	
.3	*vacat* [	

Palimpsest.
.2 *NI* 5̣ : *NI* 7̣ possible.

This tablet almost certainly records a disbursement, rather than a receipt. *o-na* is probably the plural of *o-no*, indicating a type of special payment made by the palace, probably in this as in other cases we have seen for special goods or services rendered. (*ke-do-jo* is presumably here a nominative of rubric; cf. the form of the genitive in the Mb tablet.) *o-no* payments account for the major use of **146* attested at Pylos apart from offerings. Ua 158 compares with Un 1322, the text of which is as follows.[116]

Un 1322 (Cii)

.1	] GRA [*qs*
.2	]ṇọ-[ ]ọ-no[ ] GRA 6 *ṆỊ* [*qs*
.3	de-ku-tu-wo-ḳọ[ ]o-no GRA 2 *NI* 2
.4	ị-ṭẹ-ẉẹ , o-ṇọ[ ] GRA 12
.5	we-a_2-no[ri]-no , re-po-to *1̣4̣6̣ GRA 5
.6	we-[ ]no[ ]*1̣4̣6̣ G̣ṚẠ 15̣
.7	*vestigia*

The terms *o-no* (or *o-na*) and the types of commodities – GRA, *NI* and **146* – allocated on Ua 158 are exactly paralleled in Un 1322,[117] suggesting the possibility that these tablets may be dealing with similar situations, that is *o-no* payments to craftworkers (cf. */dektu-worgōi/* 'to the net-maker' in line .3 and probably */histēwei/* 'to the weaver' in line .4). *ke-do-jo* may be some sort of merchant or craftsman to whom the palace is making payments for some reason. Now, it is not necessary that the *ke-do-jo* of Ua 158 is the same man who appears on Mb 1365, but this is likely for two reasons (of varying persuasiveness). First, the name is uncommon at Pylos: these are the only two attestations. Second, the identification of one man as the son of the other suggests that the father is someone known to the palace officials and identifiable by his name alone. But if the father receives **146* on Ua 158, why should the son contribute it on Mb 1365? A preferable explanation is that both father and son were receiving goods from the palace. (There may be an implication that the son is receiving on *account* of his father, since he is not independently named. This need not mean 'on behalf of' the father, but by right of a transaction in which the father was the principal actor. The arrangement may have been along the lines that the father would receive so much, with another further amount allocated for his son.)

We should finally note that ideogram **160* may be a variant of **146*.[118] It appears in two documents, La 628 and La 640, both of which are 'Unclear'. The amounts involved are 10+ and 13 respectively. Since these documents are in any case unclear no further account is taken of them here.

Amounts of **146* at Pylos are shown in Tables 6-18 and 6-19. Table 6-19 gives the amounts recorded in the Ma taxation tablets; Table 6-18 lists all other occurrences of **146*.[119] It should be noted that some Mb and Mn tablets are probably breakdowns of Ma records, as Killen

[116] Un 1322: For the source of the text as given here see Chapter 5 n 64.
[117] Some scholars take Un 1322 as evidence of an exchange of **146* for wheat and figs, e.g. de Fidio 1982, 134–5; and Shelmerdine 1998–1999, 332 n 81, citing Killen 1984a, 62. I understand Killen merely to be commenting that Un 1322 is a record of 'payments or allocations involving the term *o-no*' (*loc. cit.* with n 30). On Un 1322 see also Chadwick 1964; Melena 1975a; Killen 1988; Bendall 2003, 211.
[118] Duhoux 1976b, 116–18.
[119] See Shelmerdine 1998–1999, esp. 326. Note that some of the tablet numbers have changed from those appearing in *PTT* due to new joins; Shelmerdine (1998–1999, 311, 337) provides convenient lists. The figures here are taken from *PTT* I.

argues for Mn 162 and Mn 456.[120] To avoid the risk of counting them twice, we use only figures from the Ma tablets for 'overall resources';[121] the other documents are listed in Table 6-18, but not counted. Shelmerdine's identifications are on the whole followed here. [122]

Table 6-18. **146* at Pylos (except the Ma series)

	***146**
1. ***Religious disbursements***	
(1a) Offerings	
Mb 1366	2
Mn 1411 [+ 1367 and 1368?]	2+ [add 29+?]
Ua 1413	7
(1b) Banqueting	
Un 2	2
Un 6	37
Un 853	18
TOTAL 1	**68+ [97+?]**
2. *o-no payments*	
An 35	3
Ua 158	20
Un 443.1	10
Un 1322	2?
TOTAL 2	**35**
3. *Other disbursements*	
Mb 1365	4+
Mb 1376 [+] 1395	5
Mb 1378	1+
Mb 1380	1+
Mb 1381	1+
Mb 1397	1+
Mb 1402	5
Mb 1433	1+
Mb 1434	1+
TOTAL 3	**20+**
TOTAL 2+3	**55+**
TOTAL 1+2+3	**123+ [152+?]**

4. *Definite/probable tax records*	**5. *Unclear***
Mn 162	Mb 1336
Mn 456	Mb 1364
Mb 1363	Mn 1369
Mn 1370	Mb 1399+1403
Mn 1371	Mb 1400
Mb 1377	Mb 1402
Mb 1379	Mb 1404
Mb 1387	Mn 1407
Mb 1396	Mb 1429
Mb 1398	Mb 1430
Mb 1401	Mb 1431
Mn 1408	Mb 1436
Mn 1409	
Mn 1410	
Mn 1412	
Mb 1432	
Mb 1435	

Notes

Mb 1399: Unclear. Joins 1403 (Shelmerdine 1998–1999, 311, 337).

Mb 1402: Word possibly to be restored *wa-na-]ka-te*, so would be a 'personal name entry' (Shelmerdine 1998–1999, 317, 326), but considered here 'Unclear'.

In total, some 123+ units of **146* are disbursed in the preserved records, some 55% of them for religious purposes, or 64% taking the higher figure noted in 1a. Either way, religious disbursements account for over half of all disbursements of this cloth recorded at Pylos.

[120] Killen 1996a, 147.

[121] Noting that it is not necessary that all the Mb and Mn records were subsumed under the Ma series; but for the sake of the current argument it is more 'conservative' to avoid over-stating overall resources. If the figure is an underestimate, the central argument that disbursements of offerings represented only a small portion of overall resources is only strengthened.

[122] Shelmerdine (1998–1999) considers the following tablets as disbursements connected with banqueting or religion: Un 2, Un 6, Un 853 (all p. 332 n 81), and probably Mn 1411 (p. 334). Mb 1366 is seen as 'an inventory of cloth at its location of ritual use, like Ua 1413' (pp. 333–4). Despite the lack of an allative, I see no reason not to take both also as disbursement records (a more commonly attested type of document than 'inventories'); on Ua 1413 see also Palaima 1996–1997; 307–8; Nosch & Perna 2001, 473. Shelmerdine (pp. 334–5) also notes that the MNs on Mb 1433 and –1401 appear on other tablets applied to men described as '*Potnian*', but these need not be the same individuals. She further notes two tablets, Ob 1372 and –1373, recording **166+WE*, suggesting (p. 328) that **146* may be the lost ideogram on –1372. Note that amounts on Un 6 and –853 may relate to the *same* items (Killen 1999b, 350–3, esp. 352).

To compare disbursements with overall resources we need to look at the Ma series, summarised in Table 6-19. A word about the Ma tablet structure is needed.[123] Each tablet gives an assessment, sometimes followed by amounts owing or to be exempted (or both). Exemptions would not be expected to come in for that year, so are here subtracted from the total. Of the remaining figures, our present concern is with amounts so far received and amounts expected. Amounts actually received are shown in the final column, with a total at the bottom. The amount expected is obtained by adding this total to the amounts still owing (see below).

Table 6-19. **146* in the Ma series

tablet	town	assessed	owing	exempted	total actually received
Ma 90	me-ta-pa	28		4	24
Ma 120	pe-to-no	63		2	61
Ma 123	ti-mi-to-a-ke-e	24	2	1	21
Ma 124	a-pu_2-we	23		1	22
Ma 126	si-re-wa	—	3		
Ma 193	ri-jo	17	2	5	10
Ma 216	ra-wa-ra-ta_2	70	*lost*		69
Ma 221	pa-ki-ja-pi	22		1	21
Ma 222	a-ke-re-wa	23	13		10
Ma 225	pi-**82*	28		1	27
Ma 330	e-sa-re-wi-ja	42			42
Ma 333	e-ra-te-re-we	46			46
Ma 335	a-te-re-wi-ja	23			23
Ma 346	ka-ra-do-ro	18	4		14
Ma 365	ro-u-so	17		1	16
Ma 378	sa-ma-ra	24	1	3	20
Ma 393	]ẓạ-ma-e-wi-ja	28		8	20
Ma 397	a-[.]-ja	24		2	22
	TOTALS	**520**	**26+**	**29**	**468**

Notes
Ma 126: *si-re-wa* probably belongs to the district of *ro-u-so*; cf. Mn 456.
Ma 216: '69' has been restored as the amount received. This may be excessive.

468 units of **146* had actually been received by the palace at the time the Ma tablets were written, with at least another twenty-six expected, amounting to 494 units. Religious disbursements are 15% of the first figure, and 14% of the second; if the higher figure from (1a) is taken, the percentages are 21% and 20%.

However calculated, the proportion is fairly high, and it is possible that, since we (apparently) have complete records for the whole year, the figure is realistic. If so, it may be that a substantial portion, roughly a tenth to a fifth, of the cloth **146* really was earmarked for religious purposes (although it is worth noting that some four-fifths of it was not so designated). And it is important to note that figures for all disbursements are too low (25%) to account for the large amounts coming into the palace; the use of the majority of this commodity remains obscure.[124]

[123] See Shelmerdine 1973; Killen 1984b.
[124] See Killen forthcoming(b) for the suggestion that the clothing was for military use; also note Killen 1984a, 62. This explanation is accepted here as likely; but the point is that we do not have the disbursement records relating to this (unless some of the Mb disbursements are records of such issues; note an issue to a shipwright on one).

6.4.1.3 *146 AT KNOSSOS

**146* at Knossos appears mainly in the context of disbursements for offerings; there are also a few disbursements for other (including industrial) purposes, plus a taxation record, some storage documents and a number of 'Unclear' tablets. Most of the documents require little discussion, but it is useful to set out the texts here, with commentary where appropriate. We begin with the offerings records.

Definite and possible offerings records

M 719 (140)
.1 a-mi-ni-so ke-re-na , re-ne , [
.2 e-ne-si-da-o-ne , su-ja-to , **146* 1[

.1 *-na* over ⟦ ⟧ (which explains the wide spacing between *ke-re-* and *-na*). Sign at right possibly *pẹ*[, but this is very uncertain.
.2 **146* 1 over ⟦ ⟧ (perhaps ⟦*ME+RI*⟧ followed by VAS).

M 719 was encountered earlier, in the context of honey (Section 4.2.1.1), where it was noted that h. 140 and h. 103 were both involved in issuing offerings of honey and wool/textiles, possibly working together.

M 724 (—)
.1]me-no **146*
.2] *vac.*

M 724 may be an offerings record if *me-no* is the genitive of 'month' rather than the ending of another word. It is impossible to be certain, but for the present we include this with the offerings records.[125]

M 729 (—)
.1]ma-wo , **146* 1̣[
.2]po-ti-ni-ja[

.1 Trace before]*ma-wo*, possibly a divider.
.2 ⟦ ⟧ between *po-* and *-ti-*. Perhaps 1̣[after *po-ti-ni-ja*; further traces at end.

The mention of *Potnia* puts this document in the sphere of religion, whether an offering record or something else.[126]

M(1) 1645 ASHM (1938.711) (103)
.1 ka-]ra-e-ri-jo-jo , me-no
.2]-wi-jo-do *pe* **146* 1

M(1) 1645 was discussed in Section 2.2.2 where it was noted that it is likely to be an offering record since month names are never securely attested except in offerings records.[127]

An *o-no* disbursement

M(1) 559 (103)
.1 ']ke' o-no , o-na LANA 2
.2]da-wi-jo **146* 2̣

.2 Perhaps only 1.

This tablet was discussed above in Section 6.3.3.1. The appearance of *o-no* indicates a 'payment', although there is no guarantee the word was meant to apply to both lines.

---

[125] Nosch & Perna (2001, 476) agree. Text from *KT*[5].
[126] Nosch & Perna (2001, 475–6) agree. Text from *KT*[5].
[127] Nosch & Perna (2001, 476) agree. Text from *KT*[5].

An industrial disbursement

M 683 (103)

.1a] a-ze-ti-ri-ja
.1b]te-o o-nu-ke LANA 9 M 2
.2]ti-mu-nu-we *146 30

The mention of 'decorators' (*a-ze-ti-ri-ja*) indicates that M 683 records an industrial disbursement. Probably the wool in line .1b is being issued along with the thirty pieces of **146* in order for it to be decorated with 'fringe' (*o-nu-ke*).

A taxation record

The next document is shown together with a fragment which is probably from the same tablet.[128]

Nc 5100 + 8184 (133)

] M *'RI'* 8 *O* M 4

lat. inf.]2 *KE* M 10 **146* 6

Probably same tablet as Nc 8175.
O probably better than *o*. Five small stylus strokes, slightly oblique, after 4, and two others, almost horizontal, above them.

Nc 8175 (133)

e-si-[

lat. inf. o-pe[

Probably same tablet as Nc 5100.

The four ideograms recorded on Nc 5100 are all also found in the Pylos Ma series (*RI*, *KE*, *O*, **146*), suggesting, as Killen notes, a similar taxation system.[129] Syllabograms used as ideograms do not always denote the same commodities, but the conjunction of all four plus the fact that *KE* and *O* are measured by weight as they are in the Ma series suggests the same commodities are involved. As Killen has recently argued, the Ma tablets record requisitions probably for making military equipment;[130] the context of the Nc records may be similar.

Storage/delivery records

Wm 1714 (—)

.1 me-sa-ṭọ
.2]**146* 30

Wm 1816 (= 1714 b) (—)

.1 me-sa-to
.2 **1̣4̣6̣*[
inf. mut.

Wm 1817 (= 1714 c) ASHM (1941.180) (—)

sup. mut.
.1]*vest.*[
.2 **146* 30

Wm 5860 (—)

sup. mut.
.1 *vac.*[
.2 **146*[

[128] *Scribes Cnossos*, 81 considers this 'sans doute'.
[129] Killen 1984a, 62 n 31.
[130] Killen forthcoming(b).

Wm 8490 (—)
.1 *sup. mut.*
.2 **146*[

The Wm documents are labels which have traces of thick twine on their backs. Killen suggests they may have been attached to tied bales of cloth relating to the goods either in store or having been recently delivered.[131]

'Unclear' records

M 467 (—)
]2 **146* 2

Nothing can be said about the purpose of M 467.

M(1) 720 (103)
.a o-re-o-po TẸḶẠ^x[
.b ze-ne-si-wi-jo / **146* 1̣[

Shelmerdine and Weilhartner consider M(1) 720 an offering record on the basis of scribal hand (h. 103, our familiar honey and textiles scribe) and findspot, but nothing else need connect the tablet with religion (Shelmerdine rightly notes the context is ambiguous).[132] *ze-ne-si-wi-jo* is usually taken as a man's name, and *o-re-o-po* as an adjective referring to the cloth TELA,[133] although since both words are *hapax* certainty is impossible. With regard to findspot, as was noted previously, not all tablets from the Gallery of Jewel Fresco (as this one is) are necessarily associated with religion.[134] Further, h. 103 is responsible for other issues of **146* from the same area: the *o-no* and delivery records above come from F10 and F18 respectively. While these records are certainly too far away to have been filed with M(1) 720, they are both located near the area from which the Gallery of Jewel Fresco tablets come, that is the upper floor at the top of the staircase ascending from the Central Court. Since h. 103 was evidently carrying out various tasks in this area, hand and findspot are insufficient to argue for a connection with religion. It is not clear even whether the tablet refers to a collection or an issue. It could be a disbursement of any sort, including industrial, or could be a taxation record (see below).

M 757 (—)
] **146*^{2} 250[

lat. inf.] **1̣8̣1̣* 10 [
l.i. Just possibly 1̣10 rather than **1̣8̣1̣* 10, but this is highly unlikely.

The very large number on this tablet suggests it is a totalling record. Presumably it would either record recent deliveries or items in store, but the context being lost we cannot know. **181* is a circular object, possibly a belt.

L 868 [+] 5712 (—)
.a] *vacat* [ ]1̣5 [
.b] , sa-de-so , TELA^2+*PU*[ ]ẉọ **146*^{2}[
lat. inf.] *vacat* [ ]1̣1 [

---

[131] Killen 1992b, 374; 2002–2003, 101–6. Three have a different purpose: Wm 1707, –8493, –8494.

[132] Shelmerdine 1988, 348–9; Weilhartner 2005, 60. Nosch & Perna (2001) do not discuss this tablet in their account of 'cloth in the cult' so presumably do not see it as related to religion.

[133] *DMic.* II, *s.v.v. ze-ne-si-wi-jo* and *o-re-o-po*. Weilhartner (2005, 60) takes the first as a possible theonym, but there is no contextual support (as he rightly notes).

[134] *Scribes Cnossos*, 50. For the GJF not containing exclusively offerings tablets see Chapter 4 n 4.

Like M(1) 720 this tablet records both **146* and another type of cloth. Again, it is not clear whether collections or disbursements are involved.

M 7373 (—)

] *146+PE* [

↓

v.]5̣0[

r. Trace, possibly of unit, at left.

M 7373 is fragmentary and its purpose is 'Unclear'.

M 7394 + 8684 + *frr.* (3) (—)

.1]-ja TELA^2 1 [

.2]ṛẹ-ja-i **146* 3[

.1 Traces of two signs at left. Trace at right. Possibly traces of ⟦ ⟧ on *verso*.

M 7394 is also sometimes speculated on as an offerings record.[135] The word in line .2 may be the ending of a feminine plural, and proposed restorations include words both with and without cult connections (without: *ko-u-r-e-ja*, *e-ne-re-ja*;[136] with: *i-je-re-ja*[137]). The tablet is here considered 'Unclear'.

M 8170 (—)

.1] **146*^{2} 24̣[

.2]-na M 58 [

.3] *vac.* [

Probably same tablet as X 8171.

.1 Trace at left.

X 8171 (—)

.1]2̣0̣5

.2] *vest.* [

inf. mut.

Probably same tablet as M 8170.

.1]Ṃ 5 perhaps less convincing.

M 8170 and X 8171 are probably parts of the same tablet. They are of course 'Unclear'.

Summary and discussion

Table 6-20 summarises the data for **146* at Knossos.

[135] Nosch & Perna 2001, 476; Weilhartner 2005, 62; all rightly leaving the question open. M 7394 text from Godart *et al.* 1990–1991, 382.

[136] Godart *et al.* 1990–1991, 382.

[137] Nosch & Perna 2001, 476.

Table 6-20. **146* at Knossos

tablet	ideogram and number	counted as	other commodity present on tablet
1. *Offerings*			
M 719	**146* 1[	1+	
M 724	**146*	1	
M 729	**146* 1[	1+	
M(1) 1645	*pe* **146* 1	1	
TOTAL 1		**4+**	
2. o-no *disbursement*			
M(1) 559	**146* 2	**2**	LANA 2
TOTAL 1+2		6+	
3. Industrial disbursement			
M 683	**146* 30	**30**	LANA 9 M 2
4. *Tax receipt*			
Nc 5100	**146* 6	**6**	*KE, O, RI*
5. Store records			
Wm 1714	**146* 30	30	
Wm 1816	**146*[	30	
Wm 1817	**146* 30	30	
Wm 5860	**146*[	30	
Wm 8490	**146*[	30	
TOTAL 5		**150**	
6. *Unclear*			
M 467	**146* 2	2	
M(1) 720	**146* 1[	1+	TELA[
M 757	*146^2 250[	250+	**181* 10
L 868	*146^2 [	*lost*	TELA+*PU* 15
M 7373	**146+PE* [	*lost*	
M 7394	**146* 3[	3+	TELA
M 8170	*146^2 24[	24+	? M 58

Notes
M 724: No number is recorded, indicating '1'.
Wm: We restore 30 here rather than '1' on analogy with –1714 and –1817.

The offerings and *o-no* disbursements count as 'final use' (six units), of which two-thirds are offerings. A substantially larger disbursement (thirty units) is made for industrial purposes, but it is unknown what would eventually be done with the 'decorated' textiles. In terms of overall resources, the only clear 'incoming' record is Nc 5100, which records a mere six units. However, the documentation is obviously skewed. Nc 5100 is one of fifty-six Nc tablets, most of which are very fragmentary. Some of them may be parts of the same tablet (as with 5100 and 8175) but, even so, the large number of tablets suggests we are missing significant amounts of data.

The Wm store records likewise suggest substantial resources. We have in the table restored '30' rather than '1', as would normally have been done in cases where the number is lost, on analogy with the two documents where the number is preserved. This may be justified because, if it is correct that the labels were attached to bags of textiles, it is more likely than not that these bags contained more than one textile each, and it is not unlikely that all held the same number (note the industrial disbursement in M 683 is also of thirty units; it could be that the items were normally stored and distributed for processing in such amounts). We may consider the figures both with and without the restored amounts. The total issued for offerings is 6% of the lower figure and 3% of the larger one, thus fairly small.

Another source of information is M 757, which records 250+ units, more than the preserved figures in all the other documents put together. The number of units issued of offerings is a scant 2% of this figure. We cannot of course know what would have been done with the items recorded in the store records and on M 757, but it is at least clear that more of the commodity was available than is indicated by the disbursement records. It is worth noting that not only do offerings not represent a significant amount of 'overall resources' – all the disbursements taken together amount to only 2.4% of what is recorded on M 757 alone. To an extent, this figure is meaningful whatever the function of M 757. Whether it records a receipt, a disbursement or an inventory, the cloth in the record was in some way being dealt with by the palace, and thus at some point constituted an 'available resource'. We simply do not know what was being done with the majority of such resources (note there are no disbursements in banqueting contexts, unlike Pylos). This type of circumstance also highlights the impact of differential preservation on the calculations. A single broken tablet can significantly alter the Linear B account.

6.4.2 A GARMENT (**166/*166+WE*)

6.4.2.1 INTRODUCTION TO **166/*166+WE*

**166* resembles an oxhide-shaped ingot, which misled many scholars, but it represents a textile.[138] It is usually surcharged with *WE*, probably indicating *we-a$_2$-no /wehanos/* 'robe'.

6.4.2.2 **166/*166+WE* AT KNOSSOS

**166* was issued at Knossos in connection with chariots (BIG) in tablets from the RCT, and as an offering to the 'Lady of the Labyrinth'.[139] Table 6-21 summarises the data.

Table 6-21. **166/*166+WE* at Knossos

	ideogram	number	other commodities	notes
1. *Offering*	***non-RCT***			
Oa 745	*ri *166+WE*	2̣2̣[		
2. *Military*	**RCT**			
Sc 225	**166*	1	]BIG 1 EQU *MO* [	**166* on *verso*
Sc 5141	**166*	*lost*	]BIG 1 EQU [	**166* on *verso*
3. *Unclear*	***non-RCT***			
Oa 1808	**166+WE*	1		
Oa 878	**166+WE*	18	e-to-ro-qa-ta 16	

As with **146*, the data are clearly imperfect. In the RCT we have issues only for military purposes; in non-RCT contexts we have only one disbursement, involving an unusually large amount of textiles going as offerings. There is nothing to compare the figure with. There are no production records for this commodity, or any way in which overall resources might be calculated. The preserved documentation supplies an incomplete account of **166* at Knossos. It may be noted, however, that the palace had access to large numbers of textiles – for instance, Lc(1) 536 records 534 units of finished textiles (albeit not **166*) produced under the *ta-ra-si-ja* system,[140] and the 30–50 tons of wool annually gained from palace sheep was probably mostly aimed at the textile industry (as Olivier's correlation of the figures shows; see Section 6.2.2.1).

[138] Duhoux 1976b, 122–32; Olivier & Vandenabeele 1979, 152–3; Robkin 1981, 213; Shelmerdine 1998–1999, 328.

[139] Recently see Nosch & Perna 2001, 472; Weilhartner 2005, 66–7. Weilhartner (*loc. cit.*) also takes Oa 1808 as a possible offering record on the grounds of its possibly coming from G1. As discussed above, this criterion is not accepted in the present study. No text apart from the ideogram and number appear on the document.

[140] A figure which, as Olivier (1967b, 91–2) calculated, would require some 2529 units of wool; see also Nosch 2000b.

6.4.2.3 **166/*166+WE* AT PYLOS

The situation at Pylos is somewhat better, though not much. It is at least clear that **166* was produced in palace-run workshops, which could only be guessed at for Knossos. The data are summarised in Table 6-22.

Table 6-22. **166/*166+WE* at Pylos

	ideogram	no.	other commodities
1. *Religious*			
Ua 1413	**166+WE*	1 [	**146* (see Section 6.4.1.2)
Un 6.6	**166+WE*	*lost*	**146* (see Section 6.4.1.2)
2. *Industrial*			
La 626	**166*	2	]*KU* 1 *O* 1
La 640	**166*	62	**160* 13
3. Unclear			
Ob 1372	**166+WE*	1	something lost]2̣
Ob 1373	**166+WE*	10	

Again, 100% of the disbursements are for religious purposes, but again the data are manifestly incomplete. Here however, unlike Knossos, we do have at least a hint of larger resources. Although the wording is lost, La 640 can be identified as a production record since it appears in a group of tablets from Rm 6 which relate to the textile industry (Section 6.4.1.1). It may be a totalling record, so the figures from La 626 should not necessarily be added to it. In any case, the 2+ units issued as offerings amount to a scant 3% of the amount on La 640 alone. Again we do not know what the items recorded on La 640 would eventually be used for, but it is clear that the palace had access to more resources than are reflected in the offerings records.

We should note that the two Ob records, classed here as 'Unclear', are suggested by Shelmerdine as possible offerings records on the grounds that the department which generated the Ob records often dealt with offerings (although it also dealt with receipts and inventories).[141] If they are offerings records, religious disbursements would be 21% of the figure on La 640. However, no text apart from ideogram and number is preserved on these documents and we should withhold judgement as to their function.

6.4.3 *te-pa* CLOTH (TELA+*TE*)

TELA+*TE* represents the cloth known as *te-pa*.[142] It required unusually large allotments of wool to make, so must have been very large or thick.[143] *te-pa* is common at Knossos, but there are no examples of issues for religious purposes there. At Pylos, Un 6 records a number of units of TELA+*TE* issued to or contributed by a priestess and a 'Key-bearer' on the occasion of a banquet. The only other tablets on which TELA+*TE* appears are La 624 and –1393, production stint records recording forty units. The figures for Un 6 are lost, so no comparisons can be made.

6.4.4 MORE CLOTH (TELA and TELA+*PA*)

TELA and TELA+*PA* appear on PY Un 853, a land tenure record which involved obligations to contributing typical banqueting foodstuffs (Section 2.4.4). TELA without ligature appears nowhere else in the Pylos documents. TELA+*PA* appears also in stint records: La 623 (34

[141] Shelmerdine 1998–1999, 334.
[142] Killen 1966, 109; 1984a, 59.
[143] Killen 1979b, 157 with n 13.

units),[144] La 626 (1+ unit) and La 630 (1+ units), for a total of 36+ units. Un 853 thus records 100% of preserved disbursements and 3% of 'overall resources'.

It may be noted that the term *qe-te-jo*, which often appears in religious contexts, appears on a number of cloth tablets from Knossos, but it is not clear whether the term is related to religion in these instances.[145] Also note that the textile **164* appears in an offerings context only if *wo-ke* on L 698 must refer to a deity workshop (*contra* this view see Section 2.5.5).[146]

6.5 METALS

6.5.1 GOLD (**141* = AUR)

6.5.1.1 GOLD AT PYLOS

Gold appears at Pylos in various contexts. A few items in the Ta tablets, which record banqueting paraphernalia (Section 2.3.4), are made of gold; it is mentioned as inlay for two chairs (Ta 707, Ta 714), and chains for binding sacrificial victims (Ta 716).

Another instance of paraphernalia probably connected with banqueting is Tn 996, the text of which is as follows.[147]

Tn 996

.1	] , a-te-re-e-te-jo , re-wo-te-re-jo ALV 2[ ]*vacat*
.2	u-do-ro **212*^{VAS} 3 pi-a_2-ra **219*^{VAS} 3
.3	a-po-]ṛẹ-we **209*^{VAS} 2 ka-ti **206*^{VAS} 1 a-te-we AES **205*^{VAS} 7 ẠỤṚ[
.4	] **250*^{VAS} 3 po-ka-ta-ma , AUR **208*$_a^{VAS}$ 1 AES **208*$_b^{VAS}$ 3 [

Ten bronze vessels are recorded, plus at least two of gold. **208* (line .4) is a bowl with a small pedestal. The vessel ideogram in line .3 is not preserved, but the structure of the tablet makes it likely that the vases involved were *a-te-we* (**205*), tall jugs.[148] (So we would have seven bronze vessels listed, then a number of gold ones of the same type – cf. line .4.) Tn 996 comes from Rm 20,[149] a pantry serving feasting activities in Court 63.[150] It is normally interpreted as an 'inventory' but, rather than recording vessels in store, may concern an actual disbursement from the storeroom for banqueting or related activities on a specific occasion. The purpose of the record would be to ensure the items were returned.[151]

Golden vessels are also mentioned in the well-known offering tablet Tn 316, which lists thirteen vessels modified by the ideogram AUR issued to various deities (Section 2.2.3). Three

---

144 La 623 is now joined to La 625; see Melena 2000–2001a, 366–8.
145 See Hutton 1990–1991, 108; Killen 1979b, 169.
146 Nosch & Perna 2001.
147 Tn 996: The text is from Bennett 1992, 119. It is identical to *PTT* but corrects a typographical error in line .2 (i.e. **219* 3, not **219* 2) and distinguishes the different forms of **208* in line .4.
148 Vandenabeele & Olivier 1979, 252–3.
149 *Contra PoN* (I, 127), followed by Whitelaw (2001, 72), it is probable that the tablet did originate in Rm 20, rather than having fallen from an upper floor. As Palaima rightly commented, it would be 'a remarkable coincidence that a tablet with such contents fell from an upper floor into a storeroom containing pottery' (*Scribes Pylos*, 139). As he argues, if the document was stored on the upper shelves with which the room was furnished and was thrown outward subsequent to the collapse of the roof, this would explain its findspot on top of one of the upper room floor slabs. In any case, given that an origin within Rm 20 makes good sense in terms of what is now known of circulation and service patterns in this area (e.g. Bendall 2004), the issue deserves careful reconsideration.
150 The literature on this area is now extensive; see Bendall 2004 with further references.
151 For a recent discussion of Linear B vessel ideograms in banqueting contexts see Wright 2004b, 28–33. Wright (p. 31) does not seem to take Tn 996 as associated with feasting but if the tablet really does come from Rm 20 (see n 149 above) such an association would be likely. For metals in general in Linear B see Dialismas 2001b.

types of vessels are offered, of which **215*, a golden kylix, is probably the most valuable; it is given to *Potnia*, Poseidon and *do-po-ta*.[152] **213*, a simple bowl, is the most common type, offered to eight deities.[153] **216*, a handleless drinking cup or goblet, is given to Hermes and to the 'Thrice-Hero' (*ti-ri-se-ro-e*).[154]

A final religious context in which gold appears is Ae 303, which records 'sacred gold' (see Section 2.2.3).

Turning to non-religious contexts in which gold appears, there is a single record of acquisitions, in the form of contributions of gold by various officials in Jo 438, perhaps, as Chadwick suggested, in the context of raising funds to finance military activities (see Section 2.2.3). He calculates that the total of the preserved figures is M 5 N 1 (allowing for some restorations, but without taking into account all missing figures, so the estimate is on the conservative side), which is probably in the range of 5–6 kg.[155]

Finally, there is evidence for craftworkers in gold. Four goldsmiths are listed along with other craftsmen in An 207, the text of which is as follows.[156]

An 207 (H43)

.1	*deest*	
.2	*deest*	
.3	]mi[	VIR *qs*
.4	]-jo[ ]	VIR 10 [
.5	]pi-ri-je-te-re	VIR 2
.6	re-ka-ta]ne , a-de-te-re	VIR 2
.7	ṛẹ-ka[-ta-]ne , ke-ra-me-we	VIR 2
.8	re-ka-ta-ne , da-ko-ro	VIR 12
.9	wa-a_2-te-we , po-ku-ta	VIR 10
.10	a-nu-wa , ku-ru-so-wo-ko	VIR 4
.11	]kọ me-ri-da-ma-te	VIR 2
.12	]-jo , to-ko-so-wo-ko	VIR 5̣[
.13	a-pi-no[-e-wi-jo]	VIR[]1
.14	so-ro-pe-o , ra-pte-re [	VIR] 3
.15	ko-ri-si-jo ra-pte-re [	VIR *qs*
.16	ka-ro-ke-e , ra-pte-re [	VIR
.17	ra-ni-jo-ne , ra-pte-re	VIR *qs*
.18	]ka-si-da , ra-pte-re	VIR 20[

Each line gives a reference to a place (e.g. *ko-ri-si-jo* in line .15), followed by an occupational term in the plural (e.g. *ke-ra-me-we /keramēwe*(*s*)/ '[two] potters' in line .7). In line .10, four men are described as *ku-ru-so-wo-ko /khrusoworgoi/* 'goldsmiths'. The heading of the document is lost so the purpose of the list is unclear, but that at least four men existed whose primary work was in gold (bronzesmiths are carefully distinguished as *ka-ke-we*) suggests the palace (normally) had sufficient resources in the material to make it worthwhile having such specialists.[157]

It is difficult to assess exactly how rich the palace was in gold, but it is apparent that the stuff was available, although if Chadwick were correct about Jo 438, it may be that not as much was

---

[152] Vandenabeele & Olivier 1979, 210–12.
[153] Vandenabeele & Olivier 1979, 183–5.
[154] Vandenabeele & Olivier 1979, 212–16.
[155] Chadwick 1998–1999, 33.
[156] An 207: For the new text see Melena 1994–1995b, 273–4.
[157] It is also interesting, though not central to our argument here, that the status of the goldworkers does not appear to be particularly elevated. They appear mixed in with a variety of other workers – potters (.7), tailors (.14–18), and the like – and there is no evidence for their being involved in e.g. land tenure, a relatively high-status form of maintenance, as some other craftworkers are (although their presence might be masked if they were represented by name alone).

always at hand as was needed or desired. Nevertheless, it seems likely that the dedication of thirteen gold vessels, as seen in Tn 316, would have been an unusual and expensive undertaking. No comparative calculations can be done with the type of data here as have been done for other commodities, but it is worth observing that the majority of references to gold at Pylos appear in sacerdotal contexts and/or in relation to banqueting.

6.5.1.2 GOLD AT KNOSSOS

Gold is rare in the Knossos tablets. The ideogram AUR is entirely absent, with the exception of a possible new reading on X 9907.[158] However, *ku-ru-so /khrusos/* 'gold' and a compound involving it, *ku-ru-su-*56*, appear on two tablets, both recording vessels.[159] The texts are as follows.[160]

K(1) 740 (102?)

sup. mut.
.1]*vest.* [
.2 ḍi-pa AES **214*^{VAS}+*DI* 30[
.3 qe-ro$_2$ 'AES' **255* • 1ɛ̣6̣
.4 ku-ru-su-**56* • **207*^{VAS} 1
.5 pi-ri-je • *ZE* 1
.6 [· ·] 'me-no-ṇọ['
inf. mut.

.3.4.5 Large dots after **255*, before **207*^{VAS} and before *ZE*.
.6 q̣ẹ-ṛọ$_2$ possible.

K(1) 872 (102)

.1], ke-ra-a , **227*^{VAS} [
.2]me-no , ne-qa-sa-pi , **227*^{VAS} 1
.3a]-te-te , ku-ru-so , ⟦ḳụ-ṛụ-ṣọ⟧
.3b ne-]qa-sa-pi , **218*^{VAS} 3
.4 *inf. mut.*

.3a]*-te-te*: possibly]**5̣6-te-te.* , *ku-ru-so* , over ⟦ ⟧.
.3b **218*^{VAS} over ⟦ ⟧ (⟦*we* · · · *no*⟧).

**207* in K(1) 740.4 is a globular two-handled vessel with three feet.[161] Nothing necessarily relates this document to religion, although an issue of tableware may possibly have been related to banqueting,[162] as suggested above for PY Tn 996. **218* in K(1) 872 is a Vapheio cup, examples of which in gold are well attested in the archaeological record.[163] Again, a banqueting context would be possible; a connection with religion may be suggested by the presence in lines .1 and .2 of bull's head rhyta.[164]

6.5.2 BRONZE (**140* = AES)

6.5.2.1 BRONZE AT PYLOS

Pylos supplies the most extensive evidence for bronze in the extant Linear B archives. The principal records are those of the Jn series;[165] bronze also appears in the two tablets of the Ja

[158] Godart *et al.* 1992–1993, 66; also Godart *et al.* 1990–1991, 400. It is applied to what seems to be ideogram **249* (reading uncertain); see *CoMIK* IV, 210. The *Minos* articles give the ideogram as **260*; either way, it is broken and obscure.
[159]]*ku-ru-so* appears on X 1014 before a broken and obscure word *po-ro-we*[.
[160] Both from *KT*^{5}.
[161] Vandenabeele & Olivier 1979, 245–6.
[162] Wright (2004b, 31) envisions such a connection for the two tablets here.
[163] Vandenabeele & Olivier 1979, 200–5.
[164] Vandenabeele & Olivier 1979, 268–71. But for some doubts about whether rhyta were used exclusively for religious purposes in Mycenaean contexts see Bendall forthcoming(b), with further references.
[165] See Smith's thorough study (1992–1993), with further references.

series (which are probably related to the Jn tablets), in Tn 996, discussed above (Section 6.5.1.1), and indirectly in Vn 130. To begin with these last two, Tn 996 records vessels, including seven tall jugs (**205*) and three bowls (**208*) of bronze. Bronze vessels are probably also the subject of Vn 130, which records transfers of vessels from bronzeworkers at various places to the palace.[166] The tablet records fifty-nine *a-ke-a$_2$ /angeha/* 'jars' or 'pails'.

The Jn series includes two types of records, disbursements and collections. Taking the collection records first, Jn 829, to which Jn 881 might be related,[167] records a collection of 'temple bronze' from shrines in the sixteen major towns of the Pylian polity (see Section 2.2.3). The amount of bronze acquired by the palace in this document is N 200,[168] perhaps some 50 kg. Notice that in this instance we have not a disbursement for religious purposes but a collection *from* religious establishments, almost certainly for military use. Whatever the palace's overall resources in this metal, they had apparently fallen short of what the administration considered adequate at the time the document was written.[169]

The remaining eighteen Jn tablets record allocations to bronzesmiths at various settlements. Several examples of Jn documents were given in Section 2.5.4; we repeat the first few lines of one of them here.

Jn 310

.1	a-ke-re-wa , ka-ke-we , ta-ra-si-ja , e-ko-te			
.2	ti-qa-jo	AES M 1 N 2	qe-ta-wo	AES M 1 N 2
.3	a$_3$-so-ni-jo	AES M 1 N 2	ta-mi-je-u	AES M 1 N 2
&c.				

The heading reads '*a-ke-re-wa*: bronzesmiths having allotments', followed by a list of bronzesmiths with allotments. As discussed previously, the remaining Jn records have a similar pattern. In all, sixteen different towns appear, with some 228 smiths.[170] Ja 749 may be a totalling record for the set;[171] the text is as follows.

Ja 749 (S310-H2)

to-so-pa L 34 M 26

A total of M 632 is recorded in the Jn series (L 21 M 2). Thus, if Ja 749 *were* the totalling record for the series, about a third of the allotments are missing.[172] Whatever the case, the amount of bronze acquired by the palace in Jn 829 is 8% of the total attested in the Jn tablets and 5% of the amount recorded in Ja 749. The range of total allotments on individual Jn tablets is M 12 to M 78. Thus the amount collected in Jn 829 would have been sufficient to supply bronzesmiths at one or two places.[173] The amount is large enough to have made the collection worthwhile.

Finally, disbursements to *Potnian* bronzesmiths in the Jn tablets may be compared to the others. It is uncertain whether *Potnian* smiths were actually working on religious assignments but, in any case, the amount of bronze they received was small (M 38) compared to the overall

---

[166] Killen 1999d, 89. As Killen points out, one of the men on Vn 130, *a$_3$-ki-e-u* of *a-pi-no-e-wi-jo*, is almost certainly the same man who appears in Jn 605.10 as a holder of slaves connected with bronze production at the same place. (It is generally inadvisable to take persons having the same name in Linear B as the same persons without good contextual support, but here the connection is supported by both location and reference to vessels, a plausible output of bronzeworking.)

[167] Smith 1992–1993, 208.

[168] For the figure and distribution of this amount among the towns see Killen 1996a.

[169] Unless it was routine recycling of votive materials, a practice not unknown later. But the specific purpose mentioned in the heading of the tablet (for points for darts and spears) suggests otherwise.

[170] Smith 1992–1993, 210–11.

[171] E.g. Bendall 2003, 222. The other Ja tablet, Ja 1288, resembles a single entry in the Jn series.

[172] Smith (1992–1993, 171–2) argues that the set is complete.

[173] The amount extracted, some 50 kg, is not inconsiderable.

amount (M 632). Whatever it was intended for, it was 6% of the whole. It may also be noted that there were nineteen *Potnian* smiths as against some 228 others, i.e. some 8%.

6.5.2.2 BRONZE AT KNOSSOS

Bronze is rare in the Knossos records, although less rare than gold. K(1) 740, discussed above (Section 6.5.1.2), records drinking and other vessels, some of which (the 30+ *di-pa*, **214*[174]) are of bronze. Also of bronze are the sixteen(?) arm-guards in line .3.[175]

L 693 records bronze in association with textiles. The text is as follows.

L 693 (103)
.1 ri-no , / re-po-to , 'qe-te-o' ki-to , AES M 1 [
.2 sa-pa P 2 Q 1 e-pi-ki-to-ni-ja AES M 1[
.2 *-ni-* over ⟦*ja*⟧. AES over ⟦ ⟧.

A total of M 2 is recorded (perhaps about 2 kg); the tablet has no apparent connection with religion.

Oa 734 records a bronze commodity represented by **167+PE*, probably an ingot.[176]

Oa 734 (—)
]jo AES **167+PE*[

The text is broken, but again there is no apparent connection with religion. More ingots are recorded in Oa 730 and –733. It is not certain that bronze (or copper) was the metal involved, but this is likely. The texts are as follows.

Oa 730 (—)
]**167* 60 L 52 M 2
Cut at right.

Oa 733 (—)
]**167+P̣Ẹ* 10 L 6̣[

Oa 733 records ten ingots and Oa 730 records sixty. The weight given in Oa 730 is L 52 M 2, some 1562 kg on the VC values. This gives an average for each ingot of 26 kg, which compares well with archaeologically attested examples.[177] In any case, the palace clearly had substantial supplies of bronze.

Finally, several tablets record bronze in association with chariots and fittings (Sc 223, Sd 4409, Sd 4412(?), Sd 5091, So 894[178]), Ws 8497 records a bronze bath (*a-sa-mi-to*),[179] and one of the Gg tablets *may* record bronze. The text is as follows.

Gg 709 (—)
.a]-na [
.b] **209*^{VAS} 2 [
.b Trace of a sign on right edge, probably an ideogram (perhaps ẠẸṢ[).

[174] Vandenabeele & Olivier 1979, 234–9.
[175] Vandenabeele & Olivier 1979, 21.
[176] **167* alone is an ingot; ligatured with *PE* it may be an axe (although *pe* may also be an indicator of weight); see Vandenabeele & Olivier 1979, 151–4.
[177] Oxhide ingots from the Uluburun shipwreck averaged 25 kg (e.g. Pulak 1997, 235).
[178] On some of these the AES ideogram appears; on others bronze is indicated by means of the words *ka-ki-jo*, *ka-ki-ja-pi* and *ka-ko-de-ta*. Se 853 has *ka-ke*[.
[179] Vandenabeele & Olivier 1979, 176–7; cf. Olivier 1968.

This tablet was discussed above in the context of honey (Section 4.3.4.1), where it was identified as one of the records which might deal with amphorae themselves rather than vessels filled with honey. However that may be, the tablet context is obscure and the reading of AES is uncertain, so the connection with bronze is tenuous.

We may finally note that bronzesmiths are found on two records: V 958 (a list of craftsmen) and Fh 386 (an issue of oil). Bronze was clearly a commodity that the palace had access to, but there are no apparent instances of a direct use in a religious context, except for a possible connection of some bronze vessels with banqueting.

6.6 OBSCURE COMMODITIES

6.6.1 INTRODUCTION TO OBSCURE COMMODITIES

For the sake of completeness we conclude with a number of commodities which appear in religious contexts, but whose interpretation is in some way ambiguous if not entirely obscure. The majority appear on just one tablet, PY Un 219, and are represented by syllabograms used as ideograms. The remaining cases consist of one further syllabogram used as an ideogram, one ligature spelling the name of the commodity, plus a few 'ordinary' ideograms. The syllabograms and ligature do not necessarily represent the same commodities in different tablet contexts where they appear and in some cases it is demonstrable that they do not.

We will first discuss Un 219 first, along with the commodities appearing on it, then turn to the remaining commodities. All known occurrences of the signs involved are listed in Tables 6-23 and 6-24 (the first given here, the second below in Section 6.6.3). In both tables, syllabograms are usually included only where certainly or probably used as ideograms;[180] other instances are mentioned in the notes to the tables and cases where the sign is transcribed as part of a broken word are excluded.[181]

---

[180] Which is not always easy to determine, as Olivier *et al.* (1973, 12) remark.

[181] Data in these tables were compiled with reference to *Documents*, *DMic.*, Olivier *et al.* 1973, *KT*[6], *TITHEMY*, *PTT* II, *Thèbes* I, *Thèbes* III.

Table 6-23. Signs on PY Un 219

sign	Pylos, religious contexts	Pylos, non-religious contexts	Knossos	Mycenae	Thebes	Tiryns
E	Un 219*	Ub 1316 Ub 1317 Ub 1318 Un 1319*	U 5717 Xe 7437	Ge 603	—	—
KA	Un 219*	Vn 1314 An 607	—	—	—	—
KE	Un 219* Cf. Qa series	Ma set	Gg 711 Nc 5100	—	Gp 210	—
KO	Un 219*	Sh 734 Sh 735 Sh 738 Sh 739 Un 592 (adjunct)	Ce 113 Ce 8279 Ce 8346 F 7542 Ga(2) <34> Ga(2) 417 Ga 738 Ga 953* Ga 7496*	Ge 603 Ge 606 (ligature) Ge 608 (adjunct) Ue 652 (adjunct)	—	—
MA	Un 219*	—	Ga 953* Ga 5672 Ga 7496* Od 7388?	Ge 603 Ge 604	—	X 17
ME	Un 219*? see Section 4.2.3	see Section 4.2.3	—	—	—	—
O	Un 219* see Section 5.7	see Section 5.7	—	—	—	—
PE	Un 219*	La 630 Un 1319*	V 52??	Ge 602 Ge 605 Ge 606	—	
RA	Un 219* cf. Fr 1215	—	—	—	—	—
TE	Un 219*	—	—	—	—	—
U	Un 219*	—	—	—	—	—
WI	Un 219*	Wr 1332	—	—	—	—

<u>Notes</u>

* = Document appears more than once in table.

<u>*Individual tablets*</u>

Vn 1314: Reclassified from Un (Bennett 1992, 120); minor joins are reported in Melena 1992-1993a, 81 (text unchanged).

Od 7388: A possible reading *MA* is noted in the apparatus, but the ideogram is more likely to be LANA (and surely the scribe intended this, whatever he wrote).

<u>*Instances where not used as ideograms*</u>

E: *e* appears as an adjunct to cloth (KN Ln 1568) and **177* (KN U 4478); see *Documents*, 541. It stands alone in Dv 1331.b, but is probably a *lapsus* for *e<-ra>* (*DMic.* I, *s.v. e*).

KA: *ka* is used as an adjunct to the stirrup-jar ideogram **210* in KN K 700, abbreviating the name of the vessel **ka-ra-re-u* (*Documents*, 549), and is ligatured with SUS in PY Un 6 and –853. It appears as an isolated sign on KN sheep tablet Dv 1248 (with *ru*); the meaning is unclear. Finally, it appears on a stirrup-jar, MY Z 713.

KE: *ke* appears as an adjunct to vessels **202* and **222* in KN K(2) 773 (perhaps abbreviating *ke-ni-qa* or *ke-ni-qe-te-we*; *Documents*, 552), and as an isolated sign in PY Na 856 and –1041 (possibly abbreviating *ke-u-po-da*; cf. Na 527). It is ligatured with *RO_2* and **172* in KN U 746 and U 436, respectively (both discussed in Section 4.2.1.4). It also appears in As(1) 608[+]625, apparently as an adjunct to *DA* (this is more clear from the photograph and drawing [see *CoMIK* I, 222] than it is from the transcription: *ke*, written very small, is between *DA* and the number, not after the number as the transcription suggests). At Thebes, *KE* is a possible, but 'difficile', reading in Fq 187.2 (see apparatus *Thèbes* I, 73–4, 204).

KO: *ko* is used as an adjunct to cloth in KN L 8105 and perhaps abbreviates *ko-wa/wo* on KN Ap 629. It is a surcharge on **153* (PY Un 718) representing sheepskin. *ko* may be an ideogram rather than the end of a word in KN G 7525, V(2) 7527 and V 8787, but the texts are too damaged to tell. The sign also appears as an isolated erasure in KN Ga(1) 675 and PY Un 267 and Ea 421. In some cases *ko* appears as an adjunct or ligature denoting probably the same commodity as is sometimes represented by *KO* used as an ideogram (specifically in the case of coriander); such instances are included in the table.

MA: *ma* appears as an adjunct to the obscure ideogram **177* in KN U 4478 (along with *e*). It is also sometimes used in error for LANA.

ME: Note the reading in Un 219 as an ideogram is not secure – see under 6.6.2.1 below. Occurrences of *ME* at Pylos were discussed in Section 4.2.3; the syllabogram is not used as an ideogram at other sites. *me* appears as an adjunct to children in KN Ak(1) 634, –5741, probably abbreviating *me-u-jo*(*-e*) 'smaller' (*Documents*, 560).

O: Occurrences of this syllabogram used as an ideogram were discussed in Section 5.7.

PE: *pe* appears as an abbreviation of *pe-ru-si-nu-wo*/*-wa* 'last year's' in the KN D- Class tablets and several personnel records (e.g. Ak(2) 621+; Ak(3) 780+; Killen 1972, 435). It annotates cloth (e.g. KN Le 641, –647, Ln 1568+, M 1645, –7373) and TUN+*KI* (KN Ld(1) 595). It is used to measure wool at Knossos (Od(3) 1062, –1063) and mint at Mycenae (Ge 602+). It is ligatured with or accompanies wheat in numerous cases (e.g. KN F(2) 841, E 9754; cf. PY Un 1319); and is ligatured with the ingot ideogram **167* (KN Oa 733, –734). See *Documents*, 569.

RA: The only other use in connection with an ideogram is in the KN Mc series where *RA* appears to be ligatured with CAP (possibly; *Documents*, 302, 578).

TE: Is used as an ideogram only in PY Un 219. It is an adjunct to men (KN As(1) 5542, –5944) and oil (KN Fh 340), and is often ligatured with TELA (e.g. Ln 1568+) and ROTA (PY Sa 483+); see *Documents*, 584.

U: *u* is used as an adjunct to vessels (with **212* in KN K(2) 774, –775, –776; with **213* in K(2) 1810); *Documents*, 588. It appears as an ideogram only on Un 219.

WI: It is part of the ideogram **152*, indicating oxhide, and forms a part of the obscure ideogram **157* (Section 6.6.3.6). It also appears in isolation in KN E 1035 (significance unclear).

6.6.2 SIGNS ON PY UN 219

6.6.2.1 INTRODUCTION TO PY UN 219

The text of Un 219 is as follows.

Un 219 (H15)

.1 e-ke-ra-ne , tu-wo 2 *O* 1[
.2 pa-de-we , *O* 1 pa-de-we , *O* 1 [
.3 ka-ru-ke , *PE* 2 *KA* 1 *O* 6
.4 te-qi-jo-ne , *O* 1 a-ke-ti-ri-ja-i , *KA* 1
.5 a-ti-mi-te , *O* 1 da-ko-ro-i , *Ẹ* 1
.6 di-pte-ra-po-ro , *RA* 1 *O* 3 ko-ṛọ[ ] 1
.7 ạ-na-ka-te , *TE* 1 po-ti-ni-ja[
.8 e-[ ] , *U* 1 e-ma-a_2 , *U* 1 pe-[
.9 a-ka-wo-ne , *MA* 1 pa-ra-[ ] 2
.10 ra-wa-ke-ta , *MA* 1 *KO* 1 [ ]*ME* 1 *O* 1 *WI* 1
.11 *KE* 1 [ ] *vacat*
.12 *vacat*
.13 *vacat*
.14 *vacat*
.15 *vacat*
.16 *vacat*

Probably palimpsest.
.4 *te-qi-<ri->jo-ne*: cf. Fn 187.12.
.6 *-pte-* over ⟦*pe*⟧.
.7 Not *ẉạ-na-ka-te*.
.8 *pe-ṃọ*[not impossible.
.10 Last 1 on *latus dextrum*.

As Olivier observed in his important discussion of this tablet,[182] Un 219 records disbursements of commodities to various recipients (in the dative[183]), whose character can be summarised as (1) deities, (2) important officials and (3) cult servants (*desservants de sanctuaire*; see Section 2.3.3.1).[184] The theonyms include *a-ti-mi-te* 'Artemis' (line .5), *e-ma-a_2* 'Hermes' (line .8), and

[182] Olivier 1959, 175–81. The tablet has also been discussed recently by Weilhartner (2005, 166–7), but little in the past few decades has been added to Olivier's treatment.
[183] Olivier 1959, 175 n 56.
[184] Olivier 1959, 178–80; 1960, 124.

Potnia (line .7).[185] The officials include *e-ke-ra-ne* (line .1), possibly a scribal error for *e-ke-ra₂-wo-ne*, an important person (perhaps the *wanax*) on Un 718 and other documents (see Section 2.4.4),[186] and the *ra-wa-ke-ta* (line .10), thought to be the second in rank after the *wanax*. The 'cult servants' include the *ka-ru-ke* (line .3), *da-ko-ro-i* (line .5), *di-pte-ra-po-ro* (line .6), and *a-ke-ti-ri-ja-i* (line .4), all of whom figure in Olivier's 'liste-type' documents, dealing with cult and support staff at religious festivals (Section 2.3.3.1). Deities and important officials also appear in festival rations records and it is likely that Un 219 relates to a similar context even though the commodities issued are different than in other such documents. In any case, the nature of the recipients makes clear an association with religion.[187]

None of the commodities represented by a syllabogram can be identified with confidence,[188] but, as Olivier pointed out, the first commodity, which is represented by a word *tu-wo* rather than a syllabogram, is likely to be */thuwos/* 'aromatic substance' (cf. PY Un 267), an interpretation which receives support in that many of the following syllabograms are capable of interpretation as abbreviations of attested words for spices or have plausible interpretations in related contexts.[189] Olivier lists the following as reasonably secure.

KE = */kēros/* 'beeswax' (cf. *KE*+*RO₂*; but see Section 4.2.1.4)
KO = *ko-ri-ja-do-no* */koriandnon/* 'coriander' (but *KO* could also abbreviate *ko-no* */skhoinos/* 'rush'; either way aromatics would be involved)
MA = *ma-ra-tu-wo* */marathwon/* 'fennel' (attested as such at Mycenae)
ME = */meli/* 'honey' (*ME*+*RI*; but see Section 4.2.3; note reading as an ideogram in line .10 is not certain; see apparatus)

He further proposes the following as possible:

KA = */kalaminthos/* 'calamint'
TE = */terminthos/* or */terebinthos/* 'terebinth'
U = */hussōpos/* 'hyssop'
WI = *wi-ri-za* */wriza/* 'root' (cf. Un 249)[190]

This leaves a few signs unaccounted for (*E*, *O*, *PE*, *RA*), but at least two of these may also be spices. *E* appears in one of the Mycenae spice records, Ge 603, where it describes a form of rush 'ginger-grass'? (cf. *ko-no*),[191] and *O* can sometimes represent cyperus, as discussed in Section 5.7.1. Certainty is impossible but the large number of plausible possible interpretations together with the word *tu-wo* allows reasonable confidence that the commodities of Un 219 are aromatics of various sorts (plus perhaps related substances such as beeswax and honey).

Uncertainty about the units of measurement as well as interpretation of the signs makes it difficult to assess quantities in Un 219 in the way done for other commodities, but we may offer here a brief survey. The signs are addressed in turn below, with the exception of signs discussed above (*ME* in Section 4.2.3; *O* in Section 5.7 with Table 6-23, and *RA* (on Fr 1215) in Section 3.2.2 with Table 2-2), and three which warrant no further discussion. *WI* appears elsewhere on a single sealing, PY Wr 1332, which may record incoming 'roots' or may not.[192] *TE* and *U* are used as ideograms only in Un 219.

---

[185] Olivier 1959, 178–9. He also takes as possible: *Pa-de-we* (line .2, twice; perhaps a variant of *pa-de*, attested as a deity at Knossos?), *E-*[*ra*?], *Pe-*[*re-**82?].
[186] Olivier 1959, 180.
[187] Olivier 1959, 180–1; 1960, 124.
[188] Note all are counted in units, so the form of measurement provides no clue (Olivier 1959, 175 n 57).
[189] Olivier 1959, 176–8; see also *Mémoires* II, 158 n 62 (= Lejeune 1958d).
[190] Oliver 1959, 177.
[191] It may abbreviate *e-ne-me-na* (note parallel structure of line .2, where the word is written, and line .3 where *E* is used). See *Documents*, 226, 543.
[192] The sign may represent oxhide on the sealing, an interpretation unlikely to apply also to Un 219; see Olivier 1997, 75; Bendall 2003, 214; Weilhartner 2005, 169 with n 440.

6.6.2.2 *E* AS AN IDEOGRAM

We begin with cases where *E* is certainly not a spice and not used in religious contexts, then consider instances which may be comparable to Un 219. *E* appears as an ideogram at Pylos in Ub 1316, –1317 and –1318, where it abbreviates *e-ra-pe*/*pi-ja* /*elaphiai*/ 'deerskins' written on the same records. At Knossos, *E* is used as an ideogram in two documents. In U 5717 the only other (imperfectly preserved) ideogram on the tablet represents some type of animal, so *E* here may abbreviate *e-po* (see Section 2.3.2.3). However that may be, there is no reason to associate it with *E* at Pylos. The other Knossos tablet, Xe 7437, however, may be more comparable. The text is as follows.

Xe 7437 (103)

.1 [·]-ma-ta-ro[

.2 te-i-ja '*TA* 1' *E* 1 *P̣Ạ* 1̣ [

.3 ra-qa-ra [

.1]*jạ-ma-ta-ro*[possible.
.2 Small *ta* above small *e*, followed by units which probably originally totalled at least 6: only the first two were not erased or accidentally damaged; uncertain if the numerals go with *ta* and *e* together or separately. Perhaps *te-i-ja-*'*ta*' followed by *E* 2 *PA* 1̣[(cf. Ln 1568).
.3 Trace at right, possibly *wị*[.

If the reading is correct in line .2 (but see apparatus) this tablet presumably has something to do with religion, since *te-i-ja* should be /*theia*/ 'divine'. The context confirms this interpretation in PY Fr 1202, but here the context is unclear. The other two words on the document are both *hapax* and obscure. Also, if *te-i-ja-*'*ta*' were the correct reading after all (see apparatus to line .2), this would presumably be the name of a commodity. We cannot tell.

E is certainly a spice (or aromatic plant) in MY Ge 603, mentioned above, since it is used together with a form of rush.

E is probably (or possibly) also a spice in PY Un 1319, where it appears along with a number of other commodities specified only by syllabograms. The text is as follows.[193]

PY Un 1319 (Cii)

.1]-i-pụ-ma , GRA *PE* 1 [ ] A_2 4̣1̣

.2 *O PE* 2 A_2 13 *KU* 1 *E* 40 *PA* 20[ ] *PA* 6

.3 e-ri-ka-we-e GRA A_2 1 *WO* 2 re-u-ko-to , G̣ṚẠ A_2 2 *PA* 1̣ *E* 9

.4 a-ro-ka , *E* 12̣

.2 *o* <GRA> *PE* 2 not excluded; possibly]*jo*; *PA* 6 (or trace of numerals before *PA*).
.3 -*e* GRA over erasure; *PA* 1: 1 is at bottom of line, like a divider.

The function of the document is 'Unclear', but it deals with wheat and may have something to do with harvests or land tenure.[194] Since plant stuffs are involved, it is not inconceivable that *E* here is also a plant, possibly the same one as indicated in Un 219. But there is no way to determine this.

One unit of *E* is recorded in Un 219. This figure might be compared with the sixty-one units recorded on Un 1319, but apart from the fact that we cannot be certain that the same commodity is represented (or if the units represent the same 'measures') the document is in any case 'Unclear'. Nothing further can be said.

---

[193] Text as in *PTT*, but reading *O* instead of *o* in line .2, following *PoN* IV (although the apparatus of the latter also notes '*o* <GRA> *PE* 2 not excluded').

[194] For GRA in association with *PE* in land tenure contexts see Section 5.2.1. However, given the unusual structure of the present tablet (with the appearance of multiple syllabograms used as ideograms), it is uncertain whether *PE* here should be understood as an abbreviation of *pe-mo*, or as something else.

6.6.2.3 *KA* AS AN IDEOGRAM

Un 219 records two units of *KA*. The only other possible instances of the syllabogram used as an ideogram are in PY Vn 1314 and An 607. Vn 1314 is an obscure document probably dealing with medicines (cf. *pa-ma-ko /pharmakon/*? in line .1).[195] *KA* appears in line .3.A, apparently used as an ideogram, although no number appears and it is noted in the apparatus that the sign may in fact represent '100'. An 607 is also a rather obscure document, although it is clear that it deals with personnel and that the parentage of the women recorded is somehow important.[196] *KA* appears as an isolated sign in line .11, well below the other text, and not accompanied by a number. It is not entirely clear that it is being used as an ideogram here, and in any case its meaning is obscure. We may note that *KA* may sometimes abbreviate *ka-pa* (see Section 6.6.3.3) but that cannot be demonstrated for any of the cases discussed here.

6.6.2.4 *KE* AS AN IDEOGRAM

KE is collected in the PY Ma series, where it is weighed. As discussed in Section 4.2.3, a recent paper by Killen supports its identification as 'beeswax' in the Ma context,[197] but whether it means the same in Un 219 is uncertain and the fact that it is weighed in the Ma series but not in Un 219 may suggest a different commodity was intended. One unit of *KE* is recorded in Un 219, and M 149 is collected in the Ma series.

KE also appears at Pylos as part of ideogram **189* in the Qa series, which is by the same scribe, H15, as Un 219 (these being the only documents attributed to this scribe). **189* is essentially a box surcharged with *KE*. It is counted in whole units, like *KE* in Un 219, but there is no certainty the same commodity is intended. The fact that the scribe chose a different form of representation in either case might suggest that he had different goods in mind. On the other hand, the contexts in either case are similar. As noted above, Un 219 deals with deities, important officials, cult personnel and other festival support staff. The Qa series also deals with important officials and cult personnel, including possibly one of the same individuals, if *]ẹ-ke-ri-ja-wo* (Qa 1292) and *e-ke-ra-ne* refer to the same person.[198] It is conceivable that both cases relate to occasions where items were given out in the context of a festival or banquet. However that may be, we are still no closer to identifying the commodities. For the record, the Qa series records some twenty-eight to thirty-six units of **189*.

At Knossos, *KE* appears in Gg 711, possibly representing beeswax (see Section 4.2.1.4), and in Nc 5100 (Section 6.4.1.3). Three of the ideograms in Nc 5100 are the same as in the PY Ma set (*RI*, *O*, **146*), and they are measured in the same way so it may be that the same commodities were being dealt with, which would mean that *KE* here should also be beeswax. The tablet records *KE* M 10.

Finally, *KE* appears at Thebes on the upper edge of Gp 210 (Section 4.3.5, Table 4-7). The sign is isolated and there is no indication of what it represents nor why it was written on this part of the document.[199]

---

[195] Janko 1981 (but note the text has changed since he wrote; see Bendall 2003, 208, 222–3 and note to Table 6-23).
[196] Recently, see Weilhartner 2005, 172–3, with further references.
[197] Killen forthcoming(b).
[198] See Bendall 2003, 212–13, with further references. It might be mentioned in support of the identification that H15 gives the impression of being a rather unsophisticated writer – for instance, he does not seem aware of the sign ra_2, used by other scribes in writing *Enkhaliāwōn*, which may help explain his uncertainty over the spelling in Un 219 (possibly). On the Qa series see, recently, Weilhartner 2005, 136–8, also 167 *passim*.
[199] *Thèbes* I, 82, 297.

6.6.2.5 *KO* AS AN IDEOGRAM

KO and *ko* normally indicate coriander,[200] but in the PY Sh tablets *KO* is instead an abbreviation of *ko-ru-to* '(plates) of the helmet',[201] and in some of the Knossos tablets it may indicate piglets (see below and Section 2.3.2.3 *s.v.* Ce 113). We discuss the occurrences site by site beginning with Pylos.

KO is used at Pylos as an ideogram only in the Sh tablets and in Un 219, but *ko* as an adjunct appears on Un 592, the text of which is as follows.[202]

PY Un 592 (S2-H1)

.1]*kọ* AROM 8 T 8
.2]6⌋ M 2 *KAPO* 3 T 4
.3]ṣ 1 V 4 *ko* AROM 4 T 4
.4]S 1 V 3 LANA 6
.5]Ṭ 5 ra-ka , **1̣5̣4̣* 2̣1̣

The adjunct in line .4 qualifies the spice ideogram AROM, and given that *KO* is elsewhere attested as coriander (and is, as here, counted in dry measures) it is likely that the same spice is indicated here. The document records an issue for perfume manufacture and has no discernible connection with religion. It should be noted that the commodity here is measured in dry units whereas in Un 219 it appears only as a full unit (only one is counted), so it is not clear the same commodity is indicated. Given the large amount recorded in Un 592 (AROM 13 T 2) it is at least clear that the palace had reasonably substantial resources.

At Knossos, three tablets from the RCT, Ce 113, –8279 and –8346, use *KO* as an ideogram. These documents were discussed in Section 2.3.2.3, and it was noted there that although *KO* may represent coriander, it could also here be connected with pigs, standing for *ko-ro /khoiros/* 'piglet'. The tablets were listed as 'possible' banqueting records, but without much conviction, particularly as they preserve no text beyond the ideograms.

We also have *KO* in the following oil tablet, discussed briefly in Section 3.2.3.7. The text again is as follows.

KN F 7542 (—)

.1]31 *KO* 25
.2]6 ṣ OLE 9
.2 Traces at left.

The function of the tablet is 'Unclear' (taxation record? issue to a perfume manufacturer? something else?), and the meaning of *KO* is also uncertain. Note it is not weighed as coriander normally is and the amount is very large.

In the remaining cases of *KO* at Knossos, we are certainly dealing with coriander. The texts of the relevant tablets are as follows.

KN <u>Ga(2)</u> <34> (136?)

.1 pu-na-si-jo / ti-mi-ṇụ-ẉọ[
.2 *KO* T 5 [
Missing (destroyed in 1889); text from Evans' photograph of a squeeze.
.1 *ti-mi-*5̣6-wọ[* not entirely excluded.

---

[200] Adrados 1964, 134–5 (but speaking of Ga 953 and Un 219); Melena 1976a; 1976b; Foster 1977a. For uses of coriander see also Sarpaki 2001, 215–6.
[201] *Documents*, 555.
[202] Text from *PTT*; *PoN* IV now reads '10' in line .5.

KN Ga(2) 417 (136)

.A po-ni-ki-jo M 5
.B qa-mo / ko-ri-ja-do-no AROM 1

lat. inf. ta-u-na-so *KO* V 1[

KN Ga 953 [+] 955 (219)

.1 wo-de-ẉị-jo-jo , / me-ṇọ[//]ri-jo-de ,
.2 ko-no , *MA* 3 ko-ṛị[ ]2̣ pa-de-i , ko-no *MA* 2 *KO* T 1[
.3a [ ] pa-si-te-o-i ,
.3b pa-sa-ja , ko-no , [ ] a-mi-ni-so-de , *MẠ* 2 *KO* T 4

.2 Perhaps T 2̣[.
.3 Traces after *ko-no*, perhaps *ṃạ*[in .a and *ṛị*[in .b.
.3b *MA* here has the extra stroke which distinguishes LANA: probably an error.

KN Ga 7496 (219)

.1] , *MA* 1 *KO* T 2[
.2]*MẠ* 2 *KO* T 4 [
.3] *vac.* .[

.1 Trace at left (neither]*ụ* nor]*ṇọ* really convincing; perhaps part of a large]*ị* ?).
.2 Beginning of the line now damaged (text from photograph in *SM* II, pl. 62, *sub* 1633).

That *KO* here is coriander is indicated by the presence of the word in Ga(2) 417.B and (probably) in Ga 953.2.[203] Ga(2) <34> and –417 are taxation records,[204] and Ga 953 is an offerings record.[205] Ga 7496 is 'Unclear'; it is by the same scribe as Ga 953 (these are the only two documents firmly attributed to this scribe[206]) so could also be an offerings record, but we cannot be certain.

Leaving aside the 'Unclear' document, here at last we have a situation amenable to the sort of calculation made for commodities elsewhere. Ga 953 is the only (clear) disbursement record, so 100% of disbursements of coriander recorded at Knossos are for religious purposes. Amounts on the taxation records total AROM 1 T 5 V 1 (= V 91), and although the readings in line .2 of Ga 953 are uncertain (see apparatus) and some may be lost, we seem to have some T 6+ (= V 36), which is 40% of the amount on the taxation records.

Finally, at Mycenae *KO* represents coriander in Ge 603. Coriander is also recorded by means of different expressions in Ge 606 (AROM+*KO*), in Ge 608 and Ue 652 (*ko* AROM), and by means of the word written out *ko-ri-ja-da-na* or *ko-ri-a₂-da-na* on Ge 605.[207] The Ge tablets are taxation records (including assessments for taxation),[208] and are not related to religion. The possibility that Ue 652 may be a banqueting record was considered in Section 2.3.2.4, but it was concluded there that it too is more likely to be a taxation record. Since none of these records relates to religion we need not be further concerned with them here.

[203] As commonly agreed: see e.g. Killen 1962, 44; Melena 1976a. That *KO* here abbreviates coriander rather than *ko-no* is likely because the *ko-no* is already qualified as being (probably) fennel *ma-ra-tu-wo*. See also the parallel structure of lines .2 and .3b where first *MA* then coriander is offered, with the word spelled out (probably – the reading is incomplete) in line .2. See also Weilhartner 2005, 53–4. For Weilhartner's suggestions regarding *MA* and *ko-no*, see Section 6.6.2.6 below.
[204] E.g. Killen 1983d, 226–7 n 32.
[205] See recently Weilhartner 2005, 52–4.
[206] *Scribes Cnossos*, 94. However, Ga 5672, although not attributed to a hand, probably belongs with these two records; see Section 6.6.2.6 below.
[207] A possible reading *ko-ri-ja*[on Of 30.1 (Godart & Sacconi 1978, 8, 27) is now rejected (*TITHEMY*, 36).
[208] The function of the tablets was elucidated by Killen (1983d).

6.6.2.6 *MA* AS AN IDEOGRAM

MA is used as an ideogram at Pylos only in Un 219, so there is nothing to compare it with at this site.

At Knossos, *MA* is used as an ideogram in Ga 953 and –7496, one a definite and the other a probable offering record, as discussed above (Section 6.6.2.5). A further document which probably belongs with these two records, although the scribal hand is unknown, is Ga 5672, the text of which is as follows.

Ga 5672 (—)

.1	] me-no , [
.2	]*MA* 2 pa-ṣạ[-ja?
.3	] , pa-ra-[

.1 Perhaps trace of divider at left. Trace at far right.
.2]*MA*: possibly]LANA or even]*ma* (but cf. Ga 953).
.3 Trace at left:]*p̣ạ* not impossible.

As argued by Melena, support for taking this together with the other tablets is that (1) the format is similar, (2) at least one of the goods, *MA*, is the same, (3) it is, like Ga 953, almost certainly an offerings record as indicated by the word *me-no*, and (4) it may record one of the recipients attested in Ga 953, *pa-sa-ja*.[209] Altogether the three tablets record (in the surviving text) ten units of *MA*. There is nothing to compare them with, so 100% of disbursements of *MA* recorded at Knossos are certainly or probably for religious purposes and we have no evidence for overall resources.

The commodity represented by *MA* in the KN Ga records is generally taken to be fennel, attested (*ma-ra-tu-wo*) in MY Ge 602, –605 and –606, but Weilhartner has recently revived an old controversy over whether *MA* in the Ga records might not be in error for LANA.[210] If this were so, the ten units recorded here should have been included in the discussion of wool above (Section 6.3.3.1). We will consider the suggestion briefly, but it should be said at the outset that our arguments concerning wool would be unaffected either way since, given the very large amount of wool obtained annually by the palace, a mere ten extra units would not affect the figures to any significant degree. The only change to the present section would be to remove *MA* as one of the commodities used for religious offerings at Knossos (it would of course still stand at Pylos unless it were thought to represent wool too in Un 219, which seems unlikely).

The main argument in favour of *MA* representing wool rather than fennel in the Ga tablets is that the amount is too large to make interpretation as a spice plausible (Weilhartner gives the figures as some 192–288 litres on Ga 953) and that the ideogram seems actually to be written as LANA in Ga 953.3b. However, with regard to the second point, it could be that the form of the ideogram is due, as Killen argued, to a temporary lapse and the sign elsewhere in these records appears to be written correctly.[211] With regard to the first point, it may well be that the major unit of spices (cf. AROM) followed a different measure than other commodities. (For a parallel see LANA itself where, unlike other commodities measured by weight, the ideogram indicates M 3 rather than M 30.) There is no rooted objection to finding wool in the company of *KO* coriander (Ga 953.2 and .3b; see previous section), as Weilhartner rightly argues[212], but given that the word *ko-no* actually appears on this tablet and it certainly elsewhere represents */skhoinos/* it seems preferable to take it in this sense here too, as referring to (probably) fennel, rather than making it as Weilhartner does an uninterpreted adjective modifying the supposed

[209] Melena 1976a, 153–5; Weilhartner 2005, 54–5.
[210] Weilhartner 2005, 53–4; a key early discussion of the issue is in Killen 1962, esp. 43–5.
[211] Killen 1962, 44.
[212] Following Godart & Sacconi 1978, 8 (but note that the specific context they were discussing no longer pertains; see Section 6.6.2.5).

wool. Weilhartner's proposed interpretation of the tablet is not impossible,[213] but on the whole the traditional view seems more likely and is followed here. Again, the issue is not crucial for present purposes in any case.

Finally, *MA* appears in the Mycenae spice tablets (where it is universally agreed to represent fennel), but these tablets, as noted in the previous section, are not concerned with religion and require no further discussion here.

6.6.2.7 *PE* AS AN IDEOGRAM

PE is used as an ideogram at Pylos on Un 219, La 630 and Un 1319. La 630 was noted in passing in Section 6.4.4; it records a textile, TELA+*PA*, and is likely to have been a stint record. The *verso* records a small amount of an unknown commodity (the word is broken) and four units of *PE*. It is not clear what *PE* might represent in this context, nor whether it is the same commodity as on Un 219. Un 1319 was discussed above (Section 6.6.2.2). The function of the document is unclear and *PE* in this context seems to have something to do with wheat, which suggests it is not the same commodity as in Un 219 (also, it is counted in dry measures).

At Knossos *PE* may *possibly* appear on the well-known record of deity names, V 52, from the RCT. The text is as follows.

V 52 + 52 bis + 8285 (—)
.1 a-ta-na-po-ti-ni-ja 1 ụ[ ]*vest*.[
.2 e-nu-wa-ri-jo 1 pa-ja-wo-ne 1 po-se-da[-o-ne

lat. inf. ⟦e-ri-nu-we ,. pe-ṛọ ⟧ [
r.1]*vest*.[: perhaps]-*wọ*[.
l.i. *pe-ṛọ* (or *pe-ṛọ*$_2$) or *PE* 1̣.

As indicated in the apparatus, *PE* 1̣ might be read rather than *pe-ro*. But this is speculative and the occurrence is in any case isolated.

Finally, *PE* appears as one of the commodities on the Mycenae spice tablets, which are not related to religion.

6.6.2.8 SUMMARY OF SIGNS ON PY UN 219

In general, the types of calculations done for commodities in the rest of the study were not possible for those represented by ideograms on PY Un 219, the main exception being *KO* at Knossos. In most cases, there was only a single attestation in a religious context and, if the sign did appear elsewhere, it was usually uncertain whether it represented the same commodity. In a sense, one might therefore state that, as with many other commodities we have seen, in most cases 100% of the recorded disbursements were for religious purposes. Only in the case of *KO* at Knossos did records exist relating to overall resources. The amounts disbursed for religious purposes were 40% of the amounts on the taxation records.

The commodities dealt with here are rare and obscure, so that one might not expect as extensive documentation concerning them as for the other records, but even so they conform to the general pattern observed elsewhere, that religious disbursements account for the majority of all disbursements. The use of the commodities for other purposes was either not recorded or does not survive in the existing documentation.

[213] Weilhartner 2005, 54.

6.6.3 OTHER OBSCURE IDEOGRAMS

6.6.3.1 INTRODUCTION TO THE REMAINING OBSCURE IDEOGRAMS

The remaining obscure ideograms are listed in Table 6-24. We will discuss them in turn, with the exception of **132*, which appears just once, in a banqueting context, and was discussed in Section 4.2.3. We may note in passing two cases of commodities which might have been added to the table, but which appear in suspect circumstances. Ideogram **172* appears on a tablet (Gg 701) sometimes thought to be an offering record, but which need not be (see Section 4.2.1.4). A couple of commodities (*to-ka-te-ri-ja ki-wa-ra* and *pa-ta-jo*) appear on Vn 1341 from the Pylos Northeastern Building, which may, on a possible new reading, include the word *Potnia*.[214] However, the reading is very uncertain and a consensus about whether the word *Potnia* does appear has not been reached.[215]

Table 6-24. Other obscure ideograms

sign	Knossos	Pylos	Mycenae	Thebes	Tiryns
PO/po	Ce 7516 see text	see text	—	Fq 207	—
ka-po / *KAPO* (=**127*)	F(2) 841	An 616 Un 249 Un 267 Un 592	—	—	—
**132*	—	Un 2	—	—	—
**134/*190*	U 7063 U 5592 Ws 8496	—	Go 610 Oi 701 Oi 702 Oi 703 Oi 704 Oi 706 Ue 661 Wt 700	Wu 48 Wu 80 Wu 89 Wu 95 Wu 98 Uo 121 (banqueting)	X 6??
**150*	Mc series	—	—	—	—
**157*	—	An 616 Un 249 Un 267	—	—	—
**170*	C 902	—	—	—	—

<u>Notes</u>
PO: The table only includes cases where *PO/po* is used as an ideogram; but other uses are noted in the text below.
ka-po/KAPO: May appear on KN X 6030 (text broken).
****134/*190***: On TI X 6.a, **1̣9̣0* is 'just possible' (*TITHEMY*, 30).
****150***: Possible on KN C 5669, but **258* is the preferred reading (cf. *CoMIK* III, 114).

6.6.3.2 THE USE OF *PO/PO*

po is used as an adjunct to VIR (KN B 808+), TELA (KN L(5) 7380), OLE (PY Fr 1201, –1203, –1208, –1214), and a commodity indicated by *ME* (PY An 616); it is ligatured with the vessel **211* (KN Fs 8, K(1) 873) and with TELA (TH Lf 139). It represents different things in the various contexts, for instance *po-ni-ki-jo* in the oil records,[216] and probably *po-ro-ko-wo* in the ligature to **211*.[217]

---

[214] Melena 1996–1997a, 168–70; followed by Palaima 2003a, 183, 185.
[215] See Bendall 2003, 221–2 for discussion. The text is given elsewhere by Killen (1999b, 347) without reading *po-ti-ni-ja*.
[216] Foster 1977b, 61–4.
[217] See Bendall forthcoming(b) with further references.

PO is used as an ideogram in just two records, KN Ce 7516 and TH Fq 207. Ce 7516 was discussed in Section 2.3.2.3, where it was noted that *PO* might in this context (just possibly) represent 'foals'. The tablet may be a banqueting record, but was judged 'Unclear'. The Thebes Fq tablets were discussed in Section 5.3.4; the majority of Fq records deal with barley and it is unclear what *PO* might mean in this connection.[218] In any case, the Fq tablets seem to have some association with religion.

6.6.3.3 *KAPO*/*KA-PO* (= **127*)

KAPO appears both as a ligature and spelled out, *ka-po*. It usually represents /*karpos*/ 'fruit(s)', but in one context (land-holdings) may represent /*kāpos*/ 'garden' (KN F(2) 841.5).[219] In the documents with which we are concerned here, issues to perfume manufacturers at Pylos, it means 'fruit(s)'. The commodity is not used as an offering, but appears indirectly in connection with religion on Un 249, an issue to a perfumer described as *po-ti-ni-ja-we-jo*. The amounts of *KAPO* on the various tablets are given in Table 6-25.

Table 6-25. *KAPO* at Pylos

	KAPO	= V
A. to a Potnian perfumer		
Un 249	T 6	36
B. to 'ordinary' perfumers		
An 616	4	240
Un 267	2 T 5	150
Un 592	3 T 4	204
Sub-total b		**594**
TOTAL a + b		**630**

The amount of fruit issued to the *Potnian* perfumer is about 6% of the total. Consumption of *KAPO* at Pylos in connection with a perfumer connected with religion does not seem to have been a major expenditure.

6.6.3.4 **134*/**190*

It is now recognised that signs **134* and **190* represent the same commodity,[220] although what the commodity is remains to be agreed.[221] It appears exclusively, or almost exclusively, in religious contexts.[222] We will discuss first the appearances at Thebes, then Knossos and Mycenae.

**134* appears at Thebes on five sealings and one tablet, Uo 121. All of these documents are related to banqueting (Section 2.3.2.5). On the sealings, the sign appears without numbers (= '1'), and with no other text except in the case of Wu 89 which comments *a-pu-do-ke*. In Uo 121 the sign appears together with one skin, a small amount of wine, a sheep and a goat. The tablet is broken at right and if there was a number recorded after **134* it is lost. 100% of the appearances of **134* at Thebes are thus in connection with banqueting and there are no data from which to estimate overall resources.

---

[218] AGS (*Thèbes* I, 209) note that in both the KN and the TH tablet *PO* happens to be followed by the same number ('7'), which is counted in whole units. This could of course be coincidence.

[219] Killen 1994–1995b, 373.

[220] The new Thebes sealing make clear that this is the same ideogram (Piteros, Olivier & Melena 1990, esp. 163–4). A decision was taken by the CIPEM at the International Colloquium in Austin 2000 to transcribe as **134* (see Palaima *et al.* forthcoming). The likelihood of an identity was noted from the outset, but caution was rightly applied in assigning a new number (*MT* III, 57).

[221] For **134* as a kind of foodstuff see Killen 1992b, 366–7. On the various proposals see Piteros *et al.* (1990, 164–6) for a summary; also Palmer 1999, 468.

[222] Killen 2006a, 89–90.

At Knossos, **134* appears on two tablets and one sealing. U 7063 has been identified by Killen as a banqueting record (see Section 2.3.2.3); ten units of **134* appear alongside a number of sheep and an unknown quantity of wine. U 5592 records 100 or more units of **134* (the reading is uncertain) but the remaining text is lost so the purpose of the document is 'Unclear'. The sealing, Ws 8496 (from the RCT), simply records the commodity. In this it resembles some of the Thebes sealings (e.g. Wu 80, –95; Table 2-7).

At Mycenae, the contexts are more varied. Go 610 is probably a record of disbursements of **134* to a number of women,[223] possibly workers in the textile industry since two of the names appear in records of issues of wool (Oe 113, –115). Each entry books an amount of **134* given in a liquid measure (S 1 and S 2). The total is S 6 (= V 36).

The MY Oi records deal exclusively with **134*.[224] The documents list anthroponyms and occupational titles, but also deity names, particularly *Potnia*. The data are set out in Table 6-26; entries connected with religion are shown in boldface type.

Table 6-26. The Mycenae Oi tablets

Oi	RECIPIENT	**134*
701.3	**si-to-po-ti-ni-ja**	**1+**
701.4	po-ro-po-i	10
701.5	ka-na-pe-u-si	6
701.6	[. .]-ta do-ke-ko-o-ke-ne	5
701.7	[ku-wa-]no-wo-ko-i	2
702.2	**]p̣ọ-ṭị-[ni-ja?**	**3**
702.3	]ne-ja , po-po-i	5
702.4	ku-wa-]ṇọ-wo-ko-i	2
702.5	*lost*	2
703.1	]-ro-i	1+
703.2	ku-wa-no-wo-ko-i	2
703.3	[do-]ke-ko-o-ke-ṇẹ-ị	5
704.1	**po-ti-ni-ja**	**15**
704.2	ka-na-pe-u-si	6
704.3	ko-o-ke-ne-ị	*lost*
704.4	ku-wa-ṇọ[-wo-ko-i	*lost*
705.1	ị-ku-to	*lost*
705.2	re-u-ko	*lost*
705.3	ka-ra-pa-so	*lost*
705.4	[. .]-wo-ko[	*lost*
706.2	*lost*	2
706.3	]ị	1
706.4	*lost*	]1̣
708	*no surviving text*	—
	TOTAL	**75+**

Note
In cases where the figure is lost the table counts '1'.

A total of 75+ units of **134* is recorded in the Oi tablets. Three entries register amounts against figures probably related to religion: Oi 701.3 (1+), –702.2 (3) and –704.1 (15).[225] The 19+ units booked against these figures are 25% of the whole.[226] (Note the figures from Go 610 cannot be added in since they are measured differently.) It may be, however, that all of the entries should be understood to have religious associations (note *Potnia* appears at the head of each tablet), in which case 100% of the disbursements would be for religious purposes.

[223] The names are in the dative; *MT* II, 110; Killen 1992b, 366.
[224] *MT* III, 57–60; recently Weilhartner 2005, 216–18.
[225] *MT* III, 58–9.
[226] Killen 2006a, 89.

6.6.3.5 **150*

**150* appears in the Mc series at Knossos, discussed above (Section 6.2.3.1). The documents are proportional taxation records dealing with female goats (CAP^f), CORN (probably agrimi horn), **142* (probably honeycomb; Section 4.2.1.4) and **150* (unidentified). As Killen has argued, on one of the tablets, Mc 4462, one unit of **150* is allocated as an offering to the god *a-re*, Ares.[227] The text is as follows.

Mc 4462 + 5792 + 5808 + 5816 + 8450 + *frr.* (132)
.A 'ra-wo-qo-no' **150* 61 CAP^f 30 [
.B ti-]ri-to / a-re **150* 1 **142* M 26 CORN 52[

A similar situation may obtain in Mc 4454, where a unit of **150* is allocated to *da*. The text is as follows.

Mc 4454 + 4458 + *fr.* (132)
.A 'da-wa-no' **150* 29 CAP^f 16
.B u-qa-mo / *da* **150* 1 **142* M 13 CORN 26

The significance of the designation *da* is obscure – it need not refer to a theonym and may simply abbreviate the name of the man *da-wa-no* who appears in line .A as the person responsible for the payment.[228] This tablet is included merely for the sake of completeness; the nature of the allocation must be considered 'Unclear'.

Figures for the total amount of **150* collected in the Mc series are given in the totalling tablets Mc 4457 and –5107 (see Section 6.2.3.1 for the texts and discussion), one of which records 345 and the other 354 units of **150*. Taking the smaller figure (in order to be conservative, although the amounts are so similar it scarcely matters), the single unit allocated to *a-re* is a bare 0.3% of all that is collected.

6.6.3.6 **157*

**157* appears only at Pylos, on the same tablets, minus one, as *KAPO* (Section 6.6.3.2) It is uncertain what the sign represents.[229] The data are set out in Table 6-27.

Table 6-27. **157* at Pylos

	**157*
A. to a Potnian *perfumer*	
Un 249	10
B. to 'ordinary' perfumers	
An 616	28
Un 267	16
Sub-total b	**44**
TOTAL a + b	**54**

The amount issued to a *Potnian* perfumer is 19% of the total.

6.6.3.7 **170*

Ideogram **170* is attested only in KN C 902, a probable banqueting record (Section 2.3.2.3). It

[227] Killen forthcoming(a); see also forthcoming(b); Gulizio 2001; Weilhartner 2005, 62–3. For early references to *a-re* as a theonym see Melena 1972, 33 n 6.
[228] As suggested by Olivier 1967c, 331; see also Weilhartner 2005, 63.
[229] See e.g. Shelmerdine 1985, 18.

need not have any connection to the oxen with which it is recorded in the sense of being an animal-derived product, but may represent monthly dedications whatever the commodity is.[230]

6.7 CONCLUSION TO THE COMMODITIES SURVEY

This chapter concludes our survey of commodities used in connection with religion in the Linear B records. We have examined oil (Chapter 3), wine and honey (Chapter 4), various grains, figs and cyperus (Chapter 5) and animals, animal products, textiles, metals and a number of obscure commodities (Chapter 6). A summary of the conclusions is provided in Table 6-28 (given in order of their treatment in the chapters); this is intended as a reference, but is not meant to replace the more detailed accounts.

It has been noted as we progressed through the data that various anomalies arise with regard to the recording of disbursements, above all a curious lack of record-keeping in many essential areas (or at least the failure of any documents that may originally have existed to have been preserved in the archaeological record). It was frequently found to be the case that substantial proportions of 'final use' disbursements were for religious purposes, but that when overall resources could be ascertained, religious uses did not consume a majority of available goods. It was also observed that, in very many instances, most of the documentation relating to final uses was simply 'missing'. The reasons for and significance of these anomalies require consideration, as they impact on our understanding of documentation of religion and hence how the Linear B evidence for religion is to be interpreted.

In the next chapter we will draw together the data collected in Chapters 3–6 and consider what the survey tells us about the extent of resources expended for religious purposes by the Mycenaean palaces. This will lead us to enquire more generally about Linear B record-keeping as related to religion and Mycenaean administrative practices more widely.

Table 6-28. Summary of the commodities survey

LIQUID MEASURES
Oil (untreated and perfumed) • *Pylos*: A minimum of 71%, probably at least 87%, and quite possibly 100%, of disbursements for 'final use' are religious offerings. No disbursements are clearly non-religious. There are no records of how oil was obtained by the palace, but that much was available is suggested by the records of issues of raw materials to perfumers. Only perfumed oil is documented, in contrast with Knossos. • *Knossos*: Records of non-religious disbursements exist, but offerings still account for a large proportion, nearly half of 'final use' disbursements. Unlike Pylos, there are records of produce coming in, which can be used to estimate 'overall resources'. Amounts disbursed as offerings turn out to be a very small proportion of resources overall, corroborating to an extent what is suggested indirectly at Pylos.
Unguent • Unguent appears only at Pylos, and only in connection with banquets. There is no direct evidence for overall resources but, given the large scale of the Pylian perfume industry, it is likely that more resources were available than are indicated in the records. It is notable that 'ordinary' oil *never* appears on banqueting records, and unguent *only* appears on banqueting records.
Honey • *Knossos*: Final uses attested for honey are as offerings and in perfume manufacture. If only tablets definitely dealing with perfume manufacture are included in the calculations, some 67–73% of the honey disbursed was for offerings. If a few further 'probable' records are included, the range drops to 28–35%. Taxation records give some indication of overall resources. Disbursements for offerings account for some 30–40% of overall amounts on records which clearly record honey – but if Gg 521 recorded honey as well (which is uncertain, but likely) the proportion for offerings would shrink to a mere 3–4% • *Pylos*: Honey is attested with certainty only in Un 718, but is probably represented by the syllabogram *ME* in a few banqueting and perfumery records. 'Final use' disbursements in connection with banqueting are 14% of

[230] Killen forthcoming(a).

the total (the remainder being perfumery disbursements). If *KE* represents beeswax, a related product, it seems the palace could gain access to substantial resources should it wish.

- *Chania*: One of the five tablets found at Chania records offerings of honey. No data are available for overall resources but one tablet from Knossos gives data possibly related to honey for Kydonia.

Wine

- *Knossos*: In the RCT, 100% of the wine appears in connection with banqueting, but on just two records. On non-RCT tablets wine appears on one banqueting record, the Fs tablets, one possible collection record (Gm 840) and two 'Unclear' records. 100% of disbursements are in connection with religion/banqueting, but the picture may change depending on how Gm 840 is interpreted. Note that the vast majority of preserved disbursements of wine are from the RCT. Preservational factors and uncertainties over interpretation vitiate the figures.
- *Pylos*: 76% (without Vn 20) or 94% (with Vn 20) of 'final use' disbursements were for banqueting. As at Knossos, this purpose consumes the majority of documented wine, but unlike Knossos other uses (industrial, *o-no*) are attested. There is no information on 'overall resources', although there are records of vines.
- *Mycenae*: Wine appears on three tablets, one banqueting (or at least dining), one a probable delivery record, and one 'Unclear'. 100% of 'final use' disbursements are for banqueting but the amount recorded is quite small (v 12+); also, the 'banquet' in question was not necessarily a major state-organised feast such as other 'banqueting' records relate to. This may be a rare isolated instance of 'ordinary' dining. The large amount on the (probable) delivery record hints at larger resources, although it should be noted that the commodity recorded is wine related, not necessarily wine itself.
- *Thebes*: 100% of disbursements are connected with religion (whether festival rations, sacred meals or something else). There are no records of overall resources, but the approx. 860 litres recorded for the surviving disbursement records suggest access to considerable quantities.

DRY MEASURES

Wheat

- *Knossos*: Wheat reverses the situation witnessed for commodities so far, in that religious disbursements are not a significant proportion of all disbursements. Just 7% of disbursements are for religious purposes, recorded on just one tablet. The majority of disbursements are for rations. The picture for overall resources, however, is in line with the small amounts seen for other commodities, if even more extreme – religious disbursements make up just 0.2% of overall resources. The harvest records make clear that overall resources were very substantial – well over one million litres of wheat appears in the preserved documents.
- *Pylos*: The situation is similar to Knossos, with just 5% or less of wheat disbursed for religious purposes; the majority of disbursements are rations. Here, however, there are no harvest records. On the other hand, we have land tenure records.
- *Thebes*: 100% of wheat disbursements are for religious purposes. There is one attestation in connection with land tenure.
- *Observation*: At Pylos and Knossos, religious disbursements are not a significant proportion of all disbursements. The main use of wheat is as 'ordinary' rations, which are counted as 'final' disbursements, though the underlying purpose was primarily industrial.

Barley

- *Knossos*: Barley is disbursed in religious contexts and there is one ordinary rations record. For non-RCT records, 24% of disbursements are for religious purposes. For RCT records the figure may be 100%, depending on the interpretation of F(1) 193. Taking RCT and non-RCT together, nineteen tablets record 'religious' disbursements, and just one records secular rations. Either barley was not normally disbursed, or was not normally recorded, or the records have been lost or (more likely) were not kept or 'archived'. There are no records of how the commodity was obtained.
- *Pylos*: Barley appears primarily in banqueting and festival rations contexts (90%); there are also records of 'secular' rations. There are no unambiguous records of collections.
- *Mycenae*: There is one appearance only, on an offering record.
- *Thebes*: 100% of disbursements are for religious purposes; there are no records of collections. The disbursements are generally very small but are recorded on numerous tablets.
- *Observation*: Both Pylos and Knossos have non-religious disbursements for rations, but the single such disbursement preserved at Knossos is for a larger amount. This accounts for the discrepancy between 24% (Knossos) and 90% (Pylos). There are no (unambiguous) harvest records for either site; all (clear) records are of disbursements.

Flour

- Flour at all sites is disbursed in surviving Linear B records only for religious purposes. However, available resources would have been large, judging from amounts of wheat and barley recorded at Knossos and Pylos. It is inconceivable that the flour in our records was all that which existed or was used; it is more likely that flour was not normally recorded.

Figs

- *Knossos*: 100% of disbursements are for religious purposes, but probable harvest records suggest these disbursements account for only a small proportion (1.8%) of overall resources. In addition, a large number of fig trees (2044) is recorded, again suggesting substantial resources.

- *Pylos*: Unlike Knossos, religious disbursements account for a mere 2.5% of all disbursements; most disbursements are for ordinary rations, plus there are a few *o-no* records. There are no records of resources coming in, but figs appear as a major staple and the palace was clearly able to gain access to the commodity, however this was done.
- *Mycenae*: 100% of disbursements are for offerings and banqueting. There are no clear collection records.
- *Tiryns*: Figs appear on one tablet, a possible festival rations record.
- *Observation*: Viewed together with the data for wheat, it appears that a crucial factor in how much religious disbursements account for is whether a commodity was used or not for 'ordinary' rations.

Olives

- *Knossos*: Olives appear on just three disbursement records. Two (including one from the RCT) are connected with religion; the third is an ordinary rations record but the ideogram has been erased. Yet substantial amounts are recorded on harvest records – over 14,000 litres on the securely identified harvest records and nearly 75,000 litres on the definite plus probable harvest records. Amounts disbursed for religious purposes were 16% of the first amount and just 3% of the second. No records survive of what was done with the majority of olives.
- *Pylos*: Olives appear primarily in banqueting and festival rations records. There is a single instance of an issue as ordinary rations. 74% of disbursements are for religious purposes. There are no collection records.
- *Thebes*: 100% of disbursements are for religious purposes, but substantial resources are suggested by the approx. 18,600 litres of olives used as a measure of land on Ft 140.
- *Mycenae*: Olives appear on two documents, one a possible banqueting record, the other unclear but probably a delivery record. Amounts on the possible banqueting record equal 80% of the amount on the unclear/delivery record and 44% of the combined total, but since the figures derive from just two documents it is best simply to accept that such a calculation for 'overall resources' is meaningless.
- *Observation*: Knossos and Pylos are skewed in different ways. Knossos has collection records but few disbursements; Pylos has disbursement records (almost entirely religious) and no collections.

Cyperus

- *Knossos*: Cyperus appears almost exclusively in offerings and banqueting contexts; there is one industrial disbursement, for perfumery. 88% of the amounts recorded are earmarked for 'religious' purposes. There are numerous taxation and harvest records. Religious disbursements account for just 7% of overall resources. It is notable that all disbursements together account for just 8%. Again, we do not have records of what was done with the majority of the resources.
- *Pylos*: As at Knossos, disbursements are made only in connection with banqueting, offerings and perfumery. There are more perfumery records than at Knossos and 'religious' purposes account for just 15% of expenditures. Of the perfumery records, 11% of amounts disbursed were for a *Potnian* perfumer. There are no clear records of collections but the large amounts recorded in connection with the perfume industry and on some of the 'Unclear' documents hint at substantial resources.
- *Mycenae*: 100% of disbursements are for religious purposes (albeit coming from a single document). The amount disbursed is just 5% of gathered resources.
- *Thebes*: 100% of disbursements are for religious purposes. There are no records of overall resources.
- *Observation*: There is a general pattern, seen also for wheat and olives at Knossos, that where harvesting records exist, amounts disbursed for religious purposes turn out to be a small percentage of available resources.

ANIMALS

Bovines

- *Knossos*: For non-RCT tablets, bovines are recorded in one or two banqueting records, plus as working oxen and in 'Collector' flocks. The banqueting records are the only 'disbursements' (i.e. for consumption), and such records are thus 100% of all disbursements. The percentage of overall resources is either 0.9% or 13%, depending on whether C 902 is taken as a banqueting record or not. It is notable that the judgement about a single tablet makes such a significant difference. The large number of animals recorded in 'Unclear' records should also be noted. From the RCT there is one banqueting record (with a large number of animals) and a number of working oxen. The banqueting record animals are 22% of the total.
- *Pylos*: Bovines appear *only* in banqueting records, so this activity accounts for 100% of 'disbursements', but it is implausible that the 34–36 beasts recorded represent all that were available to the palace. Indirect hints at overall resources come from the some 294+ men described as cowherds (possibly ploughmen?) plus the large number of oxhides (over 1000) the palace was able to gain access to through taxation in the Ma tablets. If each man described as a cowherd were assigned just one animal, the number of those going for banqueting would be 10% of the whole; if the men were assigned a pair, the figure would be 6%. Similarly, if each oxhide implies one animal, the few disbursed for banqueting represent 3%.
- *Thebes*: Just two bovines appear, in sealings related to banqueting. There are no indications of overall resources.

Sheep

- *Knossos*: Some 80,000–100,000 sheep are recorded in records of standing flocks. Breeding flocks belonging to the deity *Potnia* appear in various records, but her flocks total just 1% of the whole and 2% if only other 'Collector' flocks are counted. The dedication of flocks shows the importance of the deity to the palace, but she was evidently not a major 'Collector'. Note that all her flocks appear in breeding records. Banqueting and fattening records come from both the RCT and elsewhere. Non-RCT tablets record 512+ sheep for banqueting and fattening – just 0.5–0.6% of the total in the standing flock records. In the RCT likewise 100% of 'disbursements' are for banqueting, and there is one fattening record. In terms of overall resources, the animals on banqueting records represent 2% of figures recorded on other tablets; taking the fattening record also into account gives 8%.

- *Pylos*: Sheep are 'disbursed' only for banqueting, but the numbers are just 1.6–1.7% of the some 10,220 recorded in standing flocks.
- *Thebes*: Sheep appear only in banqueting records, but access to wool in the Of records suggests further resources.

Goats

- *Knossos*: Goats are 'disbursed' in banqueting records, plus goats may appear in a deity flock. These animals represent 3.5% of animals in other flocks or being received in the Mc tax records. In the RCT, one tablet records a 'disbursement' for banqueting; the others are 'Unclear'.
- *Pylos*: Goats appear in banqueting and one *o-no* record. Taking these as 'final use' disbursements, banqueting accounts for 95% of the total. Banqueting disbursements are 3.7% compared with animals in standing flocks.
- *Thebes*: Goats appear only in banqueting contexts; no records relate to overall resources.

Pigs

- *Knossos*: Pigs appear in banqueting and flock records. 100% of disbursements are for banqueting. For non-RCT tablets pigs 'disbursed' for banqueting represent 3% of overall resources. For RCT records there are no figures to compare, apart from a large but erased number which may or may not pertain to pigs on Ce 162.
- *Pylos*: Pigs appear in banqueting and herd management records. One table records a flock of 190 animals belonging to *Potnia*. Animals 'disbursed' for banqueting are 24% of those in non-*Potnia* flocks, and animals belonging to *Potnia* are 32% of all animals in standing flocks. The banqueting and *Potnia* flocks together are 41% of the total of all pigs recorded in any context.
- *Thebes*: Pigs appear only in the Wu sealings; no records relate to overall resources.
- *Observation*: Compared with animals kept in standing flocks, the number of sheep and goats intended for banqueting is negligible. But it is interesting that the figure for pigs is so high. This may result from the fact that the figures for the sheep and goats refer to herds kept for secondary products (such as wool), whereas the pigs would have been intended primarily for consumption, so that only in the case of the pigs are we comparing animals with each other that were (ultimately) intended for similar purposes. There may be a hint that we are seeing something more of the 'real' situation in the percentages for pigs at Pylos.

ANIMAL PRODUCTS

Cheese

- Cheese appears in only two tablets, both at Pylos and both banqueting records. This commodity seems not to be normally recorded in Linear B, but the large numbers of sheep and goats kept in palace flocks make clear that ample sources for production were available.

Sheepskin

- The same general comments apply as for cheese. Sheepskin appears on one tablet at Pylos, and one at Thebes, both banqueting records. Sheepskin does not appear to be normally recorded in Linear B (but note that oxhide appears in large numbers at Pylos), yet the extensive flocks of sheep at Pylos again indicate availability of the resource, whether recorded or not.

Wool

- *Knossos*: Wool appears in religious contexts as offerings and in connection with deity flocks. Besides offerings, there are only two 'final' disbursement records (*o-no* payment); the offerings make up 77% of the total recorded. The vast majority of disbursements relate to transfers within the textile industry (with little or no indication of what was done with the finished textiles). The amounts used for offerings are a bare 0.07% collected for the industry (some 30–50 tons annually). Wool from deity flocks would probably also have been used for industrial purposes, but it represents a fraction (0.6%) of the main bulk. If compared only with other 'Collector' flocks (which is better), the amount is still only 2%. Deities, while clearly important since having dedicated flocks reflected high status, were not major 'Collectors'.
- *Pylos*: Wool appears in the contexts of banqueting, *o-no* payments, perfumery, and textile production (the last very poorly attested indeed, unlike Knossos, although the mention of 40 units of cloth on one of the few stint records should be noted). One of the industrial disbursements is to a *Potnian* perfumery. Of non-industrial disbursements for 'final use', wool in connection with banqueting is 39%. Taking the perfumery records into account as well (since the wool would be 'consumed', or rendered otherwise unsuitable for further use, in the processing) the *Potnian* and banqueting wool is 28%. Overall resources cannot be estimated through attestations of the wool ideogram since they are so few, but can be inferred by the large number of sheep in palace-run flocks. The amount disbursed in connection with banqueting plus to the *Potnia* perfumer is a bare 0.18% of the potential output of palace flocks. Once again religion makes up much of attested 'final use', but very little of the likely overall resources.
- *Thebes*: Wool appears only in connection with industrial processing, but three disbursements are to deities as 'Collectors'. The amounts of these disbursements as compared with the rest depend on how the lost figure for Hermes is restored. If he is allocated the same amount as the other deities (the most logical approach), deity

disbursements are 3% of the total. If, for the sake of argument, Hermes were allowed the highest figure actually attested in the series, the deity disbursements would be 12%. Following the latter procedure is of course dubious but serves to highlight the extent of the 'unknowns'.

- *Mycenae and Tiryns*: There are no clear connections with religious disbursements and some of the readings are insecure. Two 'final use' disbursement records involving *o-no* payments at Mycenae may be noted.

TEXTILES

A simple cloth: *146

- *Pylos*: Some 55% or 64% of disbursements are for religious purposes (depending on whether Mn 1411 joins –1367 and –1368), and such disbursements constitute either 14–15 or 20–21% of overall resources (again depending on the same joins). Either way, these proportions are higher than seen for any other commodity at Pylos except oil and pigs. It may be significant that both of these commodities are particularly connected with offerings (in the case of oil) and banqueting (in the case of pigs, which are primarily kept for meat). It may be that these three commodities really were allocated more commonly for religious purposes than the others seem to have been. It is further worth noting, however, that the amount of disbursements overall – both religious and non-religious – constitute only about 25% of the total resources. The use of the majority of the items is unclear.
- *Knossos*: A mere 6+ units of **146* are recorded in non-industrial disbursements, 4+ for offerings and 2 as an *o-no* payment. Offerings are thus 66% of disbursements for final use. That more cloth was available to the palace is attested by one industrial disbursement (30 units), several delivery/store documents (150 units) and a number of 'Unclear' records, including one recording 250 units. What the ultimate use of the items recorded on these documents would have been is unknown, but there are two points worth highlighting. First, large amounts of the commodity were available for use, far more than noted in the few disbursement records (of any sort), and second, the loss of data on just one tablet (that recording 250 units) can have a substantial effect on the figures.

166/*166+WE

- *Knossos*: There are three disbursement tablets, two for military purposes from the RCT and one offering record not from the RCT. The offering record has an unusually large number of items (22+). There are no records of incoming resources (including from palace workshops).
- *Pylos*: 100% of disbursements are for religious purposes, but only 2+ units are involved. One of the stint records has 62 units, suggesting larger resources; the offerings constitute 3% of this amount although the ultimate use of the textiles produced under the stint is of course unknown. Two further records which *may* be offerings records, but which are classed as 'Unclear', record larger numbers than on the two secure offerings/banqueting records (11 units), and would raise the proportion set against overall resources to 21%. Unlike Knossos, it is at least clear at Pylos that the commodity was produced in palatial workshops.

TELA, TELA+*TE* and TELA+*PA*

- TELA+*TE* is common at Knossos, but does not appear in religious contexts. At Pylos it appears once in the context of banqueting and twice on stint records. The amount on the banqueting record is lost; the stint records record 40 units.
- TELA and TELA+*PA* appear once at Pylos, in a banqueting context. TELA is unattested elsewhere, but 36+ units of TELA+*PA* appear on stint records.

METALS AND OTHER COMMODITIES

Gold

- *Knossos*: Gold is rare at Knossos and appears only on two records of vessels, which may be relevant to banqueting and libations (or may not).
- *Pylos*: Gold vessels appear, one group in a secure offerings context (Tn 316), the other possibly as part of the service ware used on the occasion of a feast (Tn 996). Also in a banqueting context, the Ta tablets record gold as furniture inlay, and there are golden chains for binding sacrificial victims. One tablet concerns 'sacred gold' involving a priestess and a number of women. Incoming gold is recorded as levies on various officials (some 5–6 kg). Four goldsmiths are attested, suggesting adequate resources to provide such specialists with work, but there are no inventory records or other clues to overall resources.

Bronze

- *Knossos*: Bronze appears at Knossos on records dealing with a bathtub and vessels, which might be relevant to banqueting(?), as breastplates, and in connection with textiles and chariots. At least seventy-one bronze ingots are recorded in tablets from the Throne Room.
- *Pylos*: 'Temple bronze' is appropriated by the palace in Jn 829, and bronze vessels appear in a possible banqueting context in Tn 996. The Jn series records disbursements of bronze to some 228 smiths at various locations, nineteen of whom are described as *Potnian*; these receive about 6% of the total amount allocated.

Obscure commodities

- It was not possible in most cases to achieve even vaguely meaningful calculations, but where possible the patterns observed were similar to those seen elsewhere.

CHAPTER 7
MYCENAEAN ADMINISTRATION AND DOCUMENTATION OF RELIGION

7.1 THE EXTENT OF RESOURCES DEDICATED TO RELIGION

In Chapters 3–6 we examined all commodities recorded in connection with religious purposes in the extant Linear B corpus. For every commodity, at each site for which relevant records were available, figures were calculated for:

1. the amount disbursed for religious purposes
2. the amount disbursed for other purposes
3. the amount of overall resources.

The aim was to attempt to determine, first, the proportion of all 'final use' disbursements represented by disbursements for religious purposes (comparing the figures derived for 1 and 2), and second, the proportion of total resources represented by amounts disbursed for religious purposes (comparing the figures derived for 1 and 3). This chapter considers the results of the survey. The data are summarised in Table 7-1, which sets out the calculations for each site. Knossos is shown with separate columns for RCT tablets and non-RCT tablets; data from Chania and Tiryns are shown in the same column because of the small number of tablets involved. Table 7-1 in a real sense marks the central outcome of the study. What can we learn from it?

Two patterns in the figures of Table 7-1 are immediately striking. First, in the great majority of cases, disbursements for religious purposes form a very *large* proportion – often 100% – of all 'final disbursements' recorded. Second, and in contrast, the proportions of disbursements for religious purposes are generally *small* in comparison with overall resources. The remainder of this chapter probes the significance of these observations.

Let us begin by exploring the patterns further, beginning with the 'final use' disbursements columns. The figures are remarkable. In forty-seven out of the sixty-six possible calculations, religious disbursements were, or could be as much as, 100% of all 'final use' disbursements, while in a further seven cases they are above 70%. Thus, in fifty-four out of sixty-six cases (82%), religious disbursements account for 70% or more of all 'final use' disbursements. What does this mean? Could it truly be the case that some 70–100% of all but a few of the commodities for which calculations were possible really was consumed for religious purposes?

The figures in the 'overall resources' columns suggest an immediate response to the contrary. In twenty-two out of the thirty-six possible calculations (61%), the figures are 5% or less (including 'negligible'). This is so even where the 'final use' disbursements column has figures of 100%, for example wine and figs at Knossos, cheese and two textiles at Pylos, and flour at both sites. Nowhere are overall resources consumed more than 41%, and most are much lower. Further, half of the fourteen figures (or ranges) above 5% include figures which

Table 7-1. Proportions of resources disbursed for religious purposes

commodity	Knossos (RCT) % of 'final use' disbursements	Knossos (RCT) % of overall resources	Knossos (non-RCT) % of 'final use' disbursements	Knossos (non-RCT) % of overall resources	Pylos % of 'final use' disbursements	Pylos % of overall resources
Liquids						
oil	n/r	n/r	12–46	6–9	71–100	11–34
unguent(?)	—	—	—	—	100	negligible
honey	—	—	28–35/67–73	3–4/30–40	14	n/a
wine	100	n/a	100	0.2	76/94	n/a
Solids						
wheat	n/r	n/r	7	0.2	4	negligible
barley	100	n/a	24	n/a	90	n/a
flour	—	—	100	negligible	100	negligible
figs	100	n/a	100	2	2.5	n/a
olives	97–100	36	100	4–16	74	n/a
cyperus	100	16	87	7	15/11◆	n/a
Animals						
bovines	100	22	100	0.8–13	100	3/6/10
sheep	100	2–8	100	0.5	100	2
goats	100	n/a	100	3	95	4
pigs	100	2	100	3	100	24/32/41
cheese	—	—	—	—	100	negligible
skins	—	—	—	—	100	negligible
wool	—	—	77	0.07	28/39	0.2
Textiles						
146	—	—	67	2–6?	55/64	14–15/20–21
166+WE	n/r	n/a	100	n/a	100	3
TELA+*TE*	n/r	n/r	n/r	n/r	100	n/a
TELA+*PA*	n/r	n/r	n/r	n/r	100	3
Metals						
gold	n/a	n/a	n/a	n/a	n/a	n/a
bronze	n/a	n/a	n/a	n/a	6◆	n/a

commodity	Thebes % of 'final use' disbursements	Thebes % of overall resources	Mycenae % of 'final use' disbursements	Mycenae % of overall resources	Chania & Tiryns % of 'final use' disbursements	Chania & Tiryns % of overall resources
Liquids						
oil	—	—	n/r	n/r	—	—
unguent(?)	—	—	—	—	—	—
honey	—	—	—	—	KH: 100	KH: n/a
wine	100	n/a	100	3?	—	—
Solids						
wheat	100	n/a	n/r	n/r	TI: n/r	TI: n/r
barley	100	n/a	100	n/a	—	—
flour	100	n/a	100	n/a	—	—
figs	—	—	n/a	n/a	TI: 100?	TI: n/a
olives	100?	2	100?	n/a?	—	—
cyperus	100	n/a	100	5	—	—
Animals						
bovines	100	n/a	—	—	TI: n/r	TI: n/r
sheep	100	n/a	—	—	—	—
goats	100	n/a	—	—	—	—
pigs	100	n/a	—	—	—	—
cheese	—	—	—	—	—	—
skins	100	n/a	—	—	—	—
wool	3(12?)◆	n/a	n/r	n/r	TI: n/r*	TI: n/r*
Textiles						
146	—	—	—	—	—	—
166+WE	—	—	—	—	—	—
TELA+*TE*	—	—	—	—	—	—
TELA+*PA*	—	—	—	—	TI: ⟦n/r*⟧	TI: ⟦n/r*⟧
Metals						
gold	—	—	—	—	TI: n/r*	TI: n/r*
bronze	—	—	—	—	—	—

Key

— = Commodity not attested

n/r = Commodity attested but not (or not clearly) in connection with religion

n/a = Commodity attested, but no meaningful calculation possible

* = Ideogram doubtful
◆ = For industrial processing
⟦ ⟧ = Ideogram possibly attested, but erased

Notes

These notes indicate for convenient reference why some figures appear with question-marks and why sometimes more than one figure (or range of figures) appears in the table; for fuller discussion see Section 6.7, Table 6-28, and individual sections for commodities at various sites.

Honey at Knossos: In the disbursements column, the first range of figures includes all probable and the second only definite perfumery records. In the overall resources column, the first range includes Gg 521, the second excludes it.

Wine at Pylos: The first figure excludes Vn 20, the second includes it.

Olives at Mycenae: A question-mark is shown because olives appear on just two documents, one a *possible* banqueting record, the other a *possible* delivery record.

Cyperus at Pylos: The first figure is for all final uses; the second gives the percentage of disbursements for perfumery going to a *Potnian* perfumer.

Bovines at Pylos: The first figure compares bovines for banqueting with oxhides received by the palace; the next two compare the same with numbers of men described as oxherds, the first assuming two animals per man, the second assuming one.

Pigs at Pylos: The first figure compares animals for banqueting with animals in standing flocks; the second compares *Potnian* flocks with other flocks; the third compares *Potnian* flocks and animals for consumption with other flocks.

Wool at Thebes: The higher figure results from restoring an unusually large amount for Hermes.

***146* at Pylos**: Disbursements for final use are either 55% or 64% depending on tablet joins; the two ranges in the overall resources column depend on the same joins.

TELA+***TE*** may be indirectly attested in the RCT (Wm 8493), but the context is not religious (*Scribes RCT*, 209).

---

could be less than 5%, depending on various factors which affected how the percentages were calculated (these in order of magnitude are: 0.8–13, 2–3/30–40, 2–6?, 2–8, 3/6/10, 4–16, 6–9). Only seven of the thirty-six possible calculations yielded proportions which must be more than 5% (7, 11–34, 14–15/20–21, 16, 22, 24/32/41, 36). So in twenty-nine out of thirty-six cases, the figures are or could be less than 5%. The overall pattern is consistent enough to give rise to a not implausible inference: that religion did not consume the majority of resources for any commodity at any site.[1]

Some minor observations support this conclusion. First, that the pattern occurs across a range of different types of commodities, overall resources for which were calculated in a variety of ways, may suggest that it is meaningful. Second, 'hazards of preservation' may tend to favour retrieval of figures from offerings records due partly to the larger numbers of tablets involved, in which case this transaction type may be over-represented. With olive oil at Pylos, for instance, it was observed (Section 3.2.2) that the care with which even small disbursements for offerings are recorded suggests that records for this activity may be more or less complete (over the given period of the administrative cycle involved), in contrast with the clearly incomplete documentation for overall resources. Further, whereas offerings records tend to book small amounts, harvest and taxation records tend to book large amounts. Hazards of preservation would affect these documents with unequal force: the loss of ten or so offerings records would not affect the figures to the extent that the loss of a single harvesting record would. We are thus likely on the whole to be underestimating overall resources.

But if this is so, and it is the case that use for religious purposes in general did not consume major proportions of palatial resources, the high percentages in the 'final use' disbursements column appear all the more striking. How may we account for the discrepancies?

[1] Although a few of the proportions might be considered 'substantial' if they do indeed reflect any sort of reality.

One obvious place to seek an answer would be in the nature of the documentation itself. It has been long observed, and is well known, that the Linear B records provide an incomplete account of Mycenaean economic (and other) activities. There are many 'gaps' in the evidence. In particular, and of special relevance here, it has often been remarked that the disbursement of finished products is rarely recorded in Linear B.[2] The quantified data provided in Table 7-1 bring this observation into sharp focus, and add a less frequently observed gloss on the phenomenon: when final disbursements *are* recorded, they tend overwhelmingly to be for religious purposes.

The bias towards documentation of disbursements related to religion may be further emphasised. At the outset of our commodities survey (Section 3.1) a broad distinction was drawn between disbursements for 'final use' and disbursements for industrial manufacture where the raw materials would be expected eventually to return to the palaces in the form of finished products. This distinction has been useful throughout the study, but a few 'grey areas' were noted and it is useful at this point to expand on and clarify them.

First, let us reiterate the distinction. Our focus has been on 'final use' in the sense that the commodity concerned is actually *consumed* in some way and would not return to the palace in any form related to its original materiality. This is not to say the palaces would not necessarily derive some benefit from such transactions – for instance, Pylos gained alum in exchange for wool and other commodities from the *o-no* payment recorded in An 35 – but the point is that the wool as such was not returned. The situation differs radically from cases where the palaces would issue wool to weavers and expect to receive back woollen textiles, particularly through the *ta-ra-si-ja* system. The question here is whether a disbursement represents 'actual expenditure' in the sense of 'real out-go'. Issues of wool where the commodity would be returned eventually in the form of textiles do not count as 'real out-go'. Now, so far we have included as 'actual expenditure' (that is, what we have been calling 'final use' disbursements) industrial transactions where the commodity would be consumed in the process, for instance oil in tanning or wool in perfumery. But such cases differ in an important way from 'final use' disbursements such as *o-no* payments and offerings, because, although consumed, the materials were used for processing products that *would* be returned to the palace (i.e. skins and perfumed oil). The case is similar for rations. Because wheat or figs disbursed as 'ordinary' rations would actually be consumed by those to whom they were issued, we have so far counted them as 'final use' disbursements. However, where the point of issuing the rations was to maintain a workforce engaged in manufacture,[3] although the rations would be *consumed*, the labour undertaken as enabled by such consumption would in a real and tangible form be 'returned' in terms of value added to raw materials. In this sense, ordinary (as opposed to festival) rations, and goods consumed in connection with industrial processing, may be grouped with disbursements for industrial manufacture rather than 'final use' disbursements.

If this revised grouping is applied to Table 7-1, the bias in the documentation appears yet more extreme. We observed above that only in twelve out of sixty-six cases did the proportion of 'final use' disbursements for religious purposes fall below 70%. The distribution of these exceptions is significant and we set them out here as follows (all cases at Knossos are non-RCT).

1. oil at Knossos (12–46%)
2. barley at Knossos (24%)
3. wheat at Knossos (7%)

[2] E.g. Halstead 1988, 525–6; 1990–1991, 360; 1992a, 62.

[3] Although some would have been for e.g. persons supplying services or employed in construction or engineering works.

4. wheat at Pylos (4%)
5. figs at Pylos (2.5%)
6. cyperus at Pylos (15/11%)
7. wool at Pylos (28/39%)
8. wool at Thebes (3[12?]%)
9. honey at Pylos (14%)
10. **146* at Knossos (67%)
11. **146* at Pylos (55/64%)
12. bronze at Pylos (6%)

In the first five cases listed, oil and barley at Knossos, figs at Pylos and wheat at both sites, the commodity concerned was used for 'ordinary' rations. It was noted at the end of Chapter 5 that a commodity's being used for rations greatly affected the proportion expended for religious purposes. This is in fact so across the board, and it is significant that where a commodity is *not* attested in connection with rations at a particular site (for instance, oil at Pylos and figs at Knossos), the 'exception' does not hold. Thus, at Pylos 'final use' disbursements of oil in connection with religion accounted for 71–100% of all disbursements, but just 11–34% of 'overall resources', and at Knossos 'final use' disbursements of figs in connection with religion accounted for 100% of all disbursements, but just 2% of 'overall resources'. We may compare cases where the same commodities were used for rations. At Knossos, oil disbursements for religious purposes were 12–46% of all disbursements and 6–9% of overall resources, while at Pylos figs for religious purposes represented just 2.5% of all disbursements and it was not possible to estimate overall resources (although an idea of the scale is gained from the large amounts issued as rations). The percentage of overall resources is (very roughly) similar in all four cases (i.e. comparatively small), but the use of a commodity for rations greatly affects whether or not religious disbursements account for a high percentage of 'final uses'.

The situation is similar for items 7 and 8 in the list, wool at Pylos and Thebes. There was an inconsistency (but for defensible reasons) in the way that wool was analysed at different sites. At Thebes, because deities appeared as 'Collectors', we included the disbursements of the Of series in our calculations for 'final use' disbursements, although it was clear that the issues were to workers for textile manufacture. At Knossos, on the other hand, issues for manufacture were excluded as 'final use' disbursements, in keeping with our ordinary practice. The calculation done for Thebes was meaningful in the sense that it indicated how much of the wool for manufacture was directed towards deity workshops, but wool going to workshops should not really count as 'final use'. Wool at Thebes thus does not constitute a 'real' exception to the 70–100% rule. On the other hand, item 7, wool at Pylos, is anomalous altogether since the few stint records which survive happen not to preserve the wool ideogram (although it probably was originally present on at least a couple of them). But the low figure arises once again mainly from the existence of industrial disbursements, in this case for perfumery (where the disbursements counted as 'final use' because the wool would be consumed), plus the presence of a few *o-no* payments. The cases are similar for items 6 and 9, cyperus and honey at Pylos. The major disbursements were for industrial processing in perfumery, so these can again be grouped with industrial manufacture. The final case, bronze at Pylos, is similar to wool at Thebes in that the calculation here compares disbursements to *Potnian* bronzesmiths as opposed to those to 'ordinary' bronzesmiths; again the context is industrial, whatever it was the smiths were actually making.

The only two real 'exceptions' to the '70 percent' rule are thus the two cases of **146* (curiously, and perhaps significantly, not a textile itself manufactured by the palace; see Section 6.4.1.1). In these two cases, the calculations were made according to our standard definition of 'final use', and amounts disbursed for religious purposes were 'genuinely' less than 70% (although still approaching this figure). In all other cases, the 'exceptions' are where a commodity was being used to supply or support industrial manufacture. Such disbursements still reflect *internal* movements of products, rather than actual and final 'out-go'. In this light, we may revise our observation that in twelve out of sixty-six cases 'final use' disbursements for religious purposes fall below 70%. If we exclude cases where the commodities were involved in industry, in only *two* out of sixty-six cases were disbursements for religious purposes less than 70% of all disbursements.

In sum, we have large percentages of disbursements for religious purposes almost across the board, but without such disbursements accounting for a majority of overall resources. This observation relates to another phenomenon witnessed in our study: that not only do religious disbursements not account for the majority of resource use, but neither in most cases do *non*-religious disbursements. In general, there is a significant discrepancy between what is recorded as available and what is recorded as disbursed. For wheat at Knossos, for example, rations even if projected *annually* still only accounted for some 33% of 'overall resources' (Section 5.2.2). What was being done with the other two-thirds of the resources? And what were the palaces doing with their manufactured products in general?

On the whole, records concerning the use of the majority of resources are simply not present in the extant archives. This lack of documentation relating to 'final use' disbursements is not confined to any particular type of commodity: it is a generalised phenomenon, calling for explanation. The pattern is too consistent to be put down to factors such as hazards of preservation alone, since it seems unlikely that preservational factors would systematically affect only this type of record. Again, that disbursements of finished products are rarely recorded in Linear B has been observed before, but Table 7-1 highlights the phenomenon through setting out the data in a systematic way and having the figures makes the problem more tangible. 'Final use' disbursements are not just impressionistically rare: they are practically non-existent – except again in the case of religion.

Now, if it is indeed the rule that 'final use' disbursements as opposed to issues for manufacture do not normally appear in the Linear B records, we need to ask why then disbursements for religious purposes *are* recorded, as seems also to be the case. The answer must have implications for our understanding of Linear B documentation relating to religion.

An initial approach to the question would be further to ask why *other* 'final uses' are generally *not* recorded. One of the most notorious 'gaps' in the Linear B evidence is the virtually complete absence of direct epigraphic evidence for trade. To an extent, the observation that disbursements of final products are almost never recorded in Linear B already goes some way towards making this 'gap' appear less 'mysterious'. It is not trade alone that is missing – nearly *all* out-go is 'missing'. If trade did appear, it would constitute an *exception* to the rule. Nevertheless, the problem of the lack of direct evidence for trade may be a useful place to start since the issue has been much discussed. In the next section we note some previous comments on the matter then go on to consider Linear B 'absences' more generally.

7.2 THE 'INVISIBILITY' OF TRADE IN LINEAR B

In our study of olive oil at Pylos (Section 3.2.2), we referred to Shelmerdine's calculation that some 2.5 times the amount of oil recorded in the Fr tablets could have been treated with the materials recorded in issues to perfumers. Shelmerdine's purpose was to attempt to determine whether a sufficient amount was produced by the palace to have been traded; she concluded, doubtless correctly, that it was.[4] Similarly at Knossos, Killen demonstrated that the extent of resources invested in the textile industry (some 30–50 tons of wool annually; see Section 6.3.3.1) suggested production on a scale such as to make it likely that textile export was a major source of Knossian wealth in imports. There is sufficient evidence in the form of Mycenaean exports abroad and foreign artefacts found in the palaces to put it beyond doubt that trade did take place and that the palaces were beneficiaries.[5] So why is trade almost never mentioned in Linear B?

Two particularly useful commentaries on the problem for our purposes here are those by Shelmerdine and Killen, each of whom lists possible reasons for the lacuna. Killen notes the following possibilities:[6]

1. that trade was essentially an occasional and marginal activity for the palaces, and the records of a single year (in some cases, indeed, probably only part of a year) would not therefore be expected to contain many references to it
2. that we do have more records of trading activity in the archives, but these are not recognisable as such
3. that there were originally more records in the archives dealing with external trade, but these, by chance, have not survived.

Under his first point, Killen discusses the possibilities that (i) trade may have been seasonal and (ii) trade may have been carried out at the sub-palatial level. He leaves the first possibility open, and rejects the second 'given what seems likely to have been the extent and in some cases also the depth of the palaces' involvement in the internal economies of the kingdoms, which makes it difficult to believe that they were not also involved in external trading activity'.[7] Possibility (2), that the records are not recognised, is also dismissed because 'in most cases records can be identified as relating to purely internal transactions'. Regarding (3), chance preservation, Killen discusses the Mycenae West Houses and notes that they yielded the only record 'at any site, of a transaction involving another Mycenaean kingdom' (MY X 508; see Section 6.3.3.4).[8] He then examines the possibility that external trade for other palaces was conducted through Mycenae, and that it is mere chance that more tablets from this site do not survive. As he points out, however, it seems on the whole difficult to accept that Mycenae would have been trading for places such as Pylos or Thebes. While keeping in mind the issue of hazards of preservation, Killen concludes that 'the absence of more records dealing with trade from the archives still remains something of a mystery'.[9]

Shelmerdine in her discussion lists the following possibilities:[10]

1. no records were kept
2. records were kept on clay, but they have not survived
3. records were kept on clay, but none had been made by the time of year the palace was destroyed
4. records were kept in some other material which has not survived
5. records were kept in a different place from the extant archives

[4] Shelmerdine 1985, 152–3.

[5] E.g. Cline 1994; 1995; Van Wijngaarden 2002, 9; Voutsaki 2001; papers in Laffineur & Greco 2005; Shelmerdine 1998a (also discussing the Linear B evidence). Whether palaces *controlled* all trade or themselves were the ship-owners is a separate issue (e.g. Sherratt & Sherratt 1991; Sherratt 2001; Shelmerdine 1998a; but see also Voutsaki 2001), but that they must have been beneficiaries is manifest partly in that they were *the* major producers for export.

[6] Killen 1985, 266–7.

[7] Killen 1985, 266–7.

[8] Killen 1985, 168–9. Note that Linear B inscribed stirrup-jars of course also give evidence for trade; see e.g. Catling *et al.* 1980; Haskell 2005; Maran 2005. The new Thebes tablets (e.g. Fq 229) make reference to a figure called *ra-ke-da-mi-ni-jo* receiving foodstuffs in a festival handouts context, but it is clear the transaction is taking place at Thebes, for consumption at Thebes.

[9] Killen 1985, 270.

[10] Shelmerdine 1985, 139.

She considers possibility (1), that no records were kept, as 'possible but unlikely. Palace records give a great deal of attention to local matters; surely they would have monitored trade in the same careful way.'[11] She agrees with Killen's point (1–ii), that the palaces must have been involved in trade, rightly noting that, 'if the palace organized the production of export goods such as oil and textiles, their disbursement would surely be a palace concern, as would the goods for which they were exchanged'. Possibility (2) is rejected because, 'given the number of extant tablets from the various palaces, it is impossible to believe not even one indication would survive'. Possibility (3), seasonality, is also considered unlikely since 'trade would not be entirely a seasonal matter like the production of goods' (but see below). She settles on possibilities (4) and (5), which are seen as overlapping 'since wherever the records were kept they might not have been on clay'. Discussing evidence for writing on perishable materials in Minoan Crete along with evidence for Mycenaean sealings, she concludes: 'I think it likely that the Mycenaeans kept their more complete, more permanent and more important records in a medium other than clay. It would hardly be surprising if international or even interregional trade qualified on all three grounds.'[12]

It is useful to bring together Killen's and Shelmerdine's lists of reasons for lacunae along with some further points. Killen's point (3) 'hazards of preservation' encompasses Shelmerdine's points (2) 'clay records have not survived' and (4) 'records on organic materials have not survived'. Killen's point (1–i) and Shelmerdine's point (3) both relate to seasonality. Killen's point (1–ii) 'trade carried out at the sub-palatial level' is not in Shelmerdine's list, although she does discuss it, as noted above, and agrees that the palaces must have been involved. The point is related to a more general observation that the absence of certain produce, such as pulses, from the Linear B documents, although attested in the archaeological record, may be due to such stuffs having been produced in the non-palatial sector,[13] and we add this possibility to our list. Shelmerdine's points (1) 'no records were kept' and (5) 'records were kept in different places' are not mentioned by Killen, but are important to include. Although Shelmerdine rejected point (1) it warrants further consideration and may even be further elaborated, since 'no records were kept' could mean more than one thing. It could mean that records were written but soon afterwards destroyed so that they do not appear in the surviving archives (so 'not kept' in the sense of 'intentionally not preserved' or 'archived'),[14] or it might mean that the records had never been written in the first place (so 'not kept' in the sense of 'never put into writing'). On the other hand, our list excludes Killen's point (2) 'trade records have not been recognised as such', as his refutation of it is decisive.[15]

A summary of the points may be given as follows.

Possible reasons for the 'invisibility' of trade in Linear B

features of the economic structure led to lacunae

1. trade was carried out at the sub-palatial level
2. goods were produced in the non-palatial sphere so do not appear in palace records

features of Linear B administration led to lacunae

3. record keeping was seasonal (depending on the seasonality of various activities)
4. records were made, but not kept (in the sense of not having been archived)

[11] Shelmerdine 1985, 139; the next four quotations are all from the same page.
[12] Shelmerdine 1985, 141. On the issue see also e.g. Driessen 1994–1995; Olivier 1996–1997; Bennet 2001.
[13] E.g. Halstead 1990–1991, 360; 1992a, 60–1, 64; 1992b, 108–9.
[14] See Killen 1984b; Halstead 1999c, 37–8.
[15] Noting again the exception of the document from Mycenae.

5. records were never made in the first place

hazards of preservation led to lacunae

6. records were kept on clay as part of the main archive but have not happened to survive
7. records were kept on clay, but outside the main archive, and thus either have not survived or have not been found
8. records were kept on perishable materials and have not survived

Let us examine the relative probability of each of the possibilities. It should be noted that these possibilities are not necessarily mutually exclusive of one another, a point we return to below. We begin with the simpler cases, so our discussion does not follow the numerical order of the list. Three of the possibilities may be dealt with at the outset; the others require a look at further comparative material and are addressed in the following section.

Beginning with possibility (3), seasonality may indeed have been a contributing factor to the invisibility of trade. Traditional overseas trade in the Mediterranean tended to be seasonal because winter sailing was hazardous, particularly for cargo-laden boats.[16] As is well known, the Linear B records were generally kept for less than a year,[17] often much less (for instance, the Knossos Fp(1) set covers six months and the Pylos records probably cover about three to five months).[18] If an activity were undertaken outside the administrative period of the existing records, no tablets relating to it might be expected (unless they had been intentionally archived, cf. possibility 4).[19] However, whether seasonality alone is a sufficient factor to explain the absence of references to trade is another matter, and we may follow Shelmerdine in rejecting it as a sole factor.

Possibility (7), 'clay records were kept elsewhere than in the main archives', is somewhat unlikely to be a reason for the absence of records relating to trade. With regard to Pylos, it has long been noted that the more important records (such as those relating to land tenure) were kept in the archives,[20] and it seems probable that records relating to something as important as trade would have been as well. Not all palaces, however, had centralised archives – Pylos is so far unique in this respect (although poor preservation at most of the other mainland sites should be kept in mind). At Knossos (and probably Thebes), the archives/deposits were decentralised, with records organised in 'bureaux' or 'departments' around the palace.[21] However, given that records were found in many different areas, it seems somewhat implausible that if clay records of trade were kept somewhere in the palace not one would survive.[22] That being said, the single record we do have of a transaction involving two different palaces (MY X 508, noted above) was found in the West House Complex at Mycenae rather than in the palace itself. The findspot of the tablet makes sense in the context of the West House Complex as a 'clearing house complex' (see below) and highlights the possibility of 'trade documents' being kept in such places. On the other hand, there are no examples from our other main example of a 'clearing house complex', the Northeastern Building at Pylos, so this does not offer a general solution.

---

[16] See e.g. Sherratt & Sherratt 1991, 357; Broodbank 2000, 92–6.

[17] Or perhaps just over a year in some cases (e.g. the PY Ma tablets, with references to payments due from the previous year).

[18] Melena 1974a; Palaima 1995b; 2001, 153.

[19] For suggested seasons for the destruction of the palaces see Melena 1974a; Chadwick 1976, 188–92; Palaima 1992a, 472; 1995b; *Scribes RCT*, 211.

[20] *Scribes Pylos*, 172.

[21] *Scribes Cnossos*; Olivier 1984.

[22] See Driessen 2001b for an important related discussion.

Possibility (6), that clay documents did not survive, is probably a contributing factor. Shelmerdine rightly observed that it seems difficult to accept that no indications would have happened to survive, but the strong effect that hazards of preservation can have were highlighted throughout our study. In many cases we observed that a single tablet or fragment was capable of radically altering the calculations. There is often said to be a 'pattern' in Linear B record-keeping, but it is important that what is usually meant by this is that 'gaps' at one site are often filled in (by us) with records from another.[23] There is nothing particularly wrong with this, so long as it is remembered what is being done. At Pylos, for instance, there is extensive documentation relating to land tenure. Nothing comparable survives at Knossos, but a few records include juridical terminology used for land tenure at Pylos,[24] suggesting Knossos had a similar type of system. If these fragments had escaped preservation, nothing at all could be said about Knossian land tenure on the epigraphic evidence and the situation would be as puzzling (for that site) as it is currently for trade. On the other hand, there are more 'gaps', and they are more strongly patterned, than can be accounted for by hazards of preservation alone, as Shelmerdine rightly observed.[25]

Our remaining possibilities are best examined in light of a wider context so we now extend the discussion beyond trade. It is useful to ask what else besides trade (and 'final use' disbursement documents in general) is 'missing' from the Linear B archives. The patterning may help give clues to possible reasons for the lacunae.

7.3 THE 'INVISIBILITY' OF MANY THINGS IN LINEAR B

In addition to trade, several other striking lacunae in the Linear B records have long been noted. For instance, Halstead has stressed the paucity of references to occupations such as pottery-making and commodities such as pulses, suggesting that the reason for such omissions (or rarity of mentions in the case of potters, since they do actually appear[26]) may be that production was carried out in the non-palatial sphere, our possibility (2).[27] As noted above, this is similar to the idea that trade was not recorded in the Linear B archives because it was carried out at the sub-palatial level, our possibility (1). The underlying suggestion in both cases is that 'not appearing in Linear B' may indicate 'non-palatial activity', implying that the extent of Linear B documentation can be taken as a measure of the extent of palatial involvement in a given sector of the economy.[28] The present study brings this view into question.

To put the matter in perspective, we may examine some further 'gaps' in the Linear B evidence. The list below highlights a number of 'suspicious lacunae', some drawn from our commodities survey and some from other sources. The list is not exhaustive, and it includes points of varying significance.

---

[23] See e.g. Palaima 2001, 152.

[24] E.g. on KN Uf(3) 835, –983, Xd 7913, F 5079(?); also TI Ef 2, –3.

[25] Note this point is not at odds with arguments made for point (7) because there specific location was being considered as a possible key factor, whereas here the issue is hazards of preservation more generally.

[26] There are at least two at Pylos, and probably four (see e.g. Palaima 1997, 410). A 'royal' potter appears in En 467.5 and Eo 371.A, designated by his name, occupation and affiliation, while a different man, designated by his name and occupation (*ke-ra-me-u /kerameus/* 'potter') appears probably as a donor of goats for a banquet in Cn 1287.4 (see Section 2.3.2.2). A further two men (they could conceivably be the same persons as the two just mentioned, but this is doubtful) are described as 'potters' in An 207.7. Also note the possibility that various types of workers are present in the records but are not recognised, for instance because they are designated by name alone (we have numerous such records) rather than by occupation. I am grateful to J.T. Killen for drawing my attention to this point.

[27] Halstead 1990–1991, 360; 1992a, 60–1, 64; 1992b, 108–9;

[28] This is commonly done; e.g. Erard-Cerceau 1988, 187–8; Halstead 1992a, esp. 58, 62, 64; Shelmerdine 1999b, 21–2.

Some suspicious lacunae in Linear B

- There are oil and grain collection records (whether taxation or 'harvest' records) from Knossos, but not from Pylos (unless PY Ua 434 is one).
- Knossos has records of disbursements of oil for non-religious purposes; Pylos does not (or at least no unambiguous cases).
- In the Pylos Fr series, oil designated *PO* is the only type ever 'inventoried', but only other types of oil are ever disbursed.[29]
- Oil does not appear in banqueting foodlists, and these do not appear to be complete 'menus' (although the use of oil for culinary purposes should not necessarily be assumed[30]).
- Only four types of animals are recorded for sacrifice. Archaeological evidence exists for sacrifice (or consumption in a religious context) of other types of animals, such as birds, yet these are never mentioned.[31]
- Only two or three tablets at Knossos record cattle for sacrifice. Also, this site in general has fewer banqueting records than Pylos, which seems at odds with the fact that Knossos was three times the size of Pylos and operated on a larger scale.[32]
- Cattle appear frequently in the banqueting records of Pylos, but *exclusively* in this context (in contrast with Knossos). On the other hand, there are records of some 290+ oxherds.[33]
- There is practically nothing at any site regarding domestic affairs or daily household organisation.
- There are no unambiguous references to 'ordinary' cooking.[34]
- Lower-level administration in general is missing.
- There are no 'workshop' records (see below).
- We have rose and sage perfumed oil at Pylos, but roses and sage do not appear in lists of perfume ingredients.
- Perishables in general are not recorded; there is an absence of fresh produce.[35]
- Only two priestesses appear at Knossos.
- Scribes do not appear at any site and there is no attested word for scribe.[36]

---

[29] The distribution of scribal duties may have something to do with this (Shelmerdine 1985), but the circumstance still appears odd.

[30] See Chapter 3 n 154.

[31] For instance, at Asine (Hägg 1981b, 93) and Agios Konstantinos, Methana (Hamilakis & Konsolaki 2004, 142). Birds do now seem to be recorded in the new Thebes tablets (e.g. *o-ni-si*; Fq 123+), but apparently as recipients of offerings or provisions rather than as sacrificial animals. Note birds are recorded among, e.g., cattle, sheep and so forth at Ugarit (Lipinski 1988, 139–40).

[32] The data are quantified in Bendall forthcoming(c).

[33] Palaima 1989; Halstead 1998–1999, 168–9.

[34] Bakers do appear (*a-to-po-qo /artopoq^{u}oi/*), but usually in the specialised festival context of the Pylos Fn tablets (Fn 50.7, with related tablets An 39.11, –427.3; see Section 2.3.3.1). I am grateful to J.T. Killen for pointing this out to me. Further mentions are on personnel records (MY Au 102) and a wool record (MY Oe 117; rations?). There is also a reference to an *a-si-to-po-qo* in the Pylos land tenure tablets (PY Eb 177, Ep 613), which may mean something like 'cook' but the interpretation of the word is dubious (a confusion of *a-to-po-qo* and *si-to-po-qo*??; *Documents*, 534; *DMic.* I, 109–10; note *si-to-po-qo* is not actually attested but is possibly to be restored in KN As(1) 608.4). In any case, since the context is land tenure, we do not see actual practice of activities. Note also the Mycenae spice records, which may relate to goods used for culinary purposes, but again we do not see the actual production. Along similar lines, Halstead (1998–1999, 171) rightly notes that 'it is highly likely that surviving texts greatly underestimate the scale of annual meat consumption by (or hosted by) the palaces'.

[35] Palmer 1999.

[36] Palaima 2003a, 153–4, 173–4.

- Land tenure tablets are rare at Knossos and other sites but common at Pylos.
- Bronzesmiths are rare at Knossos (there are only two mentions, on V(6) 958 and Fh 386), although substantial amounts of the metal was available (cf. the ingot tablets; Section 6.5.2). On the other hand, bronzesmiths are very common at Pylos (and at the same time the metal seems to have been in short supply; Section 2.2.3).
- Toponyms are recorded in different ways at Pylos and Knossos, with many of the Knossian toponyms apparently 'missing'.[37]
- Final use disbursements in general are 'missing'.

Some of the above lacunae relate to items or activities which clearly must have belonged to the palatial sector, so their epigraphic invisibility cannot be explained by their belonging to or originating in the non-palatial sector. Our possibility (2) may (indeed must) hold in some cases, but it cannot explain all of the 'gaps'. A few examples may be discussed in more detail.

Two obvious 'gaps' regarding subjects that must belong to the palatial sector are scribes and final disbursements of finished products. Scribes are, virtually by definition, 'palatial', as are manufactured goods produced in palace workshops. As noted above, since the palaces produced such goods, their disbursal must have been a matter of 'palatial concern', yet they are systematically absent from the records.

Another 'gap' is the lack of reference to domestic affairs. There are no certain references to cooks in the Linear B tablets,[38] and few if any concerning day-to-day management of palatial 'households'. The main evidence for domestic staff comes from the Pylos Ab series, where rations are issued to 'attendants' and 'bath-pourers', but there is little more.[39] Lists of foodstuffs appear all to have been for major banquets (with the possible exception of MY Ue 661; see Section 2.3.2.4), and we are 'missing' records of ordinary fare or day-to-day dining. Nor is there any indication of how kitchens were regularly supplied and organised. Yet it is difficult to accept that such activities, so intimately connected with palace daily life, were conducted through the 'non-palatial' sphere.

Apart from domestic affairs, lower-level administration in general is missing from the records. The Linear B tablets document various industries, but they do not deal with the *whole* of each industry. They concern only higher levels of administration: issues of rations and raw materials, receipts of raw materials (from both 'palatial' and 'non-palatial' sources), stints and production targets, receipts and (more rarely) storage of finished products, assessments of available labour and so forth. Not one tablet indicates how a workshop functioned on a day-to-day basis, other than recording the presence of supervisors, often with the mere purpose of indicating that they are due extra rations (for instance, the *DA* and *TA* supervisors of the Ab tablets;[40] note also the *qa-si-re-we* of the Jn tablets). These supervisors would probably have been in charge of on-the-spot management, but how they carried out palatial orders is not documented.

---

[37] As noted by Bennet (1995, 595; 1999, 135) and Driessen (2001, 98–9), some 240 TNs appear at Pylos (this figure is probably too high – the total is more likely around 200; but the point stands either way) in some 2000 m^2 of territory, while at Knossos only some 80 TNs appear although the territory controlled seems to have been some three times larger; see also Bennet 1988a, 28.

[38] See n 34 above.

[39] We might note also the oil sent 'to the attendants' on Fr 1205, which could have been oil for domestic use, but the attendants may instead have been religious staff (see Section 3.2.2). Cf. also MY Fo 101.

[40] Chadwick 1988, 171–3; for a Near Eastern example of what a more detailed work-record might look like see Postgate 1994, 236.

We may note that it used to be thought that examples of lower-level administration existed in the form of 'workshop records', but the examples do not stand up to closer scrutiny. The main proposed candidates had been the West House group at Mycenae and the Northeastern Building at Pylos. However, Shelmerdine has now shown that the Mycenae buildings were instead a sort of 'clearing house complex',[41] and the same has been argued for the Northeastern Building, which in any case was certainly not a workshop.[42] The scribes of the Northeastern Building worked together closely with the scribes of the neighbouring Archives Complex, and some of the tablets deal with polity-wide assessments and activities – this is not lower-level management we are seeing.[43] At Mycenae too the activities of the West House Complex were a direct appendage of the palace central administration (what little we know of it, given the limited surviving documentation from this site), despite the location of the buildings just outside the citadel walls. Again, it is higher-level administration that is witnessed in these documents.

A part of the reason for this absence of records relating to lower-level administration may be that Linear B scribes (as we believe) were high-status individuals – not members of a separate scribal class such as existed in many societies of the ancient Near East, but themselves the major officials undertaking administrative tasks[44] – and it is probable that literacy was confined to these higher-level officials.[45] This would suggest then our possibility (5), that no records were kept in the sense of never having been written. In this connection, comparison with some of the surviving written material from the Near East may be useful.

It is salutary to observe that many of the Linear B 'gaps' occur even in some of the much better documented periods and regions of the ancient Near East and that in these contexts too scholars have sometimes been similarly puzzled. Regarding pulses, for instance, Oppenheim once observed: 'Leguminous plants do not seem to have been of great dietary importance in Mesopotamia; in fact, they appear only rarely in first-millennium texts as against those of the Ur III period.'[46] The difficulty with the documentation here is similar to that encountered with the Linear B records. Yet rather than concluding that legumes were not 'of great dietary importance' in first-millennium BC Mesopotamia,[47] the discrepancy may be due to unusually active record-keeping regarding agricultural matters in Ur III. As Postgate notes: 'It is difficult to know if the great range of plants recorded in the Ur III texts reflects a real expansion in the crops grown, by comparison with earlier (and indeed later) times, or whether – as seems more likely – the difference is merely in the recording.'[48] Postgate puts the emphasis on the likelihood of inconsistent recording, rather than any real changes in agricultural practices, as accounting for the discrepancies and notes that, apart from medical lists, agricultural goods were only recorded when some type of legal transaction between two persons or political bodies was being undertaken. In other words, produce was not normally inventoried – it was

---

[41] Shelmerdine 1997, esp. 389–90; see also Tournavitou 1995; Varias Garcia 1999.
[42] Flouda 2000; Hofstra 2000; Bendall 2003.
[43] Bendall 2003, esp. 200–2. Palaima (2003a, 182–7) has argued that the Northeastern Building documents do represent a lower level of management, but many of the examples he cites have good parallels in the AC, and some of the building's records (e.g. the Ac tablets) deal with polity-wide assessments. Further, it is clear that the scribes were dealing with personnel carrying out labour which must have taken place outside the Northeastern Building (some of these same personnel are also documented in the AC); see Bendall 2003, 210.
[44] *Scribes Cnossos*, 135–6. For instance, Hand 1 at Pylos may be the man named *a-ko-so-ta*, one of the four Pylian 'Collectors', and thus one of the more important persons in the polity, as long advocated by Killen (pers. comm., 1995); see now Bennet 2001. On the status of scribes, see recently *Scribes RCT*, 230–2; Palaima 1987b, 504–5; 2003a, 174–7 (expressing some doubts); both with further references.
[45] On literacy and orality see e.g. *Documents* 109–10, 406; Palaima 1987b; Thomas 1984; Bennet 2007a, 2007b (for oral presentations in the Mycenaean world). The situation contrasts with that of Linear A (Schoep 2002).
[46] Oppenheim 1977, 44.
[47] Crawford (1991, 44) comments on the importance of pulses for the Sumerians from an archaeological point of view, and Oppenheim (1977, 313) notes the Sumerian role in their domestication.
[48] Postgate 1994, 170.

only (or primarily) recorded in the context of transactions.[49] The same may have been true in Mycenaean record-keeping. In general, storage records are much rarer than records of deliveries and receipts.

Some further Near Eastern 'gaps' are noted by Van de Mieroop, who comments on a bias seen in recording workshop production:[50]

> In my study of the Isin workshop, I established a sequence of five steps through which goods passed from the moment the raw materials entered the workshop until the moment the finished products left it:
> 1. delivery of raw materials
> 2. distribution of the raw materials to the craftsmen
> 3. manufacture
> 4. receipt of the finished products by workshop officials
> 5. disbursement of the finished products.
>
> Although the third step is clearly the most important of the entire sequence in the eyes of the modern scholar who would like to learn something about crafts, it is not documented in the texts.

In the Linear B documents too, the stage of actual manufacture is missing, as of course is stage 5, disbursement of finished products, our focus here. It is worth noting Van de Mieroop's further observation in the same context that the Near Eastern records do not normally give complete lists even of his stage 2, distribution of raw materials – fuel, for instance, is not recorded (it is similarly absent in Linear B), nor are items such as sage and roses for perfumery (also absent in Linear B).

The lack of Linear B records relating to 'ordinary' cooking is also sometimes paralleled in the Near East. For instance, Foster, speaking of Mesopotamia in the Sargonic Period, noted: 'Documents relating to food preparation are rare, and mostly concerned with feasts or other special occasions'.[51] This resonates with the Linear B situation where virtually all mention of 'menus' is in the context of major banquets. A parallel for the absence of scribes is seen at Ugarit, where mention of this office is similarly missing from administrative (but not other types of) documents.[52]

In general, the reason – or reasons – for record-keeping in a particular context are important. With sale records, for instance, Van de Mieroop notes that the absence (or presence) of such records need not be indicative of the importance (or otherwise) of the commodities traded, since the records were generally 'created for future purposes' and that in the case where a sale was 'final and could not be contested at a later date' there 'was no need for a written receipt'.[53] The many 'gaps' in the documentation led him to comment:[54]

> Compared to the material from other ancient civilizations the extent of the [Mesopotamian] written record is indeed enormous, but it is not unlimited. It has to be acknowledged that we are working with biased evidence concerning a limited segment of the economic activities that took place in antiquity.

---

[49] The scarcity of inventories altogether is noted by Van de Mieroop (1997, 15), who comments: '"Inventories" received a special entry in the standard Reallexikon on ancient Mesopotamian civilization, but the authors were unable to quote more than a few examples of the genre. Yet even among those many do not deserve that designation, as they are imbedded in documents that record the transfer of the property, and it is that transfer that is the primary subject matter.'

[50] Van de Mieroop 1997, 13.

[51] Foster 1993, 33.

[52] Heltzer 1999, 435

[53] Van de Mieroop 1997, 9, 17.

[54] Van de Mieroop 1997, 17. See also a useful note on the problem by Zettler (1996, 100), with further references.

This observation is important for our consideration of the similar problem in Linear B. Given the very limited scope of the Linear B documents as compared with the records of Mesopotamia at various times or of places such as Ugarit, it is unsurprising that the difficulties should be all the more formidable. Van de Mieroop notes of Mesopotamia that 'a great deal of economic activity was probably never recorded at all'.[55] The same was probably true for the Mycenaean world. It has long been observed that Linear B is biased towards the palaces and excludes the non-palatial sector, but even *within* the palatial sphere it seems a great deal was going on which was also never recorded. One implication of this is that we cannot judge whether or not a commodity or activity belonged to or had its origins in the 'non-palatial' sphere based on its non-appearance in the Linear B records. Thus, an absence of Linear B documentation cannot necessarily be taken as indicating or even suggesting that a particular activity or commodity was not under direct palatial control. In short, the extent of palatial involvement in a given sphere cannot be measured against the extent of the Linear B documentation.

When Linear B was first deciphered the detailed nature of many of the records conveyed an impression of a highly organised bureaucracy in which transactions at every level were meticulously booked and documented. This impression has persisted until relatively recently, for instance in Shelmerdine's rejection of her point (1) above, that no records were kept, as (to repeat the quote) 'possible but unlikely. Palace records give a great deal of attention to local matters; surely they would have monitored trade in the same careful way'.[56] She further comments: 'In the final analysis, it is hard to imagine that a bureaucratic system so detailed and so extensive in local matters failed to keep accounts of external business as well.'[57] This view of a detailed and extensive record-keeping system was perfectly reasonable and commonly held, but the records increasingly no longer seem as detailed and extensive as once appeared and a shift in perspective is emerging. For instance, Palaima in his classic 1987 discussion of Mycenaean sealing systems outlined six levels of transactions from high to low, on which he commented that 'the need for recording at all levels is obvious'.[58] More recently, however, he comments:[59]

> I would like to emphasize here modalities of transactions [referring to his 1987 paper] that must lie behind the records we possess, but which the central administration has no need to keep in written records. There must have been, in this still primarily oral culture with a very specialized and narrow form of literacy, considerable reliance on traditional transactional arrangements that may never have been recorded in writing.

Driessen makes statements along similar lines in the same volume, for instance: 'Ce système de gestion d'information … ne nécessite pas une opération d'enregistrement dans les provinces, mais seulement le passage de fonctionnaires itenérants collectant des impôts auprès des chefs régionaux ou locaux.'[60] His point was that we are unlikely to find administrative records in outlying settlements as had long been hoped for,[61] but the relevance for our purpose here is that written documentation was confined to palatial functionaries, and that lower-level

---

55 Van de Mieroop 2000, 42.

56 Shelmerdine 1985, 139; the next four quotes are all from the same page.

57 Shelmerdine 1985, 141.

58 Palaima 1987a, 254.

59 Palaima 2001, 154. He goes on to suggest that sealings (which do not require literacy) may have been used at some lower levels, which is possible, but it does not seem that even this could account for all 'gaps'.

60 Driessen 2001b, 118. See also Driessen 1999, 206–9, although the suggestion (p. 207) that 'proper interrelating records had to exist reflecting these different actions' may need qualification. Like Palaima, Driessen goes on to emphasise – quite rightly – the importance of the new Thebes sealings in understanding what he calls the 'Mycenaean information "super highway"' but it may be that not even something as 'lower-level' as sealings was required for the majority of transactions. (Cf. n 62 below).

61 The excavation of Nichoria, for instance, was undertaken partly in the hope of finding the first administrative documents in what was almost certainly one of the second-order centres of the polity controlled from Pylos; see McDonald & Rapp 1972; Rapp & Aschenbrenner 1978; Shelmerdine 1981.

administrative activities could be carried out without the aid of writing. Given the limited extent of Mycenaean literacy, a very likely reason for the paucity of records for lower-level administration would then indeed be our possibility (5), that 'no records were kept in the sense of never having been written'. Minor administrators did not use Linear B.[62]

That a large amount of minor administration was being carried out without being recorded in Linear B would explain a great many of the lacunae in the records, but not all of them. Trade, for instance, is still not satisfactorily explained in this way since its organisation and implementation is unlikely to have been left to minor officials; neither is the general absence of 'final use' disbursements explained since again the disposal of at least the high-status products must have been of concern to higher-level administrators at the palaces. It has been frequently noted that it is odd that we have so little documentation from so many active scribes.[63] Much information is 'missing' even at the 'higher' levels.

A further possibility to consider in this regard is of course our number (8), that records were kept on perishable materials, an explanation, as we saw above, favoured by Shelmerdine for trade. This is not the place for detailed discussion and the issue of perishable materials should remain open, but there are two points that make record-keeping on perishable materials to an extent that could explain all of our suspicious lacunae doubtful. First, there is very positive evidence for the use of perishable materials in Linear A, whereas there is a suspicious absence of such evidence for Linear B.[64] Second, while it is plausible that costly perishable materials would have been used for recording important activities such as trade, it is unlikely they would have been used for lower-level transactions, such as the quotidian supply of palace kitchens (although wood may have been a cheaper option[65]). This is not to suggest that perishable records were *never* used (the contrary is more likely), but this explanation cannot fully account for all of our 'gaps'.

We should bring in at this point the final possibility not so far considered, (4) that clay tablets were written but 'not kept' in the sense of being archived. Halstead, for instance, contemplated that hundreds or even thousands of *o-no* transaction tablets might have been 'lost' in this way.[66] That documents *were* intentionally destroyed as transaction information was updated is well known (as Halstead notes) through for instance Killen's classic discussion of the Ma tablets.[67] The point on a general level had been earlier made by Finley:[68]

---

[62] Both Palaima (2000; 2001) and Driessen (*Scribes RCT*; 2001b) have noted that sealings may have been involved in many of the lower-level transactions. There is doubtless some truth in this, but sealings deal primarily (or exclusively?) with incoming goods, and so do not entirely solve the problem. There is an interesting contrast here with Near Eastern sealings, for which the opposite seems true (Driessen 1994–1995, 242, 245). (Cf. n 60 above.)

[63] E.g. Palaima 2001, 153 (although he finds it not so odd since the scribes would have been busy in other ways).

[64] Caution should be maintained, particularly as not arguing from absence of evidence has been stressed above. Yet factors such as the fact that so much evidence for Linear A perishable materials exists (i.e. cuttlefish ink used on bowls and above all the hundreds of 'document sealings' which were attached to parchment or papyrus) and that Linear B was derived from Linear A and operated in the same physical context are suspicious. Bennett (2001a, 27–8) has questioned Driessen's (1994–1995) concept of a 'pre-archives', involving storage of temporary clay documents for eventual transferral of data onto 'permanent' records on perishable materials. He points out that many important administrative matters do appear recorded on clay and that it is not clear what economic planning further perishable records would be intended to facilitate. Elsewhere, Driessen makes the interesting suggestion that there may have been a progressive decrease in the use of perishable records by the Linear B administrators of Knossos, as the influence of Linear A bureaucratic methods, from which Linear B had been adapted, declined. He suggests that one may see earlier stages of this change in the RCT records, with later stages in the LM III A destruction levels at Knossos and later still in the documents of the LH III B mainland. See Driessen 1999, esp. 221, 225–6; *Scribes RCT*, 187, 224, 227–9; also Palaima 1990, esp. 98. This would suggest genuine differences in attitudes to record-keeping in Linear A and Linear B.

[65] Or reusable wooden diptychs with wax insets such as the one found in the Ulu Burun shipwreck (see e.g. Pulak 1997, 252–3). There is possible evidence for similar diptychs at Pylos (Shear 1998, 187–9; *PoN* I, 97–8).

[66] Halstead 1999c, 37–8.

[67] Killen 1984b.

[68] Finley 1957, 132.

> The one mistake we must not make is to assume that temporary records automatically indicate relatively insignificant operations. There was neither the antiquarian interest nor the economic interest (i.e. long-range calculations or analysis) to motivate the preservation of documents once an operation was completed or a set of relationships modified.

This recalls Van de Mieroop's comments above with regard to the documents of Mesopotamia, and it looks all the more true today with regard to Linear B. Thus, there is certainly some truth in possibility (4): Linear B documents were not normally archived in any modern sense.[69] However, it again is difficult to see this as the whole explanation. It is surely so that many (most?) records were 'temporary', but if hundreds or thousands of such records were in existence at any given time, more should have survived in what Bennet called the 'freeze-frame' snapshot of the destruction levels at various sites.[70] Possibility (4) must be at least a contributing factor in many cases since we know that records generally *were* destroyed after a transaction was complete, but whether this can explain the *general* lack of final disbursements is more doubtful.

A part of the difficulty in pinning down a precise reason for the various documentary lacunae may well be because a combination of factors is responsible, including seasonality, hazards of preservation, and the likelihood that a variety of palatial activities, even many carried out by higher-level administrators, were never recorded in Linear B in the first place. Further, different reasons might be in play in different instances. It is worthwhile considering a few examples.

Particularly with regard to things that were never recorded in Linear B, it is likely that different *underlying* reasons were responsible for the lack of record-keeping. We noted above that the absence of records for lower-level administration could be due to its being carried out by non-literate officials and supervisors, but that this cannot be true of trade in which higher-level officials would surely have had a role. However, it is possible that trade *also* was never recorded in Linear B in the first place, but for very different reasons, perhaps because it took place in circumstances that did not normally need to be recorded through such a system as the archives reveal. For instance, it may have been carried out by specialists among the elite, who may or may not have used writing.[71] Another possibility (not incompatible with the first) is that this activity, like many others, was carried out in the context of oral traditions.[72] It is clear that literacy was not deeply rooted in the Mycenaean world and the short life-span of the Linear B administrations has been rightly emphasised. Palaima points out that palatial control systems were probably grafted on to traditional set-ups and these would certainly have been based on verbal transactions.[73] The adoption of writing need not have had a major impact on those situations. Mainland populations had of course been trading long before Linear B was developed, and there may have been no need to switch to a different system purely because writing became available. It may also be that overt record-keeping in the context of trading negotiations would have been considered inappropriate. Face-to-face contact and a show of generosity to encourage good relations, rather than a display of meticulous tracking, may have

[69] See e.g. Palaima 2003a, esp. 169–71; but cf. Driessen (1994–1995, esp. 244) arguing that Linear B archives were kept on perishable materials. For archives more generally see Brosius 2003.
[70] Bennet 1988b, 510.
[71] See Killen 1979b; 1995, 216–21.
[72] Palaima 2004a, 286; see also Thomas 1984; Bennet 2004 (also 2007a; 2007b) for further comments on the importance of oral tradition in the Mycenaean world. Cf. Halstead (1988, 526) for the suggestion that exchanges were irregular or opportunistic hence not recorded. However, since the palace was producing annually it was probably trading annually. PY An 35, on the other hand, may be an example of an 'opportunistic' exchange and it is notable that this transaction *was* recorded. So the situation may be the reverse, i.e. that unusual exchanges would be *more* likely to be recorded.
[73] Palaima 2004a, 284

been more productive in such contexts.[74] Whatever the case, if it were so that activities such as trade negotiations or, for instance, law-making were rooted in oral traditions there is no reason to expect to see them in Linear B.

The absence of pulses from the records may be due to related but somewhat different reasons. Seasonality should be kept in mind as it simply may have been the wrong time of year to harvest such crops, but a more comprehensive explanation would be that neither collections nor disbursements of this commodity required the more detailed record-keeping system seen for commodities such as wheat, olives and cyperus. Pulses do not seem to have been used in such a way as to be of importance to the palace economy as was, for instance, wheat, and perhaps sufficient amounts could be grown to suit palatial needs on local lands or in palace gardens, obviating the need for detailed scrutiny. The administration of the production of this commodity need not have been recorded in Linear B if it was carried out by lower-level (but still palatial) agents. This would account for physical presence in the palaces, but absence from the records. This idea might seem again to fall into the rubric of 'not recorded = not important', yet there is something positive to suggest that pulses were not as significant for palatial economies overall as wheat was: they were not issued as rations. This is unlikely to be an effect of record-keeping disparities, because there are a great many rations records and we know what the standard foodstuffs issued to workers were: wheat, figs (at Pylos) and oil (at Knossos and Mycenae) plus barley (primarily at festivals). The only food commodities which do appear positively in the records, as already noted, are those used for rations and those in the banqueting 'menus', recalling the Near Eastern parallels mentioned above.

The point about rations is worth further emphasising. Some commodities which were not in themselves of especially high value may have become of interest because of the quantities in which, or reasons for which, they were disbursed, or both. With wheat, for instance, small amounts might be expendable, but the enormous amounts issued for rations constituted substantial outlays of resources and would be worth tracking. More importantly, the purpose behind such disbursements was crucial: the majority were to women working in the textile industries, and the textiles produced by these industries were a major source of palatial wealth. That wheat is present to the extent it is may be due not so much to an interest in *wheat* itself as a crop, but rather to an interest in the industrial production with which it was connected.[75] (But note even here the documentation is incomplete since 'final use' records for some two-thirds of the wheat at Knossos are 'missing'.) Also, the information required was complex and detailed and would have been difficult to track orally. Thus, both relative importance and the difference in the suitability or utility of writing in a given context may have been contributory factors to why wheat appears in Linear B, but pulses do not.

Potters and pottery may also be seemingly rare (although by no means unattested[76]) for different underlying reasons. There is no reason to believe that any palace was interested in (or would benefit from) producing pottery for the entire polity it controlled. All that would be required would be a workshop or two sufficient for its own needs. That at least one such workshop existed at Pylos is suggested by the appearance of a 'royal' potter in the land tenure

---

[74] This is not intended to exclude the idea of record-keeping on perishable materials – it is significant that the Ulu Burun ship (surely engaged in trade, whoever was in 'control' of it) carried wooden diptychs. Also, it is probable that PY An 35 is an example of a more straight-forward but probably *ad hoc* sort of exchange. However, there is no reason that the palaces should not have been engaged in a number of different types of transactions, operating at different levels, with a different etiquette appropriate in different circumstances.

[75] This is so of course also, to an extent, with regard to land tenure, the other main area where wheat (but as a measure of land) was recorded. Many of the persons who held leases were craftworkers, some clearly connected directly with high palace officials such as the *lāwāgetās* and the *wanax*. It is probably significant that the other major group of holders was religious officials or persons subject to religious obligations.

[76] In addition to potters at Pylos (see n 26 above) we have deliveries of vessels at Knossos, for instance of some 1800 stirrup-jars in KN K 700, and probably of amphorae in some of the Gg tablets (see Section 4.2.1.5).

records.[77] As noted above, the total number of potters in the Pylos documents is some two to four, and in fact there is a good correspondence here between the archaeological and the Linear B data since, as Whitelaw has calculated, the pottery found in the palace pantries would be the likely output of about two full-time potters.[78] There is no need to contemplate production in non-palatial workshops for palatial use. But neither on the other hand, need we envisage a palace monopoly on pottery: the 'non-palatial' sector (whatever this comprised) would have produced its own pottery.[79] The reason that we do not have records of actual production for palatial pottery would probably again be our possibility (5), that no records were kept, but this time because the 'administration' of such production, such as it was, would mostly have been carried out by the workers. Presumably the potters would have known how to go about their craft without the intervention of the Linear B scribes, and organising details of the manufacture would not have required the use of writing. Clay as a raw material is not something that would have been disbursed from palace stores, but would probably have been acquired by the potters directly, the identification of suitable deposits being part of their specialist knowledge.[80]

The absence of sage and roses from the perfumery records may be explained along similar lines.[81] Either collection of the perishables was carried out by the craftsmen themselves (perhaps drawing on specialist knowledge of suitable plants), or allocations came directly from palace gardens (or the wild) but from gatherers who did not require Linear B to conduct their activities. Commodities such as wool and oil on the other hand would have been received from palace stores and their issue to perfumers was duly recorded[82] – not necessarily, however, in this case to track the expenditure of resources, but rather with a view to receiving back the finished products from the perfumers named in the records, a point we return to below.

One major reason that things *were* recorded was to protect against embezzlement. For instance, under the *ta-ra-si-ja* system wool was tracked to ensure that the palace received back weights of textiles equal to the weight of wool that had been disbursed.[83] Where the nature of manufacture relating to an industry were different (for instance with pottery, and to an extent perfumery[84]) it may simply be that writing would be less useful as an administrative tool.

The relative value of various commodities should also be considered. Numerous scholars have commented on a bias towards recording valuable goods. Shelmerdine, for instance, notes that oil was recorded because it was precious.[85] Yet being precious on its own does not seem sufficient reason to have been recorded in Linear B. One feature of our commodities survey is that it allows the complete range of records in which a given commodity appears to be seen at a glance.[86] Gold offers an example of a precious material which is relatively rarely mentioned

[77] Palaima 1997. Galaty (1999, 78) misunderstands the nature of land tenure service obligations when he speaks of this person bargaining for and receiving land in return for his pottery. Also, he takes Tn 996 as dealing with acquisition of 'coarse utilitarian wares' from the non-palatial sector, but at least some vessels on this tablet are gold (Section 6.5.1.1).

[78] Whitelaw 2001, 65.

[79] Galaty 1999, 77.

[80] Arnold 1985, esp. 20–3, 27, 29, 31; Rice 1987, esp. 115, 120–1. See also Kiriatzi 2000; Whitbread *et al.* 2007. Cf. Galaty 1999, 78.

[81] Cf. Shelmerdine 1985, 43–4.

[82] Palmer 1999.

[83] Killen 2001a.

[84] Note that perfumery was not under the *ta-ra-si-ja* system – the specific type of production process for perfumery would make it meaningless to weigh raw materials and compare them with weights of the finished products. It seems to have been the case that a system of perquisites was in operation through participation in higher-status maintenance systems than those due to textile workers, perhaps partly to disincline the workers to cheat. See Killen 2001a.

[85] Shelmerdine 1985, 98.

[86] The database created under the direction of A. Michailidou (2001; see Dialismas 2001a) does something similar, but is not available as yet.

– there are certainly no inventories of all gold stuffs held in the palaces. A possible reason for this comparative silence is that gold and objects made of it were not moved around as much as some other commodities were. So long as gold was not involved in *transactions*, it was not vulnerable to loss or theft and need not have been recorded. It is notable that the two most prominent appearances of gold in the archives both involve transactions. PY Tn 316 deals with vessels being moved from Pylos to *pa-ki-ja-ne*, and Jo 438 deals with gold being collected from various officials.

In general, what we witness in the records is, as has long been maintained, mobilisation of resources. We see things coming into the system from various sources and, with respect to certain activities and industries (but not others), moving around *within* the system – which is doubtless partly why the Mycenaean economy looks so overwhelmingly 'redistributive'. What we do not see in general is actual expenditure, real 'out-go', with very few exceptions, the major one being with regard to disbursements for religion. The central point of the discussion above was to attempt to understand this anomaly and to put it in context. What have we learned that may be useful? In the next section we will attempt to summarise the discussion and consider how it may bear on Linear B documentation of religion.

7.4 LINEAR B DOCUMENTATION OF RELIGION

We begin by summarising possible reasons for Linear B 'gaps in the evidence' in light of the discussion above. It was emphasised that combinations of factors may be operative in particular cases, and that a good many activities and commodities may never have been recorded in the first place, but for different underlying reasons. With regard to 'gaps' occurring because the activities or commodities belonged to or originated in the non-palatial sector, it is important to be clear that this was not rejected as a possibility – indeed, it is well known that non-palatial activity was not generally recorded – but what we are particularly interested in here is why a good deal of *palatial* activity was not recorded. The list below is confined to this sector.

Possible reasons for Linear B 'gaps' in the evidence with regard to palatial activities

1. seasonality and time of year affecting, for instance
   harvest records
   lambing and shearing records
   trade
2. records not kept in the sense of never having been written, for different reasons including
   - lower-level administration being carried out by illiterate persons, affecting particularly
     household affairs
     day-to-day supervision of workshops
     lower-level management in general
   - an activity being too *important* to require detailed recording either because the details were sufficiently known or because record-keeping would have been inappropriate to the situation (e.g. in the context of trade negotiations)
   - activities being carried out by palace officials but with oral or other non-written methods of control
   - activities being carried out by special functionaries
   - focus on specific elite concerns and activities

3. focus on valuable materials and/or commodities valuable due to the purpose(s) for which they were used
4. commodities not normally inventoried but primarily recorded when they were moved or involved in transactions
5. protection against embezzlement not being a concern in the given circumstance
6. clay documents not normally 'archived' but kept only for the duration of the operation of the transaction(s)
7. general hazards of preservation (including loss of perishable materials)

The purpose of the discussion in the previous section was to attempt to understand the general absence of 'final use' disbursements in Linear B. The reason for our interest in this absence was to understand a 'presence' – why do religious purposes constitute an exception to the general rule that 'final use' disbursements were not recorded?

To an extent, there has been an assumption implicit in our examination of 'gaps' that it is these which need explaining – in other words, the expectation is for things to be recorded rather than not. It may be suggested that we should instead assume the reverse – that not being recorded was more usual and it is rather the 'presences' which require explanation. A few reasons for the 'presences' may be listed as follows. In each case it must be assumed that writing was indeed both a useful and appropriate tool for the context.

Reasons for 'presences' in Linear B

1. because the purpose of the expenditure was important (e.g. rations for textile workers)
2. because significant amounts of resources were being expended
3. to protect against embezzlement – e.g. in the case of stint and rations records
4. to ensure that obligations to the palace had been fulfilled – e.g. in the case of stint and taxation records
5. because the commodity or activity was important for social, political or economic reasons

Which of these reasons might apply to tracking of religious expenditure? One point that emerges clearly from our study is that the tracking of religious expenditures was not due to their economic significance. This might have been a natural initial supposition, given the economic nature of the Linear B records more generally, and such an impression is indeed conveyed by the large numbers of tablets involved. There is no indication, however, that religion had an inherent economic importance,[87] and Table 7-1 shows that it did not consume any significant proportion of palatial resources.

Shelmerdine once observed of the Pylos Fr tablets that 'the *principal* function of the series was not to record offerings, but to monitor the palace's supply of perfumed oil'.[88] While agreeing with the spirit of this statement, particularly as a reminder that the documents are economic records not religious texts, in the context of our commodities survey it appears less strictly speaking true. As Shelmerdine demonstrated, the palace had access to far more oil than is

[87] There does appear to be a relationship in some cases between land tenure and religion (Section 2.4), but evidence for this comes only from Pylos and even at Pylos is not necessarily general. Similarly, the appearance of deities as 'Collectors' is sometimes taken as indicative of the economic significance of religion, but as was seen previously, economic resources allocated to deities as 'Collectors' were negligible in comparison with allocations to other 'Collectors' and with overall resources (see Sections 2.5, 6.2.2.1, 6.2.3.1, 6.2.4.2 [a significant exception], 6.3.3.1, 6.3.3.3).
[88] Shelmerdine 1985, 78.

recorded in the Fr series. In other words, the series does *not* function well to monitor the palace's supply of oil, since uses of large amounts of the commodity went unrecorded. A minimum of 71% and quite possibly 100% of the oil disbursed in the Fr series was for religious offerings, but it is improbable that these disbursements accurately reflect the real uses to which perfumed oil was put. Even at Knossos, where a wider range of uses is attested, offerings are disproportionately often recorded, although the bias is less extreme. As we have now seen, the pattern occurs across the board.

The small amounts on some of the offerings records are relevant here. It is not uncommon to see amounts as small as Z 1, about 0.4 litre – but if it was important to record such small disbursements in some instances then why not in all instances? If the purpose of the Pylos Fr records really was to monitor palatial resources in oil we should expect to see every half litre meticulously accounted for, for whatever reason it had been disbursed. It seems rather that only disbursements for *some* purposes needed to be recorded: the making of religious offerings evidently being one of those purposes. In sum, it may be suggested that the main purpose of the Fr series, after all, *was* to record offerings. The economic value of the oil, while not necessarily inconsequential, seems to have had little or nothing to do with the specific reasons for keeping the records.

It would be helpful at this point to ask about other 'presences'. Our commodities survey was concerned only with those commodities which happened to appear in connection with religion. But what about those which did not? Is any pattern apparent in the remainder? The final table of our study, Table 7-2, shows all ideograms which do not occur in connection with religion, grouped according to the main types of ideograms which appear.[89]

[89] Note that Table 7-2 and Table 3-1 together should include (or refer to by commodity name) every Linear B ideogram except VIR and MUL. Also note that the two tables do not, however, constitute a complete list of all commodities appearing in Linear B, because some appear in the records by name only. However, including these would not change the overall picture and an exhaustive list is unnecessary for present purposes.

Table 7-2. Commodities not appearing in connection with religion

MILITARY		VESSELS		OTHER	
ARM	armour	*155	bowl/pannier	ARB	tree
BIG	chariot with all fittings	*200	phiale/boiling pan?	AROM	generic spice
CAPS	chariot frame	*201	tripod cauldron	CROC	saffron
CORN	agrimi horn	*202	*di-pa* – krater-like vase	*DIPTE*	robe?
CUR	wheel-less chariot	*203	*qe-to* – pithos?	LUNA	'monthly'
EQU	horse	*204	jug/ewer	*KANAKO*	safflower
GAL	helmet	*205	jug/ewer	*KAPO*	fruit?
GLA	sword	*206	hydria	*142/*172	honeycomb?
GUP	sword/dagger	*207	tripod flask	*152/*258	oxhide
HAS	spear	*208	cup/phiale?	*154	a skin?
JAC	javelin	*209	amphora	*158	a bag
PUG	sword/dagger	*210	stirrup-jar	*160	a textile?
ROTA	chariot wheel	*212	conical vase	*164	a woollen textile
SAG	arrow	*214	jar	*165	a textile?
TUN	body armour/corselet	*217	flask	*167	ingot
*180	shield?	*218	Vapheio cup	*168	bee-hive?
*245	part of a chariot?	*219	boiling pan	*169	a bed?
*246	wood for axel	*221	cup	*174	vine shoots
*253	a tyre??	*222	pithoid jar	*181	belt or thong??
*255	cuirass	*225	bath-tub	*182	pack-saddle?
*256	shield or bow??	*226	set of vessels for sacrifice	*185	bed??
		*227	bull's head rhyton	*220	footstool
		*228	ladle?		
		*229	ladle		
		*232	stunning-axe		
		*246	bath-tub		
		*250	vase		

<u>Notes</u>

<u>*General*</u>

The following unidentified ideograms are excluded: *177; *178; *179; *183; *184; *185; *189 (which may appear in a religious context in the Qa tablets); *249; *251; *252; *257; *259. *161 is an adjunct, not a commodity itself, so is also excluded.

Vessels which appear on the offering tablet Tn 316 are clearly connected with religion so are not included (*213 – bowl; *215 – kylix; *216 – chalice); the same is true for the vessel *211 containing honey offered to *pa-de* in Fs 8. *170 appears only on banqueting tablet KN C 902, so is similarly excluded, as is *248 (*NI*+CIRCULUS) which appears only on MY Ue 661. The Ta tablet ideograms listed above should arguably also be excluded since these tablets detail provisions for a feast – they are: GLA; *200; *201; *202; *204; *214; *220; *228; *232.

The detailed variations of the cloth ideogram are not shown.

<u>*Individual ideograms*</u>

***142/*172**: Honeycomb probably, but note *honey* is used as offerings (Section 4.2).

***246**: Appears twice in the table because it represents different commodities in different contexts.

A variety of commodities appears in the 'other' category (agricultural goods, textiles and so forth), but the great majority of ideograms represent military equipage or vessels. The vessels of course might be related to banqueting and/or reception activities, already well established as a central area of elite interest. Some of the vessels appear on tablets discussed above (Section 6.5), where it was suggested that disbursements on the occasions of banquets may explain for example tablets such as PY Tn 996.[90] The military equipage on the other hand has to do with warfare, which, like banqueting, is well established as a special area of Mycenaean elite interest.[91] As Driessen observed of the elite officials of Knossos, their interests were highly

[90] It may also be noted that some of the vessels are likely to have been for particular use with relation to religion, e.g. the rhyta and the set of vessels seen in *226 – although secular uses of rhyta in the Mycenaean world should not be excluded as a possibility; see Bendall forthcoming(b), with further references.

[91] See e.g. papers in Laffineur 1999. Note the issues of arms in some sense might count as 'final use' disbursements.

specialised and centred above all in the textile industry and armoury,[92] to which we may add religion, and of course banqueting.

The explanation for why 'final use' disbursements for religion appear whereas others are 'missing' must at least partly lie in this direction, that it stood alongside industrial production and military matters as an area of central concern for the palace elite. It may be noted that all of these areas of interest had not just an economic and/or practical function (e.g. defence), but were deeply rooted aspects of Mycenaean society in terms of social status, prestige, power and display. Disbursements to the gods in terms of offerings may have carried a high return-value in terms of political legitimacy and social standing, while banqueting, which has at least some connection with religion, is well established as a major arena for the manipulation and negotiation of social and political hierarchies. In this context, the extent to which religion was documented would be due in part to its cultural and symbolic significance.

This explanation, however, cannot be the whole of the picture since as we have observed there were other activities, such as trade, and commodities, such as gold, which were important but virtually never or only rarely recorded. One striking fact about offerings and banqueting records is that, as noted in Chapter 1, they appear at every site which has any significant number of Linear B documents (and even one site, Chania, which has very few). It seems to be a general Mycenaean elite attitude that religious disbursements needed to be recorded and that writing was a useful and appropriate tool for dealing with the related administration. This contrasts with the situation for trade where it has been argued that while the activity was important, writing was not considered useful for the related administration either because trade was associated with traditional oral mechanisms of control or because documentation might be inappropriate in a negotiations context (or both). If, as seems clear, however, writing was considered both useful and appropriate for administrating disbursements relating to religion, why should this have been the case? What is special about such disbursements beyond their apparent importance?

One feature that is almost unique to these disbursement records for religion as compared with all other sorts of records in the archives, both collection and disbursement records, is that they represent instances where the palaces owed something to something or someone else. The vast majority of records deal with cases where the palaces are owed something by others. Taxation, harvest and stint records for instance all function to ensure that obligations to the palaces have been met in full. With offerings records, on the other hand, the palaces are themselves under obligation. In general, the palaces recorded things to make sure that other parties fulfilled *their* obligations or requirements; here it seems things were recorded to ensure that a palace had fulfilled *its* obligations. It may be relevant in this connection that there seems to be a special transaction term, *qe-te-jo* and its variants, indicating payments due *from* the palace, and which appears very frequently in religious contexts.

It may be suggested that tablets such as the PY Fr series existed to ensure that obligations of special concern to the palatial elite had been fulfilled. This explanation could apply also to religious disbursements at Knossos, whereas disbursements of oil to workers there may have had an entirely different function: to ensure that designated persons had actually received their allotments and to protect against embezzlement. The necessity for keeping such records at Knossos but not Pylos may have partly to do with Knossian administration existing on a threefold larger scale. Pylos was a smaller operation, and it would have been easier to track

[92] Driessen 2001b, 116.

personnel through other methods.[93] Whatever the case with regard to rations, at both sites there was an evident need to record the fulfilment of important obligations to the deities.

In this connection, we may recall the curious fact observed in Section 2.2.2 that month names appear only on offerings records. There are other activities that were indeed carried out monthly – primarily the issuing of rations – but month *names* do not occur on these records. This is, as Chadwick commented, a 'strange fact' which 'has not been properly explained'.[94]

In light of our commodities survey, it may suggested that the relationship between month names and offerings records is related to an unexpected but not implausible idea, that it was only (or primarily) offerings records which were actually *archived.* In general, as noted several times above, Linear B records were not kept beyond the time at which the transactions with which they were concerned were resolved and the expected obligations fulfilled. The major exception to this rule seems to be the offerings records. The KN Fp(1) set was kept over a minimum of six months, while the PY Fr series includes at least five different words which seem to be time designations, although only one of them is actually a month name. The new Thebes tablets also record repetitively similar disbursements, although they are not monthly. In the case of the Fp(1) set, we have perhaps one of the closest examples in the Linear B corpus for documents having been actually archived in the sense of being purposefully retained in a systematic way over a period of time and in a manner such that different time periods could be distinguished from one another.[95] The scribe of the Fp(1) set would have been able to refer back and ensure that obligations had been fulfilled over a period of some half a year. Rather than tracking resources *per se* or protecting against embezzlement, what is being tracked here is the fulfilment of specific obligations to individual deities. The purpose may have been to provide certainty that such obligations had indeed been fulfilled. The records may also have been relevant to calculating current offerings – for instance, if one recipient were not due offerings regularly, but where the scribe wanted to know what had been given in the past in order to determine what was now appropriate.

There may also be evidence for the keeping of banqueting records over a series of months. The Pylos festival rations records (Fn series) include at least one one-day, one three-day and one five-day period. Unless festivals were held weekly, which seems unlikely (particularly given that one of them lasted five days), it is probable that the series was kept over at least two and probably more months. Also, the banqueting foodlists record very large amounts of foodstuffs and meat from sacrificial victims – enough for thousands of people in some instances – and in some cases may refer to events lasting a period of days (e.g. PY Un 6). There are twelve main banqueting 'menu' tablets (although Un 853 and Un 6 may refer to the same event), and again unless all of these major consumption occasions fell within the same month we are looking at records *retained* over a period of time. [96]

The suggestion that offerings and perhaps banqueting records were archived and kept in such a way that specific offerings, festival and banqueting disbursements could be identified in terms of specific time designations is consistent with the idea that the records were being kept in order to ensure the fulfilment of important obligations. This again underlines the importance such obligations had for the palatial elites, but also somewhat nuances our view of the purpose(s) behind Mycenaean record-keeping.

---

[93] Another possibility is that genuine cultural differences in traditions of allocation and uses of oil (for instance whether or not it was handed out as rations) are reflected. One might contemplate that traditions of allocation at Knossos included oil as a 'staple' (perhaps based on actual cultural preferences?) but that this was not so at Pylos.

[94] *Documents*, 407.

[95] This would suggest that the records are not after all what Driessen (1994–1995) calls 'pre-archives'. See Brosius 2003 for archives more generally.

[96] See Halstead & Isaakidou 2004; Stocker & Davis 2004; Palaima 2004b; Bendall forthcoming(a).

It was suggested in Chapter 1 that Mycenaean religion should be seen in its own context and that it may differ in fundamental ways from some of the better-documented religions of the Near East. An appreciation of the nature of the documentation of religion may begin to give us better insight into perceptions and attitudes in the Mycenaean elite world view. In tracking obligations by others to the palaces, there is an implicit implication that the palaces stood above these others. But in tracking, with care and in detail, obligations of the palaces to the gods, there is an implication that the palaces were considered beneath the deities. Whether or not the *wanax* functioned as priest as well as king (which is probable) there is some suggestion that unlike, for instance, the Egyptian pharaohs, he was not considered himself divine. In the hierarchy of obligations, gods stood above palaces and *wanaktes*.

7.5 CONCLUSION

The above conclusions may be summarised as follows. Religion did not consume a major proportion of Mycenaean palatial resources, but the disproportionate frequency with which religious expenditure was documented underlines its fundamental importance for the palatial elite. Thus, religion was economically unimportant, but culturally, symbolically and politically significant. Documentation of religion was concerned with ensuring that important obligations had been fulfilled, and Linear B was used as a tracking mechanism in part because religious affairs were attended to by higher officials who did happen to be literate and partly because writing offered them archival opportunities which they seem uniquely to have valued the advantage of exercising in the area of religion. That the documents were archived underlines the seriousness with which religious obligations were regarded and hints at how the palaces regarded themselves in relation to the gods.

The central aim of this book was to address the question of what proportion of the Mycenaean palatial economy was directed towards or invested in support for religion. The study began by defining four categories of documents in which goods and resources were disbursed or allocated for purposes connected with religion (Chapter 2). These were (1) offerings, (2) banqueting and festivals, (3) land tenure and (4) matters related to 'Collectors'. We then considered every commodity used for religious purposes at each site where relevant records existed (Chapters 3–6). In each case we compared (1) the amount of a given commodity which was disbursed for religious purposes with amounts disbursed for other 'final use' purposes, and (2) the amount disbursed for religious purposes with overall resources. The data were summarised at the end of Chapter 6 and drawn together in Chapter 7.

As we progressed through the study, various biases in the documentation became apparent. Above all, it became clear that hazards of preservation and complicating factors such as the sheer obscurity of the texts in some cases often made it difficult to achieve any meaningful calculation. Nevertheless, when the data were finally assembled (Table 7-1) a very strong pattern was apparent. Overwhelmingly, disbursements for religious purposes formed a very large proportion – almost all over 70%, many as much as 100% – of all 'final use' disbursements recorded. In almost no case, however, did religious purposes consume significant proportions of overall resources, where these could be estimated. For most commodities the proportion was less than 5%, and for many entirely negligible.[97] It was argued that this second observation may reflect a reality: that allocations for purposes connected with religion really did not consume a substantial proportion of palatial resources.

---

[97] 10% may seem 'substantial' in contrast with modern secular societies, but the point is that the majority of the Mycenaean palace economy was not being consumed in this way.

The first observation, on the other hand, was more surprising. It seemed difficult to accept that 70% or more of most commodities really was consumed for religious purposes. It was suspected that the nature of the documentation, rather than actual consumption practices, might account for the pattern and this possibility was investigated in some detail. We first observed that 'out-go' as such in the Linear B records generally seems to be missing across the board. This phenomenon had been noted before but the data had never been fully and systematically laid out. In light of the figures of Table 7-1, the problem became tangible. The question then, however, was why religion should prove an exception – why document final out-go almost exclusively with regard to religion?

With the aim of investigating a 'presence' we embarked on a consideration of 'absences', taking trade as a starting point. Several further mysterious 'gaps' were noted, and the thesis that some 'absences' in the Linear B documentation might be due to goods and services being supplied from the non-palatial sector was rejected as a general explanation (acknowledging it must have been so in some instances) because some 'gaps' existed in areas which clearly were intimately tied to palatial concerns. Similar 'gaps' in the case of some of the much better documented societies of the ancient Near East were observed and it was proposed that, as seems to have often been the case in the Near East, a great deal of economic activity was never put into writing at all. It was further suggested that different underlying reasons might be behind the lack of record-keeping, such as activities being carried out in situations where overt recording would be inappropriate (perhaps in the case of trade), or where administration was taken out by lower-level officials and supervisors who were illiterate, and/or where traditional mechanisms of authority existed, perhaps rooted in oral traditions, which were not superseded upon the adoption of writing.

An appreciation of the 'absences' was useful in understanding the 'presences'. Our final table (Table 7-2) listed ideograms which had so far not been considered in the study because the commodities concerned were not issued for religious purposes. Apart from some miscellaneous commodities, most represented military equipage and vessels, the latter perhaps connected with banqueting. This highlighted a concern on the part of the Linear B scribes with warfare, banqueting, major industries and, as noted, religion, underlining its social and symbolic significance for the palatial elite.

It was finally suggested that religious disbursement records were archived for periods of months, more or less uniquely among the Linear B documents, further underlining the importance of such disbursements for the palaces and the seriousness with which religious obligations were regarded. In sum, the significance of the religious sphere for the Mycenaean elite appears to have been due not to its economic or political power (in contrast to situations in the ancient Near East, where independent temples often had considerable economic and political importance), but rather to its critical role in the symbolic construction and maintenance of the power of the palace elite (and those who wished to be associated with this elite) and in the negotiation and expression of relative status within Mycenaean palatial society.

Finally, our study has some wider implications for Mycenaean administration more generally. In the early 1980s it was still possible to state that: 'the Mycenaean archives never tell us if they were recording virtually all economic activity in each "kingdom" or whether only a small fraction of all production and transactions came under the scrutiny of the palaces.'[98] It has now long been clear that the Linear B records do not record the majority of production and transactions in the polities, but the present study argues further that the palaces were not recording even the majority of production and transactions which did come directly under their 'scrutiny'. In particular, Linear B was not regularly used to track the disposal of palatial

[98] Halstead 1981, 309.

economic resources. It records incoming goods and internal movements of goods, above all linked with the various industries. What was 'finally' done with those goods is almost entirely absent: 'final use' disbursement records in general are 'missing', except in the case of religion. This helps explain in part why the economy appears so overwhelmingly 'redistributive' and nuances our view of the Linear B tablets as 'administrative and economic records' – they are still of course administrative, but economic concerns may not have been so central as is usually envisaged, and even where economic concerns appear paramount – for example with regard to the textile industry – the ultimate concern may have related as much to social and political factors as to economic objectives.

Above all, the palaces did not maintain 'proper' accounting systems. Not tracking out-go would be intolerable for modern institutions, but the system apparently worked, and if the palaces seemed satisfied with it this suggests that they had different objectives in terms of functionality. Such attitudes may have been fully 'rational' – in a society where divine retribution might be feared were religious obligations not fulfilled it would be rational to take care over such matters – but the careful documentation and archiving of records relating to disbursements for religious purposes had to do with symbolic capital rather than the economic importance of religion. It is questionable whether even today, in a world where most societies are dominated or at least in some way affected by a global economy, economic 'rationality' is a primary driving force in decision making rather than, for instance, psychological, political, social or indeed religious factors. Whatever may be the case today, the present study suggests that the Mycenaean palace economy was a means to an end rather than an end in itself. The final picture is of a palatial elite focused on religion, feasting, prestige-related products and warfare – a view not inconsistent with that derived from archaeological evidence for the Mycenaean world. The integration of Linear B and archaeological evidence for religion remains one of the most challenging areas of study in Aegean prehistory. It is hoped that the present study will have made some contribution to that overall project through seeking to clarify the nature of Linear B documentation of religion.

ABBREVIATIONS

1 GENERAL

The following abbreviations of commonly used forms are used in the text.

AC	Archives Complex at Pylos (Rms 7 & 8)
AN	Anthroponym
IS	Inscribed sealing
GJF	Gallery of Jewel Fresco at Knossos (G1)
KH	Khania
KN	Knossos
MN	Man's name
MU	Major unit (in Linear B measurement systems)
MY	Mycenae
NEP	North Entrance Passage at Knossos (I1–5)
PY	Pylos
RCB	Room of the Column Bases at Knossos (E1)
RCT	Room of the Chariot Tablets at Knossos (C)
TH	Thebes
THN	Theonym
TI	Tiryns
TN	Toponym
WN	Woman's name

2 REFERENCES TO AUTHORS

The following abbreviations of commonly cited groups of authors are used in the text.

AGS	Aravantinos, Godart, Sacconi (*Thèbes* I; *Thèbes* III)
POM	Piteros, Olivier, Melena (Piteros, Melena & Olivier 1990)
VC	Ventris & Chadwick (*Documents* and *Documents*[1])

3 BIBLIOGRAPHICAL ABBREVIATIONS

CoMIK I	*Corpus of Mycenaean Inscriptions from Knossos* I (Chadwick *et al.* 1986)
CoMIK II	*Corpus of Mycenaean Inscriptions from Knossos* II (Chadwick *et al.* 1990)
CoMIK III	*Corpus of Mycenaean Inscriptions from Knossos* III (Chadwick *et al.* 1997)
CoMIK IV	*Corpus of Mycenaean Inscriptions from Knossos* IV (Chadwick *et al.* 1998)
CMS I	*Corpus der Minoischen und Mykenischen Siegel* I (Sakellariou 1964)
DMic. I	*Diccionario Micénico* I (Aura Jorro 1985)
DMic. II	*Diccionario Micénico* II (Aura Jorro 1993)
Documents	*Documents in Mycenaean Greek*. Revised edition (Ventris & Chadwick 1973)
Documents[1]	*Documents in Mycenaean Greek*. First edition (Ventris & Chadwick 1956)
Flavours	*Flavours of Their Times* (Tzedakis and Martlew 1999)
KT[4]	*The Knossos Tablets*. Fourth edition (Chadwick, Killen & Olivier 1971)
KT[5]	*The Knossos Tablets*. Fifth edition (Killen & Olivier 1989)
KT[6]	*The Knossos Tablets Transliterated*. Sixth edition (Killen, Olivier & Melena forthcoming)
Mémoires I	*Mémoires de philologie mycénienne* I (Lejeune 1958)

Mémoires II	*Mémoires de philologie mycénienne* II (Lejeune 1971)
Mémoires III	*Mémoires de philologie mycénienne* III (Lejeune 1972)
Mémoires IV	*Mémoires de philologie mycénienne* IV (Lejeune 1997a)
MT II	*The Mycenae Tablets* II (Bennett 1958b)
MT III	*The Mycenae Tablets* III (Chadwick 1963)
OOT	*The Olive Oil Tablets of Pylos* (Bennett 1958a)
PM I–IV	*Palace of Minos* (Evans 1921; 1928; 1930; 1935)
PoN I	*Palace of Nestor* I (Blegen & Rawson 1966)
PoN II	*Palace of Nestor* II (Lang 1969)
PoN III	*Palace of Nestor* III (Blegen, Rawson, Taylour & Donovan 1973)
PoN IV	*Palace of Nestor* IV (Bennett *et al.* forthcoming)
PTT I	*The Pylos Tablets Transcribed* I (Bennett & Olivier 1973)
PTT II	*The Pylos Tablets Transcribed* II (Bennett & Olivier 1976)
Scribes Cnossos	*Les scribes de Cnossos* (Olivier 1967a)
Scribes Pylos	*The Scribes of Pylos* (Palaima 1988)
Scribes RCT	*The Scribes of the Room of the Chariot Tablets at Knossos* (Driessen 2000)
SM I	*Scripta Minoa* I (Evans 1909)
SM II	*Scripta Minoa* II (Evans & Myres 1952)
Thèbes I	*Thèbes. Fouilles de la Cadmée I* (Aravantinos, Godart & Sacconi 2001)
Thèbes III	*Thèbes. Fouilles de la Cadmée III* (Aravantinos, Godart & Sacconi 2002)
Thèbes IV	*Thèbes. Fouilles de la Cadmée IV* (Aravantinos, del Freo, Godart & Sacconi 2005)
TITHEMY	*TITHEMY. The Tablets and Nodules in Linear B from Tiryns, Thebes and Mycenae* (Melena & Olivier 1991)
TT II	*The Thebes Tablets* II (Chadwick & Spyropoulos 1975)

Bibliographical references

Adrados, F.R. 1964. 'Sobre el aceite perfumado: Esquilo, Agam. 96, las tablillas Fr y la ambrosía.' *Kadmos* 3: 122–48.

Adrados, F.R. 1972. 'Les institutions religieuses mycéniennes.' In Ruipérez, M.S. (ed.) *Acta Mycenaea. Proceedings of the Fifth International Colloquium on Mycenaean Studies, held in Salamanca, 30 March – 3 April 1970*. Salamanca: 170–203.

Amouretti, M.-C., Brun, J.-P. & Eitam, D. (eds.) 1993. *La production du vin et de l'huile en Méditerranée. Actes du symposium international organisé par le Centre Camille Jullian (Université de Provence-C.N.R.S.) et Le Centre Archéologique du Var* (*Ministère de la Culture et Conseil Général du Var*), *Aix-en-Provence et Toulon, 20–22 novembre 1991*). *Bulletin de Correspondance Hellénique* Suppl. 26. Athens.

Anderson, D. 1994–1995. 'Mycenaean vessel terms: evaluating the IE evidence.' *Minos* 29–30: 295–322.

Anderson, R. Forthcoming. 'Beyond belief: mind, body and ecology in the study of ancient Greek religion.'

Anderson-Stojanović, V. & Jones, E.J. 2002. 'Ancient beehives from Isthmia.' *Hesperia* 71: 345–76.

Antonelli, C. 1995. 'I santuari micenei ed il mondo dell'economia.' In Laffineur, R. & Niemeier, W.-D. (eds.) *POLITEIA. Society and State in the Aegean Bronze Age. Proceedings of the 5th International Aegean Conference / 5e Rencontre égéenne internationale University of Heidelberg, Archäologisches Institut 10–23 April 1994. Aegaeum* 12. Liège & Austin: 415–21.

Aravantinos, V.L. 1996. 'New archaeological and archival discoveries at Mycenaean Thebes.' *Bulletin of the Institute of Classical Studies* 41: 135–6.

Aravantinos, V.L. 1999. 'Mycenaean texts and contexts at Thebes: the discovery of new Linear B archives on the Kadmeia.' In Deger-Jalkotzy, S., Hiller, S. & Panagl, O. (eds.) *Floreant Studia Mycenaea. Akten des X. Internationalen Mykenologischen Colloquiums in Salzburg vom 1.–5. Mai 1995*. Vienna: 45–78.

Aravantinos, V.L, Godart, L. & Sacconi, A. 1995. 'Sui nuovi testi del Palazzo di Cadmo a Tebe.' *Rendiconti Mor. dell'Accademia dei Lincei* 6: 1–37.

Aravantinos, V.L., Godart, L. & Sacconi, A. 2001. *Thèbes. Fouilles de la Cadmée* I. *Les tablettes en linéaire B de la Odos Pelopidou. Édition et commentaire*. Biblioteca di 'Pasiphae', collana di filologia e antichità egee 1. Pisa and Rome. [= *Thèbes* I]

Aravantinos, V.L., Godart, L. & Sacconi, A. 2002. *Thèbes. Fouilles de la Cadmée* III. *Corpus des documents d'archives en linéaire B de Thèbes (1–433)*. Biblioteca di 'Pasiphae', collana di filologia e antichità egee 3. Pisa and Rome. [= *Thèbes* III]

Aravantinos, V.L., del Freo, M., Godart, L. & Sacconi, A. 2005. *Thèbes. Fouilles de la Cadmée* IV. *Les Textes de Thèbes (1–433). Translitération et tableaux des scribes*. Biblioteca di 'Pasiphae', collana di filologia e antichità egee 4. Pisa and Rome. [= *Thèbes* IV]

Arnold, D.E. 1985. *Ceramic Theory and Cultural Process*. Cambridge.

Asad, T. 1993. *Genealogies of Religion. Discipline and Reasons of Power in Christianity and Islam*. Baltimore.

Aschenbrenner, S. 1972. 'A contemporary community.' In McDonald, W.A. & Rapp, G.R. Jr. (eds.) *The Minnesota Messenia Expedition: Reconstructing a Bronze Age Regional Environment*. Minneapolis: 47–63.

Aura Jorro, F. 1985. *Diccionario Micénico*. Volume I. *Diccionario Griego–Español*. Anejo I. Consejo Superior de Investigaciones Científicas. Madrid. [= *DMic*. I]

AURA JORRO, F. 1993. *Diccionario Micénico*. Volume II. *Diccionario Griego–Español*. Anejo II. Consejo Superior de Investigaciones Científicas. Madrid [= *DMic*. II]

BAINES, J. & YOFFEE, N. 1998. 'Order, legitimacy and wealth in ancient Egypt and Mesopotamia.' In FEINMAN, G.M. & MARCUS, J. (eds.) *Archaic States*. Santa Fe: 199–260.

BARRINGER, J.M. 2001. *The Hunt in Ancient Greece*. Baltimore.

BARTONĚK, A. 2003. *Handbuch des mykenischen Griechisch*. Heidelberg.

BAUMBACH, L. 1971. 'The dilemma of the horns – an analysis of the Knossos Mc tablets.' *Acta Classica* 14: 1–16.

BAUMBACH, L. 1979a. 'Further thoughts on the Knossos Fp series.' In RISCH, E. & MÜHLESTEIN, H. (eds.) *Colloquium Mycenaeum. Actes du sixième colloque international sur les textes mycéniens et égéens tenu à Chaumont sur Neuchâtel du 7 au 13 septembre 1975*. Neuchâtel: 197–205.

BAUMBACH, L. 1979b. 'The Mycenaean contribution to the study of Greek religion.' *Studi Micenei ed Egeo-Anatolici* 20: 143–60.

BAUMBACH, L. 1983. 'An examination of the evidence for a state of emergency at Pylos c. 1200 B.C. from the Linear B tablets.' In HEUBECK, A. & NEUMANN, G. (eds.) *Res Mycenaeae. Akten des VII. Internationalen mykenologischen Colloquiums in Nürnberg vom 6.–10. April 1981*. Göttingen: 28–40.

BECK, L. & BECK, C. 1978. '*wi-ri-za* wool on Linear B tablets of perfume ingredients.' *American Journal of Archaeology* 82: 213–15.

BELL, C. 2006. *The Evolution of Long Distance Trading Relationships across the LBA/Iron Age Transition on the Northern Levantine Coast: Crisis, Continuity and Change*. British Archaeological Reports 1574. Oxford.

BENDALL, L.M. 1998–1999 [2002]. 'A time for offerings: dedications of perfumed oil at Pylian festivals.' In BENNET, J. & DRIESSEN, J. (eds.) *A-NA-QO-TA. Studies Presented to J.T. Killen. Minos* 33–34. Salamanca: 1–9.

BENDALL, L.M. 2001a. 'The economic relations of religious and political organisations and social groups in the Mycenaean world.' Unpublished Ph.D. thesis, University of Cambridge.

BENDALL, L.M. 2001b. 'The economics of *Potnia* in the Linear B tablets: palatial support for a Mycenaean deity.' In LAFFINEUR, R. & HÄGG, R. (eds.) *POTNIA. Deities and Religion in the Aegean Bronze Age. Proceedings of the 8th International Aegean Conference held at Göteborg University, 12–15 April 2000. Aegaeum* 22. Liège: 445–52.

BENDALL, L.M. 2003. 'A reconsideration of the Northeastern Building at Pylos: evidence for a Mycenaean redistributive centre.' *American Journal of Archaeology* 107: 181–232.

BENDALL, L.M. 2004. 'Fit for a king? Exclusion, hierarchy, aspiration and desire in the social structure of Mycenaean banqueting.' In HALSTEAD, P. & BARRETT, J.C. (eds.) *Food, Cuisine and Society in Prehistoric Greece. Proceedings of the 10th Aegean Round Table, University of Sheffield, January 19–21, 2001*. Sheffield Studies in Aegean Archaeology 5. Oxford: 105–35.

BENDALL, L.M. Forthcoming(a). 'How much makes a feast? Amounts of banqueting foodstuffs in the Linear B records of Pylos.' In SACCONI, A., GODART, L. & NEGRI, M. (eds.) *Proceedings of the XIIth International Colloquium of Mycenology, Rome, February 2006*. Rome.

BENDALL, L.M. Forthcoming(b). 'Does Linear B ideogram *211^{VAS}+PO* indicate a rhyton?' *Minos*.

BENDALL, L.M. Forthcoming(c). 'How much makes a feast at Knossos? Banqueting in Crete at the time of the Linear B administration.' In VLAZAKI, M. (ed.) *Proceedings of the 10th International Cretological Congress, Chania, Crete, October 2006.*

BENNET, J. 1984. 'Text and context: levels of approach to the integration of archaeological and textual data in the Late Bronze Age Aegean.' *Archaeological Review from Cambridge* 3: 63–75.

BENNET, J. 1985. 'The structure of the Linear B administration at Knossos.' *American Journal of Archaeology* 89: 231–49.

BENNET, J. 1988a. '"Outside in the distance": problems in understanding the economic geography of Mycenaean palatial territories.' In OLIVIER, J.-P. & PALAIMA, T.G. (eds.) *Texts, Tablets and*

Scribes. Studies in Mycenaean Epigraphy and Economy Offered to Emmett L. Bennett, Jr. Minos Suppl. 10. Salamanca: 19–42.

BENNET, J. 1988b. 'Approaches to the problem of combining Linear B textual data and archaeological data in the Late Bronze Age Aegean.' In FRENCH, E.B. & WARDLE, K.A. (eds.) *Problems in Greek Prehistory. Papers Presented at the Centenary Conference of the British School of Archaeology at Athens, Manchester, April 1986.* Bristol: 509–18.

BENNET, J. 1990. 'Knossos in context: comparative perspectives on the Linear B administration of LM II–III Crete.' *American Journal of Archaeology* 94: 193–211.

BENNET, J. 1992. '"Collectors" or "owners"? An examination of their possible functions within the palatial economy of LM III Crete.' In OLIVIER, J.-P. (ed.) *Mykenaïka. Actes du IX*[e] *Colloque international sur les textes mycéniens et égéens organisé par le Centre de l'Antiquité Greque et Romaine de la Fondation Hellénique des Recherches Scientifiques et l'École française d'Athènes. (Athènes, 2–6 octobre 1990). Bulletin de Correspondance Hellénique* Suppl. 25. Athens: 65–102.

BENNET, J. 1995. 'Space through time: diachronic perspectives on the spatial organization of the Pylian state.' In LAFFINEUR, R. & NIEMEIER, W.-D. (eds.) *POLITEIA. Society and State in the Aegean Bronze Age. Proceedings of the 5*[th] *International Aegean Conference / 5*[e] *Rencontre égéenne internationale University of Heidelberg, Archäologisches Institut 10–23 April 1994. Aegaeum* 12. Liège & Austin: 587–602.

BENNET, J. 1999. 'The Mycenaean conceptualization of space or Pylian geography… yet again!' In DEGER-JALKOTZY, S., HILLER, S. & PANAGL, O. (eds.) *Floreant Studia Mycenaea. Akten des X. Internationalen Mykenologischen Colloquiums in Salzburg vom 1.–5. Mai 1995.* Vienna: 131–58.

BENNET, J. 2001. 'Agency and bureaucracy: thoughts on the nature and extent of administration in Bronze Age Pylos.' In VOUTSAKI, S. & KILLEN, J.T. (eds.) *Economy and Politics in the Mycenaean Palace States. Proceedings of a Conference held on 1–3 July 1999 in the Faculty of Classics, Cambridge.* Cambridge Philological Society, Supplementary Volume 27. Cambridge: 25–37.

BENNET, J. 2004. 'Iconographies of value: words, people and things in the Late Bronze Age Aegean.' In BARRETT, J.C. & HALSTEAD, P. (eds.) *The Emergence of Civilisation Revisited.* Sheffield Studies in Aegean Archaeology 6. Oxford: 90–106.

BENNET, J. 2007a. 'Representations of power in Mycenaean Pylos: script, orality, iconography.' In LANG, F., REINHOLDT, C. & WEILHARTNER, J. (eds.) *ΣΤΕΦΑΝΟΣ ΑΡΙΣΤΕΙΟΣ. Archäologische Forschungen zwischen Nil und Istros. Festschrift für Stefan Hiller zum 65. Geburtstag.* Vienna: 11–22.

BENNET, J. 2007b. 'River of song – islands of text: Homer, Linear B and archaeology.' Paper delivered to the Sheffield Aegean Round Table 'Homer and Archaeology', 19–21 January 2007.

BENNET, J. & DAVIS, J.L. 1999. 'Making Mycenaeans: warfare, territorial expansion, and representations of the other in the Pylian Kingdom.' In LAFFINEUR, R. (ed.) *POLEMOS. Le contexte guerrier en Égée à l'âge du bronze. Actes de la 7*[e] *Rencontre égéenne internationale Université de Liège, 14–17 avril 1998. Aegaeum* 19. Liège and Austin: 105–20.

BENNETT, E.L. JR. 1950. 'Fractional quantities in Minoan bookkeeping.' *American Journal of Archaeology* 54: 204–22.

BENNETT, E.L. JR. 1956. 'The land-holders of Pylos.' *American Journal of Archaeology* 60: 103–35.

BENNETT, E.L. JR. 1958a. *The Olive Oil Tablets of Pylos. Texts of Inscriptions Found, 1955. Minos* Suppl. 2. Salamanca. [= *OOT*]

BENNETT, E.L. JR. 1958b. *The Mycenae Tablets* II. Transactions of the American Philosophical Society, New Series, Vol. 8, Pt. 1. Philadelphia. [= MT II]

BENNETT, E.L. JR. (ed.) 1964a. *Mycenaean Studies. Proceedings of the 3*[rd] *International Colloquium for Mycenaean Studies held at 'Wingspread' 4–8 September 1961.* Madison.

BENNETT, E.L. JR. 1964b. 'The find-spots of the Pylos tablets'. In BENNETT, E.L. (ed.) *Mycenaean Studies. Proceedings of the 3*[rd] *International Colloquium for Mycenaean Studies held at 'Wingspread' 4–8 September 1961.* Madison: 241–52.

BENNETT, E.L. JR. 1992. 'A selection of Pylos tablet texts.' In OLIVIER, J.-P. (ed.) *Mykenaïka. Actes du IXe Colloque international sur les textes mycéniens et égéens organisé par le Centre de l'Antiquité Greque et Romaine de la Fondation Hellénique des Recherches Scientifiques et l'École française d'Athènes (Athènes, 2–6 octobre 1990). Bulletin de Correspondance Hellénique* Suppl. 25. Athens: 103–28.

BENNETT, E.L. JR. 1996–1997. 'Junctions, restorations, and reconstructions in Pylian and related texts.' *Minos* 31–32: 135–44.

BENNETT, E.L., DRIESSEN, J.M., GODART, L., KILLEN, J.T., KOPAKA, C., MELENA, J.L., OLIVIER, J.-P. & PERNA, M. 1989. '436 raccords et quasi-raccords de fragments inédites dans *KT* 5.' *Minos* 24: 199–242.

BENNETT, E.L., MELENA, J.L., OLIVIER, J.-P., PALAIMA, T.G. & SHELMERDINE, C.W. Forthcoming. *The Palace of Nestor at Pylos in Western Messenia.* Volume IV. *The Inscribed Documents.* [= *PoN* IV]

BENNETT, E.L. JR. & OLIVIER, J.-P. 1973. *The Pylos Tablets Transcribed.* Part I. *Texts and Notes.* Incunabula Graeca 51. Rome. [= *PTT* I]

BENNETT, E.L. JR. & OLIVIER, J.-P. 1976. *The Pylos Tablets Transcribed.* Part II. *Hands, Concordances, Indices.* Incunabula Graeca 59. Rome. [= *PTT* II]

BERGQUIST, B. 1988. 'The archaeology of sacrifice: Minoan-Mycenaean versus Greek. A brief survey into two sites with contrary evidence.' In HÄGG, R., MARINATOS, N. & NORDQUIST, G. (eds.) *Early Greek Cult Practice.* Skrifter Utgivna av Svenska Institutet i Athen 38, Stockholm: 21–34.

BINTLIFF, J.L. 1977. *Natural Environment and Human Settlement in Prehistoric Greece.* British Archaeological Reports 28. Oxford.

BLEGEN, C.W. & RAWSON, M. 1966. *The Palace of Nestor at Pylos in Western Messenia.* Volume I. Part 1. *Text.* Part 2. *Illustrations.* Cincinnati. [= *PoN* I]

BLEGEN, C.W., RAWSON, M., TAYLOUR, W. & DONOVAN, W.P. 1973. *The Palace of Nestor at Pylos in Western Messenia.* Volume III. Princeton. [= *PoN* III]

BLITZER, H. 1993. 'Olive cultivation and oil production in Minoan Crete.' In AMOURETTI, M.-C., BRUN, J.-P. & EITAM, D. (eds.) *La production du vin et de l'huile en Méditerranée. Actes du symposium international organisé par le Centre Camille Jullian (Université de Provence–C.N.R.S.) et Le Centre Archéologique du Var (Ministère de la Culture et Conseil Général du Var), Aix-en-Provence et Toulon, 20–22 novembre 1991. Bulletin de Correspondance Hellénique* Suppl. 26. Athens: 163–75.

BOARDMAN, J. & PALMER, L.R. 1963. *On the Knossos Tablets. The Find-places of the Knossos Tablets. The Date of the Knossos Tablets.* Oxford.

BOËLLE, C. 2001. '*po-ti-ni-ja*: unité ou pluralité?' In LAFFINEUR, R. & HÄGG, R. (eds.) *POTNIA. Deities and Religion in the Aegean Bronze Age. Proceedings of the 8th International Aegean Conference held at Göteborg University, 12–15 April 2000. Aegaeum* 22. Liège: 403–9.

BOULOTIS, CH. 1996. 'Η Ελιά και το λάδι στις ανακτορικές κοινωνίες της Κρήτης και της Ελλάδας. Όψεις και απόψεις.' In *Ελιά και Λάδι. Δ' Τριήμερο εργασίας, Καλαμάτα, 7–9 Μαΐου 1993.* Kalatmata: 19–58.

BREMMER, J.N. 1998. '"Religion", "ritual" and the opposition "sacred vs. profane": notes towards a terminological "genealogy".' In GRAF, F. (ed.) *Ansichten griechischer Rituale, Geburtstags-Symposium für Walter Burkert.* Stuttgart and Leipzig: 9–32.

BROODBANK, C. 2000. *An Island Archaeology of the Early Cyclades.* Cambridge.

BROSIUS, M. (ed.) 2003. *Ancient Archives and Archival Tradition. Concepts of Record-Keeping in the Ancient World.* Oxford.

BRUCE, S. 2000. 'The supply-side model of religion: the Nordic and Baltic states.' *Journal for the Scientific Study of Religion* 39: 32–46.

BURKERT, W. 1985. *Greek Religion.* (Translated by J. RAFFAN.) Cambridge, Mass.

BURKERT, W. 1987. 'Offerings in perspective: surrender, distribution, exchange.' In LINDERS, T. & NORDQUIST, G. (eds.) *Gifts to the Gods. Proceedings of the Uppsala Symposium 1985. Boreas* 15. Uppsala: 43–50.

CAPITA, C. 1997. 'Reflections on the oil production in Mycenaean Greece.' In CIHO, M., NISTOR, V. & ZAHARIA, D. (eds.) *In honorem emeritae Ligiae Bârzu. Timpul Istoriei I. Memorie si patrimoniu.* Bucharest: 70–85.

CARLIER, P. 1984. *Le royauté en Grèce avant Alexandre.* Strasbourg.

CARLIER, P. 1987. 'Palais et sanctuaire dans le monde mycénien.' In LEVY, E. (ed.) *Le système palatial en Orient, en Grèce et à Rome. Actes du Colloque de Strasbourg 19–22 juin 1985.* Strasbourg: 255–82.

CARLIER, P. 1990. 'La double face de pouvoir royal dans le monde mycénien.' In NICOLET, C. (ed.) *Du pouvoir dans l'antiquité. Mots et réalités.* Hautes études du monde grèco-romain 16. Geneva: 37–52.

CARLIER, P. 1992. 'Les collecteurs: sont ils des fermiers?' In OLIVIER, J.-P. (ed.) *Mykenaïka. Actes du IXe Colloque international sur les textes mycéniens et égéens organisé par le Centre de l'Antiquité Greque et Romaine de la Fondation Hellénique des Recherches Scientifiques et l'École française d'Athènes (Athènes, 2–6 octobre 1990). Bulletin de Correspondance Hellénique* Suppl. 25. Athens: 159–66.

CARPENTER, M. 1983. '*ki-ti-me-na* and *ke-ke-me-na* at Pylos.' *Minos* 18: 81–8.

CARPENTER, M. 1984. 'Some reasons for the double version of the Pylos land-register.' *Bulletin of the Institute of Classical Studies* 31: 214.

CARRATELLI, G. PUGLIESE. 1954. 'Nuovi studi sui testi micenei.' *La Parola del Passato* 9: 215–28.

CARRATELLI, G. PUGLIESE. 1955. 'Rassegna: *The Linear 'B' Texts from Knossos.* Transliterated and edited by R. Browning.' *La Parola del Passato* 10: 220–9.

CATLING, H.W. & CATLING, E. 1984. 'The bronzes and metal working equipment.' In POPHAM, M. *The Minoan Unexplored Mansion at Knossos.* British School of Archaeology at Athens. Oxford: 203–22.

CATLING, H.W., CHERRY, J.F., JONES, R.E. & KILLEN, J.T. 1980. 'The Linear B inscribed stirrup jars and West Crete.' *Annual of the British School of Archaeology at Athens* 75: 49–113.

CHADWICK, J. 1957. 'Potnia.' *Minos* 5: 117–29.

CHADWICK, J. 1958a. *The Decipherment of Linear B.* Cambridge.

CHADWICK, J. 1958b. 'The Mycenaean filing system.' *Bulletin of the Institute of Classical Studies* 5: 1–5.

CHADWICK, J. 1963. *The Mycenae Tablets* III. Transactions of the American Philosophical Association 52.7. [= *MT* III]

CHADWICK, J. 1964. 'Pylos tablet Un 1322.' In BENNETT, E.L. (ed.) *Mycenaean Studies. Proceedings of the Third International Colloquium for Mycenaean Studies Held at 'Wingspread', 4–8 September 1961.* Madison: 19–26.

CHADWICK, J. 1966. 'The olive oil tablets of Knossos.' In PALMER, L.R. & CHADWICK, J. (eds.) *Proceedings of the Cambridge Colloquium on Mycenaean Studies.* Cambridge: 26–32.

CHADWICK, J. 1968a. 'The organization of the Mycenaean archives.' In BARTONĚK, A. (ed.) *Studia Mycenaea. Proceedings of the Mycenaean Symposium, Brno, April 1966.* Brno: 11–21.

CHADWICK, J. 1968b. 'The editing of the Mycenaean texts.' In GALLAVOTTI, C. (ed.) *Atti e Memorie del 1° Congresso Internazionale di Micenologia di Roma, 27 settembre – 3 ottobre 1967.* Incunabula Graeca 25. Rome: 486–99.

CHADWICK, J. 1970. 'Linear B tablets from Thebes.' *Minos* 10: 115–37.

CHADWICK, J. 1975. 'Who was *e-ke-ra$_2$-wo*?' In BINGEN, J., CAMBIER, G. & NACHTERGAEL, G. (eds.) *Le monde grec. Pensée, littérature, histoire, documents. Hommages à Claire Préaux.* Brussels: 450–3.

CHADWICK, J. 1976. *The Mycenaean World.* Cambridge.

CHADWICK, J. 1977. 'The interpretation of Mycenaean documents and Pylian geography.' In BINTLIFF, J. (ed.) *Mycenaean Geography*. Cambridge: 36–9.

CHADWICK, J. 1979. 'Land-holding at Pylos.' *Bulletin of the Institute of Classical Studies* 26: 130.

CHADWICK, J. 1985. 'What do we know about Mycenaean religion?' In MORPURGO DAVIES, A. & DUHOUX, Y. (eds.) *Linear B: A 1984 Survey*. Bibliothèque des cahiers de l'institut de linguistique de Louvain 26. Louvain-la-Neuve: 191–202.

CHADWICK, J. 1986. 'The semantic value of Greek ἐσχάρα.' In ETTER, A. (ed.) *o-o-pe-ro-si. Festschrift für Ernst Risch zum 75 Geburtstag*. Berlin: 515–23.

CHADWICK, J. 1987a. 'The muster of the Pylian fleet.' In ILIEVSKI, P.HR. & CREPAJAC, LJ. (eds.) *Tractata Mycenaea. Proceedings of the Eighth International Colloquium on Mycenaean Studies, held in Ohrid, 15–20 September 1985*. Skopje: 75–84.

CHADWICK, J. 1987b. 'L'économie palatiale dans la Grèce mycénienne.' In LEVY, E. (ed.) *Le système palatial en Orient, en Grèce et à Rome. Actes du Colloque de Strasbourg 19–22 juin 1985*. Strasbourg: 283–90.

CHADWICK, J. 1988. 'The women of Pylos.' In OLIVIER, J.-P. & PALAIMA, T.G. (eds.) *Texts, Tablets and Scribes. Studies in Mycenaean Epigraphy Offered to Emmett L. Bennett, Jr. Minos* Suppl. 10. Salamanca: 43–96.

CHADWICK, J. 1996–1997 [1998]. 'Three temporal clauses.' *Minos* 31–32: 293–301.

CHADWICK, J. 1998–1999 [2002]. 'Pylian gold and local administration: PY Jo 438.' In BENNET, J. & DRIESSEN, J. (eds.) *A-NA-QO-TA. Studies Presented to J.T. Killen. Minos* 33–34. Salamanca: 31–7.

CHADWICK, J. 1999. 'Linear B: past, present and future.' In DEGER-JALKOTZY, S., HILLER, S. & PANAGL, O. (eds.) *Floreant Studia Mycenaea. Akten des X. Internationalen Mykenologischen Colloquiums in Salzburg vom 1.–5. Mai 1995*. Vienna: 29–38.

CHADWICK, J., GODART, L., KILLEN, J.T., OLIVIER, J.-P., SACCONI, A. & SAKELLARAKIS, I.A. 1986. *Corpus of Mycenaean Inscriptions from Knossos*. Volume I. *1–1063*. Cambridge. [= *CoMIK* I]

CHADWICK, J., GODART, L., KILLEN, J.T., OLIVIER, J.-P., SACCONI, A. & SAKELLARAKIS, I.A. 1990. *Corpus of Mycenaean Inscriptions from Knossos*. Volume II. *1064–4495*. Cambridge. [= *CoMIK* II]

CHADWICK, J., GODART, L., KILLEN, J.T., OLIVIER, J.-P., SACCONI, A. & SAKELLARAKIS, I.A. 1997. *Corpus of Mycenaean Inscriptions from Knossos*. Volume III. *5000–7999*. Cambridge. [= *CoMIK* III]

CHADWICK, J., GODART, L., KILLEN, J.T., OLIVIER, J.-P., SACCONI, A. & SAKELLARAKIS, I.A. 1998. *Corpus of Mycenaean Inscriptions from Knossos*. Volume IV. *8000–9947 and Index to Volumes I–IV*. Cambridge. [= *CoMIK* IV]

CHADWICK, J., KILLEN, J.T. & OLIVIER, J.-P. 1971. *The Knossos Tablets. A Transliteration*. Fourth edition. Cambridge. [= KT^4]

CHADWICK, J. & SPYROPOULOS, T.G. 1975. *The Thebes Tablets* II. *Minos* Suppl. 4. Salamanca. [= *TT* II]

CHASE-DUNN, C. & HALL, T.D. 1997. *Rise and Demise. Comparing World-Systems*. Boulder & Oxford.

CHRISTAKIS, K.S. 1999. 'Pithoi and food storage in Neopalatial Crete: a domestic perspective.' *World Archaeology* 31: 1–20.

CHRISTAKIS, K.S. 2004. 'Palatial economy and storage in Late Bronze Age Knossos.' In CADOGAN, G., HATZAKI, E. & VASILAKIS, A. (eds.) *Knossos: Palace, City, State*. British School at Athens Studies 12. London: 299–309.

CHRISTAKIS, K.S. 2005. *Cretan Bronze Age Pithoi. Traditions and Trends in the Production and Consumption of Storage Containers in Bronze Age Crete*. Institute of Aegean Prehistory Monographs 18. Philadelphia.

CLINE, E.H. 1994. *Sailing the Wine-Dark Sea. International Trade and the Late Bronze Age Aegean*. British Archaeological Reports, International Series 591. Oxford.

CLINE, E.H. 1995. 'Tinker, tailor, soldier, sailor: Minoans and Mycenaeans abroad.' In LAFFINEUR, R. & NIEMEIER, W.-D. (eds.) *POLITEIA. Society and State in the Aegean Bronze Age. Proceedings of the 5th International Aegean Conference / 5e Rencontre égéenne internationale, University of Heidelberg, Archäologisches Institut 10–13 April 1993. Aegaeum* 12. Liège & Austin: 265–87.

CLINTON, K. 2005. 'Pigs in Greek rituals.' In HÄGG, R. & ALROTH, B. (eds.) *Greek Sacrificial Ritual, Olympian and Chthonian. Proceedings of the Sixth International Seminar on Ancient Greek Cult, Organized by the Department of Classical Archaeology and Ancient History, Göteborg University, 25–27 April 1997*. Stockholm: 167–79.

CONSTANTINIDOU, S. 1989. '*Xenia* and *lekhestroterion*: two Mycenaean festivals.' *Dodoni* 18: 9–25.

CRANE, E. (ed.) 1975. *Honey. A Comprehensive Survey*. London.

CRANE, E. 1983. *The Archaeology of Beekeeping*. London.

CRANE, E. 1999. *The World History of Beekeeping and Honey Hunting*. London.

CRAWFORD, H. 1991. *Sumer and the Sumerians*. Cambridge.

CHRISTAKIS, K.S. 2005. *Cretan Bronze Age Pithoi*. Institute of Aegean Prehistory Monograph 18. Philadelphia.

DALTON, G. 1967. 'Economic theory and primitive society.' In DALTON, G. (ed.) *Tribal and Peasant Economies*. New York.

D'ALTROY, T. & EARLE, T.K. 1985. 'Staple finance, wealth finance, and storage in the Inka political economy.' *Current Anthropology* 26.2: 187–206.

DAVARAS, K. 1984 [1986]. 'Μινωϊκὸ κηριοφόρο πλοιάριο τῆς Συλλογῆς Μητσοτάκη.' *Αρχαιολογική Εφημερίς* 123: 55–95.

DAY, P.M. & HASKELL, H.W. 1995. 'Transport stirrup jars from Thebes as evidence of trade in Late Bronze Age Greece.' In GILLIS, C., RISBERG, C. & SJÖBERG, B. (eds.) *Trade and Production in Premonetary Greece. Aspects of Trade. Proceedings of the 3rd International Workshop, Athens 1993*. Studies in Mediterranean Archaeology Pocket-book 134. Jonsered: 87–109.

DE FIDIO, P. 1977. *I* dosmoi *pilii a Poseidon. Una terra sacra di età micenea*. Incunabula Graeca 65. Rome.

DE FIDIO, P. 1982. 'Fiscalità, redistribuzione, equivalenze: per una discussione sull'economia micenea.' *Studi Micenei ed Egeo-Anatolici* 23: 83–136.

DE FIDIO, P. 1987. 'Palais et communautés de village dans le royaume mycénien de Pylos.' In ILIEVSKI, P.HR. & CREPAJAC, LJ. (eds.) *Tractata Mycenaea. Proceedings of the Eighth International Colloquium on Mycenaean Studies, held in Ohrid, 15–20 September 1985*. Skopje: 129–50.

DE FIDIO, P. 1992. 'Mycènes et Proche-Orient, ou le théorème des modèles.' In OLIVIER, J.-P. (ed.) *Mykenaïka. Actes du IXe Colloque international sur les textes mycéniens et égéens organisé par le Centre de l'Antiquité Greque et Romaine de la Fondation Hellénique des Recherches Scientifiques et l'École française d'Athènes (Athènes, 2–6 octobre 1990). Bulletin de Correspondance Hellénique* Suppl. 25. Athens: 173–96.

DE FIDIO, P. 1998–1999 [2002]. 'On the tracks of Aegean Bronze Age wool and weights.' In BENNET, J. & DRIESSEN, J. (eds.) *A-NA-QO-TA. Studies Presented to J.T. Killen. Minos* 33–34. Salamanca: 39–63.

DE FIDIO, P. 2001. 'Centralisation and its limits in the Mycenaean palatial system.' In VOUTSAKI, S. & KILLEN, J.T. (eds.) *Economy and Politics in the Mycenaean Palace States. Proceedings of a Conference held on 1–3 July 1999 in the Faculty of Classics, Cambridge*. Cambridge Philological Society Supplementary Volume 27. Cambridge: 15–24.

DEGER-JALKOTZY, S. 1978. *E-QE-TA. Zur Rolle des Gefolgschaftswesents in der Sozialstruktur mykenischer Reiche*. Mykenische Studien Band 6. Vienna.

DEGER-JALKOTZY, S. & PANAGL, O. 2006. *Die neuen Linear B-Texte aus Theben. Ihr Aufschlusswert für die mykenische Sprache und Kultur*. Verlag der Österreichischen Akademie der Wissenschaften. Vienna.

DEL FREO, M. 1996–1997 [1998]. 'Osservazioni su miceneo *ko-ma-we-te-ja*.' *Minos* 31–32: 145–58.

DEL FREO, M. 1999. 'Mic. *ke-re-na-i* nei nuovi testi in lineare B di Tebe.' In LA ROSA, V., PALERMO, D. & VAGNETTI, L. (eds.) *'Επὶ πόντον πλαζόμενοι. Simposio italiano di Studi Egei dedicato a Luigi Bernabò Brea e Giovanni Pugliese Carratelli, Roma, 18–20 febbraio 1998*. Scuola Archeologica Italiana di Atene. Rome: 299–304.

DEL FREO, M. 2005. *I censimenti di terreni nei testi in Lineare B*. Biblioteca di 'Pasiphae', collana di filologia e antichità egee 5. Pisa and Rome.

DIAKONOFF, I.M. 1954. 'Sale of land in Pre-Sargonic Sumer'. In *Papers Presented by the Soviet Delegation at the XXIII International Congress of Orientalists: Assyriology*. USSR Academy of Sciences. Moscow: 19–29.

DIAKONOFF, I.M. 1959. *Society and State in Ancient Mesopotamia*. Moscow.

DIAKONOFF, I.M. 1974. *Structure of Society and State in Early Dynastic Sumer*. Edited by M. DESROCHERS. Monographs of the Ancient Near East 1.3. Los Angeles.

DIALISMAS, A. 2001a. 'Appendix: the databases on the quantities recorded in Linear B tablets.' In MICHAILIDOU, A. (ed.) *Manufacture and Measurement. Counting, Measuring and Recording. Craft Items in Early Aegean Societies*. Meletemata 33. Athens: 318–34.

DIALISMAS, A. 2001b. 'Metal artefacts as recorded in the Linear B tablets.' In MICHAILIDOU, A. (ed.) *Manufacture and Measurement. Counting, Measuring and Recording. Craft Items in Early Aegean Societies*. Meletemata 33. Athens: 120–43.

DICKINSON, O.T.P.K. 1994. *The Aegean Bronze Age*. Cambridge.

DIETLER, M. & HAYDEN, B. 2001. *Feasts. Anthropological and Ethnographic Perspectives on Food, Politics, and Power*. London and Washington, DC.

DILLON, M. 2002. *Girls and Women in Classical Greek Religion*. London.

DORIA, M. 1968. *Iscrizioni dell'olio di Pilo, Cnossos, e Micene*. Istituto di Glottologia. Trieste.

DOUGLAS, M. (ed.) 1987. *Constructive Drinking. Perspectives on Drink from Anthropology*. Cambridge.

DRIESSEN, J. 1988. 'The scribes of the Room of the Chariot Tablets.' In OLIVIER, J.-P. & PALAIMA, T.G. (eds.) *Texts, Tablets and Scribes. Studies in Mycenaean Epigraphy and Economy Offered to Emmett L. Bennett, Jr. Minos* Suppl. 10. Salamanca: 123–65.

DRIESSEN, J. 1990. *An Early Destruction in the Mycenaean Palace at Knossos*. Acta Archaeologica Lovaniensia Monographiae 2. Leuven.

DRIESSEN, J. 1992. '"Collector's Items". Observations sur l'élite mycénienne de Cnossos.' In OLIVIER, J.-P. (ed.) *Mykenaïka. Actes du IXe Colloque international sur les textes mycéniens et égéens organisé par le Centre de l'Antiquité Greque et Romaine de la Fondation Hellénique des Recherches Scientifiques et l'École française d'Athènes (Athènes, 2–6 octobre 1990). Bulletin de Correspondance Hellénique* Suppl. 25. Athens: 197–214.

DRIESSEN, J. 1994–1995. 'Data storage for reference and prediction at the dawn of civilization? A review article with some observations on *Archives Before Writing*.' *Minos* 29–30: 239–56.

DRIESSEN, J. 1997. 'Le palais de Cnossos au MR II–III: combien de destructions?' In DRIESSEN, J. & FARNOUX, A. (eds.) *La Crète mycénienne. Actes de la Table Ronde Internationale organisée par l'École française d'Athènes. Bulletin de Correspondance Hellénique* Suppl. 30. Athens & Paris: 113–34.

DRIESSEN, J. 1999. 'The Northern Entrance Passage at Knossos: some preliminary observations on its potential role as "Central Archives".' In DEGER-JALKOTZY, S., HILLER, S. & PANAGL, O. (eds.) *Floreant Studia Mycenaea. Akten des X. Internationalen mykenologischen Colloquiums in Salzburg vom 1.–5. Mai 1995*. Vienna: 205–26.

DRIESSEN, J. 2000. *The Scribes of the Room of the Chariot Tablets at Knossos. Interdisciplinary Approach to the Study of a Linear B Deposit. Minos* Suppl. 15. Salamanca. [= *Scribes RCT*]

DRIESSEN, J. 2001a. 'Centre and periphery: some observations on the administration of the kingdom of Knossos.' In VOUTSAKI, S. & KILLEN, J.T. (eds.) *Economy and Politics in the Mycenaean Palace States. Proceedings of a Conference Held on 1–3 July 1999 in the Faculty of Classics, Cambridge*. Cambridge Philological Society Supplementary Volume 27. Cambridge: 96–112.

DRIESSEN, J. 2001b. 'Mécanismes de contrôle au palais de Cnossos à l'époque des tablettes en linéaire B.' *Ktema* 26: 113–20.

DUERMEIJER, G.C. 2006. 'The Lobby of the Stone Seat in the Mycenaean palace at Knossos: a department for storing and recording olive oil and a redistributive area.' *Bulletin Antieke Beschaving* 81: 1–12.

DUHOUX, Y. 1968. 'Le groupe lexical de δίδωμι en mycénien.' *Minos* 9: 81–108.

DUHOUX, Y. 1976a. *Aspects du vocabulaire économique mycénien (cadastre–artisanat–fiscalité).* Amsterdam.

DUHOUX, Y. 1976b. 'Idéogrammes textiles du linéaire B **146*, **160*, **165* et **166*.' *Minos* 15: 116–32.

EARLE, T.K. 1977. 'A reappraisal of redistribution: complex Hawaiian chiefdoms.' In EARLE, T.K. & ERICSON, J.E. (eds.) *Exchange Systems in Prehistory*. New York: 213–29.

EARLE, T.K. 2002. *Bronze Age Economics. The Beginnings of Political Economies.* Boulder & Oxford.

EARLE, T.K. & D'ALTROY, T.N. 1982. 'Storage facilities and state finance in the upper Mantaro Valley, Peru.' In EARLE, T.K. & ERICSON, J.E. (eds.) *Exchange Systems in Prehistory*. New York: 265–90.

ERARD-CERCEAU, I. 1988. 'Documents sur l'agriculture mycénienne: peut-on concilier archéologie et épigraphie?' *Minos* 23: 183–90.

EVANS, A.J. 1909. *Scripta Minoa. The Written Documents of Minoan Crete with Special Reference to the Archives of Knossos.* Volume I. *The Hieroglyphic and Primitive Linear Classes*. Oxford. [= *SM* I]

EVANS, A.J. 1921. *The Palace of Minos*. Volume I. London. [= *PM* I]

EVANS, A.J. 1928. *The Palace of Minos*. Volume II. London. [= *PM* II]

EVANS, A.J. 1930. *The Palace of Minos*. Volume III. London. [= *PM* III]

EVANS, A.J. 1935. *The Palace of Minos*. Volume IV. London. [= *PM* IV]

EVANS, A.J. & MYRES, J.L. 1952. *Scripta Minoa. The Written Documents of Minoan Crete with Special Reference to the Archives of Knossos.* Volume II. *The Archives of Knossos*. Oxford. [= *SM* II]

EVERSHED, R.P., VAUGHAN, S.J., DUDD, S.N. & SOLES, J.S. 1997. 'Fuel for thought? Beeswax in lamps and conical cups from Late Minoan Crete.' *Antiquity* 71: 979–85.

FINLEY, M.I. 1957. 'The Mycenaean tablets and economic history.' *Economic History Review* 10: 128–41. [Reprinted in SHAW, B.D. & SALLER, R.P. (eds.) 1981. *Economy and Society in Ancient Greece. Collected Essays of M.I. Finley*. New York: 199–212.]

FINLEY, M.I. 1964. 'Between slavery and freedom.' *Comparative Studies in Society and History* 6: 233–49. [Reprinted in SHAW, B.D. & SALLER, R.P. (eds.) 1981. *Economy and Society in Ancient Greece. Collected Essays of M.I. Finley*. New York: 116–32.]

FINLEY, M.I. 1985. *The Ancient Economy*. Second edition. London.

FIRTH, R.J. 1996–1997. 'The find-places of the tablets from the Palace of Knossos.' *Minos* 31–32: 7–122.

FIRTH, R.J. 2000–2001a. 'A review of the find-places of the Linear B tablets from the Palace of Knossos.' *Minos* 35–36: 63–290.

FIRTH, R.J. 2000–2001b. 'Evans' missing batch of Linear B tablets.' *Minos* 35–36: 291–314.

FIRTH, R.J. 2007. 'Re-considering alum on the Linear B tablets.' In GILLIS, C. & NOSCH, M.-L. (eds.) *Ancient Textiles: Production, Craft and Society. Proceedings of the First International Conference on Ancient Textiles, Held at Lund, Sweden, and Copenhagen, Denmark, on March 19–23, 2003*. Oxford: 130–8.

FIRTH, R.J. & MELENA, J.L. 2000–2001. 'The Knossos tablets: genesis of the 5000-series.' *Minos* 35–36: 315–55.

FLOUDA, G. 2000. 'Inscribed Pylian nodules: their use in the administration of the storerooms of the Pylian palace.' *Studi Micenei ed Egeo-Anatolici* 42: 213–45.

FORBES, H. 1993. 'Ethnoarchaeology and the place of the olive in the economy of the Southern Argolid, Greece.' In AMOURETTI, M.-C., BRUN, J.-P. & EITAM, D. (eds.) *La production du vin et de l'huile en Méditerranée. Actes du symposium international organisé par le Centre Camille Jullian (Université de Provence–C.N.R.S.) et Le Centre Archéologique du Var (Ministère de la Culture et Conseil Général du Var), Aix-en-Provence et Toulon, 20–22 novembre 1991. Bulletin de Correspondance Hellénique* Suppl. 26. Athens: 213–26.

FORBES, H. 2002. 'Prudent producers and concerned consumers: ethnographic and historical observations on staple storage and urban consumer behaviour.' In MIRACLE, P. & MILNER, N. (eds.) *Consuming Passions and Patterns of Consumption.* Cambridge: 97–111.

FOSTER, B.R. 1987. 'The Late Bronze Age palace economy: a view from the East.' In HÄGG, R. & MARINATOS, N. (eds.) *The Function of the Minoan Palaces. Proceedings of the Fourth International Symposium at the Swedish Institute in Athens, 10–16 June, 1984.* Stockholm: 11–16.

FOSTER, B.R. 1993. 'Management and administration in the Sargonic period.' In LIVERANI, M. (ed.) *Akkad. The First World Empire. Structure, Ideology, Traditions.* Padua: 25–39.

FOSTER, E.D. 1974. 'The manufacture and trade of Mycenaean perfumed oil.' Unpublished Ph.D. thesis, Duke University.

FOSTER, E.D. 1977a. 'An administrative department at Knossos concerned with perfumery and offerings.' *Minos* 16: 19–51.

FOSTER, E.D. 1977b. '*po-ni-ki-jo* in the Knossos tablets reconsidered.' *Minos* 16: 52–66.

FOSTER, E.D. 1981. 'The flax impost at Pylos and Mycenaean landholding', *Minos* 17: 67–121.

FRANCESCHETTI, A. 2001. 'Qualque osservazione sui cereali nei testi micenei.' *Ktema* 26: 145–9.

FRENCH, E.B. 2002. *Mycenae. Agamemnon's Capital. The Site in its Setting.* Stroud.

GALATY, M.L 1999. *Nestor's Wine Cups. Investigating Ceramic Manufacture and Exchange in a Late Bronze Age Mycenaean State.* British Archaeological Reports International Series 766. Oxford.

GALATY, M.L. & PARKINSON, W.A. 1999. 'Putting Mycenaean palaces in their place: an introduction.' In GALATY, M.L. & PARKINSON, W.A. *Rethinking Mycenaean Palaces. New Interpretations of an Old Idea.* Los Angeles: 1–8.

GALLAVOTTI, C. 1959. 'I documenti unguentari e gli dei di Pilo.' *Parola del Passato* 14: 87–105.

GEERTZ, C. 1973. *The Interpretation of Cultures.* New York.

GELB, I.J. 1969. 'On the alleged temple and state economies in ancient Mesopotamia.' In GIUFFRÈ, A. (ed.) *Studi in Onore di Edoardo Volterra.* Volume 4. Milan: 137–54.

GELB, I.J. 1979. 'Definition and discussion of slavery and serfdom.' *Ugarit-Forschungen* 11: 283-97.

GÉRARD-ROUSSEAU, M. 1966. 'Un document mycénien relatif à la parfumerie (PY Fr 1184).' *Antiquité Classique* 35: 207–9.

GÉRARD-ROUSSEAU, M. 1968. *Les mentions religieuses dans les tablettes mycéniennes.* Incunabula Graeca 29. Rome.

GÉRARD-ROUSSEAU, M. 1971. 'Les sacrifices à Pylos.' *Studi Micenei ed Egeo-Anatolici* 13: 139–46.

GÉRARD-ROUSSEAU, M. 1973. 'Connections in religion between the Mycenaean world and Anatolia.' In CROSSLAND, R.A. & BIRCHALL, A. (eds.) *Bronze Age Migrations in the Aegean. Archaeological and Linguistic Problems in Greek Prehistory. First International Colloquium on Aegean Prehistory, Sheffield.* London: 163–7.

GODART, L. 1968a. 'Les quantités d'huile de la série Fh de Cnossos.' In GALLAVOTTI, C. (ed.) *Atti e Memorie del 1º Congresso Internazionale di Micenologia di Roma, 27 settembre – 3 ottobre 1967.* Incunabula Graeca 25. Rome: 598–610.

GODART, L. 1968b. 'Le grain à Cnossos.' *Studi Micenei ed Egeo-Anatolici* 5: 56–63.

GODART, L. 1968c. '*kupirijo* dans les textes mycéniens.' *Studi Micenei ed Egeo-Anatolici* 5: 64–70.

GODART, L. 1969. 'La série Fh de Cnossos.' *Studi Micenei ed Egeo-Anatolici* 8: 39–65.

GODART, L. 1970. 'The grouping of place-names in the Cn tablets.' *Bulletin of the Institute of Classical Studies* 17: 159–61.

GODART, L. 1971. 'Valeur des idéogrammes OVIS^{m}, OVIS^{f}, CAP^{m}, CAP^{f}, SUS^{m}, SUS^{f}, BOS^{m} et BOS^{f} dans les tablettes de Cnossos et de Pylos.' *Κρητικά Χρονικά*, 23: 89–94.

GODART, L. 1972. 'Les tablettes de la série Co de Cnossos.' In RUIPÉREZ, M.S. (ed.) *Acta Mycenaea. Proceedings of the Fifth International Colloquium on Mycenaean Studies, Held in Salamanca, 30 March – 3 April 1970. Minos* 11–12. Salamanca: 418–24.

GODART, L. 1975. 'Il labirinto e la potnia nei testi micenei.' *Rendiconti dell'Accademia di Archeologia, Lettere e Belle Arti Napoli* 50: 141–52.

GODART, L. 1977. 'Les resources des palais mycéniens de Cnossos et Pylos.' *Les Études Classiques* 45: 31–42.

GODART, L. 1987. 'La série Fh de Cnossos, vingt ans après ...' In KILLEN, J.T., MELENA, J.L. & OLIVIER, J.-P. (eds.) *Studies in Mycenaean and Classical Greek Presented to John Chadwick. Minos* 20–22. Salamanca: 201–10.

GODART, L. 1992. 'Les collecteurs dans le monde égéen.' In OLIVIER, J.-P. (ed.) *Mykenaïka. Actes du IXe Colloque international sur les textes mycéniens et égéens organisé par le Centre de l'Antiquité Greque et Romaine de la Fondation Hellénique des Recherches Scientifiques et l'École française d'Athènes (Athènes, 2–6 octobre 1990). Bulletin de Correspondance Hellénique* Suppl. 25. Athens: 257–84.

GODART, L. 1999. 'Les sacrifices d'animaux dans les textes mycéniens.' In DEGER-JALKOTZY, S., HILLER, S. & PANAGL, O. (eds.) *Floreant Studia Mycenaea. Akten des X. Internationalen Mykenologischen Colloquiums in Salzburg vom 1.–5. Mai 1995.* Vienna: 249–56.

GODART, L., KILLEN, J.T., KOPAKA, C., MELENA, J.L. & OLIVIER, J.-P. 1990–1991. '501 raccords et quasi-raccords de fragments dans les tablettes de Cnossos post-*KT V*.' *Minos* 25–26: 373–411.

GODART, L., KOPAKA, C., MELENA, J.L. & OLIVIER, J.-P. 1992–1993. '175 raccords de fragments dans les tablettes de Knossos.' *Minos* 27–28: 55–70.

GODART, L. & OLIVIER, J.-P. 1972. '98 raccords et quasi-raccords de fragments dans les tablettes de Cnossos.' *Minos* 13: 113–29.

GODART, L. & SACCONI, A. 1978. *Les tablettes en Linéaire B de Thèbes.* Incunabula Graeca 71. Rome.

GODART, L. & SACCONI, A. 1996. 'Les dieux thébains dans les archives mycéniennes.' *Comptes Rendus de l'Académie des Inscriptions et Belles-Lettres*: 99–113.

GODART, L. & TZEDAKIS, I. 1992. *Témoignages archéologiques et épigraphiques en Crète occidentale du Néolithique au Minoen récent III B.* Incunabula Graeca 93. Rome.

GODART, L. & TZEDAKIS, Y. 2003. 'The bull in the Minoan–Mycenaean world.' In NICOLAU I MARTI, A. & TZEDAKIS, Y. (eds.) *The Bull in the Mediterranean World.* Athens.

GODDEERIS, A. 2002. *Economy and Society in Northern Babylonia in the Early Old Babylonian Period (ca. 2000–1800 BC).* Orientalia Lovaniensia Analecta 109. Leuven.

GOODY, J. & WATT, I. 1968. 'The consequences of literacy.' In GOODY, J. (ed.) *Literacy in Traditional Societies.* Cambridge: 27–68.

GRAHAM, J.W. 1987. *The Palaces of Crete.* Revised edition. Princeton.

GRIECO, A.J. 1993. 'Olive tree cultivation and the alimentary use of olive oil in late medieval Italy (ca. 1300–1500).' In AMOURETTI, M.-C., BRUN, J.-P. & EITAM, D. (eds.) *La production du vin et de l'huile en Méditerranée. Actes du symposium international organisé par le Centre Camille Jullian (Université de Provence–C.N.R.S.) et Le Centre Archéologique du Var (Ministère de la Culture et Conseil Général du Var), Aix-en-Provence et Toulon, 20–22 novembre 1991. Bulletin de Correspondance Hellénique* Suppl. 26. Athens: 297–306.

GULIZIO, J. 2001. '*A-re* in the Linear B tablets and the continuity of cult of Ares in the historical period.' *Journal of Prehistoric Religion* 15: 32–8.

GULIZIO, J., PLUTA, K. & PALAIMA, T.G. 2001. 'Religion in the Room of the Chariot Tablets.' In LAFFINEUR, R. & HÄGG, R. (eds.) *POTNIA. Deities and Religion in the Aegean Bronze Age. Proceedings of the 8th International Aegean Conference held at Göteborg University, 12–15 April 2000. Aegaeum* 22. Liège: 453–61.

GURNEY, O.R. 1990. *The Hittites.* Revised edition. London.

GUTHRIE, W.C.K. 1959. 'Early Greek religion in the light of the decipherment of Linear B.' *Bulletin of the Institute of Classical Studies* 6: 35–46.

HÄGG, R. 1981a. 'Official and popular cults in Mycenaean Greece.' In HÄGG, R. & MARINATOS, N. (eds.) *Sanctuaries and Cults in the Aegean Bronze Age. Proceedings of the First International Symposium at the Swedish Institute in Athens, 12–13 May, 1980*. Stockholm: 35–40.

HÄGG, R. 1981b. 'The house sanctuary at Asine revisited.' In HÄGG, R. & MARINATOS, N. (eds.) *Sanctuaries and Cults in the Aegean Bronze Age. Proceedings of the First International Symposium at the Swedish Institute in Athens, 12–13 May, 1980*. Stockholm: 91–4.

HÄGG, R. 1985. 'What do we know about Mycenaean religion?' In MORPURGO DAVIES, A. & DUHOUX, Y. (eds.) *Linear B: A 1984 Survey*. Bibliothéque des cahiers de l'institute de linguistique de Louvain 26. Louvain-la-Neuve: 191–225.

HÄGG, R. 1990. 'The role of libations in Mycenaean ceremony and cult.' In HÄGG, R. & NORDQUIST, G.C. (eds.) *Celebrations of Death and Divinity in the Bronze Age Argolid. Proceedings of the Sixth International Symposium at the Swedish School at Athens, 11–13 June, 1988*. Skrifter Utgivna av Svenska Institutet i Athen 4°, 40. Stockholm: 177–184.

HÄGG, R. 1992. 'Sanctuaries and workshops in the Bronze Age Aegean.' In LINDERS, T. & ALROTH, B. (eds.) *Economics of Cult in the Ancient Greek World. Proceedings of the Uppsala Symposium 1990. Boreas* 21. Uppsala: 29–32.

HÄGG, R. 1995. 'State and religion in Mycenaean Greece.' In LAFFINEUR, R. & NIEMEIER, W.-D. (eds.) *POLITEIA. Society and State in the Aegean Bronze Age. Proceedings of the 5th International Aegean Conference / 5e Rencontre égéenne internationale, University of Heidelberg, Archäologisches Institut 10–13 April 1993. Aegaeum* 12. Liège & Austin: 387–91.

HÄGG, R. 1996. 'The religion of the Mycenaeans twenty-four years after the 1967 Mycenological Congress in Rome.' In DE MIRO, E., GODART, L. & SACCONI, A. (eds.) *Atti e Memorie del Secondo Congresso Internazionale di Micenologia, Roma–Napoli, 14–20 ottobre 1991*. Incunabula Graeca 98. Rome: 599–612.

HÄGG, R. 1998. 'Ritual in Mycenaean Greece.' In GRAF, E. (ed.) *Ansichten griechischer Rituale. Geburtstags-Symposium für Walter Burkert*. Stuttgart: 99–113.

HÄGG, R. (ed.) 2002. *Peloponnesian Sanctuaries and Cults. Proceedings of the Ninth International Symposium at the Swedish Institute at Athens, 11–13 June 1994*. Skrifter Utgivna av Svenska Institutet i Athen 4°, 48. Stockholm.

HÄGG, R. & MARINATOS, N. (eds.) 1987. *The Function of the Minoan Palaces. Proceedings of the Fourth International Symposium at the Swedish Institute in Athens, 10–16 June, 1984*. Stockholm.

HALLAGER, E. 1977. *The Mycenaean Palace at Knossos. Evidence for Final Destruction in the IIIB Period*. Stockholm.

HALLAGER, E., VLASAKIS, M. & HALLAGER, B.P. 1990. 'The first Linear B tablet(s) from Khania.' *Kadmos* 29: 24–34.

HALLAGER, E., VLASAKIS, M. & HALLAGER, B.P. 1992. 'New Linear B tablets from Khania.' *Kadmos* 31: 61–87.

HALSTEAD, P. 1981. 'Counting sheep in Neolithic and Bronze Age Greece.' In HODDER, I., ISAAC, G. & HAMMOND, N. (eds.) *Pattern of the Past. Studies in Honour of David Clarke*. Cambridge: 307–39.

HALSTEAD, P. 1987. 'Traditional and ancient rural economy in Mediterranean Europe: plus ça change?' *Journal of Hellenic Studies* 107: 77–87.

HALSTEAD, P. 1988. 'On redistribution and the origin of Minoan-Mycenaean palatial economies.' In FRENCH, E.B. & WARDLE, K.A. (eds.) *Problems in Greek Prehistory. Papers Presented at the Centenary Conference of the British School of Archaeology at Athens, Manchester, April 1986*. Bristol: 519–30.

HALSTEAD, P. 1989. 'The economy has a normal surplus: economic stability and social change among early farming communities of Thessaly, Greece.' In HALSTEAD, P. & O'SHEA, J. (eds.) *Bad Year Economics*. Cambridge: 60–80.

HALSTEAD, P. 1990–1991. 'Lost sheep? On the Linear B evidence for breeding flocks at Mycenaean Knossos and Pylos.' *Minos* 25–26: 343–65.

HALSTEAD, P. 1992a. 'The Mycenaean palatial economy: making the most of the gaps in the evidence.' *Proceedings of the Cambridge Philological Society* 38: 57–86.

HALSTEAD, P. 1992b. 'Agriculture in the Bronze Age: towards a model of palatial economy.' In WELLS, B. (ed.) *Agriculture in Ancient Greece. Proceedings of the Seventh International Symposium at the Swedish Institute at Athens, 16–17 May, 1990.* Skrifter Utgivna av Svenska Institutet i Athen 4°, 42. Stockholm: 105–18.

HALSTEAD, P. 1995a. 'Late Bronze Age grain crops and Linear B ideograms **65*, **120*, and **121*.' *Annual of the British School at Athens* 90: 229–34.

HALSTEAD, P. 1995b. 'Plough and power: the economic and social significance of cultivation with the ox-drawn ard in the Mediterranean.' *Bulletin of Sumerian Agriculture* 8: 11–22.

HALSTEAD, P. 1996–1997 [1998]. 'Linear B evidence for the management of sheep breeding at Knossos: production targets and deficits in the KN Dl(1) and Do sets.' *Minos* 31–32: 187–200.

HALSTEAD, P. 1998–1999 [2002]. 'Texts, bones and herders: approaches to animal husbandry in Late Bronze Age Greece.' In BENNET, J. & DRIESSEN, J. (eds.) *A-NA-QO-TA. Studies Presented to J.T. Killen. Minos* 33–34. Salamanca: 149–89.

HALSTEAD, P. 1999a. 'Missing sheep: on the meaning and wider significance of *O* in Knossos sheep records.' *Annual of the British School at Athens* 94: 145–66.

HALSTEAD, P. 1999b. 'Surplus and share-croppers: the grain production strategies of Mycenaean palaces.' In BETENCOURT, P.P., KARAGEORGHIS, V., LAFFINEUR, R. & NIEMEIER, W.-D. (eds.) *MELETEMATA. Studies in Aegean Archaeology Presented to Malcolm H. Wiener as He Enters His 65th Year. Aegaeum* 20. Liège & Austin: 319–26.

HALSTEAD, P. 1999c. 'Towards a model of Mycenaean palatial mobilisation.' In GALATY, M.L. & PARKINSON, W.A. *Rethinking Mycenaean Palaces: New Interpretations of an Old Idea.* Los Angeles: 35–41.

HALSTEAD, P. 2001. 'Mycenaean wheat, flax and sheep: palatial intervention in farming and its implications for rural society.' In VOUTSAKI, S. & KILLEN, J.T. (eds.) *Economy and Politics in the Mycenaean Palace States. Proceedings of a Conference held on 1–3 July 1999 in the Faculty of Classics, Cambridge.* Cambridge Philological Society Supplementary Volume 27. Cambridge: 38–50.

HALSTEAD, P. 2003. 'Texts and bones: contrasting Linear B and archaeozoological evidence for animal exploitation in Mycenaean southern Greece.' In KOTJABOPOULOU, E., HAMILAKIS, Y., HALSTEAD, P., GAMBLE, C. & ELEFANTI, P. (eds.) *Zooarchaeology in Greece: Recent Advances.* British School at Athens Studies 9. London: 257–61.

HALSTEAD, P. 2005. 'Life after Mediterranean polyculture: the subsistence sub-system and the emergence of civilisation revisited.' In BARRETT, J.C. & HALSTEAD, P. (eds.) *The Emergence of Civilisation Revisited.* Sheffield Studies in Aegean Archaeology 6. Oxford: 189–206.

HALSTEAD, P. & BARRETT, J.C. (eds.) 2004. *Food, Cuisine and Society in Prehistoric Greece. Proceedings of the 10th Aegean Round Table, University of Sheffield, January 19–21, 2001.* Sheffield Studies in Aegean Archaeology 5. Oxford.

HALSTEAD, P. & ISAAKIDOU, V. 2004. 'Faunal evidence for feasting: burnt offerings from the Palace of Nestor at Pylos.' In HALSTEAD, P. & BARRETT, J.C. (eds.) *Food, Cuisine and Society in Prehistoric Greece.* Sheffield Studies in Aegean Archaeology 5. Oxford: 136–54.

HALSTEAD, P. & O'SHEA, J. 1982. 'A friend in need is a friend indeed: social storage and the origins of social ranking.' In RENFREW, C. & SHANNON, S. (eds.) *Ranking, Resource and Exchange.* Cambridge: 92–9.

HAMILAKIS, Y. 1996. 'Wine, oil and the dialectics of power in Bronze Age Crete: a review of the evidence.' *Oxford Journal of Archaeology* 15: 1–32.

HAMILAKIS, Y. 1999a. 'Food technologies/technologies of the body: the social context of wine and oil production and consumption in Bronze Age Crete.' *World Archaeology* 31: 38–54.

HAMILAKIS, Y. 1999b. 'The anthropology of food and drink consumption and Aegean archaeology.' In VAUGHAN, S.J. & COULSON, W.D.E. (eds.) *Palaeodiet in the Aegean*. Oxford: 55–63.

HAMILAKIS, Y. 2003. 'The sacred geography of hunting: wild animals, social power and gender in early farming societies.' In KOTJABOPOULOU, E., HAMILAKIS, Y., HALSTEAD, P., GAMBLE, C. & ELEFANTI, P. (eds.) *Zooarchaeology in Greece: Recent Advances*. British School at Athens Studies 9. London: 239–47.

HAMILAKIS, Y. & KONSOLAKI, E. 2004. 'Pigs for the gods: burnt animal sacrifices as embodied rituals at a Mycenaean sanctuary.' *Oxford Journal of Archaeology* 23: 135–51.

HASKELL, H.W. 1984. 'Pylos: stirrup jars and the international oil trade.' In SHELMERDINE, C.W. & PALAIMA, T.G. (eds.) *Pylos Comes Alive. Industry and Administration in a Mycenaean Palace*. Archaeological Institute of America. New York: 97–107.

HASKELL, H.W. 1997. 'Trade and production in "Mycenaean" Crete.' In GILLIS, C., RISBERG, C. & SJÖBERG, B. (eds.) *Trade and Production in Premonetary Greece. Production and the Craftsman. Proceedings of the 4th and 5th International Workshops, Athens 1994 and 1995*. Studies in Mediterranean Archaeology Pocket-book 143. Jonsered: 101–11.

HASKELL, H.W. 2005. 'Region to region export of transport stirrup jars from LM IIIA2/B Crete.' In D'Agata, A.L. & Moody, J. (eds.) *Ariadne's Threads. Connections Between Crete and the Greek Mainland in Late Minoan III (LM IIIA2 to LM IIIC). Proceedings of the International Workshop Held at Athens Scuola Archeologica Italiana 5–6 April 2003*. Athens: 205–21.

HATZAKI, E. 2004. 'From Final Palatial to Postpalatial Knossos.' In CADOGAN, G., HATZAKI, E. & VASILAKIS, A. (eds.) *Knossos: Palace, City, State*. British School at Athens Studies 12. London: 121–6.

HELLSTRÖM, P. & ALROTH, B. (eds.) 1996. *Religion and Power in the Ancient Greek World. Proceedings of the Uppsala Symposium 1993. Boreas* 24. Uppsala.

HELTZER, M. 1999. 'The economy of Ugarit.' In WATSON, W.G.E. & WYATT, N. (eds.) *Handbook of Ugaritic Studies*. Handbuch der Orientalistik I.39. Leiden: 423–54.

HERVA, V.-P. 2006. 'Flower lovers, after all? Rethinking religion and human–environment relations in Minoan Crete.' *World Archaeology* 38: 586–98.

HILLER, S. 1979. '*ka-ko na-wi-jo*: notes on interdependences of temples and bronze in the Aegean Bronze Age.' In RISCH, E. & MÜHLESTEIN, H. (eds.) *Colloquium Mycenaeum. Actes du sixième colloque international sur les textes mycéniens et égéens tenu à Chaumont sur Neuchâtel du 7 au 13 septembre 1975*. Neuchâtel: 189–95.

HILLER, S. 1981. 'Mykenische Heiligtumer: das Zeugnis der Linear B-Texte.' In HÄGG, R. & MARINATOS, N. (eds.) *Sanctuaries and Cults in the Aegean Bronze Age. Proceedings of the First International Symposium at the Swedish Institute in Athens, 12–13 May, 1980*. Skrifter Utgivna av Svenska Institutet i Athen 4°, 28. Stockholm: 95–126.

HILLER, S. 1982. 'Tempelwirtschaft im mykenischen Griechenland.' *Archive für Orientforschung* 19: 94–104.

HILLER, S. 1984. '*te-o-po-ri-ja*.' In GLOTZ, C.G. (ed.) *Aux origines de l'hellénisme. La Crète et la Grèce. Hommage à Henri van Effenterre*. Paris: 139–50.

HILLER, S. 1988. 'Dependent personnel in Mycenaean texts.' In HELTZER, M. & LIPIŃSKI, E. (eds.) *Society and Economy in the Eastern Mediterranean (c. 1500–1000 B.C.)*. Louvain: 53–68.

HILLER, S. 1992. 'Amnisos in den Tontafelarchiven von Knosos.' In SCHÄFER, J. (ed.) *Amnisos. Nach den Archäologischen, Historischen und Epigraphischen Aeugnissen des Altertums und der Neuzeit*. Berlin: 18–50.

HILLER, S. 1997. 'Cretan sanctuaries and Mycenaean palatial administration at Knossos.' In FARNOUX, A. & DRIESSEN, J. (eds.) *La Crète mycénienne. Actes de la Table Ronde Internationale organisée par l'École française d'Athènes, 26–28 mars 1991. Bulletin de Correspondance Hellénique* Suppl. 30. Paris: 205–12.

HILLER, S. 1998–1999 [2002]. '*ku-na-ke-ta*.' In BENNET, J. & DRIESSEN, J. (eds.) *A-NA-QO-TA. Studies Presented to J.T. Killen. Minos* 33–34. Salamanca: 191–6.

HILLER, S. Forthcoming. 'PY Cr 591 etc.: on palatially administrated deer.' In PALAIMA, T.G. & SHELMERDINE, C.W. (eds.) *Proceedings of the 11th International Mycenological Colloquium at Austin, Texas, 7–12 May 2000. Minos* Suppl. Salamanca.

HOCKER, F. & PALAIMA, T.G. 1990–1991. 'Late Bronze Age ships and the Pylos tablets Vn 46 and Vn 879.' *Minos* 25–26: 297–318.

HOFSTRA, S.U. 2000. 'Small things considered. The finds from LH IIIB Pylos in context.' Unpublished Ph.D. thesis, University of Texas at Austin.

HOOKER, J.T. 1979. 'The wanax in the Linear B texts.' *Kadmos* 18: 100–11.

HOOKER, J.T. 1982. 'The end of Pylos and the Linear B evidence.' *Studi Micenei ed Egeo-Anatolici* 23: 209–17.

HOOKER, J.T. 1987a. 'Minoan and Mycenaean administration: a comparison of the Knossos and Pylos archives.' In HÄGG, R. & MARINATOS, N. (eds.) *The Function of the Minoan Palaces. Proceedings of the Fourth International Symposium at the Swedish Institute in Athens, 10–16 June, 1984*. Stockholm: 313–16.

HOOKER, J.T. 1987b. 'Titles and functions in the Pylian state.' In KILLEN, J.T., MELENA, J.L. & OLIVIER, J.-P. (eds.) *Studies in Mycenaean and Classical Greek Presented to John Chadwick. Minos* 20–22. Salamanca: 257–67.

HOOKER, J.T. 1990. 'Cult-personnel in the Linear B texts from Pylos.' In BEARD, M. & NORTH, J. (eds.) *Pagan Priests. Religion and Power in the Ancient World*. London: 157–74.

HORDEN, P. & PURCELL, N. 2000. *The Corrupting Sea. A Study of Mediterranean History*. Blackwell: Oxford.

HUDSON, M. & VAN DE MIEROOP, M. 2002. *Debt and Economic Renewal in the Ancient Near East. A Colloquium Held at Columbia University, November 1998*. Institute for the Study of Long-Term Economic Trends and the International Scholars Conference on Ancient Near Eastern Economies Series 3. Bethesda, MD.

HUTTON, W.F. 1990–1991. 'The meaning of *qe-te-o* in Linear B.' *Minos* 25–26: 105–32.

IAKOVIDES, S.E. 2000 [2003]. 'Ανασκαφή Μυκηνών.' *Πρακτικά της Αρχαιολογικής Εταιρίας* 155: 63–6, pls. 32–5.

IANNACCONE, L.R. 1998. 'Introduction to the economics of religion.' *Journal of Economic Literature* 36: 1465–1496.

ILIEVSKY, P.H. 1966. 'The recipients of the Es tablets.' In PALMER, L.R. & CHADWICK, J. (eds.) *Proceedings of the Cambridge Colloquium on Mycenaean Studies*. Cambridge: 238–44.

ISAAKIDOU, V., HALSTEAD, P., DAVIS, J. & STOCKER, S. 2002. 'Burnt animal sacrifice at the Mycenaean "Palace of Nestor", Pylos.' *Antiquity* 76: 86–92.

ISAGER, S. 1992. 'Sacred and profane ownership of land. ' In WELLS, B. (ed.) *Agriculture in Ancient Greece. Proceedings of the Seventh International Symposium at the Swedish Institute at Athens, 16–17 May, 1990*. Skrifter Utgivna av Svenska Institutet i Athen, 4°, 42. Stockholm: 119–222.

JACOBSEN, T. 1976. *The Treasures of Darkness. A History of Mesopotamian Religion*. New Haven & London.

JAMESON, M.H. 1988. 'Sacrifice and animal husbandry in Classical Greece.' In WHITTAKER, C.R. (ed.) *Pastoral Economies in Classical Antiquity*. Cambridge: 87–119.

JANKO, R. 1981. 'Herbal remedies at Pylos.' *Minos* 17: 30–4.

JASINK, A.M. 1983. 'Le "tavolette dell'olio" di Pilo: considerazioni topografiche.' *Kadmos* 22: 40–53.

KAHNEMAN, D. & TVERSKY, A. 1979. 'Prospect Theory: an analysis of decision under risk.' *Econometrica* 47.2: 263–92.

KILIAN, K. 1988a. 'Mycenaeans up to date, trends and changes in recent research.' In FRENCH, E.B. & WARDLE, K.A. (eds.) *Problems in Greek Prehistory. Papers Presented at the Centenary Conference of the British School of Archaeology at Athens, Manchester, April 1986*. Bristol: 115–52.

KILIAN, K. 1988b. 'The emergence of *wanax* ideology in the Mycenaean palace.' *Oxford Journal of Archaeology* 7: 291–302.

KILIAN, K. 1990. 'Patterns in the cult activity in the Mycenaean Argolid: Haghia Triada (Klenies), the Profitis Elias cave (Haghios Hadrianos) and the citadel of Tiryns.' In HÄGG, R. & NORDQUIST, G.C. (eds.) *Celebrations of Death and Divinity in the Bronze Age Argolid. Proceedings of the Sixth International Symposium at the Swedish School at Athens, 11–13 June, 1988*. Skrifter Utgivna av Svenska Institutet i Athen 4°, 40. Stockholm: 185–97.

KILLEN, J.T. 1962. 'The wool ideogram in Linear B texts.' *Hermathena* 96: 38–72.

KILLEN, J.T. 1964. 'The wool industry of Crete in the Late Bronze Age.' *Annual of the British School at Athens* 59: 1–15.

KILLEN, J.T. 1966. 'The Knossos Lc (Cloth) tablets.' *Bulletin of the Institute of Classical Studies* 13: 105–9.

KILLEN, J.T. 1967. 'The Knossos *o-pi* tablets.' In GALLAVOTTI, C. (ed.) *Atti e Memorie del 1° Congresso Internazionale di Micenologia di Roma, 27 settembre – 3 ottobre 1967*. Incunabula Graeca 25. Rome: 636–43.

KILLEN, J.T. 1972. 'Two notes on the Knossos Ak tablets.' In RUIPÉREZ, M.S. (ed.) *Acta Mycenaea. Proceedings of the Fifth International Colloquium on Mycenaean Studies. Held in Salamanca, 30 March – 3 April 1970*. Salamanca: 425–40.

KILLEN, J.T. 1976. 'Linear B *a-ko-ra-ja/-jo*.' In MORPURGO DAVIES, A. & MEID, W. (eds.) *Papers in Greek, Italic, and Indo-European Linguistics Offered to L. R. Palmer*. Innsbruck: 117–25.

KILLEN, J.T. 1979a. 'The Linear B tablets and economic history: some problems.' *Bulletin of the Institute of Classical Studies* 26: 133–4.

KILLEN, J.T. 1979b. 'The Knossos Ld (1) tablets.' In RISCH, E. & MÜHLESTEIN, H. (eds.) *Colloquium Mycenaeum. Actes du sixième colloque international sur les textes mycéniens et égéens tenu à Chaumont sur Neuchâtel du 7 au 13 septembre 1975*. Neuchâtel: 151–81.

KILLEN, J.T. 1981. 'Some puzzles in a Mycenae personnel record.' *Zhiva Antika* 31: 37–45.

KILLEN, J.T. 1983a. 'PY An 1.' *Minos* 18: 71–9.

KILLEN, J.T. 1983b. '*TA* and *DA*.' In OLIVA, P. & FROLÍKOVÁ, A. (eds.) *Concilium Eirene XVI. Proceedings of the 16th International Eirene Conference, Prague, 31.8–4.9.1982*. Prague: 121–6.

KILLEN, J.T. 1983c. 'Mycenaean possessive adjectives in *-e-jo*.' *Transactions of the Philological Society* 209 (New series 29): 66–99.

KILLEN, J.T. 1983d. 'On the Mycenae Ge tablets.' In HEUBECK, A. & NEUMANN, G. (eds.) *Res Mycenaeae. Akten des VII. Internationalen Mykenologischen Colloquiums in Nürnberg vom 6.–10. April 1981*. Göttingen: 216–33.

KILLEN, J.T. 1984a. The textile industries at Pylos and Knossos. In SHELMERDINE, C.W. & PALAIMA, T.G. (eds.) *Pylos Comes Alive. Industry and Administration in a Mycenaean Palace*. New York: 49–63.

KILLEN, J.T. 1984b. 'Last year's debts on the Ma tablets.' *Studi Micenei ed Egeo-Anatolici* 25: 173–88.

KILLEN, J.T. 1985. 'The Linear B tablets and the Mycenaean economy.' In MORPURGO DAVIES, A. & DUHOUX, Y. (eds.) *Linear B. A 1984 Survey*. Bibliothèque des cahiers de l'Institute de linguistique de Louvain 26. Louvain-la-Neuve: 241–98.

KILLEN, J.T. 1987a. 'Notes on the Knossos tablets.' In KILLEN, J.T., MELENA, J.L. & OLIVIER, J.-P. (eds.) *Studies in Mycenaean and Classical Greek Presented to John Chadwick. Minos* 20–22. Salamanca: 319–32.

KILLEN, J.T. 1987b. 'Piety begins at home: place-names on Knossos records of religious offerings.' In ILIEVSKI, P.HR. & CREPAJAC, LJ. (eds.) *Tractata Mycenaea. Proceedings of the Eighth International Colloquium on Mycenaean Studies, held in Ohrid, 15–20 September 1985*. Skopje: 163–77.

KILLEN, J.T. 1988. 'Epigraphy and interpretation in Knossos *WOMAN* and *CLOTH* records.' In OLIVIER, J.-P. & PALAIMA, T.G. (eds.) *Texts, Tablets and Scribes. Studies in Mycenaean Epigraphy and Economy Offered to Emmett L. Bennett, Jr. Minos* Suppl. 10. Salamanca: 167–84.

KILLEN, J.T. 1992a. 'Names in *-i* on the Knossos tablets.' In OLIVIER, J.-P. (ed.) *Mykenaïka. Actes du IXe Colloque international sur les textes mycéniens et égéens organisé par le Centre de l'Antiquité Greque et Romaine de la Fondation Hellénique des Recherches Scientifiques et l'École française d'Athènes (Athènes, 2–6 octobre 1990). Bulletin de Correspondance Hellénique* Suppl. 25. Athens: 351–63.

KILLEN, J.T. 1992b. 'Observations on the Thebes sealings.' In OLIVIER, J.-P. (ed.) *Mykenaïka. Actes du IXe Colloque international sur les textes mycéniens et égéens organisé par le Centre de l'Antiquité Greque et Romaine de la Fondation Hellénique des Recherches Scientifiques et l'École française d'Athènes (Athènes, 2–6 octobre 1990). Bulletin de Correspondance Hellénique* Suppl. 25. Athens: 365–80.

KILLEN, J.T. 1992–1993a. 'The oxen's names on the Knossos Ch tablets.' *Minos* 27–28: 101–7.

KILLEN, J.T. 1992–1993b. '*ke-u-po-da e-sa-re-u* and the exemptions of the Pylos Na tablets.' *Minos* 27–28: 109–22.

KILLEN, J.T. 1993. 'Records of sheep and goats at Mycenae, Pylos and Knossos.' *Domestic Animals of Mesopotamia*, Part I. Bulletin on Sumerian Agriculture Volume 7. Cambridge: 209–17.

KILLEN, J.T. 1994. 'Thebes sealings, Knossos tablets, and Mycenaean state banquets.' *Bulletin of the Institute of Classical Studies* 39: 67–84.

KILLEN, J.T. 1994–1995a. '*a-ma e-pi-ke-re.*' *Minos* 29–30: 292–334.

KILLEN, J.T. 1994–1995b [1997]. 'Review of: Ruth Palmer, *Wine in the Mycenaean Palace Economy. Aegaeum* 10. Liège & Austin, 1994.' *Minos* 29–30: 371–3.

KILLEN, J.T. 1995. 'Some further thoughts on "Collectors".' In LAFFINEUR, R. & NIEMEIER, W.-D. (eds.) *POLITEIA. Society and State in the Aegean Bronze Age. Proceedings of the 5th International Aegean Conference / 5e Rencontre égéenne internationale University of Heidelberg, Archäologisches Institut 10–13 April 1994. Aegaeum* 12. Liège & Austin: 213–26.

KILLEN, J.T. 1996a. 'Administering a Mycenaean kingdom: some taxing problems.' *Bulletin of the Institute of Classical Studies* 41: 147–8.

KILLEN, J.T. 1996b. 'Thebes sealings and Knossos tablets.' In DE MIRO, E., GODART, L. & SACCONI, A. (eds.) *Atti e Memorie del Secondo Congresso Internazionale di Micenologia, Roma-Napoli, 14–20 ottobre 1991*. Incunabula Graeca 98. Rome: 71–82.

KILLEN, J.T. 1996–1997a. 'The find-places of the tablets from the Western Magazines at Knossos: some matters arising.' *Minos* 31–32: 123–32.

KILLEN, J.T. 1996–1997b. 'Mycenaean *te-ko-to-*(*n*)*a-pe.*' *Minos* 31–32: 179–86.

KILLEN, J.T. 1998a. 'The role of the state in wheat and olive production in Mycenaean Crete.' *Aevum* 72: 19–24.

KILLEN, J.T. 1998b. 'The Pylos Ta tablets revisited.' *Bulletin de Correspondance Hellénique* 122: 421–2.

KILLEN, J.T. 1999a. 'Mycenaean *o-pa.*' In DEGER-JALKOTZY, S., HILLER, S. & PANAGL, O. (eds.) *Floreant Studia Mycenaea. Akten des X. Internationalen Mykenologischen Colloquiums in Salzburg vom 1.–5. Mai 1995.* Vienna: 325–42.

KILLEN, J.T. 1999b. 'New readings and interpretations in the Pylos tablets.' In DEGER-JALKOTZY, S., HILLER, S. & PANAGL, O. (eds.) *Floreant Studia Mycenaea. Akten des X. Internationalen Mykenologischen Colloquiums in Salzburg vom 1.–5. Mai 1995.* Vienna: 343–54.

KILLEN, J.T. 1999c. 'Some observations on the new Thebes tablets.' *Bulletin of the Institute of Classical Studies* 43: 217–19.

KILLEN, J.T. 1999d. 'Critique: a view from the tablets.' In GALATY, M.L. & PARKINSON, W.A. (eds.) *Rethinking Mycenaean Palaces. New Interpretations of an Old Idea*. Los Angeles: 87–90.

KILLEN, J.T. 2001a. 'Some thoughts on *ta-ra-si-ja.*' In VOUTSAKI, S. & KILLEN, J.T. (eds.) *Economy and Politics in the Mycenaean Palace States. Proceedings of a Conference held on 1–3 July 1999 in the Faculty of Classics, Cambridge.* Cambridge Philological Society, Supplementary Volume 27. Cambridge: 161–80.

KILLEN, J.T. 2001b. 'Religion at Pylos: the evidence of the Fn tablets.' In LAFFINEUR, R. & HÄGG, R. (eds.) *POTNIA. Deities and Religion in the Aegean Bronze Age. Proceedings of the 8th International Aegean Conference held at Göteborg University, 12–15 April 2000. Aegaeum* 22. Liège: 435–43.

KILLEN, J.T. 2002–2003 [2007]. 'The Wm nodules from Knossos. *Minos* 37–38: 101–6.

KILLEN, J.T. 2003. 'Pylos tablet Va 482.' *Cretan Studies* 9: 63–76.

KILLEN, J.T. 2004. 'Wheat, barley, flour, olives and figs on Linear B tablets.' In HALSTEAD, P. & BARRETT, J.C. (eds.) *Food, Cuisine and Society in Prehistoric Greece.* Sheffield Studies in Aegean Archaeology 5. Oxford: 155–73.

KILLEN, J.T. 2006a. 'Thoughts on the functions of the new Thebes tablets.' In DEGER-JALKOTZY, S. & PANAGL, O. (eds.) *Die neuen Linear B-Texte aus Theben. Ihr Aufschlusswert für die mykenische Sprache und Kultur.* Verlag der Österreichischen Akademie der Wissenschaften. Vienna: 79–110.

KILLEN, J.T. 2006b. 'Conscription and corvée at Mycenaean Pylos.' In PERNA, M. (ed.) *Fiscality in Mycenaean and Near Eastern Archives. Proceedings of the Conference Held at Soprintendenza Archivistica per la Campania, Naples, 21–23 October 2004.* Studi Egei e Vicinorientali 3. Naples: 73–87.

KILLEN, J.T. Forthcoming(a). 'The language of religious texts: some fresh thoughts on old problems.' In PALAIMA, T.G. & SHELMERDINE, C.W. (eds.) *Proceedings of the 11th International Mycenological Colloquium at Austin, Texas, 7–12 May 2000. Minos* Suppl. Salamanca.

KILLEN, J.T. Forthcoming(b). 'The commodities on the Pylos Ma tablets.' In SACCONI, A., GODART, L. & NEGRI, M. (eds.) *Proceedings of the XIIth International Colloquium of Mycenology, Rome, February 2006.* Rome.

KILLEN, J.T. Forthcoming(c). 'The Linear B tablets and the Mycenaean economy.' In DUHOUX, Y. & MORPURGO DAVIES, A. (eds.) *A Companion to Linear B. Mycenaean Greek Texts and Their World.* Volume I. Louvain-la-Neuve.

KILLEN, J.T. & OLIVIER, J.-P. 1966. '388 raccords de fragments dans les tablettes de Cnossos.' In PALMER, L.R. & CHADWICK, J. (eds.) *Proceedings of the Cambridge Colloquium on Mycenaean Studies.* Cambridge: 47–92.

KILLEN, J.T. & OLIVIER, J.-P. 1968. '155 raccords de fragments dans les tablettes de Cnossos.' *Bulletin de Correspondance Hellénique* 92: 115–41.

KILLEN, J.T. & OLIVIER, J.-P. 1971. *The Knossos Tablets. A Transliteration.* Fifth edition. *Minos* Suppl. 11. Salamanca. [= KT^5]

KILLEN, J.T., OLIVIER, J.-P. & MELENA, J.L. Forthcoming. *The Knossos Tablets Transliterated.* Electronic version in progress to be used at basis for *The Knossos Tablets*, Sixth Edition. [= KT^6]

KIRIATZI, E. 2000. 'Ceramic production and technology: the LBA pottery from Toumba Thessaloniki.' Unpublished Ph.D. thesis, Aristotle University of Thessaloniki.

KNAPP, A.B. 1986. *Copper Production and Divine Protection. Archaeology, Ideology and Social Complexity in Bronze Age Cyprus.* Studies in Mediterranean Archaeology Pocket-book 42. Göteborg.

KNAPP, A.B. 1988. 'Ideology, archaeology and polity.' *Man* (New Series) 23: 133–63.

KOPAKA, K. 2001. 'A day in *Potnia's* life: aspects of Potnia and reflected "Mistress" activities in the Aegean Bronze Age.' In LAFFINEUR, R. & HÄGG, R. (eds.) *POTNIA. Deities and Religion in the Aegean Bronze Age. Proceedings of the 8th International Aegean Conference Held at Göteborg University, 12–15 April 2000. Aegaeum* 22. Liège: 15–27.

KRAMER, S.A. 1956. *History Begins at Sumer. Thirty-nine Firsts in Recorded History.* Philadelphia.

KRAMER, S.A. 1963. *The Sumerians. Their History, Culture, and Character.* Chicago.

KRISTIANSEN, K. & LARSSON, T. 2005. *The Rise of Bronze Age Society. Travels, Transmissions and Transformations.* Cambridge.

KRZYSZKOWSKA, O.H. 1997. 'Cult and craft: ivories from the Citadel House Area, Mycenae.' In LAFFINEUR, R. & BETENCOURT, P.P. *TEXNH. Craftsmen, Craftswomen and Craftsmanship in the Aegean Bronze Age. Proceedings of the 6th International Aegean Conference, Philadelphia, Temple University, 18–21 April 1996. Aegaeum* 16. Liège & Austin: 145–50.

LAFFINEUR, R. (ed.) 1999. *POLEMOS. Le contexte guerrier en Égée à l'âge du bronze. Actes de la 7e Rencontre égéenne internationale Université de Liège, 14–17 avril 1998. Aegaeum* 19. Liège & Austin.

LAFFINEUR, R. & GRECO, E. (eds.) 2005. *EMPORIA. Aegeans in the Central and Eastern Mediterranean. Proceedings of the 10th International Aegean Conference: Italian School of Archaeology, Athens, 14-18 April 2004. Aegaeum* 25. Liège & Austin.

LAFFINEUR, R. & HÄGG, R. (eds.) 2001. *POTNIA. Deities and Religion in the Aegean Bronze Age. Proceedings of the 8th International Aegean Conference held at Göteborg University, 12–15 April 2000. Aegaeum* 22. Liège.

LANDENIUS-ENEGRIN, H. 1995. 'A prosopographical study of scribal hand 103: methods, aims and problems.' In LAFFINEUR, R. & NIEMEIER, W.-D. (eds.) *POLITEIA. Society and State in the Aegean Bronze Age. Proceedings of the 5th International Aegean Conference / 5e Rencontre égéenne internationale University of Heidelberg, Archäologisches Institut 10–23 April 1994. Aegaeum* 12. Liège & Austin: 115–32.

LANG, M.L. 1964. 'The Palace of Nestor excavations of 1963. Part II: Pylos pots and the Mycenaean units of capacity.' *American Journal of Archaeology* 68: 99–105.

LANG, M.L. 1966a. 'Jn formulas and groups.' *Hesperia* 35: 397–412.

LANG, M.L. 1966b. 'Cn flocks.' In PALMER, L.R. & CHADWICK, J. (eds.) *Proceedings of the Cambridge Colloquium on Mycenaean Studies*. Cambridge: 250–9.

LANG, M.L. 1969. *The Palace of Nestor at Pylos in Western Messenia.* Volume II. *The Frescoes*. Princeton.

LANG, M.L. 1990. 'The *o-ka* tablets again.' *Kadmos* 29: 113–25.

LEGUILLOUX, M. 2003. 'The Delian chora in Classical and Hellenistic times: an island landscape planned for pastoralism.' In KOTJABOPOULOU, E., HAMILAKIS, Y., HALSTEAD, P., GAMBLE, C., & ELEFANTI, P. (eds.) *Zooarchaeology in Greece: Recent Advances*. British School at Athens Studies 9. London: 251–6.

LEJEUNE, M. 1956. 'Les tablettes pyliennes de la série Ma.' *Revue Études Anciennes* 58: 3–39. [= *Mémoires* I: 57–91]

LEJEUNE, M. 1958a. *Mémoires de philologie mycénienne. Première série (1955–1957)*. Centre National de la Recherché Scientifique. Paris. [= *Mémoires* I]

LEJEUNE, M. 1958b. 'Textes mycénien relatif aux esclaves.' *Historia* 8: 129–44. [= *Mémoires* II: 63–82]

LEJEUNE, M. 1958c [1960]. 'Prêtres et prêtresses dans les documents mycéniens.' In *Hommage à Georges Dumézil*. Collection Latomus 45. Brussels 1960: 129–39. [= *Mémoires* II: 83–9]

LEJEUNE, M. 1958d. 'De quelques idéogrammes mycéniens.' *Revue des Études Grecques* 72: 123–48. [= *Mémoires* II: 141–65]

LEJEUNE, M. 1958e. 'Les forgerons de Pylos.' *Historia* 10: 409–34. [= *Mémoires* II: 167–95]

LEJEUNE, M. 1959. '"Presents" et "absents" dans les inventaires mycéniens.' *Parola del Passato* 15: 5–19. [= *Mémoires* II: 225–40]

LEJEUNE, M. 1964. 'Observations sur l'idéogramme **146*.' In BENNETT, E.L. JR. (ed.) *Mycenaean Studies. Proceedings of the Third International Colloquium for Mycenaean Studies Held at 'Wingspread', 4–8 September 1961*. Madison 1964: 111–24. [= *Mémoires* II: 313–25]

LEJEUNE, M. 1965. 'La *damos* dans le société mycénienne.' *Revue des Études Grecques* 78: 1–22. [= *Mémoires* III: 135–54]

LEJEUNE, M. 1966. 'Le récapitulatif du cadastre Ep de Pylos.' In PALMER, L.R. & CHADWICK, J. (eds.) *Proceedings of the Cambridge Colloquium on Mycenaean Studies*. Cambridge: 260–4. [= *Mémoires* III: 105–11]

LEJEUNE, M. 1971. *Mémoires de philologie mycénienne. Deuxième série (1958–1963)*. Incunabula Graeca 42. Rome. [= *Mémoires* II]

LEJEUNE, M. 1972. *Mémoires de philologie mycénienne. Troisième série (1964–1968)*. Incunabula Graeca 43. Rome. [= *Mémoires* III]

LEJEUNE, M. 1974. 'Sur l'intitulé de la tablette pylienne En 609.' *Revue de Philologie de Littérature et d'Histoire Anciennes* 48: 247–66. [= *Mémoires* IV: 153–74]

LEJEUNE, M. 1975. 'Le dossier *sa-ra-pe-da* du scribe 24 de Pylos.' *Minos* 14: 60–76. [= *Mémoires* IV: 67–86]

LEJEUNE, M. 1976. 'Analyse du dossier pylien Ea.' *Minos* 15: 81–115. [= *Mémoires* IV: 115–52]

LEJEUNE, M. 1979. 'Sur la fiscalité pylienne Ma.' In RISCH, E. & MÜHLESTEIN, H. (eds.) *Colloquium Mycenaeum. Actes du sixième colloque international sur les textes mycéniens et égéens tenu à Chaumont sur Neuchâtel du 7 au 13 septembre 1975*. Neuchâtel: 147–50. [= *Mémoires* IV: 183–8]

LEJEUNE, M. 1997a. *Mémoires de philologie mycénienne. Quatrième série (1969–1996)*. Incunabula Graeca 99. Rome. [= *Mémoires* IV]

LEJEUNE, M. 1997b. 'Bureaucratie thébaine: intitulés et summations.' In *Mémoires* IV: 271–6.

LEJEUNE, M. 1997c. 'Sur les offrandes thébaines à Mére Terre.' In *Mémoires* IV: 279–81.

LEJEUNE, M. 1997d. 'Anatomie de la série thébaine Gp.' In *Mémoires* IV: 285–92.

LEUKART, A. 1979. 'Autour de *ka-ko na-wi-jo*: quelques critères.' In RISCH, E. & MÜHLESTEIN, H. (eds.) *Colloquium Mycenaeum. Actes du sixième colloque international sur les textes mycéniens et égéens tenu à Chaumont sur Neuchâtel du 7 au 13 septembre 1975*. Neuchâtel: 183–7.

LEVINE, T.Y. & EARLE, T.K. 1992. 'Staple finance, wealth finance and storage in the Inka political economy.' In LEVINE, T.Y. (ed.) *Inka Storage Systems*. Norman, OK: 51–61.

LINDERS, T. & ALROTH, B. (eds.) 1992. *Economics of Cult in the Ancient World. Proceedings of the Uppsala Symposium 1990. Boreas* 21. Uppsala.

LINDERS, T. & NORDQUIST, G. (eds.) 1987. *Gifts to the Gods. Proceedings of the Uppsala Symposium 1985. Boreas* 15. Uppsala.

LINDGREN, M. 1973. *The People of Pylos. Prosopographical and Methodological Studies in the Pylos Archives*. Part I. *A Prosopographical Catalogue of Individuals and Groups*. Part II. *The Use of Personal Designations and Their Interpretation. Boreas* 3.1–2. Uppsala.

LIPIŃSKI, E. 1988. 'The socio-economic conditions of the clergy in the Kingdom of Ugarit.' In HELTZER, M. & LIPIŃSKI, E. (eds.) *Society and Economy in the Eastern Mediterranean (1500–1000 B.C.)*. Leuven: 125–50.

LIVERANI, M. 2001. *International Relations in the Ancient Near East, 1600–1100 BC*. Basingstoke.

LUPACK, S. 1997. 'The role of religious personnel in Mycenaean workshops.' *American Journal of Archaeology* 101: 375.

LUPACK, S. 1998. 'The role of the religious sector in Mycenaean economics.' *Bulletin de Correspondance Hellénique* 122: 423–5.

LUPACK, S. 1999. 'Palaces, sanctuaries and workshops: the role of the religious sector in Mycenaean economies.' In GALATY, M.L. & PARKINSON, W.A. (eds.) *Rethinking Mycenaean Palaces: New Interpretations of an Old Idea*. Los Angeles: 24–34.

MAISELS, C.K. 1990. *The Emergence of Civilization. From Hunting and Gathering to Agriculture, Cities, and the State in the Near East*. London and New York.

MANN, M. 1986. *The Sources of Social Power*. Volume I. *A History of Power from the Beginning to A.D. 1760*. Cambridge.

MARAN, J. 2005. 'Late Minoan coarse ware stirrup jars on the Greek mainland. A Postpalatial perspective of the 12th century BC Argolid.' In D'Agata, A.L. & Moody, J. (eds.) *Ariadne's Threads. Connections Between Crete and the Greek Mainland in Late Minoan III (LM IIIA2 to LM IIIC). Proceedings of the International Workshop Held at Athens Scuola Archeologica Italiana 5–6 April 2003*. Athens: 415–31.

MARAN, J. & STAVRIANOPOULOU, E. 2007. 'Πότνιος Ανήρ: reflections on the ideology of Mycenaean kingship.' In DEGER-JALKOTZY, S. (ed.) *Keimelion. The Formation of Elites and Elitest*

Lifestyles from Mycenaean Palatial Times to the Homeric Period. Veröffentlichtungen der Mykenischen Kommission 27. Vienna: 285–98.

MATTINGLY, D.J. 1993. 'Maximum figures and maximizing strategies of oil production? Further thoughts on the processing capacity of Roman olive presses.' In AMOURETTI, M.-C., BRUN, J.-P. & EITAM, D. (eds.) *La production du vin et de l'huile en Méditerranée. Actes du symposium international organisé par le Centre Camille Jullian (Université de Provence–C.N.R.S.) et Le Centre Archéologique du Var (Ministère de la Culture et Conseil Général du Var), Aix-en-Provence et Toulon, 20–22 novembre 1991. Bulletin de Correspondance Hellénique* Suppl. 26. Athens: 483–98.

MCCABE, K., HOUSER, D., RYAN, L., SMITH, V. & TROUARD, T. 2001. 'A functional imaging study of cooperation in two-person reciprocal exchange.' *Proceedings of the National Academy of Sciences* 98.20: 11832–5.

MCCALLUM, L.R. 1987a. 'Decorative programs in the Mycenaean palace of Pylos. The megaron Frescoes.' Unpublished Ph.D. thesis, University of Pennsylvania.

MCCALLUM, L.R. 1987b. 'Frescoes from the Throne Room at Pylos.' *American Journal of Archaeology* 91: 296.

MCDONALD, W.A. & RAPP, G.R. JR. (eds.) 1972. *The Minnesota Messenia Expedition. Reconstructing a Bronze Age Regional Environment.* Minneapolis.

MCGOVERN, P.E., FLEMING, S.J. & KATZ, S.H. (eds.) 1995. *The Origins and Ancient History of Wine.* Philadelphia.

MEEKS, D. 1993. 'La production de l'huile et du vin dans l'Égypte pharaonique.' In AMOURETTI, M.-C., BRUN, J.-P. & EITAM, D. (eds.) *La production du vin et de l'huile en Méditerranée. Actes du symposium international organisé par le Centre Camille Jullian (Université de Provence–C.N.R.S.) et Le Centre Archéologique du Var (Ministère de la Culture et Conseil Général du Var), Aix-en-Provence et Toulon, 20–22 novembre 1991. Bulletin de Correspondance Hellénique* Suppl. 26. Athens: 3–38.

MELAS, M. 1999. 'The ethnography of Minoan and Mycenaean beekeeping.' In BETANCOURT, P.P., KARAGEORGHIS, V., LAFFINEUR, R. & NIEMEIER, W.D. (eds.) *MELETEMATA. Studies in Aegean Archaeology Presented to Malcolm H. Wiener as He Enters his 65th Year.* Volume II. Liège & Austin: 485–91.

MELENA, J.L. 1972. 'On the Knossos Mc tablets.' *Minos* 13: 29–54.

MELENA, J.L. 1974a. 'Reflexiones sobre los meses del calendario micénico de Cnoso y sobre la fecha de la caída del palacio.' *Emerita* 42: 77–102.

MELENA, J.L. 1974b. '*ku-pa-ro* en las tablillas de Cnoso.' *Emerita* 42: 307–36.

MELENA, J.L. 1975a. *Studies on Some Mycenaean Inscriptions from Knossos Dealing with Textiles. Minos* Suppl. 5. Salamanca.

MELENA, J.L. 1975b. '*po-ni-ki-jo* in the Knossos Ga tablets.' *Minos* 14: 77–84.

MELENA, J.L. 1976a. 'Coriander on the Knossos tablets.' *Minos* 15: 133–63.

MELENA, J.L. 1976b. 'La producción de plantas aromáticas en Cnoso.' *Estudios Clásicos* 78: 177–9.

MELENA, J.L. 1976c. 'Aromatic plants on the Knossos tablets. [Summary of report to the *VIth International Congress on Classical Studies* held in Madrid Sept. 1974]'. *Minos* 15: 226–7.

MELENA, J.L. 1980. 'El aceite en la civilización micénica.' In BLÁZQUEZ MARTÍNEZ, J.M. (ed.) *Producción y comercio del aceite en la Antigüedad: Primer Congresso Internacional.* Universidad Complutense. Madrid: 255–82.

MELENA, J.L. 1983a. 'Further thoughts on Mycenaean *o-pa*.' In HEUBECK, A. & NEUMANN, G. (eds.) *Res Mycenae. Akten des VII. Internationalen Mykenologischen Colloquiums in Nürnburg vom 6.–10. April 1981.* Göttingen: 258–86.

MELENA, J.L. 1983b. 'Olive oil and other sorts of oil in Mycenaean tablets.' *Minos* 18: 89–123.

MELENA, J.L. 1985. 'Notas de filología micénica VI: el silabograma **83*.' In RODRIGUEZ, A. & RODRIGUEZ, M. (eds.) *Serta gratulatoria in honorem Juan Régulo septuagenario oblata.* Volume I. *Filología.* La Laguna: 473–86.

MELENA, J.L. 1987a. 'On untransliterated syllabograms *56 and *22.' In ILIEVSKI, P.HR. & CREPAJAC, LJ. (eds.) *Tractata Mycenaea. Proceedings of the Eighth International Colloquium on Mycenaean Studies, Held in Ohrid, 15–20 September 1985*. Skopje: 203–32.

MELENA, J.L. 1987b. 'Notas de filología micénica II: qué se asienta en PY Un 1320 [+] 1442?' In BÁDENAS DE LA PEÑA, P., MARTÍNEZ DÍEZ, A., MARTÍNEZ-FRESNEDA, M.E. & RODRÍGUEZ MONESCILLO, E. (eds.) *Athlon. Satura Grammatica in Honorem Francisci R. Adrados*. Volume II. Madrid: 613–18.

MELENA, J.L. 1988. 'Notas de filología micénica I: el ideograma *142.' In OLIVIER, J.-P. & PALAIMA, T.G. (eds.) *Texts, Tablets and Scribes. Studies in Mycenaean Epigraphy and Economy Offered to Emmett L. Bennett, Jr. Minos* Suppl. 10. Salamanca: 213–17.

MELENA, J.L. 1992–1993a. '167 joins of fragments in the Linear B tablets from Pylos.' *Minos* 27–28: 71–82.

MELENA, J.L. 1992–1993b. '244 joins and quasi-joins of fragments in the Linear B tablets from Pylos.' *Minos* 27–28: 307–24.

MELENA, J.L. 1994–1995a. '28 joins and quasi-joins of fragments in the Linear B tablets from Pylos.' *Minos* 29–30: 95–100.

MELENA, J.L. 1994–1995b. '133 joins and quasi-joins of fragments in the Linear B tablets from Pylos.' *Minos* 29–30: 271–88.

MELENA, J.L. 1996–1997a. '40 joins and quasi-joins of fragments from the Linear B tablets from Pylos.' *Minos* 31–32: 159–70.

MELENA, J.L. 1996–1997b. '13 joins and quasi-joins of fragments from the Linear B tablets from Pylos.' *Minos* 31–32: 171–8.

MELENA, J.L. 1996–1997c. '19 raccords et quasi-raccords de fragments dans les tablettes de Cnossos.' *Minos* 31–32: 417–22.

MELENA, J.L. 1999. 'Some thoughts on the origin of the Knossos fragments found in 1984 at the Heraklion Museum.' In DEGER-JALKOTZY, S., HILLER, S. & PANAGL, O. (eds.) *Floreant Studia Mycenaea. Akten des X. Internationalen Mykenologischen Colloquiums in Salzburg vom 1.–5. Mai 1995*. Vienna: 363–87.

MELENA, J.L. 2000–2001a. '24 joins and quasi-joins of fragments in the Linear B tablets from Pylos.' *Minos* 35–36: 357–69.

MELENA, J.L. 2000–2001b. '63 joins and quasi-joins of fragments in the Linear B tablets from Pylos.' *Minos* 35–36: 371–84.

MELENA, J.L. Forthcoming. 'On the structure of the Mycenaean Linear B syllabary I. The untransliterated syllabograms.' In PALAIMA, T.G. & SHELMERDINE, C.W. (eds.) *Proceedings of the 11th International Mycenological Colloquium at Austin, Texas, 7–12 May 2000. Minos* Suppl. Salamanca.

MELENA, J.L. & OLIVIER, J.-P. 1991. *TITHEMY. The Tablets and Nodules in Linear B from Tiryns, Thebes and Mycenae. Minos* Suppl. 12. Salamanca. [= *TITHEMY*]

MELENA, J.L., OWENS, G. & SERRANO, M. 1990–1991. '55 raccords de fragments dans les tablettes de Cnossos.' *Minos* 25–26: 413–17.

MICHAILIDOU, A. (ed.) 2001. *Manufacture and Measurement. Counting, Measuring and Recording. Craft Items in Early Aegean Societies*. Meletemata 33. Athens.

MONROE, C.M. 2000. 'Scales of fate. Trade, tradition and transformation in the eastern Mediterranean ca. 1350–1175 BCE.' Unpublished Ph.D. thesis, University of Michigan.

MOODY, J. 1987. 'The Minoan palace as a prestige artefact.' In HÄGG, R. & MARINATOS, M. (eds.) *The Function of the Minoan Palaces. Proceedings of the Fourth International Symposium at the Swedish Institute in Athens, 10–16 June, 1984*. Stockholm: 235–41.

MORPURGO DAVIES, A. 1979. 'Terminology of work and terminology of power in Greek and Linear B.' In RISCH, E. & MÜHLESTEIN, H. (eds.) *Colloquium Mycenaeum. Actes du sixième colloque international sur les textes mycéniens et égéens tenu à Chaumont sur Neuchâtel du 7 au 13 septembre 1975*. Neuchâtel: 87–108.

MORPURGO DAVIES, A. 1999. 'The morphology of personal names in Mycenaean and Greek: some observations.' In DEGER-JALKOTZY, S., HILLER, S. & PANAGL, O. (eds.) *Floreant Studia Mycenaea. Akten des X. Internationalen Mykenologischen Colloquiums in Salzburg vom 1.–5. Mai 1995.* Vienna: 389–406.

MORRIS, C. 1990. 'In pursuit of the white tusked boar: aspects of hunting in Mycenaean society.' In HÄGG, R. & NORDQUIST, G.C. (eds.) *Celebrations of Death and Divinity in the Bronze Age Argolid. Proceedings of the Sixth International Symposium at the Swedish School at Athens, 11–13 June, 1988.* Skrifter Utgivna av Svenska Institutet i Athen 4°, 40. Stockholm: 149–56.

MORRIS, H.J. 1986. 'An economic model of the kingdom of Pylos.' Unpublished Ph.D. thesis, University of Minnesota.

MORRIS, H.J. 1987. 'Markets as a secondary means of exchange in the kingdom of Pylos.' *American Journal of Archaeology* 91: 295–6.

MORRIS, I. 2000. *Archaeology as Cultural History. Words and Things in Iron Age Greece.* Oxford.

MORRIS, S.P. 2001. '*Potnia Aswiya*: Anatolian contributions to Greek religion.' In LAFFINEUR, R. & HÄGG, R. (eds.) *POTNIA. Deities and Religion in the Aegean Bronze Age. Proceedings of the 8th International Aegean Conference held at Göteborg University, 12–15 April 2000. Aegaeum* 22. Liège: 423–34.

MOUNTJOY, P.A. 1997. 'The destruction of the palace at Pylos reconsidered.' *Annual of the British School at Athens* 92: 109–37.

MÜHLESTEIN, H. 1958. 'Einige mykenische Wörter.' *Museum Helveticum* 15: 222–6.

MURRAY, C. 1979. 'Mycenaean religion – the evidence of the Linear B tablets.' Unpublished Ph.D. thesis, University of Cambridge.

MURRAY, O. 1991. 'War and the symposium.' In SLATER, W.J. (ed.) *Dining in a Classical Context.* Ann Arbor: 83–103.

MYLONAS, G.E. 1972. *Το θρησκευτικὸν κέντρον των Μυκηνών – The Cult Centre of Mycenae.* Πραγματείαι της Ακαδημίας Αθηνών 33. Athens.

MYLONAS, G.E. 1977. *Μυκηναϊκὴ θρησκεία. Ναοὶ, βωμοὶ καὶ τεμένη – Mycenaean Religion. Temples, Altars and Temene.* Πραγματείαι της Ακαδημίας Αθηνών 39. Athens.

MYLOPOTAMITAKI, A.K. (ed.) 2002. *Οίνος Παλαιός Ηδύποτος. Το Κρητικό Κρασί από τα Προϊστορικά ως τα Νεότερα Χρόνια.* Heraklion.

NAGY, G. 1994–1995. 'A Mycenaean reflex in Homer: φορῆναι.' *Minos* 29–30: 171–5.

NIKOLOUDIS, S. 2001. 'Animal sacrifice in the Mycenaean world.' *Journal of Prehistoric Religion* 15: 11–31

NILSSON, M. 1950. *The Minoan-Mycenaean Religion and Its Survival in Greek Religion.* Second edition. Lund.

NISSEN, H.J., DAMEROW, P. & ENGLUND, R.K. 1993. *Archaic Bookkeeping. Early Writing and Techniques of Economic Administration in the Ancient Near East.* Trans. LARSEN, P. Chicago.

NOSCH, M.-L. 2000a. 'Schafherden unter dem Namenspatronat von Potnia und Hermes in Knossos.' In BLAKOLMER, F. (ed.) *Österreichische Forschungen zur Ägäischen Bronzezeit 1998. Akten der Tagung am Institut für Klassische Archäologie der Universität Wien 2.–3. Mai 1998.* Forschungen zur Archäologie Band 3. Vienna: 211–15.

NOSCH, M.-L. 2000b. 'Acquisition and distribution: *ta-ra-si-ja* in the Mycenaean textile industry.' In GILLIS, C., RISBERG C. & SJÖBERG, B. (eds.) *Trade and Production in Premonetary Greece. Acquisition and Distribution. Proceedings of the 6th International Workshop, Athens 1996.* Studies in Mediterranean Archaeology Pocket-book 154. Jonsered: 43–61.

NOSCH, M.-L. 2001a. 'The textile industry at Thebes in the light of the textile industries at Pylos and Knossos.' In RADOVA, I. (ed.) *Festschrift in Honour of A. Bartoněk.* Studia Minora Facultatis Philosophica Universitatis Brunensis 6. Brno: 177–89.

NOSCH, M.-L. 2001b. 'Entre collecteurs et travailleurs: les "responsables" dans l'industrie textile de Cnossos.' *Ktema* 26: 133–43.

NOSCH, M.-L. 2001c. 'The geography of the *ta-ra-si-ja* obligation.' *Aegean Archaeology* 4 (1997–2000): 27–44.

NOSCH, M.-L. & ANDERSON, E. 2003. 'With a little help from my friends: investigating Mycenaean textiles with the help from Scandinavian experimental archaeology.' In FOSTER, K.P. & LAFFINEUR, R. (eds.) *METRON. Measuring the Aegean Bronze Age. Proceedings of the 9th International Aegean Conference / 9e Rencontre égéenne internationale, Yale University, 18–21 April 2002. Aegaeum* 24. Liège: 197–205.

NOSCH, M.-L. & PERNA, M. 2001. 'Cloth in the cult.' In LAFFINEUR, R. & HÄGG, R. (eds.) *POTNIA. Deities and Religion in the Aegean Bronze Age. Proceedings of the 8th International Aegean Conference held at Göteborg University, 12–15 April 2000. Aegaeum* 22. Liège: 471–7.

OLIVIER, J.-P. 1959. 'Étude d'un nom de métier mycénien: *di-pte-ra-po-ro*.' *L'Antiquité Classique* 28: 165–85.

OLIVIER, J.-P. 1960. *A propos d'une 'liste' de desservants de sanctuaire dans les documents en linéaire B de Pylos*. Brussels.

OLIVIER, J.-P. 1967a. *Les scribes de Cnossos. Essai de classement des archives d'un palais mycénien.* Incunabula Graeca 17. Rome. [= *Scribes Cnossos*]

OLIVIER, J.-P. 1967b. 'La série Dn de Cnossos.' *Studi Micenei ed Egeo-Anatolici* 2: 71–93.

OLIVIER, J.-P. 1967c. '91 raccords de fragments dans le tablettes de Cnossos.' *Annual of the British School at Athens* 62: 325–36.

OLIVIER, J.-P. 1968. 'La série Ws de Cnossos.' *Minos* 9: 173–83.

OLIVIER, J.-P. 1972. 'La série Dn de Cnossos réconsidérée.' *Minos* 13: 22–8.

OLIVIER, J.-P. 1974. 'Une loi fiscale mycénienne.' *Bulletin de Correspondance Hellénique* 98: 23–35.

OLIVIER, J.-P. 1984. 'Administrations at Knossos and Pylos: what differences.' In PALAIMA, T.G. & SHELMERDINE, C.W. (eds.) *Pylos Comes Alive: Industry and Administration in a Mycenaean Palace*. New York: 11–18.

OLIVIER, J.-P. 1988. 'KN: Da–Dg.' In OLIVIER, J.-P. & PALAIMA, T.G. (eds.) *Texts, Tablets and Scribes. Studies in Mycenaean Epigraphy and Economy Offered to Emmett L. Bennett, Jr. Minos* Suppl. 10. Salamanca: 219–68.

OLIVIER, J.-P. 1994. 'L'économie des royaumes mycéniens d'après les tablettes en linéaire B.' *Les Mycéniens. Des Grecs du IIe millénaire. Les Dossiers d'Archeologie* 195: 50–65.

OLIVIER, J.-P. 1996–1997. 'El comercio micénico desde la documentación epigráfica.' *Minos* 31–32: 275–92.

OLIVIER, J.-P. 1997. 'Die beschrifteten Tonplomben.' In PINI, I. (ed.) *Die Tonplomben aus dem Nestorpalast von Pylos*. Akademie der Wissenschaften und der Literatur. Mainz: 70–81.

OLIVIER, J.-P. 2001. 'Les "Collecteurs" : leur distribution spatiale et temporelle.' In VOUTSAKI, S. & KILLEN, J. T. (eds.) *Economy and Politics in the Mycenaean Palace States. Proceedings of a Conference held on 1–3 July 1999 in the Faculty of Classics, Cambridge*. Cambridge Philological Society Supplementary Volume 27. Cambridge: 139–59.

OLIVIER, J.-P., GODART, L., SEYDEL, C. & SOURVINOU, C. 1973. *Index généraux du linéaire B.* Incunabula Graeca 52. Rome.

OLIVIER J.-P. & KILLEN, J.T. 1992. 'Errata et corrigenda à KT5 au 04/09/90.' In OLIVIER, J.-P. (ed.) *Mykenaïka. Actes du IXe Colloque international sur les textes mycéniens et égéens organisé par le Centre de l'Antiquité Greque et Romaine de la Fondation Hellénique des Recherches Scientifiques et l'École française d'Athènes (Athènes, 2–6 octobre 1990). Bulletin de Correspondance Hellénique* Suppl. 25. Athens: 457–9.

OPPENHEIM, A.L. 1977. *Ancient Mesopotamia. Portrait of a Dead Civilization.* Revised edition, completed by REINER, E. Chicago & London.

PALAIMA, T.G. 1987a. 'Mycenaean seals and sealings in their economic and administrative contexts.' In ILIEVSKI, P.HR. & CREPAJAC, LJ. (eds.) *Tractata Mycenaea. Proceedings of the Eighth International Colloquium on Mycenaean Studies, Held in Ohrid, 15–20 September 1985.* Skopje: 249–66.

PALAIMA, T.G. 1987b. 'Comments on Mycenaean literacy.' In KILLEN, J.T., MELENA, J.L. & OLIVIER, J.-P. (eds.) 1987. *Studies in Mycenaean and Classical Greek Presented to John Chadwick. Minos* 20–22. Salamanca: 499–510.

PALAIMA, T.G. 1988. *The Scribes of Pylos*. Incunabula Graeca 87. Rome. [= *Scribes Pylos*]

PALAIMA, T.G. 1989. 'Perspectives on the Pylos oxen tablets: textual (and archaeological) evidence for the use and management of oxen in Late Bronze Age Messenia (and Crete).' In PALAIMA, T.G., SHELMERDINE, C.W. & ILIEVSKI, P.HR. (eds.) *Studia Mycenaea (1988). Zhiva Antika* Monographies 7. Skopje: 85–124.

PALAIMA, T.G. 1990. 'Origin, development, transition and transformation: the purposes and techniques of administration in Minoan and Mycenaean society.' In PALAIMA, T.G. (ed.) *Aegean Seals, Sealings and Administration. Proceedings of the NEH-Dickson Conference of the Program in Aegean Scripts and Prehistory of the Department of Classics, University of Texas at Austin, January 11–13, 1989. Aegaeum* 5. Liège: 83–104.

PALAIMA, T.G. 1991. 'Maritime matters in the Linear B tablets.' In LAFFINEUR, R. & BASCH, L. (eds.) *THALASSA. L'Égée préhistorique et la mer. Aegaeum 7.* Liège: 273–310.

PALAIMA, T.G. 1992a. 'The Knossos oxen dossier: the use of oxen in Mycenaean Crete. Part I: general background and Scribe 107.' In OLIVIER, J.-P. (ed.) *Mykenaïka. Actes du IXe Colloque international sur les textes mycéniens et égéens organisé par le Centre de l'Antiquité Greque et Romaine de la Fondation Hellénique des Recherches Scientifiques et l'École française d'Athènes (Athènes, 2–6 octobre 1990). Bulletin de Correspondance Hellénique* Suppl. 25. Athens: 463–74.

PALAIMA, T.G. 1992b. 'Mycenaean scribal aesthetics.' In LAFFINEUR, R. & CROWLEY, J.L. (eds.) *EIKΩN. Aegean Bronze Age Iconography: Shaping a Methodology. Proceedings of the 4th International Aegean Conference / 4e Rencontre égéenne internationale. University of Tasmania, Hobart, Australia, 6–9 April 1992. Aegaeum* 8. Liège: 63–76.

PALAIMA, T.G. 1995a. 'The nature of the Mycenaean wanax: non-Indo-European origins and priestly functions.' In REHAK, P. (ed.) *The Role of the Ruler in the Prehistoric Aegean. Proceedings of a Panel Discussion Presented at the Annual General Meeting of the American Institute of Archaeology at New Orleans, Louisiana, 28 December 1992. With Additions. Aegaeum* 11. Liège & Austin: 119–41.

PALAIMA, T.G. 1995b. 'The last days of the Pylos polity.' In LAFFINEUR, R. & NIEMEIER, W.-D. (eds.) *POLITEIA. Society and State in the Aegean Bronze Age. Proceedings of the 5th International Aegean Conference / 5e Rencontre égéenne internationale University of Heidelberg, Archäologisches Institut 10–23 April 1994. Aegaeum* 12. Liège & Austin: 623–34.

PALAIMA, T.G. 1996a. '"Contiguities" in the Linear B tablets from Pylos.' In DE MIRO, E., GODART, L. & SACCONI, A. (eds.) *Atti e Memorie del Secondo Congresso Internazionale di Micenologia, Roma–Napoli, 14–20 ottobre 1991.* Incunabula Graeca 98. Rome: 379–96.

PALAIMA, T.G. 1996b. 'Sealings as links in an administrative chain.' In FERIOLI, P., FIANDRA, E. & FISSORE, G.C. (eds.) *Administration in Ancient Societies. Acts of Session 218 of the 13th International Congress of Anthropological and Ethnological Sciences, Mexico City July 29–August 5, 1993.* Turin: 37–66.

PALAIMA, T.G. 1996–1997. '*po-re-na*: a Mycenaean reflex in Homer? An I-E figure in Mycenaean?' *Minos* 31–32: 303–12.

PALAIMA, T.G. 1997. 'Potter and fuller: the royal craftsmen.' In LAFFINEUR, R. & BETENCOURT, P.P. (eds.) *TEXNH. Craftsmen, Craftswomen and Craftsmanship in the Aegean Bronze Age. Proceedings of the 6th International Aegean Conference, Philadelphia, Temple University, 18–21 April 1996. Aegaeum* 16. Liège & Austin: 407–12.

PALAIMA, T.G. 1999a. 'KN02–Tn 316.' In DEGER-JALKOTZY, S., HILLER, S. & PANAGL, O. (eds.) *Floreant Studia Mycenaea. Akten des X. Internationalen Mykenologischen Colloquiums in Salzburg vom 1.–5. Mai 1995.* Vienna: 437–62.

PALAIMA, T.G. 1999b. 'Mycenaean militarism from a textual perspective. Onomastics in context: *lāwos, dāmos, klewos*.' In LAFFINEUR, R. (ed.) *POLEMOS. Le contexte guerrier en Égée à l'âge du bronze. Actes de la 7e Rencontre égéenne internationale Université de Liège, 14–17 avril 1998. Aegaeum* 19. Liège and Austin: 367–79.

PALAIMA, T.G. 2000. 'The transactional vocabulary of Mycenaean sealings and the Mycenaean administrative process.' In PERNA, M. (ed.) *Administrative Documents in the Aegean and their Near Eastern Counterparts. Proceedings of the International Colloquium. Naples, February 29 – March 2, 1996*. Turin: 261–76.

PALAIMA, T.G. 2000–2001. 'Review: Aravantinos, V.L., Godart, L. & Sacconi, A. 2001. *Thèbes. Fouilles de la Cadmée* I. *Les tablettes en linéaire B de la Odos Pelopidou. Édition et commentaire*.' *Minos* 35–36: 475–86.

PALAIMA, T.G. 2001. 'The modalities of economic control at Pylos.' *Ktema* 26: 151–9.

PALAIMA, T.G. 2003a. '"Archives" and "scribes" and information hierarchy in Mycenaean Greek Linear B records.' In BROSIUS, M. (ed.) *Ancient Archives and Archival Tradition. Concepts of Record-Keeping in the Ancient World*. Oxford: 153–94.

PALAIMA, T.G. 2003b. 'Review: *Thèbes. Fouilles de la Cadmée.* Vol. I. *Les tablettes en linéaire B de la Odos Pelopidou. Édition et commentaire* by V.L. Aravantinos, L. Godart, and A. Sacconi.' *American Journal of Archaeology* 107: 113–15.

PALAIMA, T.G. 2004a. 'Mycenaean accounting methods and systems and their place within Mycenaean palatial civilization.' In HUDSON, M. & WUNSCH, C. (eds.) *Creating Economic Order. Record-Keeping, Standardization, and the Development of Accounting in the Ancient Near East*. Bethesda, MD: 269–301.

PALAIMA, T.G. 2004b. 'Sacrificial feasting in the Linear B documents.' In WRIGHT, J. (ed.) *The Mycenaean Feast. Hesperia* 73.2: 97–126.

PALAIMA, T.G. & WRIGHT, J.C. 1985. 'Ins and outs of the archives rooms at Pylos.' *American Journal of Archaeology* 89: 251–62.

PALMER, L.R. 1956. 'Military arrangements for the defence of Pylos.' *Minos* 4: 120–45.

PALMER, L.R. 1957. 'Review: Michael Ventris [†] and John Chadwick: *Documents in Mycenaean Greek*. 300 selected tablets from Knossos, Pylos and Mycenae, with comm. and vocabulary. With a foreword by Alan J. B. Wace. Cambridge Univ. Press 1956.' *Gnomon* 29: 561–81.

PALMER, L.R. 1963. *The Interpretation of Mycenaean Greek Texts*. Oxford.

PALMER, L.R. 1977. 'War and society in a Mycenaean kingdom.' In VAN EFFENTERRE, H. & MOSSÉ, C. (eds.) *Armées et fiscalité dans le monde antique. Colloques Nationaux du Centre National de la Recherche Scientifique* 936. Paris: 35–62.

PALMER, L.R. 1983a. 'Studies in Mycenaean religion.' In HÄNDEL, P. & MEID, W. (eds.) *Festschrift für Robert Muth*. Innsbruck: 283–96.

PALMER, L.R. 1983b. 'Mycenaean religion: methodological choices.' In HEUBECK, A. & NEUMANN, G. (eds.) *Res Mycenaeae. Akten des VII. Internationalen mykenologischen Colloquiums in Nürnberg vom 6.–10. April 1981*. Göttingen: 338–66.

PALMER, R. 1989. 'Subsistence rations at Pylos and Knossos.' *Minos* 24: 89–124.

PALMER, R. 1992. 'Wheat and barley in Mycenaean society.' In OLIVIER, J.-P. (ed.) *Mykenaïka. Actes du IXe Colloque international sur les textes mycéniens et égéens organisé par le Centre de l'Antiquité Greque et Romaine de la Fondation Hellénique des Recherches Scientifiques et l'École française d'Athènes (Athènes, 2–6 octobre 1990). Bulletin de Correspondance Hellénique* Suppl. 25. Athens: 475–98.

PALMER, R. 1994. *Wine in the Mycenaean Palace Economy. Aegaeum* 10. Liège & Austin.

PALMER, R. 1995. 'Wine and viticulture in the Linear A and B texts of the Bronze Age Aegean.' In MCGOVERN, P.E., FLEMING, S.J. & KATZ, S.H. (eds.) *The Origins and Ancient History of Wine*. Philadelphia: 269–85.

PALMER, R. 1998–1999 [2002]. 'Models in Linear B landholding: an analysis of methodology.' In BENNET, J. & DRIESSEN, J. (eds.) *A-NA-QO-TA. Studies Presented to J.T. Killen. Minos* 33–34. Salamanca: 223–50.

PALMER, R. 1999. 'Perishable goods in Mycenaean texts.' In DEGER-JALKOTZY, S., HILLER, S. & PANAGL, O. (eds.) *Floreant Studia Mycenaea. Akten des X. Internationalen Mykenologischen Colloquiums in Salzburg vom 1.–5. Mai 1995*. Vienna: 463–86.

PALMER, R. Forthcoming. 'Wheat and barley in Mycenaean society: 15 years later.' In SACCONI, A., GODART, L. & NEGRI, M. (eds.) *Proceedings of the XIIth International Colloquium of Mycenology, Rome, February 2006*. Rome.

PARKE, H.W. 1977. *Festivals of the Athenians*. London.

PARKINSON, W. 1999. 'Chipping away at a Mycenaean economy: obsidian exchange, Linear B, and palatial control in Late Bronze Age Messenia.' In GALATY, M.L. & PARKINSON, W.A. (eds.) *Rethinking Mycenaean Palaces: New Interpretations of an Old Idea*. Los Angeles: 73–85.

PERNA, M. 1996. 'Le tavolette delle serie Mc di Cnosso.' In DE MIRO, E., GODART, L. & SACCONI, A. (eds.) *Atti e Memorie del Secondo Congresso Internazionale di Micenologia, Roma–Napoli, 14–20 ottobre 1991*. Incunabula Graeca 98. Rome: 411–19.

PERNA, M. 2004. *Recherches sur la fiscalité mycénienne*. Études anciennes 28. Nancy & Paris.

PERPILLOU, J.-L. 1976. 'Données numériques des documents Fn de Pylos.' *Studi Micenei ed Egeo-Anatolici* 17: 65–78.

PETRAKIS, V.P. 2002–2003 [2007]. '*to-no-e-ke-te-ri-jo* reconsidered.' *Minos* 37–38: 293–316.

PINI, I. 1997. *Die Tonplomben aus dem Nestorpalast von Pylos*. Akademie der Wissenschaften und der Literatur. Mainz.

PITEROS, CHR., OLIVIER, J.-P. & MELENA, J.L. 1990. 'Les inscriptions en linéaire B des nodules de Thèbes (1982): la fouille, les documents, les possibilités d'interprétation.' *Bulletin de Correspondance Hellénique* 144: 103–84.

PLATON, N. 1971. *Zakros. Discovery of a Lost Palace of Ancient Crete*. New York.

PLATON, N. 1983. 'The Minoan palaces: centres of organization of a theocratic, social, and political system.' In KRZYSZKOWSKA, O. & NIXON, L. (eds.) *Minoan Society. Proceedings of the Cambridge Colloquium 1981*. Bristol: 273–6.

PLUTA, K. 1996–1997. 'A reconstruction of the Archives Complex at Pylos: preliminary progress report.' *Minos* 31–32: 231–50.

PLUTA, K. Forthcoming. 'The Pylos Ae series and Hand 43.' In PALAIMA, T.G. & SHELMERDINE, C.W. (eds.) *Proceedings of the 11th International Mycenological Colloquium at Austin, Texas, 7–12 May 2000*. *Minos* Suppl. Salamanca.

POLANYI, K. 1957. 'The economy as instituted process.' In POLANYI, K., ARENSBERG, C.M. & PEARSON, H.W. (eds.) *Trade and Market in the Early Empires*. New York: 243–70.

POLANYI, K. 1960. 'On the comparative treatment of economic institutions in antiquity with illustrations from Athens, Mycenae, and Alalakh.' In KRAELING, C.H. & ADAMS, R.M. (eds.) *City Invincible. An Oriental Institute Symposium*. Chicago: 329–50.

POLANYI, K. 1968. *Primitive, Archaic and Modern Economies. Essays of Karl Polanyi*. Edited by G. DALTON. New York.

POPHAM, M.R. 1991. 'Pylos: reflections on the date of its destruction and on its Iron Age reoccupation.' *Oxford Journal of Archaeology* 10: 315–24.

POPHAM, M.R. 1993. 'Review article III: Knossos.' *Journal of Hellenic Studies* 113: 174–8.

POSTGATE, J.N. 1972. 'The role of the temple in the Mesopotamian secular community.' In UCKO, P.J., TRINGHAM, R. & DIMBLEBY, G.W. (eds.) *Man, Settlement and Urbanism*. London: 811–25.

POSTGATE, J.N. 1992. *Early Mesopotamia. Society and Economy at the Dawn of History*. First edition. London.

POSTGATE, J.N. 1994. *Early Mesopotamia. Society and Economy at the Dawn of History*. Revised edition. London.

POURSAT, J.C. 1983. 'Ateliers et sanctuaires à Malia : nouvelles données sur l'organisation sociale à l'époque des premiers palais.' In KRZYSZKOWSKA, O. & NIXON, L. (eds.) *Minoan Society. Proceedings of the Cambridge Colloquium 1981*. Bristol: 277–81.

PRESTON, L. 2004. 'A mortuary perspective on political changes in Late Minoan II–IIIB Crete.' *American Journal of Archaeology* 108: 321–48.

PUHVEL, J. 1964. 'Êleutér and oinoâtis: Dionysiac data from Mycenaean Greece.' In BENNETT, E.L. JR. (ed.) *Mycenaean Studies. Proceedings of the Third International Colloquium for Mycenaean Studies held at 'Wingspread', 4–8 September 1961*. Madison: 161–70.

PULAK, C. 1997. 'The Uluburun shipwreck.' In SWINY, S., HOHLFELDER, R.L. & WYLDE SWINY, H. (eds.) *Res Maritimae. Cyprus and the Eastern Mediterranean from Prehistory to Late Antiquity. Proceedings of the Second International Symposium 'Cities on the Sea', Nicosia, Cyprus, October 18–22, 1994*. Atlanta: 233–62.

RACKHAM, O. & MOODY, J. 1996. *The Making of the Cretan Landscape*. Manchester.

RANSOME, H.M. 1937. *The Sacred Bee in Ancient Times and Folklore*. London.

RAPP, G. JR. & ASCHENBRENNER, S.E. (eds.) 1978. *Excavations at Nichoria in Southwest Greece*. Volume I. *Site, Environs and Techniques*. Ann Arbor.

REDFORD, D.B. 1992. *Egypt, Canaan, and Israel in Ancient Times*. Princeton.

REHAK, P. 1992. 'Tradition and innovation in the fresco from Room 31 in the "Cult Centre" at Mycenae.' In LAFFINEUR, R. & CROWLEY, J.L. (eds.) *EIKΩN. Aegean Bronze Age Iconography: Shaping a Methodology. Proceedings of the 4th International Aegean Conference / 4e Rencontre égéenne internationale. University of Tasmania, Hobart, Australia, 6–9 April 1992. Aegaeum* 8. Liège: 39–62.

RENFREW, C. 1979. 'Phylakopi and questions of cult in the Aegean.' *Bulletin of the Institute of Classical Studies* 26: 130–1.

RENFREW, C. 1981a. 'Questions of Minoan and Mycenaean cult.' In HÄGG, R. & MARINATOS, N. (eds.) *Sanctuaries and Cults in the Aegean Bronze Age. Proceedings of the First International Symposium at the Swedish Institute in Athens, 12–13 May, 1980*. Stockholm: 27–33.

RENFREW, C. 1981b. 'The sanctuary at Phylakopi.' In HÄGG, R. & MARINATOS, N. (eds.) *Sanctuaries and Cults in the Aegean Bronze Age. Proceedings of the First International Symposium at the Swedish Institute in Athens, 12–13 May, 1980*. Stockholm: 67–80.

RENFREW, C. 1985. *The Archaeology of Cult. The Sanctuary of Phylakopi*. British School at Athens Supplementary Volume 18. London.

RENGER, J. 1984. 'Patterns of non-institutional trade and non-commercial exchange in ancient Mesopotamia at the beginning of the second millennium B.C.' In ARCHI, A. (ed.) *Circulation of Goods in Non-Palatial Context[s] in the Ancient Near East. Proceedings of the International Conference Organized by the Instituto per gli Studi Micenei ed Egeo-Anatolici*. Incunabula Graeca 82. Rome: 31–124.

RICE, P.M. 1987. *Pottery Analysis: A Sourcebook*. Chicago.

RILEY, F.R. 1999. *The Role of the Traditional Mediterranean Diet in the Development of Minoan Crete. Archaeological, Nutritional and Biochemical Evidence*. British Archaeological Reports International Series 810. Oxford.

RILEY, F.R. 2002. 'Olive oil production on Bronze Age Crete: nutritional properties, processing methods and storage life of Minoan olive oil.' *Oxford Journal of Archaeology* 21: 63–75.

RISBERG, C. 1992. 'Metal-working in Greek sanctuaries.' In LINDERS, T. & ALROTH, B. (eds.) *Economics of Cult in the Ancient Greek World. Proceedings of the Uppsala Symposium 1990. Boreas* 21. Uppsala: 33–40.

RISCH, E. 1957. 'Mykenisch *wo-wo ko-to-no*.' *Minos* 5: 28–34.

RISCH, E. 1972. 'Le formation du mot *po-ti-ni-ja-we-jo*.' In RUIPÉREZ, M.S. (ed.) *Acta Mycenaea. Proceedings of the Fifth International Colloquium on Mycenaean Studies, Held in Salamanca, 30 March – 3 April 1970*. Salamanca: 294–300.

ROBKIN, A.L.H. 1981. 'The endogram *WE* on Mycenaean textiles **146* and **166+WE*: a proposed identification.' *American Journal of Archaeology* 85: 213.

ROUGEMONT, F. 2001a. 'Some thoughts on the identification of the "Collectors" in the Linear B tablets.' In VOUTSAKI, S. & KILLEN, J.T. (eds.) *Economy and Politics in the Mycenaean Palace States. Proceedings of a Conference held on 1–3 July 1999 in the Faculty of Classics, Cambridge*. Cambridge Philological Society Supplementary Volume 27. Cambridge: 129–38.

ROUGEMONT, F. 2001b. 'Les agents du contrôle économique dans les textes en linéaire B : le cas particulier des anthroponymes de la série Mc de Cnossos.' *Ktema* 26: 127–32.

ROUSIOTI, D. 2000. 'Did the Mycenaeans believe in theriomorphic deities?' *Journal of Prehistoric Religion* 14: 45.

ROUSIOTI, D. 2001. 'Did the Mycenaeans believe in theriomorphic deities?' In LAFFINEUR, R. & HÄGG, R. (eds.) *POTNIA. Deities and Religion in the Aegean Bronze Age. Proceedings of the 8th International Aegean Conference held at Göteborg University, 12–15 April 2000. Aegaeum* 22. Liège: 305–14.

RUIJGH, C.J. 1967a. *Études sur la grammaire et le vocabulaire du grec mycénien*. Amsterdam.

RUIJGH, C.J. 1967b. 'À propos de Myc. *po-ti-ni-ja-we-jo*.' *Studi Micenei ed Egeo-Anatolici* 4: 40–52.

RUIJGH, C.J. 1967c. 'Sur le nom de Poséidon.' *Revue des Études Grecques* 80: 6–16.

RUIJGH, C.J. 1968. 'Remarques sur les mots *we-je-we*, *we-je-ke-a*$_2$, *we-ja-re-pe* et *to-ro-qa*.' In GALLAVOTTI, C. (ed.) *Atti e Memorie del 1° Congresso Internazionale di Micenologia di Roma, 27 settembre – 3 ottobre 1967*. Incunabula Graeca 25. Rome: 699–708.

RUIJGH, C.J. 1972. 'A propos de *de-we-ro-a*$_3$*-ko-ra-i-ja*.' In RUIPÉREZ, M.S. (ed.) *Acta Mycenaea. Proceedings of the Fifth International Colloquium on Mycenaean Studies, Held in Salamanca, 30 March – 3 April 1970*. Salamanca: 441–50.

RUIJGH, C.J. 1979. 'Faits linguistiques et données externes relatifs aux chars et aux roués.' In RISCH, E. & MÜHLESTEIN, H. (eds.) *Colloquium Mycenaeum. Actes du sixième colloque international sur les textes mycéniens et égéens tenu à Chaumont sur Neuchâtel du 7 au 13 September 1975*. Neuchâtel: 207–20.

RUIJGH, C.J. 1987. '*da-ma/du-ma* δάμαρ/δύμαρ et l'abréviation *DA*, notamment en PY En 609.' In ILIEVSKI, P.HR. & CREPAJAC, LJ. (eds.) *Tractata Mycenaea. Proceedings of the Eighth International Colloquium on Mycenaean Studies Held in Ohrid, 15–20 septembre 1985*. Skopje: 299–322.

RUIJGH, C.J. 1996. 'La "déesse mère" dans les textes mycéniens.' In DE MIRO, E., GODART, L. & SACCONI, A. (eds.) *Atti e Memorie del Secondo Congresso Internazionale di Micenologia, Roma–Napoli, 14–20 ottobre 1991*. Volume 1. *Filologia*. Incunabula Graeca 98. Rome: 453–7.

RUIJGH, C.J. 1998–1999 [2002]. 'The social status of persons indicated by possessive adjectives in *–e-jo* with some linguistic observations.' In BENNET, J. & DRIESSEN, J. (eds.) *A-NA-QO-TA. Studies Presented to J.T. Killen. Minos* 33–34. Salamanca: 251–72.

RUIJGH, C.J. 1999. 'ϝάναξ et ses dérivés dans les textes mycéniens.' In DEGER-JALKOTZY, S., HILLER, S. & PANAGL, O. (eds.) *Floreant Studia Mycenaea. Akten des X. Internationalen Mykenologischen Colloquiums in Salzburg vom 1.–5. Mai 1995*. Vienna: 521–36.

RUTKOWSKI, B. 1968. *The Cult Places of the Aegean*. New Haven and London.

SACCONI, A. 1967. 'Indice topografico dei documenti nel palazzo di Pilo.' *Studi Micenei ed Egeo-Anatolici* 2: 94–102.

SACCONI, A. 1979. 'Le rôle et la valeur des idéogrammes **124* et **125* dans les textes mycéniens.' In RISCH, E. & MÜHLESTEIN, H. (eds.) *Colloquium Mycenaeum. Actes du sixième colloque international sur les textes mycéniens et égéens tenu à Chaumont sur Neuchâtel du 7 au 13 septembre 1975*. Neuchâtel: 347–52.

SACCONI, A. 2001. 'Les repas sacrés dans les textes mycéniens.' In LAFFINEUR, R. & HÄGG, R. (eds.) *POTNIA. Deities and Religion in the Aegean Bronze Age. Proceedings of the 8th International Aegean Conference held at Göteborg University, 12–15 April 2000. Aegaeum* 22. Liège: 467–70.

SÄFLUND, G. 1980. 'Sacrificial banquets in the "Palace of Nestor".' *Opuscula Atheniensia* 13.16: 237–46.

SAINER, A.P. 1976. 'An index of the place names at Pylos.' *Studi Micenei ed Egeo-Anatolici* 17: 17–63.

SAKELLARIOU, A. 1964. *Die Minoischen und Mykenischen Siegel des Nationalmuseums in Athen. Corpus der Minoischen und Mykenischen Siegel*. Volume I. Berlin. [= CMS I]

SARPAKI, A. 2001. 'Condiments, perfume and dye plants in Linear B: a look at the textual and archaeobotanical evidence.' In MICHAILIDOU, A. (ed.) *Manufacture and Measurement. Counting, Measuring and Recording. Craft Items in Early Aegean Societies*. Meletemata 33. Athens: 194–265.

SCAFA, E. 1977. 'Annotazione in margine al lessico miceneo *epo*.' *Kadmos* 16: 175.

SCHÄFER, J. 1991. 'Amnisos: harbour-town of Minos?' In LAFFINEUR, R. & BASCH, L. (eds.) *THALASSA. L'Égée préhistorique et la mer. Aegaeum 7*. Liège: 111–16.

SCHALLIN, A.M. 1997. 'Metallurgy: a divine affair?' In GILLIS, C., RISBERG, C. & SJÖBERG, B. (eds.) *Trade and Production in Premonetary Greece. Production and the Craftsman. Proceedings of the 4th and 5th International Workshops, Athens 1994 and 1995*. Studies in Mediterranean Archaeology Pocket-book 143. Jonsered: 139–72.

SCHOEP. I. 2002. *The Administration of Neopalatial Crete. A Critical Assessment of the Linear A Tablets and Their Role in the Administrative Process. Minos* Suppl. 17. Salamanca.

SHEAR, I.M. 1998. 'Bellerophon tablets from the Mycenaean world? A tale of seven bronze hinges.' *Journal of Hellenic Studies* 118: 187–9.

SHELMERDINE, C.W. 1973. 'The Ma tablets reconsidered.' *American Journal of Archaeology* 77: 261–75.

SHELMERDINE, C.W. 1981. 'Nichoria in context: a major town in the Pylos kingdom.' *American Journal of Archaeology* 85: 319–25.

SHELMERDINE, C.W. 1984. 'The perfumed oil industry at Pylos.' In SHELMERDINE, C.W. & PALAIMA, T.G. (eds.) *Pylos Comes Alive: Industry and Administration in a Mycenaean Palace*. New York: 81–96.

SHELMERDINE, C.W. 1985. *The Perfume Industry of Mycenaean Pylos*. Studies in Mediterranean Archaeology Pocket-book 34. Göteborg.

SHELMERDINE, C.W. 1987a. 'Architectural change and economic decline at Pylos.' In KILLEN, J.T., MELENA, J.L. & OLIVIER, J.-P. (eds.) *Studies in Mycenaean and Classical Greek Presented to John Chadwick. Minos* 20–22: 557–68.

SHELMERDINE, C.W. 1987b. 'Industrial activity at Pylos.' In ILIEVSKI, P.HR. & CREPAJAC, LJ. (eds.) *Tractata Mycenaea. Proceedings of the Eighth International Colloquium on Mycenaean Studies Held in Ohrid, 15–20 September 1985*. Skopje: 333–42.

SHELMERDINE, C.W. 1988. 'Scribal organisation and administrative procedures.' In OLIVIER, J.-P. & PALAIMA, T.G. (eds.) *Texts, Tablets and Scribes. Studies in Mycenaean Epigraphy and Economy Offered to Emmett L. Bennett, Jr. Minos* Suppl. 10. Salamanca: 343–84.

SHELMERDINE, C.W. 1989. 'Mycenaean taxation.' In PALAIMA, T.G., SHELMERDINE, C.W. & ILIEVSKI, P.HR. (eds.) *Studia Mycenaea (1988): Zhiva Antika*. Monographies 7. Skopje: 125–48.

SHELMERDINE, C.W. 1995. 'Shining and fragrant cloth in Homer.' In CARTER, J.B. & MORRIS, S.P. (eds.) *The Ages of Homer. A Tribute to Emily Townsend Vermeule*. Austin: 99–107.

SHELMERDINE, C.W. 1997. 'Workshops and record keeping in the Mycenaean world'. In LAFFINEUR, R. & BETENCOURT, P.P. (eds.) *TEXNH. Craftsmen, Craftswomen and Craftsmanship in the Aegean Bronze Age. Proceedings of the 6th International Aegean Conference, Philadelphia, Temple University, 18–21 April 1996. Aegaeum* 16. Liège & Austin: 387–97.

SHELMERDINE, C.W. 1998a. 'Where do we go from here? And how can the Linear B tablets help us get there?' In CLINE, E.H. & HARRIS-CLINE, D. (eds.) *The Aegean and the Orient in the Second Millennium. Aegaeum* 18. Liège & Austin: 291–9.

SHELMERDINE, C.W. 1998b. 'The palace and its operations.' In DAVIS, J. (ed.) *Sandy Pylos. An Archaeological History from Nestor to Navarino*. Austin: 81–109.

SHELMERDINE, C.W. 1998–1999 [2002]. 'The Southwestern Department at Pylos.' In BENNET, J. & DRIESSEN, J. (eds.) *A-NA-QO-TA. Studies Presented to J.T. Killen. Minos* 33–34. Salamanca: 309–37.

SHELMERDINE, C.W. 1999a. 'A comparative look at Mycenaean administration(s).' In DEGER-JALKOTZY, S., HILLER, S. & PANAGL, O. (eds.) *Floreant Studia Mycenaea. Akten des X.*

Internationalen Mykenologischen Colloquiums in Salzburg vom 1.–5. Mai 1995. Vienna: 555–76.

SHELMERDINE, C.W. 1999b. 'Administration in the Mycenaean palaces: where's the chief?' In GALATY, M.L. & PARKINSON, W.A. (eds.) *Rethinking Mycenaean Palaces. New Interpretations of an Old Idea*. Los Angeles: 19–24.

SHELMERDINE, C.W. 1999c. 'Pylian polemics: the latest evidence on military matters.' In LAFFINEUR, R. (ed.) *POLEMOS. Le contexte guerrier en Égée à l'âge du bronze. Actes de la 7e Rencontre égéenne internationale Université de Liège, 14–17 avril 1998*. *Aegaeum* 19. Liège and Austin: 403–10.

SHELMERDINE, C.W. 2001a. 'The evolution of administration at Pylos.' In VOUTSAKI, S. & KILLEN, J.T. (eds.) *Economy and Politics in the Mycenaean Palace States. Proceedings of a Conference Held on 1–3 July 1999 in the Faculty of Classics, Cambridge*. Cambridge Philological Society Supplementary Volume 27. Cambridge: 113–28.

SHELMERDINE, C.W. 2001b 'Review of Aegean Prehistory VI: the palatial Bronze Age of the southern and central Greek mainland.' In CULLEN, T. (ed.) *Aegean Prehistory. A Review*. *American Journal of Archaeology* Suppl. 1. Boston: 329–81. [First printed as: SHELMERDINE, C.W. 1997. 'Review of Aegean Prehistory VI: the palatial Bronze Age of the southern and central Greek mainland.' *American Journal of Archaeology* 101: 537–85.]

SHELMERDINE, C.W. & BENNET, J. 1995. 'Two new Linear B documents from Bronze Age Pylos.' *Kadmos* 34: 123–36.

SHELTON, K.S. 2002–2003 [2007]. 'A new Linear B tablet from Petsas House, Mycenae.' *Minos* 37–38: 387–96.

SHERRATT, A.G. 1995. 'Alcohol and its alternatives: symbol and substance in pre-industrial cultures.' In GOODMAN, J., LOVEJOY, P.E. & SHERRATT, A.G. (eds.) *Consuming Habits. Drugs in History and Anthropology*. London & New York: 11–46.

SHERRATT, A.G. & SHERRATT, E.S. 1991. 'From luxuries to commodities: the nature of Mediterranean Bronze Age trading systems.' In GALE, N.H. (ed.) *Bronze Age Trade in the Mediterranean*. Studies in Mediterranean Archaeology 90. Jonsered: 351–86.

SHERRATT, E.S. 2001. 'Potemkin palaces and route-based economies.' In VOUTSAKI, S. & KILLEN, J.T. (eds.) *Economy and Politics in the Mycenaean Palace States. Proceedings of a Conference held on 1–3 July 1999 in the Faculty of Classics, Cambridge*. Cambridge Philological Society Supplementary Volume 27. Cambridge: 214–38.

SHERRATT, E.S. 2004. 'Feasting in Homeric epic.' In WRIGHT, J.C. (ed.) *The Mycenaean Feast*. *Hesperia* 73:2. Princeton: 181–217.

SJÖBERG, B.L. 1995. 'The Mycenaean economy: theoretical frameworks.' In GILLIS, C., RISBERG, C. & SJÖBERG, B. (eds.) *Trade and Production in Premonetary Greece. Aspects of Trade. Proceedings of the 3rd International Workshop, Athens 1993*. Studies in Mediterranean Archaeology Pocket-book 134. Jonsered: 19–32.

SMITH, J.S. 1991. 'Bronzesmiths of Pylos: their place in Mycenaean economy and industry.' *American Journal of Archaeology* 95: 316.

SMITH, J.S. 1992–1993. 'The Pylos Jn series.' *Minos* 27–28: 167–259.

SNELL, D.C. 1997. *Life in the Ancient Near East 3100–332 B.C.E.* New Haven & London.

SOURVINOU, C. 1968. 'A propos de la tablette KN As 821.' *Minos* 9: 184–6.

SPECIALE, M.-S. 1999. 'La tavoletta PY Ta 716 e i sacrifici di animali.' In LA ROSA, V., PALERMO, D. & VAGNETTI, L. (eds.) *'Επὶ πόντον πλαζόμενοι. Simposio italiano di Studi Egei dedicato a Luigi Bernabò Brea e Giovanni Pugliese Carratelli, Roma, 18–20 febbraio 1998*. Rome: 291–7.

SPECIALE, M.-S. 2000. 'Furniture in Linear B: the evidence for tables.' In KARETSOU, A. (ed.) *Pepragmena H' Diethnous Kritologikou Synedriou, Irakleio, 9–14 Septemvriou 1996*. Volume A3. *Proïstoriki kai Archaia Elliniki Periodos*. Heraklion: 227–39.

SPECIALE, M.-S. 2001. 'L'industria dei profumi e l'amministrazione di Cnosso in età micenea.' *Creta Antica* 2: 149–58.

STANLEY, P.V. 1982. 'KN Uc 160 and Mycenaean wines.' *American Journal of Archaeology* 86: 577–8.

STAVRIANOPOULOU, E. 1995. 'Die Verflechtung des politischen mit dem religiösen im mykenischen Pylos.' In LAFFINEUR, R. & NIEMEIER, W.-D. (eds.) *POLITEIA. Society and State in the Aegean Bronze Age. Proceedings of the 5th International Aegean Conference / 5e Rencontre égéenne internationale, University of Heidelberg, Archäologisches Institut 10–13 April 1993. Aegaeum* 12. Liège & Austin: 423–33.

STELLA, L.A. 1958. 'La religione greca nei testi micenei.' *Numen* 5: 18–57.

STOCKER, S.R. & DAVIS, J.L. 2004. 'Animal sacrifice, archives, and feasting at the Palace of Nestor'. In WRIGHT, J.C. (ed.) *The Mycenaean Feast. Hesperia* 73.2. Boston: 59–75.

SZEMERENYI, O. 1987. 'Arcadian and Cypriot(?) ΙΕΡΗΣ and the Mycenaean antecedent.' In CONSIDINE, P. & HOOKER, J.T. (eds.) *Scripta Minora. Selected Essays in Indo-European, Greek, and Latin*. Volume III. *Greek*. Innsbruck: 1357–63.

TAYLOUR, W.D. 1969. 'Mycenae, 1968.' *Antiquity* 43: 91–7.

TAYLOUR, W.D. 1970. 'New light on Mycenaean religion.' *Antiquity* 44: 270–80.

TAYLOUR, W.D. 1983. *The Mycenaeans*. Revised edition. London.

TEGYEY, I. 1983. 'Scribe 103 at Knossos.' In OLIVA, P. & FROLÍKOVÁ, A. (eds.) *Concilium Eirene XVI. Proceedings of the 16th International Eirene Conference, Prague, 31.8–4.9.1982*. Prague: 127–32.

TEGYEY, I. 1984. 'The Northeast Workshop at Pylos.' In SHELMERDINE, C.W. & PALAIMA, T.G. (eds.) *Pylos Comes Alive. Industry and Administration in a Mycenaean Palace*. New York: 65–79.

TEGYEY, I. 1987. 'Scribes and archives at Knossos and Pylos: a comparison.' In ILIEVSKI, P.HR. & CREPAJAC, LJ. (eds.) *Tractata Mycenaea. Proceedings of the Eighth International Colloquium on Mycenaean Studies Held in Ohrid, 15–20 September 1985*. Skopje: 357–66.

TEGYEY, I. 1989. 'The Linear B tablets of the West Wing of the Palace of Knossos.' In PALAIMA, T.G., SHELMERDINE, C.W. & ILIEVSKI, P.HR. (eds.) *Studia Mycenaea (1988)*: *Zhiva Antika*. Monographies 7. Skopje: 159–66.

THOMAS, C.G. 1976. 'The nature of Mycenaean kingship.' *Studi Micenei ed Egeo-Anatolici* 17: 93–116.

THOMAS, C.G. 1984. 'Mycenaean law in its oral context.' *Studi Micenei ed Egeo-Anatolici* 25: 247–53.

THOMAS, C.G. & WEDDE, M. 2001. 'Desperately seeking *Potnia*.' In LAFFINEUR, R. & HÄGG, R. (eds.) *POTNIA. Deities and Religion in the Aegean Bronze Age. Proceedings of the 8th International Aegean Conference Held at Göteborg University, 12–15 April 2000. Aegaeum* 22. Liège: 3–14.

THOMAS, N.R. 1999. 'The war animal: three days in the life of the Mycenaean lion.' In LAFFINEUR, R. (ed.) *POLEMOS. Le contexte guerrier en Égée à l'âge du bronze. Actes de la 7e Rencontre égéenne internationale Université de Liège, 14–17 avril 1998. Aegaeum* 19. Liège and Austin: 297–312.

THOMPSON, R.J.E. 1996–1997. 'Dialects in Mycenaean and Mycenaean among the dialects.' *Minos* 31–32: 313–34.

THOMPSON, R.J.E. 1997. 'The origins of the Arcado-Cypriot dialect group.' Unpublished Ph.D. thesis, University of Cambridge.

THOMPSON, R.J.E. 1998. 'Instrumentals, datives, locatives and ablatives: the -φι case form in Mycenaean and Homer.' *Proceedings of the Cambridge Philological Society* 44: 219–50.

THOMPSON, R.J.E. 2005 [2007]. 'Two notes on Mycenaean labial stops.' *Živa Antika* 55 (*Festschrift for P.Hr. Ilievsky*). Skopje: 107–15.

TOURNAVITOU, I. 1995. *The 'Ivory Houses' at Mycenae*. British School at Athens Supplementary Volume 24. London.

TRIGGER, B.G. 2003. *Understanding Early Civilizations*. Cambridge.

TRÜMPY, C. 1989. 'Nochmals zu den mykenischen Fr-Täfelchen: die Zeitangaben innerhalb der Pylischen Ölrationenserie.' *Studi Micenei ed Egeo-Anatolici* 27: 192–234.

TRÜMPY, C. 2001. '*Potnia* dans les tablettes mycéniennes: quelque problèmes d'interprétation.' In LAFFINEUR, R. & HÄGG, R. (eds.) *POTNIA. Deities and Religion in the Aegean Bronze Age. Proceedings of the 8th International Aegean Conference held at Göteborg University, 12–15 April 2000. Aegaeum* 22. Liège: 411–21.

TZEDAKIS, Y. & MARTLEW, H. (eds.) 1999. *Minoans and Mycenaeans. Flavours of Their Times. National Archaeological Museum 12 July – 27 November 1999*. Greek Ministry of Culture. Athens. [= *Flavours*]

VAN DE MIEROOP, M. 1997. 'Why did they write on clay?' *Klio* 79: 7–18.

VAN DE MIEROOP, M. 2000. 'Review of: *Privatization in the Ancient Near East and Classical World*. Edited by Michael Hudson & Baruch A. Levine. Peabody Museum Bulletin, no. 5, the International Scholars Conference on Ancient Near Eastern Economics Series, vol. 1. Cambridge: Peabody Museum of Archaeology and Ethnology, Harvard University, 1996.' *Journal of Near Eastern Studies* 59: 40–3.

VAN DE MIEROOP, M. 2004. 'Economic theories and the ancient Near East.' In ROLLINGER, R. & ULF, C. (eds.) *Commerce and Monetary Systems in the Ancient World. Means of Transmission and Cultural Interaction*. Munich: 54–64.

VAN DE MIEROOP, M. 2005. 'Review of: *Economy and Society in Northern Babylonia in the Early Old Babylonian Period (ca. 2000–1800 BC)*. By Anne Goddeeris. Orientalia Lovaniensia Analecta 109. Leuven: Peeters, 2002.' *Journal of Near Eastern Studies* 64: 127–8.

VANDENABEELE, F. & OLIVIER, J.-P. 1979. *Les idéogrammes archéologiques du linéaire B*. Études Crétoises 24. Athens.

VAN LEUVEN, J.C. 1975. 'Aspects of Mycenaean religion.' *Bulletin of the Institute of Classical Studies* 22: 203–5.

VAN LEUVEN, J.C. 1978. 'The mainland tradition of sanctuaries in prehistoric Greece.' *World Archaeology* 10: 139–48.

VAN LEUVEN, J.C. 1979. 'Mycenaean goddesses called "Potnia".' *Kadmos* 18: 112–29.

VAN STRATEN, F.T. 1995. *Hierà Kalá. Images of Animal Sacrifice in Archaic & Classical Greece*. Religions in the Graeco-Roman World Volume 127. Leiden.

VAN WERSCH, H.J. 1972. 'The agricultural economy.' In MCDONALD, W.A. & RAPP, G.R. JR. (eds.) *The Minnesota Messenia Expedition. Reconstructing a Bronze Age Regional Environment*. Minneapolis: 177–87.

VAN WIJNGAARDEN, G.J. 2002. *The Use and Appreciation of Mycenaean Pottery in the Levant, Cyprus and Italy (ca. 1600–1200 B.C.)*. Amsterdam.

VARIAS GARCIA, C. 1999. 'The palace of Mycenae in LH IIIB2 according to the documents in Linear B: a general description.' In DEGER-JALKOTZY, S., HILLER, S. & PANAGL, O. (eds.) *Floreant Studia Mycenaea. Akten des X. Internationalen Mykenologischen Colloquiums in Salzburg vom 1.–5. Mai 1995*. Vienna: 595–606.

VARIAS GARCIA, C. Forthcoming. 'Banqueting at Mycenae: the textual evidence.' In PALAIMA, T.G. & SHELMERDINE, C.W. (eds.) *Proceedings of the 11th International Mycenological Colloquium at Austin, Texas, 7–12 May 2000. Minos* Suppl. Salamanca.

VENTRIS, M.G.F. & CHADWICK, J. 1956. *Documents in Mycenaean Greek*. First edition. Cambridge. [= *Documents*[1]]

VENTRIS, M.G.F. & CHADWICK, J. 1973. *Documents in Mycenaean Greek*. Second edition. Cambridge. [= *Documents*]

VERMEULE, E.T. 1974. *Götterkult. Archaeologica Homerica*. Band III, Kapitel V. Göttingen.

VOUTSAKI, S. 1995a. 'Value and exchange in premonetary societies: anthropological debates and Aegean archaeology.' In GILLIS, C., RISBERG, C. & SJÖBERG, B. (eds.) *Trade and Production in Premonetary Greece. Aspects of Trade. Proceedings of the 3rd International Workshop, Athens 1993*. Studies in Mediterranean Archaeology Pocket-book 134. Jonsered: 7–17.

VOUTSAKI, S. 2001. 'Economic control, power and prestige in the Mycenaean world: the archaeological evidence.' In VOUTSAKI, S. & KILLEN, J.T. (eds.) *Economy and Politics in the Mycenaean Palace States. Proceedings of a Conference Held on 1–3 July 1999 in the Faculty of*

Classics, Cambridge. Cambridge Philological Society Supplementary Volume 27. Cambridge: 195–213.

WARREN, P. 2004. 'Terra cognita? The territory and boundaries of the early Neopalatial Knossian state.' In CADOGAN, G., HATZAKI, E. & VASILAKIS, A. (eds.) *Knossos: Palace, City, State*. British School at Athens Studies 12. London: 159–68.

WEILHARTNER, J. 2003. 'Oil and honey on some of the Linear B offering tablets from Knossos: considerations about their possible application.' *Journal of Prehistoric Religion* 16–17: 46–52.

WEILHARTNER, J. 2005. *Mykenische Opfergaben nach Aussage der Linear B-Texte*. Vienna.

WHITBREAD, I.K., PONTING, M.J. & WELLS, B. 2007. 'Temporal patterns in ceramic production in the Berbati Valley, Greece.' *Journal of Field Archaeology* 32: 177–93.

WHITELAW, T.M. 2001. 'Reading between the tablets: assessing Mycenaean palatial involvement in ceramic produce and consumption.' In VOUTSAKI, S. & KILLEN, J.T. (eds.) *Economy and Politics in the Mycenaean Palace States. Proceedings of a Conference held on 1–3 July 1999 in the Faculty of Classics, Cambridge*. Cambridge Philological Society Supplementary Volume 27. Cambridge: 51–79.

WHITTAKER, H. 1997. *Mycenaean Cult Buildings*. Bergen.

WILLI, A. 1994–1995. '*do-ra-qe pe-re po-re-na-qe a-ke*: an Indo-European figure in Mycenaean?' *Minos* 29–30: 177–85.

WRIGHT, J.C. 1991. 'Religion and the role of ideology in Mycenaean society.' *American Journal of Archaeology* 95: 316.

WRIGHT, J.C. 1994. 'The spatial configuration of belief: the archaeology of Mycenaean religion.' In ALCOCK, S.E. & OSBORNE, R. (eds.) *Placing the Gods. Sanctuaries and Sacred Space in Ancient Greece*. Oxford: 37–87.

WRIGHT, J.C. 1995a. 'The archaeological correlates of religion: case studies in the Aegean.' In LAFFINEUR, R. & NIEMEIER, W.-D. (eds.) *POLITEIA. Society and State in the Aegean Bronze Age. Proceedings of the 5th International Aegean Conference / 5e Rencontre égéenne internationale, University of Heidelberg, Archäologisches Institut 10–13 April 1993. Aegaeum* 12. Liège & Austin: 341–8.

WRIGHT, J.C. 1995b. 'Empty cups and empty jugs: the social role of wine in Minoan and Mycenaean societies.' In MCGOVERN, P.E., FLEMING, S.J. & KATZ, S.H. (eds.) *The Origins and Ancient History of Wine*. Philadelphia: 287–309.

WRIGHT, J.C. (ed.) 2004a. *The Mycenaean Feast. Hesperia* 73:2. Princeton.

WRIGHT, J.C. 2004b. 'A survey of evidence for feasting in Mycenaean society.' In WRIGHT, J.C. (ed.) *The Mycenaean Feast. Hesperia* 73:2. Princeton: 13–58.

WYATT, W.F. 1962. 'The Ma tablets from Pylos.' *American Journal of Archaeology* 66: 21–41.

WYLOCK, M. 1970. 'La fabrication des parfums à l'époque mycénienne d'après les tablettes Fr de Pylos.' *Studi Micenei ed Egeo-Anatolici* 11: 116–33.

ZETTLER, R.L. 1996. 'Written documents as excavated artefacts and the holistic interpretation of the Mesopotamian archaeological record.' In COOPER, J.S. & SCHWARTZ, G.M. (eds.) *The Study of the Ancient Near East in the 21st Century*. Ann Arbor: 81-101.

INDICES

1 LINEAR B TABLETS

Page numbers in bold italic typeface indicate that the document transcription appears on the given page.

KHANIA

KNOSSOS

MYCENAE

PYLOS

THEBES

TIRYNS

2 LINEAR B SIGN-GROUPS AND SYLLABOGRAMS

3 Index of Mycenaean and other Greek words

Words are given according to the order of the English alphabet.

4 LINEAR B IDEOGRAPHIC SIGNS AND ADJUNCTS

Signs for Mycenaean measures (e.g. T, S, M, V, Z) are not indexed.

5 THEONYMS

The index includes groups, shrines, month and festival names based on theonyms, but excludes personal names. It includes only securely attested and commonly agreed deity names.